CIVIL PROCEDURE OF THE TRIAL COURT IN HISTORICAL PERSPECTIVE

BY

ROBERT WYNESS MILLAR

Emeritus Professor of Law in Northwestern University

THE LAWBOOK EXCHANGE, LTD.

Clark, New Jersey

ISBN 978-1-58477-458-7 (hardcover)
ISBN 978-1-61619-399-7 (paperback)

Lawbook Exchange edition 2005, 2014

The quality of this reprint is equivalent to the quality of the original work.

THE LAWBOOK EXCHANGE, LTD.
33 Terminal Avenue
Clark, New Jersey 07066-1321

Please see our website for a selection of our other publications and fine facsimile reprints of classic works of legal history:
www.lawbookexchange.com

Library of Congress Cataloging-in-Publication Data

Millar, Robert Wyness, 1876-1959.
Civil procedure of the trial court in historical perspective / by Robert Wyness Millar.
p. cm.
Originally published: [New York] : Published by the Law Center of New York University for the National Conference of Judicial Councils, 1952. (The judicial administration series).
Includes bibliographical references and index.
ISBN 1-58477-458-4 (cloth : acid-free paper)
1. Civil procedure—United States—History. 2.Civil procedure—Great Britain—History.
I. Title. II. Judicial administration series.

KF8840.M49 2004
347.73'5—dc22 2004040930

Printed in the United States of America on acid-free paper

THE JUDICIAL ADMINISTRATION SERIES

CIVIL PROCEDURE OF THE TRIAL COURT IN HISTORICAL PERSPECTIVE

BY

ROBERT WYNESS MILLAR

Emeritus Professor of Law in Northwestern University

PUBLISHED BY

THE LAW CENTER OF NEW YORK UNIVERSITY

FOR

THE NATIONAL CONFERENCE OF JUDICIAL COUNCILS

1952

LIBRARY OF CONGRESS CATALOG CARD NO. 52-11758

PRINTED IN THE UNITED STATES OF AMERICA

TO THE MEMORY OF

JOHN HENRY WIGMORE

TEACHER, COLLEAGUE AND
WELL-BELOVED FRIEND

"Omnia igitur divina et humana mysteria ordine reguntur ac celebrantur. Non secus et iudicium ipsum quod lapis quidam est angularis totius legalis doctrinae summo prae caeteris humanis actibus ordine regi oportet."

Maranta, Tractatus de ordine iudiciorum (ed. of 1570) Prooemium, p. 14.

"Il est aisé de comprendre que si, d'un côté, la loi sur la procédure n'est que secondaire, en ce sens qu'elle n'a d'autre objet, d'autre but que l'accomplissement de la loi civile, de l'autre, elle en est un complément nécessaire, elle lui donne seule la force et la vie."

Bellot, Loi sur la procédure civile du Canton de Genève, avec l'exposé des motifs (4th ed. 1877) p. 11.

". . . so geht eine Hauptforderung an eine Prozessgesetzgebung dahin: einen solchen Mechanismus des Verfahrens anzuordnen, in welchem die Ungleichheit der Kräfte der streitenden Theile durch zweckmässige Einwirkung der Richter und durch gestattete Beiziehung von Vertretern der Partheien so ausgeglichen wird, dass am wenigsten materielles Unrecht in formelles Recht übergehen kann."

Mittermaier, Der gemeine deutsche bürgerliche Prozess in Vergleichung mit dem preussischen und französischen Civilverfahren und mit den neuesten Fortschritten der Prozessgesetzgebung (3d ed. 1838) Vol. I, p. 19.

PREFACE

The present period is one in which the institutions of American civil justice are being subjected to scrutiny and recasting. As the 1900s opened he were a bold man who would seek to disturb, as it had become settled, the existing order in anything more than its peripheral detail. The code movement of the century just closed had spent its force, and where accepted had become largely static. Elsewhere the traditional dualism of jurisdiction was contentedly maintaining itself with only minor departure from time-honored method. But, after a first ruffling of these placid waters by the Kansas Practice Act of 1909, two events in 1912 more deeply agitated their surface. One was the appearance of the Federal Equity Rules of that year, the other the contemporaneous enactment of the innovating New Jersey Practice Act. Betokening a definitely awakened response to procedural needs, these two happenings—both now of but historical interest—pointed the way to further advance. This, though hesitant and cautious, was gradually being attained until it reached a climactic point in the Federal Rules of 1938. These Rules, as embodying the best in the State enactments and profiting by the English Rules under the Judicature Acts, have furnished a model to which State legislation, either by statute or rule of court, is already more and more conforming its procedural ideas in whole or in part. While far from perfect, the Rules in question represent by and large the nearest approach yet made, under American conditions, to the realization of a simple and effective system for the administration of civil justice.

In our latter-day reconsideration of procedural method the English Rules have unquestionably exercised a powerful influence. Indeed, there was a time prior to the advent of the Federal Rules when among those interested in procedural reform there had developed an exaggerated reverence for the modern English system. While such a feeling has now generally been succeeded by a more temperate appreciation, the acknowledged virtues of that system have often blinded us to what we owe to the builders of our own procedural institutions —have led us to forget how much of important procedural invention has come from American initiative. We need not emphasize the fused administration of law and equity which, to say nothing of its presence in Texas substantially from the outset of that State's history, had its definite introduction in the New York Code of 1848, a quarter of a century in advance of its reception in England. We can hardly make a point of this, for in Bacon's time there were those who urged such a fusion—a proposal against which he directed his eloquent pen. But there are other things upon which stress may be properly laid. Thus, the idea of a forthright judgment by default for want of appearance, arrived at in England only through a painful process in which a fictitious entry of appearance long played a part, had made itself sufficiently familiar in America even in colonial times. Thus, too, the institution of garnishment after judgment as a means of execution did not become part of the English system until the Common Law Procedure Act of 1854, although provision for it is found in Maryland of the late 1600s. Nor should we overlook the fact that an affirmative judgment in favor of a defendant establishing a set-off, unknown to the English system until the Rules of 1875, was in effect an established feature of practice in certain of the colonies, before set-off at all in common-law actions had come to recognition in England. The installation of discovery as part of the procedure in common-law actions is something which the merged administration of law and equity has since very largely deprived of importance. When it occurred, however, it was an event of decided significance. In England this step was taken by the Common Law Procedure Act of 1854, but American legislation in the same end appears as early at least as the Mississippi statute of 1828 and includes the notable Massachusetts act of 1851. Our primacy in these matters, as in various others, is undoubted. And, outside the case of such contributions to the common stock, no praise would be too great for the wisdom and inventive skill, by which from colonial times the institution of attachment on mesne process, found in germ in the custom of London, has been systematized and implanted in all our jurisdictions, whereas in England, as we shall have occasion to see, even this germ has been suffered utterly to perish.

These are achievements in which Americans can take justifiable pride. Moreover, they give us confidence in our ability to tread with sure steps the further path of reform. For, despite the signal measure of improvement already accomplished, the work of procedural betterment has many converts yet to make, much territory yet to conquer. And here significant aid can be obtained from some examination of our procedural institutions in their march to the present day. The case, therefore, is one that seems to call for a book that will briefly survey the major procedural rules employed in the courts of first instance of this country and England, viewed especially from the standpoint of their historical progression. The usefulness of such a standpoint is obvious. To the law of procedure are particularly applicable the words of Holmes, spoken of law in general, that "its form and machinery and the extent to which it is able to work out satisfactory results depend very much upon its past." In this manner of proceeding, too, we are enabled to follow, in its main lines, the course of contemporary reform and to see how far the most approved procedural ideas have come to acceptance. It is in the end of thus meeting what is an apparent desideratum that this book has been written. It confines itself to the procedure of first instance, the rules of appellate procedure having been made the subject of Professor Pound's admirable volume in the present series. Included, however, is a viewing of the processes of execution. This province of American civil procedure has developed in a manner which, for the most part, has rendered it simple and effective. Here contemporary reform is confronted with no such clamant questions as are presented by the procedure of cognition. While, therefore, except as to local detail, the matter largely falls outside the forum of current procedural debate, it is not for this reason to be subtracted from the range of our survey.

For obvious reasons our consideration of the State procedures has not troubled that of Louisiana, save in a few instances where its methods have yielded borrowings to other jurisdictions. Outside the United States, it would no doubt have been profitable to project our inquiries, beyond the modern English system, into the related procedures of English Canada and Australia, but this would have been an undertaking too large for the present account.

The text of Chapters III, IV, most of Chapter VII, and a portion of Chapter XIII, with certain lesser items, was originally part of my essay, *The Old Regime and the New in Civil Procedure,* appearing in *Law: A Century of Progress* (New York University Press, 1935). Certain other former writings of mine have been laid under contribution in varying measure, namely, *Notabilia of Civil Procedure, 1887-1937,* 50 Harvard Law Review (1937), *The Mechanism of Fact-Discovery: A Study in Comparative Civil Procedure,* 32 Illinois Law Review (1937), *Multiplying Edward Longfield: Unitary Demands and Plural Counts,* 16 Journal of the American Judicature Society (1932), and *Pleading under the Illinois Civil Practice Act,* 28 Illinois Law Review (1933). For permission to utilize this material my thanks are due to the respective editors.

The book was undertaken at the instance of Chief Justice Vanderbilt, whose support and encouragement throughout its preparation cannot be too strongly emphasized. To be recorded also is the debt which it owes to the Carnegie Corporation of New York. It is by reason of a grant from the latter that its publication has been assured, a circumstance, however, which in nowise commits the Corporation to acceptance of any of the views advanced by the author.

If I might venture to revive the fashion of an older day, I would close by saying with the editor of the English version of Finch's *Law* (1678): "Now remaineth only to extenuate the faults, either those material in the copy, or literal in the print, the first a judicious reader is able to supply, a little labour will correct the rest. He that is courteous will remit both."

ROBERT WYNESS MILLAR

Northwestern University School of Law
November 1951.

CONTENTS

Part I

GENERAL ASPECTS

Part II

SPECIFIC PHASES

CIVIL PROCEDURE OF THE TRIAL COURT IN HISTORICAL PERSPECTIVE

Part I

GENERAL ASPECTS

Chapter I

PROCEDURAL EVOLUTION AND THE ANGLO-AMERICAN SYSTEM

§ 1. Procedure as the Forerunner of Substantive Law

It has been the fortune of Anglo-American civil procedure to exemplify in a manner especially striking the truth of certain generalizations concerning the development of procedure at large. The first of these that we would mention touches the relation of procedure to substantive law. Hearken to von Jhering in his dramatic presentation of the growth of the Roman law. "Procedure," says the eloquent civilian, "belongs to the institutions of earliest development. At a time when substantive legal conceptions are visible only in the faintest of outline, procedure meets us as a figure already perfected and exact." [1] Turn then to the classic words of Sir Henry Maine: "So great is the ascendency of the law of actions in the infancy of courts of justice, that substantive law has at first the look of being gradually secreted in the interstices of procedure; and the early lawyer can only see the law through the envelope of its technical forms." [2] Looking at the history of the English law no one can doubt the spectacular realization there of the force of these observations. The procedural mechanism was what occupied the foremost place in the formative era. "In the middle ages," remarks Maitland, "one could say next to nothing about

[1] *Geist des römischen Rechts,* III, (1) (5th ed. 1906) 17 (French transl. by Meulenaere, *L'esprit du droit romain,* Vol. IV (3d ed. 1888) 15.

[2] Maine, Early Law and Custom (ed. of 1907) 389.

actions in general, while one could discourse at great length about the mode in which an action of this or that sort was to be pursued and defended."[3] The common-law forms of action were the channels through which the substantive rules came into being, the moulds which gave them shape and character. Would it be possible, for example, to divorce the history of seizin in English law from that of the old real actions,[4] the history of tort law from the actions of trespass, case and trover, the history of consideration in contract from the action of assumpsit? When the rule came to be that one whose goods had been converted and sold by another had at his command the choice of two sorts of recovery—on the one hand, a recovery of the value with interest from the time of conversion, on the other, a recovery of the amount which the converter had realized from the sale, it was only so because of the existence of trover in the first case, of assumpsit for money had and received in the other. Instances of the kind might be multiplied indefinitely. The phenomenon is one of constant recurrence throughout the formative era. Ever do we see that procedure has been the major element, substantive law the minor in the growth of the legal order, and that procedure has been signally procreative of the substantive rule. But in our law, as elsewhere, the trend of development diminishes the place of procedure and enlarges that of the substantive law. This, to be sure, is a gradual process, interrupted from time to time by hesitation and relapse. Nevertheless it is an inevitable process and ends with inversion of the early relationship between the two sets of rules. Procedure remains a necessity, but men come to the understanding that the true rôle of procedure is an ancillary one. In the household of the law procedure ceases to be the *materfamilias* and is now the handmaiden. Yet there is always a possible flicker of the old ascendancy. One recollects that to that option of the plaintiff in the case of converted goods certain American courts in the nineteenth century

[3] 2 Pollock & Maitland, History of English Law (2d ed. 1899) 562.

[4] See Maitland, The Forms of Action at Common Law (ed. of 1936) 1.

added a third manner of recovery, namely, the right to recover in assumpsit even if the defendant had not sold the converted goods. They were enabled to do so only because of the common-law action-theory of goods sold and delivered. It was the existence of the assumpsit count for goods sold and delivered that occasioned and justified this result. The phenomenon here is that of procedure reasserting its old habit of creating substantive law. This late example, of itself, would indicate how conspicuously close to the fact, in the case of our procedure, is the generalization about which we are speaking, and perhaps sets us wondering whether the procreative force of procedure has yet been wholly spent.

§ 2. Rigidity to Flexibility as a Law of Procedural Progress

A second generalization here relevant is this, namely, that as procedure develops the advance is from rigidity to flexibility. Primitive procedure is characterized by the extremest formalism. The early Roman lawsuit and that of the old Germanic system are alike in exhibiting the dominance of form. Observance of form at the outset is bound up with religious ideas and sanctions. Success or unsuccess in minutely following the form in word and act correspondingly spells success or unsuccess in the judicial proceeding, for the event signalizes the will and decision of the divine powers. Added to this is the fact that men find their safety in form. It is the beaten way, the travelled road: to depart from this is to venture into the unknown. *Via trita, via tuta.* And it comes to possess a virtue of still another character. When form is supreme no place is afforded for arbitrary decision. Apart from its religious significance, the appeal to form is an appeal to an objective standard. The subjective caprice or error of ruler or judge can have no voice in the result. Form therefore stands as a protection against the arbitrary exercise of authority. It ties the wielder of power just as it ties those subject to that power. Not far from the mark, as respects certain stages of legal development, is the celebrated epigram of von Jhering that "form is the twin sister of Liberty."[5] It is not surprising that the history of legal institutions discloses a clinging to form long after its religious association has disappeared. This is true of our own procedure as of every other. The formalism of its beginnings is the Germanic formalism of the Anglo-Saxon law tempered by the formalism of the Norman invader, notably modified by the introduction of the Norman inquest,—itself, strangely enough, an outgrowth of Germanic formalism,—and affected by the infiltration of ideas drawn from the medieval Roman law. On this basis it develops its distinctive forms—forms which imparted to its mechanism a distinctive character of rigidity. But, as in other systems, with increasing stability of the courts and growing confidence in their justice, judicial discretion becomes by degrees a surrogate of the old supremacy of form, and there is progression from rigidity to flexibility in the rules of procedure. Yet, except for the rise of the Court of Chancery and its attendant processes, many centuries pass before the progression is at all marked. Nor is it a constant progression. The introduction of written pleadings served to install a measure of rigidity wholly absent from the previous practice of oral altercation. Nor can anyone doubt that the Hilary Rules, of so recent a date as 1834, well-intentioned as they were, represented a backward step from the present standpoint. Despite halts of the kind, however, the general direction is unmistakable. But it is not until late that the progression emerges plainly to view, takes on a sweeping character, and affects the organic bases of the system. In this very lateness of its pronounced activity, the recency of its forceful manifestations, we are reminded all the more clearly that, in the present regard, also, our procedural development is conforming in impressive degree to a general principle.

§ 3. Fiction as an Agency of Procedural Development

Next to be noted is the part played by legal fiction. It is true of our own law as of the Roman that the legal fiction has

[5] *"Die Form is die . . . Zwillingsschwester der Freiheit." Op. cit.* II (2) (5th ed. 1898) 471.

made important contribution to procedural development. It is true of both that ultimately a stage is reached when men cease to depend, at least consciously, upon this aid, and direct their efforts toward discarding, as out of keeping with the spirit of the times, the fictions of preceding generations. And in the case of the Anglo-American system, the attainment of this stage is sufficiently close to our own day. In the formative era fictions serve in a sense as substitutes for enacted law. They are a means of changing the essence of a given rule, while still paying homage to the letter. They are resorted to, partly out of attachment to existing forms, partly, and more so, because of the difficulty or impossibility of obtaining legislation to effect the end in view. Just as legislation may be laudable or illaudable so may the legal fiction. But no more than in the case of legislation do the motives which impel adoption necessarily determine its ultimate usefulness. The fictions by means of which the King's Bench and the Exchequer invaded the jurisdiction of the Common Pleas were no doubt sordidly motived, but who can say that they did not ultimately redound to the benefit of English procedure? Most, however, of the fictions in our procedural history can be referred to the opposite class, or at least must be taken as representing a genuine effort at improvement. Few would question, for example, the real value for the time and place of that fiction which enabled a plaintiff, suing upon a contract made abroad, to lay his venue in the Parish of St. Mary-le-Bow in the Ward of Cheap, of that, now almost forgotten, which circumvented a technical rule of pleading by the invention of express color, of that involved in the use of plural counts in declaring upon the same substantive cause of action, of that magnificent series of fictions which placed at the plaintiff's disposal the comparatively simple action of ejectment in lieu of a perilous choice among the Procrustean real actions. But for good or ill the legal fiction abounds in our procedural history. Its rôle as a factor of procedural development was of long persistence, and, as we all know, the subsequent period of contentment with its formal product only began to terminate in the nineteenth century. Even today it has not wholly disappeared from the scene as witness the matter of plural counts referred to above. In America, though not in England, this feature continues in widespread use, despite all the reforms of pleading. Thus, though he may not be quite conscious of the fact, the practitioner who employs in his complaint variant statements of the same demand for the purpose of meeting the exigencies of proof or covering the possibilities of varying theories of recovery is making obeisance to legal fiction just as certainly as did, under somewhat different forms, his predecessor of the seventeenth century. But it is a characteristic of fiction, as it is of form, to outstay its welcome. All goes to show that in our procedure, legal fiction, albeit presenting especially picturesque outlines and lingering relatively longer than in other systems, has been the same instrumentality of procedural development encountered elsewhere.

§ 4. Singleness and Procedural Immaturity

It is further the case that in the infancy of procedure its mechanism is always so contrived as to confine the task of the deciding power, as far as possible, to the determination of a single question: each question is to be pursued free from the complication of any other. This is evidenced in the early and classical Roman law by the rule which forbade the joinder of distinct actions and which in the classical period took the form of requiring a separate formula for each separate action.[6] It is evidenced throughout the procedural methods of the Germanic law. It is in effect a means of dispensing with or reducing judicial analysis, for it casts upon the party the duty of making the analysis in advance[7]—a means fully in accord with the early notion that the judge is merely an umpire. This phenomenon looms large in the history of our law, where its manifestations are seen on every hand. The fixation of the common-law forms of action, with the necessity of the party making choice at his own peril of that which will best fit his demand, the impossibility, subject to but slight exception, of

[6] Von Jhering, *op. cit.* III (1) 20, 23 (French transl. Vol. IV, 18, 30).

[7] *Ibid.* III (1) 20 (French transl. Vol. IV, 18).

uniting separate forms of action, the inexistence in the common law, and until the statute of 1729,[8] of anything in the nature of the modern counterclaim, and, above all, the principle that the pleadings should culminate in a single issue, signally demonstrate that the system is running true to rule. So, if we look at the matter of dilatory defenses at common law and observe how they can only be presented successively and decided one by one, we are left in no uncertainty that here, again, we are meeting with the same phenomenon.

Note, however, that this primitive insistence upon singleness does not exclude the idea of third party participation in the cause. Certainly the summoning in of a warrantor to defend in the place of him against whom the suit is directed would appear to be almost as old as procedure itself. It is a recognized step in the Germanic law as well as in the Greek and Roman: sometimes, indeed, it is a duty. To the early English law the third party was no such stranger as he later became. Says Maitland of the thirteenth century cases chronicled in Bracton's Note Book: "We may be surprised at the ease with which third parties intervene of their own accord or are summoned to disclose whether they claim any right."[9] This facility of third party participation crystallizes into the institutions of voucher to warranty and receit in the case of the real actions, of aid-prayer when title to land comes in question, whether in a real or personal action, and of interpleader and garnishment in the action of detinue. The first two of these are parcel of the real actions and share their fate, but all in time fall out of use to await that process of restoration under other forms which is taking place in our own day. Why should this have been so? Why should English procedure in this respect have come to withhold advantage offered even by primitive systems? We can find the immediate causes, but, having found them, they yield no better answer than that this chapter of procedural history was due to the unthinking acceptance of procedural accident.

The characteristic of which we are speaking, this "external

[8] 9 Geo. II, c. 22, § 13.

[9] Maitland, Introduction to Bracton's Note Book (1887) 132.

apparatus of analysis" as von Jhering calls it.[10] is always bound to disappear with procedural maturity. The Roman law had got rid of it long before the time of Justinian. In our own system the influence of the matured Roman law conceptions embodied in the law of the medieval church prevented its admission, save in a minimum degree, to the processes of the Court of Chancery. For the common-law sphere, however, its disappearance has been unduly retarded, but is being gradually accomplished by latter-day reform. The changes in the pleading system, the introduction of liberality in the joinder of actions and of parties, the increasing latitude of counterclaim and cross-claim, the greater malleability of common-law judgments, and numerous other innovations, testify alike to a widening emancipation of the procedure from the thralldom of an age-old modality.

§ 5. Slowness of Procedural Progress

Finally, it is to be accepted that despite its stirring childhood, the growth of procedure in its later years is never *pari passu* with that of the law in general. Since in the case of procedure "it is not a question of moral ideas, but solely of adaptation to the end, changes in a people's mode of life and thought exercise much less influence upon procedure than upon the institutions of substantive law." [11] Of no system can this more accurately be said than of our own. When we consider that no longer ago than 1824,[12] an English court deemed itself bound to concede a trial by wager of law, that survival of a thoroughly primitive era, we are forcibly reminded of the slow pace of procedure in the general advance. Many more recent reminders might be cited. One especially notable is the fact that in Illinois, until 1934, a plaintiff in an action of trespass to land could not be required to identify the *locus in quo* beyond the statement that it was situate in the county, except by an irrational resort on the part of the defendant to the traditional common bar as a means of compelling a new as-

[10] Von Jhering, *op. cit.* III (1) 8 (French transl. Vol. IV, 8).

[11] *Ibid.* III (1) 18 (French transl. Vol. IV, 16).

[12] King v. Williams, 2 B. & C. 538, 107 E.R. 483.

signment. Nineteenth century civilization with its progress in the arts and sciences, its prodigious development of commerce and industry, was in full swing before we began seriously to unchain ourselves from procedural institutions which, however valuable in their own time and however adapted to the social conditions under which they originated, were wholly out of keeping with the contemporary needs. Laggard as had been the substantive law, its enforcement was confided to a procedure in considerable part archaic. It has been said that "only primitive procedures afford a genuine representation of the epoch to which they belong: in proportion as there are advance from origins and progress in civilization, there is an increased divergence between the rules of procedure and the conditions and exigencies of the time." [13] At the beginnings of that process of unchainment, this was assuredly true of the Anglo-American system, in spite of the fact that it never had been without some forward movement. Nowhere, indeed, has procedure ever been wholly static. On the contrary it has always exhibited a striving for improvement, more conscious perhaps, if less successful, than that appearing in other fields of law. No less, therefore, than that of the Continental systems is the history of Anglo-American procedure the history of procedural reform. But, unlike the case in those systems it was not until the middle of the nineteenth century that reform in this direction took on any vital or structural significance. Constant effort has since reduced the gap between procedural rules and substantive law demand, but that it continues to exist, wider in some jurisdictions than in others, is a fact everywhere recognized. Pursuit of this effort and the possibilities of further closing this gap are a capital concern of the present day.

[13] Chiovenda, *Le riforme processuali e le correnti del pensiero moderno* in *Saggi di diritto processuale civile* (1930) Vol. I, 381.

CHAPTER II

THE ANTECEDENTS OF THE ANGLO-AMERICAN SYSTEM

§ 1. THE ANGLO-SAXON PROCEDURE

While we know considerably less in detail of the Anglo-Saxon procedure than of the more important Germanic systems of the Continent, it is clear that, at the time of the Norman Conquest, it occupied very much the same place and in general followed much the same methods as its Continental congeners.[1] Self-help was still a very active factor, restricting narrowly the province of judicial action and influencing strongly the ways of the judicial procedure itself. Principal theaters of this procedure were the communal courts, that is to say, the courts of the hundred and of the county. Each was an assembly of landowners, presided over by an officer—usually the hundred reeve in the one case, the sheriff in the other—who was, at least nominally, a representative of the king. Indications, also, there are of private jurisdiction exercised in manorial courts by the tenants of the lord under his presidency or that of his deputy. Occasionally, and not in accordance with any system, matters of high importance were dealt with judicially by the Witenagemot, the "assembly of the wise men" of the land. In all cases, the judgment of the court was rendered by the voice of the assembly and clothed with authority by the pronouncement of the presiding officer. But, subject to what shall later be said, the judgment was not a decision of the merits of the controversy. It was merely a proof-judg-

[1] For the Anglo-Saxon courts and procedure see generally Adams, The Anglo-Saxon Courts of Law, and Laughlin, The Anglo-Saxon Legal Procedure, in Anglo-Saxon Legal Essays (1876) 1-54, 183-305; 1 Pollock & Maitland, History of English Law (2d ed. 1899) 37 *et seq.*, 2 *id.* 602 *et seq.*; 1 Holdsworth, History of English Law, (3d ed. 1922) 5-24, 2 *id.* (3d ed. 1923) 102-118; Brunner, *Entstehung der Schwurgerichte* (1872) c. XIX.

ment, determining which of the parties had the right to prove, what he was to prove, and how the proof was to be made. The proof here, as in the Germanic systems generally, was always one-sided. Thus is presented what to modern eyes might appear a paradoxical situation—that of judgment in advance of proof.

In invoking the aid of the court, the plaintiff, himself, in the presence of witnesses, summoned the defendant to appear; the summoning had to be before sunset and at the defendant's dwelling place. At the appointed time, in the presence of the assembly, the plaintiff evidences his good faith, unless the circumstances render this unnecessary, by taking a preliminary oath, the so-called fore-oath, and then asserts his claim in set words, addressed to the defendant. His assertion is not a statement of facts but of the legal conclusion which his own mind has drawn from the facts. Unless the defendant can now put forward some reason why he should not answer at the time or place or should not answer at all, he is required to make his counter-assertion, which is equally in terms of legal conclusion. In debt actions, whatever be the actual facts of the defense, the counter-assertion must always be in the form of a point-blank denial of what has been said by the plaintiff. With assertion and counter-assertion before it, the assembly proceeds to the rendition of judgment, by the effect of which either assertion or counter-assertion becomes the theme of proof. Just what principle governed the award of the proof-rôle is not at all clear, but we know that in debt actions it was ordinarily allotted to the defendant. With respect to the means of proof there appears some use of documents, at least in actions relating to land. There appears also an occasional resort to the memory of the assembly concerning matters which occurred in its presence. And in criminal cases the ordeal of fire, of cold water, of hot water or of the morsel [2] are in regular employ-

[2] "The ordeal of the morsel, or *corsnæd,* seems to have been most used by the clergy." Laughlin, *op. cit.* 302. It "was undergone by the accused undertaking to swallow a piece of barley bread, or a piece of cheese, of the weight of an ounce; in which, if he succeeded without serious difficulty, he was deemed innocent, but if he choked and grew black in the face, he was adjudged guilty." Bigelow, History of Procedure (1880) 326.

ment. But in actions touching debt and tangible property the common means of proof are oath and witnesses. The oath is either the oath of the party alone or his oath supported by that of a number of oath-helpers, varying according to the case, who swear that his oath "is clean and free from falsity." Regulation of the oath in Anglo-Saxon law seems to have been especially complicated.[8] Witnesses are of two kinds: transaction witnesses and community witnesses. Transaction witnesses are pre-appointed witnesses, persons called in to attest the sale, loan or other transaction in controversy. Community witnesses, on the other hand, are persons who because of their residence in a given neighborhood or community are presumably conversant with local situations or happenings. But neither transaction witnesses nor community witnesses depose as to facts. They merely swear to the truth of the party's assertion, just as does the party himself in the case of proof by oath. Obviously there is nothing here like what we know as evidence, directed towards influencing conviction: all is addressed to satisfying the prescribed form. And satisfy the form it must. It is not enough that the oath appears to have been taken in good conscience: it must observe to the minutest details what is appointed for word and act. Any stumbling or stammering, any variation from what has been ordained as to gesture or bodily position, is fatal: the oath is then said to have "burst," and the proving party has lost his cause. Behind this is the idea that the event has signalized divine decision: only in perfect accomplishment of the proof is seen the Deity's acceptance of the assertion sought to be proved. The name "judgment of God" is specifically given to the decision by ordeal, but the whole field of proof responds to the same notion.

Before it came to proof each of the parties had been required to give an undertaking secured by pledges that he would abide the outcome of the proof. Under the early Germanic rule it was this undertaking that enabled a successful plaintiff to obtain satisfaction of his claim, since it afforded a basis for private execution. And this rule long endured in

[8] Brunner, *op. cit.* 398.

Anglo-Saxon law. "Final judgment, when obtained, could . . . not be directly enforced. The successful party had to see to gathering the 'fruits of judgment,' as we say, for himself. In case of continued refusal to do right according to the sentence of the court, he might take the law into his own hands, in fact wage war upon his obstinate opponent."[4] To what extent, by the time of the Conquest change had come about toward evolving a judicial judgment of recovery or acquittal, according to the result of the proof, with judicial aid in its enforcement, remains a matter of conjecture. Under Roman ideas, resulting from ecclesiastical influence—the bishops and other church dignitaries commonly sat as members of the courts—it is highly probable that some development of the kind had taken place. This manner of judgment was the rule in the earliest Anglo-Norman times and there is no reason for supposing any very violent departure in this regard from the methods immediately pre-existing.

§ 2. The Norman Inquest

The procedure which the Normans carried to England was one largely shaped by the institutions of the Frankish kingdom from which they had wrested their dukedom. It was a procedure basically similar to that of the conquered country, more highly developed in some respects, more formalized in others. But it included two institutions unknown to the Anglo-Saxon law. One was the judicial duel, more commonly spoken of in English law as trial by battle; the other was the inquest. The former need not detain us. It took its place alongside the ordeals as a "judgment of God," expressly so called; it found considerable employment, also, in civil procedure, soon cut down, however, to certain cases of trial of title to land; but though enduring in letter until the nineteenth century, it ceased to be of any substantial importance after the thirteenth.[5] Very different was the case of the inquest, for it was from this in its later form that the procedure of the common law was to de-

4 Pollock, English Law before the Norman Conquest (1898) 14 L.Q.Rev. 291, 297, reprinted in Expansion of the Common Law (1904) 139, 146.

5 2 Pollock & Maitland, 632-634; 1 Holdsworth, 309-310.

rive its characteristic lineaments. Origin of the inquest is to be seen in the old institution of community witnesses. The Frankish kings had laid hold of this institution, prevailing in their dominions as in other Germanic lands, and had adapted it to a new use. Especially in the collection of revenue did it offer a potent aid, but it could be made to serve for other purposes also. So in matters relating to the revenue or to the commission of crime and to a limited extent, also, in civil controversies, it became the practice for the royal authority to summon men of the particular community who, after being sworn, were required to answer questions as to facts, likely to be within their knowledge, concerning the subject-matter under inquiry. It was not a case of their swearing to a ready-made formula, as did the original community witnesses, but of stating, under their oath, the actual facts which they were able to disclose. The result afforded the basis for appropriate further proceedings, and in the limited circle of civil controversies thus dealt with, was recognized as means of proof.[6] From the feature of questioning the institution received the name of *inquisitio* or inquest. This mode of proceeding was borrowed by the Normans and became an integral part of their procedure on the Continent. And it was this that came with them to England. There it was speedily put into application for the purposes both of administration and of justice. Striking witness in the former regard is the compilation of Domesday Book whose data were assembled from inquests held throughout the land.

One consideration must here be added. The judgment of the old popular courts, as has been seen, was merely a proof-judgment. But various causes had been contributing in the Frankish law, and resultingly in the Norman, to introduce the idea of a definitive final judgment of recovery or acquittal, consequent upon the proof-judgment. In particular, this idea prevailed in the case of the inquest, whose declaration was attended by just such a judgment,[7] but it had come to dominate generally in the prerogative justice of Frankish king and

[6] Brunner, *Entstehung*, 84, 86.

[7] *Ibid.* 125; Brunner, *Forschungen zur Geschichte des deutschen und französischen Rechtes* (1894) 242.

Norman duke. Thus it is that in Norman England, whatever may have been the case in the last days of the Anglo-Saxon procedure, the procedure of the King's Court, irrespective of the means of proof employed, is seen from the outset culminating in this manner of judgment.[8]

§ 3. Royal Justice and the Award of Writs

The Normans did not thrust their procedure upon their new subjects. On the contrary, they permitted the communal courts to carry on as before. Only in the dispensation of justice at the hands of the Crown did their own modes of proceeding come into play. And the province of this royal justice was at first a very narrow one, being confined to matters involving the lands or revenues of the King and controversies among his barons and principal men, with occasional extension to other instances as dictated by royal favor. But parcel of the royal justice was the inquest. Just as the setting on foot of an inquest was a prerogative of the ruler in the Frankish kingdom and in Normandy, so it continued to be in England. The superiority of the inquest procedure over the old formal methods of proceeding could not fail, however, to make itself evident and create a demand on the part of litigants for admission to the precincts of royal justice. Nothing could have better suited the Crown, for in acceding to the demand a means was offered not only of extending the royal authority but also, and what may perhaps have been of more immediate importance to the ruler at the time, of increasing the royal revenue by putting a money price upon that admission. Thus, following a practice which had obtained in Normandy, there began the issue by the Chancellor of royal letters known as *brevia* or writs,—and specifically as *brevia originalia* or original writs—authorizing the King's Court to take jurisdiction over the plaintiff's demand and requiring the defendant in one way or another to make answer in that court. The repeated issue of a writ based upon a given set of circumstances established a precedent for its later issue when like circumstances came to be presented and

[8] See Bigelow, History of Procedure, C. X.

thus gave rise to the recognition that an action lay under those circumstances,—created in other words a form of action cognizable in the King's Court. As might be expected under a feudal régime, these writs at first are chiefly concerned with disputes concerning land and rights arising from land ownership. That this is so in the twelfth century sufficiently appears in the book ascribed to Glanvill, but it also appears that resort to the King's justice in this sphere has ceased to be entirely optional, for it is now the law that a man cannot be compelled to answer for his free tenement without the royal writ.[9] And Bracton in the next century leaves us in no doubt that for the King's Court land relations are still the most important subject-matter of jurisdiction. Thus came into existence the real actions—actions which for a considerable period dominate the scene, but which, by reason of their formidable apparatus of technicality, will have largely fallen out of use before the time of Blackstone. But even in the twelfth century, though occasion is yet rare, a man can, by paying heavily, purchase a writ for the recovery of a debt. And the succeeding century, making more popular the invocation of royal justice and extending it to new fields, yields, through the same process of granted writ, the rest of the personal actions, some, however, as yet in embryo. As the number of writs increased, the power thus exercised by the Chancellor in their issuance came to be the subject of jealous concern on the part of the barons. To this was due a provision in Magna Charta (1215), soon, however, to be circumvented, which materially diminished the scope of the royal writ in respect of titles to land.[10] More important was the fact that by the Provisions of Oxford (1258) they exacted from the Chancellor an oath that he would seal no writs save writs of course—those, that is to say, which had attained the stage of precedent—"without the commandment of the King and his council who shall be present." The annulment of the Provisions five years later seems not to have restored the Chancellor's former freedom in this respect, for in

[9] Glanvill, Lib. XII, cc. 2, 25; 1 Pollock & Maitland, 147; Plucknett, A Concise History of the Common Law (4th ed. 1948) 338.

[10] Maitland, The Forms of Action (ed. of 1936) 41; 1 Holdsworth, 58-59.

1285 came that famous provision of the Statute of Westminster II which authorized the clerks of the chancery to make new writs in *consimili casu* with such as were already in existence. Whatever might have been the case had it been given a more liberal construction, this statute marks a definite check upon the writ-issuing power. Except for the later development under the statutory authority which gave us the action of trespass on the case and its derivatives, the tally of writs was complete, the area of common-law justice determined.

The King's Court of which we have been speaking—the *Curia Regis*—is in principle the King's Council, the group of secular and ecclesiastical dignitaries who are called upon to act as the royal advisers. But in the practice of the twelfth century "any court held in the King's name by the King's delegates is *Curia Regis*." [11] In the course of the thirteenth, however, the Council gradually throws out those definite branches which become the Courts of Exchequer, Common Pleas and King's Bench. Save for trespass and other torts of a criminal flavor, cognizable by the King's Bench, original jurisdiction over the ordinary civil controversies resides in the Common Pleas. Fiction, however, as time goes on, is instrumental in placing the other two courts on a substantial parity with the Common Pleas in this regard, except for the real actions which, until their nineteenth century abolition, belong to it alone. These are the three "superior courts at Westminster," whose individual identities come to an end only with the Judicature Act of 1873.

The development which had thus made paramount the justice of the King, operated along with lesser factors, to reduce to a position of insignificance not only the old communal courts but also the feudal courts attendant upon the Conquest, which followed like forms of proceedings. So such fragments of the Anglo-Saxon procedure as were preserved in these courts gradually perished. If we see there a good measure of the old forms in the fourteenth century there is little of them left in the eighteenth.

[11] 1 Pollock & Maitland, 153.

§ 4. The Jury

The system of writs is one of the two phenomena that furnish the key to the future development. The other is the existence in the writ procedure of the inquest as mode of proof. We say mode of proof, for it is not yet a mode of trial: its verdict for some centuries will stand much upon the same basis as proof under the older law. Other modes of proof the King's Court recognizes for civil controversies, principal of which is the judicial duel and in actions of debt that appeal to oath which, from the Norman usage, is known as "wager of law." But it is the inquest that pre-eminently distinguishes the royal procedure, and wins it the favor of litigants; soon, indeed, it will thrust these other methods into the background. Employed as an administrative instrumentality from the outset of Norman dominion, the inquest appears as a regular feature of civil litigation under the reign of Henry II: the grand assize, the petty assizes, and the *jurata,* now seen to be functioning, are all forms of the inquest.[12] It is the last mentioned of these that stamps the institution with the enduring name of jury.

We have seen how in their history the members of the jury are linked up with the community witnesses of old. It is long before they lose the character of witnesses. The early jury speaks of its own knowledge or of knowledge derived directly or indirectly from others outside of court. It is because of this recognized or presumptive knowledge that its members are chosen.[13] Like their prototypes they are still the mouthpiece of community information. In the words of Maitland's classic passage, "the verdict of the jurors is not just the verdict of twelve men; it is the verdict of a *pays,* a 'country,' a neighborhood, a community." [14] Sometimes, indeed, the jurors unite with other witnesses in their declaration.[15] Only by a slow and imperceptible process running throughout five centuries does the jury come to be solely triers of fact upon the evidence presented. The change is far advanced in the 1500s, but the

[12] 1 Pollock & Maitland, 149; 1 Holdsworth, 327 *et seq.*

[13] Thayer, Preliminary Treatise on Evidence (1898) 90 *et seq.*

[14] 2 Pollock & Maitland, 624.

[15] Thayer, *op. cit.* 97, 102.

following century will close before it can be looked upon as in all respects complete,[16] and the employment of the jury can be definitely regarded under all circumstances as a mode of trial rather than a mode of proof. But the number of the ordinary jury, notwithstanding some early fluctuation, is fixed at twelve almost from the outset of its history,[17] and the requirement of unanimity in its verdict is settled upon in the fourteenth century.[18]

§ 5. Influence of the Jury upon Procedure

As a direct outgrowth of one of the old modes of proof, the jury was a bridge from the primitive system. In the Germanic lands of the Continent the medieval influx of the Italianized Roman law broke up, with greater or less violence, the traditional procedure; in what is now Germany utterly destroyed it. In those countries the new system stands out in the sharpest of contrast with the old. But in England the case is far otherwise; for the new represents a gradual development from the old. For this we owe principal thanks to the jury, as an adaptation of a traditional form. The jury thus served to carry into the developing procedure characteristic features of the Germanic system. The old proof-judgment, remaining intact in the case of wager of law, had in the case of the jury its representative in the order commanding the sheriff that he cause twelve men to come;[19] the order "that a jury come" may, indeed, be found in records of the present day. More significant, however, is the circumstance that with the jury there was carried along the same manner of hearing as distinguished the Germanic law. The old Germanic hearing "was always an allegation-hearing, a hearing not upon the facts but upon the mutual averments of the parties, directed to the ascertainment, by judgment of the court, of the allegation to be proved."[20] So long as the jury retains its original character, so long as its members have not lost wholly the character of

16 1 Holdsworth, 334-336.
17 Thayer, *op. cit.* 85.
18 *Ibid.* 86.
19 2 Pollock & Maitland, 602, note 4.
20 Millar, The Fortunes of the Demurrer (1936) 31 Ill. L. Rev. 429, 430-431.

witnesses, this is the manner of hearing that we see in the courts of common law. And it is this circumstance that, when a different manner of hearing was called into being, left stamped upon the allegations that importance which, although diminishing, they wear even today—an importance incomparably greater than has ever been theirs in the Romanized systems of the Continent. The jury, also, brought with it the old orality of allegation: the days of oral pleading loom large in its career and their vestiges still persist. That the allegations could not well have remained oral in a literate world, without some written prologue or supplementation may be conceded, but if the principle had not been changed we might today be following some such practice in this regard as obtains in the courts of France and Germany. Just when the change occurred cannot be stated with any exactness; the indications, however, point to the middle years of the 1400s as the period of transition.[21] And, finally, when we ascribe, as we must, to the presence of the jury that distinctive discipline of allegation which appears in the common-law courts, it is to be remembered that, though its achievement has been aided by the influence of the medieval Roman law, this discipline has its roots in the crude altercation of the Germanic lawsuit, and, despite all its sophistication, is directed to a like end, that of ascertaining the precise theme of decision by the coöperative activity of the parties.

It was the existence of the jury, also, that originated our distinctive system of evidence. When it had come to pass in the evolution of the jury that the testimony of witnesses was regularly presented to the jurors on the hearing of the cause, the tradition surrounding the institution demanded that it be conveyed to them *viva voce*. Indeed, it would have been a wholly unnatural thing for such a body to proceed by the use of testimony previously taken in writing. And an even wider tradition dictated that this testimony should be heard in open court. Moreover, if we look at contemporary courts governed by the Romano-canonical law, we see reigning there, along with written evidence produced by secret examination, that

[21] 3 Holdsworth, (1923) 640 *et seq.*; Millar, *op. cit.* 444.

formal system of proof-evaluation, which considers two unexceptionable witnesses as full-proof, one as but half-proof and assigns lesser fractional values to lesser items of evidence, binding the judge by the arithmetical result even in the teeth of his own conviction. If a statute prescribed a given manner of proof for a particular case, the jury must obey it,[22] but this apart, nothing of the sort made its way into the common-law courts. And what kept it out was the jury itself. "The original character of the jury as witnesses, which had not yet become wholly effaced in the 1500s and 1600s, was a complete barrier to any reception by the common law of a rule declaring that this or that number of witnesses was essential to proof of a fact.[23] As for the further manifestations of the canonical principle in the assignment of predetermined values to items of proof, the very nature of the jury as a body of laymen forbade their admission, since these could only be applied by a trier of fact with professional training." [24] To be sure, in the field of evidence, as in the field of pleading, our law developed a discipline of its own. But this was a discipline consisting not in rules for the evaluation of proof, but in rules for regulating its admission. "The greatest and most remarkable offshoot of the jury," says Thayer, "was that body of excluding rules which chiefly constitute the 'English Law of Evidence.' " [25] It was a regimen largely in terms of exclusion, for it aimed at keeping from the jurors evidence thought likely to mislead them or to furnish an unsafe basis for their conclusion. In modern eyes it became a regimen pushed to extremes—extremes from which for a considerable time past we have been retreating.

§ 6. The Court of Chancery

Wisely or not, bounds had been set to the province of common-law justice as the effect of the Statute of Westminster II. Moreover, the equity by which in a former day the common-law judges were tempering their judgments had

[22] See Thayer, *op. cit.* 179.

[23] Citing Wigmore, Evidence, § 2032.

[24] Millar, The Formative Principles of Civil Procedure (1923) 18 Ill.L. Rev. 103-104, and as reprinted in Engelmann-Millar, History of Continental Civil Procedure (1927) 48.

[25] Thayer, *op. cit.* 180.

scarcely survived the 1200s.[26] Under these circumstances it was imperative that the ever-growing need for new and wider remedies should be met by new means. What would have happened had not this means presented itself in the rise of the Court of Chancery is an interesting subject of speculation, but we know that English law would have worn a different face. With its origin in the power residing in the King's grace to give exceptional relief to petitioners as occasion demanded, the exercise of which gradually passed to the Chancellor, the Court of Chancery emerges to view as a distinct judicial tribunal in the course of the 1400s. What called it into existence was not so much, perhaps, the necessity of supplementing the justice of the common-law courts as the interference of the great and powerful with the administration of the common-law processes. But, as the strengthened hand of the central government effaced conditions of the latter sort, the activity of the court became confined to supplying the deficiency or inadequacy of common-law remedy, to the work, in Maitland's phrase, of "composing an appendix" [27] to the common law. By the 1500s and 1600s the general lines of its jurisdiction had become fairly well drawn.[28] Despite the hostility of the Parliament and jealous opposition on the part of the common-law courts, it grew in power and constructiveness, and in the course of its career unrolled that vast body of legal principle which we know as "equity." The field of law thus existing offers an interesting parallel to the equity of the Roman praetor, which at the outset quite as sharply contrasted with the rules of the civil law which it was called upon to complement. But being administered as parcel of the general law applicable to the case in hand and not in a separate court or separate proceeding, Roman equity became absorbed by the body of that law, with the result of a coalescence so complete as to render the two sets of rules indistinguishable save as a matter of historical inquiry. Quite otherwise has been the case with the equity of the English law. Its long administration by a sepa-

[26] 2 Holdsworth, 346.

[27] Maitland, Outlines of English Legal History, in Collected Papers (1911) 495.

[28] 1 Holdsworth, 454.

rate tribunal, the general prohibition of resort to equity where there existed a remedy at law, the reluctance of the common-law courts to receive any of its principles, in short the rigid maintenance in judicature of the boundaries between the two fields of jurisdiction, imparted to English equity the character of a distinct body of law. So strongly has this character been impressed upon it that it is now too late to hope for any such fusion as occurred in the Roman system. Short of some nihilistic legal revolution, it is safe to say that, so long as the Anglo-American law endures, men will continue to speak of equitable principles as distinguished from legal. The most that we can do—and this in large measure has already been accomplished—is to provide for an administrative fusion whereby both kinds of rules may be applied by the same court in the same cause.

In the new court there developed a new manner of procedure—a procedure quite unlike that of the common-law courts. The court came into existence with an ecclesiastical aura; it was popularly known as a court of conscience;[29] its earliest Chancellors were ecclesiastical dignitaries, and their subordinates for a long period were usually men skilled in the canon law. It is not to be wondered at, therefore, that the formation of its procedure drew heavily upon the principles obtaining in the English ecclesiastical courts which had modelled their practice chiefly upon the summary procedure that the Papacy had introduced by the *Clementina saepe* of 1306. But it drew also, and in important measure, upon the procedure of the common-law courts. The development was a gradual one; its beginnings were crude and haphazard; but by the close of the seventeenth century[30] the system had been reduced to fixed principle and assigned the main features which were thereafter to characterize it. In this system there is no jury; evidence of witnesses is not heard *viva voce* but by means of written depositions taken in secret; and the plead-

[29] "And the court of the chauncerie is called of the common people the court of conscience, because that the chauncellor is not strained by rigour or forme of wordes of lawe to judge but *ex æquo* and *bono,* and according to conscience as I have said." Sir Thomas Smith, *De Republica Anglorum* (ed. Alston, 1906) 71.

[30] 9 Holdsworth, (1926) 335.

ings, while definitely regulated, have no need of the rigid discipline which rules them at common law. One might suppose that, untrammeled by the jury, the system would have taken over the canonical proof-rules, but only in small part are they suffered to affect it—"a striking evidence of the influence radiating from the courts of Westminster and of the independence of English lawyers." [81] The basic idea, however, of the court's jurisdiction,—although this will later in some sort be departed from—is that it acts *in personam* and not *in rem*—that consequently it can operate upon property rights only by compulsion of the person; and this idea finds reflection in the procedure. It is reflected in the writ of *subpoena* by which the defendant is summoned to answer under a money penalty; in the mechanism of discovery by which he is forced to make disclosure under oath; in the writ of injunction by which he is laid under direct command; and finally in the contempt process by which he is forced to obey the orders of the court. Injunction and contempt process are the means whereby the court can bend the defendant to its will, and this, after conclusion of the famous controversy between Coke and Ellesmere, even to the extent of neutralizing a judgment of the common-law court. They are the means whereby the court is enabled to give effective remedy adjusted to the particular situation and afford a compass of specific relief undreamt of in the contemporary courts of the Continent.

§ 7. External Characteristics of the Development

One salient fact in this development is the comparatively small part played by legislation. Statutes there are which from time to time influence its course, but these are aimed at what in retrospect are seen to be little more than details, however important these details may be. Nor can we except from this statement the statutory provision of 1285 which checked the flow of writs, for although its effect was to circumscribe the province of common-law judicature, this was an effect far be-

[81] Millar, The Formative Principles of Civil Procedure (1923) 18 Ill.L. Rev. 104, and as reprinted in Engelmann-Millar, History of Continental Civil Procedure (1927) 49.

yond its contemplation; all that it aimed at was to release in some measure the fetter which lay upon the hand of the Chancellor. Edward I is called the "English Justinian," but the only procedural legislation of his reign which stands out conspicuously at the present day is this very provision of the Statute of Westminster II and that other provision of the same statute to which is ascribed the origin of the bill of exceptions. Neither before nor after down to the era of reconstruction in the nineteenth century is there any procedural statute that can be regarded as epoch-making, any that affects the basic character of the system. Especially pronounced is the lack of legislative furtherance in the case of the Court of Chancery. That court, coming into existence without legislative aid, needed none either to found its procedure or to assign to that procedure its distinctive features. It is only rarely, therefore, that we can point to a legislative source for any rule of procedure in either part of the system. Not in legislation but in the activity of the courts and the bar is to be found the principal agency of the development. From the courts came that multitude of rules, which, with the few legislative exceptions, formed the body of procedure. What operated here and gave to the system the continuity which, for better or worse, was its portion was the silent progress of practice aided and fixed by judicial decision, sometimes in the later centuries, and especially in the Court of Chancery, by formal order or rule of court.

Ideas borrowed from the Romano-canonical law had influenced the common-law procedure in its infancy, but this influence had ceased by the close of the thirteenth century. The same source, through the medium of the ecclesiastical courts, had, in a later day, contributed much to the architecture of the chancery procedure. As soon, however, as the main framework had been completed, the Romano-canonical influence here, too, ceased to operate. In both cases further growth was from within, unaided by impetus from without. English civil procedure thus became a sealed book to all but Englishmen—a completely insulated system which did not look beyond itself. Even those courts in England which proceeded according to

Romano-canonical principles, the ecclesiastical courts and the Court of Admiralty, were regarded by the men of Westminster Hall as a species of oddity; they might have a procedure, but it was nothing that could be spoken of in the same breath with the general procedure of the land: certainly not a procedure from which any lessons were to be drawn. This attitude of detachment gave rise to the belief that English procedure excelled every other; the note of self-sufficiency and superiority runs throughout: we hear it from Fortescue in the fifteenth century, from Sir Thomas Smith in the sixteenth and no one can doubt that it rings sufficiently clear from Blackstone. It was only just that pride should be taken in trial by jury, as contrasted with the methods of trial in Continental countries, but this should not have blinded to the merits possessed by their systems in other respects. English procedure definitely retarded its progress by thus shutting itself off from the procedural community. For one thing, it denied admission to fructifying notions by whose aid it might have anticipated some of the principal items of present-day reform, which, brought about by experiences of utility, have done no more than put us abreast of long-standing Continental rules. And, again, it wholly foreclosed any incentive to scholarly study of its principles, and left them to the care of men who, however skilled in the practice of the law, had no glimmering of the law as a science and assuredly none of procedure as other than a mere professional tool. Had the case been otherwise, we could hardly have expected to see English lawyers, generally, sitting at the feet of Damhouder or Gaill or any other of those international figures in the world of Continental procedure, but if the genius of John Selden had been induced to irradiate the English field with the light of his cosmopolitan learning, the system would have vastly profited by the result.

Screened thus from any external contacts, certain that the paths which it had been following were the true ones, English civil procedure was, for the time being, impervious to any movement for cardinal reform. Looking abroad, we see the German States from the sixteenth century onward incessantly occupied with codes of procedure; we see the great unifying

Ordonnance civile which, thanks to the energy of a Colbert, Louis XIV adopted for his dominions in 1667; we see toward the close of the eighteenth century, the ambitious, though much too radical, procedural legislation of Frederick the Great and his successor, and the equally comprehensive but more conservative code of Austria, enacted some months after the death of Maria Theresa. But none of these efforts found echo in England. Contemporary England was not only proof against any movement of the kind; except for the interlude of the Commonwealth, no such movement is even discernible. Though Bacon, in office, had contributed distinctly to improving the details of the chancery system, his proposals for the amendment of the law, of which he has bequeathed us a sketch,[32] leave quite untouched the field of procedure, except as they make it plain that he was against any conjoined administration of law and equity.[33] The twelve years of the Commonwealth, however, witnessed strenuous demand for the reform of judicial institutions, and various projects addressed to that end. While, as a result, there ensued numerous changes now recognized as anticipations of enduring changes later to come,[34] it was only in small degree that the rules of procedure were affected. An Ordinance adopted in 1654 envisaged extensive reform of the chancery practice, but in a manner to defeat its own ends. It sought to prescribe an inflexible regimen [35] quite out of keeping with the nature of the court and the purposes of its jurisdiction, as illustrated by its requirement that all causes were to be heard on the single day for which they were set down. "It was bitterly attacked by the bar and not unjustly," says Robinson, "for it aimed with more earnestness than skill at rapidity, simplicity and cheapness." [36] The opposition, as well as its intrinsic defects themselves, rendered it ineffective and it soon became virtually a dead letter. A few of

[32] In the Advancement of Learning, Works, Vol. IX (ed. Spedding *et al.*, 1864) 311 *et seq.*

[33] *Ibid.* 323.

[34] Robinson, Anticipations under the Commonwealth of Changes in the Law, 1 Select Essays in Anglo-American Legal History (1907) 467; Inderwick, The Interregnum (1891) 201.

[35] Kerly, An Historical Sketch of the Equitable Jurisdiction of the Court of Chancery (1890) 161.

[36] Robinson, *op. cit.* 471.

its better provisions were subsequently incorporated in orders made by the Restoration Chancellor, but, this fact apart, it left no impression. For the rest need only be noted two changes made in the procedure of the common-law courts. One was the substitution of English for Latin as the language of pleading and of the record, the other the right accorded to the defendant to dispense with the use of special pleas in all actions. Both were swept away by one of the first acts of the Restoration Parliament,[37] the former, however, to be reinstated by the Act of 1731.[38] Thus, although the movement was a vigorous one, its actual accomplishment, even while the Commonwealth lasted, was but slender. With the Restoration the movement came to an end, and the system of civil procedure, like other institutions which the Republican period had agitated, resumed its wonted tenor. As the eighteenth century draws to a close we find that the legislature and the courts have made further contribution of minor improvement, but also that dissatisfaction with the ways of civil judicature has from time to time been coming to utterance. Soon is to be heard the voice of Bentham expressing that dissatisfaction with unmistakable emphasis and laying down those postulates which are in time to furnish material for reconstruction. But the era of reconstruction is yet in the distance.

[37] (1660) 12 Car. II, c. 3, §§ 4, 5.

[38] (1731) 4 Geo. II, c. 26.

Chapter III

ENGLISH CIVIL PROCEDURE IN THE EARLY NINETEENTH CENTURY

So it is that England entered the nineteenth century with the system of civil justice which this manner of growth had created. To the objective eye, a system bizarre enough despite the solid merits which lie behind its baroque façade. For the outsider, what first bewilders is the dichotomy of jurisdiction, the separate administration of common law and equity. The jurist trained in a Roman-descended system is familiar with the idea of equity, but for him it is the element that supplies the deficiencies or corrects the rigors of the legal rule in the very application of that rule; it represents the *nobile officium judicis* that prevents the legal rule from working an uncontemplated injustice, not something to be invoked collaterally to the administration of the legal rule: always it is coadjuvant and coefficient. To one so trained, how strange the phenomenon of equity being administered in a separate court, not even a court of supervisory or corrective jurisdiction; how startling the idea that, by the law of the land, a man may be the owner of a thing in one court and not in another, that, by the same token, one court, in an action pending before it, will be oblivious to a defense that another court will recognize and protect! And when he learns, resultingly, that "in many cases parties in the course of the same litigation are driven from courts of law to courts of equity and from courts of equity to courts of law," [1] acute, indeed, would be the foreign observer who could here discern the earmarks of a well-ordered system. Little wonder that a learned French magistrate, visiting the English courts in the third decade of the century, could refer to the separation as a factitious thing, and speak of the Court of Chancery as "a useless and embarrassing superfoetation,

[1] First Report of the Commissioners on the Court of Chancery (1852) quoted in Francis, The New Common Law Procedure (1854) 250-251.

adapted only to originate conflicts and a confusion of jurisdiction, detrimental to the true interests of the litigants."[2] But the notion of this separation, despite its accidental origin, had been so bred in the bone of the legal profession, as it still is to a not inconsiderable extent in America, that it wore the aspect of something dictated by nature, something integral to the processes of civil justice.

If we turn to the common-law courts, we see here a procedure, with jury trial as its nucleus, affording a striking contrast to anything known on the Continent. Its action system, comparable only to the most ancient Roman—that of the *legis actiones*—offers to the intending plaintiff a variety of pigeonholes rigidly partitioned, each for the reception of a particular manner of demand. If he chooses the wrong one, disaster may be the result. If his demand will fit in none, let him go hence; perhaps the Court of Chancery will aid him, perhaps not—it is all one to the court of common law. These pigeonholes represent the forms of action, brought into being by the royal letters known as the original writ, crystallized into precedent by the aid of the *Registrum Brevium*. Aforetime they were highly numerous: time and change have reduced their active list to a comparatively small group. Debt, covenant, assumpsit, trespass, trespass on the case, trover, detinue, replevin, ejectment, find frequent employment. A few others occasionally appear, but those named are the everyday actions, principal survivors of a once mighty host. Mark, also, that this scheme of actions, though extending to the controversies of most common occurrence, covers but a limited field of judicature. It permits a plaintiff, satisfying the requirements of legal interest, to obtain an award of money, of personal property, of real property, but beyond this it can seldom go. It can give him no preventive relief, it has no means of adjusting conflicts of rights other than in terms of recovery or non-recovery of the thing demanded, and even where it concedes specific recovery of property its processes lack a full measure of effectiveness.[3]

[2] 2 Rey, *Des Institutions judiciaires de l'Angleterre comparées avec celles de la France* etc. (1826) 19.

[3] See Langdell's fine account of the contrast of remedy between law and equity in A Brief Survey of Equity Jurisdiction (2d ed. 1908) 19 *et seq.*

Here, too, flourishes uniquely that recondite method of preparatory allegation which we call common-law pleading. Allegation in the systems of other lands is an humble servitor, dismissed when it has discharged its purely informative function; here it is lord and master, tyrannizing over the substantive law, at times trampling it under foot. The roots of its prepotence are to be found in its lineage. Alone of the Germanic nations, England has preserved the Germanic idea that the parties themselves, by their mutual averments, shall formulate in concrete terms the theme of decision. Out of the crudity of the old *thwert-ut-nay,* through coalescence of Romano-canonical borrowings with the Germanic rule that whatever is not denied stands admitted, there has long ago emerged the principle requiring the parties to plead either by way of traverse or by way of confession and avoidance. And, just as in the old Germanic system the contraposition of assertion and denial had furnished the very terms of the formula to which was addressed the oath of the party or, within the narrow sphere of witness activity, the oath of the witnesses, so here the interplay of party allegation has for centuries been evolving, in the production of issue, the theme for the sworn declaration of the twelve, themselves the descendants, through the Norman inquest, of the Germanic community witnesses. From Germanic rudiments has come the demurrer—an institution with no precise Continental counterpart—by which, on a point of law, the proceeding might often be brought to an abrupt and sometimes untimely end. As on the Continent, place has been given to preliminary defenses of fact—the dilatory pleas of the common law—although in this regard the union of Germanic and Romano-canonical ideas has engendered a sullen brood, ruled for the most part with an iron hand.

But around the central principle of progression to issue there has been contrived a discipline artificial and intricate and not always consistent with itself. The necessities of regulation have emphasized the requirement of singleness, so that the jury might not be perplexed by a multiplicity of points—a requirement alleviated in the case of the plaintiff by the use of plural counts; in the case of the defendant, from 1705 on, by the permission to plead more than one plea. Counteracted, too, it has been, by the recognition, wholly at war with the requirement itself, of the so-called general issues, no two of which have precisely the same range and which in the most commonly used actions—assumpsit and trespass on the case—utterly falsify the idea of presenting a single point for decision. Moreover, no principle dictates what matters may or may not be admitted in evidence under a given general issue: resort must be had to the arbitrary rule applying to the particular form of action. This arbitrariness is matched in the case of the replication *de injuria,* the thorny doctrines of which had come to expression in *Crogate's Case.*[4] Not much there is of exaggeration in the satirical gloss which divides the cases of this replication into those: "First, when *de injuria* may clearly be replied. Secondly, when it clearly cannot be replied. Thirdly, when it is probable that it may be replied. Fourthly, when it is probable it cannot be replied. And, fifthly, when it is altogether doubtful whether it can or cannot be replied."[5] A mingling of logic and illogic, not untinctured by tricklings of medieval scholasticism, appears throughout the whole discipline. It has yielded the special traverse with its enigmatic negation, the plea to the further maintenance of the action, the plea *puis darrein continuance;* has elaborated the learning of profert and oyer, of color, of protestation, of duplicity, of anticipation, of departure, of new assignment, of repleader, of aider, and other like positive and negative phases of enginery; has, in short, constructed an arcanum of forensic statement penetrable only by the initiate.

The very language of allegation is strange. Pleading talks with a Latin accent, barbarian not Ciceronian. When, as a result of the statute of 1731,[6] English was substituted for Latin as the medium of averment, what the practitioners largely did was to adopt as nearly literal a translation as possible of the forms of allegation theretofore employed. Hence it is that we have such expressions as "force and arms" and "breaking the

[4] 8 Coke 66b (1608).

[5] Hayes, Crogate's Case: A Dialogue In Ye Shades on Special Pleading Reform (1853) as reprinted in 9 Holdsworth, History of English Law (1926) Appendix, 430.

[6] 4 Geo. II, c. 26.

close"; hence it is that there appears such an un-English locution as that "with feet in walking" (*pedibus calcando*) the defendant wasted the plaintiff's grass. In allegation, too, legal fiction finds commodious lodgment. Witness the common counts in assumpsit solemnly averring the making and breaking of promises inexistent save in juristic metaphor; the losing and finding which every declaration in trover must charge, be the circumstances of conversion what they may or its subject a paper of pins or a thousand tons of coal; and the lease, entry, and ouster which in ejectment give impulse to the marionette figures of John Doe and Richard Roe. Fiction, indeed, is the constant substitute for what rationally should be alternative allegation, looking to the avoidance of accidents of proof; the plaintiff may state his claim in different ways, but for each variant statement is compelled to suppose a distinct happening, contrary to the fact.

Moreover, as part of its Germanic legacy, England has inherited something of the Germanic notion that in litigation the parties are acting at peril. *Ein Mann, ein Wort* has had here its echoes. All intendments are against the pleader, at least until after verdict, for, says Coke, "everie man is presumed to make the best of his owne case." [7] The possibilities of recovery from a false step were always restricted; after the change from oral to written allegation this restriction had become intensified. Thus the demurrer avails to attack faults of form as well as of substance; decision of the question of form may well end the case without inquiry into the merits. Only by the indulgence of the court in forestalling actual decision and allowing withdrawal of the demurrer, on the one hand, or an amendment, on the other, can finality be averted. So, where the action is met by a dilatory plea, if the issue of fact to which this gives rise is once decided in favor of the plaintiff, the defendant inevitably loses the cause, although he may have had a perfect defense on the merits. But if such a plea, constantly stigmatized as odious, is defeated on demurrer, the defendant is entitled to another chance. A grotesque inconsistency this, for that chance would be denied him had his plea

[7] Co. Litt. 303b.

not been one of the odious class. Amendment of allegation, however seasonably sought, is allowed none too freely, and down to the statutes of 1828 and 1833 [8] cannot be had at all once the record is made up for trial. Except in the simplest cases, the plaintiff can never be quite sure that his demand will attain the stage of trial, the defendant that some inadvertence will not see him cast *in toto*. So extreme is the intricacy, so meticulous the learning of this art of pleading, that its pursuit is generally in the hands of specialists, the so-called special pleaders under the bar—a tribe we would expect to see honored; instead, we find them esteemed by their brethren only as a useful variety of drudge.[9]

Different, however, is the picture when we look at the trial. In the *viva voce* examination and cross-examination of witnesses in open court, with their demeanor and mode of speech directly appreciable by the organs of decision, is present the method that yields all those advantages of orality, immediacy, and publicity to which contemporary Continental reform is already beginning to aspire.[10] Despite the as yet unmodified asperities of the rules of evidence, its superiority over the deposition method of the Continental courts and of certain English tribunals is too manifest for comment. This is the great virtue of the common-law system, going far to redeem it from the faults which, in other directions, it so strikingly discloses.

What, then, of the Court of Chancery? Here a Continental observer would feel more at home, encountering, as he would, a system not far removed from his own: the same absence of forms of action, a similar taking of evidence in writing, and, except when the aid of a common-law court is invoked for advisory purposes, the same mode of fact decision. Here, too, he would find the invaluable institution of discovery, descendant, like its Continental counterparts, of the Romano-canonical procedure of positions. The method of plead-

[8] 9 Geo. IV, c. 15; 3 & 4 Will. IV, c. 42.

[9] See 2 Rey, *op. cit.* at 188.

[10] See Millar, The Formative Principles of Civil Procedure (1923) 18 Ill. L.Rev. 104 *et seq.*, 150 *et seq.*, 156 *et seq.*, and as reprinted in Engelmann-Millar, History of Continental Civil Procedure (1927) 49 *et seq.*, 62 *et seq.*, 68 *et seq.*

ing, however, has peculiarities of its own. Ingress of common-law notions has furnished the demurrer and the plea. These and the answer are the pleading weapons of the defendant; but the answer is also the vehicle of discovery, and as a consequence the elements of discovery and of pleading proper have become so entangled as to cause frequent confusion. Of acting at peril there is comparatively little: false steps may usually be retrieved; but the system has its own arbitrarinesses, as evidenced by the rule that, even in the teeth of acknowledged law, the complainant is held to admit the legal sufficiency of a plea by the mere fact of taking issue upon it. The pleadings, though stopped at the replication, are of inordinate length: the tendency to repetition is exemplified by the nine parts of the bill, constituting, as commonly said, a tale thrice-told. Appalling such a document to a layman, though perhaps an excess of violence attended the reaction of John Wesley when he spoke of seeing "that foul monster, a chancery bill." [11] The taking of evidence in writing, as here practised, is a cumbersome and tedious operation; the examination of witnesses is conducted in secret by means of interrogatories and cross-interrogatories submitted by the parties, and the method involves the absurdity of cross-interrogatories formulated without knowledge either of what the direct interrogatories will contain or of what they will elicit. There is a wholly unnecessary multiplication of steps throughout; periphrasis and diffuseness mark the whole system.

In point of remedy, the chancery is able to supplement the conmon law with substantial adequacy once it attains to definitive action. But the result of its modes of progression is delay and enormous expense—delay comparable only to that of the Imperial Chamber of Justice of the Holy Roman Empire which, when the court sat at Speyer, evoked the quip *"Spirae lites spirant et non exspirant."* An interesting testimony in this respect is afforded by the case of *Godfrey* v. *Saunders*,[12] in 1770, wherein it appears that the plaintiff, after having "ex-

[11] The full quotation in Birrell, Changes in Equity Procedure and Principles, in A Century of Law Reform (1901) c. 6, 182.

[12] 3 Wils. 73, 94, 117, 95 E.R. 940, 953, 965.

hibited a bill in chancery against Saunders for an account, which hath been fruitlessly depending there for more than twelve years," turned at last to the Court of Common Pleas, seeking his remedy in the all but obsolete action of account, and, it may be added, recovered final judgment in that court in something less than two years. Even half a century later, four years time between the date of setting for hearing and the date of decree is nothing unusual; sometimes the passage of fifteen years may see a matter still undisposed of.[13] The insistence upon proceedings by way of revivor and supplement in the case of the death of any of the usually numerous parties is a constant source of addition to the normal retardation.[14] Indeed, the situation is such as to draw from an authoritative source, as late as 1839, the observation that "no man, as things now stand, can enter into a chancery suit with any reasonable hope of being alive at its termination, if he has a determined adversary."[15] And this is not a court, like the German tribunal we have mentioned, remote from the everyday life of the people. There come to it, and must come to it, the most vital questions of private property and personal relations: in point of the pecuniary value involved in individual cases it has to do with the most important segment of the judicial business of the country. But within its anaconda-like convolutions rights are smothered and die. The tragic picture painted by Dickens in creating for us the case of *Jarndyce* v. *Jarndyce* is not a misrepresentation.[16]

[13] Odgers, Changes in Procedure and the Law of Evidence, in A Century of Law Reform (1901) c. 7, 223.

[14] Bowen, in The Reign of Queen Victoria: A Survey of Fifty Years of Progress (1887) as extracted in 1 Select Essays in Anglo-American Legal History (1907) 526; Odgers, *op. cit.* at 223.

[15] The observation is that of Spence, author of the Equitable Jurisdiction of the Court of Chancery, quoted by Bowen, *op. cit.* at 529 of the Select Essays reprint.

[16] "Nobody who has read the two folio volumes I have already referred to [report of evidence taken by the Chancery Commission of 1824], nobody who has read Parkes' History of the Court of Chancery, can deny the essential truth of Jarndyce v. Jarndyce." Birrell, *op. cit.* at 192-193.

CHAPTER IV

AMERICAN CIVIL PROCEDURE IN THE EARLY NINETEENTH CENTURY

In America, by the opening of the nineteenth century, the crude administration of matters judicial obtaining in the early colonial period, characterized in Massachusetts and Connecticut by a dependence upon the Pentateuch and influenced elsewhere to a varying degree by intuitive notions of justice[1] rather than by any strict adherence to the laws of the mother country, has given way to an acceptance more or less complete of the English legal system and with it of English civil procedure. Yet desire for plainer methods, on the one hand, the more pressing because of the undeveloped state of the bar, and a certain jealousy of judicial power, on the other, have produced in the procedure modifications of not inconsiderable moment, the complete history of which even today remains unwritten.

The chancery jurisdiction which was the subject of irregular and intermittent exercise in colonial days, usually by the governor and council, sometimes by the assembly, sometimes by special courts of precarious tenure, sometimes by limited delegation to the ordinary tribunals,[2] is now, for the most part, a regular branch of judicature. Ordinarily, as in the federal judicial system, it is exercised by the same court that has common-law jurisdiction, but as a wholly distinct activity; in certain of the States, however, as in New York, the Court of Chancery is a separate tribunal. But that fear of chancery, which was influential in pre-Revolution times, has left its imprint in various quarters. In Massachusetts, Maine, and New

[1] See Reinsch, The English Common Law in the American Colonies, 1 Select Essays in Anglo-American Legal History (1907) 367-415.

[2] Wilson, Courts of Chancery in the American Colonies (1884) 18 Am.L. Rev. 226-255, reprinted in 2 Select Essays, *supra,* at 779-809; Gager, Equity, in Two Centuries Growth of American Law ((1901) c. 6, 130 *et seq.*

Hampshire this jurisdiction is granted by the legislature only in niggardly installments; anything like a complete equity jurisdiction is slow of attainment.[3] Pennsylvania, at the time of which we speak, has neither a court of chancery nor a chancery jurisdiction. Put to it, the common-law courts have done much to remedy the omission. The result is a curious anticipation of future general reforms. The assignee of a chose in action may sue in his own name; equitable defenses, such as misrepresentation and mistake, are permitted in common-law actions; an equitable title suffices in replevin and ejectment; the court, on rule to show cause, will often set aside a judgment on equitable grounds; and other phenomena of what a later day will call fusion between the two jurisdictions perforce make their appearance. But, bold as this course has been, it is not bold enough, and the lacuna which it leaves is not to be filled until the explicit grant to the courts of equitable powers by a process that begins in 1836 and is completed in 1857.[4] In Georgia, the same fear comes to different manifestation. Here a check upon the supposed arrogance of chancery is found in making issues of fact in equitable causes triable by jury as a matter of right.[5]

But Georgia has been pursuing her own way in another direction. By certain legislation of the latter years of the eighteenth century, culminating in the Judiciary Act of 1799,[6] she has provided for the conduct of all civil actions by petition setting forth the demand "plainly, fully and substantially" and by answer, on the part of the defendant, setting forth in like manner all necessary matters constituting "the cause of his defense." The effort thus displayed to assimilate common-law and equity pleading and to discard the common-law forms of action has, however, been successful only to a limited extent: the legislation has not been sufficiently definitive to pre-

[3] *Ibid.* at 136-138.

[4] Fisher, The Administration of Equity Through Common Law Forms in Pennsylvania (1895) 1 L.Q.Rev 455-465, reprinted in 2 Select Essays, *supra,* at 810-823; First Report of the Commissioners on Practice and Pleadings of New York (1848) 72-73.

[5] See T.U.P. Charlt. (1824) Pref. iv; *Ex parte* Grimball, *ibid.,* 153, 155 (1808); Hargreaves v. Lewis, 3 Ga. 162, 168 (1847); Nell v. Snowden, 5 Ga. 1, 4 (1848).

[6] Marbury & Crawford, Dig. (1802) 292; Prince, Dig. (1822) 205.

vent the courts from adhering, in large measure, to the traditional distinctions. So far as the boundaries of the common-law actions are concerned it has resulted in little more than the recognition of "petitions in the likenesses of those several forms of action." [7] But the legislation has decidedly curtailed the special pleading of the common law, for, under its terms, although the case is otherwise as to defenses in abatement, no replication is allowable to an answer on the merits: in the event of an affirmative defense the issues must define themselves from the evidence.[8] An interesting departure is thus disclosed which, under better auspices, might have materially changed the general course of reform in America.

Other jurisdictions exhibit modifications of lesser compass. To be noted for the chancery is the authorized waiver of answer under oath exemplified by the New York enactment of 1828, as also the New York rule-provision of 1839 applying, as between bill and answer, the common-law principle of admission by non-denial; especially notable the unsuccessful attempt of the Federal Judiciary Act of 1789 to install "oral testimony and examination of witnesses in open court" as the method of chancery trial—a measure which is ultimately to triumph, but in the federal jurisdiction not until 1912. On the common-law side, while recognition of the right of set-off is now universal, it is interesting to observe that Virginia has anticipated the English statute by nearly a hundred years in her provision of 1644 for this defense where the plaintiff is debtor to the defendant upon a "bill, bond or accompt." The same State, breaking with a leading principle of the common-law system, has in 1788 accorded the defendant the right to plead and demur at the same time. So, too, she has already laid the basis for that proceeding by notice and motion [9] which in after years is to become her favorite mode of conducting common-law actions. Kentucky in 1805 has originated, for actions upon bonds and notes, the proceeding by petition and

[7] Dissenting opinion of Benning, J., in Bishop v. Sanford, 15 Ga. 1, 22 (1854).

[8] Ray v. Dennis, 5 Ga. 357, 363 (1848); McLaren v. Birdsong, 24 Ga. 265, 269 (1858).

[9] Millar, Three American Ventures in Summary Civil Procedure (1928) 38 Yale L.J. 193, 213 *et seq.*

summons [10] which, although finally to perish, acquires for a time considerable vogue both within and without its native jurisdiction. An awakening recognition of the need of discovery in common-law actions has resulted here and there in remedial steps, at first for minor causes as in the case of the South Carolina summary process,[11] later for causes in general, beginning, perhaps, with the Mississippi statute of 1828.[12] Certain jurisdictions (*e.g.*, Connecticut, 1720, 1731) [13] have enlarged the common-law scope of the general issue in particular cases. Moreover, in sundry quarters place has been given to a "brief statement" (*e.g.*, Massachusetts, 1793; Maine, 1831) or notice (*e.g.*, New York, 1801; Massachusetts, 1836) accompanying the general issue, as a substitute for special pleas in bar,[14] and mention should also be made of the wide adoption of the rule that before a defendant may deny execution of the instrument sued upon he must make oath to his plea.

In America, therefore, the old régime appears with the traditional rules variously tempered. Betterment is being sought, but, apart from the not altogether prosperous experiment in Georgia, no essential change in plan or structure is being attempted; the reforms are still in the realm of patchwork. Due to the simpler organization of the courts and their officers and, in particular, to the localized administration of justice, the path of the litigant is not as difficult as it is in the mother country: certainly we hear of no such inordinate expense and delay in chancery suits as constitute the nightmare of contemporary England. Yet, after all, the general basis is the transplanted system, with its separate administration of law and equity, its artificial mode of common-law pleading, its repetitious and circumlocutory chancery processes.

10 *Ibid.* at 204 *et seq.*

11 *Ibid.* at 199-202.

12 "An Act to authorize and compel discoveries in courts of law in certain cases." Feb. 16, 1828, Mississippi Laws 1824-1838 (1838) 162-163.

13 Merrill v. Everett, 38 Conn. 40 (1871).

14 An account of the New York and Massachusetts development in this regard appears in the case last cited.

CHAPTER V

THE COURSE OF REFORM IN ENGLAND

The movement in England for reconstruction of the institutions of civil procedure may be said to have been definitively inaugurated by the celebrated speech of Brougham before the House of Commons on February 7, 1828. A commission appointed to consider reforms in the Court of Chancery had already reported some two years before,[1] but so far its labors had produced no legislative result. Behind the speech in question lay unmistakably the influence of Jeremy Bentham.[2] Brougham, while far from being converted to Bentham's extreme views on the subject, had nevertheless been an attentive listener to his demands for recasting the legal system, and profiting by his teachings, had become strongly impressed with the urgent need for improvement. In a masterly analysis of the whole situation of English justice, and in particular of its civil side, Brougham put forward his own temperate suggestions for remedy.[3] The main lines of the existing system were to be preserved intact, but it was to be purged of its most conspicuous faults and absurdities through the means on which he dwelt at length.[4] The speech was one of consummate

[1] Report by the Commissioners appointed to inquire into the Practice in Chancery (1826). The more important recommendations of this commission appear in the highly valuable work of Parkes, A History of the Court of Chancery (1828) 361 *et seq.*

[2] "The age of law reform and the age of Jeremy Bentham," says Brougham in the introduction to the published speech, "are one and the same. He is the father of the most important of all the branches of reform, the leading and ruling department of human improvement. No one before him had ever seriously thought of exposing the defects in our English system of jurisprudence." 2 Speeches of Henry, Lord Brougham (1838) 287.

[3] "He spoke for six hours, during which he exhausted a hatful of oranges—the only refreshment then tolerated by the rules of the House." Ball, Lincoln's Inn: Its History and Traditions (1947) 111.

[4] But in Bentham the speech evoked extreme dissatisfaction. "Two days afterwards, Bentham thus records his disgust and disappointment: 'Mr. Brougham's mountain is delivered and behold! a mouse. The wisdom of the reformer could not overcome the

eloquence, and ended on the note sounded in the now famous passage: "It was the boast of Augustus . . . that he found Rome of brick, and left it of marble. . . . But how much nobler will be the sovereign's boast when he shall have it to say that he found law dear, and left it cheap; found it a sealed book, left it a living letter; found it the patrimony of the rich, left it the inheritance of the poor; found it the two-edged sword of craft and oppression, left it the staff of honesty and the shield of innocence! [5]

As a result of the motion in support of which the speech was made, there came about, as regards civil procedure, the appointment of a commission to inquire "into the origin, progress and termination of actions in the superior courts of common law . . . and matters connected therewith." [6] This commission made a report in 1829 and again, more comprehensively, in 1830 and 1831.[7] A first response to the recommendations of the commission was the act of 1832,[8] establishing uniformity of initial process in the three common-law courts. This was a much needed reform, for in the course of the centuries, different causes had combined to produce a great diversity of means for citing the defendant into court.[9] A further act adopted in 1833 [10] continued the work of reform, in pursuance of the commission's recommendations, by a group of important provisions touching various phases of common-law procedure. Conspicuous among these provisions was that permitting amendments generally for the purpose of obviating the effect of variances arising at the trial. On the subject of pleading, after registering the opinion, in consonance with the ideas of the commission, that improvement would be effected if the questions for the jury were "left less at large

---

craft of the lawyer. Mr. Brougham after all is not the man to set up a simple, natural and rational administration of justice against the entanglements and technicalities of our English law proceedings.'" Dillon, Bentham and his School of Jurisprudence (1890) 24 Am.L.Rev. 727, 734.

[5] 2 Speeches *cit.* 485.

[6] *Ibid.* 486.

[7] Three additional reports were made by the commission, the fourth in 1832 dealing with arrest for debt, the fifth in 1833, dealing with the inferior courts, and the sixth in 1834, dealing with the matter of call to the bar.

[8] 2 Will. IV, c. 39.

[9] See 9 Holdsworth, History of English Law (1926) 249-250, where is reproduced the list appearing in the first report of the commission.

[10] 3 & 4 Will. IV, c. 42.

than they now are according to the course and practice of pleading in several forms," it authorized the judges to adopt rules for the purpose of making such alterations in the mode of pleading as they might deem expedient.

Product of this authority were the rules adopted at Hilary Term, 1834, the so-called Hilary Rules.[11] These contained a number of wise provisions such as the rule that multiple counts, on the one hand, or multiple pleas, on the other, were not to be allowed unless they were intended to set forth distinct subject-matters, or the rule which required the plaintiff in trespass *quare clausum fregit* to designate the *locus in quo* by name or abuttals. But the salient feature of the rules centered in the obedience to the principle enunciated in the act, that is to say, in their restriction of the former scope of the general issues. Thus, for example, in assumpsit on an express contract other than a bill of exchange or promissory note, the plea of *non assumpsit* was to operate as a denial only in point of fact of the contract alleged; where the action was upon a bill of exchange or promissory note, the plea was not to be allowed at all. So in an action on the case, the plea of not guilty was to operate as a denial only of the breach of duty or wrongful act alleged, and not of any fact stated in the inducement. In neither form of action was the general issue to support any defense in confession and avoidance. And, except in those special cases where the use of a wide general issue had been expressly authorized by statute, the same principle of substantially transforming that plea into a specific traverse was applied throughout.[12] The result obviously was one that paid homage to a central tenet of common-law pleading, but it proved to be wholly out of keeping with the practicalities of civil justice. It augmented immoderately the area of special pleading, originated a multitude of new pleading questions, exposed the litigant to a variety of new perils, and correspondingly increased the expense and delay of litigation. "Never," says Sir William Holdsworth, "was a more disastrous mistake made." [13] The sixteen volumes of Meeson and Welsby afford

[11] These rules are printed in 10 Bingh. 453-475. They appear also in 1 Chitty, Pleading, * 737-* 747.

[12] 9 Holdsworth, *op. cit.* 325.

[13] *Ibid. loc. cit.* With reference to pleading in the actions most commonly

lively testimony to the carnival of pleading intricacies developing under this regimen.

As regards the procedure of the Court of Chancery some measure of improvement was effected by General Orders of the court in 1828, mainly in response to recommendations appearing in the report of the chancery commission of 1825. Beginning in 1830, we meet with a series of acts directed toward the reform of the Court of Chancery.[14] This legislation, while largely occupied with the internal economy of the court, introduced certain specific procedural changes and included definite reinforcement of the rule-making power of the court.[15] Much re-regulation ensued in the exercise of that power: here the General Orders of 1833, 1837, 1841 and 1845 [16] are especially to be mentioned. But what had thus been accom-

employed, namely assumpsit, debt on simple contract and trespass on the case, it was said on high authority that "when the new rules compelled the use of special pleas in these actions, the technical and formal defects of the system, which previously had existed in some actions only, became extended to all and the inconvenience was increased in proportion. Special demurrers for want of form, and for objections of a technical nature, were much increased. From the necessity of specially pleading all defences to actions in most general use, new pleas were introduced; and defendants who had no real defence availed themselves of the chance of a temporary success by pleading subtle and tricky pleas to invite special demurrers for the mere purpose of delay." First Report of the Commission on Process, Practice and Pleading in the Superior Courts of Common Law, appointed in 1850 (1851) 20.

And there was little comfort in the thought that all this proceeded from the larger play given to a native dogma of the system. "The truth is," says Sir Frederick Pollock, "that a severely logical application of the assumed principles of pleading would have been intolerable even to a generation of formalists." The Genius of the Common Law (1912) 37.

14 (1830) 11 Geo. IV & 1 Will. IV, c. 36; (1832) 2 Will. IV, c. 33; (1832) 2 & 3 Will. IV, c. 111; (1833) 3 & 4 Will. IV, c. 84; (1833) 3 & 4 Will. IV, c. 94; (1934) 4 & 5 Will. IV, c. 82; (1835) 5 & 6 Will. IV, cc. 47, 82; (1840) 3 & 4 Vict. c. 94; (1841) 4 & 5 Vict. c. 52; (1842) 5 & 6 Vict. c. 103.

15 Notable is the provision in the act of 3 & 4 Vict. c. 94, § 1. This might have brought about a complete recasting of the chancery procedure, for, reciting that doubts might arise as to regulative power of the judges without the authority of Parliament, it conferred upon the Lord Chancellor, with the advice and consent of the Master of the Rolls and the Vice Chancellor, or one of them, for the period of five years, a very wide power to make rules, subject to rejection by Parliament, altering the system in respect of writs, pleading, discovery, mode of taking evidence and other specifically enumerated heads; but reform on any such scale had to await the act of 1852.

16 For these General Orders, see 1 Sanders, Orders of the High Court of Chancery (1845) 768, 774, 834, 875, 981.

plished, as regards the mode of proceeding, was of no great significance. Writing in 1841, Mr. Daniell, the author of the leading treatise on chancery practice, doubted whether the good of the changes made down to that time outweighed their evils. "Perhaps," he says, "the best solution of the question may be effected by referring the inquirer to the fact that notwithstanding the numerous alterations made of late years, and the almost entire removal from the Court of Chancery of the bankruptcy cases which formerly occupied so much of its time, the expenses and delays of the court are still complained of, at least as loudly, and apparently with as much justice as ever." [17] And while the General Orders which came four years later represented a distinct advance, they failed to still the complaints in question.

Thus the second half of the nineteenth century opened upon profound dissatisfaction with the procedure of both spheres of jurisdiction. Accordingly there was resort to two further commissions, appointed in 1850, the one to inquire into the common-law procedure, the other into that of chancery. The reports of the first mentioned commission had their sequel in the Common Law Procedure Acts of 1852,[18] 1854[19] and 1860.[20] With these enactments rough hands began to be laid upon the common-law mode of proceeding. The distinction of forms of action to a very considerable extent was now deprived of significance; the rules as to joinder of actions and of parties underwent decided liberalization; the system of allegation, while not departing from its essential bases, was so modified as to exclude all fictitious averments and demurrers for fault of form, as well as to minimize the sphere of special pleading; by leave of court a party might plead and demur at the same time to the same matter; the parties were authorized to waive trial by jury; a certain measure of equitable power was conferred upon the common-law courts, including the cognizance of equitable defenses and the elicitation of discovery both of facts and of documents; and various other

[17] Daniell, Practical Observations on the New Orders for the Regulation of the Practice and Proceedings of the Court of Chancery (1841) xv.

[18] 15 & 16 Vict. c. 76.

[19] 17 & 18 Vict. c. 125.

[20] 23 & 24 Vict. c. 126.

measures of definite improvement were installed.[21] Correspondingly, the labors of the chancery commission found response in the Chancery Practice Amendment Act of 1852.[22] The innovations which it introduced were marked and structural. Under its terms, to speak only of its more important provisions, initial process was no longer to be the writ of subpoena but a copy of the bill, with an indorsement commanding the defendant's appearance; the bill itself was now to consist merely of a narrative of the facts relied upon, with prayers for relief; discovery of facts was to be obtained by interrogatories separate from the bill; the defendant might have discovery from the plaintiff, without the use of a cross-bill, by the filing of similar interrogatories; and for the old method of taking evidence by written interrogatories and cross interrogatories there was substituted in general that of oral examination of the witness by or before an examiner, with power in the court to require examination in open court. Moreover, the court was given added authority to decide common-law questions and even a limited measure of power to make merely declaratory decrees.

Impressive as were the changes in the two systems that had thus been brought about, the administration of civil justice in England was still far from giving satisfaction. It was now not so much the matter of procedure that formed the subject of complaint as the judicial organization itself. The separate existence not only of the three common-law courts, on the one hand, and of the Court of Chancery on the other, but also of other important courts of superior jurisdiction seemed more and more to stand in the way of simplicity and directness in the disposition of civil controversies, and the ideal of a single court, with comprehensive jurisdiction, capable of adjusting its processes to the needs of the particular case, was more and more impressing itself upon the popular mind. And with the notion of such a unified court went hand in hand that of a

[21] See Day, Common Law Procedure Acts (4th ed. 1872) Introduction, 1 *et seq.*

[22] 15 & 16 Vict. c. 86. Some slight measure of improvement had been effected two years before by an act of 1850 (13 & 14 Vict. c. 35) making provision, *inter alia,* for the statement of special cases in chancery.

united administration of law and equity, under a procedure of such uniformity as the situation would admit. The continuing agitation gave rise to a new campaign for reform which opened in 1867 with a speech in the House of Commons by Sir Roundell Palmer (afterwards Lord Selborne) which brought about the appointment of a new investigating body, that known as the Judicature Commission. In 1869, this commission submitted its first and most significant report, "the report on which all the great reforms of the next few years were built. In less than twenty pages the report reviews the defects in the administration of the superior courts of England and sets forth a practical plan for a general consolidation and unification of jurisdiction and procedure." [23] A bill, prompted by the recommendations of the report, was introduced in 1870, but failed chiefly because it left the matter of regulating the procedure in an unsatisfactory state.[24] In 1873, however, a new bill, measurably removing the difficulty thus encountered, was introduced by Lord Selborne, and its passage the same year yielded the first Judicature Act. This was followed by the Judicature Act of 1875, effecting certain amendments. Under these acts the jurisdictions previously exercised by the three common-law courts, the court of chancery, and the separate courts of admiralty, probate and divorce were to be exercised by a single Supreme Court of Judicature, composed of a High Court of Justice and a Court of Appeal. For convenience of administration the former was constituted in five divisions, namely, the Chancery Division, the Queen's Bench Division, the Common Pleas Division, the Exchequer Division and the Probate, Divorce and Admiralty Division—later (in 1880) to be reduced to three by incorporating with the Queen's Bench Division the other two common-law divisions. Having thus created a unified court, the legislation in question then proceeded to accept definitely and comprehensively the principle which, a quarter of a century before, had been given the force of law by the New York Code of Procedure, namely, the conjoined administration of law and equity in the same procceed-

[23] Rosenbaum, The Rule-Making Authority in the English Supreme Court (1917) 37.

[24] *Ibid.* 38-41.

ing. Scarcely less important, however, was its recognition of the need for a greater measure of judicial control over the proceedings in the interest of economy and expedition, and its resultant enhancement, by various provisions, of the judicial directive power, "that is, the power in the judicature to direct the proper course of proceeding—the course of proceeding adapted to the nature of particular cases."[25] And a third highly important accomplishment of the acts was permanently to establish the principle that the regulation of the procedure, consistent with the statutory bases, should henceforward be entrusted to rules of court. The act of 1875 subjoined a schedule of rules, which superseding the meager schedule provided by the act of 1873, was to govern for the time being. These rules set up a system of pleading, applicable alike to causes at law and in equity, similar in general to that contemplated by the New York Code, and in other departments of procedure retained and made advance upon all the improvements which had been effected by the preceding reform legislation. The schedule of 1875 "accomplished great reforms, especially in the matter of summons, parties, pleadings and trial, but it was equally tenacious of all that promised well in the existing procedure and let much of it stand unmentioned."[26] The acts and the rules went into effect on 1 November 1875, and England thus entered upon possession of a system of judicature and procedure which exhibited many points of superiority over that of any other Anglo-American jurisdiction.

By the act of 1875, the making of rules, subject to annulment by Parliament, was committed to the judges of the Supreme Court or a majority of them which should include the Lord Chancellor. A year later, however, this power was devolved upon a Rule Committee of prescribed personnel, headed by the Lord Chancellor.[27] The Rules of 1875, with

[25] Finlason, An Exposition of our Judicial System and Civil Procedure (1877) 294.

[26] Rosenbaum, *op. cit.* 64.

[27] For legislative changes affecting the Rule Committee see Rosenbaum, *op. cit.* 21 note 1. Under the existing law the Committee consists of the Lord Chancellor, the Lord Chief Justice, the Master of the Rolls, the President of the Probate, Divorce and Admiralty Division, with four other judges named by the Lord Chancellor, and two representatives similarly appointed

various amendments, continued to govern for some eight years. But in 1883, as the result of extensive labors on the part of the Rule Committee, in response to urgent demand, they underwent a complete revision. And it is the Rules of 1883, as subsequently amended from time to time, that continue to govern the civil procedure of the Supreme Court of Judicature.

of each of the two branches of the legal profession, concurrence with the Lord Chancellor of any four members being sufficient for action. Consolidated Judicature Act of 1925 (15 & 16 Geo. V, c. 49) § 99(4).

CHAPTER VI

THE COURSE OF REFORM IN THE UNITED STATES

The first quarter of the nineteenth century had not long passed before a pronounced movement for reform on a wide scale had made its appearance on this side of the Atlantic. Its principal theater was the State of New York. "The practice of the courts of New York was modeled after that of England. Little of the comparative simplicity and directness prevailing in some of the other States was to be found in New York. It thus happened that as the burden there was felt the most, the earlier and stronger became the efforts to throw it off. Agitation began soon after a revision of the constitution of 1826, and it increased in intensity until another constitutional convention was called,"[1] that of 1846. The influence of Bentham was undoubtedly making itself felt here, too, and the great speech of Brougham, although many of the defects which he exposed either had never existed on American soil or had already been removed, could not fail to emphasize the need for improvement in any jurisdiction following the English system. Moreover, the movement was given impetus by the great wave of democratization and consequent popularization of justice which swept over the country in the wake of the Jackson administration[2]—one of the few beneficial effects of that inundation. The first attack upon the old system came in the form of two bills laid before the legislature in 1842, the one to simplify the administration of justice in the common-law courts, the other to accomplish the like result in the court of equity. These, however, failed of passage. But the consti-

[1] David Dudley Field, Law Reform in the United States and its Influence Abroad (1891) 25 Am.L.Rev. 515, 519.

[2] See Hornblower, Fifty Years of Reform Procedure, Transactions of the State Bar Association of Indiana (1898) 10.

tution of 1846, having superseded the separate courts of law and equity, by a court of general jurisdiction in both fields, made it the duty of the legislature to provide for the appointment of three commissioners "to revise, reform, simplify and abridge" pleading and practice, and report to the legislature.[3] In April 1847 a commission of three was accordingly appointed by the legislature but with the specific injunction "to provide for the abolition of the present forms of actions and pleadings in cases at common law; for a uniform course of proceeding in all cases whether of legal or equitable cognizance, and for the abandonment of all Latin and other foreign tongues, so far as the same shall by them be deemed practicable, and of any form and proceeding not necessary to ascertain or preserve the rights of the parties." [4] The commission was reconstituted in September 1847 by the naming, to fill a vacancy, of David Dudley Field [5] who became at once its dominant spirit, if not the real author of its product.[6] On the last day of February, 1848, the commission made its first report containing the draft of an act "to simplify and abridge the practice, pleadings and proceedings of the courts of this State." This, though not without a large number of amendments, was enacted into law within six weeks and went into force on July 1, 1848.[7] It was given the name of "Code of Procedure" by an act of contemporaneous adoption.[8]

The Code sought unreservedly to carry into effect the legislative directions. "Stated in fewest words, its essential features were the demolition of the forms of action, the abolition in that respect of the distinction between actions at law and suits in equity, and the substitution of one form of action for the enforcement or protection of private rights and the re-

[3] Art. VI, § 24.

[4] N.Y. Laws 1847, c. 59, Act of April 8, § 8.

[5] Hepburn, Historical Development of Code Pleading (1897) 83.

[6] "The code purports to be framed by three commissioners appointed for the purpose. Common fame asserts, and without contradiction that I am aware of, from any quarter, that Mr. David Dudley Field, who was one of them, drew the whole instrument, and may properly be regarded as its sole author." Letter of Charles O'Conor of the New York Bar to Messrs. Pope & Haskell, attorneys at law, Columbia, South Carolina, March 14, 1870, appearing in 1 Albany L.J. 302.

[7] N.Y. Laws 1848, c. 379.

[8] N.Y. Laws 1848, c. 380, § 1.

dress or prevention of private wrongs, in which one action should be determined all the rights of the parties, legal or equitable in respect of the subjects in litigation."[9] But no less important was the fact that it did away with the former systems of pleading, both at law and in equity, and replaced them with a new and uniform system which was at least intended to simplify the mode of allegation and prevent it from becoming an instrumentality for thwarting justice. The great haste which characterized both its drafting and its enactment was reflected in numerous imperfections. Its basic ideas were admirable, but it left various important matters unregulated, and the particular consequences of given provisions were not always accurately envisaged. It required an amended version adopted in 1849,[10] and amendatory acts of 1851[11] and 1852[12] to correct its more conspicuous defects. But with all its faults it opened the way to a new era of civil procedure in the Anglo-American jurisdictions.

In America the New York Code of Procedure speedily set the pattern for procedural legislation in other jurisdictions. The first decade after its adoption saw acceptance of its system in Missouri (1849), California (1850), Iowa (1851), Minnesota (1851, 1853), Indiana (1852), Ohio (1853), Washington (1854), Nebraska (1855), and Wisconsin (1856), and, save for the maintenance of the separate administration of law and equity, in Kentucky (1851) and Oregon (1854). A similar separation was re-established in Iowa by the revised code of 1860, an instrument notable for the extensive study of other systems in the course of its preparation and for its resultant distinctive character, to which the English common-law reforms of 1852 and 1854 had made important contribution. By the close of a third decade the New York system had come to number as its followers also Kansas (1859), Nevada (1861), Dakota (1862), Idaho (1864), Arizona (1864), Montana (1865), North Carolina (1868), Wyoming (1869), South Carolina (1870), Utah (1870),

[9] David Dudley Field, *op. cit.* 523.

[10] N.Y. Laws, 1849, c. 438, Act of April 11, 1849.

[11] N.Y. Laws, 1851, c. 479.

[12] N.Y. Laws, 1852, c. 392.

and Colorado (1877), with Arkansas (1868) patterning its methods upon those of Kentucky. Later accessions have been Oklahoma (1890), New Mexico (1897) and (by act of Congress) Alaska (1900). Moreover, the influence of the same system has been manifest in the codes of civil procedure adopted for the Philippine Islands, Porto Rico, the Canal Zone and the Virgin Islands.[13]

An approximation to the general system of the codes was made in the Connecticut Practice Act of 1879, but, drawing in considerable measure upon the English reforms under the Judicature Acts, this represented a distinct advance over the codes which had emanated from that of New York.

All this legislation has been the subject of amendment from time to time and very often of complete revision. In New York, itself, change has been pronounced, although without departure from more basic principles. After the Code of 1848 had undergone repeated amendment, there was adopted in 1876, with additions in 1880, a new code of civil procedure, the so-called Throop Code, extending to a much wider field of regulation than its predecessor.[14] This legislation, however, soon became the target of general criticism, chiefly because of its attempt to pursue the regulation of practice into details which should never have been dealt with by fixed provision. In short, "it was built up under a microscope." [15] Of forbidding bulk,

[13] For the period prior to 1897 we follow the chronology in Hepburn, Historical Development of Code Pleading (1897) §§ 88-122, where the history of the code adoptions appears in detail.

[14] N.Y. Laws 1876, c. 448, published as amended at the following session, in Vol. II of the Laws of 1877; N.Y. Laws 1880, c. 178; 1 Report of the Board of Statutory Consolidation on the Simplification of the Civil Practice in the Courts of New York (1915) 4. Its original statutory name, "Code of Remedial Justice," was changed in 1877 to that of "Code of Civil Procedure." N.Y. Laws 1877, c. 416, § 1.

[15] Hornblower, Revision of the Code (1896) 53 Albany L.J. 150, 152. Not altogether flattering to the intellectual calibre of its framers is the author's subjoined observation that "the commissioners went through the old code, and whenever they found the phrase 'single judge' they struck that out and put in 'one judge' and the note by the commissioners said that the phrase 'single judge' would seem to exclude married judges. This measurably recalls the doctrine of the medieval Italian jurists that a judgment, if rendered by a judge in other than a sitting position was null, because a passage in the Roman Code spoke of the "sitting judge" as the organ of judgment. Millar (1935) 29 Ill.L.Rev. 405, citing I Calamandrei, *La Cassazione civile* (1920) 158.

it introduced a host of new technicalities, frequently in relation to matters of no intrinsic importance, and in general gave rise to a thoroughly unsatisfactory situation. Agitation for revision was continuous but remained long without success. Finally it prevailed, and in 1920 the Code was superseded by the Civil Practice Act,[16] which remedied the principal objections to the former, and availing itself, among other aids, of various suggestions afforded by the English Rules, placed the civil procedure of New York on a much improved footing.

Outside of the area thus falling more especially under the aegis of the New York departure, the American jurisdictions of the present day exhibit a wide gradation of procedural method. Unique is the case of Texas. Except for some slight hesitation at the outset of its history as a republic, Texas has never known the separate administration of law and equity, and its system of pleading, by petition and answer, is a development of its own, originating, though little more than nominally, in the corresponding pleadings of the Spanish-Mexican system, and aided by reference to the principles of Anglo-American equity pleading. Of the other States within this category, two groups may be noted. In the one, while there is maintenance of the dual administration in a comparatively slight degree, a uniform system of pleading is provided, and legal and equitable causes of action, as well as legal and equitable defenses may be joined in the same suit, with resultant accomplishment of very much the same end as was sought to be attained by the New York provision for a single form of action. Here is to be placed Georgia, whose procedure represents an autonomous evolution from the simplifications contemplated by the Judiciary Act of 1799. Here, also belongs Illinois, which, long reluctant to depart very far from traditional methods, adopted in 1933 a Civil Practice Act recasting its procedure in a revolutionary manner. In the second group, the partition between law and equity is much more substantial. Whatever be the rule followed in the particular jurisdiction as to the allowance of equitable defenses in common-law actions or as to the facility of transfer from one side

[16] N.Y. Laws 1920, cc. 925, 926.

of the court to the other, there is no provision at all or none of any considerable width for the united prosecution of legal and equitable causes of action. To this group belong Massachusetts, Maine, Rhode Island, New Hampshire, Vermont, Delaware, Pennsylvania, Maryland, Virginia, West Virginia, Florida, Alabama, Mississippi, Tennessee and Michigan. The Territory of Hawaii comes within the same category.[17] But in none of these jurisdictions has the hand of reform been idle. They disclose modifications to a greater or less extent of the common-law distinctions of forms of action, sometimes their complete abandonment, simplification of the rules of pleading, often influenced by the code provisions on the subject, and in a few instances regulated by uniform provision as to both law and equity, changes in the rules relating to joinder of actions and of parties, and a multitude of other alterations looking to procedural betterment. In this class of jurisdictions it is the common-law side of the court to which reform measures have more usually been directed. Notable among these are the Massachusetts Practice Act of 1851, the Practice Act of 1912, adopted by New Jersey when it belonged to this class, the now transcended Pennsylvania Practice Act of 1915, and the Michigan Judicature Act of the same year.

In the federal sphere it was not until a recent day that the dual administration of law and equity was forsaken. A pronounced diversity in the mode of regulating the two systems marks the previous history, which in respect of the procedure at law falls into two periods. In the first period extending to 1872, the common-law procedure, as the result of the Process Acts of 1789,[18] 1792[19] and 1828,[20] except as otherwise provided by federal statute, was to be the same as that obtaining in the courts of general jurisdiction of the State wherein the federal court was sitting, while the equity and admiralty procedures were to follow the "principles, rules and usages" of courts of equity and admiralty respectively. But,

[17] This category likewise embraced the District of Columbia until the taking effect there of the Federal Rules of 1938.

[18] 1 Stat. 93.

[19] 1 Stat. 275.

[20] 4 Stat. 278, § 1.

under the Process Act of 1792, by a provision repeated in that of 1828, the prescribed procedure in each instance was made subject "to such alterations and additions, as the said courts of the United States respectively shall, in their discretion, deem expedient or to such regulations as the Supreme Court of the United States shall think proper, from time to time, by rules to prescribe to any circuit or district court concerning the same." As to common-law causes, this grant of rule-making power to the Supreme Court, although strongly reinforced for all three systems by the supplemental Judiciary Act of 1842,[21] was never availed of, and accordingly during this first period, the common-law procedure of the federal courts continued to be that of the State courts, with such modifications as were occasioned by act of Congress or effected by the lower federal courts themselves in pursuance of the power thus explicitly vested in them.[22] Except as to the matter of final process,[23] the legislation in question, unfortunately, did not allow for future improvement of the State procedures, and hence, under its terms and the later statutory extension of the Process Act of 1828 to new States, it would appear to be the case after 1828 that as to States already in the Union in 1789, that year was to be taken as the criterion of the State procedure, while as to States subsequently admitted, the condition of the State procedure at the time when, in the particular case, the act of 1828 had become applicable, was to be the norm.[24] Prior to the appearance of the code system, "little embarrassment was experienced in applying the practice thus established for the federal courts." But with adoption of the Code of 1848 in New York and its progeny in other States the case

[21] 5 Stat. 516, § 6. Other grants of regulatory power to the federal courts in general appear in the Judiciary Act of 1789, § 17 (1 Stat. 83) and the additional Judiciary Act of 1793, § 7 (1 Stat. 335). See Wayman v. Southard (1825) 10 Wheat. (23 U.S.) 1, 42.

[22] The history of this period is recounted at length in Clark and Moore, A New Federal Civil Procedure, I. The Background (1935) 44 Yale L.J. 387, 391-401.

[23] The act of 1828, in requiring execution and other final process to subscribe to the then existing State practice, made this mandate subject to the power of the court, by rule, to conform to State changes. (§ 3).

[24] Clark and Moore, *op. cit.* 400-401. The federal practice in Louisiana was governed by the special act of 1824 (4 Stat. 62).

was different. "When a generation of lawyers had grown up under these codes, knowing nothing of the common-law practice, the burden of acquiring that practice for the few cases which they had in the federal courts became intolerable." [25]

This disturbing situation led to the adoption in 1872 of the statutory provision usually known as the Conformity Act,[26] which introduced the second period of the federal common-law procedure. It established as the new rule for common-law causes "that the practice, pleadings and forms and modes of proceeding . . . shall conform, as near as may be, to the practice, pleadings and forms and modes of proceeding existing at the time in like causes in the courts of record of the State . . . any rule of court to the contrary notwithstanding." Thus there was substituted as a norm the State practice as of the time of the particular proceeding, with the resultant benefit to the federal practice of any changes that might be made from time to time in that of the State. At the same time, the statute marked the end of the trial courts' power of regulation within the compass existing under the acts of 1792 and 1828, as also, for the time being, the regulatory power of the Supreme Court. The conformity prescribed was, of course, subject to the differences arising from specific federal statutes. Moreover, the words "as near as may be" left a considerable margin for the exercise of judgment as to the closeness with which the State practice was to be followed. Accordingly, it became the accepted doctrine that literal conformity to the State practice was not required, if this would be calculated to bring about inconvenience or injustice or would conflict with the spirit of federal institutions.[27] Hence it is that the federal courts, under the act, followed their own ways in a large number of important phases of their common-law procedure and especially with relation to the conduct of the trial. A conspicuous instance of this divergency from State practice lay

[25] Amidon, D. J., in Chicago & N. W. Ry. Co. v. Kendall (C.C.A. 8th Circt.) 167 Fed. 62, 65, 66 (1909).

[26] Act of June 1, 1872, § 5, 17 Stat. 196.

[27] Indianapolis & St. Louis R. R. Co. v. Horst 93 U.S. 291, 301 (1876); Mexican Central Ry. Co. v. Pinkney 149 U.S. 194, 207, 13 S.Ct. 859 (1893); City of St. Charles v. Stookey (C.C.A. 8th Circt.) 154 Fed. 772, 778-779 (1907).

in their maintenance of the common-law method of instructing juries. As thus regulated the federal common-law system preserved its separate identity until the recent changes.

Quite different was the case in the federal equity procedure. In this field, as in that of the admiralty procedure, the rule-making power of the Supreme Court became a decisive agency of governance at an early day. The first general equity rules appeared in 1822.[28] In 1842 these were superseded by a more comprehensive series.[29] While, in the course of this regulation various not unimportant improvements had been effected, there was no serious departure from the basic lines of the traditional system. For matters to which neither their provisions nor the local rules of court applied, the Rules of 1822 prescribed the practice of the English High Court of Chancery as the canon, while the Rules of 1842, taking into account the alterations which the English chancery practice meantime had undergone, adopted that system "so far as the same may reasonably be applied consistently with the local circumstances and local convenience of the district where the court is held, not as positive rules, but as furnishing just analogies to regulate the practice." [30] By the Rules of 1842, as amended from time to time, the equity practice continued to be governed until growing recognition of its backward character brought about adoption of the Rules of 1912 [31] which became operative in 1913. The new rules, under the influence of the latter-day reform measures and especially of the contemporary English Rules, effected a radical recasting of the system. Bill and answer were stripped of every feature appertaining to discovery. The legal sufficiency of the bill was no longer to be challenged by demurrer but by motion to dismiss or by legal objection taken in the answer. Pleas were abolished. Counterclaims were substituted for cross-bills under distinctive regulation. Discovery of facts on the part of either party was now to be had by written interrogatories wholly separate from

[28] 7 Wheat. v, reprinted in Hopkins, New Federal Equity Rules (5th ed. 1925) 37.

[29] 1 How. lxi, Hopkins, *op. cit.* 43.

[30] 1 How. lxix, Hopkins, *op. cit.* 5, 61.

[31] Printed at end of 226 U.S.

the pleadings. And among the other signal changes was established the principle—a decided innovation for the federal practice—that normally witness testimony was to be taken orally in open court.

The cry to which the Conformity Act of 1872 had been a response was for uniformity of the federal common-law procedure with that of the State. But in later years with the growth of federal concerns and the vast augmentation of civil business in the federal courts, much of it affecting nation-wide private interests, practice in the federal courts was more and more losing its local character. Accordingly, for members of the profession called upon to represent their clients before the federal courts of different States the diversity of procedure was constituting a constant source of vexation. Therefore the cry was now for uniformity as among the federal courts themselves. A definite movement in this end made its appearance in 1912 through the introduction of an appropriate bill in Congress. This effort failed, but was pursued at succeeding sessions, and, save for a brief period after 1930, with untiring vigor, until it bore fruit in the act of June 19, 1934.[32] As appears, the proposal was initially aimed only at the common-law procedure. But in 1922 it was enlarged so as to permit establishment of a united administration of law and equity, and this enlargement was accepted by the act.[33] The act contains two sections, the first vesting in the Supreme Court the power to prescribe by general rules the procedure in civil actions at law, the second empowering it to unite the rules of equity procedure with those at law "so as to secure one form of action and procedure for both," but the rules resulting from the exercise of the latter power were not to take effect until after they had been reported to Congress. By order of June 3, 1935,[34] the Supreme Court signified its intention to proceed under the second section and appointed an Advisory Committee to prepare an appropriate draft of unified rules.

[32] 48 Stat. 1064, 28 U.S.C.A. §§ 723b, 723c, 1948 Revision of Title 28, § 2072.

[33] For a particular account of the movement and its progress see Sunderland, The Grant of Rule-making Power to the Supreme Court of the United States (1934) 32 Mich.L.Rev. 1116, 1117-1118; Clark and Moore, *op. cit.* 388 *et seq.*

[34] 295 U.S. 774.

After some two and a half years' labor the Committee submitted its final draft, which, with a few changes made by the court, was adopted by order of December 20, 1937.[85] Reported to Congress pursuant to the act, the ensuing rules entered into force on September 16, 1938. They remain in force subject to amendments in 1939, 1946 and 1948. Of these general importance attaches only to the two last mentioned, namely, that of December 27, 1946, effective March 19, 1948, and that of December 29, 1948, effective October 20, 1949.[86] It has been provided from the outset that the rules in question "may be known and cited as the Federal Rules of Civil Procedure." (Rule 85.)

For the unified system, an important area of regulation was that incident to the constitutional preservation of jury trial for common-law issues under the Seventh Amendment. This apart, the new rules leaned heavily on the Equity Rules of 1912. "In fact," to quote the Reporter of the Advisory Committee, "if one dared generalize, one might, I think, say that our new procedure really consists of the equity rules of 1912, applied to *all* actions and brought down to date by such new developments as have occurred since 1912."[87] Availing itself of the most important advances attained in the Anglo-American jurisdictions generally, the reconstruction thus accomplished has gone far toward realizing for the federal courts the procedural desiderata of simplicity and expedition.

But it has done more. These Rules, indeed, mark a new epoch in the American development. For their influence has signally extended itself to the States. Already their provisions have been followed in local reform to such an extent that certain of the States have taken them over almost *in toto*. And this influence is bound to continue. In any case they furnish a source for further State development, and may be regarded as establishing what will ultimately become the general type of American civil procedure.

In its later stages the American development has profited

[85] 302 U.S. 783.

[86] 329 U.S. 839; 335 U.S. 919.

[87] Proceedings of the Institute on Federal Rules at Cleveland, Ohio, July 1938, as printed in American Bar Association volume containing the Rules and these proceedings (1938) 196.

in many respects by the English example. But, on the other hand, the English reforms owe a significant debt to American pioneering. In 1879, an American writer in the English Law Magazine and Review declared that "allowing all that national intellectual pride may justly claim for English jurists and English law, I believe that no one, on either side of the Atlantic, will dispute the preponderating influence of Mr. Field and his American coadjutors in the production of the precise form of legal procedure which now prevails in England." [38] This is perhaps putting the case too strongly, but it cannot be gainsaid that the New York venture attracted much attention in England,[39] and that the apparently successful functioning of the new system with its rapid spread to other American jurisdictions afforded powerful incentive and encouragement to the English movement which resulted in the legislation of 1873. In various specific phases, too, the English development exhibits American influence. For instance, if we compare the provisions of the Common Law Procedure Act of 1854,[40] introducing discovery in common-law causes, with the corresponding Massachusetts provisions,[41] adopted three years earlier, we may be quite sure that the latter were before the eyes of the English draftsman. And that study of American institutions on the spot was not absent from English reform effort in connection at least with the Act of 1854 we may gather from a picturesque passage in an opinion of Mr. Justice Lumpkin of the Georgia Supreme Court, dated in 1855,[42] in which he refers to a visit of the English commissioners and their transmission to England of a copy of certain Georgia legislation. This American influence finds little or no mention in English writings, nor has its extent ever been precisely determined on this side of the Atlantic, but that it has contributed in no small measure to the progress of English reform may, we think, be taken as certain.

[38] Sprague, American Codification and the English Judicature Acts (1879) 5 Law Magazine & Review (4th Series) 62.

[39] See *ibid.* 64; David Dudley Field, Law Reform in the United States and its Influence Abroad (1891) 25 Am.L. Rev. 515, 525.

[40] 17 & 18 Vict. c. 125, §§ 51-57.

[41] Mass. Laws 1851, c. 233, § 98-111.

[42] Tuggle v. Wilkinson, 17 Ga. 90, 91 (1855).

In any event, the mutual influence of the English and American reforms has been a valuable factor in delivering both systems from the trammels of tradition. But, all in all, it is clear that the monument which marks the decisive break with the old order is for America the New York Code of 1848, for England the Judicature Act of 1873. For the jurisdiction which it was intended to govern, the American statute represents reform *uno ictu;* the English, in contrast, came as the result of a gradual progression. And from this fact, there can be no doubt, the modern English procedure has drawn certain distinct advantages.

Part II
SPECIFIC PHASES

Chapter VII
CONJUNCT ADMINISTRATION OF LAW AND EQUITY

Before the point of break with the old order, phenomena of fusion between the common-law and equity jurisdictions had manifested themselves both in England and America. It is familiar learning that the common-law courts had been domesticating certain equitable principles, as in the recognition of equitable estoppel, the adaptation of the action of assumpsit to demands *ex aequo et bono,* the entertainment of actions upon lost instruments, and that, on the other hand, the court of equity, more especially in America,[1] would not always withhold its hand from applying a certain measure of relief, native to the courts of the common law, if necessary, by way of supplement, to a complete disposition of the cause before it. We have noted also the situation obtaining in Pennsylvania, where the absence of a chancery jurisdiction had compelled administration of an important quota of equitable principles in common-law actions. Interesting, moreover, is the case of Texas, already mentioned, whose inhabitants, although accepting the Anglo-American law in general, had been so impressed with the procedure of petition and answer which they found in the Spanish-Mexican system as to discard virtually from the outset any separation of law and equity.[2] In England, the Chancery Practice Amendment Act of 1852 had effectively em-

[1] See 1 Story, Commentaries on Equity Jurisprudence (14th ed. by Lyon, 1918) § 105 *et seq.*

[2] Butte, Early Development of Law and Equity in Texas (1917) 26 Yale L.J. 699; Townes, Pleading in the District and County Courts of Texas (2d ed. 1913) 86, 90. The constitution of 1845 of the Texan Republic declared against the separation.

powered the Court of Chancery to deal with certain common-law questions whose decision was prerequisite to the exercise of equitable jurisdiction. And, correlatively, the Common Law Procedure Act of 1854 had bestowed upon the common-law courts, as incident to their cognizance of common-law actions, a limited degree of jurisdiction in the matter of specific performance and injunction, and had accorded place to equitable defenses in answer to common-law demands.

But in America, the case of Texas apart, fusion in any degree of fullness first came with the New York Code of 1848; in England it first came with the Judicature Act of 1873. The American statute, as its main provision in this regard, declared that "the distinction between actions at law and suits in equity, and the forms of all such actions and suits heretofore existing, are abolished; and there shall be in this State hereafter but one form of action for the enforcement or protection of private rights and the redress or prevention of private wrongs, which shall be denominated a civil action." [3] With exception made for rights of action residing in an executor, administrator, trustee of an express trust, or a person vested with express statutory authority to sue, it also declared that "every action must be prosecuted in the name of the real party in interest." [4] And these provisions in substance have been carried into the mass of the American codes.[5] The English statute proceeded differently. It explicitly faced the fact that, owing to the manner of the law's growth, the distinction between legal and equitable rules, though purely artificial, had so embedded itself in the fabric of the law as to be insusceptible of any outright abolition, and that what really was being aimed at in speaking of fusion was the concurrent administration of the two kinds of rules in the same suit when the circumstances so required. Resultingly, it enacted that "in every civil cause or matter . . . law and equity shall be administered" according to a series of detailed provisions which followed, covering the various contingencies calling for that concurrent adminis-

[3] § 62 (Code of 1849, § 69).

[4] §§ 91, 93 (Code of 1849, §§ 111, 113).

[5] Statutory references in Clark, Handbook of the Law of Code Pleading (2d ed. 1947) 82 n. 24, 158 n. 17.

tration.[6] To this was added a section regulating certain special situations involved in the change, which concluded with the significant declaration that "generally in all matters not hereinbefore particularly mentioned, in which there is any conflict or variance between the rules of equity and the rules of the common law, with reference to the same matter, the rules of equity shall prevail." [7] Thus equity, as before, was to have the last word, but now that word was to be spoken in time to foreclose the adverse word of the common law. This difference between the two statutes in the manner of approach accounts in some measure, at least, for the smoother working of the English system in the present regard.

In both systems it is clear that there may be a union of legal and equitable demands, subject to the relative provisions as to the joinder of causes of action. It is equally clear that any equitable defense—that is to say, any set of facts which, under the old order, would have been ground for an application to a court of equity to restrain the prosecution of a common-law action on the particular demand or the enforcement of a common-law judgment rendered upon it—may be the subject of direct cognizance in the action itself, either by way of answer or by way of counterclaim. But, while it is basically true of both systems that in the conduct of actions an equitable title will be given effect over the legal where no substantial reason exists to the contrary, difficulties arise under American code practice in various cases where the facts established admit of one manner of remedy when gauged by the rules of the common law and of another when gauged by the rules of equity. Here most of the American courts are strongly disposed to insist upon the consequences of the identification that the plaintiff either has or is supposed to have given to the action as one at law or in equity. This is due in part to the rigid preservation of the right of jury trial in common-law causes, and in

[6] § 24.

[7] § 25. This provision was followed in the Connecticut reform of 1879. Conn. Gen. Stat. (1949) § 7738. Maitland's minimization of its importance (Equity—ed. of 1936—16-17) is in harmony with his view of no conflict between equity and law. On this point, see the extracts in 1 Cook, Cases and Other Authorities on Equity (2d ed. 1932) 96 *et seq.*

part to the theory of the case doctrine later to be mentioned, in which regard it is put upon the ground that the allegations and proof must agree. An extreme manifestation is the statement by one court that "in order that equitable relief may be had, equitable pleadings must be interposed." [8] No such rigidity of attitude characterizes the English system. Though the precise question was in relation to different common-law remedies, note what was said by Lord Justice Scrutton in *Oakley* v. *Lyster:* [9]

> . . . I begin by ascertaining the facts in order to see whether the form in which the plaintiff is claiming is substantially right, or, if not substantially right, whether any injustice is done by giving him the real remedy which the facts justify.

And having in mind *City of Syracuse* v. *Hogan* [10] in the New York Court of Appeals, where the majority found it necessary to hold that the action was one in ejectment, although the case was such that Cardozo, J., dissenting, could consider it an action in equity to enjoin a highway obstruction, contrast the words of Lord Blackburn in *Pugh* v. *Heath:* [11]

> Some twenty years ago there might have been some difficulty, in this case, in saying whether the proper form of remedy was by ejectment at law or by a suit in Chancery; but now it is quite immaterial which of the two it is, if it can be shewn that there is a remedy, and I perfectly concur in the judgment . . . that there is a remedy in one way or the other, and it does not matter which.

It was the question of jury trial that directly produced the result in *City of Syracuse* v. *Hogan,* and it is not to be disputed that the constitutional preservation of jury trial as it existed at common law, with the statutes passed in pursuance of it, is a circumstance constantly militating against completeness of fusion. Yet in England down to 1918, and, again, from 1925 to 1932, the parties continued to have under the Judicature Acts and the relative Rules "an absolute right to a jury trial in all pure common-law actions," [12] without there arising any

[8] Home Insurance Co. v. Atchison T. & S. F. R. Co., 19 Colo. 46, 53, 34 Pac. 281, 284 (1893).

[9] [1931] 1 K.B. 148, 151.

[10] 234 N.Y. 457, 138 N.E. 406 (1923).

[11] 7 App.Cas. 235, 239 (1882).

[12] Ball, The New Procedure Rules 1932, Annotated and Explained (1932) 16, thus defines the right as existing at the date of the since abolished New

such impediment to fusion as has thus come to obtain in America. Undeniably, the different nature of the restriction upon the court's freedom of action has had much to do with the difference in outcome, but there can be little question that the American courts have often construed the entitlement in a manner sacramental rather than substantial. As part of this chapter, difficulties appear concerning the allocation of fact decision as between judge and jury where legal and equitable issues are combined. In this respect some encroachment of the jury upon the true province of the judge is here and there perceptible, but the questions emerging are still to a certain extent open and, in any event, are detrimental to a well-ordered procedure. For these questions the English system has little place; in general the discretion of the court is all-controlling.[13]

No doubt a way out of the embarrassment occasioned by the diversity in mode of trial lies in appropriate modification of the constitutional provisions, but this is not at all likely to be soon achieved. Meanwhile, the diminishing incidence of jury trial due to waiver by the parties, forwarded as this has been through introduction of the necessity for a jury demand or, more cogently, through the latter plus the exaction of a special jury fee from the demanding party, is tending to reduce obstruction in this sphere. And, obviously, in Georgia and in those few States which, like her, have extended to the parties the right of jury trial in case of equitable as well as legal issues, namely, Texas, North Carolina, and Arizona,[14] the matter of fusion, in this respect, rests upon an easier basis. But no degree of uniformity in mode of trial will yield the desired maximum of fusion until there is a complete abandonment of that overdriven insistence upon agreement between *allegata* and *probata* which characterizes too many of the American courts.

As thus appears, the general system which found its origina-

Procedure Rules, by which it was restricted in the cases falling within their scope. For the recent regulation in general of jury trial in England, see *infra,* c. XVIII, § 1.

13 Annual Practice 1949, I, pp. 626-627.

14 Statutory and other references in Clark, *op. cit.* 25 n. 62, 29 n. 71, 95 n. 52, 98 n. 59. Under its existing law Arizona exhibits, for equitable issues, the paradox of a mandatory advisory verdict: see *infra* c. XVIII, § 3.

tion in the New York Code contemplates the union of legal and equitable demands as well as of legal and equitable defenses. It obtains in most of the so-called code States and in somewhat different forms under the practice acts of Connecticut and Illinois. But in Kentucky, Iowa, Arkansas, and Oregon[15] there is followed a system of narrower compass. In these jurisdictions the court has definitely a law side and an equity side, the statute itself distinguishes between actions at law and in equity, and there may be no union of legal and equitable causes of action. On the other hand, an action at law may be met not only by an equitable defense but also by an equitable counterclaim or cross-complaint, misjoinder of causes of action is waived if not initially objected to, and provisions exist facilitating the transfer of causes from one side of the court to the other. Hence, while the door to fusion is not wide open, it is open in a decided measure, especially in view of the potentialities of the equitable cross-action.

Only slightly ajar is the door in another type of American jurisdiction. Here, apart from the possibility of transfer from law to equity or *vice versa* by formal amendment of the pleadings, concession to conjunct administration of the two systems resides solely or mainly in the authorization of equitable defenses in common-law actions. The Virginia statute of 1831 in this end remains in force without great change. Although somewhat broadened by interim amendment it is still of limited scope, but does permit an affirmative money recovery by the defendant under proper circumstances.[16] The same provision obtains in West Virginia[17] as part of the borrowed Virginia legislation. The other statutes with respect to such defenses are of a general character, exhibiting the influence of the English Common Law Procedure Act of 1854. Statutes of the kind appear in Florida,[18] Massachusetts,[19] Rhode Island,[20] Maine[21] and Maryland.[22] But just as under the Eng-

15 Bliss, Code Pleading (3d ed. by Johnson 1894) 8; Clark, *op. cit.* 82.

16 Va. Code Ann. 1942, § 6145; Va. Code Ann. 1950, § 8-241.

17 W.Va. Code Ann. 1949, § 5630.

18 Fla. Stat. 1949, § 52.20.

19 8 Mass.Ann.Laws. 1933, c. 231, § 31.

20 R.I. Gen. Laws Ann. 1938, c. 520, § 9.

21 Me. Rev. Stat. 1944, c. 100, § 18.

22 2 Md.Ann.Code (Flack, 1939) Art. 75, § 91.

lish statute it was held that the authorization extended only to such defenses as were an unconditional bar to the action,[23] so the efficacy of these American statutes has for the most part been similarly circumscribed or in any event confined to the grant of purely defensive relief.[24] In two cases at least, those of Massachusetts and Rhode Island, this limitation has come from the statute's own wording; in other cases as a result of judicial construction. The federal statute of 1915, now a matter of history, was of the same character as the majority of the State acts, but the construction given it by the United States Supreme Court in *Liberty Oil Co.* v. *Condon National Bank*,[25] stood out in brilliant relief against the usual course of State decision, and afforded a stepping-stone to the full measure of concurrent administration which was to follow. Cognate with the type of jurisdiction here in question is Pennsylvania, which without the aid of statute, and in consequence of the peculiar development already noted, continues to permit the pleading of equitable defenses in common-law actions [26] while maintaining in general the division of jurisdiction.

The events of the last hundred years, however, teach that all such partial measures are but stages on the road to ultimate merger of the two jurisdictions. Progression to that point was fairly constant among the American jurisdictions down to 1900, when Congress accepted the principle of merger for the Territory of Alaska. During the next three decades it tarried, but two recent measures have conspicuously attested its vigorous resumption. One is the Illinois Civil Practice Act of 1933, by which the State swung from a conservatism more pronounced, perhaps, than that of any other American jurisdiction to a highly modern form of procedural ideas. Prior to this statute Illinois had clung closely to the divided jurisdiction, with comparatively little modification of common-law pleading. But the statute in question, without incorporating

23 Mines Royal Societies v. Magnay, 10 Exch. 489, 156 E.R. 531 (1854); Wodehouse v. Farebrother, 5 El.&Bl. 277, 119 E.R. 485 (1855).

24 Decisions cited in 1 C.J. 1052-1053 and 1 C.J.S. 1175.

25 260 U.S. 235, 45 S.Ct. 118 (1922).

26 Highlands v. Philadelphia & Reading R. R. Co., 209 Pa.St. 286, 291, 58 Atl. 560 (1904).

the single form of action provision of the codes, has prescribed uniform rules of pleading for civil actions in general, and provided for the joinder of legal and equitable claims, on the one hand, and legal and equitable defenses, on the other, as well as for the interposition of legal and equitable counterclaims, whether the principal demand is of the one nature or the other. So that, with some comparatively minor differences from the standard code system, there is here disclosed a notable capitulation to the principle of merger.

The other measure, it is hardly necessary to say, is the Federal Rules of 1938. In the present regard the Rules, by an adaptation of the usual code provision, declare that "there shall be but one form of action to be known as 'civil action.'" They require, subject to exceptions similar to those of the codes, that all actions shall be prosecuted in the name of the real party in interest. They establish a uniform system of pleading for all civil actions, and in relation thereto authorize the joinder of legal and equitable claims, of legal and equitable counterclaims and of legal and equitable defenses to counterclaim. Moreover, while necessarily making special provision for jury trial, they provide in the matter of trial practice a uniform course of proceeding for all non-jury causes, whether involving legal or equitable issues. In short they have left no stone unturned to ensure as complete a merger of the two jurisdictions as the constitutional preservation of jury trial will permit.

Reference has been made to the influence of the Federal Rules upon the State systems. Among the products of that influence—and perhaps the most striking—is the addition of New Jersey to the jurisdictions of merger. For, by its Rules of 1948, consequent upon its Constitution of 1947, it has followed almost textually the provisions of the Federal Rules in establishing the canons just noted, abandoning thus its sedulously preserved separation of law and equity procedures.

Some American jurisdictions there remain that have not made even the minimum approach to union which consists in no more than the recognition of equitable defenses in common-law actions. Others, as has been seen, exhibit different degrees of advance in the desired direction. But in a large majority the goal has been attained and for these the work of the future lies only in perfecting application of the accepted principle. Moreover, there can be little doubt that the impressive example of the Federal Rules will powerfully accelerate the progress of the minority to that same goal.

Chapter VIII

INTRODUCTION OF THE CAUSE

§ 1. Commencement of the Suit

The story of initial process in the English common-law courts is a peculiarly complicated one in which the prevailing tendency of a former day to proceed by indirection comes to conspicuous manifestation. Upon the details of that story we need not attempt to enter, but a few of its phases require our attention. Each of the three superior courts had its own methods in the present respect. For the Court of Common Pleas, foundation of initial process was constituted by the original writ, which at one time was regularly issued as the constant practice. But in case the defendant in a personal action, upon being summoned, pursuant to the original writ, failed to appear, the primitive conception that no judgment could be rendered against a non-appearing defendant—a conception not discarded until well into the eighteenth century [1]—entailed the necessity of a series of successive writs of increasingly severe effect, for the purpose of coercing appearance, and ultimately, if the defendant remained obdurate, of visiting upon him, where statute so authorized, the extreme penalty of outlawry. Thus, failure to heed the summons was attended by a writ of attachment directed against the goods of the defendant, unless he find "safe pledges" for his appearance. If, notwithstanding the attachment, the defendant still failed to appear, there followed a writ of *distringas* or distress infinite [2] for the further seizure of his goods, as also the profits of his land, and this manner of distress could be repeated until the defendant either had made appearance or had nothing more left to be

[1] See *infra*, c. XXI, § 2(a).

[2] So called, "because it issues perpetually until he appears." Dalton, Office and Authority of Sheriffs (ed. of 1682) 160.

distrained.[3] The attachment or distress, be it noted, was limited to this purpose of compelling appearance: it in nowise operated as a security for the plaintiff's demand. "For, if the defendant appeared after an attachment or *distringas,* his goods were thereupon discharged by the court." [4] Such was the practice where the action was not deemed to involve a breach of the peace. If it did, as was true of the action of trespass among others, attachment took the place of summons at the outset. And if the sheriff returned that the defendant had nothing to be attached, or if the attachment did not produce his appearance, the plaintiff might have a writ of *capias ad respondendum* for the arrest of the defendant's person.[5] As the result, in part of fiction, but principally of legislation, notably the Statute of Marlbridge (1267),[6] the Statute of Westminster II (1285),[7] and statutes adopted in 1350 [8] and 1503,[9] the right thus to arrest the person was from time to time extended to actions other than those involving a breach of the peace, until the *capias* came to be allowable, in the words of Blackstone, "upon almost every species of complaint." [10] This being so, the course of the development brought it about that the process antecedent to the *capias* was not issued in practice, and the validity of the latter rested upon a fiction, namely, the supposition of an original writ and other antecedent process. It lay within the power of either party to require the actual drawing up of the original writ, but this occurred only in exceptional cases, as where the plaintiff sought to prosecute the defendant to outlawry. The consequence was, as regards most of the personal actions, that the suit in practice was commenced by the issuance of a *capias.*

If we turn to the King's Bench we find that here the proceeding by original writ was limited to these actions associated with the idea of a trespass, but, where an original writ was thus at command, the same commencement by *capias* was in

[3] 3 Blackstone, Comm. * 279-280.

[4] Boote, Suit at Law (4th ed. 1805) 26.

[5] *Ibid.* 63-66; Gilbert, History and Practice of the Court of Common Pleas (1737) 11-12.

[6] 52 Hen. III, c. 23.

[7] 13 Edw. I, c. 11.

[8] 25 Edw. III, Stat. 5, c. 17.

[9] 19 Hen. VII, c. 9.

[10] 3 Blackstone, Comm. * 282.

order. For the most part, however, the theoretical foundation of initial process in this court—as part of the fiction by which it drew to itself jurisdiction over causes properly belonging to the Common Pleas—was an original bill of complaint which took the place of the original writ. On this bill there was issued a precept commanding the sheriff to arrest the defendant. This precept originally was called a bill of the particular county in which the court was sitting, but became stereotyped as the bill of Middlesex after the court began to sit regularly in that county. If the defendant could not be found in Middlesex, another precept with like command, called a *latitat,*[11] and based upon the return of not found, was issued to the sheriff of the county where the defendant was likely to be found. The practice then developed, if the defendant was not in Middlesex, of suing out the *latitat* at once on the fiction of a preceding negative return to a bill of Middlesex. Accordingly, by the same manner of fiction which supposed antecedent process in the matter of the original writ, the bill of Middlesex, or, more often, the *latitat,* supposed the antecedent steps at one time followed, and so became the usual mode of commencing suit in the King's Bench, that is to say, by process, like the Common Pleas *capias,* under which the arrest of the defendant would regularly follow.

As concerns the Exchequer, whose jurisdiction over civil causes of private plaintiffs rested on the fiction that the plaintiff was the king's debtor, a *quo minus capias* corresponded to the *capias* of the Common Pleas and like it, though in a different manner, was based on the supposition of antecedent process.[12]

Down to 1725, the *capias,* on the one hand, or the King's Bench bill, on the other, involved an actual taking of the defendant into custody. But the abuses attendant upon the virtually unlimited right of arrest thus existing gave rise to the statute of that year,[13] which, limiting the right to hold to bail

[11] From the statement which it contained that the defendant "doth run up and down and secretes himself (*latitat*) in your county."

[12] As to the three courts, 3 Blackstone, Comm. *279-286; Boote, *op. cit.* 20-62; 1 Sellon's Crompton, Practice of the King's Bench and Common Pleas (Am. ed. 1813) Introd. *73-80; 1 Tidd, Practice (9th ed. 1828) cc. IV, V, VIII.

[13] 12 Geo. I, c. 29, §§ 1, 2.

to cases where the cause of action amounted to £10 [14] or upward, made necessary in those cases an affidavit on the part of the plaintiff of such cause of action. Under the terms of the statute, where the amount of the cause of action was less than the sum named or where no affidavit was filed, the defendant was not to be arrested, but was to be served personally with a copy of the process. And by an act of 1732,[15] except in cases under the statutory amount where the writ itself was to be in English, there was to be written on the copy "an English notice" [16] to the defendant advising him that he is thus served to the intent that he might by his attorney appear and make defense. Hence, to a very considerable extent, the *capias* or bill had become transformed into a mere summons to appear.

Accordingly actions came to be known as bailable and not bailable. In the former case, after arrest, the defendant could be released from custody by giving to the sheriff a bail bond conditioned for his appearance. This was called "bail below." But to make his appearance, he had further to furnish bail to the action, spoken of as "bail above" or "special bail," conditioned for the satisfaction of the judgment in case the plaintiff succeeded, or for his return to custody.[17] If, however, the action was not a bailable one, he entered what in the Common Pleas was known as a "common appearance," while in the King's Bench homage was paid to the form and resort was had to the fiction of "common bail," under which the defendant entered his appearance by putting in the fictional pledges of those imaginary characters, John Doe and Richard Roe.

The practice thus outlined obtained in England until the Uniformity of Process Act of 1832.[18] While process against the person was accordingly the ordinary mode of commencing suit in personal actions, it was always possible and occasionally even necessary or advisable to proceed by original where this was traditionally in order, or to proceed by other methods. Of the existing methods, taking into account the three courts and

[14] Increased to £ 20 by 7 and 8 Geo. IV, c. 71, § 1 (1827).

[15] 5 Geo. II, c. 27, § 4.

[16] The general change from Latin to English, resulting from 4 Geo. II, c. 26 (1731), took effect in 1733.

[17] I Sellon's Crompton, *op. cit.* * 127 *et seq.*, * 137 *et seq.*

[18] 2 Will. IV, c. 39.

the case of suits against privileged persons, no less than sixteen were enumerated by the commissioners who reported in 1829, and these did not include proceedings against attorneys, officers and prisoners.[19] But a revolution in this situation was worked by the act in question, which provided that, where it was not intended to hold the defendant to special bail, the initial process, save in one case not here material, should be a writ of summons, naming the form of action.[20] Finally, by an act of 1838 arrest on initial process was completely abolished. A defendant might still be arrested where there was probable cause to believe that he was about to leave England, but this could only occur pursuant to the order of a judge after the suit had been commenced. And this statute in terms provided that all personal actions should be commenced by a writ of summons.[21] The requirement of naming the form of action was dispensed with by the Common Law Procedure Act of 1852, which otherwise maintained the writ of summons on the same basis and in substantially the same form as under the two preceding acts.[22]

Much simpler is the chronicle of the chancery. Here the suit was normally commenced by the filing of the bill and the issuing of a subpoena *ad respondendum*.[23] At different periods in its history the court seems to have more or less countenanced the issuance of subpoena before the bill was filed,[24] but in 1705 this variation was prohibited by statute, except where the plaintiff was seeking an injunction to stay waste or to stay a suit at law.[25] By the subpoena which, down to 1833,[26] was under the great seal, the defendant was directly commanded to enter his appearance at the time appointed, under a money penalty. With various alterations from time to time in its mi-

[19] First Report of the Commissioners on Practice and Proceedings in the Superior Courts of Common Law (1829) 74.

[20] 2 Will. IV, c. 39, § 1, and No. 1 of Schedule.

[21] 1 & 2 Vict. c. 110, § 2.

[22] 15 & 16 Vict. c. 76, § 2 *et seq.*

[23] Concerning the designation of the subpoena in question as "process," see 1 Daniell, Treatise on the Practice of the High Court of Chancery (1837) 554.

[24] Barton, An Historical Treatise of a Suit in Equity (1796) 62, note; Gilbert *Forum Romanum* (ed. Tyler, 1874) 64; 1 Spence, Equitable Jurisdiction of the Court of Chancery (1846) 369.

[25] 4 Anne, c. 16, § 22.

[26] 3 & 4 Will. IV, c. 94, § 31, substituting a special subpoena seal.

nutiae, the practice remained basically unchanged until the Chancery Practice Amendment Act of 1852. This abolished the subpoena, made the filing of the bill alone the commencement of suit, and, in lieu of the old service by subpoena, required that the defendant be served with a printed copy of the bill, endorsed with a memorandum which was in effect a simple summons to appear.[27]

The difference thus existing between the common-law initial process and that of chancery necessarily disappeared under the uniform procedure established by virtue of the Judicature Acts of 1873 and 1875. The Rules of 1875 [28] provided that "every action in the High Court shall be commenced by a writ of summons," with the necessary endorsements. The summons, itself, was to be in a form which was substantially that of the common-law summons under the Common Law Procedure Act of 1852. And with no material change these provisions were carried forward into the Rules of 1883,[29] and govern the procedure of today.[30]

In the United States, the transplanted common-law procedure, although for the most part recognizing the issuance of initial process as the commencement of suit, followed no uniform pattern in this regard. In those jurisdictions more tenacious of English procedural forms, as in New York [31] and Virginia,[32] the *capias* with its concomitant of special or common bail as the case might require, was either the usual or a common method of commencing personal actions in the earlier decades of the nineteenth century. Elsewhere initial process in such actions was constituted by a writ of summons. Thus in

[27] 15 & 16 Vict. c. 86, §§ 2-5 and Schedule.

[28] 38 & 39 Vict. c. 77, First Schedule, O. II, r. 1. Following in this respect the Rules of 1873, 36 & 37 Vict. c. 66, Schedule, Rule 2.

[29] R.S.C., O. II, r. 1.

[30] Provision is still made for arrest of the defendant before judgment in certain cases where there is probable cause for believing that the defendant is about to leave the jurisdiction (Debtors Act 1869, 32 & 33 Vict. c. 62, § 6; R.S.C., O. LXIX) but this, since 1838, has been a matter wholly apart from initial process.

[31] Caines, Summary of the Practice of the Supreme Court of the State of New York (1808) 2 *et seq.;* 1 Burrill, A Treatise on the Practice of the Supreme Court of the State of New York (2d ed. 1846) 86.

[32] 1 Robinson, Practice in the Courts of Law and Equity in Virginia (1832) 120.

the New England States the suit was begun by summons,[33] usually combined with an attachment of property. For the States to be formed out of the Northwest Territory, precedent was set by the law of 1792 which recognized a writ of summons as the normal form of original process in civil actions.[34] A distinctive method of commencement obtained in Georgia where the Judiciary Act of 1799, in reiteration of antecedent legislation, provided for the commencement of suit by "petition and process," [35] which process was in effect a writ of summons. And as time went on the diminishing incidence of arrest as a step in civil proceedings was more and more rendering the method of *capias* a meaningless survival and favoring the use of the simple summons.

As opposed to this diversification on the common-law side stood the situation in equity. Here, there was in general subscription to the traditional rule of commencement, although in Virginia [36] commencement was ordinarily by the issue of subpoena before the bill was filed; in various quarters, however, a writ of summons took the place of the old subpoena.

If we look at the case in New York immediately before the Code of 1848, we see that personal actions, other than against corporations, are commenced either by *capias* or by the filing of a declaration.[37] The latter was a method introduced by statute in 1829, applicable to all personal actions except replevin, but which in practice seems to have been employed chiefly in contract actions.[38] In chancery, commencement, as we might expect, is seen to be by the filing of the bill.[39] As part of its general scheme, the Code was called upon to replace these several methods by a uniform one applicable to all civil actions. Accordingly, it provided that civil actions in courts of record "shall be commenced by the service of a sum-

[33] Mass. Act of 1784, 1 Thomas & Andrews, Perpetual Laws (1801) 199; N.H. Act of 1791, Constitution and Laws of N.H. (1805) 80; R.I. Act of 1798-1822, Public Laws of R.I. (1822) 151.

[34] Laws of the Northwest Territory 1788-1800 (Collections Ill. State Historical Society, ed. Pease, 1925) 93-94.

[35] § 8. Dig. Ga. Laws (Prince, 1822) p. 206.

[36] 2 Robinson, *op. cit.* (1835) 280.

[37] 1 Burrill, *op. cit.* 86.

[38] 2 N.Y.Rev.Stat. 1829, 347; 2 Burrill, *op. cit.* 224.

[39] 1 Barbour, Treatise on the Practice of the Court of Chancery (1843) 5.

mons." [40] With the summons in most cases was to be served a copy of the complaint [41]—a requirement discarded by the revision of 1849.[42] Under the system of the Code the summons, which was directed to the defendant, was issued not by the court but by the plaintiff or his attorney, nor was the complaint to be filed before its service. This extra-judicial summons, though in some sort a return to the methods of primitive procedure, was a radical departure from previous Anglo-American methods, and one whose wisdom is still a debatable question.

The system thus established, which, with minor changes continues to govern in New York, was followed by certain of the later American codes. These, however, have been a minority, the rest preferring to adhere to the principle of initial process emanating from the court. In any case, the jurisdictions which permit the joinder of legal and equitable causes of action exhibit today a considerable variety of methods of commencing suit. Principal of these are (*a*) the filing of complaint or petition; (*b*) the same filing accompanied by issue of process; (*c*) the service of initial process; and (*d*) the filing of complaint or service of initial process at the option of the plaintiff. The initial process is usually called a "summons," although in Iowa its statutory designation is that of "original notice," and in Texas, by inheritance from the terminology of the Spanish-Mexican system, it is known as a "citation."

In the so-called common-law jurisdictions the old method of *capias* today finds no place except as it may be authorized on special grounds inviting an actual arrest of the defendant.[43] Initial process in common-law actions is generally a writ of summons, emanating from the court, the issuance or service of which, as variously held, constitutes commencement of the suit. But commencement by the filing of a declaration is not unknown.[44] On the equity side, by the continuing general rule,

[40] N.Y. Code 1848, § 106.

[41] *Ibid.* § 109.

[42] See N.Y. Code 1849, § 130.

[43] Elsewhere such arrest of the defendant prior to judgment as is permitted by statute on special grounds is effected by process which does not displace the ordinary initial process. In a considerable number of jurisdictions, however, arrest on mesne process is altogether excluded.

[44] Mich. Stat. Ann. 1938, § 27.734.

the first step is the filing of the bill, followed by the issuance of initial process. Exceptionally, however, we encounter commencement by the issuance of the process in advance of the filing of the bill,[45] or, as an alternative to commencement in the older manner, by initial process in which the bill is inserted.[46] In certain of these jurisdictions the initial process remains a subpoena, as it did in the federal practice until the recent Rules; in others, this has been replaced by a writ of summons on a par with that employed in common-law actions.

It may be noted that in the preparation of the new Federal Rules the question arose whether the contemplated summons should be issuable as under the New York practice or should conform, instead, to the more general practice of issuance by the court. The first published draft offered two alternative rules as to the mode of commencing suit. The one provided for commencement either by service of summons and complaint or by filing the complaint and delivering the summons to the marshal, the other simply by filing the complaint, but the summons under each of the proposed rules was to be directed to the defendant and signed by the plaintiff or his attorney.[47] On further consideration, however, with the elimination of the first alternative rule of commencement, the idea of extra-judicial summons was dropped. As finally adopted, therefore, the Rules provide that the action "is commenced by filing a complaint with the court," and that thereupon summons, signed by the clerk and under the seal of the court, directed to the defendant, shall be issued and delivered to the marshal or person specially appointed, to be served, together with a copy of the complaint.[48]

Apparent from what has been said is the fact that reform in the present field has concerned itself with the direction of the process. Common-law process, under the old order, was addressed to a public officer, ordinarily the sheriff, requiring

[45] Va. Code Ann. 1942, §§ 6061, 6078, Va. Code Ann. 1950, §§ 8-45, 8-86; W.Va. Code Ann. 1949, § 5529 and note, § 5561; 12 Pa.Stat.Ann. (Purdon, 1931) § 1223.

[46] 7 Mass.Ann.Laws 1933, c. 214, §§ 7, 8.

[47] Preliminary Draft of May, 1936, Rules 3, 4, pp. 3-9.

[48] Federal Rules of Civil Procedure, Rules 3, 4.

him to summon or otherwise deal with the defendant, while in chancery the subpoena laid the command to appear directly upon the defendant. Most of the reform measures have concurred in extending the chancery principle and thus causing the initial process to be directed to the defendant himself. This was true of the English Uniformity of Process Act of 1832 in its establishment of a writ of summons for common-law causes.[49] It was true likewise of the New York Code of 1848.[50] The same manner of direction obtains under the existing English system for all civil actions, as it does under most of the American codes and the newer American legislation in general. Usually this manner of direction coincides with the rule that the process may be served by a private person, but not always so, as witness the case under the Illinois Civil Practice Act of 1933 [51] and the new Federal Rules.[52]

Another salutary tendency of modern legislation is that of causing the process to inform the defendant precisely what is required of him, as also to convey to him a warning of the consequence of disobedience. For the older command to "appear"—which the layman, as we all know, was likely to interpret as a command for his personal appearance in court—there has been generally substituted command of a more definite character, such as "to cause an appearance to be entered for you" or to "file (or serve, as the case may be) an answer to the complaint." And beginning, perhaps, with the English act of 1832,[53] there has been inclusion of specific notice in varying forms that in event of the defendant's failure to appear in the manner indicated, judgment by default may be entered against him. Thus the present English form requires the defendant to take notice that in case of failure to enter an appearance in the action "the plaintiff may proceed therein, and judgment may be given in your absence." [54] So, under the new Federal Rules the defendant is told that if he fails to serve an

[49] 2 Will. IV, § 1, and No. 1 of Schedule.

[50] § 107.

[51] § 6; Ill. Rev. Stat. 1949, c. 110, § 130; Rules of Pract. & Proc. Rule 4 (4), *ibid.* § 259.4.

[52] Rule 4(b) (c).

[53] 2 & 3 Will. IV, c. 39, § 1, and No. 1 of Schedule.

[54] O. II, r. 3, and Appendix A, Part I.

answer "judgment by default will be taken against you for the relief demanded in the complaint." [55]

Framing of the summons in the specific manner just noted may be taken therefore as an accepted canon of modern procedure. The two questions of procedural polity, however, which are susceptible of debate are first, whether the commencement of the suit should be, on the one hand, by the service of summons in advance of complaint or petition, or on the other, by the filing of complaint or petition, and, secondly, whether the summons should emanate from the court or from the plaintiff or his attorney. On the first question considerations of the advantage accruing to a plaintiff, under compulsion of taking immediate action, by allowing him to commence his suit, without waiting to draft his complaint or petition, are countered with the argument that this too readily aids the institution of unfounded suits, upon which the necessity of formally stating the claim at the outset might act as a deterrent. On the second question—one which, as above noted, was the subject of divided opinion in the preparation of the Federal Rules—there is the argument that the extra-judicial summons, with the concomitant procedure, tends to decrease expense and facilitate settlement of suits before they are brought into court, but to this is opposed the suggestion that the use of such process is capable of leading to abuses absent in the case of process under direct judicial control.

While certain States have met the first question by giving the plaintiff his choice of the two methods, the preponderance of opinion probably favors in each case answers such as have been returned by the Federal Rules. But, however these questions are resolved in particular jurisdictions, the resultant rules apparently operate satisfactorily within their respective spheres. Here and there the situation may be open to improvement, but on the whole this is one department of procedure in which the development has attained the point of adequately meeting current needs: certainly there is here no crying demand for further reform.

[55] Rule 4(b), and Appendix I, Form 1.

§ 2. Service of Process

In the English chancery procedure the subpoena *ad respondendum* was served by a private person.[56] Service of all common-law process, on the other hand, was the function of a public officer, usually the sheriff, acting by his subordinates. But the eighteenth century development materially altered this situation. The statutes of 1725 and 1732,[57] as has been seen, provided that, in non-bailable cases, that is to say, where an actual arrest was not in order, the defendant was to be personally served with a copy of the process. And since this legislation required service by an officer only in particular franchises and jurisdictions,[58] it was held that, with this exception, the service in question might be effected by any person who, having compared the copy with the original, was able to make oath to the fact of service.[59] The statutory exception was later evaded by resort to a new fiction,[60] and thus, by the opening of the nineteenth century it had come about that all non-bailable process might be served by a private person. As said by the commissioners on the practice of the superior courts, in their report of 1829, non-bailable writs "are not delivered to the sheriff to be executed; they are in fact served by the plaintiff's attorney, or those whom he employs, and the direction to the sheriff is nugatory and inconsistent with the real character of the process." [61] And for the writ of summons which they suggested as substitute, they proposed the definite rule that it "may be executed by any person who may have the charge thereof, and without the intervention of the sheriff or other officer." [62] Fruit of the commissioners' recommendations in the present connection was the Uniformity of Process Act of 1832, above mentioned, providing for the new writ of summons. The act, while not in terms adopting the proposed rule as to the agency of service, unmistakably declared for a continuance of

[56] Gilbert, *Forum Romanum* (ed. Tyler, 1874) 43.

[57] 12 Geo. I, c. 29, §§ 1, 2; 5 Geo. II, c. 27, § 4.

[58] 5 Geo. II, c. 27, § 3.

[59] 1 Tidd, Practice (9th ed. 1828) 168.

[60] First Report of the Commissioners on Practice and Proceedings of the Superior Courts of Common Law (1829) 98.

[61] *Ibid.* 97.

[62] *Ibid.* 122.

the existing practice in this regard.[63] And the Common Law Procedure Act of 1852 tacitly accepted the same method.[64] Later provision regulating the unified procedure has contented itself with prescribing that the writ shall "be served in the manner in which personal service is now made," [65] so that service by a private person remains the normal mode under the existing English system.

In the early nineteenth century practice of this country, there was divided allegiance to the English rule governing service of the chancery subpoena. Thus, in New York, it might always be served by a private person,[66] while in Virginia its service was definitely committed to the sheriff or other officer.[67] But for common-law writs agency of the officer appears to have been everywhere required, even where the process was a non-bailable *capias*. Failure to follow the English lead in the latter regard may perhaps have been due to Blackstone's Commentaries, which allow the reader to suppose that the service was always made by an officer,[68] although, in Blackstone's day, the other practice was already on foot. In New York, however, when suit was commenced by the filing of a declaration a private person was competent to serve the declaration and annexed notice to appear.[69]

With the precedent of the chancery subpoena and the statutory commencement by declaration, it was not difficult for the New York Code of 1848 to arrive at its provision that the summons was to be served "by the sheriff . . . or by any other person not a party to the action." [70] This provision has been followed in the greater number of the American codes, it being sometimes prescribed that the server shall be at least eighteen years of age. Other jurisdictions of fused procedure require that the service shall be by the sheriff or other officer, either in all cases or in most. And a provision frequently appearing, where the service is normally a matter for the officer,

[63] 2 & 3 Will. IV, c. 39, § 1.

[64] 15 & 16 Vict. c. 76, § 15.

[65] Rules of 1873, Rule 5; Rules of 1875, O. IX, r. 2; Rules of 1883, O. IX, r. 2.

[66] 1 Barbour, Chancery Practice (1843) 53.

[67] 2 Robinson, Practice in the Courts of Law and Equity in Virginia (1835) 280-281.

[68] 3 Blackstone, Comm. * 287.

[69] 2 N.Y.Rev.Stat. 1829, 347, § 1; 2 Burrill, Practice (2d ed. 1846) 224

[70] § 112.

is that the court, by order, may appoint a private person to effect the service. As for the jurisdictions of divided procedure, service of the initial writ on the common-law side continues to be the function of an officer, and in chancery, whether the initial writ on the common-law side continues to be the function of an officer, and in chancery, whether the initial writ is still a subpoena or has been transformed into a summons, conformity of practice between the two sides of the court has generally, if not everywhere, dictated that here, too, service shall be by an officer.

It may be that because of the special character of the federal system the new Federal Rules were justified in rejecting the principle of service by a private person.[71] But as concerns the State practice it would be a decided advance if this principle were everywhere accepted. As long ago as 1829 the same English commissioners of whom we have spoken observed that "this mode of service is convenient; for when the object is not to arrest the defendant, but merely to summon him, the introduction of the sheriff or his officers would be a mere incumbrance." [72] Moreover, it is in the interest not only of economy, in reducing the costs of the action, but also of efficiency. It is a matter of common knowledge, at least in populous communities, that where service is difficult to effect, the sheriff's officers are not likely to discommode themselves too greatly in order to execute the writ—a circumstance which has led in not a few quarters to the undesirable practice of bestowing a private fee upon the particular deputy in charge of the writ to stimulate his efforts. To be sure, it is sometimes said that where the service is required to be by an officer, the defendant is protected against a false return by the fact that the officer is under bond, whereas this protection would be lacking if the serving agency were a private person. But, to say nothing of the age-old employment of private service in the English chancery, the long experience otherwise with this manner of service both in England and under the American codes, has signally demonstrated

[71] See draft of April, 1937, p. 5. Service by a private person is not here specifically mentioned but was part of the rejected plan under discussion.

[72] First Report of Commissioners on Practice and Proceedings of the Superior Courts of Common Law (1829) 97.

that fear of its abuse rests on no substantial basis. What stands in the way of further extension of the principle in the State procedures is not so much any argument on the merits, as organized political opposition proceeding from the loss of fees and patronage with which it threatens the sheriff's office. But the merits of the principle are bound in time to overcome even this sort of resistance.

Another prospect of reform in connection with the agency of service concerns the use of the post-office. Suggestion in this end goes back to Jeremy Bentham.[73] The efficiency of the postal service today is such that its employment as a means of service is entitled to wider sanctioning. If we look abroad we find it to be the usual agency of service in Scotland,[74] as it is in Germany and Austria.[75] Whatever may be the view taken in particular States, it would seem to be clear, so far as concerns federal interpretation of the due process clause, that a State is at liberty to prescribe service by mail as a basis for personal judgment against its own residents, always provided that this service is regulated in such manner as to ensure that the summons or other notice will actually reach the hands of the defendant. A step in this direction was taken by Ohio in 1917 in the form of a statute authorizing the judges of the courts of common pleas, as well as the probate judges, to provide by rule for the service of process by mail, and declaring that when provision of the kind should be made, a return by the officer or person charged by law with the duty of service that a true copy of the process has been deposited in the mail, "registered or otherwise," shall be proof of residence service at the address on the envelope, provided that this was the correct residence of the party to be served and that the envelope has not been returned by the postal authorities as undelivered.[76] A more effective acting on the same principle is that disclosed by a Michigan Court Rule which was in force from 1931 to 1945.

[73] Bentham, Principles of Judicial Procedure, C. X, § 4.

[74] Millar, Civil Pleading in Scotland (1932) 30 Mich.L.Rev. 545, 556.

[75] German *Zivilprozessordnung*, §§ 193-197; Austrian *Zivilprozessordnung*, § 88. For Germany, see Shartel and Wolff, German Civil Justice (1944) 42 Mich.L.Rev. 863, 867.

[76] Ohio Gen. Code (Page, 1938) § 11297-1.

This provided that the service of summons or of declaration and notice to plead "may be made by the sheriff in the proper county by registered mail, deliverable to the addressee only, on residents of the State." Further provision was that the official return receipt, accompanied by an affidavit of the genuineness of the signature thereon and a certificate of the sheriff verifying the copy of the summons or other papers enclosed, "shall constitute *prima facie* evidence of personal service." [77] There is even less justification in service of the kind for intermediation of the sheriff than in the usual method of service, but this criticism apart, the Michigan measure, despite the fact that it was regrettably dropped in the 1945 revision of the rules, is one that commends itself to serious attention in other jurisdictions.[77a]

Reference in the Ohio statute to "residence service" points to another consideration relating to the execution of summons. While communication of the process to the defendant in person has always been the directest method of personal service, service by copy left at the defendant's abode occupies an important place as an alternative method. Indeed, at common law the summoning of the defendant under the original writ "was done either personally, or else the summons was left at his house." [78] So, also in the English chancery, under the orders of 1649 and 1661, the subpoena to answer was ordinarily to be "served personally, or left at the defendant's dwelling house or place of residence with one of that family" [79] —a rule which, applied to the copy of the bill with notice to appear, substituted for the subpoena by the Chancery Practice Amendment Act of 1852,[80] continued to obtain through-

[77] Mich. Court Rules 1931, 1933, 1945, Rule 16; Searl, Mich. Court Rules Ann. (4th ed. 1933) p. 95 and Cum. Supp. 1945, p. 25.

[77a] Important in the present connection are the recommendations of the New York State Judicial Council for the general introduction of service by registered mail as an alternative method. 4th Annual Report (1938) p. 187 *et seq.;* 8th Annual Report (1942) p. 327 *et seq.* It is to be noted that provision for service by mail exists for minor causes in a number of the States: see Report last cited, pp. 328-330.

[78] Gilbert, History and Practice of the Court of Common Pleas (1737) 10; 3 Blackstone, Comm. * 279; Dalton, Office and Authority of Sheriffs (ed. of 1682) 153.

[79] 1 Sanders, Orders in Chancery (1845) 230-231, 297.

[80] 15 & 16 Vict. c. 76, § 5.

out the history of that court. In the common-law courts, however, from the statute of 1725 [81] down to the Uniformity of Process Act of 1832, the old alternative method was not available in the ordinary mode of proceeding by non-bailable *capias* or bill: a copy of the process had to be delivered to the defendant personally. And the same was substantially true with respect to the writ of summons introduced by the last mentioned act. Nor, except in case of inability to serve the defendant personally,[82] was the rule different under the Common Law Procedure Act of 1852. And it continues thus to obtain for civil actions generally under the procedure of the Judicature Acts.[83]

In the American jurisdictions there has been and continues to be much diversity of rule in the present respect. In one,[84] at least, reading the process to the defendant in person, or offering to read it if he refuses to hear it read, is the single method prescribed. In a considerable number delivery of a copy to the defendant is required. The large majority, however, permit, as an alternative to either reading or delivery, the leaving of a copy at the defendant's place of abode. In most of these the alternative is unconditioned: the process-server is free to serve in either way. In others resort to the alternative is in some form conditioned upon inability to find the defendant in person. For some the alternative involves simply the leaving of the copy at the abode;[85] many more, patterning after the old chancery rule, require that it be left with some member of the family or household of competent age. This age is sometimes designated in the statute, usually

[81] *Supra*, p. 76.

[82] 15 & 16 Vict. c. 76, § 17.

[83] R.S.C., O. IX, r. 2.

[84] Tenn. Code Ann. (Williams, 1934) § 8662.

[85] A few statutes authorize the posting of the copy on the premises if no one is found in charge or willing to receive the copy. *E.g.*, Va. Code Ann. 1942, §§ 6041, 6062, Va. Code Ann. 1950, §§ 8-51, 8-56; W.Va. Code Ann. 1949, §§ 5519, 5537; Miss. Code Ann. 1942, § 1859. Pennsylvania permits the leaving of the copy at the defendant's place of business with some person there in charge, if the defendant's residence is not ascertained or an attempt to serve him at his residence has failed. 12 Pa.Stat.Ann. (Purdon, 1931) § 291. Colorado unconditionally authorizes the leaving of the copy at the defendant's usual place of business, "with his stenographer, bookkeeper, or chief clerk." Colo. Rules Civ. Proc., Rule 4, in Colo. Stat. Ann. 1935, Replacement Vol. I. 1941.

14, 15 or 16 years; sometimes, also, it is directed that the contents be explained to such person. The chancery pattern has been followed in the Federal Rules of 1938, under which the ordinary method of serving the individual is "by delivering a copy of the summons and of the complaint to him personally or by leaving copies thereof at his dwelling house or usual place of abode with some person of suitable age and discretion then residing therein. . . ."[86] In Illinois, where the unconditioned alternative is permitted, the residence service, however, is not complete until the officer also mails to the defendant a copy of the writ, addressed to the usual place of abode.[87] New York, again, stands apart in requiring, for resort to this manner of service, an order of court based upon a showing of inability to serve the defendant in person.[88]

Where authorized by statute, service by leaving a copy at the abode of a resident defendant is equivalent to service on the defendant personally and as such will support a personal judgment, always provided that the statutory provision has been strictly complied with.[89] To this manner of service we are accustomed in this country to apply the term "substituted service" in its strict sense, although the term, in a wider sense, is often applied outside this case. In England, however, the term "substituted service" is in standard employment as embracing any kind of service other than that of delivery of a copy of the process to the defendant in person.

What has been said above relates to service upon natural persons who are *sui juris*. Both in England and America special rules find place with reference to defendants falling outside this category, such as corporations, partnerships, unincorporated associations, municipal bodies and the like, as well as minors and persons of unsound mind.

So far we have been speaking of personal service. Of constructive service, so important a feature of the American

86 Rule 4(d).

87 Ill. Rev. Stat. 1949, c. 110, § 137.

88 N.Y. Civ. Pract. Act (Clevenger, 1950) §§ 230, 231. But a special method, not preceded by order of court, is provided for the case of a non-resident defendant engaged in business in New York. *Ibid.* § 229-b.

89 Settlemier v. Sullivan, 97 U.S. 444 (1878); Earle v. McVeigh, 91 U.S. 503 (1875); State *ex rel.* Fabrico v. Trimble, 309 Mo. 415, 274 S.W. 712 (1925).

procedure of today, the only species known to the English common-law courts was in relation to the old real actions, in which the sheriff could summon "the tenant or party by sticking up a white stick in his land" [90] and, pursuant to a statute of 1589, by proclaiming the summons on a Sunday at the door of the church or chapel of the town or parish wherein the land lay.[91] With the real actions this manner of service went out of use: in the mixed action of ejectment which in large measure took their place, service was effected by delivery of a copy of the declaration to the person in possession of the land. And our remedy of attachment as a form of provisional execution, in relation to which constructive service comes conspicuously into play, did not obtain in the English superior courts, being confined to certain local jurisdictions whose ideas of notice to the defendant were bizarre in the extreme.[92]

What is to be regarded as the archetype of the general run of American statutory provisions regulating constructive service is the English statute of 1732 [93] relating to the Court of Chancery. By this it was provided that upon affidavit being made to the satisfaction of the court that the defendant had gone out of the realm or otherwise absconded to avoid the service of process, or that upon due inquiry at his usual place of abode he could not be found so as to be served with process, the court might make an order directing his appearance at an appointed day. A copy of this order, within fourteen days after its entry, was to be "inserted in the London Gazette, and published on some Lord's day, immediately after divine service, in the parish church of the parish," in which the defendant, within thirty days before absenting himself, had had his usual abode; and within the same time a copy also was to be posted at a public place as particularly specified in the statute. In case of the defendant's failure to appear pursuant to the order, the court, on proof of the publication, might render a decree *pro confesso* against him.

[90] Dalton, Office and Authority of Sheriffs (ed. of 1682) 149.

[91] *Ibid.* 379.

[92] See *infra*, Chapter XXVI, § 1.

[93] 5 Geo. II, c. 25.

By the American statutes which reflect a development of the procedure thus prescribed, an order of court is sometimes required, sometimes not, but the affidavit and newspaper publication are standard features, variously regulated. Usually it is provided that this publication extend over a designated period or occur a stated number of times. There is at the present day nothing corresponding to the publication in church, although the posting of notice in a public place may in some quarters be part of the method. And most commonly it is required that a copy of the order, summons or notice, as the case may be, shall be sent by mail to the defendant at his last known address or place of abode, if this is available. A striking variation from this manner of proceeding against defendants who are absent from the jurisdiction appears in Louisiana as a result of Spanish law influence, and by adaptation in Kentucky, centering in the idea of a judicially appointed attorney, called in Louisiana the "curator *ad hoc*," to represent the absent defendant. In Louisiana (apart from attachment proceedings, where constructive service is effected by the posting of notice at a designated place in the court house) jurisdiction over the absentee is obtained by service upon the curator *ad hoc*.[94] In Kentucky the case is otherwise: there is an appointment of an attorney to represent the absentee, but all stress is laid upon the simultaneous entry of a so-called "warning order," calling upon the absent defendant to defend the action.[95] In neither State does the method involve any publication of notice. The representative so appointed is under the duty of communicating, if possible, with the absent defendant, and in case of his failure to appear is required to protect his rights, making such defense as the circumstances permit. Arkansas, through its following of the Kentucky code of 1854, and Texas, through its own inheritance from the Spanish law, share the same influence, in that both provide for representation of the absent defendant by an attorney similarly charged. Here, however, the appoint-

[94] La. Civ. Code 1825, Art. 57; La. Civ. Code 1870 (Dart, 1945) Art. 56; La. Code Pract. (Dart, 1942) Art. 116, 195, 254.

[95] Ky. Code Pract. in Civ. Cas. (Carroll, 1948) §§ 57-60; Brownfield v. Dyer, 7 Bush (Ky.) 505 (1871).

ment is accompanied by the usual type of service by publication.[96] No one seriously entertains the notion that newspaper publication, unaccompanied by the mailing of notice, is an effective means of conveying actual notice to the defendant. And yet, where his address is unknown or is not disclosed, this is all that constructive service demands under the general method. In view of this fact, the appointment of an attorney for the absent defendant, as under the last mentioned provisions, is an enlightened measure which deserves to be copied elsewhere.

The modern English procedure with reference to service other than directly personal within the jurisdiction places the determination of its mode largely within the discretion of the court. In the first place the Rules provide that "if it be made to appear to the Court or a Judge that the plaintiff is from any cause unable to effect prompt personal service, the Court or Judge may make such order for substituted or other service, or for the substitution for service of notice, by advertisement or otherwise, as may be just." [97] Such an order is never lightly granted and depends upon a most meticulous showing by affidavit of the asserted inability.[98] But the intention is that this manner of service "should have all the effects of personal service." [99] Again, in some ten cases specified in the general Rules (including that of relief sought against a "person domiciled or ordinarily resident within the jurisdiction"), as well as in matrimonial causes, provision is made for the allowance, by order, of service of the writ out of the jurisdiction, binding upon British subjects and persons found in British dominions, which, if it cannot be had upon the defendant personally, may take the same form of substituted service as in the case of defendants generally.[100] Here, also, the service, when effected, stands upon the same basis as per-

[96] Tex. Rev. Civ. Stat. (Vernon, 1936) Art. 2158, succeeded by Tex. Rules Civ. Proc. (Vernon, 1942) Rule 244; Ark. Stat. Ann. 1947, §§ 29-404, 29-405.

[97] R.S.C., O. IX, r. 2.

[98] O. X. For particulars, see Annual Practice 1949, I, pp. 94-95.

[99] Mellor, J., in Watt v. Barnett, 3 Q.B.D. 183, 186 (1878).

[100] O. XI, rr. 1, 6; Annual Practice 1949, I, p. 96. Some qualification exists as to the case where it is sought to effect service in Scotland or in Ireland. O. XI, r. 2.

sonal service. This is readily apparent when we note that in certain of these ten cases, as, for example, that of an action "founded on a tort committed within the jurisdiction," there is manifestly contemplated a money judgment against the defendant thus served. It is thus obvious that, under these Rules, there are many cases in which a personal judgment may be rendered on the basis of what corresponds to the American constructive service, or on the basis of personal service outside the jurisdiction.

With us, manifestly, the rôle of these two modes of service is a more restricted one. Personal service outside the State—sometimes referred to as a species of substituted service in the wider sense of that term—may afford jurisdiction over a non-resident defendant but to no greater extent than does constructive service. Whatever may be ultimately settled in State legislation and decision as to the precise limits of the State's undoubted power, within the due process clause of the Federal Constitution, to determine the effect of either sort of service as against its own residents, it is definitely established under the familiar rule of *Pennoyer* v. *Neff,*[101] subject to what later will be said, that no personal judgment can be grounded upon constructive service or upon personal service outside the jurisdiction as against a non-resident of the State. As a result, therefore, the effectiveness of constructive service or personal service outside the jurisdiction, without appearance of the defendant, is in general limited to actions which affect property or status, and so are essentially proceedings *in rem,* although in the ordinary procedure, the action in form is commonly one *in personam.*[102]

While thus, as against a non-resident defendant who does not appear, the general rule requires for personal judgment personal service within the jurisdiction, this rule admits of certain qualification. Under the circumstances and to the extent validly authorized by statute, a non-resident may be required or permitted to appoint a private person within the jurisdiction as his or its agent to receive service of proc-

[101] 95 U.S. 714 (1877).

[102] See *infra,* Chapter XXI, § 4.

ess, in which case service upon the agent may have all the effects of intra-jurisdictional service upon the non-resident in person. So, also, if the non-resident can be validly placed under the duty of appointing, either expressly or impliedly, a public official as a statutory agent for the like purpose, service upon the official may likewise afford the basis for personal judgment against the non-resident. Hence, as foreign corporations do business in the State only by its permission, they may be required as a condition of so doing business to appoint, or accept without express appointment, a public official as their agent to receive service of process in suits arising from their activities within the State. Statutes proceeding on this principle have been very generally adopted, and are held valid, under the due process clause, at least where they require the official to communicate proper notice to the non-resident defendant.[103] And of late years a notable statutory development has extended the same principle to the case of non-resident motorists in respect of actions against them to recover for injuries which they have occasioned in using the highways of the State. It is held by the United States Supreme Court that, as a State may regulate the use of its own highways, so it may condition that use on the part of a non-resident motorist by requiring him to appoint "one of its officials as his agent on whom process may be served in proceedings growing out of such use," or by declaring "that the use of the highway is the equivalent of the appointment. . . ."[104] Accordingly such provisions are consistent with due process, but only if they make it reasonable that, by communication from the official or from the plaintiff, the non-resident defendant will receive actual notice of the suit.[105] It may be added that by reason of the great volume of interstate motor tourist, coach and trucking traffic, statutes of the kind, although differing in their details, are rapidly becoming standard throughout the American jurisdictions.[106]

[103] Wuchter v. Pizzuti, 276 U.S. 13, 20-21, 48 S.Ct. 259 (1928).

[104] Hess v. Pawloski, 274 U.S. 352, 356, 357, 47 S.Ct. 632 (1927).

[105] Wuchter v. Pizzuti, *supra,* at p. 24.

[106] See Berry, Law of Automobiles (7th ed. 1935) and Cum. Supp. 1947, § 5-318 *et seq.*

In what has been said concerning service upon absent persons as a basis for personal judgment we have consistently spoken in terms of the distinction between resident and nonresident defendants pursuant to the rule of *Pennoyer* v. *Neff*. But in view of the trend of decision, and more particularly the Supreme Court case of *Milliken* v. *Meyer*,[107] decided in 1940, distinction must be made not only between resident and nonresident defendants, but also (in so far as the concept of domicile is separable from that of residence) between defendants domiciled and those not domiciled within the State. For the domiciliary is now definitely placed on a parity with the resident in the present regard. Thus, a defendant who, though not technically a resident of the State, yet has his domicile therein, stands for the instant purpose on the same basis as a resident, and is accordingly subject to service of process to the same extent as if he were a resident. "Domicile in the state," said the court in the case just mentioned, "is alone sufficient to bring an absent defendant within the reach of the state's jurisdiction for purposes of a personal judgment by means of appropriate substituted service. Substituted service in such cases has been quite uniformly upheld where the absent defendant was served at his usual place of abode in the state . . . as well as where he was personally served without the state. . . . One . . . incident of domicile is amenability to suit within the state even during sojourns without the state, where the state has provided and employed a reasonable method for apprising such an absent party of the proceedings against him." [108]

[107] 311 U.S. 457, 61 S.Ct. 339 (1940).

[108] At pp. 462, 464. In connection with this case, see 11th Annual Report of the Judicial Council of the State of New York (1945) pp. 199, 218; 15th Annual Report (1949) p. 62.

Chapter IX

JOINDER OF PARTIES

From the fact that the English common-law courts recognized only legal interests and liabilities, it followed that only those clad with the legal interest were properly joinable as plaintiffs and only those against whom the legal liability had accrued were properly joinable as defendants. With respect to rights arising from contract, these were either joint or several, dependent upon the mode of their creation. If joint, then all the promisees or obligees were required to join as plaintiffs in the action *ex contractu;* if several, they were not permitted to join, and each must bring his separate action. There was no such thing in the eyes of the common-law courts as a joint and several right: the right was either the one or the other; and consequently there was recognized no case of a contract action in the prosecution of which the promisees or obligees could join or not as they saw fit. As opposed to the right, however, the liability arising from a contract might be joint, joint and several, or several. If it was joint (and in the case of an obligation running to a plurality of promisees or obligees, this would be presumed in the absence of words making it joint and several) then all the promisors or obligors must be joined as defendants in suing upon it. If it was several, there could be no joinder of the promisors or obligors: each had to be dealt with in a separate suit. If, again, it was joint and several, it presented, so to speak, two facets: it might be treated as either joint or several at the plaintiff's election. In other words, he might sue the promisors or obligors together, in which case, conforming to the rule governing joint obligations, he must join all, or he might sue them in separate actions, precisely as if the obligation were a several one, always under the proviso that he could obtain but a single satisfaction. Hence the rule, as commonly expressed, that in the case of a joint and several obligation, the plaintiff, in a single action, may sue all or one of the promisors or obligors, but no intermediate number.

Concerning plaintiffs in actions for torts, it was basic that (apart from the case of a married woman who, until modern legislation otherwise provided, could not sue without her husband as a co-plaintiff) injuries to the person admitted of no possibility of joinder of plaintiffs: even if the injuries were inflicted at the same time and as part of the same transaction, each plaintiff was required to sue on his own account. But the rule was different where the injury was to a property interest, be it in land or chattels, or in reputation or other intangibles. Here if the interest was separate and the damage separately sustained, the persons affected must sue separately. If, however, the interest was joint all must join in suing, even if the damage was separately sustained. On the other hand, although the interest was separate, yet if a joint damage was suffered, the injured persons might sue either jointly or separately at their election. As to defendants in actions for torts the only situation which, under the common-law rules, admitted of a joinder was where the tort was one which could be considered as joint, that is to say, jointly committed by the defendants. In this case the plaintiff was at liberty to sue all or one or any intermediate number of the tort-feasors in a single action.[1]

Such were the rules of joinder, rigid and exact, which obtained in common-law actions. In decided contrast stood the case in equity. Here the primary idea was "that all persons materially interested, either legally or beneficially, in the subject-matter of a suit, are to be made parties to it, either as plaintiffs or as defendants, however numerous they may be, so that there may be a complete decree, which shall bind them all."[2] It was never possible to apply this idea without a variety of compromises, but it has always served as marking the goal to be striven for so far as the exigencies of practical justice

1 As to joinder in tort actions, see Dicey, Parties to Actions (2d Am. ed. 1886) 401, 448.

2 Story, Commentaries on Equity Pleadings (10th ed. 1892) § 72, p. 74.

would allow. Unlike the common-law courts, which could render but a single final judgment in which there could be no apportionment of recovery, as respects either plural plaintiffs or plural defendants, the court of equity could adjust its decree to suit the precise gradation of relief which the situation demanded, unhampered by any requirement that the decree affect equally all the plaintiffs or all the defendants. Nor was the precise rôle which a party occupied as plaintiff or defendant of major consequence; for his rights and liabilities could be adequately adjudicated so long as he was in the case on one side or the other. This flexibility of the equity decree manifestly operated in favor of flexibility in the joinder of parties and relieved the system from the need of translating the idea above mentioned into hard and fast rules at all comparable to those existing at common law. Certain distinctions, however, equity did make in the present field. These have been of long standing, although not reduced to precise formulation until a comparatively late day. As thus formulated by the United States Supreme Court in a series of nineteenth century decisions, they have yielded the now familiar classification of indispensable parties, necessary parties and proper parties. A party is *indispensable* in this sense if the decree sought will directly affect his interest, in which case he must be joined. But it may be that, while his presence is requisite to a complete determination of the whole matter before the court, it is possible to render a decree without directly affecting his interest: in this case he should be joined, and so is called *necessary,* but if he cannot be reached or is otherwise unavailable, the cause will proceed in his absence. And, finally, a party is *proper,* although not indispensable or necessary, when although not interested in the precise controversy initiated by the bill, he has an interest in the subject-matter which it would be more convenient to settle in the present suit than in a separate one: here he may be joined or not as the plaintiff elects.[3]

[3] Williams v. Bankhead, 19 Wall. (86 U.S.) 563, 571 (1873). This series takes its beginning in Russell v. Clark's Executors, 7 Cranch (11 U.S.) 69, 98 (1812) and includes among other cases Shields v. Barrow, 17 How. (58 U.S.) 129, 139 (1854) and Barney v. Baltimore City, 6 Wall. (73 U.S.) 280, 284 (1867).

Faced with the diversity of regulation thus existing as between common law and equity, the New York Code of 1848, in its consolidation of legal and equitable procedure, sought unification of the rules of joinder of parties by applying, as far as possible, the equitable principles to all civil actions. Respecting the union of parties in general, § 99 declared that "of the parties to the action those who are united in interest must be joined as plaintiffs or defendants; but if the consent of any one who should have been joined as plaintiff cannot be obtained, he may be made defendant, the reason thereof being stated in the complaint." Addressing itself specifically to the matter of plaintiffs, § 97 provided that, except as otherwise provided in the same title, "all persons having an interest in the subject of the action, and in obtaining the relief demanded may be joined as plaintiffs." Of the exceptions the only one still of importance was the right of a personal representative, a trustee of an express trust or a person expressly authorized by statute, to sue without joining the persons for whose benefit the suit was prosecuted (§ 93). As to defendants the Code laid down two rules, first, by § 98, that "any person may be made a party defendant who has an interest in the controversy adverse to the plaintiff," and secondly, by § 100—this on the precedent of previous New York legislation confined to the case of bills of exchange and promissory notes [4]—that "persons severally liable on the same obligation or instrument, including the parties to bills of exchange and promissory notes, may, all or any of them, be included in the same action, at the option of the plaintiff." Correlatively to this system of joinder it provided for a judgment approximating the equity decree in the rule of § 230 that "judgment may be given for or against one or more of several plaintiffs, and for or against one or more of several defendants, and it may determine the ultimate rights of the parties on each side, as between themselves."

With the revision of 1849 came two important amendments. To § 99 (becoming § 119) was added a clause recog-

[4] N.Y. Laws 1832, c. 276; First Report of the Commissioners on Practice and Pleadings N.Y. (1848) 127.

nizing the principle of representative or class actions, long obtaining in equity. And § 98 (becoming § 118) was now made to read: "Any person may be made a defendant who has or claims an interest in the controversy adverse to the plaintiff, or who is a necessary party to a complete determination or settlement of the questions involved therein." [5] As amended in these particulars, it is the provisions of the Code of 1848, with their reproduction textually or otherwise in other jurisdictions, which have furnished the standard regulation of joinder of parties in the American code procedure.

What differences from the old order were thus introduced? So far as concerns actions which prior to the codes belonged to the equity jurisdiction, no substantial change was effected, for the avowed purpose was to apply, as near as might be, the equitable principles throughout. Otherwise was the case outside purely equitable actions, although here the outcome assuredly fell short of what the framers of the Code intended. The provision calling for the joinder of those united in interest meant the maintenance of the common-law rules requiring all joint promisees to join in an action on the contract, and all those affected to join in an action of tort for injury to a joint property interest, subject, however, to the new permission to join as defendant a co-promisee or co-owner refusing to appear as plaintiff. It kept on foot, also, the common-law rule requiring all joint promisors to be joined as defendants in an action on the contract. For the case of plaintiffs change manifestly was contemplated by the provision permitting the joinder of one "having an interest in the subject of the action and in obtaining the relief demanded." The Code commissioners suggested that this would "enable a surviving partner and the representative of a deceased partner to sue together, whenever desirable"; [6] but, unfortunately, most courts have decided otherwise, in the absence of special enabling legislation.[7] As to the effect of the provision in general there has been much difference of opinion. What, precisely, in this sense,

[5] N.Y. Laws 1849, c. 438.

[6] First Report of Commissioners *cit.* 127.

[7] Pomeroy, Code Remedies (5th ed. 1929) §§ 141, 143, pp. 226, 228.

is the "subject of the action"? Does interest here necessarily mean a common interest, or will a separate interest in each plaintiff suffice? Must the relief be common to all or may the case be one in which separate measures of relief are awardable to different plaintiffs? These and similar questions have been constantly agitated, and it cannot be said that even today there is anything like uniformity of answer. In the case of defendants, as above appears, the rule of compulsory joinder is supplemented by the provision looking to permissive joinder of "any party having an interest adverse to the plaintiff." Unaided by special statutes, this has done no more than continue for equity causes the former rule applicable to these. In correspondence with their abortive suggestion as to the joinder as plaintiffs of a surviving partner and the personal representative of a deceased partner, the Code commissioners supposed that the present provision would "enable a plaintiff to exhaust in one suit his remedies against a surviving partner and the representative of a deceased partner." [8] But an attempt to do so met early frustration on the ground that, under the rule of American equity, the personal representative was liable to the creditor only after exhaustion of remedy against the survivors.[9] Legislation in many jurisdictions has here come to the rescue,[10] but the code itself has for the greater part been deemed impotent in this regard. Respecting, therefore, the matter of joint obligations in common-law actions, the code as generally construed neither widened nor narrowed the possibilities of joining defendants: as observed by a distinguished commentator, "the overwhelming weight of authority . . . has determined that . . . the common-law rules are left controlling in all legal actions." [11] Nor was any change introduced affecting the common-law rule as to parties in case of a joint tort liability: in this respect, indeed, none was needed. But a very definite advance upon the common-law rules as regards several contract liability was signalized by the provision that

[8] First Report of Commissioners *cit.* 126.

[9] Voorhis v. Childs' Executor, 17 N.Y. 354 (1858).

[10] Pomeroy, *op. cit.* § 204, p. 334.

[11] *Ibid.* § 200, p. 327.

all or any of the parties severally liable upon the same obligation or instrument might be sued together.[12]

Whatever else may have been the result of the code provisions it thus remained true under these provisions (*a*) that in the case of joint obligations, all the joint obligors must be joined as defendants; (*b*) that in the case of joint and several obligations, suit could go against all or against one, but not against any intermediate number; (*c*) that in the case of several contract liability, other than "on the same obligation or instrument," there could be no joinder of defendants, and (*d*) that no possibility was offered of an alternative joinder in respect either of plaintiffs or defendants, to provide for the situation where it was not certainly known, on the one hand, which of two or more persons was entitled to maintain the action, or, on the other, which of two or more persons was actually liable.

These shortcomings of the original code procedure were very much the same as those existing in the common-law procedure of the non-code jurisdictions. The only difference was that in some of these the original rule forbidding the joinder of defendants severally liable in respect of contract obligations had been maintained, while in others it had been modified, as in New York before the Code, by permitting the joinder of those severally liable on bills of exchange and promissory notes. But remedy for the shortcomings in question, both within and without the code area has been supplied in considerable measure. (*a*) The common law rule as to joint obligors has been mitigated by a sequence of statutes beginning even before the era of the New York Code,[13] which have sought to convert joint obligations into joint and several ones. Where these appear, most joint obligations today fall into the category of joint and several obligations, and the question of joinder is governed accordingly. (*b*) In any case, the common-

[12] As to the effect of the code provisions in general, see Pomeroy, *op. cit.* c. II, sections 5 and 6; Clark, Code Pleading (2d ed. 1947) c. 6; Phillips, Code Pleading (2d ed. 1932) c. XIV; Bliss, Code Pleading (3d ed. 1894) cc. III-VIII.

[13] *E.g.*, Ala., Act of 1818, Aiken's Dig. (1833) p. 267, § 55; Mo. Rev. Laws 1825, p. 215, § 4; Ill. Rev. Stat. 1845, c. 56, § 3, p. 299.

law rule as to defendants in actions upon joint obligations or joint and several obligations has been changed in many jurisdictions by statutes expressly permitting suit to be brought against all or any of the obligors.[14] (*c*) In the matter of several obligations most common-law jurisdictions have now gone to the extent of the code provision in permitting the joinder in respect of the same obligation or instrument. But sundry jurisdictions, both common-law and code, have gone much further in enlarging here the possibilities of joinder,[15] even to the point, as has Michigan,[16] of expressly authorizing joinder without qualification. Here too appears remedial legislation with respect to particular kinds of contacts. Especially to be noted in this regard is the case of insurance. In a considerable number of jurisdictions, under a policy of liability insurance, the person injured is by statute given a direct action against the insurer, in consequence of which, either by express provision or by necessary construction, he may join as defendants in the same suit both the insured and the insurer.[17] So, too, provisions have been adopted in different quarters, permitting an insured to bring a single action against all the insurers answerable for his loss.[18] (*d*) And, finally, the right to join defendants (and to a lesser extent) plaintiffs in the alternative has come to recognition in an important group of jurisdictions. This has been due to the influence of the English Rules, to which are owed also certain general provisions on the subject of joinder of parties recently finding place in the American picture, as will presently appear.

While the English Common Law Procedure Act of 1852 (as, indeed, did the New York Code and its progeny) took steps toward averting or mitigating the ill consequences of an error in the joinder of parties, it made no change in the regulation of the joinder itself. But with the Judicature Acts came the need for unified re-regulation of the present field. And this was accomplished in a manner more adequate and much freer

14 For such statutes see Pomeroy, *op. cit.* § 200, note 10 to p. 328; 1 Stimson, American Statute Law (1886) § 5015, p. 609.

15 See *e.g.*, Wis. Stat. 1949, § 260.17.

16 20 Mich.Stat.Ann. 1938, § 27.667.

17 See note, 96 A.L.R. 356.

18 Wis. Stat. 1949, § 260.18; Cal. Code Civ. Proc. (Deering, 1949) § 383.

from difficulties than that of the American codes. Of the Rules of 1875[19] Order XVI dealt with the subject of parties. By Rule 1 of that Order it was provided that "all persons may be joined as plaintiffs in whom the right to any relief claimed is alleged to exist, whether jointly, severally, or in the alternative" and by Rule 3 of the same Order that "all persons may be joined as defendants against whom the right to any relief is alleged to exist, whether jointly, severally, or in the alternative." And each of these Rules provided for adaptation of the judgment to the particular situation, without amendment, the one declaring that "judgment may be given for such one or more of the plaintiffs as may be found to be entitled to relief, for such relief as he or they may be entitled to," the other that "judgment may be given against such one or more of the defendants as may be found to be liable, according to their respective liabilities." It was further declared, by Rule 4, that "it shall not be necessary that every defendant to any action shall be interested as to all the relief thereby prayed for, or as to every cause of action included therein," subject to the power of the court to protect any defendant against expense or embarrassment from his being required to attend proceedings in which he had no interest. By Rule 5 it was provided that "the plaintiff may, at his option, join as parties in the same action all or any of the persons severally, or jointly and severally, liable on any one contract, including parties to bills of exchange and promissory notes." Reinforcement of the right to join defendants in the alternative appeared in Rule 6, which expressly provided that "where in any action . . . the plaintiff is in doubt as to the person from whom he is entitled to redress, he may . . . join two or more defendants, to the intent that in such action the question as to which, if any, of the defendants is liable, and to what extent, may be determined as between all parties to the action." This scheme was complemented by various other provisions including the recognition of the initial right of a trustee or personal representative to proceed without joining the beneficiaries of the trust or estate (Rule

[19] 38 & 39 Vict. c. 77, First Schedule.

7) and the recognition also of the principle of representative or class actions (Rule 9).

These provisions passed into the revision of 1883, with a few slight textual modifications but no material change. The Order in question remained Order XVI; Rule 1 retained its number; but by reason of the insertion of a new rule not here relevant, Rule 3 became Rule 4, while the numbers of the other Rules above mentioned were correspondingly changed. In 1896, Rule 1 was amended so as to give it application to joinder of causes of action, as well as joinder of parties, but this is a matter to be considered in our next chapter. Apart from this and a slight amendment in 1893 to Rule 8 (old Rule 7) which need not concern us, the provisions in question continue in force as they appeared in the version of 1883.[20]

The first American borrowing from this source seems to have been with reference to alternative joinder, when Rhode Island in 1876,[21] adopted for its common-law practice, a provision patterned upon English Rule 7 (now Rule 8), providing for the alternative joinder of defendants. Connecticut came next by including such a provision in its rules under the Practice Act of 1879.[22] A like step was taken by Wisconsin statute in 1915.[23] But in the meantime a more extensive levying upon the English rules in question had been begun by New Jersey which incorporated in its Practice Act of 1912 [24] (for common-law causes) provisions based upon the present English Rules 1 and 4. New York followed in 1920, its Civil Practice Act of that year containing similar provisions.[25] Subsequently, and in advance of federal reform, California (1927),[26] North Carolina (1931) [27] and

20 Annual Practice 1949, I, p. 229.

21 R.I. Gen. Laws 1938, c. 518, § 1.

22 Conn. Pract. Book 1879, Rule 11, § 3; Pract. Book 1934, Rule 2, § 19, p. 26.

23 Wis. Laws 1915, c. 219; Wis. Stat. 1949, § 260.11.

24 §§ 4, 6, N.J. Stat. Ann. 1939, §§ 2:27-24, 2:27-25, 2:27-38.

25 N.Y. Civ. Pract. Act 1920, §§ 209, 211. Both repealed in 1949, being embodied in a consolidated and revised version of the rules relating to permissive joinder of parties contained in a newly enacted section § 212. N.Y. Civ. Pract. Act (Clevenger, 1950). For explanation of the change, see 15th Annual Report of N.Y. Judicial Council (1949), p. 56 *et seq.*

26 Cal. Stat. 1927, pp. 477, 478, 631; Cal. Code Civ. Proc. (Deering, 1949) §§ 378, 379a.

27 N.C. Laws 1931, c. 344, p. 436; N.C. Gen. Stat. 1943 §§ 1-68, 1-69.

Illinois (1933),[28] all adopted provisions of the kind, that is to say, authorizing the joinder, as plaintiffs of persons entitled, and as defendants of persons liable, "whether jointly, severally or in the alternative." As part of this innovation, New York, California, and Illinois introduced provisions modelled upon the present English Rule 5 (defendant's interest in relief) and present English Rule 7 (specific provision as to alternative joinder of defendants in case of doubt),[29] while North Carolina accepted the substance of the last mentioned Rule.[30] It should be added that Washington in 1927,[31] modified its regulation of the joinder of plaintiffs by giving place to a provision corresponding to English Rule 1, at the same time, for the case of defendants, incorporating in substance English Rule 7, and that a Pennsylvania statute of 1937 made similar provision limited to the case of plaintiffs.[32]

This brings us to the Federal Rules of 1938. Here, by Rule 20(a), was adopted in a somewhat recast form the principle of alternative joinder of plaintiffs, on the one hand, and defendants, on the other, as appearing in the present English Rules 1, 4 and 5. Since then, under the federal influence, the principle has significantly expanded its territory. Thus, Arizona (1939), Colorado (1941), Texas (1941), New Mexico (1942), Missouri (1943), Delaware (1947)—in the separate regulation of its law and equity procedures—, and Utah (1949), have textually reproduced Federal Rule 20(a).[33] New Jersey (1948), although no stranger to the

[28] §§ 23, 24; Ill. Rev. Stat. 1949, c. 110, §§ 147, 148.

[29] N.Y. Civ. Pract. Act 1920, §§ 212, 213; both repealed in 1949, as superseded by the new § 212: see note 25, *supra;* Cal. Code Civ. Proc. (Deering, 1949) §§ 379b, 379c; Ill. Rev. Stat. 1949, c. 110, § 148(2)(3).

[30] N.C. Gen. Stat. 1943, § 1-69.

[31] 2 Wash.Rev.Stat.Ann. (Remington, 1932) and 1945 Supp. § 308.2 (Rules of Practice, 1927, Rule II, 140 Wash. xxxv).

[32] Pa. Laws 1937, p. 2072; 12 Pa. Stat.Ann. (Purdon, 1931), Pocket Part 1949 § 159.1.

[33] Ariz. Code Ann. 1939, §§ 21-512, 513 (Rules Civ. Proc., Rule 20(a); Colo. Rules Civ. Proc., Rule 20(a), Colo. Stat. Ann. 1935, Replacement Vol. I, 1941; Tex. Rules Civ. Proc. (Vernon, 1942) Rule 40(a); N.M. Stat. Ann. 1941, § 19-101(20), Rules Civ. Proc., Rule 20(a); Mo. Laws 1943, pp. 360-361, Mo. Rev. Stat. Ann. 1942, Pocket Part 1950, § 847.16(a); Del. Rules of Superior Court, Rule 20(a), Rules of the Court of Chancery,

principle, has taken the same step with but slight deviation, for its now unified system.[34] Pennsylvania (1940) has substituted for its statute of 1937 a rule of court closely approximating the federal provision,[35] and Iowa (1943)[36] has made its own adaptation of that provision. Further to be noted are Wyoming's following (1939)[37] and Maryland's substantial reception (1947)[38] of the same provision except for omission of the requirement that the joined actions arise out of the same transaction etc., as also Nevada's acceptance (1939)[39] of joint, several or alternative joinder so far as concerns defendants.

By Federal Rule 20(b) provision is made for control of the joinder thus authorized by empowering the court to order separate trials or make other orders in the end of preventing embarrassment, delay or prejudice. And this provision has generally accompanied State acceptance of Rule 20(a).

The particular phrasing of Federal Rule 20(a) will more conveniently be noticed in connection with the joinder of actions, for the unscientific commingling of the ideas of joinder of parties and joinder of demands, ushered in by the English amendment of 1896, has been carried into that provision, as it had into the pre-existing American provisions based upon English Rules 1 and 4, except those of North Carolina which are restricted to the matter of parties.

As against this permissive joinder, however, the Federal Rules provide for a compulsory joinder. While the English Rules contain no express provision looking to the compulsory joinder as plaintiffs or defendants of persons in joint interest it nevertheless remains true, under the English system, that in actions upon joint contracts, all the joint obligees must join as plaintiffs, and all the joint obligors must be joined as de-

Rule 20(a); Utah Rules Civ. Proc., Rule 20(a).

34 N.J. Rules of Civil Practice, Rule 3:20-1.

35 Pa. Rules Civ. Proc., Rule 2229, 12 Pa. Stat. Ann. (Purdon, 1931) Appendix, Pocket Part 1949.

36 Ia. Rules Civ. Proc., Rules 23, 24, 26, Ia. Code 1946, Vol. II, pp. 2146-2147.

37 Wyo. Laws 1939, c. 51, § 3, Wyo. Comp. Stat. 1945, § 3-613.

38 Md. Gen. Rules Pract. & Proc. Part 2, Subd. III, Rule 2(c) (d) (e), Md. Ann. Code (Flack, 1939) 1947 Cum. Supp. p. 2041.

39 Nev. Laws 1939, p. 32; Nev. Comp. Laws 1929, Supp. 1931-41, § 8556.

fendants.[40] The Federal Rules, on the other hand, have spoken out loud on this phase of the situation, by a provision manifestly influenced by that of the codes. Subject to the recognition of class actions and to what is in effect the former equity rule permitting the court to proceed in the absence of persons who ought to be parties but are not indispensable, it is declared by Rule 19 that "persons having a joint interest shall be made parties and shall be joined on the same side as plaintiffs or defendants. When a person who should join as a plaintiff refuses to do so, he may be made a defendant, or, in proper cases, an involuntary plaintiff."

[40] Annual Practice 1949, I, pp. 237, 262. The old rule still applies, with some exceptions, that if a joint obligor is omitted and the suit prosecuted to judgment against the other or others, the plaintiff has lost his claim against the one omitted, by the merger of the joint cause of action in the judgment. Moreover, it is open to those sued to compel the addition of the omitted joint obligor. *Ibid.* pp. 262, 379-380.

CHAPTER X

JOINDER OF DEMANDS

According to the rule of the common law, joinder of causes of action was limited to the case where all fell within the same form of action, with the two exceptions, accounted for historically, that detinue might be joined with debt and trover with trespass on the case. In chancery, there prevailed, in striking contrast, the rule which restricted the union only by the elastic test of multifariousness. In America, departure from the old rules definitely came with the New York Code of 1848. This, for its unified procedure, set up a new system of joinder—a system which, as the event has proved, was needlessly complicated and inflexible. As amended in 1852, it provided for a joinder of all claims which "arise out of the same transaction, or transactions connected with the same subject of action," and then, for claims not having this common origin, established six other classes into one of which the situation must fit before a joinder was allowable.[1] The latter regulation was especially ill-advised. Thus,

[1] Code of 1848, § 143; Code of 1849, § 167, New York Laws 1852, c. 392, p. 655.

As appearing after the amendment of 1852 the provision was the following:

"The plaintiff may unite in the same complaint several causes of action, whether they be such as have been heretofore denominated legal or equitable or both, where they all arise out of,

1. The same transaction, or transactions connected with the same subject of action.
2. Contract express or implied; or
3. Injuries with or without force, to person and property, or either; or
4. Injuries to character; or
5. Claims to recover real property, with or without damages, for withholding thereof, and the rents and profits of the same; or
6. Claims to recover personal property, with or without damages for the withholding thereof; or
7. Claims against a trustee, by virtue of a contract, or by operation of law.

But the causes of action, so united, must all belong to one of these classes, and must affect all the parties to the action, and not require different places of trial, and must be separately stated."

unless there existed the common origin indicated, it would not permit, for example, the joinder of a claim in contract with one in tort, or one for injury to character with one for injury to the person, or one for the recovery of real property with one for the recovery of personal property. Nor has the "same transaction" clause been at all a satisfactory one, for its terms and especially the expression "subject of the action" have given rise to endless difficulties of interpretation. But this group system, with variations of greater or less extent, is that which continues to be followed in most of the American code jurisdictions, including Kentucky, Arkansas and Oregon where it finds separate application to legal and equitable causes of action. An early adoption of a different system appears in the case of Iowa. Here, dating from the Code of 1851, there may be a free joinder of legal causes of action, on the one hand, or equitable causes of action, on the other, subject to the power of the court to direct separate trials.[2] Usually, however, it is a condition of the joinder, under these systems, that the several causes of action shall have identity of plaintiffs and defendants: as ordinarily provided, "they must affect all parties to the action." Sometimes it is declared that they must be consistent with each other. And, for the most part, there is further expressed the requirement that all shall be triable in the same venue.

A joinder rule of another sort obtains in Georgia. In this State, since 1861, there may be a joinder of all claims arising *ex contractu*, as of all claims arising *ex delicto*.[3] Originally applicable to legal and equitable claims as separate classes, it now, since 1887 when that separation was definitely discontinued,[4] governs the union of claims in general. Another system of which note should be taken in the present connection has been that of Texas. From an early day its courts followed a doctrine that governed the matter of joinder

[2] Ia. Code 1851, § 1751, Ia. Code Civ. Practice 1860, § 240, Ia. Revision 1860, § 2844, Ia. Code 1939, §§ 10960-10961, Ia. Rules Civ. Proc. 1942, Rules 22, 186 in Ia. Code 1946. Vol. II, pp. 2146, 2164.

[3] Ga. Code 1861, § 3185; Ga. Code 1933, § 3-113.

[4] 2 Ga.Laws 1886-7, p. 64, see Hecht v. Snook & Austin Furniture Co., 114 Ga. 921, 926, 41 S.E. 74 (1902); Ga. Code 1933, § 3-104.

by what was substantially the test of convenience in the particular case. This result appears to have been influenced by the equity test of multifariousness, not unaided by the Spanish rule in reference to cumulation of actions.[5] But now, since 1941, the matter is dealt with by certain rules of court drawn from the Federal Rules of 1938.[6]

In various jurisdictions maintaining the partition between law and equity is observable the effect upon joinder on the common-law side of provisions directed toward removal of the boundaries between the common-law forms of action. Thus, in respect of personal actions, Massachusetts since 1851 has recognized but the three divisions of contract, tort and replevin,[7] and Tennessee, since 1858, but the four divisions of contract, tort (action on the facts of the case), replevin, and detinue.[8] So Pennsylvania, under legislation of 1887,[9] has merged assumpsit, debt and covenant into a single form known as assumpsit, and trespass, trover and case into a single form known as trespass. And Vermont, by an act of 1915,[10] now knows on the common-law side only the four forms of contract, tort, replevin and ejectment. Obviously, in observance of the traditional principle of joinder within the same form of action, these measures have operated to permit the union of claims within a circle considerably wider than had been before allowable. Elsewhere in the same type of jurisdiction appear instances of a more direct widening on the common-law side. In Alabama, by successive steps from 1852 to 1917,[11] joinder is allowable so long as all the causes of action are in contract on the one hand, or *ex delicto*, on the other, with the added permission to join contract and tort claims "arising out of the same transaction, or relating to the same subject-matter." And the rule followed by Florida

5 Chevalier v. Rusk, Dallam 611 (Tex. 1844); Clegg v. Varnell, 18 Tex. 294 (1857); Hudmon v. Foster, 231 S.W. 346 (Tex. Com. App. 1921).

6 See *infra*, notes 20, 33.

7 Mass. Laws 1851, c. 233, § 1, 8 Mass.Ann.Laws 1933, c. 231, § 1.

8 Tenn. Code 1858, §§ 2746-2749; 8 Tenn.CodeAnn. (Williams 1934) §§ 8563-8566.

9 Pa. Laws 1887, p. 271, Pa. Stat. Ann. (Purdon, 1931) Tit. 12, §§ 1, 2.

10 Vt. Laws 1915, p. 176, § 1; Vt. Stat. 1947, § 1611.

11 Ala. Code 1852, § 2235; Ala. Code 1907, §§ 5328, 5329; Ala. Code 1923, § 9466, 9467; Ala. Code 1940, §§ 7-219, 220.

since 1861 [12] (except for a brief interval in the Reconstruction period when there was in force a code of the New York pattern) has been that of the English Common Law Procedure Act of 1852 later to be noted.

But the trend of more recent American reform measures has been to a completely free joinder of causes of action with identity of parties, provision being made for the severance or separate trial if the interests of justice require. New Jersey in 1912, as its first acceptance, adopted this principle for its common-law actions.[13] A provision looking, as that of Iowa, to a free joinder on each of the two sides of the court was enacted by Michigan in 1915: [14] whether it has been permitted the intended scope may perhaps be doubted.[15] A like freedom of joinder, necessarily without reference to any distinction between law and equity, was recognized by Kansas in 1909 [16] and Wisconsin in 1915.[17] Illinois, by its Civil Practice Act of 1933,[18] declared for the present principle in permitting the joinder "of any causes of action, whether legal or equitable or both." New York followed in 1935 in recasting its joinder rule so as to discard its categorical system (which had survived the Civil Practice Act of 1920) and to provide generally for the joinder of two or more causes of action whether they are such as were formerly denominated legal or equitable.[19] Finally, the Federal Rules of 1938 yielded complete adherence in the provisions of their Rule 18. Rule 18(a) permits the plaintiff or counterclaimant to "join either as independent or as alternate claims as many claims either legal or equitable or both as he may have against an opposing party," and Rule 18(b)

[12] Fla. Laws 1860-61, c. 1096, § 12; Fla. Stat. 1949, § 46.08.

[13] N.J. Laws 1912, c. 231, § 11; 1 N.J.Stat.Ann. 1939, § 2:27-37.

[14] Mich. Laws 1915, No. 314 (Judicature Act) c. VIII, § 1, p. 56, 20 Mich.Stat.Ann. (1938) § 27.591.

[15] Brewster Loud Lumber Co v. General Builders' Supply Co., 233 Mich. 633, 208 N.W. 28 (1926); Multiplex Concrete Machinery Co. v. Saxer, 310 Mich. 243, 17 N.W. (2d) 169 (1945).

[16] Kan. Laws 1909, c. 182, § 88, Kan. Gen. Stat. Ann. (Corrick, 1935) § 60-601.

[17] Wis. Laws 1915, c. 219, § 4; Wis. Stat. 1949, § 263.04.

[18] § 44(1); Ill. Rev. Stat. 1949, c. 110, § 168(1).

[19] N.Y. Laws 1935, c. 339; as revised, N.Y. Civ. Pract. Act (Clevenger, 1950) § 258.

applies this principle to the case where the establishment of one of the claims is a condition precedent to the other.

Rule 18(a) has been copied or adapted by Arizona (1939), Wyoming (1939), Colorado (1941), Texas (1941), New Mexico (1942), Missouri (1943), Maryland (1947), Delaware (1947), New Jersey (1948), and Utah (1949), and has apparently guided recent regulation (1943) in Iowa. Moreover, all these jurisdictions except Wyoming, Delaware and Iowa have likewise either reproduced or adapted Rule 18(b).[20]

Except for the wider range of the traditional equity doctrine of joinder of claims in jurisdictions where this has continued to be followed, it is apparent that the canons so far considered usually contemplate the case of joinder of claims with identity of parties. The codes in general, either expressly or impliedly, have insisted upon that identity, prohibiting such a joinder as would be in view where, for example, A proposes to unite with a claim against B a distinct claim which he has against C, or where A and B propose to unite their distinct claims against C. But of late years important change has been coming about in this respect, under the influence of the English Rules. That borrowing which we have noted in relation to the joinder of parties has introduced in a number of American jurisdictions provisions precisely contemplating a joinder of claims with diversity of parties. This will more particularly appear in the sequel, but for the moment we must transfer our attention to the English development.

In England, innovation in the field of joinder of demands began with the Common Law Procedure Act of 1852. This

[20] Ariz. Code Ann. 1939, §§ 21-507, 508 (Rules Civ. Proc., Rule 18); Wyo. Laws 1939, c. 51, § 1, Wyo. Comp. Stat. Ann. 1945, § 3-701; Colo. Rules Civ. Proc., Rule 18, Colo. Stat. Ann. 1935, Replacement Vol. I, 1941; Tex. Rules Civ. Proc. (Vernon, 1942), Rule 51; N.M. Stat. Ann. 1941, § 19-101(18), (Rules Civ. Proc., Rule 18); Mo. Laws 1943, p. 370, 3 Mo. Rev. Stat. Ann. 1942, Pocket Part 1950, §§ 847.37, 847.38; Md. Gen. Rules of Pract. & Proc., Part 2 Subd. III, Rule 2(a)(b), in Md. Ann. Code (Flack) 1947 Cum. Suppl. p. 2040; Del. Rules of Superior Court, Rule 18, Rules of Court of Chancery, Rule 18; N.J. Rules Civ. Pract., Rule 3:18-1, 3:18-2; Ia. Rules Civ. Proc., Rule 22, in Ia. Code 1946, p. 2146; Utah Rules Civ. Proc., Rule 18.

permitted the joinder, apart from replevin and ejectment, of common-law "causes of action of whatever kind, provided they be by and against the same parties and in the same rights," with power in the court to direct separate trials.[21] On this modified basis the English law remained until the Judicature Acts. For the now fused procedure the Rules of 1875 expanded the principle thus introduced in 1852 by providing that "the plaintiff may unite in the same action and in the same statement of claim several causes of action." Leave of court, however, was required for the joinder with a claim for the recovery of land of any other than a money claim in connection with the defendant's holding of the land, and for the joinder of a claim by a trustee in bankruptcy as such with one by him in any other capacity. Certain specific authorization was given for the union of joint and separate claims, as also of claims by and against an executor as such with claims by and against him personally. Separate trials might always be ordered, and the defendant was to be at liberty to move for the exclusion of any cause of action where this stood in the way of a convenient disposition of the whole.[22] These provisions, without change in substance, passed into the revision of 1883 as Order XVIII, and, with minor amendment, continue in force.

Standing alone, Order XVIII did not countenance, except to the slight degree indicated, any departure from the principle that forbade the joinder of actions with diversity of plaintiffs or defendants. Under its terms, for example, a cause of action in favor of A could not be united with a cause of action in favor of B, nor a cause of action against C with a cause of action against D. But in a case where it was sought to join a number of distinct causes of action in favor of different plaintiffs against the same defendant, the supporting contention was advanced that the very effect of permitting such a joinder attended the rules in relation to joinder of parties, in virtue of their provision (Order XVI, Rule 1) authorizing the joinder of plaintiffs "in whom any right to

[21] 15 & 16 Vict. c. 76, § 41.

[22] 38 & 39 Vict. c. 77, First Schedule, Ord. XVII.

relief is alleged to exist, whether jointly, severally, or in the alternative." In consequence of the decision of the House of Lords in *Smurthwaite* v. *Hannay* [23] denying this contention, Rule 1 was amended in 1896 so as to make it apply to joinder of actions as well as of parties. As thus amended, Rule 1 now provides that:

> All persons may be joined in one action as plaintiffs, in whom any right to relief in respect of or arising out of the same transaction or series of transactions is alleged to exist, whether jointly, severally, or in the alternative, where if such persons brought separate actions any common question of law or fact would arise; provided that, if upon the application of any defendant it shall appear that such joinder may embarrass or delay the trial of the action, the court or a judge may order separate trials, or make such other order as may be expedient, and judgment may be given for such one or more of the plaintiffs as may be found to be entitled to relief, for such relief as he or they may be entitled to, without any amendment. . . .

Although in terms affecting only the case of causes of action in favor of different plaintiffs under Rule 1, the amendment by judicial construction has been made to operate also upon Rule 4 of the same Order, relating to defendants and authorizing the joinder of all "against whom the right to any relief is alleged to exist, whether jointly, severally, or in the alternative.[24] Thus, as the effect of the amendment, both Rules now apply to joinder of causes of action as well as to joinder of parties. By its express terms, it permits, on the part of a plurality of plaintiffs, the joining of distinct claims "in respect of or arising out of the same transaction or series of transactions," where, if separate actions had been brought, a "common question of law or fact would arise." And as to claims against a plurality of defendants, the construction referred to is such as to authorize this joinder if not under precisely the same state of the case, at least under a closely similar one, namely, where they exist "in respect of or arising out of a

[23] [1894] A.C. 494.

[24] *E.g.,* Compania Sansinena de Carnes Congeladas v. Houlder Bros. & Co. Ltd. [1910] 2 K.B. 354.

set of circumstances involving a common question of law or fact."[25]

The outcome is that under the English system, not only may there be an almost unlimited joinder of causes of action by the same plaintiff against the same defendant, but place has also been given in wide measure to a joinder of causes of action with diversity of parties extending to the case of alternative joinder of distinct causes of action. This joinder is permissible so long as the united claims exhibit as between themselves that slender measure of community of origin and community of litigable question which is prescribed in the one case by the words of the amendment itself and in the other by the holdings of the courts. But, as appears, the joinder thus allowed, as also the joinder with identity of parties, is subject at all times to the power of the court to order separate trials or other separate disposition of the combined causes of action.

We have seen in connection with the joinder of parties how provisions modeled upon Rules 1 and 4 have found entrance into a considerable number of American jurisdictions. What invited this movement even more, perhaps, than the bearing of the Rules upon the joinder of parties, was the liberalization of the joinder of demands which they offered as a result of the amendment of 1896. Hence it is that nearly all the American provisions incorporated the bifactoral test for that joinder introduced into Rule 1 by the amendment. Here are to be noted, as patterning after Rules 1 and 4, New Jersey (in the now superseded Practice Act of 1912, governing common-law causes),[26] New York (Civil Practice Act of 1920),[27] California (1927),[28] Illinois (Civil Practice Act of 1933),[29] the new Federal Rules (Rule 20) and, in reliance upon the last named, Arizona (1939),[30]

[25] Annual Practice 1949, I, p. 258, summarizing the decisions as to this species of joinder.

[26] N.J. Laws 1912, c. 231, §§ 4, 6; N.J. Stat. Ann. 1939, §§ 2:27-24, 2:27-25, 2:27-38.

[27] §§ 209, 211. Repealed in 1949 and embodied in revised form in new § 212. N.Y. Civ. Pract. Act (Clevenger, 1950). And see *supra*, Chap. IX, note 25.

[28] Cal. Laws 1927, pp. 477, 631, Cal. Code Civ. Proc. (Deering, 1949) §§ 378, 379a.

[29] §§ 23, 24; Ill. Rev. Stat. (1949) c. 110, §§ 147, 148.

[30] Ariz. Code Ann. 1939, §§ 21-512, 513 (Rules Civ. Proc., Rule 20).

Pennsylvania (1940),[31] Colorado (1941),[32] Texas (1941),[33] New Mexico (1942),[34] Missouri (1943),[35] Iowa (1943),[36] Delaware (1947),[37] New Jersey, enlarging thus upon its provisions of 1912 (1948),[38] and Utah (1949).[38a] Wyoming (1939) [39] and Maryland (1947),[40] otherwise influenced by the Federal Rule, have converted the bifactoral test into a unifactoral one since they omit the requirement that the claims shall arise out of the same transaction etc.

Washington,[41] it will be recollected, has accepted (1927), the tenor of English Rule 1 but not of Rule 4, thus confining itself in the present respect to the case of joinder with diversity of plaintiffs.[42] In New York operation of the new principle was formerly embarrassed by retention of the categorical regulation with its concomitant provisions. This appears from the case of *Ader* v. *Blau,*[43] decided in 1925, which held inadmissible a joinder of distinct but alternative causes of action largely because of the continuing presence in the Civil Practice Act of the requirement, included in the categorical regulation, that the claims should arise out of "the same transaction or transactions connected with the same subject of action," and should be "consistent with each other." But in 1935 the difficulty was obviated by rejection of the categorical regulation in favor of a free joinder, as

[31] Pa. Rules Civ. Proc., Rule 2229: Pa. Stat. Ann. (Purdon, 1931), Appendix to Tit. 12, Pocket Part 1949, p. 327.

[32] Colo. Rules Civ. Proc., Rule 20, Colo. Stat. Ann., 1939, Replacement Vol. I, 1941.

[33] Tex. Rules Civ. Proc. (Vernon, 1942) Rule 40.

[34] N.M. Stat. Ann. 1941, § 19-101 (20) (Rules Civ. Proc., Rule 20).

[35] Mo. Laws 1943, pp. 360-361, 3 Mo.Rev.Stat.Ann. 1942, Pocket Part 1950, § 847-16.

[36] Ia. Rules Civ. Proc., Rules 23, 24, 26, Ia. Code 1946, Vol. II, pp. 2146-2147.

[37] Del. Rules of Superior Court, Rule 20, Rules of Court of Chancery, Rule 20.

[38] N.J. Rules Civ. Pract., Rule 3:20.

[38a] Utah Rules Civ. Proc., Rule 20.

[39] Wyo. Laws 1939, c. 51, § 3; Wyo. Comp. Stat. 1945, § 3-613.

[40] Md. Gen. Rules of Pract. & Proc., Part 2, Subd. III, Rule 2(d)(e) in Md. Ann. Code (Flack) 1947 Cum. Suppl. p. 2041.

[41] 2 Wash.Rev.Stat.Ann. (Remington, 1932) and 1945 Supp. § 308-2 (Rules of Practice, 1927, 1938, 1944, Rule 2).

[42] Note the approach to this idea in the Wisconsin provision of 1931, that "when more than one person makes a separate claim for damage against the same person or persons based upon the same alleged negligence, they may unite in prosecuting their claims in one action." Wis. Stat. 1949, § 260.12.

[43] 241 N.Y. 7, 148 N.E. 771 (1925).

has been mentioned above. In the case of Pennsylvania, as before noted in connection with the joinder of parties, a first step in the present direction had been taken by a statutory provision of 1937, corresponding to English Rule 1 and thus affecting only the matter of plaintiffs,[44]—a provision, however, which has been superseded by its rule of court of 1940, envisaging both plaintiffs and defendants and based upon the Federal Rule.[45] In Pennsylvania and Delaware the new provisions necessarily operate within the limits imposed by the separate administration of law and equity. In the majority of the adopting jurisdictions, however, it is clear that these provisions are permitted free play unhampered by either division of actions, categorical regulation or other obstructive elements. It need hardly be stressed that the joinder thus allowed, as well as free joinder with identity of parties, is generally made subject to the power of the court, in case of need, to order separate trials or other separate disposition of the combined causes of action.[46]

As the provision of the Federal Rules, judging by the influence that they have already exerted, is likely to set the specific pattern of future American legislation on the present point, it will be in order to look at its particular terms. It declares (Rule 20(a)) that:

> All persons may join in one action as plaintiffs if they assert any right to relief jointly, severally, or in the alternative in respect of or arising out of the same transaction, occurrence, or series of transactions or occurrences and if any question of law or fact common to all of them will arise in the action. All persons may be joined in one action as defendants, if there is asserted against them jointly, severally or in the alternative, any right to relief in respect of or arising out of the same transaction, occurrence or series of transactions or occurrences and if any question of law or fact common to all of them will arise in the action. A plaintiff or defendant need not be interested in obtaining or defending against all the relief demanded. Judgment may be given for one or more of the plain-

[44] Pa. Laws 1937, p. 2072, Pa. Stat. Ann. (Purdon, 1931) Tit. 12, Pocket Part 1949, § 159.1.

[45] *Supra*, note 31.

[46] For the Federal Rules, such judicial control of the joinder here in question is provided by Rule 20(b).

tiffs according to their respective rights to relief, and against one or more defendants according to their respective liabilities.

English Rules 1 and 4 of Order XVI are here represented by the combined provision in question. The clause with respect to unequal interest is based upon Rule 5 of the same Order [47] which, however, speaks in this connection only of defendants. It is to be observed that the Federal Rule, in not postulating the common question as one which would arise if separate actions had been brought, is not quite as explicit as its prototype to the effect that distinct causes of action are within its contemplation, but that this is its meaning no one can doubt.[48] Again, the same departure has rendered it necessary for the Rule to say "will arise" where the prototype, speaking in terms of hypothetical separate actions, says "would arise." In truth, neither expression is a happy one. For it cannot be known with certainty at the outset of the action what questions either of law or of fact the defendant will raise. All that we face here in any case is a probability of greater or less strength. If the Rule had qualified the common question as one which "in all likelihood will arise" or one which "is capable of arising," it would have come closer to accuracy in the present regard. Finally, however, is to be noted improvement upon the original in that the Rule does not leave to construction the case of joinder of separate causes of action in respect of defendants, but permits this upon precisely the same conditions as it does the joinder of plaintiffs.

Unquestionably it is essential to a well-ordered procedure that there should be no such combined disposition of separate causes of action as will work confusion or prejudice. But it is equally essential to avoid a plurality of suits where one will serve. And reconcilement of the two aims is not to be found in detailed rules, such as appeared in the New York Code and are still maintained by most of its progeny, but in according to plaintiffs a wide liberty of joinder and to the court discretionary powers to separate the issues for trial.

[47] See *supra,* Chap. IX, pp. 106-107.

[48] Especially as the canon of joinder established by Rule 18(a) is by a further provision of that rule made applicable to the case of multiple parties under Rule 20.

Recognition of this truth accounts for the latter-day course of the development, in which, as conspicuously appears, there has been a shifting from a hard and fast initial regulation of the joinder to a regulation confided in large measure to the judicial discretion. Some check upon the initial union there should be, and in the bifactoral test originated by the English Rules, this check seems satisfactorily afforded; certain it is, at least, that no closer relation should be here demanded.

Chapter XI

COUNTER-DEMANDS AND CROSS-CLAIMS

§ 1. Counter-Demands

Something in the nature of a claim for affirmative relief advanced by the defendant may be seen in the common-law action of replevin where he set up a right to the chattel in suit. This apart, the common law gave no place to counter-demands, except as there developed in its later history through judicial decision the limited recognition residing in the principle of recoupment. But from statute came introduction of the principle of set-off. By the English statute of 1729,[1] it was provided that in case of "mutual debts" between plaintiff and defendant, "one debt may be set against the other, and such matter may be given in evidence upon the general issue, or pleaded in bar, as the nature of the case shall require," under the restriction that to be allowable upon the general issue, notice of the set-off should be given. The provision was a temporary one but was made perpetual six years later,[2] with the added declaration, in settlement of a question meantime arising, that the right of set-off was to obtain "notwithstanding that such debts are deemed in law to be of a different nature." It was, however, subjoined that where either debt had accrued by virtue of a penalty in any bond or specialty the defense should be made the subject of a special plea in bar. The set-off thus authorized was of mutual debts, which meant that only liquidated demands fell within the terms of the statute. Moreover, to be mutual, it was necessary that the opposed demands have mutuality of parties: a several debt due C, for example, could not be set off against a demand by A and B, or a debt due B and C against a demand by A alone. Again, the statute envisaged

[1] 2 Geo. II, c. 22, § 13.

[2] 8 Geo. II, c. 24, §§ 4, 5.

the set-off as a defense and nothing more: under its terms there could be no affirmative recovery by the defendant. It has already been noticed that for America this English legislation had been anticipated in the colonial era.[3] And particularly interesting is the circumstance that Pennsylvania (1705-6), followed by New York (1714) and New Jersey (1722) had made provision for what was equivalent to an affirmative judgment in favor of the defendant where a balance was found due the latter.[4] But, whether in consequence of independent colonial enactments or by adaptation of the English provision, statutes of set-off had become universal in the American jurisdictions under the old order. Most of these admitted affirmative recovery by the defendant and certain of them extended in some sort to the allowance of unliquidated demands.[5]

Such was the case on the common-law side. A very different attitude toward the counter-demand characterized the court of equity. So far as regards the set-off of mutual debts, this principle had here come to recognition before the English statutes of set-off: indeed, it was probably from equity that the legislation had taken its inspiration. But in the sphere of chancery hospitality to the counter-demand the matter of set-off was only an incident. By means of the cross-bill, the earliest regulation of which appears to have been at the hands of Lord Keeper Sir Nicholas Bacon, in the second half of the 1500s[6]—the defendant was enabled to obtain a very wide measure of affirmative relief. Admissibility of the cross-bill was conditioned upon its relation to the original bill. The cross-bill must be a bill "touching the matter in question" in the original bill,[7] in such wise that it has

[3] *Supra,* Chap. IV.

[4] Loyd, The Development of Set-Off (1916) 64 U.ofPa.L.Rev. 541, 553 *et seq.*

[5] See *ibid.* 562. The Florida statute making the subject of set-off all mutual "debts or demands . . . whether the same be liquidated or not," which remained in force until the broadening amendment of 1941, was originally enacted Nov. 23, 1828. Dig. Fla. Laws, (Thompson, 1847) pp. 347-348. See Fla. Comp. Gen. Laws 1927, § 4326; Fla. Laws 1941, c. 20426; Fla. Stat. 1949, § 52.11.

[6] "Cross bills were at first unwillingly allowed of; the Court foresaw great inconvenience from them, and the rules relating to them were introduced by Sir Nicholas Bacon." Ward v. Eyles, Mos. 377, 382, 25 E.R. 449, 452 (1730).

[7] Mitford, Chancery Pleadings (5th ed. 1847) 97.

been considered as "a proceeding to procure a complete determination of a matter already in litigation in the court." [8] In general, therefore, a cross-bill was in order, whenever, in the case of a defendant seeking affirmative relief, the determination of his right thereto would be essential to a complete doing of justice between all the parties in respect of the matters introduced by the original bill. Shortly, the test here applicable is spoken of as that of "germaneness": the cross-bill was admissible if its matter was germane to that of the original bill. It is evident that the test was an elastic one, since minds might easily differ, in a given case, as to what was included in a complete determination of the matter of the original bill. But much in this regard had been definitely settled by judicial precedent, and it may be said that by the middle of the nineteenth century the development was progressively favoring enlargement of the compass within which the defendant might thus proceed.

In view of the obvious desirability of adjudicating, so far as consistent with practical justice, reciprocal claims in a single suit, correction of the common-law deficiency and the attainment of a uniformly applicable rule necessarily engaged the attention of reform legislation. The first decisive step in this direction appears to have been taken by the Iowa Code of 1851, which provided that the defendant might "set up by way of set-off or cross action any claim which would have been the subject of an action against the plaintiff," provided that it was matured at the time of advancement.[9] The width of this pioneer measure is especially noteworthy. The New York Code of 1848 contained no provision on the subject, but as amended in 1852, it admitted, for the prosecution of counter-demands what was given the new name of "counterclaim." [10] This contemplated a counter-demand "existing in favor of a defendant, and against a plaintiff, between whom a several judgment might be had in the ac-

[8] *Ibid.* 97-98.

[9] § 1740.

[10] New, that is to say, in the sense of a standard term. The commissioners who reported the revised Iowa statutes of 1860 refer to use of the term in 1717 in Brown's Cases in Parliament, 587. Iowa Revision of 1860, note to § 2889, pp. 524-525.

tion." And, except where the counter-demand was based upon contract and interposed in an action on contract, it fell under the requirement that the counter-demand be one "arising out of the contract or transaction set forth in the complaint, as the foundation of the plaintiff's claim, or connected with the subject of the action." For the case of contract demand against contract demand no relationship was required.[11] The rules thus laid down by the New York Code have been followed, at least in substance, by a majority of the American codes. Among other variations from its exact terms, it is often the case that the second category of the provision, that of contract demand against contract demand, is placed under the separate rubric of "set-off." Quite apart from its unnecessary restriction of the field of counter-demands, the provision has not been a fortunate one. For the particular terms in which it has sought to define the relationship required in its first category, and especially the phrase "subject of the action," much as has been the case with the similar language used by the codes in reference to joinder of causes of action, have given rise to continual diversity of interpretation. For the purpose of conforming the provision to previous holdings of its courts,[12] New York in 1877 amended it by adding the further restriction that the counterclaim must "tend, in some way, to diminish or defeat the plaintiff's recovery."[13] Thus, if the defendant sought a form of relief whose granting would not interfere in whole or in part with the granting of that claimed by the plaintiff, the counterclaim was not to be admissible. A few only of the other codes have enacted the like limitation, but some others have applied the same rule as a matter of judicial doctrine. New York, itself, has abandoned the rule along with the rest of the provision inherited from the Code, this by legislation of 1936.[14]

Iowa, in the present respect, preserved its independent position. While the revision of 1860 exhibits the influence of the New York legislation, it did not recede in substance

[11] N.Y. Laws 1852, c. 392, p. 654, amending §§ 149, 150, Code of 1849.

[12] N.Y. Code Civ. Proc. (Throop, 1880) p. 214, note to § 501.

[13] N.Y. Laws 1877, c. 416, p. 449.

[14] N.Y. Laws 1936, c. 324, repealing Civ. Pract. Act, § 266, and adding a new § 266. (Clevenger, 1950).

from the advanced stand taken in 1851. It provided for the classification of counter-demands into (1) set-off, (2) counterclaims and (3) "cross demands." By set-off, it understood a cause of action on contract or judgment, pleadable only in contract actions. Its counterclaim contemplated a cause of action "in favor of the defendants, or some of them, against the plaintiffs or some of them," otherwise defined according to the formula of the New York provision for cases other than those of contract demand against contract demand. And under the name of "cross-demand," it allowed the defense to plead a cause of action of any kind, so long as it exhibited complete mutuality of parties with the principal demand.[15] The intention was that these three classes together should cover no wider a field than the simpler provision of 1851.[16] But that there was here, however, undue differentiation, at least in nomenclature, is attested by the fact that, the relative provisions remaining the same, they were later grouped under the general head of "counterclaim," and so appeared in the Iowa Code of 1939.[17] The Iowa provisions, however, have since been recast under the influence of the Federal Rules of 1938, a matter for our later notice.

A number of the codes, in addition to provision for counterclaim, contain a separate provision for cross-complaint or cross-petition. Usually this initially proceeds from the idea of a claim by one defendant against a co-defendant, and although variously elaborated in respect of parties, excludes the matter of a claim-relation solely between the defendant and the plaintiff, and is therefore properly referable to the category of cross-claims later to be considered. But this is not always the case. A provision adopted by California in 1874 made a cross-complaint available "whenever the defendant seeks affirmative relief against any party, relating to or depending upon the contract or transaction upon which the action is brought, or affecting the property to which the action relates." [18] This was subsequently copied with or with-

[15] Ia. Code Civ. Pract. 1860, §§ 276, 282, 285, 287; Ia. Revision 1860, §§ 2880, 2886, 2889, 2891.

[16] *Ibid.* p. 526, note to § 2891.

[17] Ia. Code 1939, § 11151.

[18] Cal. Amendments to Codes 1873-1874, p. 301.

out variations, but almost always with the same formula of relationship to the principal demand, by other Western States, including Idaho, Montana, Nevada and New Mexico.[19] It is obvious, given retention of the usual form of counterclaim provision, that the field of the cross-complaint thus provided for overlaps that of the counterclaim. Apparently to avoid the duplication here involved, California in 1927 took the step of discarding for the counterclaim any requirement of relationship to the principal demand and making its sole test that of tending to diminish or defeat the plaintiff's recovery, so long as (in keeping with the received rule) it exists in favor of a defendant and against a plaintiff between whom a several judgment may be had in the action.[20] All other counter-demands, in consequence, fall under the governance of the cross-complaint provision, which in the meantime has been materially improved in sundry respects.[21]

The counterclaim, as originally regulated, contemplated a controversy between one or more of the defendants and one or more of the plaintiffs in the principal action, and not involving other parties. But a considerable number of the codes authorize the addition of new parties as defendants to the counterclaim. The commonest provision of the kind is that apparently originating in the Kentucky Code of 1851,[22] which with little or no change in wording appears in the codes of Ohio, Arkansas, Kansas, Nebraska, Oklahoma, and Wyoming,[23] if not elsewhere. This is to the effect that where a new party is necessary to the final decision of the counterclaim, the court may permit the new party to be introduced or direct

[19] Idaho Code Ann. 1949, § 5-617; Mont. Rev. Codes Ann. 1935, § 9151; 1947, § 93-3415; Nev. Comp. Laws 1929, § 8606 ("against any party to the action"); N.M. Stat. Ann. 1929, § 105-405, now superseded by N.M. Stat. Ann. 1941, § 19-101(13).

[20] Cal. Laws 1927, p. 1620; Cal. Code Civ. Proc. (Deering, 1949) § 438.

[21] *Ibid.* § 442.

[22] § 153. Ky. Laws 1850-51, p. 130. Under the present Kentucky Code the addition of new parties is by virtue of a general provision applying to cross-petitions, set-offs and counterclaims. Ky. Code Pract. in Civ. Cas. (Carroll, 1948) § 97(3).

[23] Ohio Gen. Code Ann. (Page, 1938) § 11318; Ark. Stat. Ann. 1947, § 27-1124; Kan. Gen. Stat. Ann. 1935, § 60-712; Neb. Rev. Stat. 1943, § 25-815; Okla. Stat. 1941, Tit. 12, § 276; Utah Code Ann. 1943, § 104-9-6; Wyo. Comp. Stat. Ann. 1945, § 1315.

that the counterclaim be stricken out and relegated to a separate action. Connecticut exhibits a different form of provision by which the addition of new parties is permitted as required.[24] And New York, in deserting the Code for the Civil Practice Act of 1920, incorporated therein a provision, influenced by the English Rules, countenancing and methodizing the joining of new parties as defendants to the counterclaim.[25] In those States which are equipped with a provision for a cross-complaint of the California type, this furnishes a means of proceeding against new parties along with the plaintiff or plaintiffs, if a new-party provision has not been included in the regulation of the counterclaim, provided that the counter-demand falls within the prescribed relationship.

While in most of the American common-law jurisdictions the claim of statutory set-off, in addition to the defense of recoupment, continues to be the sole manner of counter-demand finding place in common-law actions, this has undergone some interim development. It is now everywhere the rule that the defendant may have an affirmative judgment for any balance in his favor. Preponderantly the right to advance the claim remains restricted to the case where the principal demand is on contract. Some jurisdictions adhere to the rule requiring both demands to be for liquidated amounts. This is true of Massachusetts, Maine, Rhode Island, New Hampshire and Mississippi.[26] In Maryland and Michigan, however, contractual demands either liquidated or unliquidated may be set off against each other.[27] But in actions for injury to person or property because of negligence or the breach of a statutory duty, Michigan entertains a cross-declaration by which the defendant seeks to recover for negligence on the part of the plaintiff, arising out of the occurrence on which the plaintiff depends.[28] Alabama permits a setting off against each other of demands either in

[24] Conn. Gen. Stat. 1949, § 7832.

[25] N.Y. Civ. Pract. Act 1920, § 271.

[26] Mass. Ann. Laws 1933, c. 232, § 1; Me. Rev. Stat. 1944, c. 100, §§ 76, 77; R.I. Gen. Laws Ann. 1938, c. 521, §§ 1, 2; N.H. Rev. Laws 1942, c. 391, § 7; Miss. Code Ann. 1942, § 1481.

[27] Md. Ann. Code (Flack, 1939) Art. 75, § 16; Mich. Stat. Ann. 1938, § 27.826.

[28] *Ibid.* § 27.836.

contract or in tort and whether liquidated or unliquidated, but here the unliquidated demand must be one which "the law is capable of measuring accurately by a pecuniary standard." [29] Virginia, besides the set-off of mutual debts, has, since 1831, admitted, under the head of set-off, designated claims of the defendant for damages or even for equitable relief, in respect of the contract sued upon.[29a] And, by a separate provision, it permits in tort actions the setting up, under the name of "cross-claim," of a counter-demand against the plaintiff, arising from the same transaction as the principal demand.[30] West Virginia, borrowing from the code development, provides for a counterclaim representing either a demand, liquidated or unliquidated, arising out of the principal transaction, or else a liquidated contract demand.[31] In Pennsylvania, also, the term "counterclaim" has been introduced. By a statute of 1915 the defendant was entitled "to set off or set up, by way of counterclaim, any right or claim for which an action of assumpsit would lie." [32] But now this has been superseded by a rule of court of 1946 which, with some analogy to the West Virginia statute, admits as a counterclaim in assumpsit any demand that arises from the transaction of the principal demand or is contractual or quasi-contractual, expressly declaring that the counterclaim need not defeat or diminish the plaintiff's demand and may seek relief different in kind.[33]

In England the old rules on the present subject remained substantially unaffected until the Judicature Act of 1873, which explicitly empowered the court to grant the defendant any relief that it might have granted in a separate action.[34] For the counter-demand thus made generally admissible, at least where it did not amount to a technical set-off, the statutory Rules of 1873 adopted the American code term "counter-

[29] Ala. Code 1940, Tit. 7, §§ 350, 351.

[29a] Va. Laws 1830, c. 11, § 62; Va. Code Ann. 1942, §§ 6144, 6145; Va. Code Ann. 1950, § 8-239 *et seq.*

[30] Va. Code Ann. 1942, § 6097a; Va. Code Ann. 1950, § 8-136.

[31] W.Va. Code Ann. 1949, § 4977.

[32] Pa. Laws 1915, p. 483, § 14; Pa. Stat. Ann. (Purdon, 1931) Tit. 12, § 431.

[33] Rule 1031, Pa. Stat. Ann. (Purdon, 1931) Appendix to Tit. 12, 1949 Pocket Part, p. 221.

[34] 36 & 37 Vict. c. 66, § 24(3).

claim." [35] This term has been carried forward into the existing practice under the Rules of 1883. By Order XIX, rule 3, the defendant, subject to the judicial power of exclusion hereafter mentioned, "may set-off, or set up by way of counterclaim against the claims of the plaintiff, any right or claim, whether such set-off or counterclaim sound in damages or not, and such set-off or counterclaim shall have the same effect as a cross-action, so as to enable the Court to pronounce a final judgment in the same action, both on the original and on the cross-claim." And by Order XXI, rule 17, where "a set-off or counterclaim is established as a defence against the plaintiff's claim, the court or a judge may, if the balance is in favour of the defendant, give judgment for the defendant for such balance, or may otherwise adjudge to the defendant such relief as he may be entitled to upon the merits of the case."

Although on the face of these Rules there would not appear to be much occasion for distinguishing between set-off and counterclaim, the distinction is nevertheless definitely maintained, if less definitely formulated.[36] The principal reason for so strongly keeping it afoot would seem to reside in the question of costs, always of serious moment in the English system. For it makes a good deal of difference as to the incidence of costs whether a plaintiff is to be regarded as defeated in whole or in part, as he would be in the case of an established defense of set-off, or whether the case is to be regarded as one in which the plaintiff succeeds on the principal claim while the defendant succeeds on his counterclaim. Although the question has not been conclusively set at rest, the weight of authority is to the effect that the counter-demand is a matter of set-off only when it would have been set-off under the older law,[37] where, that is to say, it is for a liquidated or easily ascertainable sum, and pleaded in an ac-

[35] *Ibid.*, Schedule, Rule 20.

[36] "The framers of the Judicature Act probably intended that the existing set-off should merge in the new counterclaim. They nowhere stated what the distinction was between the two: still less did they suggest that it was to be preserved. It has, however, been found necessary to maintain it. This is perhaps unfortunate, but it was difficult to avoid it." Odgers, Principles of Pleading and Practice (11th ed. 1934) 238. See also 13th ed. (1946) 196, 197.

[37] Annual Practice 1949, I, p. 351.

tion for a sum of like description, and then only to the extent that it is a defense to the action. Obviously, the defendant may have an affirmative judgment for any excess, but this is only by way of counterclaim; up to the point, however, at which it meets the plaintiff's claim, the counterclaim, in this case, remains a matter of set-off.

In any event, it is clear, under the statute and rules, that any counter-demand is now available to the defendant by way either of set-off or counterclaim. The issues under the counterclaim may be tried separately from those of the principal demand, although apparently they seldom are.[38] The only extrinsic limitation upon the admissibility of the counterclaim is the power of the court or judge, as declared by Order XXI, rule 15, to exclude it on the ground that "the claim thereby raised ought not to be disposed of by way of counterclaim, but in an independent action." Hence, "if the defendant has any valid cause of action, legal or equitable, against the plaintiff, there is no necessity for him now to bring a cross-action, unless his counterclaim be of such a nature that it cannot conveniently be tried by the same tribunal or at the same time as the plaintiff's claim." [39]

The Rules permit the defendant to make other persons, along with the plaintiff, parties defendant to the counterclaim.[40] But when this is done, the counterclaim stands on a narrower basis than when the plaintiff alone is defendant. For here, as a result of the governing statute, the counterclaim cannot be entertained unless it seeks "relief relating to or connected with the original subject of the cause or matter." [41]

For the American jurisdictions, advance toward a wide latitude in the allowance of counter-demands, initiated by the Iowa Code of 1851, was long blocked by the almost unanimous adherence of the codes to the New York provision. Not until the English change had been in force for an ex-

[38] O. XXVI, r. 7; Annual Practice 1949, I, p. 631.

[39] Odgers, *op. cit.* 11th ed. 239, 13th ed. 190.

[40] O. XXI, rr. 11, 12.

[41] Judicature Act 1873, § 24(3); Consolidated Judicature Act 1925, § 39(1); Annual Practice 1949, I, p. 402.

tended period was that advance renewed. But within the last forty years, as a result chiefly of the English example, there has set in a pronounced tendency toward a high degree of freedom in the admission of counter-demands. In 1912, New Jersey, by its Practice Act of that year,[42] permitted the defendant in common-law actions to "set off or counterclaim any cause of action," subject to the discretionary power of the court to order separate trials or, if convenient disposition could not be had in the pending action, to strike out the counterclaim. So the Federal Equity Rules of the same year,[43] although expressly making the presentation of counter-demands arising out of the transaction in suit mandatory instead of optional, laid aside, for the rest, the old test of germaneness to the original bill, by conceding to the defendant the right to allege as a counterclaim any demand which might be the subject of an independent suit in equity. And in 1926 the same departure from the former equity practice occurred in Massachusetts.[44]

On a broader scale, manifestations of the same tendency have occurred in Arkansas (1917),[45] Illinois (1933) [46] and New York (1936).[47] In Arkansas and New York the provision is that the counterclaim "may be any cause of action in favor of the defendants or some of them against the plaintiffs or some of them," or (in New York) against "a person whom the plaintiff represents or a plaintiff and another person or persons alleged to be liable." Accompanying the Arkansas enactment is the further provision that "a set-off may be pleaded in any action for the recovery of money and may be a cause of action arising either upon contract or tort" [48]—the necessity for which is not readily apparent. Illinois has provided that "any demand by one or more defendants against one or more plaintiffs, or against

[42] N.J. Practice Act 1912, § 12; N.J. Stat. Ann. 1939, §§ 2:27-137, 2:27-141.

[43] Rule 30.

[44] Supreme Judicial Court Rules 1926, Equity Rule 6: 252 Mass. 602; Superior Court Rules 1932, Rule 32: Superior Court Rules 1932 Ann. p. 114 *et seq.*

[45] Ark. Laws 1917, no. 267, p. 1441; Ark. Stat. Ann. 1947, § 27-1123.

[46] Ill. Civ. Pract. Act, § 38; Ill. Rev. Stat. 1949, c. 110, § 162.

[47] N.Y. Laws 1936, repealing Civ. Pract. Act, § 266, and adding a new § 266 (Clevenger, 1950).

[48] Ark. Stat. Ann. 1947, § 27-1125.

one or more co-defendants, whether in the nature of set-off, recoupment, cross-bill in equity or otherwise, and whether in tort or contract, for liquidated or unliquidated damages, or for other relief, may be pleaded as a cross-demand in any action, and when so pleaded shall be called a counterclaim." [49] Both Illinois and New York give the court certain discretionary power over the counterclaim, the former to order its separate trial or possibly its severance from the principal action,[50] the latter, however, to order not only the severance or separate trial of the counterclaim, but also to strike it out without prejudice to the bringing of another action.[51]

The same direction has been taken by the new Federal Rules in following for civil actions generally the principle which had been adopted by the Equity Rules of 1912. Thus the new rules distinguish between compulsory and permissive counterclaims. With respect to the former the provision, as adopted in 1938, was that:

> A pleading shall state as a counterclaim any claim, not the subject of a pending action, which at the time of filing the pleading the pleader has against any opposing party, if it arises out of the transaction or occurrence that is the subject matter of the opposing party's claim and does not require for its adjudication the presence of third parties of whom the court cannot acquire jurisdiction. (Rule 13(a)).

The permissive counterclaim, on the other hand, emerges from the next subdivision of the same Rule:

> A pleading may state as a counterclaim any claim against an opposing party not arising out of the transaction or occurrence that is the subject matter of the opposing party's claim. (Rule 13(b)).

By the amendments of 1946 the first of these provisions underwent minor change. As a result, it now speaks of the

[49] The provision is "subject to rules," but so far no rules have been adopted concerning the counterclaim. A further provision of the Illinois Civil Practice Act is that "subject to rules the defendant may set up in his answer any and all cross-demands whatever, whether in the nature of recoupment, set-off, cross bill in equity or otherwise, which shall be designated counterclaims." § 44; Ill. Rev. Stat. 1949, c. 110, § 168.

[50] Ill. Civ. Pract. Act, §§ 44, 51; Ill. Rev. Stat. 1949, c. 110, §§ 168, 175.

[51] N.Y. Laws 1936, c. 324, amending Civ. Pract. Act, § 262.

time of "serving" rather than of "filing" the pleading in question, and makes it necessary that to except a claim from the compulsory category because of its being the subject of a pending action, the latter be pending at the time of the commencement of the principal action.[52]

It is distinctly provided that the counterclaim "may or may not diminish or defeat the recovery sought by the opposing party" and may be for relief "exceeding in amount or different in kind" from that sought by the opponent. (Rule 13(c)). Accordingly, any cause of action in favor of a defendant against a plaintiff may be advanced by way of counterclaim in any civil action, and if it falls within the category of compulsory counterclaims must be so advanced on pain of its loss.[53] In case new parties are necessary for complete relief to the counterclaimant, they are to be brought in as defendants by order of court, "if jurisdiction of them can be obtained and their joinder will not deprive the court of jurisdiction of the action." (Rule 13(h)). For any case of a counterclaim, express recognition is given to the power of the court to order its separate trial or the separate trial of any of its issues "in furtherance of convenience or to avoid prejudice." (Rule 42(b)).

The federal provisions have been taken over by Arizona (1939, 1949), Colorado (1941), New Mexico (1942, 1949); and, except that relating to permissive counterclaims, by Missouri (1943).[54] Levied upon by Florida (1941) for its com-

[52] This was the interpretation of Equity Rule 30. Texas Co. v. Borne Scrymser Co. (C.C.A. 4) 68 Fed.2d 104, 106 (1933).

[53] Federal Rules of Civil Procedure (West Publishing Co. 1947) p. 35 and Advisory Committee's note. As it now stands, Rule 13(a) reads: "A pleading shall state as a counterclaim any claim which at the time of serving the pleading the pleader has against any opposing party, if it arises out of the transaction or occurrence that is the subject matter of the opposing party's claim and does not require for its adjudication the presence of third parties of whom the court cannot acquire jurisdiction, except that such a claim need not be so stated if at the time the action was commenced the claim was the subject of another pending action."

[54] Ariz. Code Ann. 1939, and 1949 Cum. Supp. to Vol. II, §§ 21-437, 21-438, 21-439, 21-444, 21-920; Colo. Rules Civ. Proc., Rules 13(a) (b) (c) (h), 42(b), in Colo. Stat. Ann. 1939, Replacement Vol. I, 1941; N.M. Stat. Ann. 1941, and 1949 Cum. Supp. to Vol. II, §§ 19-101(13)(a) (b) (c) (h), 19-101(42)(b); 3 Mo.Rev.Stat. Ann. 1942, Pocket Part 1950, §§ 847.73, 847.74, 847.78, 847.97(b). Colorado and Missouri exhibit an unimportant

mon-law actions,[55] they have been followed in the main by Texas (1941) with the principal difference that here a demand in tort may not be counterclaimed against a demand in contract or *vice versa*.[56] And including the distinction between compulsory and permissive counterclaims, they have entered by adaptation into the recent Iowa Rules (1943).[57] Again, the federal example has undoubtedly led to the broadening by Wisconsin (1943) of its counterclaim provision, so as now to provide, though without any element of compulsion, that "a defendant may counterclaim any claim which he has against a plaintiff, upon which a judgment may be had in the action." [58] More recently the provisions in question have been followed by Delaware (1947) and Utah (1949),[59] and in part by Maryland (1947), which last named rejects the compulsory category and provides only for an optional counterclaim. The same position was initially taken by New Jersey, but has since been modified by an amendment of 1950 which introduces the element of compulsion as to "a liquidated debt or demand or a debt or demand capable of being ascertained by computation," whether or not arising out of the subject-matter of the opposing party's claim.[60]

A high degree of latitude in the admission of counter-demands would appear, therefore, to have attained solid recognition as one of the conspicuous desiderata of modern reform. According to the jurisdiction, it may be that certain proceedings will always be kept outside the ordinary rules, as *e.g.*, matrimonial causes in England; but for causes in general any initial restriction upon the admissibility of counter-demands may well be dispensed with, given the power of the court to exclude on the ground of inconvenience. In re-

---

variation in the provision of Rule 13(h).

[55] Fla. Stat. 1949, § 52.11.

[56] Tex. Rules Civ. Proc. (Vernon, 1942) Rules 97, 174.

[57] Ia. Rules Civ. Proc., Rules 29, 30, 32, 34, 186, Ia. Code 1946, Vol. II, pp. 2147, 2148, 2164.

[58] Wis. Stat. 1949, § 263.14.

[59] Del. Rules of Superior Court, Rules 13(a) (b) (c) (h), 42(b), Rules of Court of Chancery, Rules 13(a) (b) (c) (h), 42(b); Utah Rules Civ. Proc., Rules 13(a) (b) (c) (g), 42(b).

[60] Md. Gen. Rules Pract. & Proc., Part 2, Subd. III, Rules 3(a), 5(a), in Md. Ann. Code (Flack, 1939) 1947 Cum. Supp. pp. 2041, 2043; N.J. Rules Civ. Pract., Rules 3:13-1, 3:13-2, 3:13-5, 3:13-7, 3:42-2

spect of that power the Federal Rules do not go far enough: the power to order a separate trial of the counterclaim or of any of its issues, as given by Rule 42(b), stops short of being an adequate measure of control. Only when that control, in the interests of convenience, may extend to the relegation of the counterclaim to an independent action, as under the English Rules and the New York provisions, is the regulation fully consonant with the best interests of procedure.

The idea of compulsion to assert a counter-demand was not a new thing when incorporated into the Federal Equity Rules of 1912. Its earliest appearance, perhaps, was in the New Jersey statute of 1722 in relation to set-off.[61] But though foreign to the standard code regulation, as to the former practice in general, it had been accepted by a considerable number of the codes in provisions applicable, like the Federal compulsory rule, to counterclaims growing out of the same transaction as the principal demand. By some of these provisions omission to interpose the counterclaim is made a bar to its subsequent prosecution in a separate action;[62] others merely attend the omission with deprivation of costs in the later action.[63] The soundness of the idea of compulsion in this regard is by no means self-evident. Both for the Roman and the Germanic law,[64] the maxim *Invitus agere nemo cogatur* represents a firmly imbedded principle and one generally accepted by their modern derivatives. To be sure, certain exceptions have been widely admitted, as in the case of the action for declaratory judgment, but these exceptions have been induced by much more cogent reasons than obtain in the present situation. Over against the argument based upon the economic and social gain proceeding from the enforced disposition of mutual controversies in a single suit is to be set the consideration that that enforced disposition disturbs the parity which ought to exist between the parties. Fundamentally, the holder of a right of action is free to

[61] See Loyd, The Development of Set-Off (1916) 64 U.ofPa.L.Rev. 541, 560.

[62] *E.g.*, Cal. Code Civ. Proc. (Deering, 1949) § 439.

[63] *E.g.*, Ind. Stat. Ann. (Burns, 1933), Replacement Vol. II, 1946, § 2-1019; Wyo. Comp. Stat. 1945, § 3-1314.

[64] Wetzell, *System des ordentlichen Civilprocesses* (3d ed. 1878) 98.

assert it when and where he chooses, limited only by the requirements of the law with respect to jurisdiction. To compel him, because sued by the person against whom that right exists, to assert it in the pending action, is to lessen the liberty of assertion which he otherwise would enjoy, and to create an inequality of advantage as between him and his opponent, who has brought his action in the full exercise of his liberty of assertion. Certainly a rule of compulsion extended to every allowable counterclaim cannot be regarded as defensible. If a compulsory rule is ever justifiable it is only when the counterclaim operates by way of defense to the principal claim. Just as a defendant may not with impunity withhold a defense, so we may without violence to the traditional maxim deny him the right to withhold a counterclaim if this in whole or in part is of a defensive nature. This would appear to indicate the proper line of division between compulsory and permissive counterclaims. But it is not the line of division adopted by the Federal Rules under which the distinction is between counter-demands which arise out of "the transaction or occurrence" on which the plaintiff rests his claim and those which do not. Suppose on the one hand, the ordinary case of set-off: B, let us say, is indebted to A in the sum of $500 upon a promissory note, and A is indebted to B in the sum of $1000 for goods sold and delivered. One would imagine that if we are to have a compulsory rule this would be the very case to which it would be appropriate, for recovery by B would here as part of its effect wholly cancel A's claim. Yet under such a rule as the federal one, B would be perfectly free to reserve his counter-demand for a separate action. Suppose, on the other hand, that A and B have engaged in the exchange of properties, each giving to the other as part of the transaction, a mortgage on the property conveyed to the mortgagor, and that in each case the mortgaged property is so ample a security for the mortgage indebtedness that no question of a deficiency will arise. Suppose, further, that after the maturity of both mortgages, each remaining unpaid, A sues to foreclose the mortgage executed by B on property X, not asking for any personal judgment against B.[65] Under the principle thus accepted by the Federal Rule, B would be compelled, through the medium of a counterclaim, to seek foreclosure of the mortgage executed by A on property Y, although he might have excellent reasons for not wanting to do so until a later time, and simply because both claims, affecting entirely different pieces of property arose out of the same transaction. Clearly, then, there should be no compulsion where the two claims thus aim at unconnected relief. Accordingly, if we are to have a compulsory counterclaim at all, it would be in order to invoke here the formula, elsewhere injudiciously used in another bearing, and restrict the compulsory counterclaim to the case where it "tends to diminish or defeat the plaintiff's recovery."

§ 2. Cross-Claims

The right of a defendant to advance against a co-defendant a claim concerning the subject matter of the suit was something wholly unknown to the common-law system, but was recognized in equity, where, like the right to advance a counter-demand against the plaintiff, it was effectuated by means of a cross-bill. This right was not expressly conceded in the pattern set by the New York Code, but in general was allowed, at least in respect of equitable demands, by virtue of the provision empowering the court, by its judgment, to determine the rights of the defendants as between themselves. For the incident procedure resort was had to the former equity practice, the vehicle of presentation being variously termed a counterclaim, a cross-complaint, a cross-petition or a cross-bill. Nevertheless certain of the codes incorporated express provision on the subject. Apparently the first was that of Kentucky, which, by an amendment of 1857, permitted the answer to be made a cross-petition "when a

65 This is the sort of case in which, by the New York decisions of an older day, reflected in other jurisdictions, the counterclaim was not allowable because it did not interfere with the plaintiff's recovery. See Nat. Fire Insurance Co. v. McKay, 21 N.Y. 191 (1860); Lipman v. Jackson Architectural Works, 128 N.Y. 58, 27 N.E. 975 (1891). But under the Federal Rules, as noted, interference with the plaintiff's recovery is not essential to the maintenance of the counterclaim.

defendant has a cause of action against a co-defendant, or a person not a party to the action, and affecting the subject matter of the action." [66] This provision was followed in the Iowa revision of 1860,[67] and subsequently entered into the statutes of Arkansas.[68] Seemingly traceable to the same source is a Utah provision obtaining before the Rules of 1949 which, however, contemplated only a claim by one defendant against another, without alternative.[69] In Kentucky, itself, the provision has since been materially remodelled, and, as it now stands, it permits a cross-petition as well to a plaintiff in his capacity of defendant to a set-off or counterclaim. In the case of a defendant the cross-petition lies against a co-defendant or a person not a party to the action or against both, upon a cause of action that affects or is affected by the principal one.[70] But in Arkansas the provision retains the original Kentucky dimension. Note should be taken of the Wisconsin provision dating from 1898, by which, according to its present tenor, "a defendant or a person interpleaded or intervening may have affirmative relief against a co-defendant, or a co-defendant and the plaintiff, or part of the plaintiffs, or a co-defendant and a person not a party, or against such person alone." The relief in question, however, "must involve or in some manner affect the contract, transaction or property which is the subject matter of the action or relate to the occurrence out of which the action arose." [71] As appears, these statutes deal expressly with the case of a claim by one defendant against another. Besides this type of provision there exists the type originating in the California provision of 1874,[72] which authorizes a cross-complaint by a defendant against "any party," including of course the plaintiff, but which furnishes an instrumentality for the prosecution of a claim by a defendant against a co-defendant, where this ex-

[66] Ky. Laws 1857-58, c. 5, Vol. I, p. 2.

[67] Ia. Revision 1860, § 2892; Ia. Code 1939, § 11155—superseded by Ia. Rules Civ. Proc., Rules 33, 34, Ia. Code 1946, Vol. II, pp. 2147-2148.

[68] Ark. Code Pract. in Civ. Cas. 1868, § 108, Ark. Stat. Ann. 1947, § 27-1134.

[69] Utah Code Ann. 1943, § 104-9-7.

[70] Ky. Code Pract. in Civ. Cas. (Carroll, 1948) § 96.

[71] Wis. Stat. 1898, § 2656*a*; Wis. Stat. 1949, § 263.15.

[72] *Supra,* p. 127.

hibits the prescribed relationship to the principal demand. Another manner of provision occurs in the Illinois Civil Practice Act of 1933 which, as part of its counterclaim regulation, permits the assertion of "any demand by one or more defendants . . . against one or more co-defendants," not requiring here any more than in the case of a counter-demand, any relationship to the principal claim.[73]

Under the English Rules the counterclaim is never allowed against a co-defendant except as a co-party with the plaintiff.[74] For the rest, the Rules restrict the right of a defendant to proceed, in the plaintiff's action, against a co-defendant within a narrow category. That is to say, the right is admitted only to the same extent and upon the same grounds as against a person not a party to the action, to proceed for contribution, indemnity or kindred relief, under the so-called "third-party procedure," of which we shall speak in a later place. The present case is assimilated also to the claim against the outsider in point of procedure, since, in common with the latter, the medium of presentation is a notice, accompanied by a copy of statement of claim or indorsed writ.[75]

Culmination of the American development in the present regard are the provisions of the Federal Rules, which, by Rule 13(g), as originally adopted, declare that a pleading may state as a cross-claim any claim by one party against a co-party arising out of the transaction or occurrence either of the original action or of a counterclaim therein. Such cross-claim may include a claim that the party against whom it is asserted is or may be liable to the cross-claimant for all or part of a claim asserted in the action against the cross-claimant. And, by subdivision (h) of the same Rule, the addition of new parties is authorized precisely as in the case of a counterclaim.

The same manner of regulation has since entered into various State jurisdictions. The provision of Rule 13(g) has

[73] Ill. Civ. Pract. Act, § 38; Ill. Rev. Stat. 1949, c. 110, § 162.

[74] Odgers, Principles of Pleading and Practice (11th ed. 1934) 243-244, (13th ed. 1946) 193-194.

[75] O. XVIA, r. 12; Annual Practice 1949, I, p. 325.

found place textually in South Dakota (1939), Arizona (1939), Colorado (1941), Texas (1941), New Mexico (1942) and Missouri (1943), and substantially in Florida (1941)—for its common-law actions—as well as in Iowa, with retention here of the old name of "cross-petition." Rule 13(g) has also been followed by New Jersey (1948), but without the requirement as to the origin of the cross-claim imposed by the model. All these jurisdictions other than South Dakota have accepted, in addition, the provision of Rule 13(h), with or without some modification.[76]

By the federal amendments of 1946, the scope of the cross-claim under Rule 13(g) was widened by making it available in respect also of a claim "relating to any property that is the subject matter of the original action." [77] As thus amended, the provision was followed by Delaware (1947), Maryland (1947) and Utah (1949), these also adapting Rule 13(h).[78]

Apart from the intrinsic merit of the federal regulation, especially in its express encompassment of the claim for relief over, it has performed a decided service in the interest of accurate terminology. For in lieu of the varied terms previously employed in the present case, most of which apply to the assertion of the defendant's claim against the plaintiff, it has definitely set its seal upon the word "cross-claim." It has thus started this term well on its way to becoming a standardized one in denoting the assertion, within the plaintiff's action, of the claim of one defendant against another.

[76] S.D. Code 1939, § 33.0912; Ariz. Code Ann. 1939, §§ 21-443, 21-444; Colo. Rules Civ. Proc., Rule 13(g) (h), in Colo. Stat. Ann. 1939, Replacement Vol. I, 1941; Tex. Rules Civ. Proc. (Vernon, 1942) Rule 97(e) (f); N.M. Stat. Ann. 1941, § 19-101(13) (g) (h); 3 Mo.Rev.Stat. 1942, Pocket Part 1950, §§ 847.77, 847.78; Fla. Stat. 1949, § 52.11(7) (8); Ia. Rules Civ. Proc., Rules 33, 34, Ia. Code 1946, Vol. II, pp. 2147-2148; N.J. Rules Civ. Pract., Rules 3:13-6, 3:13-7.

[77] Federal Rules of Civil Procedure (West Publishing Co. 1947) pp. 35-36, and note of Advisory Committee, p. 36.

[78] Del. Rules of Superior Court, Rule 13(g) (h), Rules of Court of Chancery, Rule 13(g) (h); Md. Gen. Rules Pract. & Proc., Part 2, Subd. III, Rule 3(b) (c), in Md. Ann. Code (Flack, 1939) 1497 Cum. Supp. pp. 2041, 2042; Utah Rules Civ. Proc., Rule 13(f) (g). The amendment has also been incorporated in the Arizona and New Mexico provisions: see 1949 Cum. Supp. to Vol. II of each of the codes.

CHAPTER XII

THIRD-PARTY PARTICIPATION

§ 1. INTERVENTION

The readiness with which the infancy of common-law judicature permitted the entrance of third parties into litigation has already been remarked.[1] This attitude left an especially definitive imprint upon the old real actions. Here we encounter, among other instances of third-party participation, a species of intervention, in the so-called proceeding of *receit.* Thus, in an action against the owner of the lesser estate, a reversioner or remainderman, upon proper prayer to be received, might be admitted to defend his "freehold or inheritance," whereupon, as it is said, "two actions concur, one between the demandant and the tenant, and the other between the tenant by receit and the demandant." [2] But this was the sole instance of voluntary intervention recognized by the common-law procedure, after it can be spoken of a system, and with the passing of the real actions, it retained nothing of the kind. As for the classic system of chancery procedure, this was all but negative in the present regard. Baron Gilbert, indeed, speaks of the *tertius interveniens,* but it is apparent that the intervention which he has in view was accomplished by means of a separate suit and not through admission of the intervenor as a party to the pending cause.[3]

[1] *Supra,* Chapter I, § 4.

[2] Booth, Nature and Practice of Real Actions (1701) 69. See also 2 Reeves, History of the English Law (ed. Finlason, 1869) 63; Stearns, A Summary of the Law and Practice of Real Actions (2d ed. 1831) * 102.

[3] Gilbert, *Forum Romanum* (ed. Tyler, 1874) 47-48. Here the formative period of chancery seems to have followed the doctrine of the Roman Rota, rather than that of any other canonical source. For, in the view of the former, intervention represented an "independent action which, instituted before the court of the pending cause, was directed against both parties to that cause and led to a judgment binding upon both." Weismann, *Hauptintervention und Streitgenossenschaft* (1884) 14, 17.

Under the orthodox equity rule, "strangers to a cause cannot be heard therein either by petition or motion, except in certain cases arising from necessity, as when the pleadings contain scandal against a stranger, or where a stranger purchases the subject of litigation pending the suit, and the like. . . . Creditors who are allowed to prove debts, and persons belonging to a class on whose behalf suit is brought, are regarded as quasi parties, and of course may have a standing in court." [4] So in the case of *cestuis que trustent,* "a court of equity will sometimes, as a matter of indulgence, and to prevent further delay and expense, allow them (if they wish) to bring forward their claims by petition, in order to have their interests ascertained and their rights protected." [5] Again, when property, real or personal, had been the subject of sequestration, either on mesne or final process, a third person, claiming an interest in the property, was permitted to come in either by motion or petition, and pray for an examination *pro interesse suo,* to the end that he might have proper relief; and the like proceeding obtained where a third person claimed property in the possession of a receiver.[6] Beyond this, the classic system did not go. But on the basis thus appearing, there occurred in the nineteenth century that development at the hands of the American courts, and especially those of the Federal system, which has led to the acceptance of voluntary intervention as an everyday feature of equity practice, however variant its compass in different jurisdictions.

Meanwhile provisions had been adopted quite generally in common-law jurisdictions extending the right of third-party intervention in special cases of property litigation, such as those of attachment, replevin and detinue. And the American codes had made place for the proceeding as a general measure. The year 1851 marks the appearance of two very similar provisions of the kind. The Iowa Code of that year

[4] Bradley, J., in Anderson v. Jacksonville P. & M. R. Co., 2 Woods 628, 1 Fed.Cas. No. 358 (1873).

[5] Story, Equity Pleadings (10th ed. 1892) § 208.

[6] 1 Daniell, Chancery Practice (1937) 644 and note (h); 2 *id.* (1840) 720; Krippendorf v. Hyde, 110 U.S. 276, 283, 285, 4 S.Ct. 27 (1884).

laid down the rule that "in actions for the recovery of property any person not a party thereto, on showing himself interested in the subject matter of the suit, may be allowed to appear as defendant therein." [7] And the New York Code, by an amendment of the same year, incorporated the provision that "when, in an action for the recovery of real or personal property, a person, not a party to the action, but having an interest in the subject thereof, makes application to the court, to be made a party, it may order him to be brought in by the proper amendment." [8] That one of these influenced the other is plain. The Iowa enactment preceded that of New York by some months,[9] and the internal evidence, also, would seem to point to it as the original. But whichever is entitled to primacy, both envisage the case from the standpoint of equity practice, as an enlargement of the circle of parties to the original controversy and both restrict the proceeding to actions for the recovery of property. This manner of provision, on the New York model, has had a large following among the codes, and in general, although with occasional verbal change, remains restricted to actions for the recovery of property. Usually, however, it is associated, either as part of the same statutory section or otherwise, with a provision having its source in the original New York Code, which either requires or permits the court to cause the bringing in of new parties whose presence is necessary to a complete determination of the controversy. In varying measure this provision has contributed to extend the ambit of intervention beyond actions for the recovery of property, on the ground that the intervenor's presence is thus necessary. Indeed, in Missouri, while it still lacked an intervention statute, the allowance of intervention appears to have been justified in respect of a money demand without other authority than the presence of such a provision.[10] And in Indiana the

[7] Iowa Code 1851, § 1684.

[8] N.Y. Laws 1851, c. 479, p. 883, Code of Procedure, § 122.

[9] The Iowa Code was adopted Feb. 5, 1851, the New York amendment, July 10, 1851.

[10] Zeitinger v. Hargadine-McKittrick Dry Goods Co., 298 Mo. 461, 250 S.W. 913 (1923); see also State v. Hudson, 86 Mo.App. 501 (1901). But in 1943, as will later appear, Missouri adopted intervention provisions based upon those of the Federal Rules.

two provisions in conjunction suffice to extend the intervention practice to any species of civil action.[11]

In New York, itself, legislation has widened the scope of the intervention provision. By successive amendments of the Code, that provision assumed the form in which it passed into the Civil Practice Act of 1920, dropping the old restriction to actions for the recovery of property and requiring the court to cause the applicant to be made a party to the pending action when "he has an interest in the subject thereof, or in real property the title to which may in any manner be affected by the judgment, or in real property for injury to which the complaint demands relief." [12] These terms, however, were interpreted as not extending to the case where the pending action was one for the recovery of money only [13]—a rule which survived until the changes of 1946 hereafter noted. Here also is to be mentioned the distinctive Connecticut provision which declares that "if a person not a party shall have an interest or title which the judgment will affect, the court on his application, shall direct him to be made a party." [14]

But the codes also disclose a type of intervention statute quite different from the Iowa-New York legacy of 1851. California here broke the path by legislation of 1854. Inspired by the civil-law rule obtaining in Louisiana,[15] it provided that "any person shall be entitled to intervene in an action who has an interest in the matter of litigation, in the success of either of the parties to the action, or an interest against both. An intervention takes place, when a third person is permitted to become a party to an action between other persons, either by joining the plaintiff in claiming what is sought by the complaint, or by uniting with the defendant in resisting the claims of the plaintiff, or by demanding anything ad-

[11] Zumbro v. Parnin, 141 Ind. 430, 40 N.E. 1085 (1895); Dodd v. Reese, 216 Ind. 449, 24 N.E. 2d 995 (1940).

[12] N.Y. Civ. Pract. Act, § 193, prior to the changes of 1946.

[13] Bauer v. Dewey, 166 N.Y. 402, 60 N.E. 30 (1901); 12th Report of Judicial Council, State of N.Y. (1946) 221.

[14] Conn. Gen. Stat. 1949, § 7829.

[15] Smith v. Gale, 144 U.S. 509, 518, 12 S.Ct. 674 (1892). See La. Code Pract. 1825, Art. 389, as amended by act of April 7, 1826, § 10; La. Code Pract. (Dart, 1942) Art. 390.

versely to both the plaintiff and defendant."[16] Under this provision intervention was not merely a developed form of the equity doctrine of parties, but an independent institution,[17] with three different trajectories, comprising, that is to say, what in Continental law is known as "accessory intervention" (intervening (*a*) in aid of one party or (*b*) the other) and "principal intervention" (intervening (*c*) against both parties).[18] Moreover, it did not restrict itself, as did the other mode of regulation in its usual form, to actions for the recovery of property. The California example was followed by the Iowa revision of 1860,[19] and subsequently set the pattern for legislation in other Western States, particularly those of the Pacific coast. Its share of the field, in the code system, is perhaps somewhat larger than that of the other type of provision. It has even passed outside the code area to find place in the legislation of Alabama.[20] And while the provision has not been enacted in Texas, the scope of intervention there, as a result principally of early Louisiana influence,[21] is not far removed from that of its terms. The codes have not disseized the courts of the old, albeit narrow, powers attaching to the equitable jurisdiction, to entertain in equity causes, the applications of third persons, such as creditors and claimants against a receiver, even though the exercise of such powers may not come within the terms of the particular intervention provision, as when this envisages intervention only in actions for the recovery of property. In most cases an application of the kind is not designated as an intervention, since the applicant does not become a true party, remaining on the basis of a quasi party, but, whether it is or not, the statute, where necessary, finds itself supplemented by the powers here in question. And, as regards the other side of the court, in jurisdictions where the intervention provision speaks of actions

16 Cal. Laws 1854, p. 73, Cal. Dig. Laws (Wood, 1857) Art. 808.

17 Pomeroy speaks of it as creating "a new division of the procedure." Code Remedies (5th ed. 1929) § 308, p. 461.

18 Chiovenda, *Principii di diritto processuale civile* (3d ed. 1923) 601-602, 1102.

19 Ia. Revision 1860, § 2930.

20 Ala. Code 1940, Tit. 7, § 247.

21 Legg v. McNeill, 2 Tex. 428 (1847); Pool v. Sanford, 52 Tex. 621 (1880); Tex. Rules Civ. Proc. (Vernon, 1942) Rule 60.

for the recovery of property, there usually obtain special provisions authorizing intervention in attachment proceedings.

In the federal system, where the antecedent judicial development had resulted in permitting intervention on a wide scale in equity causes, the Equity Rules of 1912 formulated the principle that "any one claiming an interest in the litigation may at any time be permitted to assert his right by intervention, but the intervention shall be in subordination to, and in recognition of, the propriety of the main proceeding." [22] Formulation in the same terms appears in a Florida statute of 1931.[23] The principle finds like formulation with extension to common-law causes in the Michigan Judicature Act of 1915, whose provision makes it applicable "either at law, or in equity." [24]

In applying the rule thus laid down, the federal courts continued to recognize the distinction previously drawn by the decisions between cases in which the intervention was to be regarded as depending on the discretion of the court and those in which it was to be considered a matter of right. Most cases fell within the former class, but where refusal to allow the intervention would amount to "a practical denial of certain relief to which the intervenor is fairly entitled," [25] there was an absolute right to intervene. Instances of the latter sort would be where a fund was before the court which might be dissipated before the applicant could otherwise assert his interest in it,[26] or where he was a member of a class not adequately represented by the appearing parties.[27] Accordingly, in the redaction of the new Federal Rules, this distinction was preserved. And now, for civil actions in general, the Rules recognize the two classes of intervention of right and permissive intervention. Under their provisions intervention is of right "(1) when a statute of the United States confers an unconditional right to intervene; or (2) when the represen-

[22] Rule 37.

[23] Fla. Laws 1931, c. 14658, § 9; Fla. Stat. 1949, § 63.09.

[24] Mich. Jud. Act, c. 12, § 11; Mich. Stat. Ann. 1938, § 27.663.

[25] Credits Commutation Co. v. U.S., 177 U.S. 311, 316, 20 S.Ct. 636 (1900).

[26] Vicksburg S. & P. Ry. Co. v. Schaff (C.C.A. 5) 5 Fed.2d 610 (1925).

[27] Whittaker v. Brictson Mfg. Co. (C.C.A. 8) 43 Fed.2d 485 (1930); Palmer v. Bankers' Trust Co (C.C.A. 8) 12 Fed.2d 747 (1926).

tation of the applicant's interest by existing parties is or may be inadequate and the applicant is or may be bound by a judgment in the action; or (3) when the applicant is so situated as to be adversely affected by a distribution or other disposition of property [originally "in the custody of the court or of an officer thereof," now, as amended in 1946] which is in the custody or subject to the control or disposition of the court or an officer thereof." (Rule 24(a)). It is permissive, on the other hand, "(1) when a statute of the United States confers a conditional right to intervene; or (2) when an applicant's claim or defense and the main action have a question of law or fact in common." In this regard it is provided that "in exercising its discretion the court shall consider whether the intervention will unduly delay or prejudice the adjudication of the rights of the original parties." (Rule 24(b)).

It is observable that the new provisions have omitted the requirement of the former Equity Rules that "the intervention shall be in subordination to, and in recognition of the propriety of the main proceeding." This requirement was always difficult to interpret and occasionally worked injustice.[28] The wisdom of its rejection by the new Rules is not open to doubt. Whatever salutary effect it possessed is sufficiently retained in directing the court to take into consideration delay or prejudice to the principal action in the matter of permissive intervention.

The federal provisions *mutatis mutandis* have been followed by Arizona (1939, 1949), Colorado (1941), New Mexico (1942, 1949), Missouri (1943), Delaware (1947), New Jersey (1948) and Utah (1949).[29] New York (1946) now explicitly recognizing the right to "intervene in an ac-

[28] See 2 Moore's Federal Practice (1938) 2373 *et seq.*, 4 *id.* (2d ed. 1950) 108 *et seq.*, where the cases are considered.

[29] Ariz. Code Ann. 1939, and 1949 Cum. Supp. to Vol. II, §§ 21-527, 21-528; Colo. Rules Civ. Proc., Rule 24(a)(b), in Colo. Stat. Ann. 1939, Replacement Vol. I, 1941; N.M. Stat. Ann. 1941, and 1949 Cum. Supp. to Vol. II, § 19-101(24)(a)(b); Mo. Rev. Stat. 1942, 1950 Pocket Part to Vol. III, § 847.21; Del. Rules of Superior Court, Rule 24(a)(b), Rules of Court of Chancery, Rule 24(a)(b); N.J. Rules Civ. Pract., Rules 3:24-1, 3:24-3; Utah Rules Civ. Proc., Rule 24(a)(b).

tion including but not limited to an action for the recovery of money," has also taken these provisions as pattern, with minor variations, except that intervention of right, by a borrowing from the former statute, is expressly made to include the case "when the applicant has an interest in real property, the title to which may in any manner be affected by the judgment, or in real property for injury to which the complaint demands relief." [80] In South Dakota (1939) whose statute was of the California type, the Federal Rule has been influential to the extent of causing to be added to the type-grounds of intervention the third ground of the federal intervention of right, namely, the applicant being adversely affected by the distribution or other disposition of property in the custody of the court or its officer.[81] Similarly, the Pennsylvania rules on the subject (1940) accept this as one of their four grounds of intervention. As their other grounds they permit intervention (1) where the applicant would have been under a duty of indemnification in respect of the judgment, (2) could have been joined as an original party, or (3) has a legally enforceable interest which may be affected by the determination of the action, whether he would be bound by the judgment or not. It is to be noted that here the old requirement that the intervention shall be "in subordination to and in recognition of the propriety" of the principal action is retained to the extent of giving the court discretionary power to refuse the application where the contrary is the case.[82]

In the present field the American development has incurred no indebtedness to the modern English system. There, except for probate and divorce causes and admiralty causes *in rem,* which in this respect have the benefit of inheritance from the practice of the former ecclesiastical and admiralty courts, intervention is very sparingly admitted. "Generally," it is said, "in common law and chancery matters a plaintiff who conceives that he has a cause of action against a defend-

[80] N.Y. Civ. Pract. Act, § 193-b, the former § 193 being repealed.

[81] S.D. Code 1939, § 33.0413.

[82] Pa. Rules Civ. Proc., Rules 2327, 2329, in Pa. Stat. Ann. (Purdon, 1931) Appendix to Tit. 12, 1949 Pocket Part.

ant is entitled to pursue his remedy against that defendant alone. He cannot be compelled to proceed against other persons whom he has no desire to sue." [33] But, by a provision of the Rules (O. XII, r. 25), taken over from the Common Law Procedure Act of 1852, it is open to a third person, in an action for the recovery of land, to appear and defend by leave of court, "on filing an affidavit showing that he is in possession of the land either by himself or by his tenant." Moreover, there is a general provision (O. XVI, r. 11) giving authority to the court to add the names of any parties "who ought to have been joined or whose presence before the Court may be necessary to enable the Court effectually and completely to adjudicate upon and settle all questions involved in the cause or matter." Under this general provision it is clear that in a class suit a member of the class may intervene on the ground that he is not adequately represented. So, too, intervention may be had by one whose property interest would be directly and legally affected by the judgment.[34] To these cases may be added that of an action for specific performance "where third persons have an interest in the manner in which the contract should be performed." [35] But in all such cases the applicant must meet the very terms of the Rule. Before intervention can be permitted, it is necessary to "find either that he 'ought to have been joined' or that 'his presence before the Court may be necessary to enable the Court effectually and completely to adjudicate upon and settle all the questions involved in the cause or matter.' " [36]

[33] Annual Practice, 1949, I, p. 253.

[34] Moser v. Marsden, [1892] 1 Ch. 487, C.A.; Dollfus Mieg et Campagnie S.A. v. Bank of England, [1950] 2 All E.R. 605.

[35] Annual Practice 1949, I, p. 254. This addition rests upon Dix. v. Great Western Ry. Co., 55 L.J. Ch. 797, 54 L.T. 830, 34 W.R. 712 (1886), where by indenture three persons, D, O and J, had conveyed to the company certain parcels of land belonging to them respectively, and the company had made a separate covenant with each to build a road on the land thus acquired. D having brought an action for specific performance against the company, it was held that O and J ought to be added as parties defendant, for without their presence complete adjudication was not possible, this principally on the ground that "these two persons may possibly entertain very different views from the plaintiff as to the line of the road, and the mode of making it." Approved in McCheane v. Giles [1902] 1 Ch. 911, 915-916.

[36] McCheane v. Gyles, *supra,* at 917.

§ 2. Medial Interpleader

Third-party participation may also result from an application of the principle upon which moves, by way of independent suit, the equitable remedy of interpleader. Latter-day procedural reform, that is to say, has set its seal of favor upon means of affording the defendant, sued by one of two rival claimants of the debt or property in question, opportunity to call upon the other to come into the cause and litigate his claim with the plaintiff. This, indeed, was the procedural device employed in a former day in the common-law action of detinue: here the defendant in a limited category of cases, where he claimed no interest in the chattel in suit, was entitled to cause the summoning in of a third-party claimant of the chattel, by "garnishment," if the third party had not yet commenced action, by "interpleader," if he had.[37] In England this common-law remedy, which in the meantime had become obsolete, was revived and extended by a statute of 1831. Under this it was made available to the defendant in any action of assumpsit, debt, detinue or trover, upon his showing by affidavit or otherwise that he claimed no interest in the subject-matter of the action, that the right thereto was claimed by or supposed to belong to a third party who either had sued or was expected to sue in that regard, that the defendant did not collude with the third party, and was ready to place the subject-matter of the action at the disposition of of the court.[38] And by way of supplement, a provision of the Common Law Procedure Act of 1860 declared that the proceeding was in order "though the titles of the claimants . . . have not a common origin, but are adverse to and independent of one another." [39]

The Rules of 1875, under the Judicature Acts, accepted the practice thus established and extended it to other common-law actions.[40] But by the Rules of 1883 the institution was explicitly regulated, although without substantial depar-

[37] 2 Story, Equity Jurisprudence (14th ed. 1918) §§ 1111-1113, based upon 3 Reeves, History of English Law (2d ed. 1787) 448 *et seq.* The common-law remedy also had some application outside of detinue, but in no other personal action. Story, § 1114.

[38] 1 & 2 Will. IV, c. 58, § 1.

[39] 23 & 24 Vict. c. 126, § 12.

[40] Rules of 1875, O. I, r. 2.

ture from the former basis. The remedy of interpleader, whether by way of independent action, or as a defensive measure, was to be open to any one who is "under liability for any debt, money, goods, or chattels, for or in respect of which he is, or expects to be, sued by two or more parties . . . making adverse claims thereto." In any case showing is required of the applicant, substantially as under the medial interpleader act of 1831, of absence of interest on his part, non-collusion, and willingness to surrender the subject-matter. The provision of 1860 dispensing with the necessity of a common origin for the claimants' titles likewise finds place for interpleader in general. The medial form of the remedy is not separately dealt with, except in the provision definitely recognizing it, that "where the applicant is a defendant, application for relief may be made at any time after service of the writ of summons." [41]

In the United States, the English statute of 1831 appears to have suggested similar legislation, namely, the Pennsylvania provision, enacted in 1836,[42] this, however, with a background in previous judicial practice,[43] and directly the Virginia statute of 1849.[44] Reception of the same institution of medial interpleader in the American code legislation, however, dates from 1851, as the result of provisions adopted in Iowa and in New York. The Iowa Code of that year gave to the defendant the right to "obtain the substitution in his place of any person not already a party who claims the money or property which is the subject matter of the action." This was to be done upon affidavit of the defendant stating the facts, denying collusion with the third party, and offering to pay the money or deliver the property as should be directed by the court, followed by a rule to show cause directed against the plaintiff and the third party.[45] The New

[41] Rules of 1883, O. LVII, rr. 1-4. Order LVII also includes the subject of sheriff's interpleader.

[42] Pa. Stat. Ann. (Purdon, 1931) Tit. 12, § 581. It had been adopted the previous year for the District Court for the City and County of Philadelphia. *Ibid.*, note to § 581.

[43] See Coates v. Roberts, 4 Rawle 100, 110 (1833); McMunn v. Carothers, 2 Am.L.J. 133 (1848).

[44] Va. Code 1849, c. 152, § 1, Va. Code Ann. 1950, § 8-226; see Dickeschied v. Exchange Bank, 28 W.Va. 340, 344 (1886).

[45] Iowa Code 1851, §§ 1685, 1686.

York provision, which came as an amendment to the Code already in force, granted the remedy to a defendant "against whom an action is pending upon a contract, or for specific real, or personal property." Such defendant, it declared, "may at any time, before answer, upon affidavit that a person not a party to the action, and without collusion with him, makes against him a demand for the same debt or property, upon due notice to such person and the adverse party, apply to the court for an order to substitute such person in his place, and discharge him from liability to either party, on his depositing in court the amount of the debt, or delivering the property, or its value to such person as the court may direct; and the court may, in its discretion, make the order." [46]

The New York form of provision was that which more usually prevailed in the subsequent code legislation. With or without more or less variation it is now characteristic of the American code system. Under different forms similar recognition of medial interpleader obtains in a number of States outside of the code area. For the whole, considerable diversity is to be noted as to the kinds of action affected. An important quota of jurisdictions follows the original New York rule in making the remedy available in actions on contract or for the recovery of specific real or personal property;[47] others restrict it to actions on contract or for the recovery of specific personal property,[48] or actions on contract or for the recovery of personal property,[49] without the appellative. Other specifications are actions "for the recovery of money . . . or for the recovery of the possession of personal property" [50] and actions "for debt or for specific property or for the conversion thereof." [51] Sometimes, again, it is available in

[46] N.Y. Laws 1851, c. 479, Code § 122. Here, as in the case of intervention, the Iowa provision antedated that of New York by a few months.

[47] *E.g.*, N.C. Gen. Stat. 1943, § 1-73; N.D. Rev. Code 1943, § 28-0224; Minn. Stat. 1945, § 544.12.

[48] *E.g.*, Cal. Code Civ. Proc. (Deering, 1949) § 386; Idaho Code Ann. 1949, § 5-320; Mont. Rev. Codes Ann. 1947, § 93-2825.

[49] Ohio Gen. Code (Page, 1938) § 11265; Ark. Stat. Ann. 1947, § 27-817; Kan. Gen. Stat. (Corrick, 1935) § 60-418.

[50] W.Va. Code 1949, § 5702.

[51] Wis. Stat. 1949, § 260.19.

any action [52] or in any action at law to recover money.[53] Iowa which, by the Code of 1851, apparently allowed the measure in any action for money or property, retreated from this stand by a provision of the Revision of 1860,[54] which in altering the form of the existing provision, confined its application to actions "upon contract for the recovery of personal property," and on this basis it remained until the widening effected by the Iowa Rules of 1943 under the influence of the Federal Rules of 1938.[55] In New York the Code section was in 1877 changed in terms so as to apply to "an action to recover upon a contract, or an action of ejectment, or an action to recover a chattel," [56] and in this form it passed into the Civil Practice Act of 1920.[57] It had also in 1877 incorporated the provision, likewise passing into the Civil Practice Act, that if the defendant disputed his liability or asserted some interest in the subject-matter, then instead of applying for discharge, he was to apply for an order joining the third party claimant or claimants as co-defendants. This principle, opening the way for a medial proceeding, akin to an original bill in the nature of a bill of interpleader, has since, by an act of 1939, been given further development in relation to actions "to recover specific personal property, including certificates of stock, bonds, notes or other securities or obligations, exceeding fifty dollars in value, held by the defendant within this state, or to enforce a vested or contingent interest therein or lien thereon," as also with respect to actions "to recover damages in conversion for the alleged wrongful detention" of such specific personal property. There is provided in this connection a carefully detailed procedure, by means of which all claims, of which the defendant has notice, as well as his own, if any, and whether the several claims are adverse or not, may be adjusted in the pending action.[58]

[52] Va. Code Ann. 1950, § 8-226.

[53] 8 Mass.Ann.Laws 1933, c. 231, § 40.

[54] Ia. Revision 1860, § 2767.

[55] Ia. Code 1939, § 11002; Ia. Rules Civ. Proc., Rules 35, 36, in Ia. Code 1946, Vol. II, p. 2148.

[56] N.Y. Laws 1877, c. 416, N.Y. Code Civ. Proc. (Stover, 6th ed. 1902) § 820.

[57] N.Y. Civ. Pract. Act 1920, § 287.

[58] N.Y. Laws 1939, c. 804, N.Y. Civ. Pract. Act (Clevenger, 1950) § 287-b *et seq.*

In general, however, the medial interpleader of the State jurisdictions does not go beyond the case where the defendant, disclaiming interest in the subject-matter of the action, seeks only to be relieved from his position as stakeholder. And usually the proceeding is regarded as a substitute for the independent equitable remedy and governed by the same rules as to the character of the rival claims which apply to that remedy.[59] But certain jurisdictions, with California[60] taking the lead, have removed the fetters of orthodox equity doctrine by allowing the defendant thus to proceed in respect of the conflicting claimants "although their titles or claims have not a common origin, or are not identical, but are adverse to and independent of one another," which phraseology, it will be observed, reflects that of the English Common Law Procedure Act of 1860.

Either in addition to or in the absence of general provision for medial interpleader there variously appear among the States provisions granting this manner of remedy in statutory garnishment proceedings, as well as in cases involving particular transactions, such, especially, as actions against a bank to recover the amount of a money deposit. Here, too, is to be noted the effect of the Uniform Warehouse Receipts Act[61] and the Uniform Bills of Lading Act.[62] The one provides that the warehouseman, the other that the carrier, may have the remedy of interpleader, either as an original suit or "as a defense to any action brought against him." As a result the enactment of one or both of these measures has served to introduce a limited measure of the medial principle in jurisdictions lacking any general provision on the subject. Also to be taken into account, in the absence of any statutory provision on the subject, is the possibility which may exist under local practice of invoking the defensive remedy by means of counterclaim. While, according to orthodox equity practice, interpleader was an original proceeding, there are American instances where the use of a cross-bill

[59] 4 Pomeroy, Equity Jurisprudence (4th ed. 1919) § 1329.

[60] Cal. Code Civ. Proc. (Deering, 1949) § 386.

[61] § 17: 3 U.L.A. (1922) 29.

[62] § 20: 4 U.L.A. (1922) 37.

seeking relief by way of interpleader, though criticized, has been tolerated.[63] And under the reformed procedure, the counterclaim should ordinarily be available for the purpose without the support of special provision. Indeed, the Supreme Court of the United States in *Liberty Oil Co.* v. *Condon National Bank,*[64] in effect approved utilization of the medial principle on much narrower premises, namely, under the general authority given by the act of 1915 for the pleading of equitable defenses in actions at law.

In the federal sphere, however, the medial principle has since made pronounced advance. Succeeding interpleader legislation of 1917, 1925 and 1926, an act of 1936[65] extended the remedy by bill of interpleader or bill in the nature of a bill of interpleader to the case where the claimants were citizens of different States and the money or property was of the value of $500 or more. A further condition of jurisdiction was the deposit of the subject-matter in the registry of the court or the giving of bond by the applicant to secure compliance with the future order of the court in the premises. The statute adopted almost literally the language of the California Code dispensing with the need for common origin and identity of the conflicting claims. Moreover, what especially interests us here is its express provision that in any action at law the defendant might invoke this manner of relief, by setting up as an equitable defense, in accordance with the statute of 1915, "any matter which would entitle him to file an original or ancillary bill of interpleader, or bill in the nature of interpleader in the same court or any other United States District Court against the plaintiff in such action at law and one or more adverse claimants. . . ."[66]

Now, with the disappearance of the old distinction between actions at law and suits in equity under the Federal Rules of 1938, and in consequence of the corresponding revi-

[63] Foss v. First Nat. Bank of Denver (C.C., D.Colo.) 1 McCrary 474, 3 Fed.Cas. 185, 190 (1880); Curtis v. Williams, 35 Ill. App. 518, 527 (1890).

[64] 260 U.S. 235, 43 S.Ct. 118 (1922).

[65] 49 Stat. 1096, 28 U.S.C.A. § 41 (26) as of 1947.

[66] See Chafee, The Federal Interpleader Act of 1936 (1936) 45 Yale LawJ. 963, 969 *et seq.*, 982, 988-990.

sion of the statute in 1948,[67] the relief in question is available under the statute in any civil action in which its jurisdictional terms are met.

But a further widening of the remedy has been effected under the Federal Rules. By Rule 22(1) it is provided that "persons having claims against the plaintiff may be joined as defendants and required to interplead when their claims are such that the plaintiff is or may be exposed to double or multiple liability." Here, too, the old requirement of common origin and identity of the claims in question is laid aside by the use of the California formula. The principle of the bill in the nature of a bill of interpleader comes to recognition in the provision that it is not an objection to the proceeding that "the plaintiff avers that he is not liable in whole or in part to any or all of the claimants." And the medial form, in full measure, is sanctioned by the declaration that "a defendant exposed to similar liability may obtain such interpleader by way of cross-claim or counterclaim." The provisions of the Rules in this regard are in nowise to limit those relating to the joinder of parties. And by Rule 22(2) the remedy thus provided for is declared to be in addition to that given by the act of 1936, but actions under the act are to be conducted in accordance with the Rules. It is apparent that actions falling outside the terms of the act are governed by the rules applicable to civil causes in general in respect of jurisdiction, venue and process, in contradistinction to the exceptional rules of the act.[68]

Rule 22(1) with or without minor adaptation has been followed in Arizona (1939), South Dakota (1939), Colorado (1941), Texas (1941), New Mexico (1942), Missouri (1943), Delaware (1947), New Jersey (1948), and Utah (1949).[69] It also finds reproduction in the Iowa Rules

[67] U.S.C. 1948, Tit. 28, §§ 1335, 2361, effective September 1, 1948, and reviser's notes, pp. 1838, 1913.

[68] See 2 Moore's Federal Practice (1938) 2198-2200, 3 *id.* (2d ed. 1948) 3009 *et seq.*

[69] Ariz. Code Ann. 1939, § 21-521; S.D. Code 1939, § 33.0412; Colo. Rules Civ. Proc., Rule 22, Colo. Stat. Ann. 1939, Replacement Vol. I, 1941; Tex. Rules Civ. Proc. (Vernon, 1942) Rule 43; N.M. Stat. Ann. 1941, § 19-101(22); Mo. Rev. Stat. 1942, 1950 Pocket Part to Vol. III, § 847.18: Del. Rules of Su-

(1943).[70] Arizona, however, has concurrently retained its previous provision for medial interpleader of the code type, applicable in actions upon contract or for specified personal property.[71] The influence of the federal provision is further apparent in the regulation of medial interpleader by the Pennsylvania rules (1941), especially in their extension of the remedy to all cases of exposure of the defendant to double or multiple liability, in removal of the necessity that the defendant shall be a mere stakeholder, and in excluding also the requirements of privity between the parties and of common origin and identity of the claims.[72]

§ 3. Third-Party Impleader [73]

In the voucher to warranty of the common-law practice of real actions means were open to a defendant claiming a freehold estate in the land in suit, whereby he might cause to be summoned his warrantor and cast upon him the burden of defending the action. Should the plaintiff obtain judgment, the defendant was entitled in the same cause to recover over against his warrantor in the form of a judgment "to have land of him of the value of the land lost by reason of his warranty." [74] This principle had been of wider application in its Germanic origins, but in the crystallization of the English common-law system it was given no place outside of the real actions. And with the obsolescence and subsequent dis-

perior Court, Rule 22, Rules of Court of Chancery, Rule 22; N.J. Rules Civ. Pract., Rule 3:22; Utah Rules Civ. Proc., Rule 22.

70 Ia. Rules Civ. Proc., Rules 35, 36, in Ia. Code 1946, Vol. II, p. 2148.

71 Ariz. Code Ann. 1939, § 21-522.

72 Pa. Rules Civ. Proc., Rule 2302 *et seq.*, in Pa. Stat. Ann. (Purdon, 1931), Appendix to Tit. 12, 1949 Pocket Part.

73 For the bringing in of the third party here in question a satisfactory term is wanting. The English designation "third party procedure," followed as "third-party practice" by the Federal Rules, is lacking in definiteness, inasmuch as it might equally well be applied to intervention and interpleader. The term "impleader," sometimes used, also is inexact, since there is technically an "impleader" in any case of an added defendant. "Third-party impleader," as employed in the Advisory Committee's note to Federal Rule 14, while still falling short of precision, makes a much closer approach.

74 Booth, The Nature and Practice of Real Actions (1701) 43; 1 Reeves, History of the English Law (ed. Finlason, 1869) 422; Stearns, A Summary of the Law and Practice of Real Actions (2d ed. 1831) *131-132.

placement of the real actions, it disappeared altogether from the English scene. Here, therefore, as in other cases in which he had a right to relief over against a third person, the unsuccessful defendant, however his task in the matter might be lessened by the fact that he had given notice of the suit to the third person thus liable over, was relegated to his separate action against the latter. But in the current of latter-day reform the principle immanent in the old proceeding of voucher to warranty has been laid hold of for the creation of a more generalized procedural device similarly aimed at dealing with the third party in the original cause. This process began with the English Judicature Act of 1873, which empowered the court to grant to the defendant, in addition to all proper affirmative relief against the plaintiff, "all such relief relating to or connected with the original subject of the cause or matter . . . claimed against any other person, whether already a party to the same cause or matter or not, who shall have been duly served with notice in writing of such claim pursuant to any Rule of Court or any Order of the Court, as might properly have been granted against such person if he had been made a defendant to a cause duly instituted by the same defendant for the like purpose." [75] The vigor of this provision was but feebly reflected in the Rules of 1875. They granted permission thus to apply for leave to call in the third person by notice in two cases, first, "where a defendant is or claims to be entitled to contribution or indemnity, or other remedy or relief over," and, secondly, "where from any other cause it appears to the Court or a Judge that a question in the action should be determined not only as between the plaintiff and defendant, but as between the plaintiff, defendant, and any other person, or between any or either of them." [76] But they did not contemplate the rendition of any judgment in the same cause against the person thus called in. Their object simply was "to bind the third party conclusively by the judgment given as between the plaintiff and the original de-

[75] 36 & 37 Vict. c. 66, § 24(3); Consolidated Judicature Act 1925, 15 & 16 Geo. V, c. 49, § 39(1)(b).

[76] Rules of 1875, 38 & 39 Vict. c. 77, First Schedule, O. XVI, r. 17.

fendant," [77] leaving the latter to his independent action against the third party for indemnity or other relief over. This fault, however, was repaired by the revision of 1883 which, expressly providing for judgment against the third party, in favor of the notifying defendant, to be rendered in the pending action,[78] more adequately implemented in this respect the provision of the statute. On the other hand, the revision very materially reduced the scope of the institution by confining it to the case of "contribution or indemnity," claimed by the defendant against a third person, including another defendant.[79] But this narrowing was not to endure. By amendments of 1929, which incidentally made the Rules concerning the present matter the subject of a separate Order (O. XVIA) instead of parcel of the general order (O. XVI) relating to parties, this so-called third-party procedure, so far as concerns the ambit of its application, was restored very much to what it had been prior to 1883. Specifically, as the case now stands under the change thus effected, the procedure in question is applicable where the defendant claims against a person not already a party to the action or against another defendant:

> (*a*) that he is entitled to contribution or indemnity, or
>
> (*b*) that he is entitled to any relief or remedy relating to or connected with the original subject-matter of the action and substantially the same as some relief or remedy claimed by the plaintiff, or
>
> (*c*) that any question or issue relating to or connected with the said subject-matter is substantially the same as some question or issue arising between the plaintiff and the defendant and should properly be determined not only as between the plaintiff and the defendant but as between the plaintiff and the defendant and the third party or between any or either of them. (O. XVIA, r. 1).

The remedy thus given to a defendant is now expressly made available to the plaintiff as defendant to a counterclaim. (O. XVIA, r. 13). As before, judgment may be rendered against the third party in the pending action. (O.

[77] Mellish, L. J., in Treleaven v. Bray, 45 L.J. Ch. 113, 114 (1875).

[78] O. XVI, former rr. 50-52.

[79] O. XVI, former rr. 48, 55.

XVIA, rr. 6, 7, 9). Apart from the case of default on the part of the third party and resulting admission of liability, it is for the court, on application for directions, to say as to "the mode and extent in or to which the third party shall be bound or made liable by the decision or judgment in the action," and the court is empowered to enter such judgment as the nature of the case may require, as between the defendant and the third party, it being, however, provided that there shall be no execution without leave on the judgment against the third party until the defendant has satisfied the judgment rendered against him in favor of the plaintiff. (O. XVIA, rr. 5, 6, 8, 9). Moreover, it is now provided that the defendant or the third party may be granted such relief or remedy as might have been granted if the third party had been a defendant in an action brought against him by the present defendant. (O. XVIA, r. 9(1)). And, by a provision which in essence dates back to 1911, there is expressly recognized the right of the third party, in his turn, to call in another against whom he seeks relief over. (O. XVIA, r. 11).[80] As has been seen, the defendant is entitled to pursue the third-party procedure against either an outsider or a co-defendant; the only procedural difference between the two cases is that, when the claim is made against another defendant, no leave is required for the issuance of the notice, and no appearance to the notice is necessary. (O. XVIA, r. 12).

In the United States the path in the present direction appears to have been broken by the admiralty practice. On the heels of a predisposing District Court decision,[81] there was added in 1883 to the Admiralty Rules a provision (Rule 59) in reference to bringing in new parties in suits for damage by collision, sufficiently broad to permit the assertion by the claimant or respondent of a claim for relief over. And this was succeeded in 1920 by the present Admiralty Rule 56 which expressly provides for the bringing in at the instance of the claimant or respondent in any suit, whether

[80] This was characteristic of the primitive Germanic institution. At common law the vouching over might continue "to the fourth degree, but no farther." Stearns, Real Actions (2d ed. 1831) * 131.

[81] The Hudson (S.D.N.Y.) 15 Fed. 162 (1883).

in rem or *in personam,* of "any other vessel or person (individual or corporation) who may be partly or wholly liable to the libelant or to such claimant or respondent by way of remedy over, contribution or otherwise, growing out of the same matter." [82] Apart from this development, it is to be noticed that here and there, in the State procedures, some measure of relief over against a third party has been recognized as grantable to the defendant under general provisions in relation to parties or cross-actions.[83] And in Texas, by a distinctive practice of judicial origin, the right of a defendant to obtain relief over in the pending cause (although latterly within more restricted limits than at the outset) had been solidly established without specific statutory aid, long before adoption of the court rule hereafter mentioned.[84]

But a definite current of express legislation on the subject is seen setting in with the Wisconsin statute of 1915, which provided that a defendant showing by affidavit that, if held liable in the action, he would have a right of action against a third person not a party to the action for the amount of the recovery against him might, upon notice to the third party and the opposing party, apply for an order making such third person a defendant to the action, which order the court was given discretionary power to make.[85] In its present form the provision is that "a defendant, who if he be held liable in the action, will thereby obtain a right of action against a person not a party may apply for an order making such person a party defendant and the court may so order." [86] The claim thus entertainable is to be asserted by

[82] For this admiralty development, see Cohen, Impleader: Enforcement of Defendant's Rights against Third Persons (1933)) 33 Col.L.Rev. 1147, 1167-1169; 1 Benedict, American Admiralty (5th ed. 1925) § 349 *et seq.;* 1 Moore's Federal Practice (1938) 749 *et seq.;* 3 *id.* (2d ed. 1948) 450 *et seq.*

[83] *E.g.,* Gregg v. City of Wilmington, 155 N.C. 18, 70 S.E. 1070 (1911); Guthrie v. City of Durham, 168 N.C. 573, 84 S.E. 859 (1915); Bowman v. City of Greensboro, 190 N.C. 611, 130 S.E. 502 (1925); Harding v. Kentucky River Hardwood Co., 205 Ky. 1, 265 S.W. 429 (1924); McMillan v. Spencer, 162 Ga. 659, 134 S.E. 921 (1926).

[84] McCormick, Revival of the Pioneer Spirit in Texas Procedure (1940) 18 Tex.L.Rev. 426, 431. See Courchesne v. Santa Fé Fuel Co. (Ct. Civ. App.) 155 S.W. 684 (1913); Coombs v. Jackson (Ct. Civ. App.) 238 S.W. 992 (1922); Barton v. Farmers' State Bank (Comm. App.) 276 S.W. 177 (1925).

[85] Wis. Laws 1915, c. 219, § 6, p. 22.

[86] Wis Stat. 1949, § 260.19.

means of cross-complaint served upon the third party and its adjudication is regulated by the court under the power to make such orders "for the determination of the rights of the parties as shall be just." [87] In its interpretation of the third-party provision the Supreme Court of Wisconsin has recognized the propriety of two judgments in the action, one as between the plaintiff and the original defendant and the other as between the original defendant and the third person, notwithstanding that the latter judgment may be a contingent one, not effectuable until the discharge of the defendant's liability to the successful plaintiff.[88]

In 1922, New York, by an amendment to the Civil Practice Act, similarly inspired by the English example, made provision for bringing in a non-party claimed to be liable in whole or in part to one of the parties to the action in respect of the claim made against the latter.[89] As amended the following year, it declared that "where any party to an action shows that some third person, not then a party to the action, is or will be liable to such party wholly or in part for the claim made against such party in the action, the court, on application of such party, may order such person to be brought in as a party to the action and direct that a supplemental summons and a pleading alleging the claim of such party against such person be served upon such person and that such person plead thereto, so that the claim of such moving party against such person may be determined in such action, which shall thereupon proceed against such person as a defendant therein to such judgment as may be proper." [90] In this form the provision stood until 1946, when it was revised and amplified. Under its present terms—wherein is in some measure discernible the influence of Federal Rule 14 shortly to be mentioned—a defendant, after the service of his answer, "may bring in a person not a party to the action

[87] Wis. Stat. 1949, § 263.15.

[88] Scharine v. Huebsch, 203 Wis. 261, 234 N.W. 358 (1931); Wait v. Pierce, 191 Wis. 202, 210 N.W. 822 (1926).

[89] 2 N.Y. Laws 1922, c. 624, p. 1670, amending Civ. Pract. Act, § 193, the latter now repealed (1946) in favor of a new § 193.

[90] N.Y. Laws 1923, c. 250, pp. 445-446.

who is or may be liable to him for all or a part of the plaintiff's claim against him, by serving as a third-party plaintiff upon such person a summons and a copy of a verified complaint. The claim against such person . . . must be related to the main action by a question of law or fact common to both controversies, but need not rest upon the same cause of action or the same ground as the claim asserted against the third-party plaintiff." The impleaded defendant is entitled to assert against the plaintiff any defenses which the third-party plaintiff has to the plaintiff's claim and the plaintiff to assert against the impleaded defendant, subject to the latter's right of defense and counterclaim, any claim assertable against him had he been originally joined as a defendant. The same right of impleader inures to the plaintiff as defendant to a counterclaim. And in all cases the impleaded defendant, under the same principles, may implead another non-party. Among other features of the amendment is notable the wide range of discretion over the proceeding, once instituted, given to the court in the avoidance of undue delay in the main action or prejudice to any of the parties. No more than in Wisconsin had any difficulty been experienced in New York in entering against the third party a judgment contingent upon the satisfaction by the original defendant of the plaintiff's claim,[91] but this practice is now strengthened by the express declaration of the revised provision that "the court shall proceed to such judgment or judgments as may be proper."[92]

A like combination of the action over with the original suit is envisaged by the Pennsylvania statute of 1929, which provided for the suing out by any defendant of a writ of *scire facias* to bring in as an additional defendant "any other person alleged to be liable over to him for the cause of ac-

[91] First Nat. Bank v. Bankers' Trust Co., 151 Misc. 233, 271 N.Y.S. 191 (1934). And see also cases cited in Cohen, Impleader: Enforcement of Defendant's Rights against Third Parties (1933) 33 Col.L.Rev. 1146, 1157 note 56.

[92] N.Y. Laws 1946, c. 971, N.Y. Civ. Pract. Act (Clevenger, 1950) § 193-a. For the motivation of the change—which involved substitution of § 193-a for the related clause of the former § 193—see 12th Annual Report of the N.Y. Judicial Council (1946) p. 199 *et seq.*

tion declared on, or jointly or severally liable therefor with him." The suit was then to continue "according to equitable principles, although at common law, or under existing statutes, the plaintiff could not properly have joined all such parties as defendants." [93] Subsequent amendments included an attempt in 1937 to follow the English provision as to the calling in of a third person where identical questions existed between him and the original defendant, on the one hand, and between the plaintiff and the original defendant, on the other.[94] But in 1939 the statute in question was suspended by the going into effect of the chapter of the new Rules of Civil Procedure "governing joinder of additional parties," which provided for the initiation of the proceeding by petition and otherwise re-regulated it.[95] In 1942, however, the relative provisions were recast, and now by means of a praecipe for an appropriate writ, accompanied by complaint, the defendant as of course "may join as an additional defendant any person not a party to the action who may be alone liable or liable over to him on the cause of action declared upon or jointly or severally liable thereon with him." Pleading and procedure as between the moving party and the additional defendant are to be the same as if they were respectively plaintiff and defendant. No pleadings, however, are to be filed between the additional defendant and any party other than the moving party, except that the additional defendant may counterclaim against the plaintiff. The assertion by an original defendant of a counterclaim against the plaintiff precludes the original defendant from joining an additional defendant unless the counterclaim is founded upon the "transaction, occurrence or series of transactions or occurrences out of which the original cause of action arose." And no counterclaim may be asserted by an additional defendant which is not so founded. Any defendant added by the procedure in question is entitled in like manner to implead another person not already a party to the action.[96]

[93] Pa. Laws 1929, p. 479, Pa. Stat. Ann. (Purdon, 1931) Tit. 12, § 141.

[94] Pa. Laws 1937, p. 2118; Pa. Stat. Ann. (Purdon, 1931) 1949 Pocket Part, § 141.

[95] Pa. Rules Civ. Proc., Rule 2252 *et seq.* of 1939.

[96] Pa. Rules Civ. Proc., present Rule

In 1933, the Municipal Court of Chicago which, under the act creating it, has extensive authority to regulate its own practice by rules of court adopted certain rules patterned very closely upon those of the English Supreme Court prior to the amendments of 1929, providing for impleader in case of a defendant's claim to "contribution or indemnity over" against a third person or a co-defendant.[97] These continued in force until their revision in 1940, as presently to be noted.

A high point in the acceptance of this institution by American practice was attained by inclusion of provisions on the subject in the Federal Rules of 1938. Rule 14(a) as originally adopted, permitted a defendant *ex parte* or on notice to the plaintiff, according as he acts before or after the service of his answer, to move "for leave as a third-party plaintiff to serve a summons and complaint upon a person not a party to the action[98] who is or may be liable to him or to the plaintiff for all or part of the plaintiff's claim against him." The person thus served (known as the third-party defendant), in addition to making defense, was given the right to put forward any counterclaim or cross-claim "against the plaintiff, the third-party plaintiff, or any other party," in accordance with the Rule governing counterclaims and cross-claims. "The third-party defendant," it was provided, "may assert any defenses which the third-party plaintiff has to the plaintiff's claim," and "is bound by the adjudication of the third-party plaintiff's liability to the plaintiff, as well as of his own to the plaintiff or to the third-party plaintiff." If the third-party defendant could have been joined originally as a defendant by the plaintiff, the plaintiff was entitled to amend his pleadings so as appropriately to assert his claim against such third-party defendant. The third-party defendant in turn was entitled to proceed under the Rule as against any other person not a party to the action, in respect of the latter's liability over to him or liability to the third-party plaintiff.

2251 *et seq.*, in Pa. Stat. Ann. (Purdon, 1931) Appendix to Tit. 12, 1949 Pocket Part.

97 Civil Practice Rules of Municipal Court of Chicago 1933, Rules 38-45.

98 It is always open to a defendant to assert against a co-defendant a claim for relief over, but this is done by means of a cross-claim under Rule 13(g).

By Rule 14(b) the right to bring in a third party as thus provided was extended to the case of a counterclaim asserted against the plaintiff; here the plaintiff as defendant to the counterclaim assumes the rôle of third-party plaintiff.

Certain important changes were effected in Rule 14(a) by the amendment of 1946. The Rule, it will be observed, gave the proceeding to the defendant not only in respect of a person not a party to the action liable over to him, but also—this on the precedent of the Admiralty Rules—in respect of such a person liable to the plaintiff. Relevant to the latter liability was the provision concerning the plaintiff's amendment of his pleadings. But since, as had been repeatedly held, the plaintiff could not be compelled to assert his claim if he did not choose to do so, the impleading of the third-party defendant on the ground of his liability to the plaintiff might well become an idle gesture. Accordingly it was deemed advisable to discard this feature, and appropriate change in this regard was made by the amendment. Again, under the amendment, besides asserting against the plaintiff any defenses which the third-party plaintiff has to the plaintiff's claim, the third-party defendant "may also assert any claim against the plaintiff arising out of the transaction or occurrence that is the subject matter of the plaintiff's claim against the third-party plaintiff." And the plaintiff, on his part, is entitled to assert any claim against the third-party defendant arising from the same source, with the right in the latter to defend, counterclaim or cross-claim as in other cases. In addition, the amendment excised the provision concerning the binding effect of adjudication upon the third party, inasmuch as, stating a rule of substantive law, it was not properly within the scope of the Rules.[99]

Under the federal regulation, as under other provision for this institution, it is apparent that as the claim for relief over involves a separate cause of action, the court is here called upon to render separate judgments, whether as part of the

[99] Note of Advisory Committee, containing detailed explanation of the amendment. Federal Rules of Civil Procedure (West Publishing Co., 1947) pp. 37-40. See also Clark, Code Pleading (2d ed. 1947) 417.

same judgment-order or not. So, too, it is manifest that where the liability of the third-party defendant to the third-party plaintiff depends upon the discharge of the latter's liability to the principal plaintiff, the judgment against the third-party defendant, if rendered before that discharge, must be so framed that it is not executory until the discharge has been effected.

Rule 14 in its original form found acceptance in Arizona (1939), Colorado (1941) and New Mexico (1942).[100] With some slight adaptation it has been given place in Missouri.[101] It has been followed in Texas (1940-41) with little change, except that the measure is not to be "applied in tort cases, so as to permit the joinder of a liability or indemnity insurance company, unless such company is by statute or contract liable to the person injured or damaged," or in any case so as to run counter to the rules relating to venue.[102] And, with the studies looking to its amendment, it has contributed appreciably to the New York legislation of 1946.[103] Influence of the original Rule also appears in the procedure of the Municipal Court of Chicago, which in 1940 substituted for its previous rules on the subject a single rule embodying among other changes the Federal formula then designative of the third person thus to be called in.[104] In its amended form, moreover, Rule 14 has been substantially followed in Maryland (1947), has entered with minor adaptation into the procedures of Delaware (1947) and New Jersey (1948), and has been taken over verbatim in Utah (1949).[105] The amendment has also been incorporated (1949) in the previously adopted Arizona and New Mexico provisions.[106]

100 Ariz. Code Ann. 1939, §§ 21-446, 21-447; Colo. Rules Civ. Proc., Rule 14, in Colo. Stat. Ann. 1935, 1941 Replacement Vol. I; N.M. Stat. Ann. 1941, § 19-101 (14).

101 Mo. Rev. Stat. 1942, 1950 Pocket Part to Vol. III, § 847.20.

102 Tex. Rules Civ. Proc. (Vernon, 1942) Rule 38.

103 See 12th Annual Report of the N.Y. Judicial Council (1946) particularly pp. 212-213.

104 Civil Practice Rules of the Municipal Court of Chicago 1940, Rule 25.

105 Md. Gen. Rules Pract. & Proc. Part 2, Subd. III, Rule 4, Md. Ann. Code (Flack, 1939), 1947 Cum. Supp. pp. 2042-2043; Del. Rules of Superior Court, Rule 14, Rules of Court of Chancery, Rule 14; N.J. Rules Civ. Pract., Rule 3:14; Utah Rules Civ. Proc., Rule 14.

106 See 1949 Cum. Supp. to each of the two annotated codes.

One is tempted to wonder why the development of the present institution should have been deferred to so late a day in the modern movement for procedural reform. Considerations of economy attaching to the use of a single suit where otherwise a plurality of separate proceedings would be necessary, together with the better opportunity for doing accurate justice when all the parties and matters involved are before the court, render it an accessory of civil procedure which no well-ordered system should be without. Any possibility that it may cause confusion by reason of a complex of controversies is effectively guarded against by vesting in the court a full measure of discretion, if not to refuse the application in the first instance, certainly to separate the conjoined controversies for trial and determine the order of their trials, as well as to take all other steps of directive control necessary to avoid prejudice to the several parties.

Chapter XIII

PLEADING

§ 1. The American Codes and the English Rules

Object of pleading reform in England and America has been the achievement of a system emancipated, on the one hand, from the artificialities of the common law and, on the other, from the prolixity of chancery. The Hilary Rules of 1834 sought improvement of the common-law system by a depuration of its basis, but this, in the main, led only to enhanced difficulty in its workings. And while certain fragmentary advances were made by the earlier legislation in this country, and more decided progress effected by the English Common Law Procedure Act of 1852 and the Chancery Practice Amendment Act of the same year, it is to the New York Code of 1848, for America, and the Rules under the Judicature Acts of 1873 and 1875, for England, that we must look as establishing the prevailing types of present-day pleading.

Under the American code system, the plaintiff's cause of action and demand for relief are stated in the pleading known generally as the "complaint," in some jurisdictions as the "petition." Provision is made for a "demurrer," but this is limited to attack upon faults of substance particularly designated in the statute. Factual defenses are stated in an "answer." If the answer contains new matter, a "reply" is called for by most of the codes; in others the interposition of a reply depends upon leave of court; and in a few the pleadings stop with the answer. As a rule, any permissible counterclaim is stated in the answer, in which case a "reply to counterclaim" is usually in order. Defenses to the jurisdiction or in abatement, not available on motion or demurrer, are generally to be combined in the single answer with defenses on the merits, but in a few jurisdictions their presentation is either required or permitted to be by way of preliminary answer.[1]

In England, the plaintiff sets forth his cause of action and claim for relief in a "statement of claim."[2] The defendant, on his part, interposes a "defence" or "counterclaim" or "defence and counterclaim" as the case may be. The succeeding step, if in order, is a "reply." Originally, under the Rules, this might be delivered without leave of court; later, leave, in general, was required; and now, since 1933, the requirement is again omitted.[3] The reply, however, does not necessarily close the pleadings; it is open to the parties by leave of court to plead further, but occasion for so doing seldom arises. In 1883 the demurrer ceased to obtain. Instead, the point of law is raised in the answering pleading. But, where the legal insufficiency of the statement of claim or other pleading is so "plain and obvious" as to admit of no hesitation in recognizing it, a motion to strike out the pleading will be entertained.[4] Again, it is expressly provided that "no plea or defence shall be pleaded in abatement." Accordingly, such objections as were formerly the subject of dilatory pleas are now advanced by motion or by what is in effect a motion, though this may take the form of a summons to set aside service, to strike out parties, to stay proceedings, or the like.[5]

The two systems concur in exacting directness and brevity of allegation. By the usual American code provision the facts are to be stated "in ordinary and concise language without repetition"; by the English Rules, "every pleading shall contain, and contain only, a statement in a summary form of the facts on which the party pleading relies for his claim or defence."[6] They concur also in requiring the allegation of

[1] Clark, Handbook of the Law of Code Pleading (2d ed. 1947) 210 *et seq.*, 601-604, 687 *et seq.*

[2] In a large class of cases the statement of claim may come by way of special indorsement of the writ of summons. O. III, r. 6.

[3] Rules 1875, 38 & 39 Vict. c. 77, First Schedule, O. XXIV, r. 1; present O. XXIII, r. 1, and note in Annual Practice 1949, I, p. 440, *et seq.*

[4] Annual Practice 1949, I, p. 445, note to O. XXV, r. 1. The words "plain and obvious" come from Hubbuck v. Wilkinson [1899] 1 Q.B. 90, 91 (C.A.) there cited.

[5] O. XXI, r. 20, and notes in Annual Practice 1949, I, p. 406, II, p. 3197 *et seq.;* O. XII, r. 30.

[6] O. XIX, r. 4.

facts as distinguished from evidence and as distinguished from legal conclusions. Under the English Rules, with the permission to make affirmative allegations in the alternative, the use of the old method of plural counts for the variant statement of the same substantive cause of action has completely disappeared; to a considerable extent, however, it lingers under the American codes. Here alternative allegation in this regard is far from being everywhere admitted to recognized standing.[7] So far as concerns the interaction of the pleadings, both systems follow the Germanic principle of the common law that whatever is not denied stands admitted. Thus both accept generally the common-law rule prescribing advance by way of traverse or by way of confession and avoidance, but in neither is there any sharp application of the rule, or, resultingly, any insistence upon the definitive production, by the pleadings themselves, of literally formulated issues such as characterized the common-law system. The issues are there, but except in simple cases, their exact formulation, just as in the old chancery pleading, usually demands some interpretative activity on the part of the court.

For the purpose of ensuring good faith in the allegations, most of the codes have had resort to sworn pleadings; in some the requirement is a general one; in others—and this is the more usual rule—it is applied as a measure of party election: if either chooses to verify his own pleading then each subsequent pleading must be verified.[8] No requirement of the kind obtains in England; there, however, a check upon unfounded denial exists in the power of the court to compel payment by the offending party of the extra costs thus occasioned.[9] The American rule is of doubtful efficacy. For one thing, it tends to reduce the oath to a mere matter of convention and to favor the unscrupulous litigant at the expense of his conscientious opponent; furthermore, it offers an unneces-

[7] The situation as of 1947 is described in Clark, *op. cit.* at 255-256.

[8] For details see *ibid.* at 215-220.

[9] O. XXI, r. 9. Provisions of the kind have latterly found entrance into American legislation: see Conn. Gen. Stat. 1949, § 7821; Conn. Pract. Book 1934, p. 51, § 122; Mich. Court Rules 1931, 1933, 1945, Rule 17, §§ 10, [11], Searl, Mich. Court Rules Ann. (4th ed. 1933) p. 97 and 1948 Cum. Supp. p. 28; Ill. Civ. Pract. Act 1933, § 41; Ill. Rev. Stat. 1949, c. 110, § 165.

sary obstacle to the presentation of inconsistent defenses, for which, by the consensus of enlightened opinion, opportunity should always be afforded. The English rule, on its part, is hard to operate, since its application involves in each case a particular inquiry into the matter of the extra expense arising from the denial. But its mere presence has a salutary influence and, on the whole, it is much to be preferred to the other.

The fact has often been emphasized that the judges upon whom devolved the early administration of the New York Code were generally unsympathetic to its innovations and construed its provisions so narrowly as to prevent it from fully accomplishing the objects at which it was aimed. Illustrative of this unreceptive temper is the story related of the judge in a New York rural county, before whom, soon after the taking effect of the code, there came on for hearing a demurrer to a complaint, based on the objection that the plaintiff had failed to state a cause of action. The question turned on the meaning of the complaint's allegations. At that time the relative code provision, after requiring the facts to be stated concisely, contained the additional words: "and in such a manner as to enable a person of common understanding to know what is intended." [10] After listening to counsel and carefully reading the complaint, the judge handed it to his bailiff. "John," he commanded, "read over this complaint!" The bailiff silently read the pleading. "John," pursued the judge, "do you understand it?" "Yes, your Honor," replied the bailiff. "Very well," said the judge, "I don't understand it, but John does. The demurrer will be overruled." Certain it is that the code procedure entered upon its career in an atmosphere of unfriendliness, and the result was a crystallization of pleading doctrine which not only perpetuated certain of the old evils, but also developed technical difficulties unknown to the former régime. And while a later generation of judges, not thus biased by their training, has done much by way of correction, the system is still marked to a certain extent by the imprint of its early vicissitudes.

Detail we must forego, but it is safe to say that, although

[10] Code of 1848, § 120; Code of 1849, § 142.

the statutes themselves are in some degree to blame, the standard set by these inauspicious beginnings largely explains why the American codes have not succeeded as well as the English Rules in reducing pleading to that purely ancillary position which it ought to occupy in the procedural scheme. There is commonly too strong an insistence upon exactness of statement in the allegation of cause of action and defense and, as before suggested, too rigid an application of the rule against variance between allegation and proof. The test of prejudice worked to the opponent of the party at fault is too apt to be overridden by considerations of the regularity of the record. Amendments, to be sure, are liberally allowed, but save in a few jurisdictions, the power to amend the pleadings stops with the trial court.[11] Where this is the case it is still possible for a judgment to be reversed by an appellate court because of a fault in the pleadings alone, without regard to the evidence or to the question of prejudice *vel non* to the opposite party. The English system, in contrast, has virtually attained the position that a fault in pleading, however substantial, will not be permitted to affect the result if it has produced no actual injury. This is accomplished in part by the power of amending available at all stages of the proceeding, but in greater degree by the difference in judicial attitude which in an earlier place we have had occasion to observe. In comparison with the American event, the welcome at once extended by the English bench to the new system was as sunlight to shadow, and old prepossessions were not allowed to stand in the way of its successful functioning. Hence, if a party's claim or defense is supported by the evidence, he has little to fear from slips in his pleadings, for in practical effect everything depends on the case made at the trial.[12] It may be a question whether this does not go too far in a direction opposite to the traditional one: certainly, criticisms of the looseness of modern English pleading from time to time come to expression.[13] But for the present, at least, this looseness is endured in the interests of substantial justice.

[11] See Clark, *op. cit.* at 727-728.

[12] See Fifoot, English Law and its Background (1932) 161-163.

[13] See Clydesdale Bank v. Paton [1896] A.C. 381 and other cases cited in Keigwin, Cases in Code Pleading

§ 2. Reforms in the Non-Code Area Prior to the Federal Rules of 1938

Standing apart from the system of the codes, though not without experiencing to some extent their influence, the rules of pleading for the separate administration of law and equity in the so-called common-law jurisdictions have exhibited their own quota of reform measures. Activity in this direction became pronounced about the middle of the century, in the wake of the New York innovation. Especially notable in this regard for the common-law side is the Massachusetts reform embodied in the Practice Act of 1851, which remains the substantial basis of the existing common-law procedure of that State. This laid down for the declaration the principle that "only the substantive facts necessary to constitute the cause of action shall be stated, without unnecessary verbiage, and with substantial certainty," substituted for the pleas of the former system in personal actions an answer, restricted the plea of general issue to real and mixed actions, and provided that an answer in avoidance should "set forth, in clear and precise terms, each substantive fact intended to be relied upon." [14] The same period witnessed general reforms of pleading in Alabama (1852), Maryland (1856), Mississippi (1857) and Tennessee (1858) in the like end of ensuring simplicity and brevity of allegation and foreclosing formal objections.[15] After this the movement lost impetus, so far as regards matters other than those of detail, and long remained in abeyance. But within the last forty years there set in a significant revival. Here come into view the New Jersey Practice Act of 1912, with the rules thereunder, legislation of 1915 in Pennsylvania and Vermont, and the Michigan Judicature Act of 1915, followed by the rules of 1931 and 1933. All these enactments, for common-law actions, established allegation on a basis approximating that of the codes or the English Rules. In New Jersey and Vermont a "complaint"

(1926) 497, note 3; Lord Parker in Banbury v. Bank of Montreal [1918] A.C. 626, 709-710.

14 Mass. Laws 1851, c. 233. §§ 2, 20, 27.

15 See Hepburn, Historical Development of Code Pleading (1897) 144, 146-149.

superseded the common-law declaration, an "answer" the common-law plea or pleas, while in Pennsylvania a "statement of claim" and an "affidavit of defense" became the respective instruments of allegation. Michigan retained the name "declaration," but for the statement thus designated, discloses the outright adoption of the principle of notice-pleading,[16] and provided for an answer as the vehicle of defensive allegation. In all three jurisdictions provision was made in varying terms for further pleadings, limited, however, in Pennsylvania to a "reply." New Jersey, Michigan and Pennsylvania abolished the demurrer *eo nomine,* and provided that the corresponding objection to the statement of the plaintiff's demand might be taken by a motion to strike out (New Jersey) or to dismiss (Michigan) or by a preliminary affidavit of defense (Pennsylvania), or might be included in the general defensive pleading. They likewise abolished pleas to the jurisdiction or in abatement, referring the relative objection to an appropriate motion (New Jersey), to the affidavit of defense (Pennsylvania), or to either an appropriate motion or to the answer (Michigan). Vermont, on the other hand, retained the demurrer; here dilatory defenses in point of fact apparently were to be included in the answer.[17]

In Vermont and Michigan the measures thus instituted basically hold place today. But the case has been otherwise in New Jersey and Pennsylvania. In New Jersey the régime of this legislation was a transient one, succeeded, as it has been, by the plenary reform of 1948, largely modelled upon the unified procedure of the Federal Rules. In Pennsylvania the system, as it emerged from the legislation of 1915, has been much changed by the Rules of Civil Procedure, adopted under the act of 1937. The general character of allegation remains the same, but the terms "statement of claim" and "affidavit of defense" have been discarded in favor of the

16 See *infra,* § 4 of the present Chapter.

17 New Jersey: Former Rules of Supreme Court, Rule 30 *et seq.* in N.J. Stat. Ann. 1939, Appendix to first vol. of Tit. 2, p. 450 *et seq.;* Mich. Court Rules 1931, 1933, 1945, Rules 17, 19, 23-25, Searl, Mich. Court Rules Ann. (4th ed. 1933) and 1948 Cum. Supp., p. 26 *et seq.;* Pa. Stat. Ann. (Purdon, 1931) Tit. 12, §§ 383-386, 411, 471, all suspended by Pa. Rules Civ. Proc.

more common "complaint" and "answer." To some extent the canons of allegation have been influenced by those of the Federal Rules, but in most respects the Pennsylvania rules have followed their own way. Thus, defenses to the jurisdiction may be raised by petition, and, remarkably enough, the demurrer has been reinstated.[18] While primarily adopted for common-law causes, the rules reach over into equity, for it is provided that such of them as are here applicable "shall prevail over any existing equity rules which are inconsistent therewith." [19]

Nor in the present place should mention be omitted of the simplified pleading incident to the procedure by notice of motion, obtaining for common-law causes in Virginia. This has a long history, but became an important factor in the mid-century period of activity above mentioned, when (1849) it was made available in actions on contract for the recovery of money. Commencing, however, in 1912, its application was extended until, by legislation of 1919, it became authorized for common-law actions in general. This mode of proceeding dispenses with a declaration, allows the facts on which the plaintiff grounds his claim for relief to be stated in the motion in any adequate manner and permits the defendant to allege his defense either by appropriate plea or pleas or by an informal statement in writing. The advantages which it offers to a plaintiff are such that it has now become much the more usual method of prosecuting common-law actions.[20] The same method obtains in West Virginia, but the only general class of cases to which it is there applicable is that of the Virginia Code of 1849, namely, actions on contract for the recovery of money.[21]

On the equity side importance attaches in the present re-

[18] Pa. Rules Civ. Proc., Rule 1017, Pa. Stat. Ann. (Purdon, 1931), Appendix to Tit. 12 in 1949 Cum. Pocket Part.

[19] Pa. Equity Rule 92, 1940, 1941, in Appendix *cit.*, p. 179; Vt. Stat. 1947, § 1613.

[20] Va. Code Ann. 1942, § 6046; Va. Code Ann. 1950, § 8-717 *et seq.;* Millar, Three American Ventures in Summary Civil Procedure (1928) 38 YaleL.J. 193, 213 *et seq.;* Arnold, Simonton and Havighurst, Report etc. (1929) 36 W.Va.L.Q. 1, 67 *et seq.* See also Chisholm v. Gilmer, 299 U.S. 99, 57 S.Ct. 65 (1936).

[21] W.Va. Code Ann. 1949, § 5524.

gard to the Federal Equity Rules of 1912. These reduced the bill of complaint to a form resembling that of the code complaint and abolished both demurrers *eo nomine* and pleas. Any defense in point of law arising on the face of the bill was to be made by motion to dismiss or in the answer, and the answer similarly was to be the vehicle of any defense previously raisable by plea, provision being made for the advance disposition at the court's discretion of defenses of either sort.[22] Michigan in 1915 acceded to the same principle in relation to the presentation of these defenses, its abolition of the demurrer and dilatory pleas extending to equity as well as common-law causes. Florida, in its Chancery Act of 1931, exhibits a like yielding to the influence of the Federal Equity Rules.[23] Maryland's abolition of pleas in equity[24] would seem to have been due to that influence, while the Pennsylvania Equity Rules of 1924 disclose a close approximation to the federal change in disestablishing both the demurrer and the plea and transferring the function of the former to a "preliminary answer,"[25]—a step, however, now obsolete in view of the changes attendant upon the new Rules of Civil Procedure.

But most sweeping for the period under scrutiny have been the changes in the field of allegation introduced by the Illinois Civil Practice Act of 1933 which, as has been seen, effected in large measure the conjunct administration of law and equity. Down to this time, Illinois had been adhering, perhaps more faithfully than any other American jurisdiction, to the canons of common-law pleading as they existed before the Hilary Rules. And, except for the mutations of discovery incident to change in the law of evidence,[26] it continued in substantially full allegiance to the orthodox principles of equity pleading. But the enactment in question accomplished a complete revolution in these respects. In the unified system of allegation which it set on foot the technical

22 Rules 25, 29, 30.

23 Fla. Laws 1931, c. 14658, §§ 22, 33, 34; Fla. Stat. 1949, §§ 63.22, 63.33, 63.34.

24 Md. Ann. Code (Bagby, 1924), Art. 16, § 173; Md. Ann. Code (Flack, 1939) Art. 16, § 179.

25 Pa. Rules of Equity Practice 1924, Rules 15, 48.

26 See *infra*, Chapter XIV, § 1.

forms of common-law and equity pleading are wholly disestablished. There is a "complaint" on the part of the plaintiff, an "answer" on the part of the defendant, and a "reply" in case of affirmative allegations in the answer. Allegation in the alternative is permitted as is also alternative demand for relief. Here, too, the demurrer *eo nomine* is abolished; in lieu thereof the objection may be made by motion to dismiss or to strike out, or, at least as regards complaint and counterclaim, in the answering pleading. Certain dilatory defenses, even where not apparent on the face of the complaint, may be the subject of motion to dismiss, but any factual defense of the kind may be advanced by preliminary answer or included in the answer in chief.[27]

§ 3. The Federal Rules of 1938

A unified system of pleading was necessarily an integral feature of the reform instituted by the Federal Rules of Civil Procedure of 1938. Accordingly, for all civil actions, these provide for a "complaint" and an "answer," with a "reply" allowable only as against a counterclaim or when ordered by the court. There may also be an "answer" to a cross-claim. The only other pleadings permitted are the "third-party complaint" and the "third-party answer." [28] (Rule 7). The complaint or other pleading setting forth a claim for relief, it is declared, "shall contain (1) a short and plain statement of the grounds upon which the court's jurisdiction depends, unless the court already has jurisdiction and the claim needs no new grounds of jurisdiction to support it, (2) a short and plain statement of the claim showing that the pleader is entitled to relief, and (3) a demand for judgment for the relief to which he deems himself entitled. Relief in the alternative or of several different types may be demanded." (Rule 8(a)). Defenses are likewise to be stated "in short and plain terms." (Rule 8(b)). And these injunctions are reinforced by the further provision that "each averment of a pleading shall be simple, concise, and direct." (Rule 8(e)). The an-

[27] §§ 32 *et seq.*, 43, 45, 48, 50(4); Ill. Rev. Stat. 1949, c. 110, §§ 156 *et seq.*, 167, 169, 172, 174(4).

[28] See *supra*, Chapter XII, § 3.

swer is governed by the usual rule of admission by failure to deny; but its own averments are to be taken as denied or avoided where no reply is in order. (Rule 8(d)). Equiparated to denial, substantially as under the codes, is the statement of lack of knowledge or information sufficient to form a belief. A general denial is in order but only when the pleader intends in good faith to controvert all the allegations of the opposing pleading. (Rule 8(b)). Defenses in avoidance must in all cases be affirmatively pleaded. In case of mistake of designation as between defense and counterclaim, the court "on terms, if justice so requires, shall treat the pleading as if there had been a proper designation." (Rule 8(c)). In respect both of attack and defense, provision is made for alternative or even hypothetical allegations: "a party may set forth two or more statements of a claim alternately or hypothetically, either in one count or defense or in separate counts or defenses." And he may "also state as many separate claims or defenses as he has regardless of consistency." (Rule 8(e)). The wisdom of this last is especially apparent when we recall the vexatious chapter on the subject of consistency of defenses in the chronicles of the American codes.[29] There are certain regulations concerning the character of allegations in special instances, which include the requirement that in averments of fraud or mistake the constitutive circumstances shall be stated with particularity, as also, in keeping with reform elsewhere, the allowance of generality of allegation in pleading official

[29] These, for the most part, have been interpreted as excluding inconsistent defenses. No chapter in the history of the American codes is more conspicuous for jejune dialectic than that relating to the present matter. Enforcement of the requirement of consistency has come to involve distinguishing between kinds of inconsistency. (See Clark, Handbook of the Law of Code Pleading (2d ed. 1947) 629-632). The inquiry in each case, as it arises, is whether the facts stated in the defenses are "so inconsistent that the facts stated in one must necessarily be false if the facts stated in the other are accepted as true (Hart-Parr Co. v. Keeth, 62 Wash. 464, 114 Pac. 169 (1911))—whether they are "so inconsistent as to be incompatible" (Advance-Rumely Thresher Co. v. Terpening, 58 Mont. 507, 193 Pac. 752 (1920)). And this inquiry naturally will necessitate an examination of the allegations in question to see whether they contain any element of legal conclusion, for the presence of this may avert the imputation of objectionable inconsistency (see Hart-Parr Co. v. Keeth, *supra*). For a highly cogent argument in opposition to the usual code interpretation, see McAlpine v. Fidelity & Casualty Co. of New York, 134 Minn. 192, 158 N.W. 967 (1916).

documents or acts, judgments, and the performance of conditions precedent. (Rule 9(b) (c) (d) (e)). And with particular bearing upon the defense of the statute of limitations, it is provided that "for the purpose of testing the sufficiency of a pleading," averments of time, as well as those of place, shall be considered material. (Rule 9(f)).

"Demurrers, pleas, and exceptions for insufficiency of a pleading shall not be used." (Rule 7(c)). The first preliminary draft of the Rules, while recognizing a preliminary motion for the purpose of presenting objections to service, venue and jurisdiction, required "every other objection in point of law or fact, whether in abatement or bar," to be made in the answer—subject to appropriate provision in reference to motion for judgment after the close of the pleadings, motion for summary judgment, and motion to particularize a pleading or to strike out impertinent or scandalous matter.[80] It thus gave no place to any direct substitute for a demurrer as a preliminary instrumentality of defensive objection in point of law, calling in question the sufficiency of the statement of claim. But this failed to meet with the favor of the profession, habituated as it had been to the use of just such an instrumentality. Accordingly, in the draft of April, 1937, and in the Rules as adopted the proposal in question was rejected. Instead, it was provided that all defenses were to be made in the responsive pleading, "except that the following defenses may at the option of the pleader be made by motion: (1) lack of jurisdiction over the subject matter, (2) lack of jurisdiction over the person, (3) improper venue, (4) insufficiency of process, (5) insufficiency of service of process, (6) failure to state a claim upon which relief can be granted," which motion is to be made in advance of pleading. To these the amendments of 1946 added a further defense, viz., "(7) failure to join an indispensable party." In respect of the sixth defense there is thus yielded a preliminary objection in point of law, equivalent to the general demurrer of the older systems. Question having arisen as to whether the measure authorized

80 Preliminary Draft of Federal Rules of Civil Procedure, May, 1936, p. 29, Rule 16.

a "speaking demurrer," that is to say, support of the legal objection by extrinsic facts, the amendments of 1946 here interpose the provision that if "matters outside the pleading are presented to and not excluded by the court," the motion is to be treated as one for summary judgment and disposed of accordingly.[31] (Rule 12(b)).

Concerning the second, third, fourth and fifth of the defenses thus enumerated, the requirement emerges that all intended to be relied upon, if presented by motion, must be advanced at the same time by being included in the one motion, otherwise no advantage can be taken of any of them by motion. (Rule 12(g)(h)).[32] And highly significant for these defenses, whether presented by motion or by answer, is the declaration that "no defense or objection is waived by being joined with one or more other defenses or objections in a responsive pleading or motion." (Rule 12(b)). This completely does away with the subtleties attaching to the doctrine of special appearance, for, there being no waiver, there is now no conclusive submission to the jurisdiction over the person produced by the joining of objection thereto with defenses of other sorts.[33] The seven defenses of the provision in question, whether made in a pleading or by motion, are to be heard and determined before trial on the application of any party, unless the court otherwise orders. (Rule 12(d)).

Other motions in advance of responsive pleading, as originally provided, were the motion for "a more definite statement" or for a bill of particulars, and the motion to strike from a pleading "redundant, immaterial, impertinent or scandalous matter." The amendments of 1946, however, discarded the bill of particulars altogether, restricted the mo-

[31] See the Advisory Committee's note to the Amendment. Federal Rules of Civil Procedure (West Publishing Co. 1947) p. 29 *et seq.*

[32] See 1 Moore's Federal Practice (1938) 648, 660-662; 2 *id.* (2d ed. 1948) 2260.

[33] "A defendant need no longer appear specially to attack the court's jurisdiction over him. He is no longer required at the door of the federal court-house to intone that ancient abracadabra of the law, *de bene esse*, in order by its magic power to enable himself to remain outside even while he steps within." Orange Theatre Corporation v. Rayherstz Amusement Corporation (C.C.A. 3) 139 Fed.2d 871, 874 (1944). See also other cases cited in 2 Moore, *op. cit.* (2d ed. 1948) 2262-2263.

tion for a more definite statement to the case where the pleading "is so vague or ambiguous that a party cannot reasonably be required to frame a responsive pleading," and added to the target of the motion to strike the case of "any insufficient defense." (Rule 12(e)(f)). In this last mentioned use the motion thus becomes tantamount to the old demurrer to a defense.

After the pleadings are closed, it is in order for either party to move for judgment on the pleadings. On the same principle as now governs the case of a motion to dismiss for failure to state a claim, the adduction of extrinsic facts, as the provision is now amended, may operate to convert this motion into one for summary judgment. (Rule 12(c)). Defenses and objections not presented either by motion or in answer or reply are waived, except that failure to state a proper claim or a legal defense, or failure to join an indispensable party may be later urged, and necessarily that objection to the jurisdiction of the subject-matter always remains open. (Rule 12(h)).

The Rules contain liberal provision for amendment of the pleadings. A pleading may be amended as of course at any time before a responsive pleading is served, or in case no responsive pleading is in order, and the suit is not yet on the trial calendar, within twenty days after service of the pleading to be affected. In other cases, amendment may be made only by order of court or written consent of the adverse party. (Rule 15(a)). In the matter of amendment to harmonize the pleadings with the evidence, it is provided that "when issues not raised by the pleadings are tried by express or implied consent of the parties, they shall be treated in all respects as if they had been raised in the pleadings." In such case conformity may be brought about by amendment even after judgment, "but failure so to amend does not affect the result of the trial of these issues." (Rule 15(b)). A further important provision as to amendment is that "whenever the claim or defense asserted in the amended pleading arose out of the conduct, transaction, or occurrence set forth or attempted to be set forth in the original pleading, the amendment relates back to the date of the original pleading." (Rule 15(c)). The principal object here is to obviate the harsh and scholastic doctrine, which in case of an amendment after the statute of limitations had run on the claim, treated deviation from the original statement in almost any material particular as the averment either of a new cause of action or of a cause of action for the first time, and thus as bringing the claim with the bar of the statute. The doctrine in question, whose barbarity has been the means of defeating countless just claims throughout the American jurisdictions, especially in personal injury cases, is of peculiarly American origin and growth. It has no foundation in the common law which, on the contrary, proceeded on the benign principle that, where possible, amendment would be allowed to save the claim from the operation of the statute,[34] and assuredly has no recognition in modern England. Although the Supreme Court of the United States had already come to temper the severity of the doctrine,[35] it is nevertheless a happy circumstance that the influential Federal Rules, following the lead of certain State jurisdictions,[36] have sought definitely to lay the axe to this product of a misdirected legal astuteness.

It is noteworthy, also, that the Rules have very properly discounted the *ad captandum* provision of the codes with reference to the verification of the pleadings. They declare that "except when otherwise specifically provided by rule or statute, pleadings need not be verified or accompanied by affidavit." This, however, is attended with the provision,

[34] Bearcroft v. Hundred of Burnham, 3 Lev. 347, 83 E.R. 723 (1695); Maddock *q.t.* v. Hammet, 7 T.R. 55, 101 E.R. 851 (1796); Jones v. Corry, 6 Bingh. N.C. 247, 133 E.R. 97 (1840); Craufurd v. Cocks, 6 Exch. 287, 155 E.R. 551 (1851); Carne v. Malins, 6 Exch. 803, 155 E.R. 770 (1851); Cowburn v. Wearing, 9 Exch. 207, 156 E.R. 88 (1853). In Jones v. Corry, *supra,* Erskine, J., is reported as saying that "the courts have allowed amendments to prevent the statute of limitations from attaching, but I never heard of their refusing an amendment in order to give effect to that statute," and Maule, J., that "the right to amend should be indulgently viewed, where the statute of limitations is likely to apply."

[35] See Maty v. Grasselli Chemical Works, 303 U.S. 197, 58 S.Ct. 507 (1938).

[36] Ill. Civ. Practice Act 1933, § 46; Ill. Rev. Stat. 1949, c. 110, § 170; Ala. Code 1940, Tit. 7, § 239, dating from 1907 (Ala. Code 1907, § 5367). *Cf.* 2 Wash.Rev.Stat.Ann. (Remington, 1932) § 308-3(4) (S.C. Rule III) dating from 1931.

strengthened over the corresponding one of the former Equity Rules, that the signature of the attorney (required whenever the party is thus represented) "constitutes a certificate by him that he has read the pleading; that to the best of his knowledge, information, and belief there is good ground to support it; and that it is not interposed for delay." (Rule 11). It might have been expected that, in accordance with the English system and some State legislations, the Rules would have taken the further step, in the present connection, of imposing costs upon the offending party, in case of unfounded denials, by way of reimbursement [37] to the other for the expense of making proof of the allegations so denied, but, as regards the pleadings, no such provision appears.

With the slightest of adaptation to the local practice the Federal Rules on the subject of pleading have been adopted in Arizona (1939), Colorado (1941) and New Mexico (1942).[38] They have also been extensively borrowed from in Missouri (1943).[39] Significant indebtedness to their provisions is likewise exhibited by South Dakota (1939) and Texas (1940).[40] In some measure, too, they have contributed to the Pennsylvania Rules (1946).[41] And, with the amendments of 1946, to which Arizona and New Mexico added their accession in 1949,[41a] they have largely entered into the procedures of Delaware (1947), New Jersey (1948) and Utah (1949), in the case of Delaware being availed of separately for its still distinct law and chancery systems.[42] So, too, they have been much drawn upon by Florida (1949) for its recent common-law rules, yielding also certain aid to its contemporaneous equity rules.[42a]

[37] See *supra*, § 1 of the present Chapter.

[38] Ariz. Code Ann. 1939, § 21-401 *et seq.;* Colo. Rules Civ. Proc., Rule 7 *et seq.*, Colo. Stat. Ann. 1935, Replacement Vol. I, 1941; N.M. Stat. Ann. 1941, § 19-101(7) *et seq.*

[39] 3 Mo.Rev.Stat. 1942, Pocket Part 1950, § 847.32 *et seq.*

[40] S.D. Code 1939, § 33.0901 *et seq.;* Tex. Rules Civ. Proc. (Vernon, 1942) Rule 45 *et seq.*

[41] Pa. Rules Civ. Proc., Pa. Stat. Ann. (Purdon, 1931), Appendix to Tit. 12, Cum. Pocket Part 1949; see in particular Rules 1019, 1023, 1030, 1032.

[41a] See 1949 Cum. Supp. to Vol. II of each of the Arizona and New Mexico annotated codes before cited.

[42] Del. Rules of Superior Court, Rule 7 *et seq.*, Rules of Court of Chancery, Rule 7 *et seq.;* N.J. Rules Civ. Pract., Rule 3:7 *et seq.;* Utah Rules Civ. Proc., Rule 7 *et seq.*

[42a] Fla. Common Law Rules, Rule 8 *et seq.*, Equity Rules, Rule 33.

§ 4. Some General Observations

It is to be noted that so much of the reform measures under survey as is directed toward requiring the union of different kinds of defenses in the single answer, in lieu of their presentation *seriatim*, represents a manifestation of that principle of eventuality or concentration which has a history of many centuries on the European Continent.[43] While there is always room for debate as to the extent to which it should go, the validity of the principle as a means of telescoping what would otherwise be separate and successive stages of the proceeding, and thus expediting its final disposition, is now axiomatic in procedural polity. The manner in which this principle was accepted in the first draft of the Federal Rules recalls the statute of the Holy Roman Empire adopted in 1654, by which it was "prescribed that all defenses of whatsoever kind, whether dilatory or peremptory, save only those declinatory of the forum (or, as we would say, pleas to the jurisdiction) were to be pleaded together 'on pain of preclusion.'"[44] But the Rules as adopted and as they now stand are characterized by a less plenary acceptance of the principle. And particularly is this so in their recognition of the preliminary defense of "failure to state a claim upon which relief can be granted." In this regard their measure of allegiance to the principle stops short of that obtaining under the English Rules, because of the difference in the character of the preliminary attack. On the other hand, that measure has not been attained in various of even the later State reforms, and has been exceeded by none; the traditions of the demurrer practice have been too strong.

Retention of the preliminary objection in point of law is accompanied in most of the later American reforms by abolition of the demurrer. This step has had its origin in the influence of the English Rules. What has been largely overlooked, however, on our part is that in discarding the demurrer, the

[43] Millar, The Formative Principles of Civil Procedure (1923) 18 Ill.L. Rev. 1, 25 *et seq.*, and as reprinted in Engelmann-Millar, History of Continental Civil Procedure (1927) 28 *et seq.*

[44] *Ibid.* 29(31).

English Rules have not provided for a preliminary test of the legal sufficiency of the statement of claim in any true sense. They require in general that the point of law be taken in the answering pleading. To be sure, they also give place to a motion to strike out when the pleading is frivolous or vexatious, or when it discloses "no reasonable cause of action or answer" [45] but the latter condition is one, which as before indicated, exists only when the insufficiency is "plain and obvious," not "requiring argument and careful consideration." [46] The motion, therefore, is a very different thing from the old weapon. But the American measures in this respect, including the Federal Rules, have proceeded otherwise. Most of them permit the objection to be taken in the answering pleading; all, however, concur in extending the absolute right to raise beforehand all objections of the kind going to substance, by way usually of motion. Hence the motion is made an outright substitute for the demurrer. The English Rules, remarked Chitty, J., "could not have intended to abolish demurrers by the right hand and restore them by the left." [47] But this is precisely what has been done in America. It is no wonder that courts seeking to identify the instrumentality of objection are led to speak of a "motion to dismiss—or a motion to strike—in the nature of a demurrer." In these circumstances the so-called abolition of the demurrer means nothing but verbal achievement. Why it should have been supposed that expulsion of the name, accompanied by retention of the thing, would betoken progress is difficult to understand. The prevailing liberality of amendment has everywhere stripped the term "demurrer" of any sinister import that it may once have had. And since a notion to strike, to dismiss, for judgment, or the like may proceed on many grounds other than of the legal insufficiency of the opposing pleading, the dropping of the term is detrimental to exactness of procedural terminology and, in consequence, to clarity of procedural thought. Highly significant, we think, is the restoration of the demurrer *eo nomine* under the recent Pennsylvania rules.

[45] O. XXV, rr. 1, 4.

[46] Hubbuck v. Wilkinson [1899] 1 Q.B. 86, 91; Annual Practice 1949, I, p. 445.

[47] Republic of Peru v. Peruvian Guano Co., 36 C.D. 489, 495 (1886).

Liberal as the allowance of amendment has generally become, the traditional canon which demands agreement between allegation and proof has not altogether ceased in America to produce miscarriage of justice. The New York Code of 1848 initiated the provision, common to the code systems in general, that no variance was to be deemed material unless it had prejudicially misled the opposite party in point of the merits. But as part of the same provision it was declared that where the allegation of cause of action or defense was unproved "in its entire scope and meaning," the case was to be deemed not that of variance, but of "failure of proof." [48] Whether the deviation should be assigned to one category or the other was a question upon which there could scarcely be unanimity of judicial opinion: what one court might regard as variance only, another might easily view as going to affect the "scope and meaning" of the statement of claim or defense as an entirety. And the decisions, accordingly, reflect this uncertainty in the application of the provision. If the deviation is looked upon as a variance in this technical sense, then by the usual rule no advantage can be taken of it, unless there has been objection to the reception of the evidence. Regularly there should be amendment to conform the pleading to the proof, but formal amendment is frequently presumed or altogether dispensed with. On the other hand, if the deviation is regarded as a "failure of proof," then, for the most part, the absence of objection will not prevent reversal of a judgment based upon the discrepant evidence. And in these respects the practice followed in the common-law jurisdictions, although not using the term "failure of proof," is not essentially different from that obtaining under the code provision. But a very considerable inroad upon the "failure of proof" rule appears in the doctrine, obtaining in certain of the code states, that if the parties, without objection, proceed "to the trial of an issue not presented by the pleadings, it amounts to a consent to try such issue." [49] This

[48] Code of 1848, § 147.

[49] Hanson v. Kline, 136 Ia. 101, 113 N.W. 504 (1907); Erickson v. Fisher, 51 Minn. 300, 53 N.W. 638 (1892); Bennett v. Snyder, 147 Ark. 206, 227 S.W. 402 (1921). And see Ia. Rules

doctrine has found favor with the Federal Rules which, it will be recalled, provide that issues extraneous to the pleadings "tried by express or implied consent of the parties" shall be treated as though raised in the pleadings. (Rule 15(b)). A decided advance is thus marked, on the assumption that failure to object to the evidence suffices to constitute implied consent. The value of the provision also to some extent depends upon the construction of the term "issue" to include every matter of fact on which there must be a finding, even though the new evidence has not been contradicted, and is thus not the subject of an issue in the technical sense. Whether, on the whole, it goes far enough is a question which only much longer experience of its administration will definitely answer. There may prove to be occasion for regret that the Rules did not retain the wider provision appearing in the preliminary draft of 1936, which declared that "during a hearing or trial the pleadings shall be deemed amended to conform to all evidence that is received without objection." [50]

It has been commonly the case in the American jurisdictions that, in obedience to inherited rule, the pleadings are required to state all the essential factual elements of cause of action or defense. Exemplification of this is the code provision that the complaint shall contain "a statement of the facts constituting the cause of action." [51] Statement of these elements sometimes squares with the idea of notice to the opposite party; sometimes, however, it transcends that idea. The difference between the two things is readily apparent by reference to the classic common-law case of the biting dog. Here the elements of the cause of action are (1) the keeping of the animal by the defendant; (2) its propensity to bite mankind; (3) knowledge on the part of the defendant of the dog's vicious propensity; and (4) the injury to the plaintiff. To state a cause of action, therefore, would require a statement of each of the four elements. Yet, if the third element, that of *scienter*, is omitted, is not the defendant, nevertheless,

Civ. Proc., Rule 249, in Ia. Code 1946, Vol. II, p. 2171, probably based on the Federal provision.

[50] Preliminary Draft of Rules of Civil Procedure, May 1936, p. 39, Rule 22(b).

[51] N.Y. Code of 1848, § 120.

reasonably informed of the nature of the claim? That the strict application of the traditional principle may be attended with injustice is a commonplace of our procedural history. A basic question, therefore, from the standpoint of procedural polity, is whether the office of a pleading, in respect of its statement of fact, should be regarded as fulfilled when notice is adequately given, regardless of the coincidence of this with a statement of the essential elements of cause of action or defense. It is, of course, with reference to the statement of claim that this question assumes particular importance.

The question is one which has not been satisfactorily met by the recent reform measures. Thus the Illinois Civil Practice Act of 1933 provides that "no pleading shall be deemed bad in substance which shall contain such information as shall reasonably inform the opposite party of the nature of the claim or defense which he is called upon to meet," [52] but, at the same time, calls for a "plain and concise statement of the pleader's cause of action," [53] constantly speaks elsewhere in terms of "cause of action," [54] and in its section abrogating, *inter alia,* the distinction in pleading between law and equity, expressly declares that "this section shall not be deemed to affect in any way the substantial averments of fact necessary to state any cause of action either at law or in equity." [55] What is yielded, therefore, is not a solution, but a conflict of two inconsistent ideas, which still awaits solution at the hands of the State Supreme Court. So, in the recent Texas Rules, it is prescribed that a relief-claiming pleading shall contain "a short statement of the cause of action sufficient to give fair notice of the claim involved." [56] There, in a less accentuated form, is the same combination of two irreconcilable principles. For, if a cause of action is to be stated, this may require more than "fair notice of the claim," and, conversely, if "fair notice of the claim" is all that is necessary, the pleader, on occasion, is authorized to stop short of stating a cause of action. The dilemma is not aided by the collateral

[52] Ill. Civ. Pract. Act, § 42(2); Ill. Rev. Stat. 1949, c. 110, § 166(2).

[53] *Ibid.* § 33(1); c. 110, § 157(1).

[54] See *ibid.* §§ 24, 43, 44, 46, 48; c. 110, §§ 148, 167, 168, 170, 172.

[55] *Ibid.* § 31; c. 110, § 155.

[56] Tex. Rules Civ. Proc. 1940 (Vernon, 1942) Rule 47.

provision affirming that "an allegation" is not objectionable on the ground of its being evidentiary or by way of legal conclusion "when fair notice to the opponent is given by the allegations as a whole," [57] for this concerns the sufficiency of individual allegations and does not extend to the case where the allegation of an essential element is wholly omitted. Nor are we in much better case when we turn to the Federal Rules. The Rules, to be sure, speak in terms of "claims" rather than of "causes of action," but this of itself decides nothing. Concerning relief-claiming pleadings, the provision is that they shall contain "a short and plain statement of the claim showing that the pleader is entitled to relief." (Rule 8(a)). Does this dispense with stating all the essential elements? If the provision had stopped with requiring "a short and plain statement of the claim," there would be little doubt that the answer must have been in the affirmative. But the addition of the participial clause "showing that the pleader is entitled to relief" is disturbing. A very fair argument could be made to the effect that the pleading would not show entitlement to relief if it omitted an essential element of what we have been accustomed to speak of as the cause of action, even though not necessary to conveying adequate notice of the claim, because in the absence of that element there could be no recovery. At any rate it would not be altogether inaccurate to say that there are two schools of interpretation among the federal courts. On the one hand, we find it declared to be "axiomatic that a plaintiff must state facts sufficient to show a cause of action," [58] or, of the instant case, that the question presented is "whether the present complaint alleges facts sufficient to constitute a cause of action or merely conclusions of the pleader." [59] On the other hand, it is said that "the function of the complaint is to afford fair notice to the adversary of the nature and basis of the claim asserted and a general indication of the type of litigation involved," [60] that "a generalized summary of the case that affords fair notice is all

[57] *Ibid.* Rule 45.

[58] Pelelas v. Caterpillar Tractor Co. (S.D. Ill.) 30 Fed.Supp. 173, 177 (1939).

[59] Guth v. Texas Co. (C.C.A. 7) 145 Fed.2d 820, 821 (1944).

[60] Continental Collieries, Inc. v. Shober, Jr. (C.C.A. 3) 130 Fed.2d 631, 635.

that is required,"[61] or, again, that "it is necessary only to allege sufficient facts to apprise the opposing party of the nature of the claim which will be proved."[62] That facts must be stated, rather than legal conclusions unsupported by facts, seems to be for the most part accepted,[63] although conclusions either of fact or of law have been deemed sufficient if they meet the test of fair notice.[64] But whether the facts thus required need only be such facts as afford adequate notice of the claim,[65] or (omitting mention of "cause of action") must be "definite facts upon which a judgment might be based,"[66] is a matter on which unanimity is lacking.[67] The Rules, manifestly, have not provided the desired solution of the present question.

The solution, we think, is to be found in the frank and unqualified acceptance by statute or rule of court, as the case may be, of the principle that, so far as regards the statement of facts, no more should be asked of a pleading than that it give adequate notice of the claim or defense, whether the essential elements thus fall to be stated or not. This is what has been contended for by the exponents of notice-pleading;[68] this is of the essence of Pound's fifth postulate in his memorable ground plan of procedural reform.[69] It is the course definitely adopted by Michigan in 1915 with respect to the declaration in common-law causes,[70] in the light, perhaps, of a certain application of the same principle by rule of the Mu-

[61] Securities & Exchange Commission v. Timetrust, Inc. (N.D. Cal.) 28 Fed.Supp. 34, 41 (1939).

[62] Van Dyke v. Broadhurst (M.D. Pa.) 28 Fed.Supp. 737, 740 (1939).

[63] See Washburn v. Moorman Mfg. Co. (S.D. Cal.) 25 Fed.Supp. 546 (1938); Foley-Carter Insurance Co. v. Commonwealth Life Insurance Co. (C.C.A. 5) 128 Fed.2d 718 (1942).

[64] Mails v. Kansas City Public Service Co. (W.D. Mo.) 51 Fed.Supp. 562, 565 (1943).

[65] Hirshhorn v. Mine Safety Appliances Co. (W.D. Pa.) 54 Fed.Supp. 588, 591 (1944).

[66] Fleming v. Dierks Lumber & Coal Co. (W.D. Ark.) 39 Fed.Supp. 237, 240 (1941).

[67] For the cases in general, see 2 Moore's Federal Practice (2d ed. 1948) 1647 *et seq.*

[68] See Whittier, Notice Pleading (1918) 31 Harv.L.Rev. 501, and other articles cited by Clark, Code Pleading (2d ed. 1947) 56.

[69] Pound, Some Principles of Procedural Reform (1910) 4 Ill.L.Rev. 491, 497.

[70] Sunderland, The Michigan Judicature Act of 1915 (1916) 14 Mich.L. Rev. 551, 553; Isaacs, Logic. v. Common Sense in Pleading (1918) 16 Mich.L.Rev. 589. See also Mich. Court Rules Ann. (Searl, 1933) and 1948 Cum. Supp., Rule 19.

nicipal Court of Chicago in 1909.[71] Moreover, the principle in question is in substance that which governs in the Continental systems, where, except for the prayer, the written pleadings are informational only.[72] The English Rules, it is true, continue to prescribe that a pleading shall state, in summary form, "the material facts on which the party pleading relies for his claim or defence." [73] But if one looks at the forms of pleading annexed to the Rules, it is seen that this requirement has been translated in so lenient a fashion as to be in keeping with the idea of notice-pleading.[74] In any case, the different attitude of the English system, as it is actually practiced, in placing all emphasis on the evidence even to the disregard of the pleadings, makes the paper rule assume a very different complexion from what its counterparts have worn in our systems.

With the establishment of adequate notice as a test for the factual content of a pleading, the idea of notice should be carried a step farther. In the existing situation there frequently arises the question of the legal theory upon which the party is proceeding. Here, again, it is in relation to the complaint that the question becomes of particular importance. Under the old order the question has not been wholly unknown on the common-law side; more often it has arisen in chancery. Yet, after all, the traditional practice never gave wide occasion for its occurrence. The methodology of that practice, in itself, went far toward identifying the theory of the action. The distinction between common-law and equity causes of action manifested by the form of suit was an initial factor of identification; and the distinction between the common-law forms of action, with the use of multiple counts and established forms of allegation largely removed any doubt as to the theory or theories in the case of common-law causes. Different, however, has been the case in the channelless procedure of the new order. Here, manifestly, the statement of the facts

[71] See Whittier (1910) 4 Ill.L.Rev. 512-513.

[72] See Millar, Some Comparative Aspects of Civil Pleading under the Anglo-American and Continental Systems (1926) 12 A.B.A.J. 401, 402-403,

[73] O. XIX, r. 4.

[74] See O. XIX, r. 5, and Annual Practice 1949, Appendix C to Rules, particularly Secs. V, VI.

qua facts, or even in conjunction with the prayer for relief (though consideration of this in the present connection is usually discountenanced) will not always identify the theory upon which the plaintiff is seeking to proceed. And yet identification may become necessary for various reasons, as in determining whether the action is legal or equitable; in determining in respect of the statute of limitations, for example, whether the action is in contract or in tort; in determining, in respect of the measure of damages, which one of several principles, appurtenant at common law to different forms of action is to find application. In such cases the courts, groping for means of identification, are disposed to attach importance to the *manner* in which the facts are stated, with reference to its greater or less approximation to the modes of allegation of the old system. From this has arisen the so-called "theory of the case" doctrine [74a] which in its strictest form of application confines the plaintiff, for all purposes, to that which has been discovered to be the theory of his complaint. Latent in this is the idea that the defendant is entitled to notice of that theory, even though that notice is to be gathered only from inference. Where such strictness of application obtains or where the decisions leave the matter in doubt, it has thus been the common practice for a plaintiff to use a plurality of counts setting forth the facts in such variant modes as are adapted to the possible different theories of recovery. This practice obviously is at war with the intent of the codes and represents in effect a continued employment of one of the fictitious devices of the common-law system, but has been tolerated as a measure of valuable prophylaxis. Referring to this practice, as obtaining in New York, the Committee on Law Reform of the Association of the Bar of the City of New York in 1931 advanced the following proposal:

> A party shall no longer be permitted to plead several causes of action or counterclaims arising out of a single transaction or connected set of facts, but shall be required to make a single statement of the transaction or facts, followed by a statement of the various

[74a] See Clark, Code Pleading (2d ed. 1947) 259 *et seq.*

> legal theories upon which he claims to be entitled to recover under those facts. He may demand one or more kinds of relief warranted by the facts and legal theories pleaded, whether legal or equitable or both. He shall not be required to elect as between the various theories, but a verdict shall be rendered upon each separate claim, unless the court shall dismiss the action or direct a verdict as to such claim. If there are different measures of damage for the various legal theories pleaded, he shall be entitled to recover the highest measure of damages on any of the theories proven.[75]

The proposal was urged, according to the Chairman of the Committee, because "it was thought expedient to eliminate the practice of pleading the same transaction in two or more different forms, depending on different legal theories. . . . We could see no reason why . . . a plaintiff should not set forth the facts once and for all, and then state as many legal theories as he thought the facts would enable him to support. This would get the complaint down to a realistic basis." [76]

Whether the Committee had any knowledge of the Scottish system of pleading we do not know, but the fact is that this has long followed a method which precisely corresponds to the Committee's suggestion. In its institution of "pleas in law," we find the very formulation of legal theory thus desired. For each of the parties is required to append to his unitary statement of facts a "concise note of the legal propositions" upon which he rests his claim or defense.[76a] Thus the plaintiff's *condescendence* (in combination with the *conclusions* of the summons equivalent to the American complaint) and the defendant's pleading, the *answers to the condescendence*, each consists, first, of a statement of the facts in numbered paragraphs, and, secondly, of a *note of pleas in law*, also in numbered paragraphs, briefly identifying the legal basis of the party's case.[77] And reference to Continental pro-

[75] Tentative Proposals for Changes in Civil Procedure and Practice, formulated by the Committee on Law Reform of the Association of the Bar of the City of New York (June, 1931) 14.

[76] Dayton, A Program of Legal Reform in the United States (1931) 16 The Consensus, no. 3, p. 21.

[76a] Mackay, Manual of Practice in the Court of Session (1893) 194. See also Maclaren, Court of Session Practice (1916) 312-313.

[77] As to the Scottish system, see Mil-

cedure discloses analogous practices. In the French, Italian and Spanish systems,[78] to go no further, the parties are required to set forth their grounds of law as well as of fact. In none of them is the technique as well-ordered as in the Scottish system, but the principle is exactly the same. Nor is it without relevance that the English Rules have recently taken a limited step in the like direction by providing in patent actions "for the delivery of statements . . . setting out all the contentions whether of fact or law . . . upon which the parties respectively intend to rely." While these statements do not take the place of the pleadings, they would appear to stand in much the same relation to the pleadings as does a bill of particulars in our own systems. At any rate, the recognition of the principle of notice of the legal theory is here unmistakable.[79]

But, it may be urged, the need of that notice is present only in systems where there is danger of defeat by application of the theory of the case doctrine, and that if this doctrine be wholly repudiated the question solves itself. In a considerable number of the State jurisdictions, to be sure, it is usually considered that the plaintiff is entitled to recover on any theory to which the facts alleged, as supported by proof, are found to give rise.[80] This is the case in England, and in the extremer form of concurrently overlooking an associated variance between pleading and proof. Referring to the old rule which permitted a passenger injured by negligence of a carrier to sue either in contract or in tort, Lord Esher, M.R., said in 1895: "At the present time a plaintiff may frame his claim in either way, but he is not bound by the pleadings, and if he puts his claim on one ground and proves it on another he is

lar, Civil Pleading in Scotland (1932) 30 Mich.L.Rev. 545, 709, at 562 *et seq.*, 577 *et seq.*, 740-742. The reforms of the Scottish procedure instituted in 1934 have in nowise affected this mode of proceeding. *Cf.* Thomson and Middleton, Manual of Court of Session Procedure (1937) 76-78.

[78] France: 2 Glasson and Tissier, *Traité théorique et pratique d'organisation judiciaire, de compétence et de procédure civile* (3d ed. 1926) no. 487, p. 460; Italy: *Codice di procedura civile,* 1940, Art. 163; Spain: *Ley de enjuiciamiento civil,* 1881, Art. 524, 548.

[79] O. LIIIA, r. 21A(2) (amendment of 1936). See Millar, A Septennium of English Civil Procedure, 1932-1939 (1940) 25 WashingtonU.L.Q. 525, 532.

[80] See Clark, *op. cit.* 261-363.

not now embarrassed by any rule as to departure." [81] And again, we are told, in 1918, by Lord Parker in the House of Lords, although by way of disparagement of the system, that this "permits a plaintiff to set up at the trial, without amending his pleadings, a case other than that put forward in the statement of claim. . . . There are pleadings, it is true, but the pleadings are, for all practical purposes, disregarded. . . . The judge has no longer to deal with a case formulated on the pleadings, but to make up his mind whether on the facts proved there is any and what case at all." [82] The Federal Rules have not attempted any express regulation of the point, but apparently, without any such cavalier treatment of the pleadings, aim at the like result of entitling the plaintiff to any relief warranted by the facts proved, regardless of the theory on which the action was prosecuted. It has been said by an authoritative interpreter of the Rules, in his judicial capacity, that under their provisions, "after trial judgment must be given according to the right of the case, whether the correct legal theory has been presented or not." [83]

It is certain, however, that, if we envisage a well-balanced system, the need for notice of the legal theory is not thus obviated. The rule just referred to may be very well for the claimant, but is it entirely just to the opposite party? Plainly it puts him under a severe disadvantage. Concededly, it means that every statement of claim carries with it every possible theory which can find support in the facts alleged, or even of the facts to be proved. No one can doubt that preparation on the law may be quite as arduous a task as preparation on the facts; sometimes, indeed, more arduous. And yet, as the case stands, we are calling upon the defendant to prepare on the law for eventualities which he may never be required to meet. If he fails to be armed at all points, he may be unjustly overthrown by a wholly unexpected development in point of theory which he is not ready to answer. Nor is the possibility

[81] Kelly v. Metropolitan Ry. [1895] 1 Q.B. 944, 946 (C.A.).

[82] Banbury v. Bank of Montreal [1918] A.C. 626, 709-710.

[83] Clark, J., in Atwater v. North Am. Coal Corporation (C.C.A. 2) 111 Fed.2d 125, 126 (1940).

foreclosed of a judgment being affirmed on appeal on a theory which had never had any ventilation at all in the court below. But, quite apart from the hardship thus imposed upon the claimant's adversary, the rule in question does not touch the case where identification is required in advance of trial, as where it should become necessary to distinguish between a claim in contract and a claim in tort for the purpose of determining whether, under the State practice, there may be a preliminary attachment of property or the holding of a defendant to bail. Here the court is compelled to ascertain the theory as best it can by scrutiny of the complaint; if the pleading is negative in this regard, how can there be any proper ascertainment? Then, too, after judgment there may exist the right to body execution if the claim is in tort as distinguished from contract. Unless the governing statute requires some specific finding as a basis for this manner of execution, identification can only be collected from the plaintiff's allegations. For it would be out of the question to apply here the rule under discussion. To say that, if the facts proved were consistent with a claim either in contract or in tort, the judgment would be regarded, for the present purpose, as a tort judgment would be repelled as a shocking proposition.

Plainly, therefore, notice should be given of the legal basis of recovery. The means of accomplishing this desideratum have been indicated by the New York proposal. Accordingly, with a statement of facts measured as to its sufficiency by the criterion of reasonable notice, the plan would be to append to it, in one or more concisely worded propositions (numbered if more than one), a statement of the legal theory or theories upon which the pleader intends to rely. Thus notice of the facts and notice of the theory would be coördinate parts of the pleading. Amendment of the statement of theory would be on the same basis as amendment of the statement of facts. And as regards the situation at the trial this would be in nowise different from that which now exists under the practice which permits different theories to be presented by different counts of the complaint.

Undoubtedly such a plan involves a certain break with traditional method, but if we stop to consider that the new order has stripped away the old factors of identification without putting anything in their place, it is seen that what is here sought to be done is something that was very largely done by the old order in a different way. The measure would afford a satisfactory solution of a troublesome problem and would be easily administered. Fairness to the opposite party, economy of the court's time, and accuracy of result alike argue for its adoption.

CHAPTER XIV
DISCOVERY AND INSPECTION

§ 1. DISCOVERY OF FACTS

One of the few blemishes that Blackstone permitted himself to impute to the common-law system was its lack of any means of discovery.[1] Elicitation of evidence from the adversary could be had only in the Court of Chancery by the means which it had developed for the purpose under the influence of Romano-canonical principles, particularly as applied in the English ecclesiastical courts. For discovery of facts the system thus patterned after employed, beginning in the 1200s, so-called "positions," consisting of affirmative propositions, to be categorically answered by the adversary under oath. These in the classic Romano-canonical procedure were wholly distinct from the pleadings, but in the English ecclesiastical procedure the libel (or complaint) on the one hand, and the positions of the plaintiff, on the other, were united in such wise that the libel served both as a statement of claim and as the positions of the plaintiff. Nevertheless, in that procedure, as in every other variation of the classic system, the answers to the positions were separate from the answers to the libel as a statement of claim.[2] This feature it is important to notice because its principle, ignored in the chancery development, came to acceptance in the course of nineteenth century reform.

In the chancery system the place of the ecclesiastical libel was taken by the bill of complaint. Of its familiar nine parts, as the procedure assumed a settled form, the *stating part*

1 3 Blackstone, Commentaries, * 382.

2 For an account in some detail of the Romano-canonical system, see Millar, The Mechanism of Fact-Discovery: A Study in Comparative Civil Procedure (1937) 32 Ill.L.Rev. 261, 266-276. It is from the Anglo-American part of the same article, 32 Ill.L. Rev., 437-453, that § 1 of the present chapter, in so far as it deals with the situation prior to the Federal Rules of 1938, has been largely drawn.

contained a narrative of the facts upon which the plaintiff relied, the *charging part* contained the charges of evidence upon which primarily he sought to elicit the defendant's declaration, and the *interrogating part* (first appearing as a distinct element toward the close of the seventeenth century)[3] was composed of specific interrogatories addressed to the defendant. What most nearly corresponded to the Romano-canonical positions was the charging part, but the correspondence was not exact, for it was the duty of the defendant to answer every material element of the bill. Nevertheless it is clear that however the correspondence might define itself in the particular case, the allegations of the bill served in the quality of positions: here, as in the case of the ecclesiastical libel, the positions, to use the word of Baron Gilbert were "flung" into the written complaint.[4]

From the common law chancery had borrowed the demurrer and the plea. Accordingly, by the one, the defendant might contest the plaintiff's right to discovery in point of law, by the other in point of fact. In the absence of successful contest, the defendant was required to put in his answer, and in this to make the requisite disclosure, that is to say, the equivalent of the answers to the Romano-canonical positions. But the answer was also a vehicle of defense to the plaintiff's claim for substantive relief. Thus, unlike the case in the parent system, "in chancery these two things, so different in their nature, are indiscriminately blended in the answer."[5]

Again, there was no way in which the answer, agency as it thus was of defensive allegation, could embody positions addressed to the plaintiff, no way therefore in which the defendant through the answer could effect disclosure from the plaintiff. This was another marked deviation from the ecclesiastical prototype wherein the defendant, as well as the plaintiff, was free, as a routine measure, to address positions to his adversary, in support of any affirmative allegation. The sole method

[3] Langdell, Summary of Equity Pleading (2d ed. 1883) 63, note 1.

[4] Gilbert, *Forum Romanum* (ed. Tyler, 1874) 89.

[5] Langdell, *op. cit.* 65. See also the passage in Hare, A Treatise on the Discovery of Evidence by Bill and Answer in Equity (2d Am. ed. 1849) no. 223.

by which the defendant in chancery could obtain discovery from the plaintiff was the exhibition of a cross-bill—in effect the institution of a new proceeding. The reason for this lay in the conception that the disclosure-compelling power was an emanation of the royal authority: "a party can only be compelled to answer in chancery by a writ of subpoena under the great seal; and, as the only way provided by law of obtaining that writ is by filing a bill, defendants are compelled to seek discovery in that mode." [6]

Only in a few cases was the plaintiff under the duty of making oath to the bill, but the defendant was normally required to put in his answer under oath. In relation to the effect of the sworn answer there found application a fragment of the Romano-canonical legal proof theory [6a] employed in a peculiar manner. While in general proceeding by the common-law rules of evidence and thus by the principle of free evaluation of the proof, yet the Court of Chancery took occasion to depart from that principle with respect to the statements of the answer. Accordingly, it was the established rule that a denial in the answer, sworn to positively and not merely on belief, could be overcome only by the testimony of two witnesses or an equal quantum of proof represented by the testimony of one witness and corroborating circumstances.[7] Whatever else the chancery system was to transmit to the reformed procedure of discovery this baleful rule was everywhere to disappear with the abandonment of that system.

Insufficiency of the answer in point of disclosure was challenged by means of exceptions. Although in the Romano-canonical system failure or refusal to answer a given position meant that this position was affirmed, without reference to any other independent position, this principle of *pro tanto* confession was never accepted by the chancery. For enforcement of the duty to answer and to put in a sufficient answer it em-

[6] Langdell, *op. cit.* 200.

[6a] Which had as its core the rule that testimony of two unimpeachable witnesses was necessary to the proof of a given fact. See Millar, The Formative Principles of Civil Procedure (1923) 18 Ill.L.Rev. 1, 96, and as reprinted in Engelmann-Millar, History of Continental Civil Procedure (1927) 42.

[7] 2 Daniell, A Treatise on the Practice of the High Court of Chancery (1840) 404-406.

ployed the contempt power against the defendant's person, and if this exercise of the power proved ineffectual then the bill in its entirety might be taken as confessed against him.[8] This was "the crude and drastic substitute of the chancery for the discriminating method of the Romano-canonical system . . . by which the positions were taken as confessed only to the extent that the opposite party had failed to make answer." [9]

The Court of Chancery thus granted discovery as an aid to the prosecution, or (by way of cross-bill) to the defense, of a claim for substantive relief falling within its peculiar jurisdiction. But it granted discovery also as an aid to the conduct of proceedings pending elsewhere, recognizing for the purpose bills whose sole object was the obtaining of discovery. Hence either party to an action in a common-law court might exhibit a bill in the Court of Chancery for the purpose of discovering material evidence to be used in the trial of that common-law action. As in other cases the disclosure was made by the defendant's answer. But as there was here no claim for substantive relief to defend against, the answer did not present that double character noted above. And in view of the purpose in hand, the putting in of a sufficient answer terminated the proceeding.[10]

That the methods thus appearing were complicated, difficult and expensive is now a commonplace of our procedural history. Such as they were, however, they represent the system which, with some minor adaptations, found lodgement in America and which continued to rule in both countries awaiting the impact of nineteenth century reform.

It was America, rather than England, that initiated this course of reform. The first step was the extension to the common-law courts of the power to compel discovery. A limited exercise of this power applicable to minor causes appears in South Carolina as early at least as 1800.[11] So in 1809 Ken-

[8] 1 Daniell, *op. cit.* (1937) 684-685.

[9] Millar, *Ficta Confessio* as a Principle of Allegation in Anglo-American Civil Procedure (1928) 23 Ill.L.Rev. 215, 231.

[10] Langdell, *op. cit.* 204; 1 Maddock, A Treatise on the Principles and Practice of the High Court of Chancery (4th Am. ed. 1832) *218.

[11] See Millar, Three American Ventures in Summary Civil Procedure (1928) 38 Yale L.J. 199-200.

tucky conferred such a power upon justices of the peace for certain of the petty causes falling within their jurisdiction.[12] But perhaps the first emergence of discovery as a feature of the ordinary common-law procedure dates from Mississippi legislation of 1828.[13] As a means of invoking the granted power this adopted the expedient of an equitable petition for discovery filed as a step in the common-law cause itself. The petition was to be upon oath, an order directing the discovery was to follow, and the discovery was to be made in writing. Refusal or neglect to make the discovery entailed confession of the facts in relation to which discovery was prayed. A statute similar in terms, but expressly providing for the incorporation of interrogatories in the petition, was enacted by Missouri in 1835 [14] and by Arkansas in 1837.[15] In 1836 Connecticut [16] vested like power in the common-law courts, but provided for initiation of the interstitial proceeding by motion filed under leave of court. The motion was to set forth the facts upon which discovery was sought, and, upon oath or affirmation of the moving party as to his belief in their truth, the opposite party was to plead, answer or demur to the motion as to a bill in chancery. Other jurisdictions proceeded directly to the unincumbered use of interrogatories in the common-law action. The Virginia statute of 1831 [17] was of this type. It provided for the filing by either party of interrogatories addressed to the other, and for an order to answer the interrogatories when it had been made to appear "by oath of the party filing the same or otherwise," that they were material, pertinent, and such as the interrogated party would be bound to answer on a bill in chancery. For failure to answer or evasive answering the interrogated party was rendered liable, as the court might direct, to attachment and enforced answer in open court and, if he was defendant, to judgment by default, or, if plaintiff, to

[12] Act of 1 February, 1809: 4 Littell, Statute Law of Kentucky (1814) p. 35.

[13] Act of 16 February, 1828: Hutchinson, Mississippi Code (1848) pp. 865-866.

[14] Act of 17 March, 1835, §§ 10-14: Rev. Stat. of Missouri (1835) pp. 462-463.

[15] Act of 18 December, 1837, §§ 93-97: Rev. Stat. of Arkansas (1937) c. 116, p. 632.

[16] Act of 2 June, 1836: Pub. Stat. Laws of Connecticut (1836-37) c. 3.

[17] Act of 16 April, 1831, c. 11, § 68: Virginia Laws 1830-31, p. 65.

dismissal of his action. This act was copied by Alabama in 1837[18] and, with insignificant change, by Georgia in 1847.[19] Another departure of the same kind was that contained in the Massachusetts Practice Act of 1851.[20] Under its terms the interrogatories whose filing was open to either party, were to be supported by an affidavit stating that the interrogating party had reason to believe that he would derive some material benefit in the action from the discovery sought and showing that he was not thus proceeding for the purpose of delay; and the respondent normally was to answer in ten days. Failing proper answer and compliance with an order directing that such answer be made, the party at fault might be penalized by nonsuit or default judgment, according as he was plaintiff or defendant.[21]

But much more important and far-reaching was the measure adopted by the New York Code of 1848 in connection with its establishment of a single form of procedure. A statute of the previous year had authorized the parties in all civil proceedings, that is to say, in both the then separate common-law and equitable jurisdictions to examine each other as witnesses at the trial.[22] Maintaining this principle, the Code expanded it into the rule that such an examination might be had either before or at the trial. If before trial it might take place by way of deposition upon commission, or be had before a judge of the court or a judge of the county court. Oral examination before trial was thus made to replace in its entirety the hitherto prevailing chancery method of fact-discovery by bill and answer. A party refusing to testify was to be subject, like any other witness, to the contempt process and in addition "his complaint, answer, or reply may be rejected," a contuma-

[18] Act of 23 December, 1837: Aiken, Digest Supp. (1841) pp. 111-112.

[19] Act of 17 December, 1847: Georgia Laws, pp. 197-198; 1 Cobb, Digest (1851) p. 465.

[20] Act of 22 May, 1851: Massachusetts Laws 1851, c. 233, §§ 98-111, pp. 718-720.

[21] A matter apart is the early use of interrogatories in Louisiana and Texas. In the former case we meet *eo nomine,* though in modified form, the French interrogatory on facts and articles (Code of Practice 1825, § 347 *et seq.*); in the latter, the initial influence of the Spanish procedure (see Act of 18 December, 1837, § 7: 2 Laws of the Republic of Texas (1838) p. 95).

[22] New York Laws 1847, c. 462, pp. 630-631; First Report of Commissioners on Practice and Pleadings N.Y. (1848) pp. 244-245.

cious plaintiff being thus exposed to dismissal of his action and a contumacious defendant to judgment against him by default.[23] When we consider that at this period the party was still disqualified as a witness under the general rules of evidence, the significance of the steps thus taken cannot be too highly appreciated.

It was this very matter of the party's disqualification that had lent to the chancery procedure of discovery its commanding importance. And in the removal of this disqualification lay a capital means of easing the road to fact-discovery. If now, we return to England, we note a beginning in this direction in 1843, when by Lord Denman's Act [24] it was provided that any defendant in a chancery proceeding might be examined as a witness on behalf of any plaintiff or co-defendant. Following the County Courts Act of 1846 [25] which had made the parties competent witnesses for and against each other in these inferior tribunals, came in 1851 [26] the great change in the English law of evidence, when by the Evidence Act of that year the same principle was extended to all courts of justice. America was not slow to conform. The first statute introductive of the new principle appears to have been a Connecticut act of 1849 [27] perhaps inspired by the English County Courts Act. After the English act of 1851, however, the movement for the change became widespread and not many years had passed before the innovation had become the rule in all the American jurisdictions.[28] Thus the specific instrumentalities of discovery on both sides of the Atlantic became everywhere supplemented by the right of either party to examine his opponent at the trial or hearing. With it there lessened the need for interlocutory means of discovery—a fact which in those American jurisdictions which had retained the chancery system, with the peril for the plaintiff attaching to the sworn answer, led to

[23] Code of Procedure 1848, § 343 *et seq.* As to the Code's supersession of the chancery method, see Glenny v. Stedwell, 64 N.Y. 120 (1876).

[24] 6 & 7 Vict. c. 85, § 1.

[25] 9 & 10 Vict. c. 95, § 83.

[26] 14 & 15 Vict. c. 99, § 2.

[27] Act of 27 June, 1848: Public Acts of Connecticut 1848, c. 80, p. 71, adopting revision of statutes; Rev. Stat. of Connecticut (1849) tit. I, c. 1, §§ 141, 142, p. 86; 2 Wigmore, Evidence (3d ed. 1940) § 577, note 4.

[28] See 2 Wigmore, *op. cit.* §§ 576, 577.

this system largely falling into disuse. Nevertheless, the need remained present in a still important measure, especially for causes of a common-law nature, in view of the fact that the change *per se* did not enable the party to examine his adversary in advance of the trial. Accordingly, the matter of interlocutory discovery was still one that strongly engaged attention in the process of reform.

In England that process moved at a distinctly slower pace than it had in America. By the Chancery Practice Amendment Act of 1852,[29] however, the old chancery methods were made the subject of a definite recasting. It was here provided that the bill, instead of following the traditional pattern, should contain "as concisely as may be a narrative of the facts, matters and circumstances on which the plaintiff relies, set forth in numbered paragraphs, with a prayer for relief, but should not contain any interrogatories for the examination of the defendant." The plaintiff, if he sought disclosure from the defendant, was to present written interrogatories for examination of the latter. The defendant was entitled to raise the question of his duty to answer by demurrer or plea. And the answer, it was declared, "may contain, not only the answer of the defendant to the interrogatories . . . , but such statements material to the case as the defendant may think it necessary or advisable to set forth therein." If no disclosure was required by the plaintiff, the defendant was free to set forth his defense by demurrer, plea or answer as the case might be.[30] It is apparent that, although the interrogatories are here separated from the bill, the answer is still the appointed medium both of discovery and of defensive allegation and "discovery and defence are still as inseparable as ever." [31] But a notable improvement was effected by the act in its removal of the necessity of proceeding by way of cross-bill when the defendant sought discovery from the plaintiff. While he retained the right so to proceed if he chose, he was now enabled, instead (but only after a sufficient answer where answer had been required by the plaintiff), to present "written interrogatories

[29] 15 & 16 Vict. c. 86.

[30] §§ 10, 12, 13, 14.

[31] Langdell, Discovery under the Judicature Act 1873, 1875 (1898) 12 Harv.L.Rev. 167.

for the examination of the plaintiff, to which shall be prefixed a concise statement of the subjects on which a discovery is sought." These the plaintiff was required to answer in the same manner as if they had been contained in a bill for discovery.[32] Failure to answer under the new practice was governed by no other or different principle from that which had previously obtained. In case a defendant at fault withstood the contempt process, the bill might be taken as confessed against him, although in view of the greater facility for proving his case now accorded the plaintiff by the changed rules of evidence, it appears that this measure was seldom invoked.[33]

English reform then took the further step, already a familiar one in America, of conferring the power to compel discovery upon the common-law courts. This occurred by the Common Law Procedure Act of 1854.[34] By this legislation (which exhibits unmistakably the influence of the Massachusetts act of 1851), it was provided that in all causes in the three superior courts of common-law, either party, by judicial leave, might deliver to the other "interrogatories in writing upon any matter as to which discovery may be sought," to be answered by affidavit in writing within ten days. Application for the order was normally to be made upon affidavit stating the moving party's belief that he would derive material benefit from the discovery, that he had a good cause of action or defense and, if defendant, that the discovery was not sought for delay. For enforcement of the duty to answer resort was had to the contempt power: the party omitting, without just cause, to answer was to be deemed guilty of a contempt of court. But it was also provided that in case of such omission, the court or judge might "direct an oral examination of the interrogated party, as to such points as they or he may direct." And submission to this examination might be similarly enforced.[35]

On the basis thus appearing the interlocutory fact-discovery mechanism of the English courts stood until the Judicature Acts. In the now fused procedure there was no occasion for

[32] 15 & 16 Vict. c. 86, § 19.

[33] 1 Daniell, Pleading and Practice of the High Court of Chancery (3d Am. from 3d Eng. ed. 1865) 499-500.

[34] 17 & 18 Vict. c. 125.

[35] § 51 *et seq.*

other than uniformity of method in the present field. For principal instrumentality was taken as model in a general way that obtaining under the Common-Law Procedure Act of 1854. By the Rules of 1875,[86] it was provided that either side might "deliver interrogatories in writing for the examination of the opposite party or parties . . . with a note at the foot thereof, stating which of such interrogatories each of such persons is required to answer." For the delivery leave of court was required if it came after the close of the pleadings, otherwise not. The interrogatories might be challenged for scandal, irrelevancy, immateriality, lack of good faith or on any other ground, by motion to strike out. Answer was required to be made by affidavit, and in this objections to answering might be taken.[87] The sufficiency of any answer was to be determined on motion or summons. In case of failure to answer or insufficiency of the answer, the court or a judge was authorized to enter an order requiring the interrogated party to answer or to answer further, either in writing or by *viva voce* examination as might be directed. Failure to comply with such an order was to subject the offender to attachment of his person; moreover, if a plaintiff, his action might be dismissed for want of prosecution, or if a defendant, he might be treated as without defense.[88] These provisions passed into the revised Rules of 1883 with but slight change. By the revision leave to deliver was required in all cases, except in actions based upon fraud or breach of trust. It was provided that on application to deliver, the court in determining the necessity of a given interrogatory is to "take into account any offer, which may be made by the party sought to be interrogated to deliver particulars, or to make admissions, or to produce documents relating to any matter in question." And in lieu of the former motion to strike out interrogatories was substituted a motion to set aside on the ground of unreasonableness or vexatiousness, or to strike out for prolixity, oppressiveness, unnecessariness or scandal.[89] Since 1883 certain further modifications have

[86] 37 & 38 Vict. c. 77, First Schedule.

[87] See, however, Fisher v. Owen, 8 Ch.D. 645, 654, C.A. (1878).

[88] 37 & 38 Vict. c. 77, First Schedule, O. XXXI, rr. 1-10, 19, 20.

[89] R.S.C. 1883, O. XXXI, rr. 1-11, 20-26.

come about. In particular, leave of the court or of a judge has been made necessary in all cases and provision has been introduced requiring (unless judicially dispensed with) submission of a copy of the proposed interrogatories to the opposite party before hearing of the application for leave. All reference to the motion to set aside or to strike out has been discarded and any objections to the interrogatories are now to be taken in the answering affidavit.[40]

Meanwhile in America, the principle of oral examination before trial established by the New York Code of 1848 had constantly won ground with the march of the code system in general. Today, there are still a few States which offer nothing more than the old chancery method, albeit more or less modified in scope and form—a method seldom resorted to in practice for the reason already indicated; fewer still in which the chancery method having disappeared, no other interlocutory means have been substituted. In general, however, means variously regulated are provided in the form of written interrogatories either annexed to the pleadings or filed separately, oral examination pursuant to order of court or oral examination by way of deposition, it sometimes being the case that the moving party has a choice of means.[41] The oral examination, by the deposition method, is the means more commonly obtaining.[42] It has usually the highly important advantage of permitting the examination for discovery to extend not only to the adversary but also to third person witnesses. Formerly the value of this institution was not always properly appreciated in the jurisdictions possessing it, perhaps as has been suggested, because in this form its statutory authority was frequently present under the rubric of "depositions" rather than of "discovery." [43] But more recently there has been a quickened interest in the examination thus conducted. Exemplification of this appears in its admission to the Michigan practice in 1931,[44] as also in the fact that in Illinois,

[40] R.S.C., present O. XXXI, rr. 1, 2, 6.

[41] The various statutes as of 1932 are collected in Ragland, Discovery before Trial (1932) Appendix, 267-391; see also in the same work pp. 25-26.

[42] Ragland, *op. cit.* 23, 241 *et seq.*

[43] *Ibid.* 23.

[44] Mich. Court Rules 1931, 1933,

where it had long been applicable to chancery causes, it was in 1933 made part of the apparatus of discovery in the unified procedure established by the Practice Act of that year.[45] So, too, as presently to be noted, it has found place in the Federal Rules of 1938.

In the federal sphere, so long as there remained a distinct common-law side of the court, this was virtually without any means of interlocutory fact-discovery. For under the régime of the Conformity Act, its provisions were held not to render available the interlocutory discovery processes of the State courts, on the ground that the specific federal provisions on the subject of witness testimony impliedly excluded the use of such processes.[46] In equity the relative method until February 1, 1913, was the old chancery one of bill and answer, with certain modifications, but unchanged in principle. As elsewhere it was not in frequent use and for the same reason. But by the Federal Equity Rules of 1912, this time-honored method was discarded. Instead was adopted a method patterned directly upon that of the English Rules. As a result the bill of complaint no longer contained any charges of evidence or interrogatories; in essence it consisted of narrative and prayer.[47] The answer was similarly restricted, setting out only a statement of the defense, unless there was a counterclaim to be included.[48] But either party after filing his pleading was authorized as a separate matter to "file interrogatories in writing for the discovery by the opposite party of facts and documents material to the support or defense of the cause." The filing required no leave of court if occurring not later than twenty-one days from the joinder of issue. Answers to the interrogatories were to be made in writing and under oath. Opportunity was afforded the interrogated party to file written objections to the interrogatories, before being required to answer. The court was given power to enforce answers by appropriate or-

1945, Rule 41, Searl, Mich. Court Rules, Ann. (4th ed. 1933) 283, and 1948 Cum. Supp. 86; 3 Searl, Mich. Pleading and Practice (1934) § 1376, p. 375.

45 Ill. Rules Pract. & Proc. 1933, Rule 19; Ill. Rev. Stat. 1949, c. 110, § 259.19; *ibid.* c. 51, § 24.

46 *Ex parte* Fisk, 115 U.S. 713, 5 S.Ct. 724 (1885); Hanks Dental Association v. International Tooth Crown Co., 194 U.S. 303, 24 S.Ct. 700 (1904).

47 Rule 25.

48 Rule 30.

der, and failure to comply with such order subjected the party at fault to substantially the same consequences as under the English Rules, that is to say, attachment of his person, and, if a plaintiff, dismissal of his bill, if a defendant, deprivation of his right to defend.[49]

With the adoption, however, of the Federal Rules of 1938 came a re-regulation of fact-discovery, now made applicable to civil causes in general, definitely revealing a discriminating assay of the past development. The Rules provide for the taking by any party of the testimony of any person, party or nonparty "by deposition upon oral examination or written interrogatories for the purpose of discovery or for use as evidence in the action or for both purposes." The provision in its original form required leave of court prior to service of answer, but, under the amendments of 1946, leave is now required only where notice of the taking is served by the plaintiff within twenty days after commencement of the action. Either sort of deposition is to be taken upon the service of notice as prescribed, before some officer authorized by law to administer oaths (foreign depositions being otherwise specially regulated) or, since the amendments, "before a person appointed by the court in which the action is pending." The parties, however, may stipulate in writing to take the deposition before any person and upon any notice. The case of oral examination normally contemplates attendance of both parties, but it is provided that a party served with notice of such examination, instead of thus participating, "may transmit written interrogatories to the officer, who shall propound them to the witness and record the answers verbatim." Where written examination is proposed, a copy of the interrogatories is to accompany the service of notice, and provision is also made for the service of cross, re-direct and re-cross interrogatories. Choice of method is open to the moving party, but, either being proposed, the court upon motion and for good cause may require that the examination be conducted by the other method. This, however, is but one phase of the extensive control over the proceeding vested in the court, which includes the power, upon

[49] Rule 58.

a like showing, to prevent the taking of the deposition altogether, to terminate an examination once begun, to change the time and place of the examination, to limit its subject-matter or scope and, in a proper case, to take specified measures by way of ensuring the secrecy of the proceeding. When completed the deposition, in accordance with the usual practice, is to be filed in a sealed envelope with the clerk of the court, and it is further required that notice of the filing be given by the moving party to all the other parties in the cause. (Rules 26, 28, 29, 30, 31).

Concerning the scope of the proceedings for discovery, the rule followed in the chancery system restricted the party to inquiry into matters relating to his own side of the controversy, forbidding excursion into the evidence by which that case was proposed to be met. The interpretation of this rule and whether and to what extent it should be adhered to have been vexed questions in the later development, as a result of which have come much conflict of decision, and some enlarging legislation in the State jurisdictions.[50] Under the Equity Rules of 1912, there was a sharp division of view as to the limit of inquiry in the interrogatory practice, although more generally the chancery rule was that which was followed.[51] Now, for the federal courts, the matter has been settled—and to all appearances definitely—by the new Rules, which, as amended in 1946, sweepingly declare that, unless otherwise ordered by the court in its control of the examination, "the deponent may be examined regarding any matter, not privileged, which is relevant to the subject matter involved in the pending action, whether it relates to the claim or defense of the examining party or to the claim or defense of any other party, including the existence, description, nature, custody, condition, and location of any books, documents, or other tangible things and the identity and location of persons having knowledge of relevant facts. It is not ground for objection that the testimony will be inadmissible at the trial if the testimony sought appears

[50] See Ragland, *op. cit.* Chap. XV.

[51] Dobie, Handbook of Federal Jurisdiction & Procedure (1928) 725; Clephane, Handbook of Equity Pleading & Practice (1926) 80.

reasonably calculated to lead to the discovery of admissible evidence." (Rule 26(b)). It is obvious that this provision enables the moving party to inquire very widely into his opponent's case. It would appear also that, although not without some State precedent,[52] it breaks more completely with tradition by permitting him to ascertain the names of his opponent's witnesses; this, however, is not to be taken in any absolute sense if, under the particular circumstances, the judicial discretion should otherwise dictate.[53]

In addition, there is made available to any party as a separate means of fact-discovery the optional use of written interrogatories addressed to the opposite party, much as under the Equity Rules of 1912. The interchange of these interrogatories, however, occurs by service instead of filing as under the Equity Rules, and no leave of court is now required for initiation of the proceeding, except (under the amendments of 1946) where the service takes place within ten days after commencement of the action. These amendments *inter alia* also expressly give this examination by interrogatories the same scope as the examination by deposition. (Rule 33).

Refusal of a party or other witness to answer, on deposition, after being directed to do so by the court in whose district the deposition is being taken, "may be considered a contempt of that court." And, whichever of the three methods is under employment, in case of refusal on the part of "any party or an officer or managing agent of a party" to obey an order of court, as provided for, requiring him to answer designated questions, the court is at liberty "to make such orders in regard to the refusal as are just." In particular, it is empowered to make an order that the fact in question be taken as established for the purposes of the action in accordance with the moving party's claim, an order disentitling the offending party to support or oppose designated claims or defenses, or to introduce designated items in evidence, or an order striking out pleadings or parts thereof, staying proceedings pending obedience, dismissing the action in whole or in part or rendering

[52] See 6 Wigmore, *op. cit.* § 1856c note 1.

[53] See cases cited in 4 Moore's Federal Practice (2d ed. 1950) 1077 *et seq.*, 2268-2269.

judgment by default. In lieu of such orders or in addition thereto, it is also empowered to direct the arrest of the disobedient party or agent. (Rule 37 (a) (b)).

With its origin apparently in the Hilary Rules of 1834,[54] a measure which found acceptance in the New York Code of 1848 [55] and resultingly in a large number of the American States as well as in the Federal Equity Rules of 1912,[56] is that which enables a party to call upon his adversary to admit the genuineness of a material document. In England the measure was given place in the Common Law Procedure Act of 1852 [57] and in the Chancery Amendment (Lord Cairns') Act of 1858,[58] and, having been embodied in the English Rules of 1875,[59] underwent significant extension by the Rules of 1883. It was now made applicable further to the case of any specific evidentiary fact mentioned in the notice by which the request to admit was advanced, the admission in this case, however, to be only for the purposes of the particular controversy.[60] With some variations concerning the effect of the admission, the measure in this widened form was subsequently adopted in New Jersey (1912),[61] Massachusetts (1917),[62] New York (1920),[63] Wisconsin (1927),[64] Michigan (1931)[65] and Illinois (1933).[66] In its widened form, also, it has found place in the Federal Rules, which provide that admission may thus be requested "of the genuineness of any relevant documents described in and exhibited with the request or of the truth of any relevant matters of fact therein set forth." (Rule 36(a)).

[54] Reg. Gen. Hil. T., 4 Will. IV, reg. 20, 1 Chitty, Pleading (11th Am. ed. 1851) * 736; 9 Wigmore, *op. cit.* § 2596.

[55] Code of 1848, § 342.

[56] Rule 58.

[57] 15 & 16 Vict. c. 76, §§ 117-119.

[58] 21 & 22 Vict. c. 27, § 7.

[59] 37 & 38 Vict. c. 77, First Schedule. O. XXXII, rr. 2-4.

[60] R.S.C. 1883, O. XXXII, rr. 2-9.

[61] N.J. Pract. Act 1912, § 18, N.J. Stat. Ann. 1939, § 2:27-161, now superseded by Rules Civ. Pract. of 1948.

[62] Mass. Laws 1917, c. 194, and, as amended, 8 Mass.Ann.Laws 1933, 1949 Cum. Supp., c. 231, § 69.

[63] N.Y. Civ. Pract. Act 1920, § 323, now repealed and included in substance in the wider provisions of present § 322 (Clevenger, 1950).

[64] Wis. Laws 1927, c. 316, and, as amended by Supreme Court orders, Wis. Stat. 1949, § 327.22.

[65] Mich. Court Rules 1931, 1933, 1945, Rule 42, § 2 (§ 4 revision of 1945), Searl, Mich. Court Rules (4th ed. 1933) 284, and 1948 Cum. Supp. 89.

[66] Ill. Rules Pract. & Proc. 1933, Rule 18; Ill. Rev. Stat. 1949, c. 110, § 259.18.

By further provision the effect of the admission in either case is confined to the pending action. (Rule 36(b)).

Usually the penalty for unjustified failure or refusal to make the admission has been restricted to the imposition of the expense of proof thus unnecessarily occasioned. In Massachusetts and Wisconsin, however, an ignoring of the notice is attended by constructive admission of the fact in question,[67] and in England, by an amendment of 1937 to the Rules,[68] albeit confined to the case of documents, failure to give notice of non-admission within the prescribed period results in admission of the genuineness, unless it is otherwise ordered. The Federal Rules have followed their own path in this regard. Under their provisions the matter, of whichever sort, specified in the request is to be deemed admitted, unless within the prescribed time the party to whom the request is directed serves upon the moving party either (1) a sworn statement specifically denying the matter in question or setting forth in detail why he cannot truthfully admit or deny that matter, or (2) as added by the amendments of 1946, "written objections on the ground that some or all of the requested admissions are privileged or irrelevant or that the request is otherwise improper in whole or in part." If, after a sworn denial, the matter is proved by the moving party, then unless good reason existed for the denial, or the admission was unimportant, there follows the penalty of costs, that is to say, the moving party is entitled to an order requiring the other to pay the reasonable expense of proof, including attorney's fees. (Rule 37 (c)).

The federal regulation thus outlined of the field of fact-discovery, as also of the associated fields of discovery and inspection of documents and non-documentary inspection, to be considered in the further course of the present chapter, has been taken over with little variation by Arizona (1939, 1949), Colorado (1941), New Mexico (1942, 1949), Delaware (1947), New Jersey (1948) and Utah (1949), and has been largely availed of by South Dakota (1939) and Maryland (1941).[69] Parts of that regulation have been adopted in

[67] Ragland, *op. cit.* 195 *et seq.*, 204.

[68] O. XXXII, r. 2 (1937).

[69] Ariz. Code Ann. 1939, and 1949 Cum. Supp. to Vol. II, § 21-701 *et seq.*;

Missouri (1943) and to a lesser extent in Texas (1940-41).[70] And Florida, providing by a statute of 1947 that depositions may be taken and used "for the same purposes and according to the same procedure" as under the Federal Rules, has since for common-law actions effectively supplemented this provision in respect of discovery in general by extensive borrowings from the Federal Rules, appearing in its Common Law Rules of 1949.[71]

In following the course of the development above outlined one is struck by certain phenomena of what appears to be reversion, however unconscious, to the principles of the medieval Italian procedure from which the chancery had mediately borrowed. Severance of the discovery mechanism from the pleadings is the most striking manifestation of that reversion. Yet it is signalized also by the bestowal of the right to discovery equally upon both of the parties as a matter of course. In a third respect that reversion is likely to be much more evident than it has been in the past: we refer to the *pro tanto* confession for failure to answer a given item of inquiry. Apart from certain limited and partial application, in recent years, of the relative principle in the special practice of notice to admit, its only recognition, previously to the Federal Rules, had been in a few American jurisdictions (Louisiana, Texas, Arizona),[71a] that recognition being traceable to modern civil law influence. It is therefore particularly interesting to note that, as before appears, it has come to acceptance in the Federal Rules, as dictating one of the consequences which the court may attach to a contumacious failure to answer on examination either by the deposition method or the independent written interrogatory. And a final manifestation relates to that

---

Colo. Rules Civ. Proc., Rule 26 *et seq.* in Colo. Stat. Ann. 1935, 1941 Replacement Vol. I; N.M. Stat. Ann. 1941, and 1949 Cum. Supp. to Vol. II, § 19-101(26) *et seq.;* Del. Rules of Superior Court, Rule 26 *et seq.*, Rules of Court of Chancery, Rule 26 *et seq.;* N.J. Rules Civ. Pract., Rule 3:26 *et seq.;* Utah Rules Civ. Proc., Rule 26 *et seq.;* S.D. Code 1939, § 36.0601 *et seq.;* Md. Gen. Rules Pract. & Proc., Part 2, Subd. I (Depositions), Subd. II (Discovery) in Md. Code Ann. (Flack, 1939), 1947 Cum. Supp. p. 2029 *et seq.*

[70] Mo. Rev. Stat. 1942, 1950 Pocket Part, § 847.85 *et seq.;* Tex. Rules Civ. Proc. (Vernon, 1942) Rules 167, 169, 170, 209.

[71] Fla. Laws 1947, c. 24041, Vol. I, p. 832; Fla. Stat. 1949, § 91.30; Fla. Common Law Rules 1949, Rule 20 *et seq.*

[71a] The Arizona provision which

same special practice of notice to admit. For it is difficult to escape the reflection that this practice is in its form something of a return to the original method of the Romano-canonical system in demanding categorical answers to the detached affirmative assertions constituted by the positions.

§ 2. Discovery and Inspection of Documents

Small opportunity was afforded by the common law for the discovery and inspection of documents. Nor could we expect to find the case otherwise in a system which gave no general right to require production, even at the trial, of documents in the possession of the opposite party. As to sealed instruments upon which the claim or defense directly rested there was a right to inspect for pleading purposes through the institution of profert and oyer. Upon the technical averment in the pleading that the instrument was brought into court (*profert in curia*), the pleader's opponent, to enable him to make proper answer, was entitled, in the days of oral pleading to hear (oyer) the instrument read, in later times to inspect it or obtain a copy. The only other possibility of inspection originally existing was where there was a right to inspect independently of the suit: the instances given are those of corporate and manorial records. In the eighteenth century, however, especially under the liberal influence of Lord Mansfield, the right to inspect became decidedly widened, at least where the document could be considered as in a sense the common property of both parties. But after Lord Mansfield's time retrogression set in, and the ground lost in consequence was never quite recovered until the advent of ameliorative legislation.[72]

In chancery discovery of documents was obtainable through the mechanism primarily addressed to the discovery of facts. That is to say, if discovery of documents was sought, the bill included a charge, complemented by appropriate interrogatories, that certain documents relating to the plaintiff's case were in the possession or control of the defendant. It was ad-

was in force prior to the federally influenced Rules of 1939 apparently dated from the Revised Statutes of 1887, § 1859.

72 6 Wigmore, Evidence (3d ed. 1940) § 1858; 1 Tidd, Practice (9th ed. 1828) 589 *et seq.*

visable for the plaintiff to specify or describe the documents as well as he could, but in any case it was sufficient to refer to them as certain books, papers, documents, or writings relating to the allegations or charges of the bill.[73] This charge the defendant was obliged to answer in the same manner as charges of evidence generally. If thus he could be made to admit upon oath the possession or control of a relevant document, then upon motion he could be required to produce it and submit it to the plaintiff's inspection. But only where such admission was made, with the relevancy of the document appearing from bill and answer, was the plaintiff entitled to the production.[74] Such was the classic chancery practice. Variations of it were introduced in the later chancery development. Thus the Chancery Practice Amendment Act of 1852 [75] provided that even though no answer by way of discovery had been required of the defendant, the court might make an order for the production of relevant documents. This involved the plaintiff taking out a summons for the hearing of the application, and, if necessary, the entry of an order requiring the defendant to make an affidavit as to the documents in his possession, admission of possession on the part of the defendant, however, being still requisite before production could be ordered.[76] And under the Federal Equity Rules of 1912, the written interrogatories there provided for applied to the discovery of documents as well as facts, the court being empowered upon motion to make all orders appropriate "to effect the inspection or production of documents in the possession of either party and containing evidence material to the cause of action or defense of his adversary." [77]

In the course of reform an obvious remedial measure was to confer upon the common-law courts an adequate power with respect to documentary inspection and discovery. Here New York seems to have led the way. By a statute of 1828,[78]

[73] Langdell, Summary of Equity Pleading (2d ed. 1883) 244

[74] *Ibid. loc. cit.*

[75] 15 & 16 Vict. c. 86, § 18.

[76] 2 Daniell, Pleading and Practice in the High Court of Chancery (3d Am. from 3d Eng. ed. 1865) 1372 *et seq.*

[77] Rule 58.

[78] N.Y. Rev. Stat. 1829, Pt. III, c. I, tit. III, §§ 21, 22 (Vol. II, p. 199).

to an extent confirmatory of previous judicial rulings,[79] it gave the Supreme Court this power to be exercised according to rules of court, under governance of the "principles and practice of the court of chancery in compelling discovery." According to the resulting rules, either party, on petition, was to be entitled to such documentary discovery and production from the other as was necessary to enable the petitioner to draft his pleadings or prepare for trial.[80] And the same practice was by later legislative action made to obtain in other common-law courts.[81] In England, the Evidence Act of 1851[82] provided that, on application, an inspection was to be allowed of all documents relating to the action in the custody or control of the opposite party. But this conferred a right of inspection only, not of discovery.[83] A right of discovery came three years later with the Common Law Procedure Act of 1854[84] which provided that, upon proper affidavit made on belief by either party, the other might be ordered to answer by affidavit stating what documents he had in his possession or power relating to the matter in dispute or what he knew as to their custody, and whether and on what ground he objected to the production of any such document, the court being empowered to make such further order in the premises as should be just.

The New York Code, as amended in 1849,[85] authorized the court to "order either party to give to the other, within a specified time, an inspection and copy, or permission to take a copy, of any books, papers and documents in his possession, or under his control, containing evidence relating to the merits of the action, or the defence therein," but made no provision for the discovery of such documents.

In this regard, however, the Code did not supersede the discovery authorized by the statute of 1828[86] which, although established for common-law actions, continued to be available for the unified procedure until change was made by the Code

[79] See Townsend v. Lawrence, 9 Wend. 458 (1832).

[80] 1 Burrill, Practice (2d ed. 1846) *450.

[81] *Ibid.* *450 note b.

[82] 14 & 15 Vict. c. 99, § 6.

[83] Hunt v. Hewitt, 7 Exch. 236, 155 E.R. 931 (1852).

[84] 17 & 18 Vict. c. 125, § 50.

[85] Code of 1848, § 342; Code of 1849, § 388.

[86] Hoyt v. Am. Exchange Bank, 8 How.Pr. 89 (1853).

of 1876.[87] During this period some of the courts permitted the examination before trial to be utilized for the discovery of documents, while others did not.[88] The Code of 1876 [89] altered the situation by providing an exclusive method for the discovery, on petition, of documentary evidence, with which substantially disappeared any right to make the oral examination available for the purpose.[90] The provisions of the Code, in an improved form, entered into the Civil Practice Act of 1920,[91] and with amendment and supplementation regulate the existing New York procedure.[92]

The absence from the Code of 1848-49 of any provision other than for inspection undoubtedly accounts for the fact that in the larger number of the code States the relative provision is likewise restricted to inspection. Looking, therefore, at the situation in State jurisdictions as a whole, as it existed prior to the recent ameliorative borrowings by certain of them from the Federal Rules, we find that in a few of those retaining the separate administration of law and equity the case has not materially advanced from what it was at common law, and that in a large majority of the jurisdictions there is a statutory right to inspect documents, but that a right to discovery in the true sense is given recognition, through means of greater or less effectiveness only in a relatively small number.[93] Here and there the right to inspect may find supplement by turning to account the oral examination before trial for the purpose of discovering what documents are in the adversary's possession,[94] as was sometimes done in the former practice of New York, but this is usually discountenanced. (Nevertheless, as we shall presently see, it was to become the method of the Federal Rules). Under the governing statutory provisions,

[87] 2 Wait, N.Y. Practice (ed. of 1873) 527, 551.

[88] *Pro:* Brevoort v. Warner, 8 How. Pr. 321 (1853); Brett v. Bucknam, 32 Barb. 655 (1860); *contra:* Houseman v. Sterling, 61 Barb. 347 (1872); De Bary v. Stanley, 6 Daly 412 (1874).

[89] § 803 *et seq.*

[90] See *e.g.,* Singer v. Nat. Gum & Mica Co., 211 App.Div. 758, 208 N.Y.S. 1 (1925).

[91] § 324.

[92] *Id.* as of 1949 (Clevenger, 1950); N.Y. Rules Civ. Pract., Rule 140 *et seq.*

[93] See the statutes in Ragland, Discovery before Trial (1932) Appendix, and the later summary of statutes in 6 Wigmore, *op. cit.* (1940) note 1 to § 1859 and 1947 Pocket Supp.

[94] Ragland, *op. cit.* 179.

failure or refusal to comply with the order for inspection or discovery, while it may entail punishment for contempt, or loss of the cause, almost always is attended with the right of the court to exclude the document when offered in evidence by the offending party.[95]

In the federal system, under the dual administration of law and equity, inspection in common-law causes remained on its common-law basis, for the statute concerning production of documents, although the question had long been unsettled, was finally construed by the Supreme Court as referring to production at the trial.[96] Discovery and inspection were obtainable in equity, and while, after the Equity Rules of 1912, resort to a bill to discover evidence for use in a common-law cause was rarely seen, it was entirely in order.[97] All this has been changed by the Rules of 1938. For the unified procedure it is here provided that upon motion and notice the court may "order any party to produce and permit the inspection and copying or photographing, by or on behalf of the moving party, of any designated documents, papers, books, accounts, letters, photographs, objects, or tangible things, not privileged, which constitute or contain evidence . . . and which are in his possession, custody, or control." According to the original text, the evidence in question was to be evidence "material to any matter involved in the action," but now, since the amendments of 1946, it is evidence "relating to matter within the scope" prescribed for examination by deposition. (Rule 34). Failure to comply with the order is subject to the same consequences as is refusal to obey an order to answer on examination by deposition or independent written interrogatories. (Rule 37(a)(b)).[98] What is thus provided for is production and inspection. For discovery of documentary evidence we must turn to the rules relating to depositions. Here the ambit of the examination, whether by oral or written interrogatories, is expressly made to extend to "the existence, description, nature, custody, condition and location of books, documents or

[95] See 6 Wigmore, *op. cit.* § 1859*e*.

[96] Carpenter v. Winn, 221 U.S. 533, 31 S.Ct. 683 (1911).

[97] Sinclair Refining Co. v. Jenkins Petroleum Process Co., 289 U.S. 689, 53 S.Ct. 736 (1933).

[98] *Supra*, p. 215.

other tangible things." (Rule 26 (b)). Any doubt as to whether like discovery may be effected by means of independent written interrogatories under Rule 33 has been removed by amendment in 1946, equiparating the scope of such interrogatories to that of examination by deposition.

A highly controversial question arising under the Rules concerns the extent to which a party may have discovery of written or oral statements of witnesses obtained by his adversary's counsel or memoranda of evidence made by the latter, in preparation for trial. After numerous decisions of the lower federal courts, not at all of a uniform complexion,[99] the question came before the Supreme Court in the now celebrated case of *Hickman* v. *Taylor*,[100] decided in January, 1947. The court held that under the Rules the discovery of written statements secured from witnesses was a matter resting in the discretion of the trial court upon proper cause shown. But as to oral statements made to counsel "whether presently in the form of his mental impressions or memoranda," the standards of the profession forbade that discovery should be granted under ordinary conditions. The court concedes the possibility of circumstances existing which would justify the production of such matters, the burden to show which would necessarily rest upon the party seeking discovery, but refers to this as a "rare situation." It concludes by saying that "when Rule 26 [the deposition rule] and the other discovery rules were adopted, the Court and the members of the bar in general certainly did not believe or contemplate that all the files and mental processes of lawyers were thereby opened to the free scrutiny of their adversaries. And we refuse to interpret the rules at this time so as to reach so harsh and unwarranted a result." [101]

The method of documentary discovery, as distinguished from inspection, thus provided by the Federal Rules, while a

[99] See Ilsen, Recent Developments in Federal Practice and Procedure, in Federal Rules of Civil Procedure (West Publishing Co. 1947) 298; Wolfe, The Federal Discovery Rules (1948) 19 Pa. Bar Association Quarterly, 144, 147.

[100] 329 U.S. 495, 67 S.Ct. 385.

[101] Said Mr. Justice Jackson in his concurring opinion, joined in by Mr. Justice Frankfurter: "I can conceive of no practice more demoralizing to the Bar than to require a lawyer to write out and deliver to his adversary an account of what witnesses have told him." P. 516.

notable advance over previous federal practice, is unnecessarily clumsy in requiring the moving party, seeking discovery of documents in the hands or under the control of his adversary to proceed by an examination of the latter. Much simpler, more direct and less expensive are the means provided by the English Rules. Under this system any party, without filing an affidavit may apply for an order directing any other party to the cause "to make discovery on oath of the documents which are or have been in his possession or power, relating to any matter in question therein." On such application the court may direct the discovery to be made by affidavit. But alternatively it may require the party addressed to deliver to the moving party a list of the relevant documents. In case of either affidavit or list the documents disclosed are to be specified in two schedules, the first embracing those which the party addressed is willing to produce, the second those which he objects to producing. Accordingly the items of the one sort are open to inspection of the moving party forthwith, while those of the other sort become similarly available to him, if and when the objections noted are overruled.[102] This method in essence has found entrance into the Rules under the Illinois Civil Practice Act of 1933.[103] It was also, in essence, sought to be established by a proposed provision in the first preliminary draft of the Federal Rules, which, on the precedent of the Ontario Rules, contemplated the listing on written request without a preliminary order of court.[104] It is to be seriously regretted that this proposal, in some form, has not met acceptance in the Rules.

§ 3. Non-Documentary Inspection

At common law, "in most real actions after the demandant hath counted, the tenant may demand the view of the land" which is the object of the action or out of which issues that object.[105] This "view by the party" was granted in order that

[102] R.S.C., O. XXXI, r. 12 *et seq.*

[103] Ill. Rules 1933, Rule 17; Ill. Rev. Stat. 1949, c. 110, § 259.17.

[104] Preliminary Draft of Federal Rules, May 1936, Rule 37 and note, pp. 67-68.

[105] Booth, Nature and Practice of Real Actions (1701) 37; Stearns, A

the tenant might be made certain as to the land in question, and preceded most of his pleading steps. It represented, however, the only thing in the nature of an inspection of property before trial known to the common law. In chancery the case was quite otherwise: here inspection of real or personal property was allowable "whenever fairness seemed to demand it." [106]

In England, the Common Law Procedure Act of 1854 [107] effectively supplied the common-law deficiency by providing for inspection by the party or his witnesses "of any real or personal property, the inspection of which may be material to the proper determination of the question in dispute." And now, under the Rules of the Supreme Court, the court is empowered in any cause or matter to make an order for the "inspection of any property or thing, being the subject of such cause or matter, or as to which any question may arise therein," as well as to authorize entry into premises in the possession of any party, and also the taking of samples and the making of any observations or experiments, "necessary or expedient for the purpose of obtaining full information or evidence." [108]

The American State jurisdictions present various types of statutes and rules of court bearing upon the present subject, but in the aggregate fall far short of the progress attained in England. Some of these, particularly in the West, are confined to the case of mining property, others permit inspection and survey of land in general, while those that allow inspection of real and personal property without restriction constitute a disappointing minority.[109] As for the federal system, this knew no inspection of the kind, other than in equity, until the Rules of 1938. Under their terms, it will be recalled, disclosure may be elicited of any "tangible things." (Rule 26 (b)). Similarly the provision as to inspection extends to "objects, or tangible things." Moreover, it continues with the declaration that the court may "order any party to permit entry

---

Summary of the Law and Practice of Real Actions (2d ed. 1831) *110; Stephen, Pleading (1824) 83.

[106] 6 Wigmore, *op. cit.* § 1862.

[107] 17 & 18 Vict. c. 125, § 58.

[108] R.S.C., O. L, r. 3.

[109] See the summary of statutes in 6 Wigmore, *op. cit.* and 1947 Pocket Supp., § 1862 note 8.

upon designated land or other property in his possession or control for the purpose of inspecting, measuring, surveying or photographing the property" or what, originally spoken of as "any designated relevant object or operation thereon," is now, under the amendment of 1946, denoted as "any designated object or operation thereon within the scope of the examination permitted by Rule 26(b)." (Rule 34).

Another sort of inspection, particularly the subject of current attention, is examination of the person, as in the case of a plaintiff in a personal injury action to determine the extent of the injury. The justice of permitting such an examination, as a safeguard against extravagant or fraudulent claims, is sufficiently obvious, but has had to face objection based upon an exaggerated notion of the sanctity of the person. On the question of the judicial power to order such an examination independently of legislative authority there has been no unanimity of opinion.[110] But statutes or rules of court appear in a number of States expressly giving such authority.[111] The Federal Rules have likewise acquiesced here in a definite procedural need. Envisaging the case where either the physical or the mental condition of a party is in controversy, they enable the court, on motion, "to order him to submit to a mental or physical examination by a physician." The order is to "specify the time, place, manner, condition and scope of the examination and the person or persons by whom it is to be made." (Rule 35(a)). By the further terms of the provision the person examined is entitled on request to a copy of a detailed written report of the examining physician, but availing himself of this entitlement he, in turn, must on request deliver to the moving party a like report of any examination otherwise made in respect of the same physical or mental condition. Ob-

[110] 8 Wigmore, *op. cit.* and 1947 Pocket Supp., § 2220, decisions cited in note 13; Ragland, Discovery before Trial (1932) 191.

[111] See the statutes cited in 8 Wigmore, *op. cit.* and 1947 Pocket Supp., § 2220 note 13. The only English provision on the subject appears to be 31 & 32 Vict. (The Regulation of Railways Act 1868) c. 119, § 26, relating to a person seeking to recover for injury occasioned by an accident on a railway, and authorizing an order in the relative proceedings that such person be examined by a duly qualified medical practitioner not being a witness on either side.

taining thus the report of the examination ordered, or taking the deposition of the examining physician, constitutes a waiver of any privilege on the part of the examined party as to the testimony of any physician otherwise examining him. (Rule 35(b)). The means of enforcing the order, as all other orders for non-documentary inspection, are the same as in the case of inspection of documents, except that in the present case the disobedient person is not subject to arrest. (Rule 37(b)(2)). The validity of the Rule in question has been upheld by the United States Supreme Court, although persistence of the idea that such a measure runs counter to the policy of the law in protecting the inviolability of the person caused the decision to be by a divided voice.[112]

As part of their adherence to the federal pattern in the field of discovery, Arizona (1939), South Dakota (1939), Colorado (1941), Maryland (1941), New Mexico (1942), Missouri (1943), Delaware (1947), New Jersey (1948), Utah (1949), and (for common-law actions) Florida (1949) have placed inspection of property on the basis of that pattern, as has Texas less completely. So, also, all of these, except Texas, follow the federal provision as to physical and mental examination with or without some variation from the pattern.[113]

[112] Sibbach v. Wilson & Co., 312 U.S. 1, 655, 61 S.Ct. 422 (1941).

[113] Ariz. Code Ann. 1939, §§ 21-736, 21-738; S.D. Code 1939, § 36.0601 *et seq.;* Colo. Rules Civ. Proc., Rule 35, in Colo. Stat. Ann. 1935, Replacement Vol. I, 1941; Md. Gen. Rules Pract. & Proc., Part 2, Subd. II, Rules 4, 5, Md. Ann. Code (Flack, 1939) Cum. Supp. 1947, p. 2038; N.M. Stat. Ann. 1941, § 19-101 (35); Mo. Rev. Stat. 1942, 1950 Pocket Part to Vol. III, § 847.86, 847.87; Del. Rules of Superior Court, Rule 35; N.J. Rules Civ. Pract., Rule 3:35, as amended in 1949; Utah Rules Civ. Proc., Rule 35; Fla. Common Law Rules, Rules 27, 28; Tex. Rules Civ. Proc. (Vernon, 1942) Rules 167, 168.

Chapter XV

THE PRE-TRIAL HEARING

Recognition of a preliminary hearing with the object, in greater or less compass, of preparing the cause for the decisive hearing is nothing new in the history of civil procedure. What may be classed as an episode of the kind occurred in both the Greek and Roman law. A notable example of a different character was afforded by the German common-law system which prevailed in most of the German States from the 1500s down to the unifying federal code of 1877: here the preparation involved decision as to the theme of proof, the burden of proof and the time within which proof was to be made—a decision which, unless reversed by interlocutory appeal, was binding for the future course of the proceeding. And in modern Continental procedure stand out the preparatory hearings respectively provided for by the Austrian and German systems, variant in ambit as they are, as well as that contemplated by the Italian Code of Civil Procedure of 1940. But nothing of the sort was known to the Anglo-American law until the English Rules of 1883 established the institution of summons for directions, whereby there was devolved upon the masters of the court authority to make certain interlocutory orders looking to the preparation of the cause for trial.[1] At first the issuance of such a summons was a matter of choice with the plaintiff, but it was later made compulsory except in certain special

[1] A quite distinct manner of preparation is that provided for under the Code of Civil Procedure adopted in 1908 for British India. In its system, the court "at the first hearing of the suit" is to ascertain from each party whether he admits or denies such of his adversary's allegations of fact as are not already admitted or denied in the pleadings, and to this end may examine the parties, or any person accompanying them, or their pleaders, able to answer "any material questions relating to the suit." Upon ascertaining "upon what material propositions of fact or of law the parties are at variance," the court at the same first hearing is required "to frame and record the issues on which the right decision of the case appears to depend." Code Civ. Proc.—Act V of 1908 (ed. Sarkar, 8th ed. by Mukerji, 1934) First Schedule, O. X, O. XIV, r. 1.

classes of cases. The authority of the master has been increasingly widened and at the present day covers an extensive field of preparation. Thus he regulates discovery and inspection of documents, interrogatories for the discovery of facts, inspections of real and personal property, admissions of facts and documents as elicitable under the Rules, makes orders as to pleadings and particulars, determines the question of jury trial where that arises, directs the time and place of trial and registers an estimate of the time which the trial will require. He may appoint the court expert provided for by a rule of 1934, and has certain powers in relation to the evidence, that is to say, he may limit the number of expert witnesses and provide under proper circumstances for evidence by affidavit or for examination of witnesses before an examiner or commissioner, or for the proof of particular facts by statements on information and belief, or by production of documents or entries in books. He also records any consent of the parties limiting or excluding the right of appeal. And, as a consequence of certain recent legislation in relation to contribution among tortfeasors, he may order that in case of a claim of contribution as between tortfeasors sued together, a written offer of contribution be treated as a notice of payment into court, and so entail the same consequences as such notice with reference to the matter of costs.[2] It thus appears that there is little or nothing calculated to clear the way for the actual trial of the cause that falls outside the master's authority.

In 1912, New Jersey, patterning upon the English summons for directions, as it then existed, sought to install, under the name of "preliminary reference," a similar system in its then Supreme Court—the court of general common-law jurisdiction—with court commissioners taking the place of the English masters. But the effort proved unsuccessful under local conditions and subsequently dwindled to the recognition of authority in the court to refer interlocutory motions to its commissioners, all of whom, by the currently existing law, had to be judges of the lesser Circuit Court—an

[2] R.S.C., O. XXX. For a more detailed description, see Millar, A Septennium of English Civil Procedure, 1932-1939 (1940) 25 Wash.U.L.Q. 525, 533-536.

authority, moreover, which appears to have been seldom availed of.[3] The New Jersey experiment apart, American progress in the present direction has been identified with the development of that preliminary consideration of the cause usually before the court itself, which has come to be known as the "pre-trial hearing." This seems to have had its inception in a practice, definitely dating from 1932, adopted by the Circuit Court of Wayne County, Michigan, which has its seat in Detroit. The practice in essence involved the maintenance of law and chancery pre-trial dockets, on which were placed all causes commenced in the court, after their arrival at issue. Call of the pre-trial docket was in order some weeks before the cause would ordinarily be reached for trial, and attendance of counsel on the call was in principle made mandatory. As each case was thus called before a judge of the court, there ensued an informal conference between court and counsel at which the usual subjects of consideration were (1) the state of the pleadings and the question of their amendment so as properly to present the case, (2) the possibility of procuring reciprocal admissions and agreement upon the facts, and (3) the chances of settlement. On the termination of the conference, the court was under the duty of preparing a "pre-trial report," for filing in the cause, in which was minuted the results of the conference, including a notation of the time required for trial, as ascertained in the course of the discussion.[4] So successful did the venture prove in simplifying and expediting the proceedings at the trial and in ridding the dockets of causes which could be disposed of without trial,[5] that it soon came to attract nation-wide attention. As a result it was copied, through local rule of court, in other quarters of which

[3] *Cf.* Rules 61-65 of 1912 (N.J. Laws 1912, pp. 395-396) and Rules 92-95 as of 1939, N.J. Stat. Ann. 1939, Tit. 2, 2-1 to 2-23, Court Rules, pp. 459-460 (all now superseded by Rules Civ. Pract.). And see Mutual Discount Corp. v. Nagy, 111 N.J.L. 592, 169 Atl. 185 (1933).

[4] Cooper, Pre-Trial Procedure in the Wayne County Circuit Court, appearing in the Sixth Annual Report of the Judicial Council of Michigan (1936) 63 *et seq.;* Pre-Trial Procedure in Wayne Circuit (1933) 16 Jour.Am. Jud.Soc. 136 *et seq.;* Sunderland, Theory and Practice of Pre-Trial Procedure (1937) 21 Jour.Am.Jud.Soc. 125, 130.

[5] See Cooper, *op. cit.* 72-75.

are to be particularly mentioned the metropolitan centers of Boston [6] (Superior Court for Suffolk County, 1935), Cincinnati (Common Pleas Court of Hamilton County, 1936) [7] and Los Angeles (Superior Court of Los Angeles County, 1937).[8] But much more emphatic recognition of its value came with its incorporation in 1938 in the new Federal Rules.[9] On this point it was provided (Rule 16) that:

> In any action, the court may in its discretion direct the attorneys for the parties to appear before it for a conference to consider
> (1) The simplification of the issues;
> (2) The necessity or desirability of amendments to the pleadings;
> (3) The possibility of obtaining admissions of fact and of documents which will avoid unnecessary proof;
> (4) The limitation of the number of expert witnesses;
> (5) The advisability of a preliminary reference of issues to a master for findings to be used as evidence when the trial is to be by jury; [10]
> (6) Such other matters as may aid in the disposition of the action.

It is further provided that there shall be an order recording the outcome of the hearing, which order "controls the subsequent course of the action, unless modified at the trial to prevent manifest injustice." The court, moreover, is given

[6] Pre-Trial Procedure Adopted for Boston (1935) 19 Jour.Am.Jud.Soc. 11; Cox, Pre-Trial and Conciliation Lists (1935) Bar Bulletin (Boston) No. 99, p. 1; 12th Report of Judicial Council of Mass. (1937) 22 Mass.L.Q., Supp. No. 1, p. 10.

[7] "Preview" Procedure in Cincinnati Court (1936) 20 Jour.Am.Jud.Soc. 53.

[8] Trying Cases on their Merits in Los Angeles (1937) 20 Jour.Am.Jud. Soc. 249; Bowron, The Pre-Trial Calendar (1938) 13 Los Angeles Bar Assoc. Bulletin, 252, 254; Pre-Trial Challenges Lawyers' Influence (1939) 23 Jour.Am.Jud.Soc. 69, 71.

[9] Of surpassing importance with reference to the antecedents and desirability of the pre-trial hearing is the notable report of the Committee on Pre-Trial Procedure, Section of Judicial Administration of the American Bar Association, Proceedings, American Bar Association 1938, p. 534 *et seq.*, adopted by the Association in July, 1938. For discussion of its recommendations and its effect, see Minimum Standards of Judicial Administration (ed. Vanderbilt, Judicial Administration Series, 1949) c. V.

[10] Rule 53 permits reference to a master in a jury action "when the issues are complicated," and provides that the master's findings "upon the issues submitted to him are admissible as evidence of the matters found and may be read to the jury," subject to any objections to the report in point of law.

authority to establish by rule a pre-trial calendar for jury or non-jury actions or for both.

Sometimes as written or substantially so, sometimes with more or less modification, this Rule has found acceptance in more, perhaps, of the State jurisdictions than any other of the Federal Rules. Examples of its closer following are afforded by Pennsylvania (1938), Wisconsin (1939), Arizona (1939) and New Mexico (1942),[11] of its basic utilization, commonly omitting the item concerning preliminary reference to a master, by Connecticut (1939), Montana (1939), Texas (1940), Illinois (1941) and New Jersey (1948).[12]

Obviously under the federal provision attainment of results depends upon the voluntary coöperation of counsel. This is in marked contrast with the wide range of authority quite independent of any such coöperation exercised, in the corresponding proceeding, by the English master. It would seem that the undoubted value of the institution, as it exists in America, would be enhanced if the court were enabled "on the pre-trial to play a part beyond that of merely eliciting and recording consent of counsel to this or that step,"[13] and the proceeding made to take on some measure at least of the same authoritarian aspect as obtains in the English system. In the first place, attendance of counsel should everywhere, in express terms, be made compulsory, as under the Michigan practice. In the matter of the pleadings, the court should have the power to direct an amendment even against the will of the party. Compulsory amendment is not a new thing even in America.[14] It should also be open to the court to require the parties to indicate, for their mutual information, the means of proof which they intend to employ at the trial, and to enter

[11] Pa. Rules Civ. Proc., Rule 212, Pa. Stat. Ann. (Purdon, 1931) Appendix to Tit. 12, Cum. Pocket Part 1949, p. 196; Wis. Stat. 1949, § 269.65; Ariz. Code Ann. 1939, § 21-453; N.M. Stat. Ann. 1941, § 19-101(16).

[12] Conn. Pract. Book (1934) p. 57, Rules for Trial Court, § 147A, insertion of Nov. 27, 1939; Mont. Rev. Codes Ann. 1947, § 93-4905; Tex. Rules Civ. Proc. (Vernon, 1942) Rule 166; Ill. Rev. Stat. 1949, c. 110, §§ 182a, 259.23A; N.J. Rules Civ. Proc., Rule 3:16.

[13] Millar, A Rule for Pre-Trial Hearing (1940) 28 Ill.Bar.Jour. 201, 202.

[14] See Millar, The Formative Principles of Civil Procedure (1923) 18 Ill.L.Rev. 1, 19, and as reprinted in Engelmann-Millar, History of Continental Civil Procedure (1927) 21.

at this stage any order in relation to discovery of facts or documents which would have been proper on specific notice and motion for the purpose. The court, moreover, should be empowered to exercise here the same power as at the trial with respect to limiting the number of expert witnesses, irrespective of party-consent.[15] And at this stage, too, if it becomes evident that the cause is one that could advantageously be disposed of by motion for summary judgment, it should lie with the court to set the cause down for hearing as on such motion, making necessary provision for the advance filing of the appropriate affidavits.[16] These are some of the matters which, in addition to the specific possibilities under the Federal form of provision, ought to find place in a hearing of the present character. Trend in such a direction appears inevitable as the institution, even in its present somewhat embryonic form, continues more and more to demonstrate its worth as a factor of procedural efficiency.

The Michigan practice and other local rules which have copied it, as also the Connecticut Rule, include conciliation as a proper subject of consideration at the pre-trial hearing. The Federal Rule, on the other hand, is wholly silent on the point. In this it appears to have proceeded wisely. For important as is the affording of an opportunity for conciliation with the aid of the court, the pre-trial hearing under discussion is no place for it. With the prospect before their eyes that the cause may be terminated by a settlement, counsel are not likely to bestow the same care and attention upon analyzing their procedural needs as if it were certain that the cause is to proceed to trial. The aim of clearing the ground for trial can only be blunted and confused if pursued in conjunction with proposals for compromise. And, on the part of the court, the arbitral frame of mind induced by presiding over such proposals is hardly favorable to a purely legal consideration, along clear-cut lines, of the procedural exigencies of the cause. Unquestionably, place should be given to an opportunity for con-

[15] The right so to limit on the trial is widely recognized. 6 Wigmore, Evidence (3d ed. 1940) § 1908.

[16] See the two forms of rule suggested in Millar, A Rule for Pre-Trial Hearing, *supra*, at 202-204.

ciliation as a step in the cause, but this clearly should be the subject of a separate proceeding in advance of the pre-trial hearing and confined to that subject alone. The pre-trial hearing under discussion should, therefore, proceed on the assumption either that conciliation has failed or that it is not desired.

Under the English practice, as above noted, the summons for directions is heard by the master. In 1932, as part of the so-called "New Procedure" then adopted, the hearing in causes falling within this system, was to be before a judge instead of the master. It was thought that the change would be in the interest of expedition, doing away with any appeal from the master to the judge and enabling the judge to obtain an acquaintance with the cause before it came on for trial. In the working of this plan, however, it turned out that oftener than otherwise the judge before whom the cause was tried was not the judge who had heard the summons. Moreover the levy upon the judicial time made by this preliminary hearing was such as to interfere seriously with the other business of the court and especially to occasion pronounced arrears in the trial of non-jury cases. As a result of the ensuing dissatisfaction, the New Procedure was abolished in 1937, and the hearing of the summons for directions reverted to its original place before the master.[17] Apart from the unsuccessful experiment in New Jersey, the American development has centered upon a hearing before the judge.[18] For one thing, in probably most jurisdictions constitutional difficulties stand in the way of vesting in a master or commissioner definite judicial power such as is exercised by the English master. Then, again, even if no such barrier existed, the traditions of American civil justice are such as to incline the bar against entrusting the present function to anyone less in stature than a judge. It may be that the same considerations of speed with economy of judicial administration which brought about the English reversion of

17 See Millar, The "New Procedure" of the English Rules (1932) 27 Ill.L. Rev. 363; Millar, A Septennium of English Civil Procedure, 1932-1939 (1940) 25 Wash.U.L.Q. 525-528.

18 But see Hale, Pre-Trial Procedure in Wisconsin (1932) 15 Jour.Am.Jud. Soc. 180. Hearing before a judge, however, was part of the American Bar Association's recommendations of 1938. Minimum Standards of Judicial Administration, *cit.* c. V.

1937 will one day force a change, at least in the case of metropolitan courts, but for a long time to come the American institution is likely to remain on its present basis as a hearing before a judge of the court.[19]

[19] Of the literature on the subject of the pre-trial hearing since the adoption of the Federal Rules see in particular Murrah, Pre-Trial Procedure—Some Practical Considerations (1940) 26 A.B.A.J. 592; Laws, Pre-Trial Procedure under the Federal Rules (1941) 12 Mo.BarJour. 95; Pre-Trial Clinic, sponsored by the Committee on Pre-Trial Procedure of the Judicial Conference of Senior Circuit Court Judges (1944) 4 F.R.D. 35-82, and report of the same committee, *ibid.* 83-103; Shafroth, Pre-Trial Techniques of Federal Judges (1944) 4 F.R.D. 183. Useful in the present connection is the list of articles appearing in the bibliographic index contained in Federal Rules of Civil Procedure (West Publishing Co. 1947) pp. 264-265. Importance attaches, moreover, to the book of Nims, Pre-Trial (1950) "published under the joint sponsorship of the Committee on Pre-Trial Procedure of the Judicial Conference of the United States and of the Council of the Section of Judicial Administration of the American Bar Association."

CHAPTER XVI

MOTIONS FOR SUMMARY DISPOSITION ON THE MERITS

§ 1. THE MOTION FOR SUMMARY JUDGMENT

Before the Hilary Rules of 1834 the English common law system tolerated to a considerable extent the wholly indefensible practice of pleading, for the purpose of delay, pleas which were altogether unfounded in fact, so-called "sham pleas." Favorite types of plea used in this end were those of judgment recovered or accord and satisfaction. Certain cases of sham pleas, however, fell outside the toleration. Such were pleas made "the subject of indecorous jesting" or otherwise absurd on their face, as where there was pleaded a judgment recovered in the Court of Piepoudre at Bartholomew's Fair;[1] and these could be treated as nullities without much ado. But such also were pleas, plausible enough in aspect, which by departing from the more or less tolerated simple types, threatened to involve the plaintiff in undue trouble and expense.[2] In this case, if the court had reason to believe that the plea was not interposed in good faith, it would proceed summarily to set it aside on affidavit of its untruth and allow judgment to go forthwith for the plaintiff. There was no real question of interference with the normal trial of facts, for if the plea were actually sham the traditions of the bar naturally forbade any insistence by counsel upon carrying the dishonesty further.[3]

[1] Blewitt v. Marsden, 10 East 237, 103 E.R. 765 (1808).

[2] These impermissible pleas are described at length in 1 Chitty, Pleading (11th Am. ed. 1851) * 542-* 543.

[3] On the general subject of sham pleas, see Stephen, Pleading (1824) 444; Chitty, *op. cit.* * 541 *et seq.*; 9 Holdsworth, History of English Law (1926) 306. The contemporary attitude toward this practice is curiously evidenced by what fell from Lord Ellenborough in a case involving a plea of this character. "If sham pleas are used," said he, "they must not be new and fantastic, and framed to deceive the parties who are to reply to them. If pleaders wish to be as mischievous as their ancestors, they must be as dull; we must have no novelties." Phillips v. Bruce, Hil. T. 1817, cited in note to Idle v. Crutch, 1 Chitty

With its roots apparently in this manner of disposition, there originated in America the practice of requiring the defendant, usually in actions on contract and after affidavit of claim on the part of the plaintiff, to interpose with his plea an affidavit of merits as a condition of his right to defend. This practice—an early instance of which was owed to an agreement of the Philadelphia bar in 1795 [4] and another to a New York rule of court in 1808 [5]—found acceptance in various jurisdictions, and, since in the absence of the affidavit the plaintiff was entitled to judgment forthwith, proved a useful means of cutting off groundless defenses. But a factor operating against the general acceptance of the practice was the coming into existence of the code with its provision for verification of the pleadings. In its original form the affidavit of merits required only the statement, by way of conclusion, of the defendant's belief that he had a good defense on the merits, occasionally supplemented by a statement that he had been so advised by counsel. In some jurisdictions, however, there appeared the added requisite, in varying language, that it state the nature of the defense. This was the case in Illinois from 1907 to the going into effect of the Civil Practice Act of 1933.[6] It was also the case under the Delaware statute in force prior to the Rules of 1947, and a former Supreme Court Rule of the District of Columbia.[7] But in any event, under this practice, the court did not look further than the face of the affidavit. Even where the nature of the defense was required to be disclosed, there was no inquiry into the evidentiary facts underlying the defendant's statements.[8] And it is

Rep. 524, 526 (1819). Speaking of the situation in the time of Lord Kenyon, the predecessor of Lord Ellenborough as Chief Justice, Lord Campbell tells us that "sham pleas, which had become much multiplied, were, by a threat to ask *who had signed them,* restrained to 'judgment recovered' or 'a horse given in satisfaction,'" Lives of the Chief Justices of England, c. XLIV.

[4] Andrews v. Blue Ridge Packing Co., 206 Pa. 370, 373, 55 Atl. 1059, 1060 (1903); Vanatta v. Anderson, 3 Binn. 417, 423 (1811).

[5] 3 Johns. 542.

[6] Act of Feb. 12, 1853, § 3, Ill. Laws 1853, p. 173, regulating practice for Cook County; Practice Act of 1871, § 36, Ill. Laws 1871, p. 344; Practice Act of 1907, § 55, Ill. Laws 1907, p. 455.

[7] See Clark and Samenow, The Summary Judgment (1929) 38 Yale L.J. 423, 457, 460.

[8] Thus, with respect to the District

precisely this which differentiates the older practice from the later development identified today with what we know as the motion for summary judgment.

In England, by a statute of 1855, a measure analogous to the American one was applied in the narrow field of actions on bills of exchange and promissory notes. Here was contemplated the filing by the plaintiff of an affidavit showing service of the writ of summons, indorsed *inter alia,* with a statement of his demand, including a copy of the instrument sued on. This imposed upon the defendant the necessity of applying for leave to defend, which might be granted on the defendant paying into court the sum demanded or upon affidavits satisfactory to the judge, disclosing "a legal or equitable defence, or such facts as would make it incumbent on the holder to prove consideration, or such other facts as the Judge may deem sufficient to support the application," and the granted leave might be subjected to terms.[9] In this different manner of treatment from the American provisions in respect of the defendant's duty lay the kernel of future advance. It was left; however, to the English Rules under the Judicature Acts to set the institution on the way to attain a maximum of advantage. By Order XIV of the Rules of 1875 [10] a plaintiff, who had by special indorsement of the writ of summons under Order III, Rule 6, conveyed initial notice of his claim to the defendant, was entitled, upon an affidavit verifying the claim and stating his belief that there was no defense to the action, to call upon an appearing defendant to show cause why judgment should not be rendered against him. And the court or judge was empowered to order such judgment unless the defendant by affidavit or otherwise should satisfy it that "he has a good defence to the action on the merits, or disclose

of Columbia rule which went to the extent of requiring the defendant to state specifically "in precise and definite terms, the grounds of his defense," it was said by the Supreme Court of the District that this "does not mean a defence in all its details of incident and fact, but the foundation of the defence. . . . It was never contemplated that this rule required a party to follow his case through all the lights and shadows of the evidence in it." Nat. Metropolitan Bank v. Hitz, 1 MacAr. & M. (11 D.C.) 198, 200 (1879).

[9] 18 & 19 Vict. c. 67.

[10] This was based on Rule 7 of the Rules of 1873 (36 & 37 Vict. c. 66, Schedule) which were superseded before going into effect.

such facts as the Court or Judge may think sufficient to entitle him to be permitted to defend the action." To fall under Order III, Rule 6, and thus to come within the incidence of the proceeding, the case had to be one of a liquidated demand for the recovery of money on a contract express or implied, simple or under seal, on a statute, on a guaranty when the demand against the principal was a liquidated one, or on a trust.[11] By the Rules of 1883 and subsequent amendments, especially those of 1933, the proceeding was materially improved both in point of incidence and otherwise. As the case now stands, Order XIV, Rule 1, provides that:

> Where the defendant appears to a writ of summons specially indorsed with or accompanied by a statement of claim under Order III, Rule 6, the plaintiff may on affidavit made by himself or by any other person who can swear positively to the facts, verifying the cause of action and the amount claimed (if any liquidated sum is claimed), and stating that in his belief there is no defence to the action except as to the amount of damages claimed if any, apply to a Judge for liberty to enter judgment for such remedy or relief as upon the statement of claim the plaintiff may be entitled to. The Judge thereupon, unless the defendant shall satisfy him that he has a good defence to the action on the merits or shall disclose such facts as may be deemed sufficient to entitle him to defend the action generally, may make an order empowering the plaintiff to enter such judgment as may be just, having regard to the nature of the remedy or relief claimed.

Though thus in terms conferred on the judge, authority to deal with the motion falls in practice within the province of the master.[12] As the result of changes in Order III, Rule 6, prior to 1933, the proceeding had been extended to certain actions by a landlord to recover possession of leased premises and to actions for the recovery of specific chattels. But the effect of the 1933 extension was to make it applicable broadly to actions of any kind in the King's Bench Division, except those for libel, slander, malicious prosecution, false imprisonment, seduction or breach of promise of marriage and actions

[11] 38 & 39 Vict. c. 77, First Schedule, pp. 780, 790.

[12] See O. LIV, r. 12.

in which fraud is alleged by the plaintiff.[13] In addition, an amendment of 1937 brought within its compass actions in which was claimed "possession of any property forming a security for the payment of money." Moreover, by an independent Order (O. XIVA), adopted in 1927, a similar form of proceeding had been authorized in actions for specific performance in the Chancery Division. The general provision under Order XIV is likewise available in the Chancery Division (though not often employed) but, owing to the wording of the 1933 amendment, only, as it would appear, where the cause is one falling within the scope of the proceeding as it existed before that amendment, or coming within the increment of 1937.[14]

The defendant may discharge the burden of showing entitlement to defend by affidavit, or, exceptionally, the court may allow him in this end to be examined on oath.[15] Practically, however, the character of evidence to be adduced by the defendant rests in the discretion of the master.[16] There is also discretionary power to permit a reply affidavit.[17] The burden is discharged when a triable issue of fact is made to appear and is equally discharged when a disputable question of law is presented. But the defendant's showing "must condescend upon particulars" and disclose such "an extent of definite facts," [18] as will enable the court to determine whether the test of the Rules has been met. This test is satisfied by something less than the positive disclosure of an unquestionable defense, since what it calls for is the showing either of a good defense or of facts sufficient to entitle him to defend. Hence "as a general principle, where a defendant shows that he has a fair case for defence, or reasonable grounds for setting up a defence, or even a fair probability that he has a *bona fide* defence, he ought to have leave to defend." [19] The leave to defend may be either as to the whole or part and may be either

[13] See the terms of the present O. III, r. 6: Annual Practice 1949, I, pp. 17-18.

[14] Annual Practice 1949, pp. 19, 184; R.S.C., O. V, r. 5A.

[15] R.S.C., O. XIV, r. 3.

[16] Annual Practice 1949, I, p. 195.

[17] *Ibid.* p. 190.

[18] Lord Blackburn in Wallingford v. Mutual Society (H.L.) 5 App.Cas. 685, 704 (1880).

[19] Annual Practice 1949, I, p. 208.

unconditional or upon "such terms as to giving security or time or mode of trial or otherwise as the Judge may think fit." [20]

The high value of this institution, as a means of suppressing defenses whose only purpose is that of delay, a value abundantly demonstrated by the English experience from the outset, did not fail to impress the latter-day American reform movement. Profiting by the transatlantic example, various American jurisdictions, prior to the advent of the new Federal Rules, adopted provisions patterned in greater or less degree upon those of the English Rules. Here may be noted New Jersey (1912), Michigan (1915, 1931), New York (1921), Connecticut (1928), Massachusetts (1929), Rhode Island (1929), Wisconsin (1931), Illinois (1933), and California (1933).[21] Among other variations from each other and from the English Rules, these provisions, with such amendment as they have undergone, exhibit considerable diversity as to the field of application. Thus the New Jersey provision from the beginning, until superseded by the Rules of 1948, applied only to actions for recovery of liquidated demands upon contract, judgment or statute. Similarly the Michigan provision has applied only to actions in general arising upon contract, judgment or statute. Limited originally to the case of liquidated money demands upon contract or judgment, the New York provision has since been extended, and in the main by an amendment of 1932, to six other classes of actions, Accordingly, it is now applicable, summarily stated, in actions (1) to recover a debt or liquidated demand arising on con-

[20] R.S.C., O. XIV, rr. 3, 4, 6.

[21] Citation of the American provisions in question, as inclusive of later amendment: *New Jersey:* Until superseded by Rules of 1948, N.J. Stat. Ann. 1939, §§ 2:27-124 *et seq.*, Rules of Supreme Court 1938, Rules 80-91; *Michigan:* Mich. Stat. Ann. 1938, § 27.989, Mich. Court Rules 1931, 1933, 1945, Rule 30, Searl, Mich. Court Rules Ann. (4th ed. 1933) p. 224 and 1948 Cum. Supp. p. 60; *New York:* N.Y. Rules Civ. Pract. (Clevenger, Annual Practice 1950) Rules 113, 114; (a statute of 1936 here extended the procedure to mandamus actions, N.Y. Laws 1936, c. 763); *Connecticut:* Conn. Pract. Book (1934) p. 34, Rules for Trial Court, §§ 52-57; *Massachusetts:* Mass. Ann. Laws 1933, c. 231, § 59B; *Rhode Island:* R.I. Gen. Laws Ann. 1938, c. 524, § 1; *Wisconsin:* Wis. Stat. 1949, § 270.635; *Illinois:* Ill. Rev. Stat. 1949, c. 110, §§ 181, 259.15, 259.16; *California:* Cal. Code Civ. Proc. (Deering, 1949) § 437c: (while adopted for the Superior Courts in 1933, the California provision originated in 1925 as one applicable to the Municipal Courts —see McCabe, Summary Judgment (1938) 11 So.Cal.L.Rev. 436, 438).

tract; (2) to recover a debt or demand on a judgment for a sum of money; (3) to recover on a statute a sum of money other than a penalty; (4) to recover an unliquidated debt or demand for a sum of money arising on contract; (5) to recover possession of a specific chattel with or without a claim for hire or damages; (6) to enforce or foreclose a lien or mortgage; (7) for specific performance of a written contract for the sale or purchase of property, including alternative and incidental relief; and (8) for an accounting arising on a written contract. The Connecticut provision struck out initially for a fairly comprehensive field, since it allowed the proceeding in case of liquidated demands on any contract (exclusive of demands on quasi-contact), on a money judgment, on a statute, and on guaranty where the claim against the principal was a liquidated one, and, further, in actions to recover specific chattels with or without a claim for their withholding, to quiet title to real estate, to enforce or foreclose a lien, and to discharge any claimed invalid mortgage, lien, caveat or *lis pendens*. It remains on this basis except for the exclusion in 1934 of actions to enforce or foreclose liens. The Massachusetts and Rhode Island provisions from the outset have been sufficiently conservative; both are restricted to contract actions for the recovery of liquidated demands. Wisconsin commenced with restriction to liquidated demands on contract or judgment. In 1934, however, it enlarged this field to embrace certain further classes of actions, similar to those added by the New York amendment of 1932, but including also actions for the recovery of real property, and finally in 1941, apparently under the influence of the Federal Rules, discarded restriction altogether, providing for the use of the institution "in any civil action or special proceeding." In California the statute in its original form gave the proceeding only in "an action to recover upon a debt or upon a liquidated demand including an action to enforce or foreclose a lien or mortgage," but in 1939 added the cases of "an action to recover an unliquidated debt or demand for a sum of money only arising on a contract express or implied in fact or in law or to recover possession of specific real or personal property or for specific performance of a contract in writing for the sale or purchase of property, or for an accounting arising on a written contract." The Illinois provision permitted application only in actions on contract, on money judgments, or for the recovery of possession of land, with or without rent or mesne profits, or of specific chattels. Considered as confined to the case of common-law actions, this provision was amended in 1941 so as to bring equitable actions of the same description within the compass of the proceeding. There is no unanimity among the provisions in question as to the stage of the cause at which the motion may be made. Rhode Island requires the motion to be filed with the declaration. Connecticut and Massachusetts follow the English system of permitting it at any time after appearance, while Wisconsin and Illinois, by their silence on the present point, seem to take the same position. But in New York and California the motion is not in order until after answer, and in Michigan not until after the cause "shall be at issue." Postponing the motion until the answer has come in may perhaps lead to a better development of the facts and an easier ascertainment of the existence *vel non* of a triable issue, but, as against this, it may detract considerably from the expedition which the proceeding is designed to effect.

In the English practice the proceeding is quite definitely directed toward overthrowing a defense because of its lack of *bona fides*. It does not aim at testing the legal sufficiency of a defense which is clearly advanced *bona fide*. Accordingly, if the validity of the defense rests upon an arguable question of law, that question will not be dealt with on the application, and leave to defend will be given.[22] The same is by no means generally true under the American provisions above noted. The Michigan Rule is explicit to the contrary; if it appears to the court from the mutual affidavits and depositions that the applicant is entitled to judgment "as a matter of law, without deciding any controverted question of fact," judgment is to be entered accordingly. So also is the Connecticut Rule, which declares that "if the court shall be of opinion that the only question or questions arising are *bona fide* questions of law, it shall file its

[22] Annual Practice 1949, I, p. 209.

finding so stating and that the defendant has no defense on the merits." It is then open to the defendant to file, within an extendible period of ten days, "a pleading appropriate to test such question or questions of law." Failure to file the pleading or failure to prevail on it is to result in judgment for the plaintiff. And while the New York Rule contains no expression on the point, it has been construed as applicable "even though an important question of law has to be determined." [23] The same result apparently obtains under the California statute.[24] So, under the other provisions in reference, not expressly regulating the matter, it is probably safe to say that the usual course is to consider the determination of *bona fide* questions of law as within the province of the hearing.

Again, certain of these American provisions are characterized by a closer regulation of the affidavits than appears in the English Rules. In England, all that Order XIV requires of the affidavit for the plaintiff, apart from the statement of belief in the lack of defense, is that it be one "verifying the cause of action and the amount claimed (if any liquidated sum is claimed," made on personal knowledge of the facts. And while, as has been seen, the defendant is required to deal particularly with the facts of the defense, the provision itself is expressed in general terms, namely, that he shall satisfy the court that "he has a good defence to the action on the merits or shall disclose such facts as may be deemed sufficient to entitle him to defend the action generally." On the other hand, the New York and Wisconsin provisions require that the applicant's affidavit shall set forth evidentiary facts, and also call for the showing of relative documentary support. The Michigan Rule is decidedly detailed in the present regard. It requires that the affidavit verifying the cause of action "shall set forth

[23] Coutts v. J. L. Kraft & Bros. Co., 119 Misc. 260, 196 N.Y.S. 135, 137 (1922), aff'd in memo. 206 App.Div. 625, 198 N.Y.S. 908 (1923); Rotenbach v. Young, 119 Misc. 267, 196 N.Y.S. 220 (1922) aff'd in memo. 206 App.Div. 775, 200 N.Y.S. 946 (1923); Kennilwood Owners' Association v. Wall, 148 Misc. 67, 264 N.Y.S. 135 (1932). *Contra:* Munoz & Co. v. Savannah Sugar Refining Corp., 118 Misc. 24, 193 N.Y.S. 422 (1922).

[24] Bank of America Nat. Trust & Savings Association v. Casaday, 15 Cal.App.2d 163, 59 Pac.2d 444 (1936); Ware v. Heller, 63 Cal.App.2d 817, 148 Pac.2d 410 (1944).

with particularity the facts upon which the plaintiff's cause of action is based," shall have attached sworn or certified copies of all papers (with exceptions named) upon which the plaintiff relies, and "shall not consist of conclusions but of such facts as shall be admissible in evidence and shall show affirmatively that the affiant, if sworn as a witness, can testify competently thereto." It expressly permits two or more affidavits to be used, if all the facts are not within the personal knowledge of one person. And it provides that the affidavit of merits shall be drawn in the same manner. If given facts are known only to persons whose affidavit has not been procurable "by reason of hostility or otherwise," this circumstance may be shown in the affidavit presented, with a statement of the affiant's belief as to what such persons would testify to, whereupon the court is empowered, if it sees fit, to grant a continuance for the purpose of procuring their affidavits, depositions or answers to interrogatories. With but slight change, the Michigan provisions in this regard have been followed by Illinois. And, though differently framed, the California provision expressly insists upon particularity, permits plurality of affidavits and requires it to appear that the affiant, if sworn as a witness, could competently testify to the facts stated.

Most salient, however, of the innovations upon the English practice lay in making the remedy available to the defendant as well as the plaintiff within the same circle of actions. This consisted in the first place in putting the remedy at the command of a defendant prosecuting a counterclaim, which was done by New York and Illinois in 1933 and by Wisconsin in 1934. But Michigan in 1931 led the way to the bolder measure of enabling the defendant to employ the proceeding defensively, upon a successful showing of the absence of a question of fact and his entitlement to judgment as a matter of law. This idea was taken over by the New York and Wisconsin amendments of 1933 and 1934 respectively, which provide for rendition of judgment for the defendant, if he is able to make it appear by his affidavit that his defenses are sufficient to defeat the action, unless the plaintiff shows such facts as entitle him to a trial. California adopted a similar plan by an amendment of 1939, whereby the defendant was entitled to judgment upon affidavit or affidavits showing that "the action has no merit," if the opposite party was unable to make the prescribed disclosure of facts deemed sufficient to present a triable issue of fact. Illinois followed in 1941 by the statutory provision that the defendant "may move for a summary judgment or decree in his favor as to all or any part" of the plaintiff's action, under the same procedure as is prescribed for the case of a like motion by the plaintiff or counterclaimant.

When it came to the adoption of the new Federal Rules, there had been thus in the State development prior to 1938 abundant American experience upon which to draw for a new moulding of the institution, whose well-demonstrated success both in England and America inevitably called for its inclusion here. The regulation which ensued initiated the radical step of rendering the proceeding applicable in every class of action without restriction. And on State precedent it explicitly placed within the province of the hearing the determination of questions of law, specifically dealt with the form of the affidavits for and against, and permitted employment as an instrumentality both of offense and defense.

As thus methodized, the motion is available, on the one hand, to any "party seeking to recover upon a claim, counterclaim, or cross-claim or to obtain a declaratory judgment," and, on the other, to any "party against whom a claim, counterclaim, or cross-claim is asserted or a declaratory judgment is sought." In the one case, it is in order, by the original terms of the provision, at any time after service of the answering pleading, now, by these terms as amended in 1946, at any time after the "expiration of 20 days from the commencement of the action or after service of a motion for summary judgment by the adverse party." In the other case it is in order at any time after the movant's appearance. It may be made with or without supporting affidavits and may be addressed to the whole or any part of the demand. (Rule 56(a), (b)). Service of the motion must be had at least ten days before the time which is specified for the hearing, and opposing affidavits may be served before the hearing day. It is then provided that the judgment sought shall be rendered forthwith, if the pleadings, depositions and admissions on file, together with the affidavits, if any, show that there is no genuine issue as to any material fact and that the moving party is entitled to judgment as a matter of law. As originally provided, the genuine issue thus referred to was to be "except as to the amount of damages." In other words, where there was such an issue as to damages, no summary judgment was possible. This exception was eliminated by the amendments of 1946 which, instead, provided that "a summary judgment, interlocutory in character, may be rendered on the issue of liability alone, although there is a genuine issue as to the amount of damages." (Rule 56(c)). The supporting and opposing affidavits are governed as to character (Rule 56(e)) by substantially the same discipline as appeared first in the Michigan Rule and, as in the latter, there is provision for opportunity, by means of continuance, to procure proof presently unavailable. Here, however, this opportunity is confined to the opposing party, it being declared that if it appears from his affidavits "that he cannot for reasons stated present by affidavit facts essential to justify his opposition, the court may refuse the application for judgment or may order a continuance to permit affidavits to be obtained or depositions to be taken or discovery to be had or may make such other order as is just." (Rule 56(f)). Influenced also by the Michigan Rule is the penalizing of affidavits presented "in bad faith or solely for the purpose of delay," by the imposition upon the offending party of the reasonable expenses occasioned to the other through their filing, as well as by subjection of the offending party or his attorney to the contempt power. (Rule 56(g)). A provision altogether new contemplates the case where, on the motion, "judgment is not rendered upon the whole case or for all the relief asked and a trial is necessary." In this event, the court from an examination of the pleadings and evidence and interrogation of counsel is required, if practicable, to "ascertain what material facts exist without substantial controversy," and to make an order specifying such facts, "including the extent to which the amount of damages or other relief is not in controversy, and directing such further proceedings in the action as are just." And the facts so specified are to be deemed established on the trial of the cause. (Rule 56(d)).

The federal provisions have found lodgement in Arizona (1939, 1949), New Mexico (1942, 1949), Delaware (1947), Florida (1949), Utah (1949), and with minor variations in Colorado (1941) and New Jersey (1948).[25] They have also influenced in important measure the provisions adopted in Maryland (1947).[26]

Whatever doubts there may be as to the wisdom of deferring, by hard and fast precept, the motion of the plaintiff (or corresponding claimant), absent a like motion by the adverse party, until the expiration of twenty days from the commencement of the action, there can be none as to the other features thus embodied in the Federal Rule. The steps progressively taken on both sides of the Atlantic to broaden the province of the motion find their logical culmination in the removal of all restrictions as to the kind of causes in which it may find application. Enlargement of its incidence in another direction so as to make it the theater of debatable questions of law is a decided departure from the original purpose of striking at the lack of *bona fides* in the defense, but, if the question is one summarily determinative of the claim in whole or in part, there can be no gainsaying the convenience of the theater or the wholesome abridgement of the proceedings thus occasioned. Specific regulation of the contents of the affidavits is obviously desirable both as a guide to the litigants and as a means of economizing the judicial time. And throwing the procedure open to either side of the controversy is a measure distinctly subserving, as between the parties, that equality of advantage and opportunity the maintenance of which in the fullest degree

[25] Ariz. Code Ann. 1939, and 1949 Cum. Supp. to Vol. II, §§ 21-1210 to 21-1216; N.M Stat. Ann. 1941, and 1949 Cum. Supp. to Vol. II, §§ 19-101(56); Del. Rules of Superior Court, Rule 56, Rules of Court of Chancery, Rule 56; Colo. Rules Civ. Proc., Rule 56, Colo. Stat. Ann. 1935, 1941 Replacement Vol. I; N.J. Rules Civ. Pract., Rule 3:56; Fla. Common Law Rules, Rule 43, Equity Rules, Rule 40; Utah Rules Civ. Proc., Rule 56.

[26] Md. Gen. Rules Pract. & Proc. Part 2, Subd. IV, Rules 1-7, in Md. Ann. Code (Flack, 1939), 1947 Cum. Supp. p. 2044.

should be a cardinal tenet of every well-regulated procedural system.

§ 2. The Motion for Dismissal on Summary Issues

Akin to the motion for summary judgment proper is a measure incorporated in the Rules under the New York Civil Practice Act of 1920,[27] and finding subsequent adoption, with some variation in detail, in Michigan (1931)[28] and Illinois (1933),[29] which enables the defendant in the case of certain designated defenses to proceed by way of motion to dismiss, even where the defense is not apparent on the face of the complaint or declaration and involves the determination of a controverted question of fact. In such case the defensive facts are set up by affidavit and issue formed by means of counter-affidavit. Unless, under the existing rules, the situation calls for a jury trial, the issue of fact may be summarily tried by the court, although in this respect New York follows one mode of regulation and Michigan and Illinois another. The defenses here envisaged are a selected group, some of which are essentially in abatement, some in bar, but with the common characteristic of representing a short objection to the prosecution of the demand. Specifically these defenses in all three jurisdictions are (1) lack of jurisdiction of the subject-matter, or (2) of the person, (3) absence, on the plaintiff's part, of capacity to sue, (4) pendency of another action, (5) former judgment, (6) statute of limitations, (7) release, (8) statute of frauds and (9) non-accrual of the cause of action because of the defendant's infancy or other disability, to which Michigan in 1933 added the defense of assignment or other disposition of the cause of action by the plaintiff before suit.

The New York Rule provides that the court may either determine the motion itself, or "may direct that the questions of fact . . . be tried by a jury or referee, the findings of which shall be reported to the court for its action." Here, while the

[27] N.Y. Rules of Civ. Pract., Rules 107, 108.

[28] Mich. Court Rules 1931, 1933, 1945, Rule 18, Searl, Mich. Court Rules Ann. (4th ed. 1933) p. 118 and 1948 Cum. Supp. p. 32.

[29] Ill. Pract. Act 1933, § 48, Ill. Rev. Stat. 1949, c. 110, § 172.

rule itself contains nothing mandatory on the point, it has been held that where the defendant is constitutionally entitled to a jury trial, the issue should thus be sent to a jury.[80] A further alternative provided by the Rule is that of overruling the motion, with permission to the defendant to allege the same facts in the answer. In Michigan and Illinois, on the other hand, the provision is that "if disputed questions of fact are involved the court may deny the motion without prejudice, and shall so deny it, if the action is one at law and the opposite party demands that the issue be submitted to a jury." This, in Illinois, is followed by the express declaration of what in Michigan seems to follow by implication, namely, that unless the defense has been decided on the motion, it may be raised in the answer, as may any defense of the kind not raised by the motion. Thus, with reference to the jury issue on the motion, it is seen that the New York procedure contemplates a jury trial specially addressed to that issue, with a verdict confined to the ambit of the motion and furnishing the basis of its decision, whereas in Michigan and Illinois, if there must be a jury trial, the motion-proceeding comes to an end with the motion's denial, and the parties are remitted to the ordinary course of proceeding.

New York and Michigan accord to the plaintiff the benefit of the same manner of proceeding, in respect of defenses not appearing on the face of the pleading, as against a counter-demand advanced by the defendant. Here the Michigan Rule, after providing for the defendant's motion, simply says that "a similar motion may be made by the plaintiff in case of recoupment, set-off or cross-bill under similar circumstances."[81] New York, again, has a special rule recognizing a motion, supported by affidavit, for a judgment dismissing a counterclaim and specifying the defenses which may be thus presented. These are the same *mutatis mutandis* as those available on the defendant's motion with omission of lack of jurisdiction of the person and addition of the defense "that the counterclaim is

[80] Herzog v. Brown, 217 App.Div. 402, 216 N.Y.S. 134 (1926). See also Barker v. Conley, 276 N.Y. 43, 195 N.E. 677 (1935).

[81] Mich. Court Rules 1931, 1933, 1945, Rule 18, § 2.

not one which may be properly interposed in the action." The hearing is to be governed by the same provisions as apply to the defendant's motion.[32] Illinois, however, gives no place to a step of the kind on the part of the plaintiff.

With its nearest analogue, perhaps, in the use of the plea of the classic chancery system [33] there has been here contrived a mode of proceeding which has manifest claim to a more general acceptance. It supplements usefully the motion for summary judgment which, it need not be emphasized, is abortive in the presence of a triable issue of fact, however uncomplicated. In the case of a simple and speedily determinable issue such as is usually presented by the specified defenses, there is the best of reasons for providing the short cut to decision which is offered by the practice in question.[34]

[32] N.Y. Rules of Civ. Pract., Rule 110.

[33] See Herzog v. Brown, *supra*.

[34] *Cf.* with the practice in question that prescribed by the California statute of 1939, under which, when by his answer the defendant pleads the statute of limitations, former judgment, another action pending "or any other defense not involving the merits of the plaintiff's cause of action, but contituting a bar or ground of abatement to the prosecution thereof, the court may, upon the motion of either party, proceed to the trial of such special defense or defenses before the trial of any other issue in the case." The same rule applies in respect of an answer to a counterclaim. Cal. Code Civ. Proc. (Deering, 1949) § 597.

Chapter XVII

VOLUNTARY DISMISSAL[1]

"It has always been a recognized principle of the English law, on the equity as well as on the common-law side of the court, that a plaintiff is not bound to prosecute a suit or action to a finish because he has begun it. But on the contrary he is at liberty to abandon it without losing the right of action on which it is founded, and he may enforce that right subsequently on paying the costs of the former proceeding."[2] Some restriction upon that liberty, however, there long has been, and the progress of procedural reform, from considerations of fairness to the defendant, has been marked by the tendency to increase restriction by advancing the stage of the cause at which there may be a withdrawal as a matter of right.

By the original rule of the common law the plaintiff might elect to submit to a nonsuit even after the return of a verdict, but this was changed by a statute of the year 1400, which declared that "if the verdict pass against the plaintiff, the same plaintiff shall not be nonsuited."[3] It thus became and remained the common-law rule that the taking of a nonsuit was open to the plaintiff at any time before verdict. In the Court of Chancery the plaintiff enjoyed a kindred freedom. There was here established at an early day the general rule that a plaintiff was at liberty to dismiss his bill without prejudice at any time before the pronouncement of decree[4]—a rule, however, which ad-

[1] The term "dismissal" comes from the chancery practice, where it was applied to any decretal termination of the cause in the defendant's favor. His voluntary withdrawal of the suit was a dismissal "without prejudice." At common law "nonsuit" was the term used for an equivalent withdrawal, while the term "discontinuance," although involving the same idea, had a more technical connotation. In modern practice, under the fused administration of law and equity, the terms are used interchangeably, although "dismissal" is favored in the American jurisdictions and "discontinuance" in England.

[2] Earl Carpenter & Sons Co. v. New York, New Haven & Hartford RR. Co., 184 Mass. 96, 99, 68 N.E. 28 (1903).

[3] 2 Hen. IV, c. 7.

[4] 2 Daniell, Chancery Practice (1840) 355.

mitted of exception, in the court's discretion, when the dismissal would work some prejudice to other parties in the cause above and beyond that occasioned to the defendant by being thus rendered subject to a renewal of the litigation.[5] And this regulation of voluntary dismissal was parcel of the acceptance of the English practice in the American chancery jurisdictions.

The process of narrowing the plaintiff's liberty in the present regard began in America. In the first quarter of the nineteenth century, Massachusetts, without the aid of statute, cut off the right to submit to a nonsuit with the opening of the trial: after that point the matter rested in the discretion of the court.[6] The same rule soon met with judicial approval in Maine [7] and New Hampshire,[8] and at a much later period was to be adopted in substance by a statute of Rhode Island.[9] Elsewhere there appeared before the middle of the century statutes enacting the more conservative change of forbidding the nonsuit after the jury had retired to consider its verdict. Where these began it is difficult to say, but Tennessee had legislation of the kind as long ago as 1801.[10] This rule, indeed, is that which continues to govern in a considerable quota of the common-law jurisdictions, and, with the increasing number of common-law cases tried by the court without a jury, has usually been supplemented, as a result of statute or judicial decision, by fixing either the submission to the court of a cause so tried, or the court's announcement of its decision, as the point before which the nonsuit must be taken. Of other forms of provision in these jurisdictions there should be mentioned that of Maryland [11] prior to the Rules of 1941, which required that the plaintiff act before argument on the facts, and that of Michigan [12] which in any civil action prevents him from act-

[5] Bank of the State of South Carolina v. Rose, 1 Rich.Eq. (S.C.) 292, 294 (1845); Pullman's Palace Car Co. v. Central Transportation Co., 171 U.S. 138, 18 S.Ct. 808 (1898).

[6] Haskell v. Whitney, 12 Mass. 47 (1815); Locke v. Wood, 16 Mass. 317 (1820).

[7] Proprietors of Kennebec Purchase v. Davis, 2 Me. 352, 356 (1823); Theobald v. Colby, 35 Me. 179, 180 (1853).

[8] Judge of Probate v. Abbot, 13 N.H. 21 (1842).

[9] R.I. Gen. Laws 1938, c. 523, § 1.

[10] Tenn. Laws 1801, c. 6, § 58 (Revisal of Public Acts, 1809, p. 280).

[11] Md. Ann. Code (Flack, 1939) Art. 75, § 183.

[12] Mich. Stat. Ann. 1938, § 27.1081.

ing without the consent of the defendant, "whenever the defendant shall have entered upon his defense to the action in open court." On the chancery side the initiative seems to have been taken in England where, by the General Orders of 1845, any voluntary dismissal of the bill after the cause had been set for hearing was made equivalent to a dismissal on the merits.[13] In the American chancery jurisdictions of the present day, the original rule basically recognizing the plaintiff's right to dismiss down to the pronouncement of decree still commands some allegiance. Departures have variously appeared, as in Michigan, where the provision already mentioned applies to civil actions generally; in Massachusetts, where the rule would seem to follow in the main that of the common-law side in denying the right after the opening of the hearing;[14] and in Alabama, where a rule of court patterned upon the English Order of 1845 has been succeeded by a rule restricting the dismissal as of course to the period before answer or cross-bill.[15] So, in New Jersey and Delaware, prior to the current Rules, it had been provided, in the one case by statute and in the other by rule of court, that when the hearing has commenced and the taking of proofs has begun, the right to voluntary dismissal ceases except upon good cause shown and special order of court.[16]

The New York Code of 1848 failed to deal with the subject. It was not until the Code of 1876 that New York had any statutory provision in the present regard, and this,[17] following a rule of the Supreme Court adopted in 1858,[18] did no more than forbid a nonsuit "after the cause has been committed to the jury." So the rule remains in New York, submission marking the same point in case of a trial before the court or a ref-

[13] 1 Daniell, Chancery Practice (3d Am. ed. 1865, from 3d Eng. ed.) 799.

[14] Kempton v. Burgess, 136 Mass. 192 (1883); Hollingsworth & Vose Co. v. Foxborough Water Supply District, 171 Mass. 450, 50 N.E. 1037 (1898).

[15] Ala. old Chancery Rule 28, in Ala. Code 1928, p. 1943; present Equity Rule 75, in Ala. Code 1940, Tit. 7, p. 1105.

[16] N.J. Stat. Ann. 1939, § 2:29-50; Del. Chancery Rule 79 (1917), Allied Chemical & Dye Corporation v. Steel & Tube Co., 14 Del. Ch. 368, 371, 127 Atl. 414 (1925).

[17] N.Y. Code Civ. Proc. 1876, § 1182.

[18] Schintzuis v. Lackawanna Steel Co., 224 N.Y. 226, 231, 120 N.E. 137 (1918).

eree.[19] The Kentucky Code of 1851 required the plaintiff to act "before final submission" of the cause to the jury or the court,[20] and this manner of restriction has been adopted by a considerable group of other States. A different form of provision which also commands an important number of adherents was that of the California Practice Act of 1851 which permitted a voluntary nonsuit "at any time before trial." [21] This has generally been interpreted as meaning "before the opening of the trial," but California, itself, has held otherwise, considering that "trial" signifies a determination of the issue and that the plaintiff, accordingly, is at liberty to act until there is a final submission for such determination.[22] By the Indiana Code of 1852 [23] the barring point was fixed as the retirement of the jury; in case of trial by the court, however, not the submission for decision but the announcement of the court's decision was made the point in question, and provision of this kind has not been without its own followers. In general, it may be said that these three types of rules share most of the ground in the code area.[24]

A factor which has entered into the situation is the increase of opportunity in modern procedure for the assertion of counter-demands. So far as concerns the cross-bill in equity, the only definite instance of such opportunity under the old order, the classic chancery rule, in general, imposed here no restriction upon the plaintiff because of the exhibition of a cross-bill and left the defendant free to proceed with his claim for affirmative relief notwithstanding dismissal of the original bill. Little need therefore existed for any legislation governing the chancery courts in this connection.[25] But the case was otherwise on

[19] N.Y. Civ. Pract. Act (Clevenger, 1950) §§ 457, 469.

[20] Ky. Code of Pract. in Civ. Cas. 1851, § 412, 1 Ky.Laws 1850-51, p. 169.

[21] Cal. Pract. Act 1851, § 148, Cal. Laws 1851, c. 5, p. 73.

[22] See MacDermot v. Grant, 181 Cal. 332, 334, 184 Pac. 396 (1919), and other cases in note, 89 A.L.R. 13, 53-54.

[23] Ind. Code 1852, § 363, 2 Ind.Rev. Stat. 1852, p. 120.

[24] Highly informative as to the different rules in the present regard are the notes in 89 A.L.R. 13 and 126 A.L.R. 284.

[25] But see the Illinois statute dating from 1845 (Rev. Stat. 1845, c. 21, § 28) which, after a cross-bill had been filed, forbade voluntary dismissal of the original bill without consent of the defendant. This was superseded by the kindred provision in the Civil Practice Act of 1933.

the common-law side, once there had come to recognition the right of the defendant, under a plea of set-off, to recover an affirmative judgment against the plaintiff. Accordingly, statutes were adopted in many quarters taking away the plaintiff's absolute right in respect of a nonsuit after a plea of set-off had been filed. And legislation of this sort continues to obtain in the common-law jurisdictions of today.[26] In the code area the question obviously involves the effect of a counterclaim upon the plaintiff's right to dismiss. In the absence of statutory provision on the point the question has been variously answered,[27] but more usually such provision exists. This, for the most part, is either to the effect that the plaintiff's right of dismissal is precluded by the presence of a counterclaim, unless of course he obtains the defendant's consent to the dismissal,[28] or else that his dismissal of the principal action does not affect the defendant's right to prosecute his counterclaim to judgment.[29]

More recently the rule abridging the plaintiff's absolute right by requiring him to act before the opening of the trial has found acceptance in the Illinois Civil Practice Act of 1933; after that point, it provides, he may dismiss only by specially regulated order of court or by stipulation entered into by the defendant. And, after a counterclaim has been filed, the dismissal in no case can be effected without the defendant's consent.[30] But, far as this manner of rule has departed from those of the old order, more energetic measures had already appeared. By the English Rules of 1875 it was provided that "the plaintiff may, at any time before receipt of the defendant's statement of defence, or after the receipt thereof before taking any other proceeding in the action (save any interlocutory application), by notice in writing" discontinue the action or any part thereof. But, unless applied for within the time thus limited, there was to be no discontinuance without leave, which

[26] *E.g.*, Vt. Stat. 1947, § 1656; Mich. Stat. Ann. 1938, § 27.833; Mass. Ann. Laws 1933, c. 232, § 8.

[27] See cases cited in 15 L.R.A. (N.S.) 341.

[28] *E.g.*, Cal. Code Civ. Proc. (Deering, 1949) § 581; 2 Wash. Rev. Stat. (Remington, 1932) § 408; N.D. Rev. Code 1943, § 28-0801.

[29] *E.g.*, Ohio Gen. Stat. (Page, 1938) § 11587; Ky. Code of Pract. in Civ. Cas. (Carroll, 1948) § 372; Okla. Stat. 1941, Tit. 12, § 685.

[30] § 52; Ill. Rev. Stat. 1949, c. 110, § 176.

the court was empowered to grant before, at, or after the hearing or trial.[81] This rule, carried into the revision of 1883 without substantial change, is that which governs today.[82] The revision, however, added the provision, embodying a result previously reached by judicial decision, that in case of such discontinuance, any counterclaim "may nevertheless be proceeded with." [83] The meaning of "other proceeding in the action" is not altogether clear and has given rise to some question, but the width accorded it is evidenced by the recognition that the delivery of a reply or of an amended statement of claim comes within its terms.[84]

The precedent thus set by the English practice has influenced the provisions on the subject contained in the new Federal Rules. These, free from the difficulty of interpretation just noted, are even more stringent than the English. They lay down the general rule that the plaintiff may dismiss his action without order of court by filing either a notice of dismissal or a stipulation of dismissal signed by all the parties who have appeared in the action. The notice as originally prescribed was to be filed at any time before service of the answer; now by amendment of 1946 it is to be filed "at any time before service by the adverse party of an answer or of a motion for summary judgment, whichever first occurs." (Rule 41(a)(1)). Except as thus provided, "an action shall not be dismissed at the plaintiff's instance save upon order of the court and upon such terms and conditions as the court deems proper." (Rule 41(a)(2)). In case of a counterclaim, "the action shall not be dismissed against the defendant's objection unless the counterclaim can remain pending for independent adjudication by the court." (*Ibid.*) And, on suggestion proceeding from certain State legislation,[85] with reference to the matter of a second dismissal, it is also provided that "a notice of dismissal oper-

81 38 & 39 Vict. c. 77, First Schedule, O. XXIII.

82 O. XXVI, r. 1.

83 O. XXI, r. 16; Annual Practice 1949, I, p. 404.

84 Annual Practice, 1949, I, p. 458.

85 Alabama provides that two nonsuits are equivalent to a verdict for the defendant (Ala. Code 1940, Tit. 7, § 254) and Minnesota and North Dakota that there may be no second dismissal without the defendant's written consent or an order of court on notice and cause shown. Minn. Stat. 1945, § 546.39; N.D. Code 1943, § 28-0801.

ates as an adjudication upon the merits when filed by a plaintiff who has once dismissed in any court of the United States or of any state an action based on or including the same claim." (Rule 41 (a) (1)).

The federal pattern has been accepted by Arizona (1939, 1949), Colorado (1941), Delaware (1947), New Jersey (1948) and Utah (1949), and for the most part by New Mexico (1942, 1949). For common-law actions it has been followed by Florida (1949), and to a large extent by Maryland (1941).[86]

[86] Ariz. Code Ann. 1939, and 1949 Cum. Supp. to Vol. II, § 21-915, 21-917, 21-918; Colo. Rules Civ. Proc., Rule 41 (a) (c) (d), in Colo. Stat. Ann. 1935, Replacement Vol. I, 1941; Del. Rules of Superior Court, Rule 41 (a) (c) (d), Rules of Court of Chancery, Rule 41 (a) (c) (d); N.J. Rules Civ. Pract., Rules 3:41-1, 3:41-3, 3:41-4; Utah Rules Civ. Proc., Rule 41 (a) (c) (d); Fla. Common Law Rules, Rule 35 (a) (c) (d); N.M. Stat. Ann. 1941, and 1949 Cum. Supp. to Vol. II, § 19-101 (41) (a) (c) (d); Md. Gen. Rules Pract. & Proc., Part 3, Subd. III, Rule 1, in Md. Ann. Code (Flack, 1939) Cum. Supp. 1947, pp. 2049-50.

Chapter XVIII
MODE OF TRIAL

§ 1. Waiver of Jury Trial

Apart from the survival of certain of the older methods of trial,[1] never applicable to other than special situations and already substantially obsolete in the 1700s, decision of issues of fact by a judge unaccompanied by a jury, with or without the consent of the litigants, was something to which the common law gave no place. In England, the Common Law Procedure Act of 1854 first made it possible for the parties in the superior courts to waive a jury by consent and commit the decision of fact-issues to the judge alone, this, however, only when the court or judge "should think fit to allow such trial." [2] In America the right to waive jury trial in common-law actions generally was given recognition at a much earlier day, although its beginnings are obscure. It came to definite acknowledgement by the Supreme Court of the United States in 1819.[3] In the federal system, however, it was long hampered, until legislation came to the rescue,[4] by the artificial rule, drawn from the inexistence of the right at common law, that a judgment based upon decision of the issues of fact without a jury could not be reviewed on writ of error.[5] In New York the right seems to have been first admitted for certain inferior tribunals, but, by the Constitution of 1846, it was declared that

[1] *Viz.*, trial by inspection, by certificate, or *per testes:* see 3 Blackstone, Commentaries, * 331 *et seq.*

[2] 17 & 18 Vict. c. 125, § 1. By the act of 1846 establishing the new County Courts it had been provided that trial of issues of fact was to be by the judge, subject to the right of either party to require jury trial on demand, where the amount of the claim exceeded £ 5 and to the discretionary power of the judge to order jury trial where less than such amount was claimed. 9 & 10 Vict. c. 95, §§ 69-71.

[3] Bank of Columbia v. Okely, 4 Wheat. (17 U.S.) 235, 244 (1819).

[4] For this legislation, see 3 Moore's Federal Practice (1938) 3026-3027.

[5] Guild v. Frontin, 18 How. (59 U.S.) 135 (1855); Campbell v. Boyreau, 21 How. (62 U.S.) 223 (1858); Flanders v. Tweed, 9 Wall. (76 U.S.) 425 (1869).

"a jury trial may be waived by the parties in all civil cases in the manner prescribed by law." [6] Pursuant to this authority the Code of 1848 provided that the waiver might be effected (a) by failing to appear at the trial, (b) by written consent or (c) by oral consent in open court [7]—a provision which in 1849 was amended so as to require the assent of the court in other than actions on contract.[8] In its amended form, with or without some variation, this provision has had a wide following in the code States. Today the rule is universal throughout the United States that waiver of jury trial is permissible, assent of the court being called for or not according to the particular regulation. Effectuation of the waiver finds itself differently governed in different jurisdictions. Many of the code States adhere to provisions patterned upon the New York Code of 1849; and such provisions may or may not be construed as excluding a waiver unmistakably evidenced in some other manner;[9] more and more there has been coming into favor the simple rule, which found early enunciation in the Iowa Code of 1851,[10] that unless a party demands trial by jury, the trial will be by the court. To a very considerable extent this is the canon now followed in New York.[11] It is the canon obtaining throughout in numerous other State jurisdictions, and the one adopted by the new Federal Rules. Usually the demand is to be made in writing, but in at least one jurisdiction (Texas)[12] it must be advanced in open court. There is no uniformity as to the time of the demand; sometimes it is to be made at the filing of complaint or appearance; sometimes at a specified later stage of the cause before trial. In regulating this matter of waiver the Federal Rules, in respect of any issue triable by jury as of right, provide for a demand in writing to be served not later than ten days after the service of the last pleading directed to the issue sought to be tried, and declare that the failure to serve and file such demand constitutes a waiver of

[6] Art. I, § 2.

[7] N.Y. Code of 1848, § 221.

[8] N.Y. Code of 1849, § 266.

[9] Not so construed in New York. Baird v. Mayor etc. of New York, 74 N.Y. 382, (1878).

[10] Iowa Code 1851, § 1772.

[11] N.Y. Civ. Pract. Act (Clevenger, 1950) § 426.

[12] Tex. Rules Civ. Proc. (Vernon, 1942) Rule 216.

trial by jury. (Rule 38(b) (d)). When demand is thus made, the trial must be by jury, unless the parties otherwise consent or the court finds that the right to jury trial is inexistent. In the absence of demand, the court nevertheless has discretion to order a jury trial. (Rule 39(a) (b)). These federal provisions, with or without some variation, have been copied in Arizona, Colorado, Delaware and Utah.[13]

The necessity of an explicit demand as a condition of jury trial has done much toward diminishing the incidence of that mode of trial. But in a large number of jurisdictions resort to the jury has been much more definitely discouraged by requiring the demanding party to pay or deposit a special jury fee. And with slight exception it is held that such a measure is one of competent regulation and therefore does not contravene the constitutional right to jury trial.[14]

Supplementing earlier reference to the latter-day regulation of civil jury trial in England,[15] it should be here mentioned that except for the power given by the Rules of 1883 to dispense with a jury in any matter "requiring any prolonged examination of documents or accounts, or any scientific or local investigation" which cannot conveniently be made with a jury, the right to jury trial in common-law actions remained on its former basis until 1918. It was then cut down to the small group of cases directly to be noted in connection with legislation of 1933, but in 1925 was restored to its previous ambit. Apart from the exception introduced by the short-lived New Procedure Rules (1932-1937),[16] the right so stood until the Administration of Justice (Miscellaneous Provisions) Act of 1933,[17] which resumed the 1918 restriction. Then in 1939,

13 Ariz. Code Ann. 1939, §§ 21-908, 21-910, 21-911, 21-912; Colo. Rules Civ. Proc., Rules 38(b) (d), 39(a) (b), in Colo. Stat. Ann. 1935, Replacement Vol. I, 1941; Del. Rules of Superior Court 1947, Rules 38(b) (d), 39(a) (b); Utah Rules Civ. Proc. 1949, Rules 38(b) (d), 39(a) (b).

14 See note, 32 A.L.R. 865.

15 *Supra,* Chapter VII, p. 68.

16 For the New Procedure Rules, see Ball, The New Procedure Rules 1932, Annotated and Explained (1932) 16; Millar, A Septennium of English Civil Procedure, 1932-1939 (1940) 25 WashingtonUniv.L.Q. 525-527.

17 (1918) 8 & 9 Geo. V, c. 23, § 1; (1920) 10 & 11 Geo. V, c. 78, § 3; (1933) 23 & 24 Geo. V, c. 36, § 6. And see Jackson, The Incidence of Jury Trial During the Past Century (1937) 1 Modern L.Rev. 132, 139 *et seq.*

under the stress of the war emergency, the right altogether disappeared for the time being; jury trial was not to be awarded "unless the court or a judge is of opinion that the case ought to be tried by jury." [18] But, pursuant to an Order in Council, this provision ceased to operate as of April 1, 1947,[19] and the right to jury trial is again governed by the act of 1933, under which it exists where, on application by any party, "the court or a judge is satisfied that (a) a charge of fraud against that party; or (b) a claim in respect of libel, slander, malicious prosecution, false imprisonment, seduction or breach of promise of marriage, is in issue . . . unless the court or a judge is of opinion that the trial thereof requires any prolonged examination of documents or accounts or any scientific or local investigation which cannot be conveniently made with a jury"; otherwise the award of a jury rests in the judicial discretion.[20] By the Rules of 1875 the party to avail himself of the right of jury trial was required to give notice to that effect,[21] and, under varying legislation, claim of this mode of trial has since been essential to its award.[22]

§ 2. Modifications of the Jury as a Trial Body

Although provision is commonly made for a jury of less than twelve in courts of inferior or limited jurisdiction, retention of the common-law number is the general American rule for the ordinary civil procedure. But departures exist. Thus Florida [23] provides for a jury of six and Utah [24] for a jury of eight in all civil cases, while Virginia [25] declares for a jury of five where a value of less than $300 is involved and of seven in all other cases. So, also, there is encountered provision for a jury of six with the right of either party to increase the number to twelve upon paying an additional jury fee.[26] And various forms of provision occur authorizing deviation from the pre-

[18] 2 & 3 Geo. VI, c. 78, § 8(1)(2).

[19] Addenda to Annual Practice 1946-47.

[20] 23 & 24 Geo. V, c. 36, § 6(1).

[21] 38 & 39 Vict. c. 77, First Schedule, O. XXXVI, rr. 3, 4.

[22] See O. XXXVI, rr. 1, 6; Annual Practice 1949, I, pp. 622, 630.

[23] Fla. Stat. 1949, § 54.14.

[24] Utah Code Ann. 1943, § 48-0-5.

[25] Va. Code 1942, § 6012; Va. Code Ann. 1950, § 8-193.

[26] *E.g.*, Colo. Rules Civ. Proc. 1941, Rule 48.

scribed number by agreement of the parties. An unusual instance of the kind is the Virginia statute permitting by consent a jury of three persons, one chosen by each of the parties and the third selected by the two thus chosen.[27]

More extensive departure from the common law is apparent when it comes to the number of jurors necessary to a verdict. The common-law rule of unanimity has been abandoned in many quarters, in favor of a designated majority concurrence. Most of the jurisdictions thus proceeding have settled on a majority of three-fourths,[28] although a considerable number have provided for a five-sixths majority.[29] The latter is the rule recently adopted in New York and New Jersey.[30] One jurisdiction at least (Montana) fixes the necessary majority at two-thirds.[31] Texas, while not subscribing to a majority verdict in general, provides that in case of the disability of any of the jurors selected, a verdict may be returned by the others if as many as nine remain competent to act.[32]

Both the departure from unanimity and from the common-law number come about under the terms of the State constitutions. Neither is possible in the federal system, since the Seventh Amendment forbids.[33] It should be added that, just as in the case of deviation from the prescribed size of the jury, numerous provisions are to be found in the State statutes authorizing and regulating the return of a verdict by less than the whole number of jurors pursuant to consent of the parties.

Of late years there has been widespread adoption of means to prevent the necessity of declaring a mistrial in case one or

[27] Va. Code, *loc. cit.*

[28] Ariz. Code Ann. 1939, § 21-1003; Cal. Code Civ. Proc. (Deering, 1949) § 618; Idaho Code Ann. 1947, §§ 2-104, 10-217; Ky. Rev. Stat. 1948, § 29.330; La. Code Pract. (Dart, 1942) § 527; Miss. Code Ann. 1942, § 1801; Mo. Rev. Stat. Ann. 1942, § 719; Ohio Gen. Code Ann. (Page, 1938) § 11420-9; Okla. Const. Art. II, § 19; Ore. Const. Art. VII, § 5 [18]; Utah Code Ann. 1943, § 104-24-27.

[29] Minn. Stat. 1945, § 546.17; Neb. Rev. Stat. 1943, § 25-1125; N.M. Stat. Ann. 1941, § 19-101(48)(b); Wash. Rev. Stat. (Remington, 1932) § 358; Wis. Stat. 1949, § 270.25.

[30] N.Y. Laws 1937, c. 120, N.Y. Civ. Pract. Act (Clevenger, 1950) § 463-a; N.J. Laws 1948, c. 120, N.J. Stat. Ann. 1939, Cum. Pocket Part 1949, §§ 2:27-233.1 to 233.4.

[31] Mont. Const. Art. III, § 23.

[32] Tex. Rules Civ. Proc. (Vernon, 1942) Rule 292, from Rev. Civ. Stat. (Vernon, 1936) Art. 2204.

[33] American Publishing Co. v. Fisher, 166 U.S. 464, 17 S.Ct. 618 (1897); Thompson v. Utah, 170 U.S. 343, 350, 18 S.Ct. 620 (1898).

more of the jurors should die or become incapacitated in the course of the trial—a necessity productive of unfortunate consequences where the trial has already consumed much time. The shortest cut to a remedy would be to allow the remaining jurors to render a verdict if there is left a specified majority of the original members, as is contemplated by the Texas provision. This, however, is not constitutionally possible where a unanimous verdict is required, and does not appear to have commended itself to those jurisdictions constitutionally permitting a designated majority verdict. Accordingly, the means in question have usually taken the form of provision for the selection of alternate jurors to sit with the regular jury and hear the trial proceedings, so that any vacancy in the regular jury caused by misfortune can be filled forthwith and the trial proceed without other interruption. Commonly the authority given is for the selection of one or two alternates as the court may deem proper, but there is also encountered provision for the definite selection of two and sometimes, again, of one only. With the precedent, therefore, of many State enactments of the kind, as well as that of the federal statute of 1932[34] applicable to criminal causes, the Federal Rules of 1938 have adopted this method of proceeding by means of alternate jurors. They provide that "the court may direct that one or two jurors in addition to the regular panel be called and impanelled to sit as alternate jurors. Alternate jurors in the order in which they are called shall replace jurors who, prior to the time the jury retires to consider its verdict, become unable or disqualified to perform their duties . . . An alternate juror who does not replace a principal juror shall be discharged after the jury retires to consider its verdict." Accompanying are provisions placing the alternates on the same basis as the regular panel as to their drawing, qualifications and the like, as well as awarding to each party an additional peremptory challenge for use only as against the alternates. (Rule 47(b)). In this form the measure has been followed by Arizona (1939), Florida (1939), Delaware

[34] 47 Stat. 380.

(1947) and Utah (1949), and in the main by Colorado (1941).[85]

A different mode of providing like remedy had its introduction in Michigan,[86] and has since been adopted in Massachusetts and New Jersey.[87] This consists in giving the court authority to impanel at the outset a jury of not to exceed fourteen persons, who sit together and hear the cause. Envisaging the possibility of some circumstance occasioning the removal of any of the jurors, the relative measures, despite certain differences in phrasing, establish the rule that if, in any event, more than twelve are left at the time when the case is to go to the jury, then there are drawn by lot from this group (in Massachusetts excepting the foreman) the names of one or two, as the case may be, so as to reduce the jury to twelve persons who become the deliberating and deciding body. This method, which has so far weathered constitutional objection,[88] deserves more extensive acceptance. For it offers a very decided superiority over the method of proceeding by alternates. In the latter the strong probability always is against occasion arising to call any of the alternates into service, and these, in consequence, are not likely to give the same degree of attention to the evidence as if they felt from the outset the responsibility of regular jurors. In the Michigan method, on the other hand, each one of the fourteen has the same chance as any of the others of becoming part of the jury of decision, all are equally charged with responsibility until the close of the judge's charge, and there is no factor operating to lessen the degree of attention on the part of any one of them during the progress of the trial.

[85] Ariz. Code Ann. 1939, § 21-938; Fla. Stat. 1949, § 54.15 (adopted by Laws 1939, c. 19030, § 1; Del. Rules of Superior Court (1947) Rule 47(b); Utah Rules Civ. Proc. (1949) Rule 47(b); Colo. Rules Civ. Proc. (1941) Rule 47(b).

[86] Mich. Stat. Ann. 1938, § 27-1071. This method made its first appearance for criminal cases. *Ibid.* § 28-1041. In 1935 it was adopted for criminal cases in New Jersey. N.J. Stat. Ann. 1939, §§ 2:91-A1 to 2:91-A3.

[87] Mass. Laws 1945, c. 428, § 1, 8 Mass.Ann.Laws 1933, Cum. Supp. 1949, c. 234, § 26B; N.J. Rules Civ. Pract. 1948, Rule 3:47-2.

[88] State v. Dollow, 117 N.J.L. 560, 189 Atl. 915 (1937), supporting by a majority vote the New Jersey criminal provision; Com. v. Bellino, 320 Mass. 635, 71 N.E.2d 411 (1947), upholding the Massachusetts statute.

In England there has been no departure from the requirement of unanimity in the verdict. Nor has there been adoption of any measure comparable to the selection of alternate jurors; usually in case of death or disability there is consent to proceed with the remaining jurors. In point of number, the emergency legislation of 1939 provided that where a jury was allowed, it need not consist of more than seven persons."[39] But under the Order in Council terminating this legislation, the jury has reverted to its common-law number since January 1, 1948.[40]

§ 3. Trial of Equity Causes and Issues

In two of the American jurisdictions—Georgia[41] and Texas[42]—the basic rule of the classic chancery procedure which assigned to the judge the decision of fact, as well as of law, has never obtained; in two others—Tennessee[43] and North Carolina[44]—although originally obtaining, it has been set aside. In these jurisdictions either party is entitled to demand a jury trial of equity issues of fact with the same binding force attaching to the verdict as in the case of common-law issues. In a fifth jurisdiction—Arizona—it has been held that the State constitution (adopted in 1912) gave an absolute right of jury trial to either party in equity as well as common-law causes, but did not prevent establishment of the rule, especially under a statute of 1921, that as to equity causes, the verdict should be an advisory one.[45] In 1939, as part of an extensive following of the Federal Rules of 1938, there was adopted a provision cor-

[39] 2 & 3 Geo. VI, c. 78, § 7(1).

[40] Addenda to Annual Practice 1946-47.

[41] *Ex parte* Grimball, T. U. P. Charlton, 153, 155 (1808); Hargraves v. Lewis, 3 Ga. 162 (1847); Nell v. Snowden, 5 Ga. 1 (1848); Ga. Code 1933, § 37-1101 *et seq.*

[42] Tex. Const. Art. V, § 10.

[43] By statute in 1846: see James v. Brooks, 6 Heisk. (53 Tenn.) 150 (1871). Excepted are matters of complicated accounting and cases under special statutory provisions. Tenn. Code Ann. (Williams, 1934) §§ 10574, 10579.

[44] As a result of the Constitution of 1868: see Lee v. Pearce, 68 N.C. 80 (1873); Worthy v. Shields, 90 N.C. 192 (1884); Wilson v. Bynum, 92 N.C. 717 (1885). And see also N.C. Const. Art. I, § 19, Art. IV, §§ 1, 13; N.C. Gen. Stat. 1943, § 1-172.

[45] Ariz. Const. Art. 2, § 23; Brown v. Greer, 16 Ariz. 215, 141 Pac. 841 (1914); Mounce v. Wightman, 30 Ariz. 45, 243 Pac. 916 (1926); Donahue v. Babbit, 26 Ariz. 542, 227 Pac. 995 (1924).

responding to Federal Rule 39, which embodies the principle of the discretionary advisory jury for equity issues. This notwithstanding, the State continues to exhibit the anomaly of an advisory verdict demandable of right.[46]

Elsewhere there obtains the traditional canon of trial by the court, subject here and there to statutory exceptions for special cases.[47] But as the English chancellor always had the power to direct an issue for jury trial as a means of aiding in the decision of the cause, this also has become the general American rule. In the old practice the direction was effectuated by a so-called "feigned issue"; that is to say, through the medium of an action of assumpsit, instituted in a court of law, upon a fictitious contract of wager as to the existence of the fact in question, with the verdict of the jury certified back to the Court of Chancery. This mode of proceeding, however, has everywhere been replaced either by the direct certification of the issue for common-law trial or else, and especially in those jurisdictions ceasing to maintain the divided administration of law and equity, by the submission of the issue to a jury sitting with the court of the cause. In the classic system, while the court in its decree very generally followed the jury's verdict, it was not bound to do so: the verdict was advisory only. Such continues to be the rule in most of the American jurisdictions. But in a small minority including Massachusetts,[48] Connecticut,[49] New Hampshire [50] and Minnesota,[51] although the court is free to direct or not an equitable issue to be tried by jury, the

[46] Ariz. Code Ann. 1939, §§ 21-907 *et seq.*, 21-1010. See Brooks v. Brooks, 60 Ariz. 119, 132 Pac.2d 431 (1942). And see also Clark, Handbook of the Law of Code Pleading (2d ed. 1947) 98, note 59.

[47] Apart from the case of exceptions relating to particular actions, there is to be noted the peculiar provision obtaining in Virginia (Va. Code 1942, § 6121; Va. Code Ann. 1950, § 8-213) and West Virginia (W.Va. Code Ann. 1949, § 5610) by which either party is entitled to jury trial of an issue of fact arising under a chancery plea as distinguished from an answer. Here the verdict is binding, which is not true in these jurisdictions of the verdict on ordinary issues out of chancery.

[48] Crocker v. Crocker, 188 Mass. 16, 73 N.E. 1068 (1905).

[49] Conn. Gen. Stat. 1947, § 7974; Conn. Pract. Book 1934, Rule 15, §§ 152, 153, pp. 57, 58. *Cf.* Nowsky v. Siedlecki, 83 Conn. 109, 113, 75 Atl. 135 (1910); Dzubin v. Dzubin, 121 Conn. 646, 186 Atl. 652 (1936).

[50] Berry v. Merrill, 85 N.H. 525, 161 Atl. 34 (1932).

[51] First Nat. Bank of Lakefield v. Quevli, 182 Minn. 238, 234 N.W. 318 (1931).

verdict of the latter, in point of conclusiveness, stands on the same footing as in actions at law. The federal courts succeeded both to the power to direct jury trial in equity cases and to the principle that its verdict was no more than advisory. Under the fused procedure of the new Rules, however, the matter has undergone some re-regulation. With power in the court to direct trial by jury in any case where it is not a matter of right, the advisory principle is made applicable to all such cases, unless the court, by consent of the parties, orders, as it may do except when, in an action against the United States, a statute provides for trial without a jury, that the verdict shall have the same effect as in jury trial of right. (Rule 39(c)). Arizona (1939), Colorado (1941), New Mexico (1941), Delaware (1947), New Jersey (1948) and Utah (1949) have adopted corresponding provisions.[52]

By a rather remarkable coincidence the modern English development seems to have come to the same result as that small minority of American jurisdictions noted above, in departing from the principle of advisory verdict. The Chancery Amendment Act of 1858 [53] displaced the old device of feigned issues by making it lawful for the Court of Chancery to cause any question of fact "to be tried by a special or common jury before the court itself," and rendering the "powers, jurisdiction and authority" of the court in that regard the same as those of a common-law court. This was supplemented by an act of 1862,[54] which authorized the direction of any such issue for trial in a common-law tribunal, if convenience should so dictate, the determination being otherwise governed by the provisions of the preceding statute. And now, under the Rules of the Supreme Court, as they have existed since 1875,[55] while

[52] Ariz. Code Ann. 1939, § 21-913; Colo. Rules Civ. Proc., Rule 39(c); N.M. Stat. Ann. 1941, § 19-101(39)(c); Del. Rules of Superior Court, Rule 39(c); N.J. Rules Civ. Pract., Rule 3:39-1; Utah Rules Civ. Proc., Rule 39(c). As regards Arizona the statement here included from the Federal provision that "in all actions not triable of right by a jury the court . . . may try any issue with an advisory jury" does not seem to adjust itself happily to the situation in that State where, as before seen, trial by jury is constitutionally of right in equity causes, although the verdict is but advisory.

[53] 21 & 22 Vict. c. 27, §§ 3, 4.

[54] 25 & 26 Vict. c. 42, §§ 2, 3.

[55] 38 & 39 Vict. c. 77, First Schedule, O. XXXVI, r. 27; present O. XXXVI, r. 3.

it is always open to the court to direct trial by jury of a cause, or of an issue in a cause, assigned to the Chancery Division, it does not appear that a verdict thus reached has any different effect from a verdict in a common-law action. There is no explicit statement on the point, but the act of 1858 would seem to stand in the way of regarding the verdict as merely advisory. By the present practice, when jury trial is thus directed it does not occur in the Chancery Division: the cause or issue is transferred for trial to the King's Bench Division.[56]

That other basic rule of the classic chancery system, which prescribed that evidence should be taken in writing, had little claim to survival as against the superior advantages of oral testimony in open court, and accordingly retains small foothold in the Anglo-American systems. In England, the original practice of taking such evidence in secret on written interrogatories gave way, under the Chancery Practice Amendment Act of 1852,[57] to that of oral examination by or before examiners at the instance of either party, or if neither party desired so to proceed, to that of evidence by affidavit, with the affiants subject to oral cross examination and re-examination by or before an examiner and to re-examination on behalf of the party filing the affidavit. The old rule of secrecy was relaxed to the extent of providing that the examination in all cases should be had "in the presence of the parties, their counsel, solicitors or agents." This method continued in force[58] until the Judicature Acts, when by the Rules of 1875 there was established the present principle that subject to certain exceptions, including a limited use of affidavit evidence, the witnesses in all civil cases "shall be examined *viva voce* and in open court."[59] In the United States the change to oral evidence has an older history. For the federal system the Judiciary Act of 1789[60] provided "that the mode of proof by oral testimony and examination of witnesses in open court" should obtain in equity causes. But this rule "ceased in 1802 to be an absolute one

[56] Annual Practice 1949, I, pp. 629, 630-631.

[57] 15 & 16 Vict. c. 86, § 28 *et seq.*

[58] See Birrell, Changes in Equity, Procedure, and Principles, in A Century of Law Reform (1901) 190, 195.

[59] 38 & 39 Vict. c. 77, First Schedule, O. XXXVII, r. 1; present O. XXXVII, r. 1.

[60] § 30, 1 Stat. 88.

except in certain districts . . . ; it mostly failed of observance, was in effect superseded in 1842, and underwent repeal in 1874."[61] Except by agreement of the parties, the old method of written interrogatories was followed until 1861, when the Supreme Court by rule definitely substituted the method of oral examination before an examiner—a provision qualified in 1893 by enabling the court to permit the evidence in whole or in part to be adduced orally in open court on final hearing.[62] But it was left to the Equity Rules of 1912[63] to effectuate the change sought by the act of 1789, in finally establishing as a general rule that "in all trials in equity the testimony of witnesses shall be taken orally in open court." And with the fused administration of law and equity under the new Rules, the provision now is that in all trials the testimony shall be so taken unless otherwise provided in the Rules. (Rules 43(a)). In contrast to the federal tardiness stands the case in most of the State jurisdictions. The New York constitution of 1846 opened the way for the uniformity in the matter of trial prescribed by the Code of 1848 by declaring that "the testimony in equity cases shall be taken in like manner as in cases at law."[64] With the spread of the code its uniformity of trial procedure necessarily called for oral testimony in open court as the general rule for all civil actions. But apart from jurisdictions of the fused procedure, there was early adoption of the change, either as a mandatory general method (thus Massachusetts, 1852[65]) or as a method available to the parties (Michigan, 1846[66]; Illinois, 1849[67]). Today, under varying regulations, it is commonly the case in the jurisdictions of divided administration, that resort may be had to oral testimony in open court, at least as an alternative mode of pro-

[61] Millar, *Ficta Confessio* as a Principle of Allegation in Anglo-American Civil Procedure (1928) 23 Ill.L.Rev. 215, 235 note 93, citing 2 Street, Federal Equity Practice (1909) § 1625 *et seq.*

[62] 2 Street, *op. cit.* § 1627.

[63] Rule 46.

[64] Art. VI, § 10.

[65] Mass. Laws 1852, c. 312, § 85, "unless the court for special reasons shall otherwise direct"; Parker v. Nickerson, 137 Mass. 487 (1884).

[66] Mich. Rev. Stat. 1846, c. 90, § 57, p. 362; 1 Mich. Laws 1869, p. 381; Enslow v. Township of Albion, 27 Mich. 4 (1873).

[67] Ill. Laws 1849, p. 133.

ceeding, even though, as in Alabama[68] and Virginia,[69] this may occur only on the direction of the court, or, as in Tennessee,[70] either on such direction or by consent of the litigants, or, as in West Virginia,[71] by agreement and leave of court. A few jurisdictions there are, however, that maintain a closer adherence to the older method, usually effectuable through oral examination before a master, commissioner or examiner.

§ 4. Administration of the Issues

Except for the special form of procedure obtaining in the action of account,[72] the common-law trial was a trial of the issues *en bloc;* with but slight qualification, separate trial of different jury issues in the same action was not admissible.[73] In chancery, on the other hand, although normally the issues in chief were dealt with together, the flexible character of the procedure and the absence of a jury left the court free to deal with the issues in such manner as it deemed most expedient. But in the current of modern reform along with the necessity of separating jury from non-jury issues, occasioned by the administrative fusion of law and equity, the matter of separating issues along other lines has come to express regulation either as incident to other procedural changes or as directly dictated by considerations of utility. Apart from its implicit separate trial of legal and equitable issues, nothing on the point appears in the New York Code of 1848, save the provision that, where a jury trial was not required, the

[68] Ala. Code 1923, § 6574, succeeded by Equity Rule 56, Ala. Code 1940, Tit. 7, p. 1094.

[69] Va. Code 1942, § 6228a; Va. Code Ann. 1950, § 8-310.

[70] Tenn. Code Ann. (Williams, 1934), Cum. Pocket Supp. to Vol. VI, 1949, § 10564.

[71] W.Va. Code Ann. 1949, § 5672.

[72] In account the normal jury issue was the question of liability to account. If that was determined in favor of the plaintiff, there followed the interlocutory judgment of *quod computet,* after which the cause was sent to auditors to take and state an account. But in the case of a disputed question of fact arising before the auditors the issue was certified for jury determination. See Locke v. Bennett, 7 Cush. (61 Mass.) 445, 447 (1851).

[73] The qualification concerns only the case where the plaintiff's action was met in part by dilatory defense, in part by defense in bar, as where there was a dilatory plea to one count of the declaration and a plea in bar to another, or where one of several defendants pleaded a dilatory plea and the other or others pleaded in bar.

court might nevertheless order the issues, or "any specific question of fact involved therein, to be tried by a jury." [74] The Iowa Code of 1851 seems to have initiated legislation in the present regard by providing that in the case of united causes of action, "the court, to prevent confusion therein, may direct all or any portion of the issues joined therein to be tried separately," [75] and that in any case the court in its discretion might allow "a separate trial between the plaintiff and any or all of several defendants." [76] Similar to the second of these provisions was that added in the same year to the New York Code, which spoke of "a separate trial between a plaintiff and any of the several defendants." [77] By the Revision of 1860, the Iowa law went decidedly further, providing that "where in any controversy there are several issues," the court was authorized to direct the separate trial of all or any of such issues.[78] This might well have been followed in New York also. Instead, the New York Code of 1876, as amended in 1877, contained the provision that "a separate trial, between the plaintiff and one or more defendants, of some or all of the issues of fact, or one trial of some or all of the issues of law, or a change in the order of disposition of the issues, may be directed by the court, in its discretion." [79] That this was regarded as applying only to the case of a plurality of defendants would seem to be evidenced by the enactment in 1907 of a provision permitting the court in its discretion to "order one or more issues to be separately tried prior to any trial of the other issues in the case." [80] The results thus reached in the two jurisdictions in question substantially obtain in their present-day legislations.

The Iowa and New York provisions are the repository upon which other code jurisdictions, so far as they expressly regulate the present matter, have generally drawn. In these, however, there has been but little resort to a full-dress provision to the effect that any or all of the issues in any cause may

[74] N.Y. Code 1848, § 209.
[75] Ia. Code 1851, § 1751.
[76] *Ibid.* § 1768.
[77] N.Y. Laws 1851, c. 479, amd'g § 258, Code of 1849.
[78] Ia. Revision 1860, § 3025.
[79] N.Y. Laws 1877, c. 416, amd'g § 967, Code of 1876.
[80] N.Y. Laws 1907, c. 526, adding § 973.

be separately tried.[81] More common is the provision for separate trials in the case of a plurality of defendants. Provision for separate trial of united causes of action finds scattering place in the American jurisdictions generally—and here is to be recalled its association with liberalized rules of joinder [82]—as does provision directed to the separate trial of counterclaims. But absence of legislation in this field is no criterion of the actual procedure, for, quite independently of statute or rule, the courts frequently exercise the power of separating issues for trial, even on the common-law side of divided jurisdictions. Without statutory aid, this practice, for example, has been upheld in Virginia [83] and New Hampshire [84] in respect of common-law trials. And before the recent Federal Rules the Supreme Court of the United States had itself conceded the propriety of so proceeding "in exceptional instances where there are special and persuasive reasons" for departing from the traditional common-law practice.[85]

One of the cogent considerations impelling exercise of such a power is that, where there are several defenses, the establishment of one may suffice to bring the action to an end, and thus avoid the necessity of entering upon the others. This, in jurisdictions permitting dilatory and peremptory defenses to be pleaded together, leads to provisions enabling the court to direct that the dilatory defenses be tried first.[86] This, too, has prompted the California statute of 1939, providing for the separate and preliminary trial of certain special defenses set up in the answer, namely, the defenses of the statute of limitations, prior judgment, or another action pending, or (as it is rather inaccurately put) "any other defense not involving the merits of the plaintiff's cause of action, but constituting a bar thereto or ground of abatement to the prosecution thereof." [87] But it is obvious that the part of wisdom lies in

[81] But see, *e.g.,* Mo. Rev. Stat. Ann. 1942, § 1102.

[82] See *supra,* Chapter X.

[83] Dixon Livery Co. v. Bond, 117 Va. 656, 86 S.E. 106 (1915).

[84] Owen v. Weston, 63 N.H. 599 (1885).

[85] Miller v. American Bonding Co., 257 U.S. 304, 308, 42 S.Ct. 98 (1921).

[86] Wis. Stat. 1949, § 270.07(2); Ill. Civ. Pract. Act 1933, § 43(3), Ill. Rev. Stat. 1949, § 167(3).

[87] Cal. Code Civ. Proc. (Deering, 1949) § 597.

expressly bestowing on the court a general discretionary power with relation to any or all of the issues such as was ultimately done in the Iowa and New York legislations and under their influence in some of the other code jurisdictions. Sweepingly of this character is the power of the court in the modern English procedure, where, since the Rules of 1875, there has governed the general provision, subject to the right of the party to jury trial, so far as this has obtained, and to some exceptions elsewhere appearing, that "the court or a judge may, in any cause or matter, at any time or from time to time, order that different questions of fact arising therein be tried by different modes of trial, or that one or more questions of fact be tried before the others." [88] And the Federal Rules of 1938, followed by Pennsylvania (1938), Arizona (1939), Colorado (1941), New Mexico (1942), Maryland (1947), Delaware (1947), New Jersey (1948) and Utah (1949)[89] have inevitably taken the same direction of comprehensive authorization by providing that "the court in furtherance of convenience or to avoid prejudice may order a separate trial of any claim, cross-claim, counterclaim, or third-party claim, or of any separate issue or of any number of claims, cross-claims, counterclaims, third-party claims, or issues." (Rule 42(b)).

With the presence in the same cause of both legal and equitable issues the matter of administration (except in those few jurisdictions which give the right of jury trial as to both) extends to the determination of the mode of trial. Here, in the light of procedural tradition and the constitutional preservation of jury trial, the basic notion manifestly is that the one sort should be tried by jury and the other sort by the court, and this obvious allocation sometimes comes in differing form

[88] 38 & 39 Vict. c. 77, First Schedule, O. XXXVI, r. 6; present O. XXXVI, r. 7. The text of the latter is the same as that of the 1875 Rule, except that, as designative of the question of fact, "in any cause or matter" has been substituted for "in any action."

[89] Pa. Rules Civ. Proc., Rule 213(b), in Pa. Stat. Ann. (Purdon, 1931) Appendix to Tit. 12, 1949 Cum. Pocket Part; Ariz. Code Ann. 1939, § 21-290; Colo. Rules Civ. Proc., Rule 42(b); N.M. Stat. Ann. § 19-101(42)(b); Md. Gen. Rules Pract. & Proc., Part 2, Subd. III, Rule 5, Md. Ann. Code (Flack, 1939) Cum. Supp. 1947, p. 2043; Del. Rules of Superior Court, Rule 42(b), Rules of Court of Chancery, Rule 42(b); N.J. Rules Civ. Pract., Rule 3:42-2; Utah Rules Civ. Proc., Rule 42(b).

to particular statutory expression.[90] But application of the idea is not always easy, since it becomes complicated by a variety of considerations, including the difficulty of assigning a particular issue to one class or the other, the relation in which a given issue stands to others, and the manner in which the issue arises. The commonest situations in which this duality of issues makes it appearance are where there is a union of legal and equitable demands in the complaint, where an equitable defense or counterclaim is pleaded to a legal demand, and where a legal defense or counterclaim is interposed in an equitable action. In the first of these situations, whether the conjoined legal and equitable claims arise out of the same or different sets of facts, the rule usually followed, consonant with the basic notion, accords to each of the parties a right to jury trial as to the legal claim, leaving the equitable claim to trial by the court. But in the case of origination in the same set of facts, this rule finds frequent qualification. Thus in New York, and in at least one other jurisdiction, where both claims are in respect of the same wrong, the plaintiff by uniting them, is taken to have lost his right of jury trial as to the legal claim, although the defendant's right to that mode of trial remains unaffected.[91] Elsewhere, in such a case, it is very often sought, by surveying the complaint as a whole, to characterize it as legal or equitable, by the application of variously worded tests, and grant or withhold jury trial, according as its legal or equitable aspect appears to be in the ascendant.[92] Where the situation is that of an equitable defense to a legal demand, there is a clearer-cut diversity of view. In New York and a few other States an equitable defense, so long as it can be treated purely as a defense, stands on the same footing as any

[90] See, *e.g.*, Ind. Stat. Ann. (Burns, 1933), Replacement Vol. II, 1946, § 2-1204; Conn. Gen. Stat. 1947, § 7936; Wis. Stat. 1949, § 270.07(1).

[91] Di Menna v. Cooper & Evans Co., 220 N.Y. 391, 115 N.E. 993 (1917); Cogswell v. New York, New Haven & Hartford RR. Co., 105 N.Y. 319, 11 N.E. 518 (1887) (claims in respect of the same *cause of action*); Dunlap v. Seattle Nat. Bank, 93 Wash. 568, 161 Pac. 364 (1916) (similarly speaking of *cause of action*). See further Ehrle v. Sutton Place Apartments, 137 Misc. 122, 241 N.Y.S. 386 (1930).

[92] As in Towns v. Smith, 115 Ind. 480, 16 N.E. 811 (1888); State *ex rel.* v. Wm. Cameron & Co. Inc., 147 Okla. 1, 294 Pac. 104 (1930); Norback v. Board of Directors, 84 Utah 506, 37 Pac.2d 339 (1934).

other defense and the issues thereunder go to the jury.[93] But here enters the chimerical distinction between the presentation of the obstacle to recovery by way of defense, on the one hand, and by way of counterclaim on the other. If, under the local procedure it is properly presented by counterclaim, then it falls outside the rule and is a matter of equitable cognizance, with the issues triable by the court.[94] In by far the most jurisdictions, however, the rule is otherwise: all equitable defenses, as such, as well as all equitable counterclaims are governed, in respect of the relative issues, by the equity manner of trial.[95] And nowhere is there dissent in the case of the equitable counterclaim. In the further situation above noted, that of a legal defense or counterclaim advanced against an equitable demand, the preponderant voice denies any right to a jury trial.[96] But admission of the right is not rare, as a matter of reasoning from general premises, especially when the issue is one involving title to land; [97] and here, again, New York stands apart from most of its sister jurisdictions, since it gives statutory recognition to that right, in respect of any admissible counterclaim advancing a legal demand which could have been the subject of a separate action.[98] Under the new Federal Rules there is no waiver of jury trial by inclusion in the complaint of a claim for equitable relief. The provision of Rule 38(b) is explicit that any party "may demand a trial by jury of any issue triable of right by a jury," and Rule 38(c) declares that he may in his demand "specify the issues which he wishes so

[93] Susquehanna Steamship Co. v. A. O. Anderson & Co. Inc., 239 N.Y. 285, 146 N.E. 381 (1925); Gill v. Pelkey, 54 OhioSt. 348, 360, 43 N.E. 991 (1896). Clark, Handbook of the Law of Code Pleading (2d ed. 1947) 104 note 76, refers to this exceptional rule as obtaining also in Missouri and Minnesota. See also note, Ann. Cas. 1913D, 168.

[94] In the Susquehanna case the distinction is sought to be made according as the matter does or does not require an affirmative judicial pronouncement for the defendant's "complete protection." But, as has been pointed out, the defendant is sufficiently protected in such cases by sustaining the defendant's claim as a defense: the affirmative judicial pronouncement is "a mere idle ceremony." Cook, Equitable Defenses (1923) 32 Yale L.J. 645, 653-654. And see Clark, *op. cit.* 105 note 77, 625-627; *id.* Trial of Actions under the Code (1926) 11 Corn. L.Q. 482, 493 *et seq.*

[95] Clark, Handbook *cit.* 105-110.

[96] Notes, Ann. Cas. 1914C, 852; 89 A.L.R. 1391.

[97] See, *e.g.*, Capell v. Moses, 36 S.C. 559, 15 S.E. 711 (1892); Pankey v. Ortiz, 26 N.M. 575, 195 Pac. 906 (1921).

[98] N.Y. Civ. Pract. Act (Clevenger, 1950) § 424.

tried; otherwise he shall be deemed to have demanded trial by jury for all the issues so triable." And while the Rules contain no express statement on the point, it is clear that an issue presented under an equitable defense or an equitable counterclaim interposed against a legal demand continues to be governed by the former federal rule [99] applicable to the case of equitable defenses, and is for decision by the court. On the other hand, where a legal counterclaim is advanced in an equitable action, the provision in question, like the New York statute, unmistakably gives the right to jury trial as to the legal issues arising thereunder.[100] Of the federal provisions just mentioned both have been followed by Arizona (1939), Colorado (1941), Delaware (1947) and (with minor adaptation of Rule 38(b)) Utah (1949), while Rule 38(c) finds reproduction in New Mexico (1942).[101]

Accompanying the separation of the issues for trial, whether so expressed in the relative legislation or not, is the authority to determine the order in which they are to be tried. As between legal and equitable issues, priority is ordinarily given to the latter. Thus a Connecticut rule of court provides that, where some of the issues are put to the jury, the remaining issues are to be tried first, unless the court otherwise directs.[102] So, too, in the case of equitable defenses the Supreme Court of the United States has expressed the view that these should be disposed of before proceeding to others,[103]—a proper measure where, as in most cases, the sustaining of the equitable defense would bring the suit to an end.[104] But it is obvious that the determination cannot be regulated by any hard and fast rule. The relation of the issues to each other and to the cause as a whole must here always be the touchstone, and the application of this must ultimately be left to the judicial discretion. And, if the court should choose to submit both the legal and

[99] Liberty Oil Co. v. Condon Nat. Bank, 260 U.S. 235, 43 S.Ct. 118 (1922).

[100] Judson v. Buckley (S.D.N.Y.) 31 Fed.Supp. 246 (1940).

[101] Ariz. Code Ann. 1939, §§ 21-908, 21-909; Colo. Rules Civ. Proc., Rule 38(b) (c); Del. Rules of Superior Court, Rule 38(b) (c); Utah Rules Civ. Proc., Rule 38(b) (c); N.M. Stat. Ann. 1941, § 19-101(38)(c).

[102] Conn. Pract. Book 1934, Rule 15, § 149, p. 57.

[103] Liberty Oil Co. v. Condon Nat. Bank, *supra*.

[104] As in Ross v. Service Lines, Inc. (E.D. Ill.) 31 Fed.Supp. 871 (1940).

equitable issues to the jury as might well be the case, particularly where their identification as of one or the other class is in doubt, that discretion will permit it to do so, and, except in the few jurisdictions where the jury result would be binding in its entirety, to treat the ensuing verdict on the equitable issues as advisory only.[105]

In England questions arising from the presence of legal and equitable issues in the same cause, do not seem to have been of frequent occurrence. Under the Judicature Acts certain causes are assigned to the respective Divisions of the High Court. Accordingly it has been held in substance that, if in an action instituted in the Chancery Division the plaintiff unites with his equitable claim a legal demand or the defendant interposes a legal counterclaim, the question of allowing a jury trial of the legal demand, even though under the existing rule he would have had a clear right to jury trial, had he asserted that demand by way of independent action, becomes a matter for the judicial discretion.[106] As to equitable defenses to common-law demands it is to be noted that when these were first introduced by the Common Law Procedure Act of 1854, it does not appear that these defenses were dealt with, as a matter of trial, any differently from other defenses. Nor does the general practice under the Judicature Acts seem to have been otherwise, despite the undoubted power of the court under the Rule before quoted to provide for the separate trial of an equitable issue without a jury. And on this point it is important to notice that the provision of the Administration of Justice Act of 1933,[107] admitting the right of jury trial only in respect of a charge or claim in a limited class of cases—a provision which again controls after cessation of the war emergency suspension of the right—expressly declares that this shall be without prejudice to the power of the court or judge under the Rules in reference to the trial by different modes of different questions of fact arising in an action, and

105 See Fed. Reserve Bank v. Idaho Grimm Alfalfa Seed Growers' Association (C.C.A. 9) 8 Fed.2d 922 (1925). Cert. denied 270 U.S. 646, 46 S.Ct. 347 (1926).

106 Gardner v. Jay, 29 C.D. 50 (1885); Lynch v. MacDonald, 37 C.D. 227, C.A. (1887); Kinnaird v. Field [1905] 2 Ch. 361, C.A.; Annual Practice 1949, I, pp. 628-629.

107 23 & 24 Geo. V, c. 36, § 6.

that the requirement of trial by jury "shall have effect only as respects questions relating to any such charge or claim."

§ 5. References

At common law the action of account, in the sending of the cause to auditors to take and state an account, furnishes the only instance there of what may be spoken of as a reference, and this, as before appearing,[107a] was not a reference involving the trial of any issue of fact. The early history of American procedure, however, discloses certain instances of a widened power, in this regard, of the common-law courts. One was parcel of the development in New England of the peculiar action of book account or book debt. In this action, the introduction of which is ascribed to acquaintance with a similar proceeding made in Holland, on the part of some of the early colonists,[108] the parties were permitted to testify, contrary to the rules of the common law, but what particularly interests us here is that there was no jury trial on the merits: the cause was referred for trial to one or more auditors, upon whose report, when approved, the court entered judgment.[109] Subject to this manner of trial, the action obtains today in Connecticut and Vermont.[110] The same desire of simplifying decision led Massachusetts in 1817 to establish a qualified mode of reference in common-law actions generally where there was involved "an investigation of accounts or an examination of vouchers." Here there was no displacement of jury trial, but the report of the auditors was to be "given in evidence to the jury, subject, however, to be impeached by evidence from either party." [111] The procedure thus adopted not only remains in force, and in a notably broadened form in the State of its

107a *Supra,* note 72.

108 "The action in book account is founded in a kind of moral necessity. . . . The principles of it, I believe, were introduced into this country from Holland, by the first settlers of New England." *Per* Brainard, J., in Beach v. Mills, 5 Conn. 494, 497 (1825). "It is supposed that the substitute of this form of action was brought to New England by a dissenting English minister from Holland, not long after the arrival of the pilgrims." McLaughlin v. Hill, 6 Vt. 20, 26 (1834).

109 Hall v. Armstrong, 65 Vt. 421, 26 Atl. 592 (1893).

110 Conn. Gen. Stat. 1949, §§ 7936, 8168 *et seq.;* Reiley v. Torkomian, 78 Conn. 649, 63 Atl. 516 (1906); Vt. Stat. 1947, § 1948; Hall v. Armstrong *supra.*

111 Mass. Laws 1817, c. 142; Holmes v. Hunt, 122 Mass. 505, 513, 520 (1877).

origin,[112] but, as presently to be seen, has been strongly influential elsewhere, especially in the federal system. A further instance of departure from common-law method, which, curiously enough, resembles the proceeding in book account, in being apparently traceable to the law of Holland, appears in New York. There tradition of the method employed during the Dutch régime prompted enactment in 1768 of a statute authorizing the court, where the trial of a cause would probably "require the examination of a long account, either on one side or the other," to refer the cause to referees whose report, if confirmed, would become the basis of judgment, thus without any resort to jury trial. And, with some slight interruption, this statutory rule continued to prevail in substance during the pre-code period of the New York procedure.[113]

As opposed to the situation at common law stood the extensive power of the High Court of Chancery to call upon its masters and other officers for assistance in adjudication and to refer to them a great variety of matters for hearing and report. To the power thus exercised, whatever may be the case in particular code jurisdictions, have succeeded those jurisdictions in which the administration of law and equity remains divided in whole or in part. Accordingly the master has been "usually employed to take and state accounts, to take and report testimony and to perform such duties as require computation of interest, the value of annuities, the amount of damages in particular cases, the auditing and ascertaining of liens upon property involved, and similar services." [114] By the general rule it is not competent for the court to refer to a master the general hearing on all the issues without the consent of the parties,[115] but in some jurisdictions statutes exist under which such a general reference is authorized independently of the parties' consent.[116]

In New York's organization of the code procedure it was but natural that this should continue in some form the State's

[112] Mass. Ann. Laws 1933, c. 221, § 56.

[113] Steck v. Colorado Fuel & Iron Co., 142 N.Y. 236, 238-240, 253-254, 37 N.E. 1 (1894).

[114] Kimberly v. Arms, 129 U.S. 512, 523, 9 S.Ct. 355 (1889).

[115] *Ibid.* 524.

[116] See R.I. Gen. Laws 1938, c. 528, § 17; Vt. Stat. 1947, § 1935; Ill. Civ. Pract. Act 1933, § 61, Ill. Rev. Stat. 1949, c. 110, § 185.

time-honored rule as to references in case of accounts. Hence, in addition to permitting references in all cases with the consent of the parties, the Code of 1848, as revised in 1849, provided[117] that, without the consent of the parties, unless the investigation would require the decision of difficult questions of law, the court may "direct a reference in the following cases: (1) where the trial of an issue of fact shall require the examination of a long account on either side;[118] in which case the referees may be directed to hear and decide the whole issue, or to report upon any specific question of fact involved therein; or (2) where the taking of an account shall be necessary for the information of the court, before judgment, or for carrying a judgment or order into effect; or (3) where a question of fact, other than upon the pleadings, shall arise, upon motion or otherwise, in any stage of the action." This provision, with variation here and there but without basic change, became in consequence the standard one in most of the code jurisdictions. In certain of these, including California, Minnesota, Nebraska and Idaho, it was held unconstitutional, as an infringement of the right of jury trial, so far as regards causes in which that right had existed. In the majority, however, it has been supported.[119] Another question which has arisen is whether the statutory provision is exclusive in the sense that it divests the court of its power of directing references in equity causes other than those coming within its terms.[120] This question New York answered in the affirmative, it being declared that neither in equitable nor in legal actions "can a compulsory reference be ordered unless the trial will require the examination of a long account."[121] And the greater number,

[117] Code of 1848, § 226; Code of 1849, § 271.

[118] See the limitation placed upon this provision in its subsequent New York history. Steck v. Colorado Fuel & Iron Co., *supra*.

[119] Russell v. Alt, 12 Idaho 789, 88 Pac. 416 (1907), and note, 13 L.R.A. (N.S.) 146.

[120] Note, 126 A.L.R. 314.

[121] Thayer v. McNaughton, 117 N.Y. 111, 114, 22 N.E. 562 (1889). The court adds that "in equity actions the reference may be of the whole issues, or any one of them, or to report upon specific questions of fact." The distinction thus made between legal and equitable actions resulted from the recasting of the original provision by the Code of 1876-1877 (Code Civ. Proc. § 1013): see Barnes v. West, 16 Hun 68 (1878). The recast provision has been carried into the present law. Civ. Pract. Act, § 466.

perhaps, of the code jurisdictions take the same view.[122] No doubt this accords with the intention of the original framers of the provision, but, to speak only of New York, if the equity power had been retained, it would, in considerable part, have rendered unnecessary the detailed provisions respecting references for particular purposes appearing in the present statutes and rules. The minority view, on the other hand, allows the court to exercise the traditional equity power alongside that conferred by the statute. It should be added that a few of the code States, instead of adhering to the original New York model, proceed on a basis, at once broader and narrower, by simply providing for the compulsory reference for trial of the issues in any cause not triable by jury.[123]

The Massachusetts statute of 1817 was speedily copied by Maine (1821) [124] and New Hampshire (1823).[125] In later years it set the pattern for variously expressed legislation in a large number of other jurisdictions, including Texas,[126] Michigan,[127] New Jersey,[128] Mississippi,[129] West Virginia,[130] Geor-

122 See note, 126 A.L.R. 314.

123 Ohio Gen. Code Ann. (Page, 1938) § 11476; Wyo. Comp. Stat. Ann. 1945, § 3-2502.

An anomalous manner of reference obtains in North Carolina, where the right of jury trial extends to equity causes. It is provided that a compulsory reference may be directed in three cases corresponding to those of the original New York provision, and in matters involving a complicated question of boundary or requiring a personal view of premises, as also in equity causes. The statute, however, declares that the reference "does not deprive either party of his constitutional right to a trial by jury of the issues of fact arising on the pleadings, but such trial shall be only upon the written evidence taken before the referee." N.C. Gen. Stat. 1943, § 1-189. Under this practice the referee's findings cannot go to the jury. Bradshaw v. Hilton Lumber Co. 172 N.C. 219, 90 S.E. 146 (1916). And it is held that "a party who would preserve his right to a jury trial in a compulsory reference must object to the order of reference at the time it is made, and on the coming in of the report of the referee, if it be adverse, he should seasonably file exceptions to particular findings of fact made by the referee, tender appropriate issues on the facts pointed out in the exceptions and raised by the pleadings, and demand a jury trial on each of the issues thus tendered." Marshville Cotton Mills, Inc. v. Maslin, 200 N.C. 328, 329, 156 S.E. 484 (1931). One would be disposed to think that at this rate the party earns his right to jury trial.

124 Howard v. Kimball, 65 Me. 308, 327 (1876).

125 Perkins v. Scott, 57 N.H. 55, 77 (1876).

126 Tex. Rev. Civ. Stat. (Vernon, 1936) Art. 2292, dating from 1846; Tex. Rules Civ. Proc. (Vernon, 1942) Rule 172.

127 Mich. Stat. Ann. 1938, §§ 27.1056, 27.1061, dating from 1846.

128 N.J. Stat. Ann. 1939, §§ 2:27-178, 2:27-179.

129 Miss. Code. Ann. 1942, § 1541.

130 W.Va. Code Ann. 1949, § 5685.

gia [181] and the District of Columbia,[182] confined, as the archetype originally was, to matters of account.[183] But in Massachusetts, itself, the institution, in the course of time, took on a wider scope. In 1856, by a separate provision, the proceeding was made applicable to actions of contract, tort or replevin for report by the auditor or auditors "upon such matters therein as may be directed" by the court. The two provisions were subsequently combined so as to permit the appointment of one or more auditors "to hear the parties, examine their vouchers and evidence, state accounts, and report upon such matters therein as may be ordered by the court," and this, it is now provided, may be done in any civil action.[184] In this process of amendment, also, the original provision that the report was to be "subject to impeachment" before the jury was re-phrased so as to make it "*prima facie* evidence" in that connection.[185] Thus it had become a general means calculated "to relieve the courts from making personal examination of details and to simplify and elucidate the issues to be tried," [186] and as such, is today widely applied even to some extent in cases involving the negligent operation of motor vehicles.[187]

Besides leading to adoption of statutes in other jurisdictions restricted to matters of account, the Massachusetts statute in

[181] Ga. Code, 1933, §§ 10-102, 10-402 *et seq.*

[182] D.C. Code 1940, §§ 16-102, 16-103; Eichberg v. U.S. Shipping Bd. Emergency Fleet Corporation, 51 App. D.C. 44, 273 Fed. 886 (1921). Here the statute has become of small importance in view of the larger opportunity afforded by the Federal Rules.

[183] A provision of this type was included in the Illinois Practice Act of 1907 (§ 69—Laws 1907, p. 457) but was superseded in 1933 by a provision of the Civil Practice Act permitting reference without jury trial in "any action at law in which matters of account are in controversy" (Civ. Pract. Act, § 61; Ill. Rev. Stat. 1949, c. 110, § 185), the validity of which still remains to be determined.

The manner of statute mentioned in the text was declared unconstitutional in Rhode Island (Francis v. Baker, 11 R.I. 103 (1875), and in Vermont the same result had been reached in respect of a similar statute not restricted to matters of account. Plimpton v. Town of Somerset, 33 Vt. 283 (1860).

[184] Mass. Gen. Stat. 1860, c. 121, § 46; Holmes v. Turner's Falls Co., 150 Mass. 535, 538-540, 23 N.E. 305 (1890); Mass. Rev. Laws 1901, c. 165, § 55; Mass. Ann. Laws 1933, c. 221, § 56.

[185] Mass. Gen. Stat. 1860, c. 121, § 46. The change was apparently made in the light of Allen v. Hawks, 11 Pick. (28 Mass.) 358 (1831).

[186] Lorell v. Commonwealth Thread Co., 280 Mass. 243, 246, 182 N.E. 364 (1932).

[187] See Cook v. Farm Service Stores, Inc., 301 Mass. 564, 17 N.E. 2d 890 (1938).

its broader aspect has had a pronounced influence upon the federal procedure. In *Ex parte Peterson,*[138] decided by the United States Supreme Court in 1920, a federal district court, sitting in New York, had, in an action at law upon a contract, with a contract counterclaim pleaded, appointed an auditor "to make a preliminary investigation as to the facts; hear the witnesses; examine the accounts of the parties, and make and file a report . . . with a view to simplifying the issues for the jury; but not to finally determine any of the issues in this action; the final determination of all issues of fact to be made by the jury on the trial." Over challenge, the court upheld the validity of this order in an interesting opinion by Mr. Justice Brandeis, in which reference is made to the Massachusetts origin and development of the practice in question. "The report," it said, "will, unless rejected by the court, be admitted at the jury trial as evidence of facts and findings embodied therein; but it will be treated, at most, as *prima facie* evidence thereof." [139] For the federal system, it noted, the Seventh Amendment stands in the way of a compulsory reference with power to determine the issues, "but no reason exists why a compulsory reference to an auditor to simplify and clarify the issues and to make tentative findings may not be made at law, when occasion arises, as freely as compulsory references to special masters are made in equity. . . . The inherent power of a federal court to invoke such aid is the same whether the court sits in equity or at law." [140] This decision, therefore, in no sense confining the ambit of such a reference to matters of account, opened the way for the broad reception of such a proceeding in the new Federal Rules. Accordingly, in their regulation of references to masters (under which term as here used are included referees, auditors and examiners) the Rules provide that:

> A reference to a master shall be the exception and not the rule. In actions to be tried by a jury, a reference shall be made only when the issues are complicated; in actions to be tried without a jury, save in matters of account, a reference shall be made only

[138] 253 U.S. 300, 40 S.Ct. 543 (1920).

[139] Pp. 310-311.

[140] P. 314.

> upon a showing that some exceptional condition requires it. (Rule 53(b)).

And, with respect to the the master's report in jury cases, they declare:

> In an action to be tried by jury the master shall not be directed to report the evidence. His findings upon the issues submitted to him are admissible as evidence of the matters found and may be read to the jury, subject to the ruling of the court upon any objections in point of law which may be made to the report. (Rule 53(e)(3)).

These provisions textually or substantially have entered into the recent reforms in Arizona (1939), Colorado (1941), New Mexico (1942) and Utah (1949).[141] So, too, this regulation of the evidentiary effect of the master's findings has been given place in New Jersey (1948).[142] It is clear that, whether by a close following of the federal provisions or not, the particular modification of jury trial which we have been discussing, with the prestige of the Federal Rules behind it, is destined to a larger place than it now occupies in the State jurisdictions generally.

It has been noticed that the standard code provisions permit references for trial in all civil actions by consent of the parties. And there is probably no American jurisdiction in which statute or rule does not admit in some form of the same manner of reference. It was formerly the federal doctrine that the master's findings of fact on a consent reference in equity were entitled to greater weight than on a compulsory reference.[143] But this doctrine has been discarded by the Rules of 1938 in the provision that "the effect of a master's report is the same whether or not the parties have consented to the reference." (Rule 53(e)(4)).[144] Under the rule more usually

141 Ariz. Code Ann. 1939, §§ 21-1102, 21-1109; Colo. Rules Civ. Proc., Rule 53(b), (e)(3); N.M. Stat. Ann. 1941, § 19-101(53)(b), (e)(3); Utah Rules Civ. Proc., Rule 53(b), (e)(3).

142 N.J. Rules Civ. Pract., Rule 3:53-5(c).

143 Kimberly v. Arms, 129 U.S. 512, 524, 9 S.Ct. 355 (1889).

144 Followed in Ariz. Code Ann. 1939, § 21-1110; Colo. Rules Civ. Proc., 1941, Rule 53(e)(4); N.M. Stat. Ann. 1941, § 19-101(53)(e)(4); N.J. Rules Civ. Pract. (1948) Rule 3:53-5(d); Utah Rules Civ. Proc., Rule 53(e)(4).

followed in the American jurisdictions, a reference for trial of the issues, no less than any other reference, contemplates a report of the officer which has no vitality until confirmed by the court: on this manner of reference, therefore, judgment follows only when directed by the court after its approval of the report. But in a number of the code States, by a rule proceeding from the original New York Code,[145] the report of a referee to hear and determine the issues as a whole requires no confirmation: it "stands as the decision of the court," and judgment follows as upon such decision. Thus, under the existing New York practice, the filing of the report, except in special cases, authorizes immediate entry of judgment, as the report directs, by the clerk of the court.[146]

In England the basic regulation of the matter of references is contained in the Consolidated Judicature Act of 1925.[147] Subject to rules and to any right of jury trial, section 88 of the Act permits references for inquiry and report in respect of any question arising in any cause or matter. Section 89 deals with references for trial and authorizes such a reference, in respect of the whole cause or matter or any question or issue of fact arising therein, to a special referee or arbitrator agreed upon by the parties or to an official referee or officer of the court, under any one of three conditions. These are "(*a*) if all the parties interested who are not under disability consent: or (*b*) if the cause or matter requires any prolonged examination of documents or any scientific or local investigation, which cannot in the opinion of the Court or a judge be conveniently made before a jury or conducted by the Court through its other ordinary officers: or, (*c*) if the question in dispute consists wholly or in part of matters of account." The effect of the officer's report under this section resembles that under the New York practice: the report is "equivalent to the verdict of a jury," and, subject to the terms of the order of reference, the officer has the same power to direct that a judgment be entered as a judge of the court.[148] From his judg-

[145] N.Y. Code 1848, § 227.

[146] N.Y. Civ. Pract. Act (Clevenger, 1950) § 470; N.Y. Rules Civ. Pract. (*ibid.*) Rule 198.

[147] 15 & 16 Geo. V, c. 49.

[148] *Ibid.* § 90(2); O. XXXVI, r. 50; O. XL, r. 2; Annual Practice 1949, I, p. 666.

ment an appeal lies, differently regulated, according to the kind of referee and the Division of the court in which the reference has occurred. In the case of a special referee the appeal goes to the judge only in the Chancery Division; in the other two Divisions it goes to a Divisional Court.[149] But where the judgment is one directed by an official referee then, by statute, the appeal, lying on a point of law only, goes directly to the Court of Appeal.[150]

149 O. LIXA, r. 2.

150 Administration of Justice Act 1932, 22 & 23 Geo. V, c. 55, § 1; Annual Practice 1949, I, p. 1373.

Chapter XIX
TRIAL BY JURY

§ 1. Examination of Jurors on the Voir Dire

What strikes most forcibly the American lawyer who attends an English jury trial is the absence of any preliminary examination of the prospective jurors,[1] for the purpose of ascertaining whether or not there is ground for challenge, such as in some form he has been accustomed to in his home jurisdiction. Yet both systems have in their background the common-law rule in reference to examination of jurors on the *voir dire*. This rule, however, contemplated in strictness such as examination only after a challenge had been interposed and in support of the challenge, and the extent of examination permitted was of a decidedly circumscribed character. The books, nevertheless, are not precisely voluble on the subject. All that Coke says is that "if the cause of challenge touch the dishonor or discredit of the juror, he shall not be examined upon his oath, but in other cases he shall be examined upon his oath, to informe the triors." [2] And Blackstone contents himself with a paraphrase of the same statement in saying that "a juror may himself be examined on oath of *voir dire, veritatem dicere,* with regard to such causes of challenge as are not to his dishonour or discredit; but not with regard to any crime, or anything which tends to his disgrace or disadvantage." [3] As to the scope of interrogation the leading case at common law is that of *Peter Cook,* tried for high treason

[1] There is the same absence in the Canadian provinces. For Ontario, note the observations of Mr. Justice Riddell in Rex v. Harri, 69 D.L.R. 647, 648 (1922): "No, you cannot question him, you can challenge for cause, and the matter will then be tried, but you cannot question a juryman. We have no such system as obtains in some of the American courts . . . We have never introduced into this Province the practice which seems to be common in the United States; we have followed the English practice."

[2] Co. Litt. 158b.

[3] 3 Blackstone, Comm. * 364. The triors were the two persons appointed to try the fact in the case of a challenge to the favor—a practice which is still recognized in England and to some extent in a few of the American jurisdictions.

in 1696. Here it was ruled that, while previous expression of belief in the prisoner's guilt would be a good ground of challenge if independently proved, the juror, himself, might not be asked as to such expression, this for the reason, strange as it may appear to us today, that such a prejudgment would show "a scandalous misbehaviour . . . not fit to be required to be disclosed." In answer to the contention that a juror might be asked "any question that does not make him guilty of any offence or crime, or liable to any punishment," it was said by Lord Chief Justice Treby: "You may ask upon a *Voyer Dire* whether he have any interest in the cause; nor shall we deny you liberty to ask whether he be fitly qualified, according to law, by having a freehold of sufficient value; but that you can ask a juror or a witness every question that will not make him criminous, that is too large." Mr. Justice Powell, however, was of opinion that such a question might be asked in a civil case.[4] In 1821 the rule thus laid down disallowing such a question in a criminal case, was reaffirmed by the King's Bench, on motion for new trial, in *King* v. *Edmonds,*[5] an indictment for conspiracy.

Although in *Peter Cook's Case,* the question referred to, as well as certain questions permitted to be answered, were put before any formal challenge was made, and some indication of the same thing appears elsewhere in the State Trials,[6] it is clear that these instances involved departure from established rule, for the statement of Coke plainly implies that any examination shall be after challenge,—and this deviation was definitely discountenanced in the later practice. The necessity of precedent challenge is expressly recognized by the Jurors Act of 1825[7] which, referring to a challenge for matter of general disqualification, declares that "the person so challenged shall and may be examined, on oath of the truth of the said matter." In *King* v. *Edmonds, supra,* while the report of the trial does not disclose a challenge before the putting of the questions, the court, on the motion for new trial, speaks

[4] 13 How. State Trials, 311, 344-346 (1696), *sub nom.* Anon. 1 Salk. 153, 91 E.R. 141.

[5] 4 B. & Ald. 471; 1 State Trials (N.S.) 785 (1821).

[6] See Trial of Francis Francia, 15 How. State Trials, 898 (1717).

[7] 6 Geo. IV, c. 50, § 50.

of "what has been called a challenge . . . made on the ground of opinions" etc. of whose expression "it was proposed to obtain the proof, by questions put to the jurymen themselves." [8] More explicitly the challenge is insisted upon in *Queen* v. *Stewart* (1845).[9] There counsel for the prisoner, charged with larceny from a tradesman, sought to inquire of each juror whether he was a member of a certain association for the prosecution of those committing frauds upon tradesmen. Alderson, B., declined to permit it, saying: "It is quite a new course to catechise a jury in this way . . . I cannot allow you to cross-examine the jury . . . If you like to challenge absolutely you may do so." So, also, in *Regina* v. *Dowling* (1848),[10] counsel for the prisoner having asked that one of the jurors be sworn on the *voir dire* in order that he might be examined "with a view to a challenge, if necessary," Earle, J., refused the application, considering it to be "a very unreasonable thing that a juryman should be cross-examined, without your having received any information respecting him." It is from these cases that we must discover the warrant for the English practice, for civil cases on the subject seem to be completely lacking. Whatever differences may have existed as to the range of questioning between civil and criminal cases, it is perfectly plain, notwithstanding the informality appearing in the case of Peter Cook and to some extent elsewhere in the State Trials, that the common-law rule provided for no preliminary examination in advance of challenge, and that such *voir dire* examination of jurors as was permitted occurred only after challenge and in support of challenge.

In the modern English practice challenges continue to be possible, but very seldom are interposed,[11] and only in the rare

[8] At p. 490 of 4 B. & Ald.

[9] 1 Cox C. C. 174 (1845).

[10] 3 Cox C. C. 509 (1848)

[11] "In selecting the jury in the English courts, the challenge of a juror is almost as rare as the challenge of a judge in the United States. A chairman of quarter sessions said to us, when questioned on the subject: 'I have been on the bench for six years —3,300 indictable offenses are tried in my court in a year—I remember only two or three challenges in my life, and not one during the last three years.' We talked to more than one practitioner at the criminal bar who acknowledged that he had never seen a juror challenged for any reason, either by the Crown or by the defense.' Lawson and Keedy, Criminal Procedure in England (1910) 1 Jour. Am.Inst.Cr.Law&Criminology 595, 609. Professor Lawson, co-author of the article just cited is referred to as say-

event of a challenge can there be any *voir dire* examination of the juror. As a basis for any challenge the party is obliged to rely upon such outside information as he can obtain, the list of jurors being always accessible to him in advance. The theory today is the same as stated by Peake at the opening of the nineteenth century, in his work on Evidence: "The pannel," he says, "is made out and known to the parties long before the trial; they have an opportunity of inquiring as to the characters and course of life of the persons named in it; and if they find anything which destroys the competency of a juror, they may be prepared to prove it." [12]

There can be no doubt that the common-law rule excluding the *voir dire* examination except in support of a definite challenge was that which at first usually prevailed in the United States.[13] The fact above noted of some precedent for irregular preliminary questioning may have aided in its displacement, but the democratizing influences of the early and middle 1800s had undoubtedly much to do with the change. In any event it came to be accepted in most of the American jurisdictions, whether on the theory of a constructive challenge or not,[14] that a preliminary questioning of the jurors on the *voir dire,* for the purpose of ascertaining whether a challenge would be in order, was a definite right of the parties. And along with this change there was usually recognized a much wider field of inquiry than was permitted at common law. That revolution in the latter regard was well on its way at an early day is sufficiently attested by the trial of Aaron Burr in 1807, where Chief Justice Marshall had no difficulty in allow-

ing on another occasion that "he was informed by one of the judges that only one instance of a challenge had come under his observation during a period of fourteen years." Editorial by J. W. G. in the same volume of the journal cited, at pp. 533-534. Such being the case in criminal proceedings, it can be imagined how much rarer challenges are in civil actions. And see R. D. Moore, Voir Dire Examination of Jurors—The English Practice (1928) 16 Georgetown L.J. 438, 449 *et seq.*

[12] Peake, Evidence (ed. of 1808) *134 (Am. ed. 1812) 141.

[13] See *e.g.,* State v. Baldwin, 1 Treadw. (S.C.) 289 (1813); State v. Flower, Walker (1 Miss.) 318 (1829); King v. State, 5 How. (6 Miss.) 730, 734 (1841); State v. Creasman, 10 Ired. L. (N.C.) 395, 397 (1849); Crippen v. People, 8 Mich. 117, 126 (1860).

[14] See People v. Larubia, 69 Hun 197, 23 N.Y.S. 579 (1893); People v. Rendigs, 123 Misc. 32, 46, 205 N.Y.S. 133, 145 (1924).

ing extensive examination of jurors as to their previous opinion of the guilt of the accused.[15] But the preliminary examination prior to challenge did not everywhere attain with ease its present-day prevalence. Thus in New Jersey it was not until a statute of 1911 that the old rule was discarded in civil cases; [16] here, however, it continues even now to be followed in criminal cases other than prosecutions for murder.[17] So, also, in Alabama [18] and Minnesota,[19] we find long persistence of the old rule, though qualified by the holding that the court might in its discretion permit the pre-challenge examination; it was left, however, for comparatively recent legislation (Alabama (1923); [20] Minnesota (1927)[21]) to make such examination a right of the parties.

In a number of jurisdictions the statute defines the questions that may be put on the preliminary examination. Thus in Massachusetts it was provided by a statute, dating in substance from 1807,[22] that "the court shall on motion of either party in a suit, examine on oath a person who is called as a juror therein, to learn whether he is related to either party, or has any interest in the cause, or has expressed or formed an opinion, or is sensible of any bias or prejudice therein; and the party objecting to the juror may introduce any other competent evidence in support of the objection." In 1887 this was amended so as to include the provision that alternatively the "examination may be made by the parties or their attorneys under the direction of the court," [23] and as thus amended continues in force.[24] But the amendment has not altered the prac-

15 Trial of Aaron Burr, ed. Robertson, Vol. I (4 *Causes célèbres,* 1875) p. 406 *et seq.*

16 Lamble v. State, 96 N.J.L. 231, 114 Atl. 346 (1921); N.J. Stat. Ann. (1939) § 2:92-4.

17 State v. Calabrese, 107 N.J.L. 115, 151 Atl. 781 (1930); State v. Burns, 135 N.J.L. 386, 52 Atl.2d 160 (1947); N.J. Stat. Ann. (1939) § 2:92-10; N.J. Rules Crim. Pract. 1948, Rule 2:7-2(b).

18 Bales v. State, 63 Ala. 30 (1879); Kansas City, Memphis & Birmingham RR. Co. v. Whitehead, 109 Ala. 495, 19 So. 705 (1895); Jarvis v. State, 138 Ala. 17, 34 So. 1025 (1903).

19 State v. Smith, 56 Minn. 78, 57 N.W. 325 (1894).

20 Ala. Code 1940, Tit. 30, § 52; Ala. Code 1923, § 8662. See Mays v. State, 218 Ala. 656. 120 So. 163 (1929); Nix v. City of Andalusia, 21 Ala.App. 439, 109 So. 182 (1926).

21 Minn. Stat. 1945, §§ 546.10, 631.26; Minn. Laws 1927, c. 281.

22 Mass. Pub. Stat. 1882, c. 170, § 35: see 2 Mass.Gen.Laws to 1822 (1823) c. 140, § 9, p. 190.

23 Mass. Laws 1887, c. 149.

24 Mass. Gen. Laws 1932, c. 234, § 28; 8 Mass.Ann.Laws 1933, and Cum. Supp. 1949, c. 234, § 28.

tice under the statute. The questions are usually put by the court and confined to those of the statute. Other questioning remains in the court's discretion, and this discretion, as said *per* Mr. Justice Holmes, "is exercised wisely by not going beyond the usual questions, unless something appears which makes it proper to go further." [25] Certainly the party is not given "the right to submit the juror to an inquiry in the nature of a cross-examination, in order to ascertain if he could not elicit something tending to show bias or prejudice on the part of the juror." [26] With some textual variation the provision in its original Massachusetts version appears elsewhere, notably in Maine,[27] Rhode Island,[28] South Carolina [29] and Virginia.[30] In all these jurisdictions the duty of questioning is thus devolved upon the court. In West Virginia [31] the statute similarly defining the questioning provides that "either party in any action or suit may and the court shall on motion of such party" conduct the examination. All agree on the three heads of relationship, interest and bias, as subjects of the examination, but Virginia and West Virginia are silent as to the matter of previous opinion, and the latter includes ascertainment of "whether he is a qualified juror." It is apparent that a provision of the kind, for its effect in saving time and preventing unnecessary interrogation depends upon the mode of its administration, since if the statutory enumeration is looked upon merely as designating heads of inquiry and not as indicating the particular mode of questioning, the widest sort of inquiry might be allowable. Whatever may be the actual practice elsewhere under these statutes, Massachusetts furnishes an impressive example of close delimitation of the field of inquiry

[25] Com. v. Poisson, 157 Mass. 510, 512, 32 N.E. 906 (1893). To the same effect: Com. v. Cero, 264 Mass. 264, 162 N.E. 349 (1928).

[26] Com. v. Burroughs, 145 Mass. 242, 243, 13 N.E. 884 (1887).

[27] Me. Rev. Stat. 1844, c. 100, § 102.

[28] R.I. Gen. Laws 1938, c. 506, § 35.

[29] S.C. Code 1942, § 637.

[30] Va. Code 1942, § 6000; Va. Code Ann. 1950, § 8-199. The provision also appears in Wisconsin, but with a proviso thoroughly calculated to neutralize its salutary operation, namely, that nothing which it contains "shall be construed as abridging in any manner the right of either party in person or through his attorneys to examine any person so called in regard to his qualifications as fully as if this section did not exist." Wis. Stat. 1947, § 270.16.

[31] W.Va. Code Ann. 1949, § 5646.

under firm judicial control of the examination, from which other jurisdictions might usefully profit.

More commonly, however, there is no statutory provision regulative of the examination, and in the State jurisdictions, although occasionally the actual practice may not differ widely from that of Massachusetts,[32] it is most commonly true that the questioning is left to the parties. The extent to which the court may interfere and itself question the jurors varies greatly, and sometimes is of a limited character. Thus in the leading Illinois case on the subject, where the trial court declined to permit examination except "through the mouth of the court," this was held to be error. It was said that while the court may also examine the jurors if it sees fit, "such reasonable examination by counsel should always be allowed as will enable the court to see that the jurors stand indifferently between the parties and are possessed of the requisite qualifications, and also to enable counsel to challenge for cause, if cause exists, or to exercise the right of peremptory challenge, when in their judgment it is deemed necessary or advisable." [33]

In the federal courts, on the other hand, there has been uniformly recognized a greater measure of judicial control over the examination. The practice has differed in different districts, being more or less influenced by the local State practice, but conduct of the examination by the court itself has been sufficiently common. In October, 1924, the Conference of Senior Circuit Judges made the explicit recommendation that "examination of prospective jurors shall be by the judge alone. If counsel on either side desires that additional matter be inquired into, he shall state the matter to the judge, and the judge, if the matter is proper, shall conduct the examination." [34] Rules to this effect were subsequently adopted by various District Courts,[35] and from the decisions of the Circuit Courts of Appeal in which the practice thus prescribed came

[32] See Von Moschzisker, Trial by Jury (2d ed. 1930) § 120.

[33] Donovan v. People, 139 Ill. 412, 415-416, 28 N.E. 964 (1891).

[34] Recommendations of Judicial Conference of Senior Circuit Court Judges, October 1924, 10 A.B.A.J. (1924) 875.

[35] R. D. Moore, Voir Dire Examination of Jurors—II. The Federal Practice (1928) 17 Georgetown L.J. 13, 14.

in question, it seems clear that, so long as the judge's power is exercised with reasonable regard to the rights of the parties, the method is entirely approvable; certainly there was recognized no right to insist upon direct questioning by counsel.[86] The Federal Rules of 1938 have not followed the text of the recommendation; their provision is that "the court may permit the parties or their attorneys to conduct the examination of prospective jurors or may itself conduct the examination. In the latter event, the court shall permit the parties or their attorneys to supplement the examination by such further inquiry as it deems proper or shall itself submit to the prospective jurors such additional questions of the parties or their attorneys as it deems proper." (Rule 47(a)). It is of course evident that under the Rule the court if it chooses may itself conduct the examination throughout. But the Rule's emphasizing of the matter of direct questioning by counsel in making its permitted use the first alternative tends to carry the implication that of the two methods it is the preferred one. Assuredly, to the judge who has been trained in the usual State practice it offers an easy road to relinquishing his true function and abdicating that command of the situation which is his under common-law tradition. We do not believe that the well-nigh unlimited method of persistent questioning, so prevalent in some of the State courts is ever likely to become the practice in the federal courts, but a closer adherence of the Rule to the Circuit Judges' recommendation would have more effectually closed the door to any danger of the kind. It is, we think, most unfortunate that the Rule should not have been in terms of the recommendation or at least have been so framed as to place the emphasis upon examination by the court.

The Rule in question has been adopted in Arizona (1939), New Mexico (1941), and (with minor change) New Jersey (1948) and Utah (1949).[87]

Much as we may admire the English system of selecting

[86] *Ibid.* 14. See the cases there cited in note 3 and particularly Falter v. U.S. (C.C.A. 2) 23 Fed.2d 420, 426 (1928).

[87] Ariz. Code Ann. 1939, § 21-937; Colo. Rules Civ. Proc. (1941) Rule 47(a); N.M. Stat. 1941, § 19-101(47)(a); N.J. Rules Civ. Pract. (1948) Rule 3:47-1; Utah Rules Civ. Proc. (1949) Rule 47(a).

juries, and free as we are constitutionally to adopt it, the practice of preliminary questioning is probably too firmly entrenched with us to be easily dislodged, nor can it be denied that good reason exists in favor of its retention. But it imperatively demands such regulation as will prevent it from being attended with the abuses which in many quarters have become conspicuously evident. In criminal causes, as everyone knows, the examination of one juror after another is often so protracted as to amount to a shocking tax upon the public treasury, as well as to an unjustified retardment of the proceedings. And while this phase of abuse is much less felt in civil cases, the examination here in a large quota of the State jurisdictions not seldom involves an inexcusable waste of time. Offensive, moreover, to the dignity of the citizen called for jury service and degrading to jury trial itself is the interminable cross-examination to which he is all too frequently subjected. If an accused is entitled to the presumption of innocence, why should not a juror be entitled to the presumption of impartiality, if he is able to assert that impartiality by his answer to general questions?[88] The presumption may, and in a proper case should, be overcome, but not by a process which is in effect that of making the juror a witness against himself. It appears to us that the desired ends of regulation should be met by the Massachusetts rule of general questions, with the conduct of the examination wholly in the hands of the court. Counsel here, as in the Federal practice, should be entitled to suggest further questions. The putting of them, however, should rest in the discretion of the court, which would be controlling unless there definitely appears some reason why that discretion has been wrongly exercised.

§ 2. Withdrawing the Case from the Jury

Under the common-law principle apportioning the respective functions of judge and jury, it obviously follows that on the trial the matter may be withdrawn from the jury's decision if it appears that no legally relevant evidence has been

[88] On this point, see the observations of Bay, J., in State v. Baldwin, 1 Treadw. (S.C.) 289, 320 (1813).

adduced by the plaintiff. The classic common-law method of invoking this rule was by *demurrer to the evidence,* which challenged the legal sufficiency of the evidence to maintain the plaintiff's case in the same manner as was challenged by demurrer the sufficiency of a pleading. The demurrer was in writing and contained a full statement of the evidence in question, which was thus made a matter of record. Following joinder in demurrer by the defendant, the jury was discharged, except as it might be retained to assess contingent damages, and the determination of the issue rested solely with the court. Coke tells us that the demurrer was thus applicable when there was shown "any matter of record, or deeds or writings, or any sentence in the ecclesiastical court, or other matter of evidence, by testimony of witnesses, or otherwise . . ." [39] It was as to oral evidence that doubt and difficulty arose.[40] In 1779 the rule as to admissions effected by the demurrer was stated by Lord Mansfield in *Cocksedge* v. *Fanshaw* [41] to be that "by the demurrer, the defendant admits every fact which the jury *could* have found upon the evidence." But in 1793 came the well-known case of *Gibson* v. *Hunter,*[42] decided by the House of Lords. Here the opinion of the judges, *per* Lord Chief Justice Eyre, was that, in the case of oral testimony which was "loose and indeterminate" or circumstantial, the defendant could not be required to join in demurrer unless there was specific admission in the demurrer of the fact which such evidence conduced to prove. In other words, on such a demurrer, unless, perhaps, the plaintiff voluntarily joined, there could no longer be any inquiry as to whether a jury could have found the fact; if the evidence at all conduced to prove the fact, the fact had to be admitted of record. It is apparent that this rule rendered the demurrer to the evidence an instrumentality

[39] Co. Litt. 72a.

[40] Middleton v. Baker, Cro. Eliz. 752, 78 E.R. 983 (1600); Wright v. Pindar, Aleyn, 18, 82 E.R. 892 (1646), *sub nom.* White v. Pyndar, Styles 22, 82 E.R. 499.

[41] 1 Doug. 119, 132, 99 E.R. 80 (1779). More expansively, Mr. Justice Buller in the same case says that "the demurrer admits the truth of all facts, which, upon the evidence stated, *might* be found by the jury in favour of the party offering the evidence." P. 134. The judgment for the plaintiff which followed was subsequently affirmed by the Exchequer Chamber and the House of Lords.

[42] 2 H. Blackstone 187, 207-208, 126 E.R. 499 (1793).

which, in cases of parol testimony, a defendant could seldom use without stating himself out of court: as aptly said by Professor Thayer [43] the case was a "death blow" to demurrer to evidence in England.

But it is evident from *Gibson* v. *Hunter* that even before its date the use of the demurrer to evidence had been markedly on the decine.[44] Various new developments in procedure had indirectly contributed to this end.[45] Notable, however, is the fact that the courts had begun to exercise the power of *directing verdicts* for insufficiency of the evidence. We find as early as 1725 Lord Chief Justice Eyre of the Common Pleas directing a verdict for the defendant on the ground of absence of proof of a material element of the plaintiff's cause of action.[46] But the plaintiff could always escape such a direction by moving for a nonsuit, even until the return of the verdict itself.[47] With its roots in this right of the plaintiff, and originating, apparently, in the courts' inclination against peremptorily foreclosing the plaintiff by a directed verdict, there became established a practice which dispensed with affirmative action of the plaintiff in seeking a non-suit—a practice which is especially manifest after the middle of the 1700s. When, that is to say, it seemed to the court that the plaintiff had not presented evidence legally sufficient to maintain the action, it was usual for the court to direct a *nonsuit*.[48] This nonsuit to all appearances was a compulsory one. But in theory it was not so. It was at the option of the plaintiff to submit or not to the nonsuit,[49] but his consent was taken as present un-

[43] Thayer, Preliminary Treatise on Evidence (1898) 235.

[44] In the opinion of the judges, it is said: "The questions . . . arise upon a proceeding, which is called a demurrer to evidence, and which, though not familiar in practice, is a proceeding well known to the law." P. 205.

[45] See Thayer, *op. cit.* 237, 241 *et seq.*

[46] Syderbottom v. Smith, 1 Strange 649, 93 E.R. 759 (1725).

[47] *Supra,* Chapter XVII.

[48] "When the jury are sworn, it becomes the duty of the plaintiff's counsel to enter upon his case; and it is incumbent upon him not only to prove by evidence *every fact* that is necessary to support it, but the facts, when proved, must be such as in point of law are sufficient to maintain an action; for if he fails in either of these respects, he will, under the direction of the judge, be nonsuited . . ." 1 Sellon's Crompton, Practice of the Courts of King's Bench and Common Pleas (Am. ed. 1813) *463.

[49] Lord Ellenborough in Minchin v. Clement, 1 Barn.&Ald. 212, 106 E.R. 93 (1818); Lord Denman, C. J., in Dewar v. Purday, 4 Nev.&Man. 633 (1835).

less he expressly objected.[50] If he did object, then the court had no alternative but to give directions in favor of the defendant. This manner of nonsuit,[51] as that which was the result of the plaintiff's expressly voluntary act, left the plaintiff free to renew his action. But it differed from the expressly voluntary nonsuit in the fact that, as it rested on the court's view of the law, the plaintiff was at liberty to move to set it aside on the ground that that view was a mistaken one.[52] On plain principles the right to direct a verdict existed also as against the defendant where the latter had the burden of proof, but here there was no avenue of escape such as the nonsuit offered to a plaintiff. Capstone of the practice thus indicated appears in the statement of the Exchequer Chamber in *Ryder* v. *Wombwell* in 1868 that "there is in every case . . . a preliminary question which is one of law, viz., whether there is any evidence on which the jury could properly find the question for the party on whom the onus of proof lies. If there is not, the judge ought to withdraw the question from the jury and direct a nonsuit if the onus is on the plaintiff or direct a verdict for the plaintiff if the onus is on the defendant." [53]

The present-day English law has long since forgotten the demurrer to the evidence. A judgment of nonsuit was recognized by the Rules of 1875,[54] but the relative provision was repealed by the Rules of 1883, and there is no longer any such thing as a nonsuit in the proper sense of the term.[55] "But the word is still sometimes used to denote the act of the Judge

[50] Garrow, B., in Elworthy v. Bird, 13 Price 222, 147 E.R. 972 (1824).

[51] See the instructive article of Demarest, Nonsuits Old and New (1903) 65 Albany L.J. 363.

[52] "I take the distinction to be, that where the counsel for the plaintiff asks to be nonsuited, they cannot afterwards move to set it aside; but where the judge orders it without their concurrence, I think they are not precluded, although they do not object at the time." Graham, B., in Ward v. Nason, 9 Price 291, 147 E.R. 96 (1821).

[53] L.R. 4 Exch. 32, 38-39 (1868).

[54] 38 & 39 Vict. c. 77, First Schedule, O. XLI, r. 6, providing that such a judgment, unless otherwise directed, shall have the same effect as a judgment upon the merits for the defendant, subject to be set aside upon terms in case of mistake, surprise or accident.

[55] Fox v. Star Newspaper Co. [1898] 1 Q.B. 636, [1900] A.C. 19 (H.L.). "The substance is," said Halsbury, L. C., in the House of Lords, that when it [the case] once comes into court, and when the plaintiff offers no support to his action, there must be a verdict for the defendant." P. 20.

when he withdraws the case from the jury and directs judgment to be entered without (or in spite of) their verdict, or in non-jury cases when he enters judgment for the defendant without calling upon him to prove his defence." [56] In essence, therefore, what remains to the modern English practice is the equivalent of the directed verdict, translated, through simplification of the procedure, into a directed judgment.

In America the demurrer to the evidence found acceptance as part of the procedure in various jurisdictions. The United States Supreme Court originally approved the rule of admission applied in *Cocksedge* v. *Fanshaw*,[57] but subsequently, through Mr. Justice Story, it gave adherence to the rule of *Gibson* v. *Hunter*,[58] and even expressed the opinion that "the demurrer is allowed or denied by the Court in the exercise of a sound discretion under all the circumstances of the case." [59] Some of the States followed the rule of *Gibson* v. *Hunter* [60] (in most cases with resulting unsuccess of the demurrer); others applied the easier rule and did not compel a stated admission of the adverse inferences from parol evidence.[61] Conspicuous among the latter was Virginia which contrived its own peculiar practice in the present regard. It apparently being usual to defer the demurrer until both sides had completed their evidence, this practice, as described by Conway Robinson (1832), was to "put all the evidence on both sides in the demurrer, and then to consider the demurrer as if the demurrant had admitted all that could reasonably be inferred by a jury from the evidence given by the other party, and waived all the evidence on his part which contradicts that offered by the other party, or the credit of which is impeached,

[56] Odgers, Principles of Pleading & Practice (13th ed. 1946) 269; Annual Practice 1945, p. 1592N; *id.* 1949, I, p. 1645.

[57] Pawling v. U.S. 4 Cranch (8 U.S.) 219 (1808).

[58] Young v. Black, 7 Cranch (11 U.S.) 565 (1813); Fowle v. Common Council of Alexandria, 11 Wheat. (24 U.S.) 320 (1826).

[59] Young v. Black, *supra,* at 568.

[60] *E.g.,* Copeland v. New England Insurance Co. 2 Pick. (39 Mass.) 135 (1839); Dormady v. State Bank, 2 Scam. (3 Ill.) 236 (1840); Sawyer v. Fitts, 2 Port. (Ala.) 9 (1835); Duerhagen v. U.S. Insurance Co. 2 Serg.& R. (Pa.) 185 (1816).

[61] *E.g.,* Lewis v. Few, 5 Johns. (N.Y.) 1 (1809); Shields v. Arnold, 1 Blackf. (Ind.) 109 (1820); Andrews v. Hammond, 8 Blackf. (Ind.) 540 (1847); Dangerfield v. Paschal, 11 Tex. 579 (1854).

and all inferences from his own evidence which do not necessarily flow from it."[62] The practice in question passed over into West Virginia[63] where it took on the added distortion of permitting the court in certain circumstances to decide the demurrer on the preponderance of the evidence.[64] In both these States the institution, as thus malformed, seems to hold place in present-day procedure;[65] elsewhere the demurrer to the evidence is nowadays generally of rare occurrence.[66] It should be added, however, that the term "demurrer to the evidence" is in many quarters loosely applied to any challenge of the legal sufficiency of an opponent's case. In particular, it is the fashion in a number of jurisdictions, to apply the term to the contention which seeks to attain a directed verdict against the plaintiff for insufficiency of his evidence.[67] This, for example, is what was in view in the Supreme Court case of *Van Stone* v. *Stillwell & Bierce Mfg. Co.*, where we read that "a general demurrer to the evidence was interposed by the plaintiff in error at the close of the testimony offered by the plaintiff be-

[62] 1 Robinson, Practice in the Courts of Law and Equity in Virginia (1832) 351. See also Patteson v. Ford, 2 Gratt. 18, 28 (1845).

[63] Muhleman v. Nat. Insurance Co. 6 W.Va. 508 (1873). It seems also to have attained some recognition in Indiana. Strough v. Gear, 48 Ind. 100 (1874).

[64] Carlin, Anomalous Features of Demurrers to the Evidence in West Virginia (1921) 27 W.Va. L.Q. 236, at 245 *et seq.*

[65] See H. A. Seinsheimer Co. v. Greenaway, 159 Va. 528, 166 S.E. 539 (1932); Metropolitan Life Ins. Co. v. Myers, 161 Va. 822, 172 S.E. 279 (1934); Fink v. Scott, 108 W.Va. 456, 152 S.E. 3 (1930); Finance Co. of America v. Bailey, 106 W.Va. 651, 146 S.E. 723 (1929). See also Carlin, *op. cit.* at 236, where under date of 1921 there is recorded, from a reading of the West Virginia decisions, "the impression that the practice of demurring to the evidence in this State, instead of being obsolescent, is becoming even more popular."

[66] Notice, however, Hopkins v. Nashville, C. & St. L. Ry. 96 Tenn. 409, 34 S.W. 1029 (1896), where a demurrer to evidence conforming to orthodox principles was successfully employed. Apparently as the result of this case, which seems to indicate that the demurrer to evidence was then the sole method, under the Tennessee practice, of challenging the sufficiency of the plaintiff's evidence in advance of verdict, the demurrer entered upon a new life—the court in Greenlaw v. Louisville & N. R. Co. 114 Tenn. 187, 86 S.W. 1072 (1905) saying that its use "now prevails quite generally"—until the decision in Tyrus v. Kansas City, Ft. S. & M. R. Co. 114 Tenn. 579, 86 S.W. 1074 (1905) definitely established the practice of directed verdicts.

[67] Instances: Macklin v. Fogel Construction Co. 326 Mo. 38, 31 S.W.2d 14 (1930); Rusco v. De Good, 127 Kan. 708, 275 Pac. 201 (1929); Smith v. Dunbar Co. 125 Okla. 215, 257 Pac. 282 (1927); Clough & Molloy, Inc. v. Shilling, 149 Md. 189, 131 Atl. 343 (1925).

low . . ." [68] But this so-called "demurrer" is without the incidents and consequences of the common-law institution. It does not set out the evidence in writing and, if overruled, does not hinder the opponent from going on with his evidence to the jury.

It is easily seen how the English practice of nonsuit at the trial, viewed superficially, could suggest the idea that the compulsory nonsuit was authorized at common law.[69] It is therefore not surprising to find this manner of practice installed by early judicial decision in New York [70] and in an important quota of other State jurisdictions.[71] To the same practice statutory recognition was extended by Pennsylvania in 1836 [72] and Connecticut in 1852.[73] But as many, if not more, of the State jurisdictions set their faces strongly against the compulsory nonsuit, holding literally to the basic common-law notion of the nonsuit as the result of the plaintiff's voluntary act.[74] This view was shared by the United States Supreme Court which in 1828 definitely held against the power of the trial court to order a nonsuit without the consent of the plaintiff [75]—a rule

[68] 142 U.S. 128, 133, 12 S.Ct. 181 (1891).

[69] Thus it is said in the Tennessee case of Bacon, Assignee v. Parker, 2 Overton 54 (1809), where the court declined to admit the practice of compulsory nonsuit: "Here, as well as in North Carolina, in common cases, the Court never compels a nonsuit, or gives judgment to that effect, but with the consent of the party nonsuited. In England, the practice is understood to be, that the Court will order a judgment of nonsuit to be entered, whenever it clearly perceives the plaintiff fails in proving his case, supposing his evidence to be true; or where no evidence is given on his part."

[70] Pratt v. Hull, 13 Johns. 334 (1816); Labar v. Koplin, 4 N.Y. 547 (1851).

[71] Among these were South Carolina: Clason v. Bird, 2 Brev. 370 (1810); Maine: Inhabitants of Sanford v. Emery, 2 Me. 5 (1822); Kentucky: Hanks v. Roberts, 3 J. J. Marsh. (26 Ky.) 298 (1830); Iowa: Eddy v. Wilson, 1 G. Greene 259 (1848); New Hampshire: Stickney v. Stickney, 21 N.H. 61 (1850); California: Ringgold v. Haven, 1 Cal. 108 (1850); Wisconsin: Hunter v. Warner, 1 Wis. 141 (1853); Georgia: Tison v. Yawn, 15 Ga. 491 (1854); Ohio: Ellis & Morton v. Ohio Life Ins. & Trust Co. 4 OhioSt. 628 (1855).

[72] Pa. Laws 1836, p. 76, applicable to the District Court of Philadelphia, extended generally in 1863. Pa. Stat. Ann. (Purdon, 1931) note to § 245, Tit. 12.

[73] Cook v. Morris, 66 Conn. 196, 210, 33 Atl. 994 (1895); Conn. Laws 1852, c. 4, § 1.

[74] Representative are Smith v. Seaton, Minor (Ala.) 75 (1822); French v. Smith, 4 Vt. 363 (1827); Ringo v. Field, 1 Engl. (6 Ark.) 43 (1845); Morgan v. Ide, 8 Cush. (62 Mass.) 420 (1851).

[75] Elmore v. Grymes, 1 Pet. (26 U.S.) 469 (1828); D'Wolf v. Rabaud, 1 Pet. (26 U.S.) 476 (1828).

which was consistently maintained in the federal courts until the Conformity Act of 1872 [76] operated to introduce the local State practice. The New York Code of 1848 passed the practice of compulsory nonsuit *sub silentio,* nor has subsequent legislation in that State materially affected the court's power thus to proceed, although the term nonsuit has to a pronounced extent given way to that of dismissal.[77] The practice in question, testing the sufficiency of the plaintiff's evidence substantially in the same manner as the motion to direct a verdict presently to be examined, has won important ground since the first half of the 1800s and has found place in many of the newer codes.[78] Moreover, it has been substantially adopted by the Federal Rules of 1938 which include in Rule 41(b) the provision that:

> After the plaintiff has completed the presentation of his evidence, the defendant, without waiving his right to offer evidence in the event the motion is not granted, may move for a dismissal on the ground that upon the facts and the law the plaintiff has shown no right to relief.[79]

This provision has been copied by Arizona (1939), Colorado (1941), New Mexico (1942), Delaware (1947), Florida (1949), Utah, (1949), and (with some modification) New Jersey (1948).[80]

In a very few jurisdictions the motion for a compulsory nonsuit comes too late, if made, at least for the first time, after the introduction of evidence in defense: [81] generally,

[76] *Supra,* Chapter VI.

[77] See N.Y. Civ. Pract. Act (Clevenger, 1950) §§ 441, 459; Demarest, Nonsuits Old and New (1903) 65 Albany L.J. 363, 368 *et seq.*

[78] *E.g.,* Oregon: Comp. Laws Ann. 1940, § 6-201; Washington: 2 Rev.Stat. Ann. (Remington, 1932) § 408; Idaho: Code Ann. 1949, § 10-705; Montana: Rev. Codes Ann. 1947, § 93-4705; North Dakota: Rev. Code 1943, § 28-0801.

[79] An amendment of 1946 to Federal Rule 41(b) relates only to nonjury cases and regulates the matter of findings of fact, where on a motion for involuntary dismissal there is involved some exercise of the court's function of trier of the facts. Federal Rules of Civil Procedure (West Publishing Co., 1947) and note of Advisory Committee, p. 94.

[80] Ariz. Code Ann. 1939, § 21-916; Colo. Rules Civ. Proc. 1941, Rule 41 (b)(1); N.M. Stat. Ann. 1941, § 19-101(41)(b); Del. Rules of Superior Court, Rule 41(b), Rules of Court of Chancery, Rule 41(b); N.J. Rules Civ. Pract., Rule 2:41-2; Fla. Common Law Rules, Rule 35(b); Utah Rules Civ. Proc., Rule 41(b).

[81] Lyon v. Sibley, 32 Me. 576 (1851); Bragdon v. Appleton Mut.

however, it is in order down to the submission of the case to the jury. Moreover, there is considerable authority to the effect that the motion is waived, if after its overruling the defendant proceeds to the introduction of evidence: this waiver, however, does not preclude a motion to direct a verdict on all the evidence.[82] Normally, the compulsory nonsuit, as the nonsuit at common law, leaves the plaintiff free to renew his action, but this rule is not without exception in some States, where as a result of judicial decision [83] or statute,[84] distinction is made between nonsuits with and without prejudice to the renewal of the action. This very distinction, moreover, has found place in the Federal Rules as part of Rule 41 (b) (and accordingly in the borrowing jurisdictions) in the provision that, unless the court otherwise specifies, the dismissal on motion of the defendant for failure to show a right to relief upon the facts and the law "operates as an adjudication upon the merits." [84a] The Rule in question primarily contemplates a non-jury trial, but applies also to jury trials,[85] although here ordinarily the motion would be replaced by one for a directed verdict. Thus applying, it would seem that under the Rules, the plaintiff in a proper case could escape a directed verdict, if the court in its discretion saw fit to order in its stead a dismissal without prejudice at the close of all the evidence.

Most common, however, of the methods of withdrawing the case from the jury is the *directed verdict*. But, despite its common-law roots, establishment in America of the court's power thus to proceed has not been without struggle. The early practice in Pennsylvania declined to admit it,[86] as did

---

Fire Ins. Co. 42 Me. 259 (1856); Nowell v. Basnight, 185 N.C. 142, 116 S.E. 87 (1923); Bennett v. Agricultural Ins. Co. 51 Conn. 504 (1884) applying statute now § 7977, Gen. Stat. 1949.

82 Union Insurance Co. v. Smith, 124 U.S. 405, 8 S.Ct. 534 (1888); Bogk v. Gassett, 149 U.S. 17, 13 S.Ct. 738 (1893).

83 Brett v. Marston, 45 Me. 401 (1858); Cartin v. South Bound RR. Co. 43 S.C. 221, 20 S.E. 979 (1895); Morrow v. Atlanta & Charlotte Air Line Ry. Co. 84 S.C. 224, 66 S.E. 186 (1909); Ordway v. Boston & M. RR. 69 N.H. 429, 45 Atl. 243 (1899).

84 N.Y. Civ. Pract. Act (Clevenger, 1950) § 482.

84a The Rule expressly excludes a dismissal for lack of jurisdiction or for improper venue.

85 3 Moore, Federal Practice (1938) p. 3045; Ohlinger, Federal Practice, Replacement Vol. 3-A (1948) p. 48.

86 Von Moschzisker, Trial by Jury (2d ed. 1930) § 293.

that in Virginia,[87] Kentucky[88] and Missouri.[89] In Georgia the power was absent as late as 1884,[90] and in Tennessee it was not definitely recognized until 1905.[91] And, even within comparatively recent years, it has been the subject of specific legislative attack. In Virginia where, although the power had been judicially declared "not in accordance with the practice in this State,"[92] the procedure was tending toward its recognition,[93] a statute of 1912 struck in and expressly forbade the court to give "a peremptory instruction directing what verdict the jury shall render."[94] While this has prevented the exercise of the power as such, it has been in substance evaded by the awkward expedient, derived from the previous practice, of permitting the trial court in a proper case to strike out the evidence, thus leaving none to go to the jury.[95] Again, in Wisconsin a statute of 1923, in maladroit terms, sought to prohibit the direction of a verdict, but this was unequivocally held unconstitutional.[96] A lesser form of attack appears in statutes of Minnesota (1913) and North Dakota (1921),[97] which required the court to deny a motion for directed verdict upon objection of the opposite party, but left it free to give judgment for the moving party, if the situation so required, on

[87] Martin v. Stover, 2 Call 514 (1801).

[88] Reed v. Bragg, 5 J. J. Marsh. (28 Ky.) 620 (1831).

[89] Scoggin v. Wilson, 13 Mo. 80 (1850); Chambers v. McGiveron, 33 Mo. 202 (1862). So also the early practice of Texas, Reynolds v. Williams, 1 Tex. 311 (1846).

[90] Manning v. Mitchell, 73 Ga. 660 (1884).

[91] Tyrus v. Kansas City, Fort S. & M. R. Co. 114 Tenn. 579, 86 S.W. 1074 (1905).

[92] Hargrave's Admr. v. Shaw Land & Timber Co. 111 Va. 84, 90, 68 S.E. 278 (1910). "In Virginia the practice has been either to demur to the evidence in a proper case, or to ask an instruction directing a verdict upon a hypothetical case—that is, to tell the jury if they believe so and so their verdict should be for the plaintiff, or the defendant, as the case may be." Burks, Pleading and Practice (1913) § 273, p. 506, quoted in Small v. Virginia Railway & Power Co. 125 Va. 416, 424, 99 S.E. 525 (1919).

[93] Graham, Directing Verdicts (1910) 16 Va.LawReg. 401, 403; an editorial in the same volume of the Register, at 384-385, speaks of a "growing practice on the circuits in this State."

[94] Va. Laws 1912, c. 27, p. 52; Va. Code Ann. 1942, § 6003; Va. Code Ann. 1950, § 8-218.

[95] Barksdale v. Southern Ry. Co. 152 Va. 604, 148 S.E. 683 (1929).

[96] Thoe v. Chicago, Milwaukee & St. Paul Ry. Co. 181 Wis. 456, 195 N.W. 407, 29 A.L.R. 1280 (1923).

[97] Matz v. Martinson, 127 Minn. 262, 149 N.W. 370 (1914); First Nat. Bank of Ashley v. Strauss, 50 N.D. 71, 194 N.W. 900 (1923); note, 29 A.L.R. 1287.

his subsequent motion for judgment notwithstanding the verdict. In both these States, however, wiser counsels have since prevailed and the objectionable feature thus presented has disappeared under subsequent legislation.[98]

Concerning the latter day development of the directed verdict it is finally to be noted:

(*a*) There has generally passed away the idea once held that any evidence, however slight, is enough to carry the case to the jury—the so-called scintilla doctrine—and there is now general recognition of the test, variously phrased, that to be sufficient for this purpose the evidence must be such as, if it stood uncontradicted, would justify a jury, acting as reasonable men, in finding a verdict for the plaintiff.[99]

(*b*) The rule has come to be followed by most courts that, under a similar test, a verdict may be directed generally in favor of the party having the burden of proof [100]—which signifies that in a proper case the plaintiff may be its beneficiary,—although here a minority stumbles against the question of credibility of witnesses, and particularly that of interested witnesses, which they maintain is always a matter for the jury.[101]

(*c*) While, basically speaking, the question of preponderance of the evidence ought to lie outside consideration in passing on the motion for a directed verdict, it is the federal doctrine that if the evidence is so overwhelming on the side of the moving party as to leave no room for doubt as to the fact and imperatively requires the setting aside of a verdict for the opponent, the case is one for a directed verdict.[102] As said

[98] See Minn. Stat. 1945, § 605.06; N.D. Rev. Code 1943, § 28-1510.

[99] 9 Wigmore, Evidence (3d ed. 1940) § 2494, p. 296 *et seq.*

[100] *Ibid.* § 2495, pp. 305-306; see also Sunderland, Directing a Verdict for the Party Having the Burden of Proof (1913) 11 Mich.L.Rev. 198

[101] *E.g.,* Giles v. Giles, 204 Mass. 383, 90 N.E. 595 (1910); Wooden v. Durfee, 46 Mich. 424, 9 N.W. 457 (1881); King & King v. Porter (Tex. Civ. App.) 256 S.W. 627 (1923); Second Nat. Bank of Pittsburg v. Hoffman, 229 Pa. 429, 78 Atl. 1002 (1911); Anniston Nat. Bank v. School Committee of Durham, 121 N.C. 107, 28 S.E. 134 (1897).

[102] People's Savings Bank v. Bates, 120 U.S. 556, 7 S.Ct. 679 (1887); Southern Pacific Co. v. Pool, 160 U.S. 438, 16 S.Ct. 338 (1896); Delaware, Lackawanna & Western RR. Co. v. Converse, 139 U.S. 469, 11 S.Ct. 569 (1891); Empire State Cattle Co. v. Atchison, Topeka & Santa Fe Ry. Co. 210 U.S. 1, 28 S.Ct. 607 (1908).

by the Supreme Court in *Pennsylvania R. Co.* v. *Chamberlain* (1933), the rule is that "whenever in the trial of a civil case the evidence is clearly such that if a verdict were rendered for one of the parties the other would be entitled to a new trial, it is the duty of the judge to direct the jury to find according to the views of the court." [103] The same rule obtains in many of the State courts,[104] here sometimes phrased as giving place to the direction in the case where the weight of the evidence is so "decidedly preponderating" as to require a verdict for the opponent to be set aside.[105] Usually, however, the cases where the rule is applied are those in which the contradictory evidence consists of mere surmise or is otherwise of an insubstantial character. Yet in New York the whole distance bade fair to be traversed by a statute of 1921 which provided in terms that "the judge may direct a verdict when he would set aside a contrary verdict as against the weight of the evidence." [106] But a very distinct retreat from this stand is disclosed by an amendment of 1949 which substituted the formula that "the court may direct a verdict when it would be required to set aside a contrary verdict for insufficiency of the evidence." [106a] This would appear substantially to revert to the orthodox rule obtaining in perhaps the larger quota of jurisdictions, as notably exemplified by England [107] and Massachusetts,[108] which in effect holds that whether or not a verdict for the opponent would be set aside as against a preponderance of the evidence is a question alien to the inquiry on a motion for a directed verdict and that if there is proper evidence on both sides this must go to the jury.[109]

[103] 288 U.S. 333, 343, 53 S.Ct. 391.

[104] *Ibid. loc. cit.*

[105] See 26 R.C.L. 1068; the pre-statute cases in New York of Leinkauf v. Lombard, 137 N.Y. 417, 33 N.E. 472 (1893) and Hemmens v. Nelson, 138 N.Y. 517, 34 N.E. 342 (1893); also Eagle Loan & Inv. Co. v. Starks, 116 Okla. 151, 243 Pac. 725 (1926).

[106] N.Y. Laws 1921, c. 372, § 3; N.Y. Civ. Pract. Act (Clevenger, 1948) § 457-a, subd. 1.

[106a] N.Y. Laws 1949, c. 604; N.Y. Civ. Pract. Act (Clevenger, 1950) § 457a, Subd. 1; see 15th Annual Report, Judicial Council of the State of New York (1949) pp. 249-250, 278 *et seq.*

[107] Dublin, Wicklow & Wexford Ry. Co. v. Slattery, L. R. 3 App.Cas. 1155 (1878).

[108] Niland v. Boston Elevated Ry. Co. 208 Mass. 476, 94 N.E. 703 (1911).

[109] See the observations in 9 Wigmore, Evidence (3d ed. 1940) § 2494, pp. 298-299, maintaining the unsoundness of applying to the motion to direct the test of setting aside the verdict as against the overwhelming weight of the evidence.

(*d*) Originating apparently in New York [110] there has appeared the rule that where both parties move for direction of the verdict, this is treated as tantamount to a submission of the case to the court, subject to the right of each to submit specific questions of fact for answer by the jury. This rule, despite its illogical character, has had a major following in the State courts,[111] and was definitely adopted by the United States Supreme Court in decisions of 1895 and 1908.[112] Fortunately it has been discarded by the Federal Rules of 1938 which provide in this regard that "a motion for a directed verdict which is not granted is not a waiver of trial by jury even though all parties to the action have moved for directed verdicts." (Rule 50(a)). This has set in a current against the practice, exemplified by its rejection on the part of New York itself through an amendment of the Civil Practice Act in 1940,[113] following the federal provision.[113a]

(*e*) Under the general rule the motion to direct on the part of the defendant may be made at the close of the plaintiff's evidence, but its overruling cannot be questioned on review, unless it is renewed at the close of all the evidence, since there is always the possibility that the plaintiff's evidence may be strengthened by that coming from the other side. The same consideration has led to the rule in some quarters that a motion to direct, as distinguished from a motion for compulsory nonsuit, cannot properly be made until both sides have rested.[113b]

[110] Koehler v. Adler, 78 N.Y. 287 (1879).

[111] Notes, 18 A.L.R. 1433; 69 A.L.R. 633; 108 A.L.R. 1315.

[112] Beuttell v. Magone, 157 U.S. 154, 15 S.Ct. 566 (1895); Empire State Cattle Co. v. Atchison, Topeka & Santa Fe Ry. Co. 210 U.S. 1, 28 S.Ct. 607 (1908).

[113] N.Y. Laws 1940, c. 749; N.Y. Civ. Pract. Act (Clevenger, 1950) § 457-a, subd. 2.

[113a] The federal provision has been followed also by Arizona (1939), Colorado (1941), New Mexico (1942), Missouri (1943), Delaware (1947), New Jersey (1948) and Utah (1949). Ariz. Code Ann. 1939, § 21-1014; Colo. Rules Civ. Proc., Rule 50(a) in Colo. Stat. Ann. 1935, Replacement Vol. I, 1941; N.M. Stat. Ann. 1941, § 19-101 (50)(a); 3 Mo.Rev.Stat. 1942, Cum. Pocket Part 1950, § 847.112; Del. Rules of Superior Court, Rule 50(a); N.J. Rules Civ. Pract., Rule 3:50; Utah Rules Civ. Proc., Rule 50(a). In New Jersey, however, by amendment (1949) of Rule 3:50 the motion for a directed verdict has been superseded by a motion for judgment.

[113b] Dunbar v. Fant, 170 S.C. 414, 170 S.E. 460 (1933); Cantor v. Reserve Loan Life Ins. Co. 161 S.C. 198, 159 S.E. 542 (1931); Kaley v. Van Ostrand, 134 Wis. 443, 114 N.W. 817 (1908); Thoe v. Chicago, Milwaukee

§ 3. The Charge to the Jury

Inseparable from jury trial at common law was the salutary power of the judge in charging the jury to comment upon the evidence, always making it plain, however, that his views thus expressed were in no sense binding upon the jurors. In England this power has been retained in the fullest measure, but the chronicle of jury trial in the United States tells a different story. Here the judge has been widely stripped of that power. Initiative in this regard appears to have been taken by a North Carolina statute of 1796 as a consequence of an embittered dispute between the judges and leading members of the bar.[114] This was followed in the same year by a constitutional provision of Tennessee to like effect, forbidding the judges to charge juries with respect to matters of fact.[115] The movement thus inaugurated gathered impetus under that wave of democratization which reached its height about the middle of the nineteenth century, until State after State had succumbed to the ill-starred innovation.[116] In result the case is that the common-law rule in question has been preserved only in the federal courts (not, however, without some measure of trammeling judicially imposed in more recent years)[117] and, either by retention[118] or, in a few late instances presently

---

& St. Paul Ry. Co. 181 Wis. 456, 195 N.W. 407 (1923).

[114] Johnson, Province of the Judge in Jury Trials (1928) 12 J.Am.Jud. Soc. 76, 78; Hogan, The Strangled Judge (1930) 14 J.Am.Jud.Soc. 116, 120; Clark, The Supreme Court of North Carolina (1892) 4 Green Bag 457, 472.

[115] Tenn. Const. 1796, Art. V. § 5; Johnson, *op. cit.* 80; Sunderland, The Problem of Trying Issues (1926) 5 Tex.L.Rev. 18, 32.

[116] Data as to the progress of the departure appear in the articles just cited of Johnson, Hogan and Sunderland.

[117] See 9 Wigmore, Evidence (3d ed. 1940) § 2551, pp. 507-508.

[118] Here to be mentioned are New Jersey, New York, Pennsylvania, Connecticut, Rhode Island, Vermont, New Hampshire and Minnesota. See Johnson, *op. cit.* at 77 note 9. Utah is also included in this writer's enumeration, under the citation of People v. Lee, 2 Utah 441 (1878) and is likewise assigned to the present group by Minimum Standards of Judicial Administration (ed. Vanderbilt, 1949) 229. But, while the court may state the evidence (Utah Code Ann. 1943, § 104-24-14; Utah Rules Civ. Proc. 1949, Rule 51), it is very doubtful whether the power to comment as under the Lee case has here survived: see Hawley v. Corey, 9 Utah 175, 33 Pac. 695 (1893); State v. Green, 77 Utah 580, 6 Pac.2d 177 (1931); State v. Parker, 104 Utah 23, 36, 137 Pac.2d 626, 632 (opinion of Wolfe, C. J.). Indeed, it is explicitly stated in the cited rule that "the court shall not comment on the evidence in the case." Again, it is not altogether clear that Minnesota can be regarded as squarely falling within this group:

to be mentioned, by restoration, in a small minority of the State jurisdictions. Elsewhere the judge is restrained from commenting on the evidence. In certain of the States he may summarize the evidence for the benefit of the jury, but without expressing any opinion as to its effect.[119] More usually he is not permitted to go beyond charging on the law, and the jurors are left without that help contributable by the judge in evaluating the facts and applying the legal rule, which is properly their due. For, here, the judge, in the words of Sir Matthew Hale, is able "in matters of fact to give them a great light and assistance by his weighing the evidence before them, and observing where the question and knot of the business lies, and by shewing them his opinion even in matters of fact; which is a great advantage and light to laymen," [120] it being always made clear to them that the judge is thus acting for their assistance only and that the decision rests with them alone. Of the prohibition of judicial comment on the evidence thus so extensively imposed, it has been justly said that this "has done more than any other one thing to impair the general efficiency of jury trial as an instrument of justice." [121]

The movement responsible for the prohibition had not fully expended its force in recent years. This is seen in the adoption or reaffirmation of the restrictive rule by a number of constitutions and statutes, exemplified by its inclusion in the Arizona constitution of 1912 [122] and its maintenance in the Delaware constitutional amendment of 1951.[123] But that for some time past there has been a definite movement in the opposite direction no one can doubt. Retention of the common-law

---

see Pressley Fruit Co. v. St. Louis M. T. & S. Ry. Co. 130 Minn. 121, 153 N.W. 115 (1915) cited by Johnson, and State v. Taran, 176 Minn. 182, 222 N.W. 906 (1929).

119 Massachusetts furnishes perhaps the foremost example of this manner of charge. It was there established by the statute of 1860 which abrogated the power of charging on the facts—a statute which, it is said, is owed to the animus of Benjamin F. Butler (later the Civil War general of that name) directed against certain of the judges: see Hale in 11 Mass.L.Q. No. 2, p. 57 (Jan. 1926). But this method long antedates the Massachusetts statute as a concomitant of the prohibition of comment. For that matter, it was conceded by the North Carolina and Tennessee provisions of 1796 above noted.

120 History of the Common Law (4th ed. 1792) 292, quoted in Quercia v. U.S. 289 U.S. 466, 469, 53 S.Ct. 698.

121 9 Wigmore, *op. cit.* § 2551, p. 505.

122 Ariz. Const. 1912, Art. 6, § 12.

123 Del. Const. 1897, Art. IV, § 22; Amendment, May 14, 1951, of Art. IV, § 19.

rule in the federal courts and in a few of the State jurisdictions has afforded a solid point of support for the advocacy of its general reinstatement, which of late has made itself widely heard. And this opposite movement has already yielded concrete results. Michigan having revived the common-law power of comment for criminal trials by a statute of 1927,[124] adopted a like measure for civil trials by a rule of court dating from 1931, under which the judge may "make such comment on the evidence, the testimony and the character of the witnesses as in his opinion the interests of justice may require." [125] California, by a constitutional amendment of 1934 [126] opened the way for such a revival which, although not yet enacted for civil causes, was effected for criminal causes by a statute of 1935.[127] Revival for criminal trials also obtains in the Territory of Hawaii under legislation of 1932.[128] Another convert of the current movement is New Mexico which, by a rule of court effective in 1934, applicable to both civil and criminal causes, provided that the judge, informing the jurors that they are the sole judges of all questions of fact, "may make such comment on the evidence and the credibility of any witness as in his opinion is necessary for the proper determination of the cause." [129] This rule, with separate enunciation for the two classes of causes, now stands embodied in the code of the State.[130] And in Wisconsin, of late years, without the aid of statute or rule of court, it has come to be the doctrine of the Supreme Court that the judge may "properly state to the jury his opinion as to what the evidence proves," if he makes it clear that this opinion is not binding upon them.[130a] There was restoration also of the old rule in Colorado, but this proved evanescent. In 1931 the Supreme Court of Colorado, upon

[124] Mich. Laws 1927, No. 175, p. 321; Mich. Stat. Ann. 1938, § 28.1052.

[125] Mich. Court Rules 1931, 1933, 1945, Rule 37, § 9; Searl, Mich. Court Rules Ann. (4th ed. 1933) p. 252, and Cum. Supp. 1948, p. 73.

[126] Cal. Const. Art. VI, § 19, Amendment of Nov. 6, 1934.

[127] Cal. Laws 1935, c. 718, p. 1942; Cal. Penal Code (Deering, 1949) § 1127.

[128] Haw. Laws 1932, 2d Sp. Sess., Act 24, p. 60; Haw. Rev. Laws 1945, § 10123.

[129] N.M. Trial Court Rules, 70-106, 70-107, 38 N.M. p. xvii.

[130] N.M. Stat. Ann. 1941, § 19-101 (51)(e)(f), § 42-1117.

[130a] Branigan v. State, 209 Wis. 249, 256, 244 N.W. 767 (1932); Jessner v. State, 202 Wis. 184, 191, 231 N.W. 634 (1930).

which had been conferred a general rule-making authority, adopted a rule granting the right to comment on the evidence by reference to the federal practice. This rule was upheld by a divided court in *Kolkman* v. *People*[131] in the same year. While the cause was pending decision in the Supreme Court, the legislature modified the act in reference to the rule-making power by providing that no rule should be adopted permitting comment on the evidence. Although the majority opinion, at least *obiter,* asserted an inherent rule-making power, independent of the statute, the court did not stand out against the legislature. For in 1941 the rule in question was superseded and in its stead was adopted one reverting to the former practice of no comment.[132] The result is an unfortunate one, but we may indulge the hope that it is no more than a temporary check to a movement so strongly in keeping with the intelligent conduct of jury trials.

To a very large extent, in the State jurisdictions, the common-law orality of the charge has also disappeared: the instructions must be given in writing, either as a matter of course or upon request of one of the parties.[132a] The evils of the written instruction have been often pointed out. Based for the most part upon more or less partisan drafts presented by counsel,[133] and commonly consisting of a series of separate hypotheses, elaborated in winding sentences and studied with technical expressions, it is seldom comprehended by the ordinary juror, even if he is disposed to apply his mind to its confusing contents. The consequence is not only to deprive the jury of direct and plain-spoken guidance as to the applicable rules of law, but also to develop a new species of special pleading (for so it has been aptly called) fertile in engendering error, to which the appellate courts apply none too elastic a yardstick. But an important mitigation of the ill consequences attending the ironclad rule of written instructions lies in the provision found in

[131] 89 Colo. 8, 300 Pac. 575 (1931).

[132] Colo. Rules Civ. Proc. 1941, Rule 51, in Colo. Stat. Ann. 1935, Replacement Vol. I, 1941.

[132a] On this point, see Minimum Standards of Judicial Administration, *cit.* 231.

[133] Indeed, in some jurisdictions the statute makes it imperative that the judge give or refuse a requested instruction in the precise language of the request. *E.g.,* Ala. Code 1940, Tit. 7, § 273; Wis. Stat. 1949, § 270.21; N.D. Rev. Code 1943, § 28-1412.

a number of jurisdictions, establishing as an equivalent the stenographic taking down and transcribing of the charge by an official reporter.[184] To this extent the charge becomes an oral one, but it usually suffers from the fettering traditions of the written practice, particularly in the staccato reproduction of counsel's drafts, and unless accompanied by the right of judicial comment on the evidence it is at best an oral charge of a lame and handicapped character. The two things—orality and comment—belong together as they did at common-law, and jury trial in the American jurisdictions will continue to lack a full measure of adequacy until the two are everywhere united.

Another disfigurement which common-law jury trial has undergone in a very substantial group of States is that which prescribes that the charge of the court precede the closing arguments of counsel.[185] This, again, is a device manifestly originating in the desire to diminish the authority and influence of the judge. It enables counsel to make his argument a vehicle of criticism, masked or otherwise, of the court's view of the law and tends to undermine whatever impression the instructions have left upon the minds of the jurors.[186] It conduces to setting the instructions, in point of weight, on a parity with the ob-

[184] See *e.g.*, Ala. Code 1940, Tit. 7, § 272; Wis. Stat. 1949, § 270-21; 2 Wash.Rev.Stat. (Remington, 1932) § 308-4 (Rule IV), § 339.

[185] It appears from Minimum Standards of Judicial Administration, *cit.*, 233-234, that this practice obtains in some twenty States there named. Sometimes it is legislatively recognized, sometimes not. One finds its recognition by statute or rule of court in at least the following jurisdictions: Arizona: Code Ann. 1939, § 21-1017; Arkansas: Stat. Ann. 1947, § 27-1727; Colorado: Rules Civ. Proc. 1941, Rule 51; Idaho: Code Ann. 1948, § 10-206; Kansas: Gen. Stat. Ann. (Corrick, 1935) § 60-2909; Kentucky: Code Pract. in Civ. Cas. (Carroll, 1948) § 317; Montana: Rev. Codes Ann. 1947, § 93-5101; Nebraska: Rev. Stat. 1943, § 25-1107; Nevada: Comp. Laws 1929, § 8766 (on demand of either party); New Mexico: Stat. Ann. 1941, § 19-101(51)(c), § 42-1113; Oklahoma: Stat. 1941, Tit. 12, § 577; South Dakota: Code 1939, § 33.1307; Texas: Rules Civ. Proc. (Vernon, 1942) Rule 275; Utah: Code Ann. 1943, § 104-24-14, Rules Civ. Proc., Rule 51; Washington: 2 Rev.Stat. (Remington, 1932) § 339; Wyoming: Comp. Stat. Ann. 1945, § 3-2408.

[186] "My observation has been that where arguments are given last, a great deal of time is spent by counsel in attempting to explain, controvert or limit the legal propositions put to the jury in the form of instructions which, in many cases, result in the jury being confused as to the law which the Court has previously given them." T. Blake Kennedy, The Wyoming Practice and Procedure Act (1947) 2 Wyo.L.J. 11, 15-16.

servations of counsel, as parcel of the arguments in the case, and robs the charge of the solemnity which ought to appertain to it as the final word of the judge. What a contrast is thus presented to the federal practice! In the latter, to borrow the words of Judge Soper, the atmosphere of the courtroom "is one of partisanship conflict, until the judge sums up at the end . . . Then the judge speaks as the representative of the law and its authorized expositor; he speaks, and for the first time in the trial the conflict is stilled, and every one is aware that an impartial official, the one unbiased person in the court room best qualified to pass judgment, is striving to sort out the tangled skeins of controversy and simplify the issues, so that the jury may pass upon them with understanding." [187]

Moreover, the practice under criticism is thoroughly illogical for, after all, the charge is or should be a charge on the case as a whole, and may even have occasion to include instructions concerning the very arguments of counsel—an illogic underlined now and then [188] by express recognition of the right to charge again after the arguments. Such advantage as the departure may yield counsel in enabling him to know precisely the court's view of the law is thoroughly illusory; in the absence of that precise knowledge he can and does shape his argument to cover the eventualities of the charge in point of law; and in any case such advantage cannot outweigh the harm which this practice otherwise works. Perhaps in the march toward restoring jury trial to its salutary common-law basis even this departure from principle may one day find itself excised.

§ 4. The Verdict

The books of the common law teach that verdicts were of two sorts, general and special. The general verdict was that which passed upon the several issues produced by the pleadings; the special verdict, originating as a means of averting the risk of the barbarous attaint, found the facts in specie, as

[187] Soper, The Charge to the Jury (1940) 24 J.Am.Jud.Soc. 111, quoted by Chesnut, Instructions to the Jury, Judicial Administration Monographs A.B.A. (Series A, 1942) p. 38.

[188] See Neb. Rev. Stat. 1943, § 25-1107; Nev. Comp. Laws 1929, § 8766.

established by the evidence, leaving the conclusion of law to the court. The procedural advantages attending the special verdict, however, were outweighed by the technical rules that governed it and especially by the requirement that it find every element of fact, not admitted by the pleadings, which was a necessary constituent of the basis for judgment, whether such element had been a point of controversy or not. Obviously such a finding could hardly be expected from a lay jury unaided, and accordingly the practice was such that "when it is agreed that a verdict of that kind is to be given, the jury merely declare their opinion as to any fact remaining in doubt; and then the verdict is adjusted without their farther interference. It is settled, under the correction of the judge, by the counsel and attornies on either side, according to the state of facts as found by the jury, with respect to all particulars on which they have delivered an opinion, and with respect to other particulars, according to the state of facts which it is agreed that they *ought* to find upon the evidence before them." [139] At best, however, "there was so much technical nicety required in framing a special verdict, that it required great skill, and some good fortune, to be able to raise the real question on it." [140]

But the English courts long before the opening of the nineteenth century had been employing various devices for the purpose of keeping a proper rein upon the general verdict and preventing it from going contrary to law. There was the practice of entering the verdict found for the plaintiff, with leave reserved to the defendant to move for the entry of a nonsuit or of a verdict in his favor; of entering a nonsuit with leave reserved to the plaintiff to move for a verdict.[141] The reservation in such cases apparently depended on the consent of counsel, and where it contemplated a verdict other than the one found, it proceeded also on the theory of at least an implied consent on the part of the jury.[142] There was also the practice

[139] Stephen, Pleading (1824) 113.

[140] Lord Blackburn in Dublin, Wicklow & Wexford Ry. Co. v. Slattery, L. R. 3 App.Cas. 1155, 1204-1205 (1878) noted by Thayer, Preliminary Treatise on Evidence (1898) 243, note 1 to 241.

[141] Smith, Action at Law (11th ed. 1873) 162, 180-181; Kerr, Action at Law (1854) 196, 205; Thayer, Judicial Administration (1915) 63 U.of Pa.L.Rev. 599 *et seq.*

[142] Smith, *op. cit. loc. cit.;* Mead v. Robinson, Barnes (3d ed.) 451, 94

of taking the verdict subject to a special case stated by agreement of counsel.[143] The last mentioned expedient operated to supersede special verdicts, except where it was intended to carry up the case by writ of error, since the record would show the special verdict, whereas, down to the Common Law Procedure Act of 1854,[144] in the case of the reservation nothing of this would appear of record.[145] Then, again, beginning perhaps about the opening of the nineteenth century, the reports disclose a practice which does not seem to have had the attention of the books—the practice, that is to say, of putting special questions to the jury and directing a general verdict in accordance with the judge's view of the legal effect of the answers.[146]

But chiefly due to the persisting fear of the judge exceeding his province, devices of the kind had scant attraction for the formative era in America. To be noted, however, is the recognition in Pennsylvania, dating from a statute of 1825, of a limited power of making the verdict subject to a reserved question,[147] as also the practice, said to be not uncommon in Massachusetts in the early 1800s, of taking a general verdict subject to the opinion of the court,[148] and some existence in the early Virginia practice of a general verdict subject to the opinion of the court on specific points or on an agreed case.[149] Mention should also be made of the provision incorporated in the New York code in 1852, authorizing the direction of a verdict subject to the opinion of the court.[150] These measures, in a circumscribed manner, permitted the court, in a proper case, to enter a judgment contrary to the verdict, dictated not by the state of the pleadings, but by the state of the evidence. Further

E.R. 999 (1743); Treacher v. Hinton, 4 B.&Ald. 413, 106 E.R. 988 (1821).

143 Smith, *op. cit.* 162-163; Stephen, *op. cit.* 114.

144 17 & 18 Vict. c. 125, § 32.

145 Lord Blackburn in Dublin, Wicklow & Wexford Ry. Co. *supra,* at 1205; 1 Sellon's Crompton, Practice of the Courts of King's Bench and Common Pleas (Am. ed. 1813) *474.

146 *E.g.,* Leonard v. Baker, 1 M.&S. 251, 105 E.R. 94 (1813). This in later times appears on the criminal side. Rex v. Jameson, 60 J.P. 602 (1896).

147 Dalmas v. Kemble, 215 Pa. 410, 64 Atl. 559 (1906).

148 Karlowski v. Kissock, 275 Mass. 180, 182, 175 N.E. 500 (1931).

149 1 Robinson, Practice in the Courts of Law and Equity in Virginia (1832) 373-374; McMichen v. Amos, 4 Rand. 134 (1826); Dejarnatte v. Allen, 5 Gratt. 499 (1849).

150 § 265 of 1851 (§ 220 of 1848) as amended in 1852, Laws 1852, c. 392, p. 658.

progression in the same direction has come in later years. The New York provision was brought to improved expression in the Code of 1876[151] in terms subsequently embodied in the Civil Practice Act of 1920,[152] empowering the judge, when the case presents only questions of law, to direct the jury to render a verdict, subject to his opinion, or to set aside a verdict already rendered and direct judgment to be entered for either party, with like effect as if such a direction had been given at the trial. In 1912 New Jersey made provision for reserving questions of law and submitting the case to the jury upon alternative propositions of law as to the right to relief or damages and for judgment accordingly.[153] And in Massachusetts, where the early practice above mentioned had fallen into disuse, a statute of 1915, taking the view that express assent of the jury was here a necessary element, provides for reservation, by such assent, of the question of law and for entry of the verdict pursuant to the court's determination of that question.[154] But by far the most trenchant advance in relation to judicial control of the verdict, and one embracing a much wider circle of jurisdictions, has proceeded from the numerous group of statutes and rules of court which have adopted the statutory motion presently to be considered, for judgment notwithstanding the verdict on the basis of the evidence.[155]

The special verdict, as at common law, was accepted in most of the American jurisdictions,[156] but, although nominally retained in a number of these, has now generally fallen into disuse. Statutory provision exists in various States for what is known as a special verdict, which, at least in practice, is usually composed of answers to questions submitted.[157] But, except as

151 § 1185.

152 § 461. This provision remained in effect until 1949, when it was repealed as having become superfluous. N.Y. Laws 1949, c. 604: see 15th Annual Report, Judicial Council of the State of New York, 247, 265, and *infra,* § 6 of the present Chapter, p. 334.

153 N.J. Laws 1912, c. 231; N.J. Stat. Ann. 1939, § 2:27-227.

154 Mass. Laws 1915, c. 185; Mass. Ann. Laws 1933, c. 231, § 120.

155 *Infra,* § 6 of the present Chapter.

156 The Georgia constitution of 1777 (Art. XLI), however, provided that "the jury shall be judges of law, as well as of fact, and shall not be allowed to bring in a special verdict." Noted in Scott, Fundamentals of Procedure (1922) 95 note 72.

157 See Clementson, Special Verdicts and Special Findings (1905) 171 *et seq.,* 188 *et seq.*

will appear, this retains as a rule the infirmity of the common-law institution in its rigid requirement as to encompassing the facts. From an early day, however, there emerged the distinctive practice, established in most of the New England States by judicial usage and elsewhere resting on statute,[158] by which the jury is required to answer special interrogatories in connection with its return of a general verdict. The special findings thus attained control the general verdict in such wise that, if a material inconsistency is present, they afford the basis for a judgment contrary to that verdict. This method finds employment in the greater number of the States,[159] and has been adopted by the Federal Rules of 1938. (Rule 49(b)).

But much more satisfactory in its results than the general verdict coupled with special findings is a comparatively recent development of the statutory special verdict. This has consisted in overcoming the requirement of the common-law special verdict that, outside of pleading admissions, there be a finding of all the facts disputed or undisputed, essential to support the judgment. England has had no difficulty on this score. Since the Judicature Acts, the practice is there well established, as an alternative to the general verdict, of taking the jury's answers to specific questions directed to it by the judge and rendering judgment on the basis of these answers, without reference to the doctrines of the common-law special verdict. In America, however, the more rigid notions of the domain of jury trial, consequent upon its constitutional preservation, have not permitted so direct a solution. But under its special verdict statute, Wisconsin, betimes, had advanced by judicial decision to the position that the verdict would not be impaired by the omission of a fact which, although not admitted by the pleadings, had not been disputed in the evidence.[160] In 1897, with reference to a similar statute, providing for a verdict "upon special issues," Texas produced the true key to the situation by foreclosing appellate attack on the ground of an omitted finding, unless there had been, on the part of the complaining

[158] *Ibid.* 16 *et seq.*, 24.

[159] See *ibid.* 24 *et seq.*

[160] McNarra v. Chicago & N. W. Ry. Co. 41 Wis. 69 (1876); Williams v. Porter, 41 Wis. 422 (1877); Hutchinson v. Chicago & N. W. Ry. Co. 41 Wis. 541 (1877); Ward v. Busack, 46 Wis. 407, 1 N.W. 107 (1879).

party, a written request for the submission of the particular point, and by providing that in the absence of such request there should be deemed to be a finding by the court on the point, in such manner as, if sustained by the evidence, would support the judgment.[161] Ten years later Wisconsin remodeled its special verdict statute by availing itself of the Texas principle in the skilfully drafted provision that "whenever any special verdict shall be submitted to a jury and there is omitted therefrom some controverted matter not brought to the attention of the court by request but essential to sustain the judgment, such matter of fact shall be deemed determined by the court in conformity with its judgment and the neglect or omission to require a finding by the jury on such matter shall be deemed a waiver of jury trial *pro tanto* and a consent that such omitted fact be determined by the court." [162] Thus the Texas practice of verdict "upon special issues" and the Wisconsin special verdict, both subsequently improved in other directions, have signally contributed to the value of jury trial.[163] In both States the practice is extensively used, in Wisconsin, as we are told,[164] particularly in personal injury cases. Michigan in 1931 adopted the like practice, borrowing the Wisconsin provision.[165]

At common law, as we know, the general verdict represented the jury's pronouncement on the formulated issue or issues. If, for example, to an action of debt on a bond the defendant had pleaded *non est factum,* and the jury decided in favor of the plaintiff, the verdict when spoken in court may well have

[161] Tex. Laws 1897 (Sp. Sess.) c. 7. In substance now incorporated in Tex. Rules Civ. Proc. (Vernon, 1942) Rule 279.

[162] Wis. Laws 1907, p. 571, now rewritten in Wis. Stat. 1949, § 270.28.

[163] For a detailed study of the practice in both States, see Green, A New Development in Jury Trial (1927) 13 A.B.A.J. 715, reprinted in Judge and Jury (1930) 350. It is here pointed out that the suggestion for the Texas amendment of 1927 came from Gaines, C. J., in Silliman v. Gano, 90 Tex. 637, 39 S.W. 559 (1897). Green, at 717 (359). See also in this connection, McCormick, Jury Verdicts upon Special Questions in Civil Cases (1942) Judicial Administration Monographs, A.B.A. Series A, p. 72, and for the Wisconsin practice in general, Werner, Special Verdicts v. General Verdicts (1930).

[164] 3 Bryant, Wisconsin Pleading and Practice (2d ed. 1931) § 470.

[165] Mich. Court Rules 1931, 1933, 1945, Rule 37, § 7, Searl, Mich. Court Rules Ann. (4th ed. 1933) and Cum. Supp. 1945.

been: "We find for the plaintiff and assess his damages at such and such a sum," but when entered of record it appears as a specific finding on the issue, viz., "the jurors . . . say upon their oath that the within mentioned writing obligatory is the deed of the within named C.D. as the within written A.B. has within declared against him," followed by the requisite assessment of damages.[166] In case of a plurality of issues the same principle self-evidently applied. Thus the general verdict, as a preface to its fixation of the amount of recovery if the event so required, was always in legal effect a finding or series of findings meeting the issue or series of issues developed by the pleadings, in the precise terms of those issues. Now, though in the reformed pleading the issues are seldom formulated in the concrete fashion of the common law, they are necessarily extractable from the pleadings and are or should be distinctly stated by the judge to the jury. If, then, the jury is asked to return, instead of a verdict in terms of a general finding for one party or the other, a verdict consisting of categorical affirmative or negative answers to specific questions framed in terms of the issues, as drawn by the judge from the pleadings, along with an answer to a question as to the amount of recovery should the preceding answers so require, there can be no doubt that we have here a general verdict fully corresponding to that of the common law. This idea has been laid hold of in North Carolina, where under a provision regulating the drafting of the issues "arising upon the pleadings," it has been put into successful application as the usual method of taking a verdict for more than half a century.[167] The method is one that ought to be open everywhere, and without statutory aid, for it entails the utilization of common-law principles that have nowhere been displaced.

To be underlined is the step taken by the Federal Rules of

[166] 1 Richardson, Attorney's Practice in the Court of King's Bench (1792) 184.

[167] Green, *op. cit.* 716, 777 *et seq.* (Judge and Jury, 355 *et seq.*, 360 *et seq.*) See also McCormick, *op. cit.* 73-76. An excellent demonstration of the method appears in Porter v. Western N. C. R. Co. 97 N.C. 66, 2 S.E. 581 (1887). The rule referred to originated in 1871 as a rule of court (65 N.C. 705; Green, *op. cit.* 716 (358), but with some variation of expression has since become statutory. Gen. Stat. 1943, § 1-200.

1938. These turned to account the Wisconsin and Texas principle by a provision in which, perhaps, the North Carolina practice was not without influence. Applying the principle both to issues of fact arising upon the pleadings and those arising upon the evidence, it declares that:

> The court may require a jury to return only a special verdict in the form of a special written finding upon each issue of fact. In that event the court may submit to the jury written questions susceptible of categorical or other brief answer or may submit written forms of the several special findings which might properly be made under the pleadings and evidence; or it may use such other method of submitting the issues and requiring the written findings thereon as it deems most appropriate. The court shall give to the jury such explanation and instruction concerning the matter thus submitted as may be necessary to enable the jury to make its findings upon each issue. If in so doing the court omits any issue of fact raised by the pleadings or by the evidence, each party waives his right to a trial by jury of the issue so omitted unless before the jury retires he demands its submission to the jury. As to an issue omitted without such demand the court may make a finding; or, if it fails to do so, it shall be deemed to have made a finding in accord with the judgment on the special verdict. (Rule 49 (a)).

The Federal Rule has been followed textually or nearly so by Arizona (1939), Colorado (1941), Maryland (1941), North Dakota (1943), Delaware (1947), New Jersey (1948), and Utah (1949), and in substance by Iowa (1943).[168]

As has been indicated the English procedure of today is much freer from apparatus in the present regard than is the American. With the opportunity afforded by the Common Law Procedure Act of 1854 [169] to bring error on a special case, the common-law special verdict in civil cases had lost the remaining reason for its retention.[170] Nor does the English law

[168] Ariz. Code Ann. 1939, § 21-1008; Colo. Rules Civ. Proc., Rule 49(a), in Colo. Stat. Ann. 1935, Replacement Vol. I, 1941; Md. Gen. Rules Pract. & Proc., Part 3, Subd. III, Rule 7, in Md. Ann. Code (Flack, 1939), Cum. Supp. 1947, p. 2052; N.D. Rev. Code 1943, § 28-1502; Del. Rules of Superior Court 1947, Rule 49(a); N.J. Rules Civ. Pract. 1948, Rule 3:49-1; Utah Rules Civ. Proc. 1949, Rule 49(a); Ia. Rules Civ. Proc. 1943, Rule 205.

[169] *Supra,* note 144 of the present Chapter.

[170] It has, however, been retained in the criminal procedure. See Queen v. Dudley, 14 Q.B.D. 273, 280 (1884).

recognize anything such as our general verdict coupled with special findings. Indeed, although use of a somewhat similar practice appears in certain of the earlier cases,[171] it was later decided that the judge had no right to question the jury as to the grounds of its general verdict.[172] Where the judge, as he may, instead of permitting the jury to return a general verdict, directs the jury to answer specific questions—questions, be it noted, which normally are not drafted by counsel but are the judge's own, although it is open to counsel to propose others [173] —the result is sometimes spoken of as a special verdict.[174] But the circumstance that there may have been some matter not determined by admission in the pleadings or by the jury's answers cannot affect the judgment, so long as the matter had not been controverted. An omission of that kind, with us, would be harmless under such a practice as that obtaining in Wisconsin and Texas and established by the Federal Rules. Elsewhere, it may well be that there would be applied to the case the traditional principles of the common-law special verdict, and the omission, if concerning a material though wholly undisputed matter, would be fatal to the judgment.[175] Certain provisions of the Rules [176] contribute to the English result, but this seems mainly to have been brought about by the general attitude of bench and bar since the Judicature Acts in looking to the substance rather than the form. For America, however, the more trammeled conditions of jury trial make hopes for the future dependent upon a wider acceptance of the principle which we have seen ultimately turned to account in the Federal Rules.

§ 5. The Motion in Arrest and its Congeners

The paramount importance attaching to the pleadings at common law brought into existence a highly organized system of attack upon the verdict grounded upon faults of pleading.

171 *E.g.*, Cotterill v. Tolly, 1 T.R. 665, 99 E.R. 1304 (1787).

172 Mayor and Burgesses of Devizes v. Clark, 3 Ad.&El. 506, 111 E.R. 506 (1835); Arnold v. Jeffreys [1914] 1 K.B. 512.

173 Odgers, Principles of Pleading and Practice (13th ed. 1946) 272.

174 Wharton, Law Lexicon (14th ed. 1938) p. 945.

175 See *e.g.*, Hodges v. Easton, 106 U.S. 408, 1 S.Ct. 307 (1882); Standard Sewing Machine Co. v. Royal Ins. Co. of Liverpool, 201 Pa. 645, 51 Atl. 354 (1902); Ward v. Gradin, 15 N.D. 649, 109 N.W. 57 (1906).

176 O. XXXVI, r. 39; O. XL, r. 10; O. LVIII, r. 4.

This system reflected the intricacy and complexity of the pleading method itself, but its essence lay in the circumstance that, as the verdict decided only the facts in issue and the only facts in issue were those made so by the pleadings, the fault of the pleadings in this regard, if sufficiently serious, would operate to vitiate the verdict. After the Statute of 1585 [177] faults of substance only could be here regarded, and faults, moreover, which had survived the curative effect of the other statutes of jeofails. Accordingly, there was the *motion in arrest of judgment,* open to the defendant and proceeding because of error apparent in the record. As regards the pleadings, its principal ground was the failure of the declaration to state a legally sufficient cause of action or, occasionally, the confession of a sufficient defense in a bad replication.[178] This, unless the fault was aided by express averment of the opposite party, was supportable or not pursuant to the dictates of the esoteric principle of aider by verdict, moving upon the twin pinions represented by the change in the rule of construction of allegation after verdict and the ascertainment of a basis for inference within the issue.[179] Open to the plaintiff was the *motion for judgment non obstante veredicto,* resting on the contention that the defendants' plea had expressly confessed [180] the plaintiff's cause of action as alleged in his declaration, without stating a legally sufficient defense, this also being affected by the prin-

177 27 Eliz. c. 5.

178 Other pleading faults thus assailable were error in the form of action apparent on the face of the declaration, misjoinder of counts and apparent defect of parties.

179 The classic statement is that of Serjeant Williams in his notes to Saunders' Reports (1 Wms. Saund. 5th ed. 1845, p. 228a): "Where there is any defect, imperfection, or omission in any pleading, whether in substance or form, which would have been a fatal objection upon demurrer; yet if the issue joined be such as necessarily required on the trial proof of the facts so defectively or imperfectly stated or omitted, and without which it is not to be presumed, that either the judge would direct the jury to give, or the jury would have given the verdict, such defect, imperfection or omission, is cured by the verdict by the common law."

180 In the later common-law development in England, when the case was that of a plurality of issues, one or more found for the plaintiff and one or more for the defendant, the equivalent of an express confession in the defective plea was regarded as present, if the cause of action had been proved on another issue or if an express confession of the cause of action appeared in a companion plea, the issue under which had been found for the plaintiff. Gwynne v. Burnell, 6 Bing.N.C. 453, 133 E.R. 175 (1840); Couling v. Coxe, 6 D.&L. 399 (1848).

ciples of aider, though in lesser degree. Each of these aimed at a judgment for the moving party instead of the judgment which normally would have followed the verdict.[181] Then there was the *motion for repleader,* a sort of poor relation of the other two, founded upon such an immateriality of the issue as fell outside the scope of either, having only the modest goal of setting on foot a new series of pleadings starting with the displacement of that one which had initiated the fault, and contemplating a new trial of the rejuvenated issue. It was open to the party against whom the verdict had been rendered, but only when he was not responsible for initiating the fault. On the other hand, the party successful in the verdict might be sufficiently apprehensive of the effect of the immateriality to seek its reform, in which case the motion for repleader was open to him, whether or not his was the responsibility for initiating the fault. Finally there should be mentioned the *motion for a venire de novo* which was the appropriate vehicle of objection to defects disclosed of record in the verdict itself, and which, as a consequence, became a means of pleading-attack in the one case where a general verdict had gone for the plaintiff upon a plurality of counts one or some of which, less than all, were assailed as insufficient in law. As the term implies, the motion, if successful, resulted in a new trial.

The motion in arrest and the motion for judgment *non obstante* have played a considerable part in the early stages of American procedure, and are retained in most of the common-law jurisdictions.[182] Neither was mentioned in the New York Code of 1848 or has been in any subsequent New York legislation. At the present day the motion in arrest finds statutory recognition in a few of the unitary procedure States,[183]

[181] It should be noted that the judgment for the defendant because of failure to state a sufficient cause of action did not prevent the plaintiff from successfully maintaining a new action with a remedied declaration, for the cause of action here stated was not the same as that originally alleged.

[182] Maine, however, has abolished the motion in arrest in civil cases (Rev. Stat. 1944, c. 100, § 52) while Massachusetts and Rhode Island restrict its use to the case where it is based on a lack of jurisdiction of the court. Mass. Ann. Laws 1933, c. 231, § 136; R.I. Gen. Laws Ann. 1938, c. 522, § 1.

[183] Ariz. Code Ann. 1939, § 21-1308; Conn. Gen. Stat. 1949, §§ 8007, 8332, Practice Book 1934, p. 73, Rule 229; Ga. Code 1933, § 110-702 *et seq.;* Ind. Stat. Ann. (Burns, 1933) 1946 Replace-

while in a number of others it is employed without such recognition.[184] So, too, in some of the code jurisdictions, the motion for judgment *non obstante* is permitted its common-law function without statutory aid.[185] But a decisive step was taken by the Kentucky Code of 1851 in its institution of a fusion between the two motions through the logical provision, in full correspondence with common-law principle, that "where, upon the statements in the pleadings, one party is entitled by law to judgment in his favor, judgment shall be so rendered by the court, though a verdict has been found against such party."[186] This manner of provision is one which commended itself to further adoption, and borrowed by Ohio for its Code of 1853[187] and there retained, it is today present also in the legislation of Indiana, Kansas, Nebraska, Oklahoma and Wyoming in substantially the same terms and in somewhat variant terms in that of Oregon, Alaska and Iowa.[188] Kentucky, too, preserves its provision, although not in quite the original form.[189] The motion for judgment on the pleadings which thus has come into use is by no means restricted to a motion after verdict: it is commonly open at any time after conclusion of the pleadings, and accordingly combines the function of the demurrer with that of the common-law motions here in question. Thus in New York, while the early stages of the code

ment Vol. II, § 2-608; N.C. Gen. Stat. 1943, § 1-25; Tex. Rules of Civ. Proc. (Vernon, 1942) Rule 321. Like recognition obtained in Missouri (Mo. Rev. Stat. Ann. 1942, §§ 1171, 1172) until 1943 when both the motion in arrest and the motion for judgment *non obstante veredicto* were abolished and their functions transferred to a motion for new trial or an innominate motion for relief. Mo. Laws 1943, p. 389, § 120; Mo. Rev. Stat. Ann. 1942, 1950 Cum. Pocket Part for Vol. 3, § 847.120.

184 See *e.g.*, Quimby v. Boyd, 8 Colo. 194 (1884); Messenger v. Woge, 20 Colo.App. 275, 78 Pac. 314 (1904); Brickman v. S. Carolina RR. Co. 8 S.C. 173 (1876).

185 *E.g.*, Baxter v. Irvin, 158 N.C. 277, 73 S.E. 882 (1912); Barnes v. Rodgers, 54 S.C. 115, 31 S.E. 885 (1899); Hurt v. Ford, 142 Mo. 283, 44 S.W. 228 (1898); King v. Kaw-Mo. Wholesale Grocer Co. 188 Mo.App. 225, 175 S.W. 77 (1915).

186 Ky. Code Pract. in Civ. Cas. 1851, § 424, reënacted in Code 1854, § 416.

187 Ohio Laws 1853, p. 120; Code 1853, § 384.

188 Ohio Gen. Code Ann. (Page, 1938) § 11601; Ark. Stat. Ann. 1947, § 29-111; Ind. Stat. Ann. (Burns, 1933) 1946 Replacement Vol. II, § 2-2503; Kan. Gen. Stat. Ann. 1935, § 60-3119; Neb. Rev. Stat. 1943, § 25-1315; Okla. Stat. 1941, Tit. 12, § 698; Wyo. Comp. Stat. Ann. 1945, § 3-3603; Ore. Comp. Laws Ann. 1940, § 6-707; Alaska Comp. Laws Ann. 1949, § 55-9-47; Ia. Rules Civ. Proc. 1943, Rule 243.

189 Code Pract. in Civ. Cas. (Carroll, 1948) § 386.

procedure show judicial recognition extended to the equivalent of the common-law motions,[190] it was provided in 1908 that "if either party is entitled to judgment upon the pleadings, the court may upon motion at any time after issue joined give judgment accordingly." [191] Carried into the Civil Practice Act of 1920, this provision was so widened as to permit the motion to take into consideration admissions outside the pleadings and to be made "at any stage of an action or appeal." [192]

So far, however, as the motion for judgment is applied after verdict and remains restricted to the pleadings and so far as the common-law motions are retained, the determination of the motion under traditional rules rests solely upon the contents of the pleadings, without reference to the evidence at the trial. But provisions as to amendment are now everywhere so liberal, that it is today probably true generally, that the evidence may be looked at in order to ascertain whether the fact omitted or defectively alleged was actually a subject of controversy. If so the matter may be set right by appropriate amendment, should no injustice thus be occasioned to the opponent. On the other hand, if the fact in question was neither alleged nor the subject of proof, the matter ordinarily would be beyond the reach of mere amendment. For such a case, the English Common Law Procedure Act of 1852 permitted the party whose pleading was alleged or adjudged to be defective, on motion in arrest or motion for judgment *non obstante veredicto,* to suggest the existence of the fact in question, which suggestion was then to be pleaded to by the opposite party, and the issue or issues thus arising to be tried in the ordinary way; if the existence of the fact should be admitted or found in his favor, the suggesting party was to be entitled to such a judgment as would have followed had the fact been originally stated in the pleading attacked, otherwise the sustained motion would result in a judgment for the assailant.[193] This has been followed in substance by a statutory provision in Florida.[194]

[190] See Burnham v. De Bevorse, 8 How.Pract. 159 (1853); Mallory v. Lamphear, 8 How.Pract. 491 (1853).

[191] N.Y. Laws 1908, c. 166.

[192] N.Y. Civ. Pract. Act (Clevenger, 1950) § 476. See also Rules Civ. Pract., Rule 112 (Clevenger, *op. cit.* p. 15-87).

[193] 15 & 16 Vict. c. 76, §§ 143, 144.

[194] Fla. Stat. 1949, § 54.27.

An alternative provision in Florida [195] and a provision in Illinois [196] have gone much further in mitigating the common-law effect of a sustained motion in arrest: under their terms the sustaining of the motion may signify only a new trial on amended pleadings. The same was true of the Missouri procedure prior to the changes of 1943: [197] how far it has been affected by the repeal of the applicable statute and the abolition of the motion in arrest [198] as such it is difficult to say. While at common-law, the sustaining of a motion in arrest for fault in the pleadings normally resulted in a judgment of *nil capiat,* viz., that the plaintiff take nothing by his writ and go thereof without day,[199] yet the court, with respect to the motion in general, was not without a certain amount of discretionary power; [200] and it may be a question whether, even in the absence of statutory authority, and apart from an ascertainment that the fact omitted or defectively alleged had been definitely dealt with in the evidence, an American court of the present day, if convinced that the plaintiff actually had a good course of action, could not on a sustained motion in arrest or its reformed equivalent, where the interests of justice so required, direct an amendment and new trial without too much violence to orthodox principle.

The Federal Rules give no place to either of the two common-law motions. The motion for judgment on the pleadings which they recognize is one made in advance of the trial. (Rule 12(c)). [201] If an objection on the ground of failure to state a claim for relief, or to join an indispensable party, on the one hand, or to state a legal defense, on the other, were not advanced until after verdict (lack of jurisdiction of the subject-matter apart), it would apparently be considered as waived under the provisions of Rule 12(h).

[195] *Ibid., loc. cit.*

[196] Ill. Civ. Pract. Act 1933, § 56; Ill. Rev. Stat. 1949, c. 110, § 180.

[197] Mo. Rev. Stat. Ann. 1942, § 1172, now repealed.

[198] See *supra,* note 183 of the present Chapter.

[199] Kierle v. Shriver, 11 Gill & J. (Md.) 405 (1841).

[200] See Butcher v. Metts, 1 Miles (Pa.) 233 (1836).

[201] While, as affecting a pre-verdict motion, the point falls outside the present inquiry, it is interesting to note that the amendments of 1946, by way of settling the practice, provided that if matters outside the pleadings are entertained on the motion, the motion is to be treated as one for summary judgment. Federal Rules of Procedure (West Publishing Co. 1947) pp. 27, 31.

The common-law judgment of repleader for mere immateriality of the issue continues its existence in most of the common-law jurisdictions, as well as in some other quarters.[202] Elsewhere its substance is generally present, without the old designation, in the form of an order for amendment of the pleadings, and the award of a new trial. As for the motion for a *venire de novo,* this has long been simply a species of motion for new trial, as it had in effect become in the later days of common-law pleading in England.[203]

In the modern English law the names of these motions have wholly disappeared from the working procedural vocabulary. Under the Rules, the question of a failure to state a cause of action or a defense in the pleadings would be, after verdict, translated into a question of whether or not a proper cause of action or defense had appeared in the evidence, for the generally applicable principle is that "if the issue of fact can be fairly determined upon the existing evidence, they [the parties] may of course amend." [204] In a case of the kind, therefore, (although none has been found in the reports) the matter would be resolved by the canons governing insufficiency of the evidence. In a very clear case of such insufficiency, the trial judge apparently would have power, with or without motion, to direct a judgment in favor of the party unsuccessful in the verdict.[205] But if the matter were not free from doubt, then the judge would be required to enter judgment on the verdict, and the recourse of the unsuccessful party would be by motion in the nature of an appeal addressed to the Court of Appeal, which would have plenary power to render a judgment contrary to the verdict, or, if the situation so required, to direct a new trial on amended pleadings.[206]

202 See 49 C.J. p. 580, § 812 *et seq.*

203 See Watkin Williams, Introduction to the Principles and Practice of Pleading (1857) 197.

204 *Per* Lord Atkin in Bell v. Lever Bros., Ltd., [1932] A.C. 161, 216.

205 See observations of Phillimore, L. J., in Skeate v. Slater's, Ltd. [1914] 2 K.B. 429, 444 (C.A.).

206 O. XL, r. 10; O. LVIII, r. 4; Winterbotham, Gurney & Co. v. Sibthorp, [1918] 1 K.B. 625 (C.A.).

§ 6. The Motion for Judgment on the Evidence notwithstanding the Verdict

Mention has already been made of the common-law practice of causing a verdict to be rendered subject to a reserved question, and of certain American developments toward the same end. But in the past half century American attention has been markedly directed to a different type of regulation in the field of verdict-control, usually conditioned upon the circumstance that a motion to direct a verdict has been previously made. Its instrumentality is commonly spoken of as a motion for judgment notwithstanding the verdict, in analogy to the common-law motion of that name, it being, however, sharply distinguished from the latter by the fact that it is actuated by the state of the evidence, instead of the state of the pleadings.[207] In this development Minnesota seems to have taken the lead by a statute of 1895,[208] under which, following the denial of a motion to direct, "the trial court, on motion made that judgment be entered notwithstanding the verdict, or on motion for a new trial, shall order judgment to be entered in favor of the party who was entitled to have a judgment directed in his or its favor." The same provision was taken over by North Dakota in 1901.[209] In 1905 Pennsylvania effected an improvement of its reserved question practice by adopting substantially the same rule applicable to "a point requesting binding instructions . . . reserved or declined." [210] Wisconsin and Washington attained to a similar regulation without statutory aid, the one in 1903,[211] the other in 1906.[212] Between the time last mentioned and the advent of the Federal Rules of 1938, legislation of the present pattern made its appearance in a number of other States. Thus Michigan

207 Valuable in this regard are the Notes (1935) 34 Mich.L.Rev. 93 and (1936) 13 Tex.L.Rev. 206.

208 Minn. Laws 1895, c. 320, Minn. Stat. 1945, § 605.06.

209 N.D. Laws 1901, c. 63.

210 Pa. Laws 1905, No. 198, Pa. Stat. Ann. (Purdon, 1931) Tit. 12, § 681; Dalmas v. Kemble, 215 Pa. 410, 64 Atl. 559 (1906).

211 Muench v. Heinemann, 119 Wis. 441, 96 N.W. 800 (1903); Hay v. City of Baraboo, 127 Wis. 1, 105 N.W. 654 (1906).

212 Roe v. Standard Furniture Co., 41 Wash. 546, 83 Pac. 1109 (1906). See also the previous case of Casey v. Jamison, 35 Wash. 478, 77 Pac. 800 (1904).

(1915),[213] Wyoming (1915),[214] South Dakota (1921),[215] California (1923),[216] Idaho (1931),[217] Texas (1931),[218] Illinois (1933),[219] and Ohio (1935),[220] all accepted this manner of proceeding. Various of these statutes either by their original terms or by amendment extend the rule so as to authorize a like judgment where the jury has been discharged for failure to agree upon a verdict; sometimes, as in Pennsylvania and Michigan, this is the result of a separate enactment.[221] Apparently in deference to the older practice, the Michigan statute, followed by that of Illinois, requires reservation of the motion to direct. All proceed on the basis of an actual motion to direct previously made, except those of Texas and Ohio, both of which are content with the existence of such a situation as would have supported a motion to direct. But the principle established by the Minnesota and Pennsylvania statutes is identical throughout.[222] The value of the authority which thus vests in the court is self-evident. If, for example, the defendant moves for a directed verdict and the court sustains the motion, then the verdict is directed and judgment goes for the defendant. If, on the other hand, there is a denial of the motion, followed by a verdict for the plaintiff, and the court becomes

213 Mich. Laws 1915, p. 366; Mich. Stat. Ann. 1938, § 27-1461.

214 Wyo. Laws 1915, c. 134; Wyo. Comp. Stat. Ann. 1945, § 3-3605.

215 S.D. Laws 1921, c. 181; S.D. Code 1939, § 33.1705.

216 Cal. Laws 1923, c. 366; § 1; Cal. Code Civ. Proc. (Deering, 1949) § 629.

217 Idaho Laws 1931, c. 27; Idaho Code Ann. 1949, § 10-224.

218 Tex. Laws 1931, c. 77, § 1; Tex. Rules Civ. Proc. (Vernon, 1942) Rule 301.

219 Ill. Civ. Pract. Act 1933, § 68(3); Ill. Rev. Stat. 1949, c. 110, § 192(3). Whether Rules Civ. Pract. & Proc. 1933, Rule 22 (§ 259.22), operates to dispense with the necessity of reservation appears to be still an open question.

220 Ohio Laws 1935, p. 413; Ohio Gen. Code Ann. (Page, 1938) § 11601.

221 Pa. Stat. Ann. (Purdon, 1931) Tit. 12, § 684; Mich. Stat. Ann. 1938, § 27-1471.

222 A cognate statute but one of a different description is that enacted in 1919 in Virginia, where direction of a verdict is forbidden. This provides that where a verdict is set aside by a trial court as contrary to the evidence, or without evidence to support it, a new trial shall not be granted if there is sufficient evidence before the court to enable it to decide the case on its merits, but final judgment shall be entered as to the court seems right. Va. Code Ann. 1942, § 6251; Va. Code Ann. 1950, § 8-352. As construed by the Supreme Court this gives the court no power to pass on disputed facts but operates only in the absence of evidence to support the verdict. W. S. Forbes & Co. v. Southern Cotton Oil Co. 130 Va. 245, 108 S.E. 15 (1921).

convinced that the motion should have been allowed, it is manifestly logical that here, too, there should be a judgment in favor of the defendant, for thus the parties are put in the position which would have been theirs had the court not committed the error of failing to sustain the motion.

While it is true that this measure operates to cut off the pre-existing right of new trial in the cases to which it is applicable, yet, properly viewed, it trenches no more upon the province of the jury than would direction of a verdict in the first place. Nevertheless the Supreme Court of the United States in 1912 came to an opposite conclusion. In the well-known case of *Slocum* v. *New York Life Insurance Co.*[223]—an action originating in the Federal Circuit Court, sitting in Pennsylvania, where, after the trial court had declined the defendant's request for binding instructions, verdict and judgment had gone for the plaintiff, and the Circuit Court of Appeals, pursuant to the Pennsylvania statute, under which the appellate tribunal had the same power as the trial court in the present regard, had directed the entry of judgment for the defendant—it was held that such a mode of proceeding, in depriving the plaintiff of the benefit of a new trial, ran counter to the Seventh Amendment. But more than twenty years later another decision of the court—that of *Baltimore & Carolina Line Inc.* v. *Redman* [224]—went far toward repairing the damage thus wrought to the principle in the federal forum. The statute here in question was the New York provision, which, as has been seen, dated basically from 1852, enabling the judge, where only questions of law are involved, to cause the verdict to be returned subject to the opinion of the court. The defendant having moved for dismissal, as also for a directed verdict, on the ground of insufficiency of the evidence, the trial court had allowed the jury to return a verdict subject to the court's opinion, and then, in conformity with the verdict, rendered judgment for the plaintiff. On review the Circuit Court of Appeals agreed with the defendant as to the insufficiency of the evidence and reversed the judgment, but considered that under the *Slocum* case it could give no direction other than

[223] 228 U.S. 364, 33 S.Ct. 523 (1913). [224] 295 U.S. 654, 55 S.Ct. 890 (1935).

that for a new trial. This, the Supreme Court held, was wrong: the direction should have been for dismissal as authorized under the statute. The situation was not governed by the Slocum case, because here, instead of a denial by the trial court of the defendant's motions, there was express reservation of decision of the motions—a course which the court considered to be in consonance with common-law practice, "well established when the Seventh Amendment was adopted." That it may be a question whether this common-law practice did not depend upon at least the constructive consent of the jury is a circumstance not adverted to by the court. And to what extent the force of the decision is affected by the court's observation that no objection was taken to the proceedings in relation to the reservation and that "they must be regarded as having the tacit consent of the parties" remains a matter of conjecture. But these doubts have since become purely academic through the court's adoption of the Rules of 1938. By these it is provided that "whenever a motion for a directed verdict made at the close of all the evidence is denied or for any reason is not granted, the court is deemed to have submitted the action to the jury subject to a later determination of the legal questions raised by the motion"; that within ten days after verdict or a discharge of the jury without verdict, a party who has moved for a directed verdict may move for the setting aside of the verdict and any judgment entered thereon, and for judgment in accordance with his motion to direct; that a motion for new trial may be joined with this motion either concurrently or in the alternative, and that "if a verdict was returned the court may allow the judgment to stand or may reopen the judgment and either order a new trial or direct the entry of judgment as if the requested judgment had been directed," a direction for a like judgment or for a new trial being in order if no verdict had been returned. (Rule 50(b)).[225] Thus, by the use of the words "is deemed

[225] It should be noted that it has been held by the Supreme Court that where the motion for judgment notwithstanding the verdict is coupled with a motion for new trial, it is the duty of the trial court to rule on each motion, that the sustaining of the motion for judgment does not impliedly overrule the motion for new trial, and that when the court has failed to rule specifically on the motion for new trial, the case must go back for its

to have submitted . . . subject to a later determination" etc., homage is paid to the theory of reservation, and the artificial expedient so contrived is all that, on the face of things, stands between the principle invoked and the violation of the Seventh Amendment found in the Slocum case. But unrealistic as is this means, no one can doubt that the principle itself, with its highly beneficial results, is now secure in the federal tribunals.[225a]

The provision of the Federal Rules has given new impetus to the advance of the principle in the State jurisdictions. It found echo, either verbatim or substantially so, in Arizona (1939), New York (1940), New Mexico (1942), North Dakota (1943, in substitution for its former statute); Missouri (1943), Delaware (1947), Florida (1949) and Utah (1949).[226] Further recognition of the principle under the federal influence appears in Maryland (1941), South Carolina (1942) and Iowa (1943).[227]

In New York, however, certain modifications of the adopted provision were introduced by legislation of 1949. Particularly of interest is the discarding of the formal allegiance to the reservation theory expressed by the "deemed" clause of the Federal Rule. There is accordingly recognized the right of the court to act on the party's motion without regard to any ques-

ruling on this motion. Montgomery Ward & Co. v. Duncan, 311 U.S. 243, 61 S.Ct. 189 (1940). The court has also decided that, unless the appropriate motion is made below, after denial of a motion for directed verdict, the appellate court is without power to direct the entry of a judgment notwithstanding the verdict. Cone v. West Virginia Pulp & Paper Co. 330 U.S. 212, 67 S.Ct. 752 (1947).

225a Retention of the words in question has been against the advice of the Advisory Committee, which in its 1946 report recommended the elimination as wholly unnecessary of what it properly calls an "awkward fiction." Report of Proposed Amendments etc. June 1946, p. 64.

226 Ariz. Code Ann. 1939, § 21-1015 (Rules Civ. Proc., Rule 50(b)); N.Y. Laws 1940, c. 749, N.Y. Civ. Pract. Act (Clevenger, 1948) § 457-a, subd. 3; Colo. Rules Civ. Proc. 1941, Rule 50(b), in Colo. Stat. Ann. 1935, Replacement Vol. I, 1941; N.M. Stat. Ann. 1941, § 19-101 (50)(b), (Rules Civ. Proc., Rule 50(b)); N.D. Rev. Code 1943, § 28-1510; Mo. Laws 1943, p. 387, § 113, 3 Mo.Rev.Stat. 1942, 1950 Cum. Pocket Part, § 847.113; Fla. Common Law Rules 1949, Rule 40(b); Utah Rules Civ. Proc. 1949, Rule 50(b).

227 S.C. Rules Pract. for Circt. Courts, Rule 79, in S.C. Code 1942, Vol. I, p. 1428; Ia. Rules Civ. Proc. 1943, Rule 243(b), in Ia. Code 1946, Vol. II, p. 2170; Md. Gen. Rules Pract. & Proc., Part 3, Subd. III, Rules 4, 8, in Md. Code Ann. (Flack, 1939), 1947 Cum. Supp., pp. 2050, 2052; see also p. 2085.

tion of reservation express or implied. Only where the court acts on its own motion is reservation of moment, and here it must always be express.[227a]

§ 7. The Motion for New Trial [228]

Apart from the award of a *venire facias* for error apparent of record, the early common law discloses various instances of new trials granted on the ground of misconduct of jurors.[228a] But new trials in the wider sense, particularly with reference to matters of evidence, are not recorded before the 1600s. The first case in the books appears to be that of *Wood* v. *Gunston,*[229] decided in 1655, where a new trial was granted on the ground of excessive damages. We are told by Lord Mansfield, speaking in 1757, that "for a good while after this time, the granting of new trials was holden to a degree of strictness, so intolerable, that it drove the parties into a court of equity, to have, in effect, a new trial at law of a mere legal question . . . And therefore of late years, the courts of law have gone more liberally into the granting of new trials, according to the circumstances of the respective cases," [230] acting, as Blackstone has put it, on the maxim that "where justice is not done upon one trial, the injured party is entitled to another." [231] With this end in view the motion for new trial developed into a widely applicable institution of the common-law practice as a means of challenging and remedying prejudicial errors in the trial not appearing in the record itself. The common-law rules as to grounds passed into the American practice and have been

[227a] N.Y. Laws 1949, c. 604; N.Y. Civ. Pract. Act (Clevenger, 1950) § 457-a, subd. 2, 3; 15th Annual Report, Judicial Council of the State of New York (1949) 245 *et seq.*

[228] Our order of treatment in postponing consideration of the motion for new trial until after that of the other post-verdict motions departs from the order of the common-law writers, consequent upon the common-law rule by which the making of a motion in arrest of judgment or a motion for judgment n. o. v. operated as a waiver of a motion for a new trial. Modern developments have made it more logical to follow the order here observed.

[228a] 3 Blackstone, Comm. * 387-388; Thayer, Preliminary Treatise on Evidence (1898) 169, 171.

[229] Style 466, 82 E.R. 867. In Bright v. Eynon, 1 Burr. 390, 394, 97 E.R. 365 (1757) Lord Mansfield, referring to Wood v. Gunston, says that "the reason why this matter cannot be traced further back is 'that the old report books do not give any accounts of determinations made by the Court upon motions.' "

[230] Bright v. Eynon, *supra,* 394, 395.

[231] 3 Blackstone, Comm. * 388.

retained in substance both in the common-law jurisdictions and under the codes. Today, therefore, there is little difference on this score among the Anglo-American jurisdictions in general.

The numerous grounds thus assignable may concern any angle of the trial proceedings. Most familiar are those maintaining that the court erred in admitting or excluding evidence, or in charging the jury, that the jury was at fault in returning a verdict contrary to law or against the evidence, or assessing too large or too small an amount of damages, that there was misconduct on the part of jurors, or of the opposite party or his counsel, or that since the return of the verdict there has been discovered material evidence which could not with reasonable diligence have been produced at the trial. In many of the codes there is an enumeration of grounds, but the jurisdictions thus ruled disagree as to whether such enumeration excludes resort to other grounds recognized by the common law.[232]

At common law, according to the practice of the Court of King's Bench, the party successful in the verdict took out a rule *nisi* for judgment expiring in four days from the date of its entry. The motion for new trial normally had to be made within these four days.[233] In the Common Pleas there was also a four-day period for the motion somewhat differently initiated.[234] But where the ground was that of newly discovered evidence, the courts exercised discretion as to granting further time.[235] Indeed, it was said in 1790 that it was "never too late to move for a new trial on discovery . . . if you apply in due time after the discovery is made."[236] In America, this ground apart, the motion is generally required to be made at the verdict term, unless otherwise regulated by statute or rule of court. But such regulation is abundant and diversified:

[232] See 39 Am.Jur. *s. v.* New Trial, § 27; 46 C.J. *s. v.* New Trial, § 27.

[233] 1 Sellon's Crompton, Practice of the Courts of King's Bench and Common Pleas (Am. ed. 1813) *478 *et seq.*, *484; 2 Tidd, Practice of the Courts of King's Bench and Common Pleas (9th ed. 1828) 912; Heiskell v. Rollins, 81 Md. 397, 398 (1895).

[234] 1 Sellon's Crompton, *op. cit.* *478; 2 Tidd, *op. cit. loc. cit.*

[235] Willis v. Bennett, Barnes 443, 94 E.R. 995 (1737).

[236] Lofft, 160, 98 E.R. 587 (reports of cases from Easter, 12 Geo. 3, to Michaelmas, 14 Geo. 3, published 1790).

it ascends the scale, ranging from two days after verdict in Washington [237] to sixty days in Wisconsin.[238] A number of jurisdictions have in common the rule requiring the motion to be made within thirty days after verdict "unless unavoidably prevented." [239] Ten days after verdict, or ten days after judgment are rules also favored. This last is the one adopted by the Federal Rules of 1938. (Rule 59(b)). When change is thus made from the common-law requirement that the motion and its decision precede the judgment, it is usually provided that enforcement of the judgment be suspended either automatically or upon special order of court, pending decision of the motion. As at common law, the motion grounded upon newly discovered evidence stands on a somewhat different basis with respect to time. An enlarged time is here frequently assigned. A fairly common provision—apparently originating in the Kentucky Code of 1851 [240]—permits application for new trial on this ground, by petition on which summons issues, filed not later than the second term after discovery. The original provision barred the application if not made within three years after the final judgment. This period is still retained in Kentucky,[241] but commencing, it would seem, with the Ohio Code of 1853,[242] the period is more usually fixed at one year. The Federal Rules originally provided by Rule 59(b) that the motion be made before the expiration of the time for appeal, but since the amendments of 1946, Rule 59(b) regulates only the ordinary motion for new trial, and the motion on the ground of newly discovered evidence, now governed by Rule 60(b), is presently in order within a reasonable time not more than one year from the date of the judgment.[243]

237 Wash. Rev. Stat. (Remington, 1932) § 402.

238 Wis. Stat. 1949, § 270.49.

239 Kan. Gen. Stat. 1935, § 60-3003; Ky. Code Pract. in Civ. Cas. (Carroll, 1948) § 342; Neb. Rev. Code 1943, § 25-1143; Ohio Gen. Code (Page, 1938) § 11578; Okla. Stat. 1941, Tit. 12, § 653. These statutes, except that of Kansas, require that the motion be made at the term as well as within the three days.

240 Ky. Code Pract. in Civ. Cas. 1851, § 385.

241 Present Ky. Code (Carroll, 1948) §§ 340, 344.

242 Ohio Code Civ. Proc. 1853, § 301.

243 Federal Rule 59(b) as it originally stood has been followed in Arizona, Code Ann. 1939, § 21-1305, and Colorado, Stat. Ann. 1935, Replacement Vol. I, 1941, Rule 59(b). Both 59(b) and 60(b) in their present form, with or without some variation,

The motion for new trial is usually said to be addressed to the discretion of the court. This was fully true at common law,[244] where there was no means of reviewing the decision of the motion, which could not come in question on writ of error.[245] It continues to be true today, but the decision is now subject to review to a greater or less extent. There is, to be sure, a difference between a motion raising a pure question of law and one which involves what is sometimes inaccurately called "error of fact," as where it urges that the verdict is against the weight of the evidence. In some jurisdictions the error purely of law is accordingly said to fall outside the sphere of discretion.[246] With respect to errors of law not productive of manifest injustice, it would seem in accord with common sense, whether we speak of discretion or not, that no such error should warrant the grant of a new trial. And this, indeed, was the rule of the common law. But in 1835, the English Court of Exchequer, in the matter of evidence, "announced a rule which in spirit and in later interpretation signified that an error of ruling created *per se* for the excepting and defeated party a right to a new trial." [247] This doctrine obviously appealed to that point of view which sought to restrict the power of the court as against that of the jury. Accordingly it found a wide following in the United States as to errors of law in general, and continues to influence the practice in many quarters. Statutory provisions seeking its correction have not been too successful, and American procedure in considerable degree still suffers from the legacy of the so-called "Exchequer rule." Its elimination is not an easy task. Over and above legislative

---

not, however, affecting this particular matter, have been followed in New Mexico, Stat. Ann. 1941, Cum. Supp. to Vol. II, 1949, § 19-101(59)(b), 19-101(60)(b); Delaware, Rules of Superior Court 1947, Rules 59(b) and (in part) 60(b); New Jersey, Rules Civ. Pract. 1948, Rules 3:59-2, 3:60-2; and Utah, Rules Civ. Proc. 1949, Rules 59(b), 60(b).

[244] See Edmondson v. Machell, 2 Term Rep. 4, 100 E.R. 2 (1787).

[245] The motion for new trial waived the right to a writ of error. 1 Holdsworth, History of English Law (3d ed. 1922) 226.

[246] *E.g.*, Buck v. Buck, 122 Minn. 463, 468, 142 N.W. 729 (1913); Loftus v. Metropolitan Street Ry. Co. 220 Mo. 470, 481, 119 S.W. 942 (1909); Wetter Bros. v. Otto, 179 Ia. 873, 882, 162 N.W. 12 (1917); Bonner v. Pullman Co. 160 S.C. 531, 541, 159 S.E. 382 (1931).

[247] 1 Wigmore, Evidence (3d ed. 1940) § 21, p. 367. The case in question was Crease v. Barrett, 1 Cr.M.&R. 919, 149 E.R. 1353.

measures, it is to be accomplished, as Professor Wigmore has pointed out, only by a change of spirit in the administration of justice.[248] But it is not too much to hope that here a complete reversion to the salutary doctrine of the common law will one day come about, and that in this matter of new trials, the controlling principle will be everywhere recognized, as it always has been in certain jurisdictions, that "if . . . upon the whole case justice has been done between the parties, and the verdict is substantially right, no new trial will be granted, although there may have been some mistakes committed at the trial." [249]

In England the career of the "Exchequer rule" came to an end under the Judicature Acts, with the Rules of 1875 which provided that a new trial was not to be granted for misdirection or the improper admission or rejection of evidence, unless in the opinion of the court "some substantial wrong or miscarriage has been thereby occasioned in the trial of the action." Carried into the revision of 1883, this provision remains in substance a part of the Rules now in force.[250] Unlike the case in certain American courts construing similar provisions,[251] that here in question has been so interpreted as to give full effect to its words. Accordingly, a new trial on the ground of the errors mentioned will be denied "if the respondent can satisfy the Court that no substantial wrong or miscarriage has been thereby occasioned." [252]

At common law the motion was addressed to and decided by the court *en banc,* and the early stages of American procedure disclose a similar practice in various jurisdictions. But the distinctive form of judicial organization developed here in the first half of the 1800s, with its emphasis upon the decentralized administration of trial justice and review of errors

[248] Wigmore, *loc. cit.,* where the matter is luminously dealt with at length.

[249] McLanahan v. Universal Insurance Co. 1 Pet. (26 U.S.) 170, 183 (1828), opinion by Mr. Justice Story.

[250] 38 & 39 Vict. c. 77, First Schedule, O. XXXIX, r. 3; present Rules, O. XXXIX, r. 6. The revision likewise restricted the award of a new trial "because the verdict of the jury was not taken upon a question which the judge at the trial was not asked to leave to them." And the Rule now speaks in terms of the Court of Appeal.

[251] 1 Wigmore, *op. cit.* § 21, p. 373.

[252] Odgers, Principles of Pleading and Practice (13th ed. 1946) 284.

by a separate tribunal of appellate jurisdiction,[253] has generally brought it about that the motion in first instance is passed upon by the trial judge. Some remains of the former practice, however, continue to exist in a few of the older States, notably in Maine, where the Supreme Judicial Court hears and determines motions for new trial in causes tried before one of its own judges in the exercise of its original jurisdiction. In New York the motion is addressed to the trial judge and normally decided by him in accordance with the usual rule, but a certain resemblance to the former practice is suggested by the provision which gives him discretion in jury cases, on the application of the party aggrieved, to order that the motion in first instance be heard by the court to which an appeal could be taken from the judgment.[254]

In England, as part of the reform instituted by the Judicature Acts, it was provided by the act of 1873 that every motion for new trial was to be heard before a Divisional Court.[255] This consisted usually of three judges of the Division to which the action belonged. Since, under other provisions of the act, judgment preceded the motion, the motion thus came to be virtually an appeal to the Divisional Court.[256] It was therefore but logical that the further step should be taken, as it was by the amendatory act of 1890, of providing that the motion "shall be heard and determined by the Court of Appeal and not by a divisional court of the High Court." [257] And it is now declared by the Rules that the motion "shall be brought before the Court of Appeal in like manner as an appeal, and on the hearing of such application the Court of Appeal shall have all such powers as are exercisable by it on the hearing of an appeal." [258]

A recent writer, criticizing the narrowness of view with respect to motions for new trial obtaining in the federal

[253] See Pound, Organization of Courts (1940) 122, 247.

[254] N.Y. Civ. Pract. Act (Clevenger, 1950) § 550.

[255] 36 & 37 Vict. c. 66, § 48.

[256] In 1877 it was said: "Thus, in all cases now the application must be to set aside the judgment; and, whatever the ground of the application, it must be against the decision of the judge, and is really an appeal." Finlason, An Exposition of our Judicial System and Civil Procedure (1877) 363.

[257] 53 & 54 Vict. c. 44, § 1.

[258] R.S.C., O. XXXIX, r. 2.

courts, has strongly urged the substantial adoption of the English system. "The need," he says, "for developing the motion for new trial into a simple method of appeal is as great in this country as it was in England. The necessary reform can be achieved by the simple expedient of directing that the motion be heard by a bench of judges or by an appellate court. Our whole scheme of arguing motions for new trial before single trial judges is anomalous—the product of historical accident—and should be abolished." [259] The argument is a captivating one, because manifestly the change would eliminate one stage of the proceeding and produce a speedier judgment. But what as to the element of discretion which is the very marrow of the motion? Is the appellate bench in the same good position to exercise it as the trial judge? Compare the two under the existing system. The trial court "is more fully possessed of the case, has opportunities of observing the witnesses, their demeanor upon the stand, and the hundred other minor incidents of a jury trial which may tend to satisfy it of the justice or injustice of the verdict. A court of review, revising its rulings, sees nothing in the case beyond the bald statements in the bill of exceptions, and is bound to pass upon the questions involved as abstract propositions of law." [260] And what is true of the bench in its function of revision would gather no aid from the fact that it was acting initially. At common law it was not altogether unusual for the trial judge to sit as one of the bench passing on the motion. In any case the bench frequently sought his views on the matter. We are told by a commentator on the Judicature Acts, speaking of the previous practice, that "as a general rule, if the judge who tried the case was 'satisfied' with the verdict on the evidence, it was allowed to stand, but if he was not 'satisfied' with it, then it was set aside," and, again, that, in this matter of evidence, the trial judge "was always referred to and his opinion deferred to by the court." [261] Whatever advantages are offered by the present English system, they are confined to pure questions

[259] Blume, Motions for New Trial in the Federal Courts (1941) 25 Jour. Am.Jud.Soc. 109, 112.

[260] Brown, D. J. (later of the Supreme Court) in Rowe v. Matthews (C.C.E.D. Mich.) 18 Fed. 132, 134 (1883).

[261] Finlason, *op. cit.* 360, 361.

of law, and even then the appellate bench is not provided with the same atmosphere as the trial judge in determining the prejudiciality of the error. Moreover, turning the motion into an appeal would involve the abandonment of the informal presentation of the materials for decision which obtains in many jurisdictions, and, unless there be radical recasting of appellate procedure in general, or for this phase of it in particular, would everywhere require that such presentation be made by bill of exceptions, case-made, or other formal means appropriate to appeal. Historical accident or not, the present method has virtues which are absent from both the old practice and the modern English. The saving of time by the latter cannot outweigh the merits of the existing practice in promoting the interests of substantial justice.

"So far as a new trial goes beyond the necessity of its use," said the learned Mr. Justice Doe, "so far it is an unnecessary injustice and an unmixed evil." [262] Thus is expressed the thought which has brought about departure from the common-law rule, based upon the idea of the indivisibility of the verdict, that a new trial must be a new trial of all the issues, even if the motivating error affected them only in part. That rule forbade a new trial as to less than all the issues, but also, in general, as to less than all the parties. The departure in the sense of permitting the award of a new trial, limited to particular, clearly severable issues, whether between the same parties, or involving only some of the parties, was recognized in Massachusetts as early as the 1830s,[263] and had come to prevail in many of the American jurisdictions prior to the turn of the century. Since then, by force of statute or rule of court, the number of adherent jurisdictions has undergone significant increase. Thus Kansas (1909), New Jersey (1912), Arizona (1913), and Michigan (1931), are seen extending such a power to the trial court,[264] while

[262] Lisbon v. Lyman, 49 N.H. 553, 600 (1870).

[263] Winn v. Columbian Insurance Co. 12 Pick. (29 Mass.) 279 (1831); Bicknell v. Dorion, 16 Pick. (33 Mass.) 478 (1835); Boyd v. Brown, 17 Pick. (34 Mass.) 453 (1835); Robbins v. Inhabitants of Townsend, 20 Pick. (37 Mass.) 345 (1838).

[264] Kan. Laws 1909, c. 182, § 307, Kan. Gen. Stat. Ann. 1935, § 60-3004; N.J. Pract. Act 1912, Schedule A, Rules

Mississippi (1918), North Dakota (1927) and Illinois (1933) have spoken in this regard with reference to the powers of the appellate court,[265] as did also Maryland (1914, 1920) and Colorado (1929) [266] prior to enlargement by their recent Rules. In 1931 the principle was accepted by the Federal Supreme Court,[267] and finds place in the Rules of 1938 in the formula that "a new trial may be granted to any or all of the parties and on all or part of the issues." (Rule 59 (a)). Further State acceptance in the words or under the influence of this formula has occurred in Arizona (1939), Colorado (1941), Maryland (1941), New Mexico (1942), Missouri (1943), Delaware (1947), New Jersey (1948), and Utah (1949).[268] Although applicable in general to any case of plurality of issues where there may be separation without occasioning injustice, the measure in question plays an especially useful part where the error is one affecting only the quantum of damages.

Departure from the old rule has occurred in England, also, but it was deferred until the Judicature Acts. In restricting, as above mentioned, the award of a new trial for misdirection or improper rulings on evidence to the case of some substantial wrong or miscarriage, the Rules of 1875 further provided that if such wrong or miscarriage affected part only of the matter in controversy, the court might give final judgment as to part thereof and direct a new trial as to the other

---

72, 73, Rules of Supreme Court 1938, Rules 131, 132; Ariz. Rev. Stat. 1913, §§ 597, 598; Mich. Court Rules 1931, 1933, Rule 47, § 2, Searl, Mich. Court Rules Ann. (4th ed. 1933) p. 306.

[265] Miss. Rules of Supreme Court 1918, Rules 12, 13: 161 Miss. 905, 906 (1931); N.D. Laws 1927, c. 214, N.D. Rev. Code 1943, § 28-2729; Ill. Civ. Pract. Act 1933, § 92(1), Ill. Rev. Stat. 1949, c. 110, § 216(1).

[266] Md. Laws 1914, cc. 149, 248, Laws 1920, c. 229, Md. Code Ann. (Flack, 1939) Art. 5, §§ 25, 26; Colo. Supreme Court Rules 1929, Rule 54, 85 Colo. xxix, in accord with the decision in Plains Iron Works v. Haggott, 72 Colo. 228, 210 Pac. 696 (1922).

[267] Gasoline Products Co. v. Champlin Refining Co. 283 U.S. 494, 51 S.Ct. 513 (1931).

[268] Ariz. Code Ann. 1939, § 21-1304; Colo. Rules Civ. Proc. 1941, Rule 59(a), in Colo. Stat. Ann. 1935, Replacement Vol. I, 1941; N.M. Stat. Ann. 1941, § 19-101(59)(a); Mo. Laws 1943, p. 388, 3 Mo.Rev.Stat.Ann. 1942, 1950 Cum. Pocket Part, § 847.115; Delaware, Rules of Superior Court 1947, Rule 59(a); N.J. Rules Civ. Pract. 1948, Rule 3:59(1); Utah Rules Civ. Proc. 1949, Rule 59(a); Md. Gen. Rules Pract. & Proc., Part 3, Subd. III, Rule 10, Md. Ann. Code (Flack, 1939) 1947 Cum. Supp. p. 2053.

part only.[269] And, by a separate provision, it was declared that "a new trial may be ordered on any question in an action, whatever be the grounds for the new trial, without interfering with the finding or decision upon any other question." [270] With the interim change in the former to make it apply also where the error in question affects "some or one only" of the parties, these provisions remain substantially the same in the present Rules.[271]

A related aspect of new trial procedure is that dealt with by the Supreme Court of the United States in *Dimick* v. *Schiedt*.[272] Although denied in England,[273] the power of the court in a proper case to refuse a new trial on condition of the plaintiff remitting an appropriate amount from that of the verdict has long been well established in the State courts, as also in the federal practice. But the question whether the court has a corresponding power, where the amount of the verdict is deemed inadequate, to condition the denial of the motion upon the defendant's consent to an increase of the amount, stands very differently. That power has come to definite recognition in New Jersey and Washington (in the one by judicial decision,[274] in the other by statute in accord with judicial decision),[275] as also by a Massachusetts statute of 1945, providing that "a verdict shall not be set aside solely on the ground that the damages are inadequate until the parties have first been given an opportunity to accept an addition to the verdict of such amount as the court adjudges reasonable." [276] Moreover, it is not without considerable support elsewhere; [277] in particular, its exercise in a special form is involved in the peculiar double option practice currently obtaining in Wisconsin.[278]

[269] 38 & 39 Vict. c. 77, First Schedule, O. XXXIX, r. 3.

[270] *Ibid.* O. XXXIX, r. 4.

[271] O. XXXIX, rr. 6, 7; Annual Practice 1949, I, pp. 740, 745.

[272] 293 U.S. 474, 55 S.Ct. 296 (1935).

[273] By the House of Lords in Watt v. Watt [1905] A.C. 115.

[274] Gaffney v. Illingsworth, 90 N.J.L. 490, 101 Atl. 243 (1917).

[275] Wash. Laws 1933, c. 138, § 2, 2 Wash. Rev. Stat. Ann. (Remington, 1932) 1940 Pocket Part, § 399-1, following Clausing v. Kershaw, 129 Wash. 67, 224 Pac. 573 (1924).

[276] Mass. Laws 1945, c. 578, § 1; Mass. Ann. Laws (1933), 1949 Cum. Supp. c. 231, § 127.

[277] Note (1934) 44 Yale L.J. 318 325. See also Note (1934) 32 Mich.L. Rev. 538, and Carlin, Remittiturs and Additurs (1942) 49 W.Va.L.Q. 1, 24 *et seq.*

[278] The essence of this practice, as

In the federal case just mentioned, existence of the power was squarely put in issue as a matter of federal practice. The action was one for personal injuries in which, with a verdict for $500, the trial court allowed a motion for new trial on the ground of inadequate damages, unless the defendant would consent to an increase of the amount to $1500. That consent was given and the motion accordingly denied. There being no consent on the part of the plaintiff, it was considered by the Circuit Court of Appeals [279] that the action of the trial court contravened the Seventh Amendment. Dividing by five to four, the Supreme Court approved this result. It held that whatever instances of the exercise of such a power may have appeared earlier in its history, the common law in its later development and at the time of the adoption of the Constitution "forbade the court to *increase* the amount of damages awarded by a jury in actions such as that here under consideration," that the practice in question was not a corollary of the recognized *remittitur* practice, and that in consequence it must be regarded as violative of the Seventh Amendment. It is to be hoped that the cogent considerations to the contrary adduced in the dissenting opinion of Mr. Justice Stone will ultimately come to prevail. There is no convincing reason why the *additur* (for so it has conveniently been called) should not be governed by the same considerations as the *remittitur*. The fact that in the one case the jury has reached and gone beyond the amount finally incorporated in the judgment, while in the other the jury has not reached that amount, presents a difference purely superficial, for in the case of *remittitur*, no less than that of *additur*, it is the jury's estimate which is the subject of interference by consent of the party whom this interference adversely affects.

applicable in the case of unliquidated damages, where the court deems the award wholly inadequate, is to give the plaintiff the option to accept, as an alternative to a new trial, such an increased amount as is found by the court "to represent the least amount that an unprejudiced jury would probably find" in the premises, and to give the defendant the option either to consent to such increase or move for a new trial. Risch v. Lawhead, 211 Wis. 270, 278, 248 N.W. 127 (1933). See also Campbell v. Sutliff, 193 Wis. 370, 214 N.W. 374 (1927); Heinlich v. Tabor, 123 Wis. 565, 102 N.W. 10 (1905); and Note (1933) 18 Ia.L.Rev. 404, 407.

[279] Schiedt v. Dimick, 70 Fed.2d 558 (C.C.A. 1st, 1934).

CHAPTER XX

INFLUENCE OF JURY PROCEDURE ON TRIAL BY THE COURT

Otherwise than in the exceptional case where an issue was directed out of chancery for advisory decision, there was nothing in the classic chancery procedure precisely corresponding to the common-law verdict. Hence, when it came to the rule that in common-law causes a jury might be waived and trial had before the court itself, the analogies of the chancery procedure failed, and resort was had to the analogies of trial by jury. The early American practice in this regard contemplated a statement by the judge of his conclusion as a basis for judgment, and applied to it the term "finding." Thus, for example, we observe the Missouri Supreme Court in 1826 holding that the evidence "did not warrant the finding and judgment of the court." [1] Thus, too, by the New York Judiciary Act of 1847, it was declared that "the finding of the judge . . . shall in all respects have the same effect as a verdict of a jury." [2] And by successive and constant use the term "finding" became subsequently fixed in the American procedural vocabulary, as signifying in a trial by the court, initially of a common-law action, the counterpart of the verdict in a jury trial.

But the New York Code of 1848, in harmony with its basic purpose of uniting the administration of law and equity, proceeded on the theory that there should be no difference in the mode of trial of fact by the court, whether this was of common-law issues in virtue of waiver of jury, or of equitable issues pursuant to the court's traditional power. For the case, then, of any trial of fact by the court, it provided that "its decision shall be given in writing . . . In giving the decision, the facts found shall be first stated, and then the conclusion of

[1] Lee v. Collins, 1 Mo. 587 (1826). [2] N.Y. Laws 1847, c. 280, § 80.

law upon them. Judgment upon the decision shall be entered accordingly." [3] This requirement of separate statement of findings of fact and conclusions of law, although eliminated for the time being by an amendment of 1949,[4] nevertheless furnished the original of one of the two principal types of provision which came to prevail throughout the code jurisdictions. The other, making the findings conditioned upon request, probably takes its inception in the Kentucky Code of 1851. The latter declared that "upon trials of questions of fact by the court, it shall not be necessary for the court to state its finding, except generally, for the plaintiff or defendant, unless one of the parties requests it, with a view of excepting to the decision of the court upon the questions of law involved in the trial; in which case it shall state in writing the conclusions of facts found, separately from the conclusions of law." [5]

Accordingly, a majority of the code jurisdictions adhere to the first type, requiring that in all cases there be a special finding in the sense that the conclusions of fact and of law must be separately stated.[6] A numerous minority prefer the second type, and require such a statement only upon request, being content otherwise with a general finding for one party or the other.[7] Most of these are faithful to the archetype in

[3] N.Y. Code 1848, § 222. The following contemporary observations by Hurlbut, J., in Doke v. Peek, 1 Code Rep. 54-55 (1848) are not without interest in the present connection. "Since the Code took effect, a trial by the court is very different from what it used to be. Before the Code, it was only necessary to say, I find for the plaintiff or defendant. Now, I should say to the party in whose favor I decided, I find for you on all, or some of the issues, draw up a special verdict, serve it on the adverse party, and within 20 days I will settle it—that would be the practice at *Nisi Prius;* it could not be expected of a Judge that he is to prepare a special verdict . . . A Judge will not draw the special verdict, but will require the party in whose favor he decides, to draw the special verdict, and to attend before him on notice to the adverse party to settle same."

[4] N.Y. Code 1849, § 267,

[5] Ky. Code 1851, § 374.

[6] Alaska Comp. Laws Ann. 1949, § 55-7-92; Ark. Stat. 1947, § 27-1744; Cal. Code Civ. Proc. (Deering, 1949) § 632; Colo. Rules Civ. Proc., Rule 52(a), in Colo. Stat. Ann. 1935, 1941 Replacement Vol. I; Idaho Code Ann. 1949, § 10-303; Ia. Rules Civ. Proc. 1943, Rule 179, in Ia. Code 1946, Vol. II; Minn. Stat. 1945, § 546.27; Mont. Rev. Codes Ann. 1947, § 93-5303; N.M. Stat. Ann. 1941, § 19-101 (52(B)); N.C. Gen. Stat. 1943, § 1-185; N.D. Rev. Code 1943, § 28-1602; S.C. Code 1942, § 649; S.D. Code 1939, § 33.1403; Utah Rules Civ. Proc. (1949) Rule 52(a); Wash. Rev. Stat. (Remington, 1932) § 367; Wis. Stat. 1949, § 270.33.

[7] Ariz. Code Ann. 1939, § 21-1028; Ind. Stat. Ann. (Burns, 1933) Replacement Vol. II, 1946, § 2-2102; Kan. Gen. Stat. Ann. 1935, § 60-2921; Ky. Code

identifying the request as for the purpose of excepting to the decision in point of law.[8] Some variants from these types may be noted. Thus Connecticut [9] and Nevada [10] call only for findings of fact, the one upon request, the other unconditionally, Hawaii [11] requires a decision in writing, stating reasons, while in New York (where the original rule, departed from in 1849, was subsequently reaffirmed and then more than once modified) the present provision, dating from 1936, is that "the decision of the court may be oral or in writing and, except where a nonsuit is granted, must state the facts which it deems essential." [12]

In general the code jurisdictions apply the provision to trials of either common-law or equitable issues. A few confine its operation to the former. This is true of Kentucky,[13] Missouri [14] and Washington.[15] Among the non-code States are found provisions of a similar character for the governance of law actions. Vermont requires a finding of facts,[16] Alabama provides for such a finding on request,[17] while Pennsylvania,[18] Rhode Island [19] and Tennessee [20] in substance agree upon findings of fact and conclusions of law pursuant to request. New Jersey prior to its Rules of 1948 had provided by rule for a finding of the facts and, upon request, rulings of law.[21] Now, with unification of the procedure, it follows the Federal Rule, presently to be mentioned, in unqualifiedly requiring separately stated findings of fact and conclusions of law.[22]

Pract. in Civ. Cases (Carroll, 1948) § 332; 3 Mo.Rev.Stat. 1942, 1950 Cum. Pocket Part, § 847.114(b), conclusions of law here unnecessary; Neb. Rev. Stat. 1943, § 25-1127; Ohio Gen. Code Ann. (Page, 1938) § 11421-2; Okla. Stat. 1941, Tit. 12, § 611; Ore. Comp. Laws Ann. 1940, § 5-502; Tex. Rules Civ. Proc. (Vernon, 1942) Rule 296; Wyo. Comp. Stat. Ann. 1945, § 3-2423.

8 Indiana, Kentucky, Nebraska, Ohio, Oklahoma, Wyoming.

9 Conn. Gen. Stat. 1949, § 7975, Conn. Pract. Book (1934) §§ 232, 233.

10 Nev. Comp. Laws 1929, §§ 8783, 8784.

11 Haw. Rev. Laws Ann. 1945, § 10107.

12 N.Y. Civ. Pract. Act (Clevenger, 1950) § 440.

13 Deep v. Farmers' Nat. Bank, 247 Ky. 801, 57 S.W.2d 1002 (1933).

14 Fitzpatrick v. Weber, 168 Mo. 562, 68 S.W. 913 (1902)

15 Soboda v. Frederick Nolf & Co. 91 Wash. 446, 157 Pac. 1100 (1916).

16 Vt. Stat. 1947, § 2121.

17 Ala. Code 1940, Tit. 7, § 262.

18 Pa. Stat. Ann. (Purdon, 1931) Tit. 12, 1949 Cum. Pocket Part, § 689.

19 R.I. Gen. Laws Ann. 1938, c. 526, § 6.

20 Tenn. Code (Williams, 1934) § 8811.

21 N.J. Rules of Supreme Court 1938, Rule 113.

22 N.J. Rules Civ. Pract. 1948, Rule 3:52-1.

Whether specifically provided or not by the governing legislation, it is always open to the parties to present requests for particular findings of fact, which the court marks or otherwise identifies as held or refused. In this is seen a reflection of counsel's coöperation in the framing of a common-law special verdict. The conclusions of law, again, are an echo of the court's charge to the jury.[23] As exponent of the law the court is in a sense instructing itself as trier of the facts.[24] These conclusions are thus subject to much the same regimen as instructions to the jury. Accordingly the parties are usually at liberty to present requests for particular conclusions of law, variously styled in this regard as "propositions of law," "declarations of law," or even "instructions," and to require that they be passed upon by the court.

[23] Although in England conclusions of law in this sense are unknown, the two-sided character of the trial judge's function, has prompted, where he has gone wrong on the law, the occasional use of the expression that he "has misdirected himself" (see *e.g.*, Sanatorium Ltd. v. Marshall [1916] 2 K.B. 914)—an expression strongly criticized by Lord Shaw in the House of Lords case of Herbert v. Fox, 85 L.J.K.B. 441 (1916).

[24] A too literal application of this idea disclosed by the reports has provided a museum piece of judicial absurdity. In Touchard v. Crow, 20 Cal. 150, 163-164, the action, said the Supreme Court of California, *per* Field, J., "was tried by the court without the intervention of a jury. Of course, in such cases the court not only performs the peculiar and appropriate duty of deciding the law, but also discharges the functions of a jury, and passes upon the facts. The counsel of the appellants, impressed, as it would seem, with this dual character, requested the court to charge itself as a jury, and handed in certain instructions for that purpose. The court thereupon formally charged that part of itself which was thus supposed to be separated and converted into a jury, commencing the charge with the usual address, 'Gentlemen of the jury,' and instructing that imaginary body, that if they found certain facts they should find for the plaintiff, and otherwise for the defendants, and that they were not concluded by the statements of the court, but were at liberty to judge of the facts for themselves. The record does not inform us whether the jury thus addressed differed in their conclusions from those of the court. These proceedings have about them so ludicrous an air that we could not believe they were seriously taken, but for the gravity with which counsel on the argument referred to them. If counsel, when a case is tried by the court without a jury, desire to present for consideration certain points of law as applicable to the facts established or sought to be established, upon which the court might be called upon to charge a jury, were there a jury in the case, the proper course is to present them in the form of propositions, preceding them with a statement that counsel makes the following points, or contends as follows. The mode adopted in the present case, though highly original, is not of sufficient merit to be exalted into a precedent to be followed." See Note (1921) 15 Ill. LawRev. 621.

In the federal sphere the act of 1865,[25] which provided for trial by the court in jury-waived cases, made it the rule in such cases that "the finding of the court upon the facts, which finding may be either general or special, shall have the same effect as the verdict of a jury." In equity cases reliance continued to be placed upon the decree itself in conjunction with the pleadings and evidence, as disclosing the basis of decision, until 1930 when the Supreme Court added to the Equity Rules of 1912 a new rule providing that "in deciding suits in equity . . . the court of first instance shall find the facts specially and state separately its conclusions of law thereon; and the findings and conclusions shall be entered of record . . ." [26] So the case stood until the Rules of 1938 which, after much debate, centering in the question of providing a uniform canon of review in common-law and equity cases, took the same course in the now united administration as the greater number of the codes, by providing that "in all actions tried upon the facts without a jury, the court shall find the facts specially and state separately its conclusions of law thereon and direct the entry of the appropriate judgment." (Rule 52(a)).[27]

In the same Rule it is also declared that "requests for findings are not necessary for purposes of review." This provision has since commended itself to State adoption in a number of quarters.[28]

The requirement of special findings of fact has introduced a new chapter of procedural complications. Superficially it appears of easy application. But it renews the embarrassment frequently experienced in pleading of determining the true line of distinction between evidentiary or probative facts on the one hand, and ultimate facts on the other, for obviously it is only the latter which are to form the subject of special findings of fact. Again, inadvertent inconsistencies between different findings in the action frequently arise to plague the reviewing court. Moreover, the decisions time and again disclose instances

[25] 13 Stat. 501.

[26] Equity Rule 70½, adopted June 2, 1930.

[27] By amendment of December 27, 1946, the Rule was expressly made to apply also to the case of trial "with an advisory jury."

[28] See the Colorado, Iowa and Utah provisions cited in note 6, *supra,* and N.J. Rules Civ. Pract. 1948, Rule 3:52-1.

of confusion between the finding of fact and the conclusion of law, where what has been set down as the one turns out, upon appellate analysis, to be properly classifiable as the other. But the most serious disadvantage attending this practice proceeds from the analogy to the common-law special verdict which, as has been seen,[29] demands the statement of all the facts essential to support the judgment. In dealing with the federal statute of 1865, the Supreme Court of the United States had occasion to observe that the statute "provides for two kinds of findings in regard to the facts, to wit, general and special. This is in perfect analogy to the findings of a jury, for which the court is in such cases substituted by the consent of the parties. In other words, the court finds a general verdict on all the issues for plaintiff or defendant, or it finds a special verdict. This special finding . . . is not a mere report of the evidence, but a statement of the ultimate facts on which the law of the case must determine the rights of the parties; a finding of the propositions of fact which the evidence establishes and not the evidence on which those ultimate facts are supposed to rest." [30] This represents the commonly accepted doctrine. Accordingly, on the model of the special verdict, it is the general rule, in the application of the requirement of special findings of fact, that these must meet all the material issues and embrace every material fact necessary to the support of the judgment which follows. Unlike the case at common law the aid of inference may usually be invoked to eke out the deficiencies of direct statement, and there is otherwise significant departure from the common-law rigidity of construction. But, nevertheless, where special findings are required, the total omission from them of a basic fact, even if this fact has been established by the evidence, will generally operate to overturn the judgment. Some effort has been recently made to avert such a consequence. Thus the New York amendment of 1936 includes the provision that the "decision shall not be deemed to be the verdict of a jury." [31] Whether this will yield adequate prophylaxis remains a matter of conjecture. Much more promising,

[29] *Supra,* Chap. XIX, § 4.

[30] Norris v. Jackson, 9 Wall. (76 U.S.) 125, 127 (1869).

[31] N.Y. Civ. Pract. Act (Clevenger, 1950) § 440.

however, is the expedient adopted by the Missouri revision of 1943. Prompted evidently by the rule applicable to the recent statutory special verdict practice, this declares that "all fact issues upon which no specific findings are made shall be deemed found in accordance with the result reached." [32] This provision, manifestly, is one that commends itself to wider acceptance.

Michigan and Illinois of late years have wholly emancipated themselves from the practice in question. Both these States formerly had statutes providing for special findings of fact and conclusions of law in common-law actions, although Illinois had consistently refrained from applying the special verdict idea to the findings of fact.[33] But in 1931-1933 Michigan provided by rule of court that, while the judge was to file a written opinion, "no special findings of fact shall be required, but it shall be sufficient for the trial judge to find generally for or against the several parties." [34] And Illinois, by its Civil Practice Act of 1933, provided that "no special findings of fact or propositions of law shall be necessary in any case at law tried without a jury to support the judgment or as a basis of review." [35] So, too, in Maryland, where, although there is no review of the facts in case of a common-law trial of the kind, "prayers for instructions" had been required as a basis for reviewing questions of law,[36] the rules of 1941 have altogether dispensed with the necessity for such requests, in favor of a brief statement by the court of the grounds of its decision and the method of determining any damages awarded.[37]

Nothing in the nature of special findings has ever been required in the English practice of non-jury trial. The Common Law Procedure Act of 1854, which instituted this manner of trial in the superior courts, spoke of the judge's conclusion

[32] Mo. Laws 1943, p. 388, 3 Mo.Rev. Stat. 1942, 1950 Cum. Pocket Part, § 847.114(b).

[33] See *e.g.*, Tarjan v. National Surety Co. 268 Ill. App. 232 (1932).

[34] Mich. Court Rules 1933, Rule 37, § 11(b)(c), Searl, Mich. Court Rules Ann. (4th ed. 1933) p. 252.

[35] Ill. Civ. Pract. Act, 1933, § 64(2), Ill. Rev. Stat. 1949, c. 110, § 188(2).

[36] Md. Ann. Code (Flack, 1939) Art. 5, § 10; Turner v. Eagan, 116 Md. 35, 81 Atl. 877 (1911).

[37] Gen. Rules Pract. & Proc. 1941, Part 3, Subd. III, Rule 9(a), in Md. Ann. Code (Flack, 1939), 1947 Cum. Supp. p. 2053.

as his "verdict," and provided that it "shall be of the same effect as the verdict of a jury, save that it shall not be questioned upon the ground of being against the weight of the evidence" [38]—a prohibition which has since disappeared.[39] The existing practice does not speak of either a "verdict" or a "finding" on the part of the judge. "In non-jury cases he gives judgment at the conclusion of counsel's speeches, stating his reasons." [40] The statement may be of the most informal character, or his reasons may appear from his rulings or observations in the course of the trial.

As against the disadvantages attending the employment of special findings must be weighed their usefulness in furnishing a clearly determined basis of review. In their absence the appellate tribunal, unless afforded more than the usual concurrence of coöperation on the part of counsel, may be compelled to do much groping in the record to ascertain precisely what are the questions which it is called upon to decide. This consideration unquestionably occasioned the addition of 1930 to the Federal Equity Rules [41] and is responsible for the present Federal Rule on the subject. It has been suggested by way of accounting for the absence of similar mechanism in the English practice that the courts "are not faced with the problem of crowded appellate dockets or of voluminous trial records," that the high cost of appeals keeps down their number, and that the discretionary power in determining whether the trial shall be with or without a jury "places a different emphasis upon the review of findings." [42] While these matters may not be without influence, we think that the real explanation lies in the modern English disposition to reduce procedural apparatus to a minimum, as contrasted with the American inclination, repeatedly seen in previous chapters, toward the inclusion of fettering devices for fear of one thing or another. Whether, discounting their disadvantages, the presence of special findings is advisable as a basis of review is a question that must

[38] 17 & 18 Vict. c. 125, § 1.

[39] See notes to O. LVIII, r. 1, in Annual Practice 1949, I, p. 1314 *et seq.*

[40] Odgers, Principles of Pleading and Practice (13th ed. 1946) 274.

[41] Clark and Stone, Review of Findings of Fact (1937) 4 Univ.of Chicago L.Rev. 190, 205.

[42] *Ibid.* 206, 216.

be answered, first, in the light of the judicial organization and the particular burdens cast upon appellate tribunals, and, secondly, in that of the possibility of contriving other means of identifying the points of dispute for the benefit of the reviewing court—means that will not enter into the judgment itself, but leave it free to stand or fall on the pleadings and evidence.[43]

Some further analogy to jury procedure is to be noted. It is always open to the party to test the sufficiency of his opponent's evidence. This, under principles more nearly resembling the common-law method than that of the separate equity procedure, is done in various ways as prescribed by the particular practice,[44]—by motion for a finding in the party's favor, by the submission of a peremptory proposition of law, or, in the case of a defendant, by motion for nonsuit or dismissal. The appropriate motion is even spoken of as a motion to direct a verdict,[45] and is sometimes termed a demurrer to the evidence.[46] Again, there may be occasion for the employment of a motion in arrest of judgment.[47] But the strongest imprint of jury procedure on the post-finding stage of non-jury trial comes from the motion for new trial. That motion is at all times available on proper grounds, although its ambit is materially cut down by the circumstance that the judge is himself the trier of the facts and by the greater latitude conceded to him in the management of the evidence. In the separate equity procedure there was no motion for new trial *eo nomine*. Its nearest equivalent was the petition for rehearing or, under special circumstances, a

[43] Contending for such means, Professor Sunderland, in his admirable article on special findings, points to the New York amendment of 1852 (N.Y. Code, § 268) which, instead of requiring special findings and conclusions prior to judgment, provided for inclusion by the trial judge of a brief specification of the facts found and his conclusions of law in the settlement of a case prepared for the purpose of appeal, and also to the construction of the Kentucky statute (Albin Co. v. Ellinger & Co. 103 Ky. 240, 44 S.W. 655) as similarly postponing the findings until after judgment. Sunderland, Findings of Fact and Conclusions of Law in Cases where Juries are Waived (1937) 4 Univ.of ChicagoL.Rev. 218, 230-232. To these may be added the practice under the former Missouri statute: see Fruin v. O'Malley, 241 Mo. 250, 145 S.W. 437 (1912).

[44] On this topic see 64 C.J. p. 1210 *et seq.*

[45] See *e.g.*, E. E. Alley Co. v. Ball, 102 Fla. 1034, 136 So. 704 (1931).

[46] See *e.g.*, Windus v. Bodecker, 132 Kan. 857, 297 Pac. 702 (1931).

[47] See Alexander v. Alexander, 140 Ind. 555, 38 N.E. 855 (1894).

bill of review. Now in most systems of the unitary procedure the motion for new trial applies alike to common-law and equity cases, thus replacing for the latter the old mode of correction, by an instrumentality whose principles are chiefly drawn from common-law sources.

CHAPTER XXI

THE JUDGMENT

§ 1. THE JUDGMENT IN GENERAL

Under the old régime there existed an inveterate contrast between the judgment at law and the decree in equity. The latter was flexible, adjusting itself to the multiform contingencies of decision in the particular case; the former, reflecting the limited manner of relief afforded by the common-law courts, was always "simple and absolute," [1] always in stereotyped form of affirmative or negative adjudication. Again, equity was always free to enter decretal orders from time to time in the progress of the suit, making, if need be, final disposition of part of the cause, while retaining the residue for further adjudication. The common law, on the other hand, although settling various interim matters by interlocutory judgment, knew but a single final judgment, regardless of the number of parties or causes of action involved, and this unitary judgment must go for or against all the plaintiffs and in other than tort actions, with slight exception, for or against all the defendants. Moreover, unlike equity, the common law afforded no means, within the suit, of determining any controversy arising between the defendants. This situation is no longer typical. Change in the direction of assimilating the two types of judgment has necessarily accompanied the advent of concurrent administration of legal and equitable rules; change, too, has come about in the purely common-law judgment, the better to adapt it to the ends of justice. By the original New York Code there was introduced for causes in general the rule theretofore obtaining in chancery that "judgment may be given for or against one or more of several plaintiffs, and for or against one or more of several defendants, and it may determine the ultimate rights of the parties on each side as

[1] Finlason, An Exposition of our Judicial System etc. (1877) 107.

between themselves."[2] Frequently with the addition that the court may grant to the defendants any affirmative relief to which they may be entitled, this departure, which has been followed in most of the American codes, is usually supplemented with the further provision, issuing from a New York amendment of 1849,[3] which authorizes the court, in the case of a plurality of defendants, "to render judgment against one or more of them, leaving the action to proceed against the others, whenever a several judgment may be proper." Such provisions naturally operate in correlation with the regulation of joinder of parties and of causes of action. In some jurisdictions, indeed, they have latterly been reinforced by explicit provision in connection with that regulation, as will presently appear. So, too, their application is subject to the prevailing substantive law rules as to joint rights and several rights, on the one side, and joint obligations, joint and several obligations, and several obligations, on the other—a tangled field into which a measure of order has been introduced by other statutory provisions governing particular aspects of the ensuing problems. Authority to enter a fractional judgment is variously conceded in cases beyond that of a plurality of defendants. In particular, diversely phrased provisions appear in many jurisdictions, under which judgment may be given for an uncontested part of the claim, without prejudice to a continued prosecution of the action in respect of the residue. Thus Kentucky has had since 1854 the rule which, in its original phrasing, declared that, "if only a part of the plaintiff's claim is controverted by the defendant's answer, judgment may at any time be rendered for the part not controverted."[4] Another example is the Ohio amendment of 1879, providing that "judgment may be taken, as upon a default, for so much of the plaintiff's demand as is not put in issue by the answer upon any or all of the causes of action, without prejudice to the rights of the plaintiff as to that portion of his demand disputed."[5] And of recent years provisions of this character have received

[2] § 230.

[3] N.Y. Laws 1949, c. 438, § 274, pp. 669-670.

[4] Ky. Code Pract. in Civ. Cas. 1854, § 410; Ky. Code Pract. in Civ. Cas. (Carroll, 1948) § 380.

[5] Ohio Laws 1879, p. 78, Ohio Gen. Code (Page, 1938) § 11592.

an important accession through the installation in sundry jurisdictions of the procedure for summary judgment [6] which invariably permits this manner of fractionized recovery.

The direction thus taken in America toward imparting to the common-law judgment, so far as permitted by the nature of the rights involved, that malleability which was always characteristic of the equity decree has likewise been that of the English procedure under the Judicature Acts, and the result attained differs but little from that in the most advanced of the American jurisdictions. Rules 1 and 4 of Order XVI [7] concerning the joinder of parties (from which American reform has extensively borrowed) subjoin to their principal precepts clauses relating to the rendition of judgment. As to plaintiffs the subjoined clause provides that, without amendment, judgment may be given "for such one or more of the plaintiffs, as may be found to be entitled to relief, for such relief as he or they may be entitled to." As to defendants the subjoined clause correspondingly provides for judgment "against such one or more of the defendants as may be found to be liable, according to their respective liabilities." There exists also a series of provisions (including those relating to summary judgment) permitting the rendition of judgment for an admitted or undefended part of a claim or, in case of default, for a failure to disclose a right to defend, against one or more of a larger number of defendants, the right being reserved to the plaintiff to prosecute his action to further judgment for the residue of his claim or against the remaining defendants.[8] In the case of counterclaims, moreover, the court often exercises the power to render separate judgments on the original and counter demands.[9] A controversy between a defendant and a third person called in or between co-defendants, as one in respect of contribution or indemnity, may find adjudication in the principal judgment,[10] but would seem regularly to be the subject of a separate judgment.[11] In general, however, the

[6] *Supra,* Chap. XVI, § 1.

[7] *Supra,* Chaps. IX and X.

[8] O. XIII, rr. 4, 7; O. XIV, rr. 4, 5; O. XXVII, rr. 3, 6, 9, 12.

[9] Annual Practice 1949, I, pp. 404-405, note to O. XXI, r. 17.

[10] *Cf.* 3 Seton, Forms of Judgments and Orders (1901) 2142.

[11] O. XVIA, rr. 6, 9, 12(2).

wider latitude of joinder of parties and of causes of action than is permitted in most of the American jurisdictions enables the single judgment to have a correspondingly wider scope. But, as with us, the plasticity of the judgment is necessarily held in check by considerations relating to the severability of the demand. And to a greater extent than is commonly true in America the traditional common-law rule as to joint liability has here preserved an influence. For in the case of such liability, with certain exceptions, the rendition of judgment against one of a plurality of defendant contractors, even though not partners, is still held to release the others on the traditional theory of merger.[12] Indeed, it was not until the act of 1935 that the same effect ceased to attach in all cases of joint tort liability.[13]

That reinforcement of the American provisions respecting plural parties which was referred to above is parcel of the levy made upon the English Rules 1 and 4 of Order XVI in the field of joinder of parties. Of the jurisdictions participating in this borrowing, prior to the Federal Rules of 1938, three, New York, California and Illinois, took over the subjoined judgment clause as to plaintiffs, while the two former adopted the subjoined clauses for both plaintiffs and defendants.[14] Both clauses later found place in the Federal Rules.

In these Rules is reflected the antecedent progress made both in England and America toward the general end of adapting the judgment to procedural needs. They contain three principal provisions bearing on the present matter. First, in connection with the permissive joinder as patterned after the English Rules, there appear in a combined sentence of Rule 20(a) the two subjoined clauses above mentioned, it being provided that "judgment may be given for one or more of the plaintiffs according to their respective rights to relief, and against one or more defendants according to their respective liabilities."

12 Annual Practice 1949, I, pp. 379-380, where the exceptions are noted.

13 Law Reform (Married Women and Tortfeasors) Act, 25 & 26 Geo. V, c. 30, § 6-(1)(a). This statute also introduced the principle of contribution among tortfeasors. § 6-(1)(c).

14 N.Y. Civ. Pract. Act (Clevenger, 1948) §§ 209, 211, repealed in 1949, the matter in question now appearing as part of § 212: see *supra,* Chapter IX, note 25; Cal. Code Civ. Proc. (Deering, 1949) §§ 378, 379a; Ill. Civ. Pract. Act 1933, § 23, Ill. Rev. Stat. 1949, c. 110, § 147.

Secondly, Rule 54(b), as originally adopted, provided for the case of a plurality of claims that "the court at any stage, upon a determination of the issues material to a particular claim and all counterclaims arising out of the transaction or occurrence which is the subject matter of the claim, may enter a judgment disposing of such claim," terminating the action with respect thereto and allowing the action to proceed as to the remaining claims. On the ground that this formulation left too much room for piecemeal litigation and failed to foreclose all controversy as to whether the cause had been definitely terminated as to a particular claim,[15] the amendments of December 27, 1946 substituted the provision that "when more than one claim for relief is presented in an action, whether as a claim, counterclaim, cross-claim, or third-party claim, the court may direct the entry of a final judgment upon one or more but less than all of the claims only upon an express determination that there is no just reason for delay and upon an express direction for the entry of judgment," and that, in the absence of such determination and direction, an adjudication of less than all the claims is not to terminate the action as to any of the claims, and is to be subject to revision until adjudication of all the claims. Thirdly, a fractional judgment, in consonance with the principle obtaining in the usual summary judgment practice, is provided for by Rule 56 which enables "a party seeking to recover upon a claim, counterclaim, or cross-claim or to obtain a declaratory judgment" to move for a summary judgment in respect of his demand "upon all or any part thereof" (Rule 56(a)), and extends a corresponding right to the party defending to move for summary judgment as to all or any part of the demand. (Rule 56(b)).

Prior to the amendment mentioned these provisions had been taken over integrally by Arizona (1939), New Mexico (1942) and Colorado (1941), which two first named have also acceded to the amendment, Arizona with a minor adjustment.[16] Since

[15] See note of Advisory Committee, Federal Rules of Civil Procedure (West Publishing Co. 1947) p. 121.

[16] Ariz. Code Ann. 1939, §§ 21-512, 21-1202, 21-1210, 21-1211, and Cum. Supp. 1949 to Vol. II; Colo. Rules Civ. Proc., Rules 20(a), 54(b), 56(a), 56(b), in Colo. Stat. Ann. 1935, Replacement Vol. I, 1941; N.M. Stat. Ann. 1941, §§ 19-101(20(a)), 19-101(54(b)), 19-101(56(a), 56(b)), and Cum. Supp. 1949 to Vol. II.

the amendment they have been followed by Delaware (1947), New Jersey (1948) and Utah (1949).[17] Texas (1941) and Missouri (1943) have each copied Rule 20(a).[18] Rule 54(b) in its amended form has found place in Maryland (1947).[19]

§ 2. Judgments by Default

(*a*) *Occasion for Default.*—The primitive conception of a lawsuit as an activity involving coöperation of the parties forbade the rendition of a judgment against a defendant who had declined to appear.[20] Apart from the special rules attending the old real actions, this motion continued to cramp procedure in England much longer than on the Continent. Like other systems, however, the common-law procedure sought relief from the restriction by resort to measures directed toward coercing the defendant's appearance, employing for the purpose that complex variety of process which we have already had occasion to notice.[21] If all the appropriate measures, successively used, were attended with failure, even though there had been actual service of process, no judgment could be rendered against the defendant in a personal action.[22] Emergence from this condition first came about by a statute of 1725, which, limiting actual arrest of the person to matters of £10 or more, provided that in case of the defendant's failure to appear, after personal service of process, it should be lawful for the plaintiff, upon affidavit of such service, "to enter a common appearance or file common bail for the defendants, and to proceed thereon, as if such defendant or defendants had entred his, her or their appearance, or filed common bail; any law or usage to the contrary notwithstanding." [23] Thus

17 Del. Rules of Superior Court, Rules 20(a), 54(b), 56(a)(b); N.J. Rules Civ. Pract., Rules 3:20-1, 3:54-2, 3:56-1, 3:56-2; Utah Rules Civ. Proc., Rules 20(a), 54(b), 56(a)(b).

18 Tex. Rules Civ. Proc. (Vernon, 1942) Rule 40; Mo. Laws 1943, pp. 360-361, 3 Mo. Rev. Stat. Ann. 1942, 1950 Cum. Pocket Part, § 847.16(a).

19 Md. Gen. Rules Pract. & Proc., Part 2, Subd. III, Rule 6(a), Md. Ann. Code (Flack, 1939) 1947 Cum. Supp. p. 2043.

20 Millar, The Formative Principles of Civil Procedure (1923) 18 Ill.L.Rev. 1, 4-5, and as reprinted in Engelmann-Millar, History of Continental Civil Procedure (1927) 6-7.

21 *Supra,* Chap. VIII, § 1.

22 1 Robinson, Practice in the Courts of Law and Equity in Virginia (1832) 166.

23 12 Geo. I, c. 29, § 1.

coercion was laid aside in most cases, but only by making formal obeisance to the old notion. And it was not until the Common Law Procedure Act of 1852 that this vestige of outworn tradition was finally relinquished.[24]

Similar prepossessions characterized the chancery. "By the ancient constitution of the court no bill could be taken *pro confesso,* unless an appearance had been entered. In order, therefore, to obtain an appearance a long chain of process was employed, ending in a sequestration of the defendant's property . . . the plaintiff was without remedy where he could not serve the defendant with process; and where he did serve him, he could only have him committed and detained until he cleared his contempt by entering his appearance." [25] Subpoena, attachment, attachment with proclamations, serjeant at arms and, finally, sequestration, such were the steps that might have to be gone through in the effort to force an appearance. But all this might still prove unavailing. Unless the defendant had been thus induced to enter his appearance, the plaintiff, even after sequestration, was faced with the rule that without appearance there could be no decree *pro confesso.* A very considerable measure of relief, however, was introduced by that statute of 1732 which came under our attention in connection with service by publication. For the case of the defendant who had "gone out of the realm or otherwise absconded to avoid being served" with process, it permitted a decree *pro confesso* to be entered against him upon the plaintiff's fulfillment of the conditions as to published notice which it prescribed, and, for the case of the defendant who, taken into custody and brought before the court, upon process, refused or neglected to enter his appearance, it provided that the court "may appoint a clerk in court [26] or attorney of such court to enter an appearance for such defendant . . . and such proceedings may thereupon be had in the cause, as if the party

[24] 15 & 16 Vict. c. 76, § 26.

[25] 1 Hoffman, Practice of the Court of Chancery (1834) 184, 185.

[26] One of the "sixty clerks" who at this time were officials of the court. "Every suitor in the court of Chancery must appoint a clerk in court, who was supposed to act as his solicitor in court, to advise his private solicitor, and from whom copies of the pleadings must be obtained." 9 Holdsworth, History of English Law (1926) 370.

had actually appeared." [27] It was not until 1845 that a similar substitute was devised for the case of actual service. By the Chancery Orders of that year the plaintiff was relieved from the necessity of attaching the defendant who had failed to appear after due service of the subpoena, and instead was authorized to cause the defendant's appearance to be entered by the Record and Writ Clerk of the court, upon proper affidavit of the service.[28] But it was still a matter of appearance entered *for* the defendant, and "this ghost of the old rule lingers down to the very last days of the High Court of Chancery." [29]

In colonial America the slow development of the legal profession and the preponderant influence of the laity upon the institutions of justice made it comparatively easy to disregard the notion which, in the present regard, had handicapped the common-law procedure in the mother country. Accordingly, it is not surprising to find a Massachusetts Bay statute of 1692-93 providing that if upon "summons duly served, and affidavit thereof made in court, the defendant do not appear by himself or his attourney lawfully authorized, judgment shall pass against him by default"—a result made subject by an act of 1697 to his right to move for a trial "before the jury be dismist"; [30] or a Pennsylvania statute of 1700 which, requiring the plaintiff to take oath in open court to his belief in the justness of his cause, provided that "if the party complained against shall nevertheless refuse to appear, the plaintiff shall have judgment against defendant by default." [31] Similarly, though by a different course of proceeding, Virginia, through legislation beginning in 1645, relieved the defendant "from the necessity of appearing when he had no defense to make." [32] With provisions such as these in its background there

[27] 5 Geo. II, c. 25, § 2.

[28] 1 Daniell, Chancery Practice (3d Am. from 3d Eng. ed. 1865) 451-452; Gen. Orders 1845, Ord. XXIX, Sanders, Orders in Chancery (1845) Vol. I, Pt. II, p. 995.

[29] Millar, *op. cit.* 7(9).

[30] Acts and Resolves of the Province of Massachusetts Bay, Vol. I, 1692-1714 (1869) p. 75. The first mentioned act was repealed by advice of the Privy Council, on a ground not here in question, but reappeared in an improved form in the act of 1697. *Ibid.* p. 286.

[31] 2 Pa. Stat. at Large, 1682-1801, p. 128.

[32] 1 Robinson, *op. cit.* 166.

was no likelihood that the future American practice in common-law actions could fail to be wholly emancipated from the old notion. The case was not altogether the same in the chancery procedure, sparingly admitted in the colonial era. Here was a system which, because of its complex nature, could not well be managed without professional assistance, and which offered small room for such directness as could be applied to the administration of simple common-law claims. As a result there was a closer clinging to the English rules of procedure. Yet even here, by the opening of the 1800s, the practice probably everywhere had advanced to the position of allowing a decree *pro confesso* merely for failure to appear after due service of process, without concerning itself with the need of a fictitious appearance. While numerous other simplifications in the field of process were generally introduced, nevertheless some remnants of the old notion are still to be seen after that time. Thus in New York, if, instead of proceeding to a decree *pro confesso* for the failure of the defendant to appear, the plaintiff had elected to have him attached—as he might to ensure that he would be later amenable to compulsion in the matter of his answer,—and the defendant then brought into court had refused or neglected to enter his appearance, the court, by statute, was to cause his appearance to be entered for him, substantially as under the English statute of 1732.[33] And this remained the rule until the adoption of the Code.

With the Judicature Acts in England and the codes and kindred legislation in America, there disappeared the slender allegiance to the primitive notion persisting in chancery. It is safe to say that among the Anglo-American jurisdictions, including those retaining chancery as a separate system, there is none that still considers appearance of the defendant as essential to the rendition of a judgment by default.

Failure to answer after appearance, like failure to appear, is today a normal ground for judgment by default. This was

[33] See 1 Hoffman, *op. cit.* 123, 187-188; 1 Barbour, Practice of the Court of Chancery (1843) 80. Other instances of the kind appear, for example, in Delaware (Act of 1806, Del. Laws (1816) Vol. IV, 1806-1813, c. 21, § 4) and Virginia (1 Rev.Code 1819, p. 218, § 115, 2 Robinson, *op. cit.* (1835) 328.

the case at common law, where a failure to plead after appearance usually resulted in such a judgment, known as a judgment of *nil dicit*. Indeed, in the common-law practice, whether the default resided in the failure to appear voluntarily or in failing to plead after a voluntary appearance, the judgment was always prefaced by a rule to plead, and therefore was technically one of *nil dicit*. But in the American common-law practice, for the case of non-appearance, the rule to plead was frequently dispensed with, and the situation accordingly was spoken of simply as that of a judgment by default. And, even in the later days of common-law procedure in England, it was usual to speak of a judgment by default as distinguished from a judgment of *nil dicit*.[34]

In the classic English chancery practice, on the other hand, the mere failure to put in an answer after appearance could not result in a decree *pro confesso*. For, unlike the common-law plea, the answer was a vehicle of discovery, and such discovery might well be indispensable to establishment of the plaintiff's right to relief. Hence it was open to the plaintiff to compel an answer, and in this end he had recourse to the same chain of process which was applicable to compelling appearance before the statute of 1732. If a decree *pro confesso* had not been entered under the statute—for the defendant may have voluntarily appeared or other reasons might be present for not invoking the statute—it was the rule that a decree *pro confesso* might be rendered upon attainment of the last step in the sequence of process, that of sequestration, though here the sequestration was not to be executed.[35] This was the only instance of a decree *pro confesso* for want of an answer in the classic practice. But important changes in this respect were made by the Orders of 1845. These provided for an order taking the bill as confessed, if the court saw fit, upon no more than the return of an attachment upon the person of a defendant who had failed to answer after appearance. If for any reason an attachment or later process could not be thus executed, then the defendant was to be deemed "to have

[34] See Watkin Williams, Introduction to the Principles and Practice of Pleading (1857) 201.

[35] Rowley v. Ridley, 2 Dick. 622, 624-625 (1784).

absconded to avoid or to have refused to obey the process of the Court." In that case provision was similarly made for taking the bill as confessed against him upon the court being satisfied that he ought to be so deemed.[36] The old method of compelling an answer still survived, although the steps in the process had in the meantime been materially shortened, and survived even the radical reforms introduced by the Chancery Practice Amendment Act of 1852,[37] which largely disestablished the answer as a means of discovery.[38] But in consequence of these changes it could be said in 1857 that "the practice of taking bills *pro confesso* will now very rarely be sanctioned by the Court." [39]

The situation was quite different in the United States. Here the regulation of chancery practice, long before the change in the rule of evidence which tended to place the chancery answer upon a basis similar to that of the common-law plea, usually allowed a decree *pro confesso* for the defendant's failure to answer. In adopting a rule to this effect for the New York chancery practice, Chancellor Kent said in 1814: "If an answer be essential, as in bills for discovery, an answer can be compelled by the process for contempt; but there is no need of this when the bill is for relief, and states sufficient ground. All that is wanted is admission of the facts; and if the defendant has appeared, and will not answer, he ought to be concluded in the same manner as he is by neglect to plead to a declaration at law." [40] Elsewhere is seen statutory authority for so proceeding, with the provision that cause might be later shown to permit a defense. Such was the case in Virginia under a statute of 1788 which provided that upon the defendant's failure to file his answer within the time prescribed, the plaintiff might have such a decree *nisi,* taking the bill for confessed.[41] Similarly, the first Federal Equity Rules, those of 1822, provided that if the defendant failed to answer within

[36] 1 Daniell, Chancery Practice (3d Am. from 3d Eng. ed. 1865) 477, 502; Gen. Orders 1845, Ord. LXXVI, LXXVII, LXXVIII, Sanders, Orders in Chancery (1845) Vol. I, Pt. II, pp. 1006-1007.

[37] 1 Daniell, *op. cit.* 499.

[38] *Supra,* Chap. XIV, § 1.

[39] 1 Daniell, *op. cit.* 500.

[40] Caines v. Fisher, 1 Johns. Ch. 8, 9-10 (1814).

[41] Act of 2 Jan. 1788, Laws 1787-88, c. 9, § 2, 12 Henning & Mumford's Stat. p. 464.

three months after the appearance day, "the plaintiff may proceed to take his bill for confessed, and the matter thereof shall be decreed accordingly; which decree shall be absolute unless cause be shown at the term next succeeding that to which the process shall be returned served." [42]

A decree *pro confesso* for want of an answer after due service of process was thus the general rule of the American chancery practice. And, unlike the turn the matter had taken in England after the Chancery Practice Amendment Act of 1852, this practice more especially commended itself when the change in the rules of evidence relieved plaintiffs from depending upon the answer as a means of discovery and enabled them, under statutory provisions, to elect for an answer not under oath. Both for failure to appear and failure to answer the normal course was to enter orders of default as the defaults occurred, on the basis of which in a proper case a decree *pro confesso* would follow.[43]

Now, under the unitary procedure in England and America, it is everywhere the rule that failure to put in the proper defensive pleading entails a judgment by default substantially as was the case in the English common-law system. And the same is true of the practice in those American jurisdictions which retain the divided administration of law and equity, whether the cause in question is of one kind or the other.

But default may be occasioned by omissions other than failure to appear or to answer. At common law it might occur by failure to file a pleading subsequent to the plea, or to take

[42] Rule VI, 7 Wheat, (20 U.S.) vi-vii.

[43] It will be observed that in dealing with the English chancery system we have not used the term "default" with reference to failure to appear in the cause or to answer. For neither of these omissions where they resulted in a decree *pro confesso* was technically known as a default. The "default" of that system consisted in the failure of the defendant to appear at the hearing, and this originally resulted not in a decree *pro confesso* absolute, but in a decree *nisi*, that is to say, one binding upon the defendant unless he could show cause to the contrary. 2 Daniell, Chancery Practice (1840) 621-622; 1 Whitehouse, Equity Practice (1915) § 196, p. 374, note 35. In the later history of the system, by the Orders of 1841, the decree *nisi* was turned into an absolute one. 2 Daniell, *op. cit.* (3d Am. from 3d Eng. ed. 1865) 995, 1019. The same practice of decrees *nisi* for failure to appear at the hearing entered into the American chancery procedure (Whitehouse, *loc. cit.*) but this very generally came in the course of time to apply, on the common-law analogy, the term "default" to these omissions which entailed a decree *pro confesso*.

other prescribed pleading steps. Latter-day procedure has undoubtedly enlarged the circle of such default-attended omissions. Thus failure to verify an answer where verification is required, failure to file an affidavit of merits or other affidavit necessary to support the defense, or failure to answer interrogatories, produce documents or otherwise make discovery are all instances which may, according to the particular system, invite the rendition of a judgment by default.

(*b*) *Ascertainment of the Recovery.*—At common law the default admitted every well-pleaded allegation of the facts constituting the cause of action and consequently that something was due the plaintiff; allegations of damage it did not admit, and these remained to be proved. In the comparatively few cases where the amount due was an integral part of the cause of action, as in an action of debt upon an unconditional obligation to pay a definite sum, a judgment of recovery could be entered forthwith. But the case of other money demands required an interlocutory judgment which fixed the liability, but left the ascertainment of its amount to further proceedings. If the demand was upon a bill of exchange, promissory note or other instrument as to which the amount could be arrived at by mere calculation there became established in the latter part of the 1700s the practice of referring the matter to a prothonotary in the Common Pleas or to the master in the King's Bench to make the necessary computation as the basis for final judgment.[44] Where, however, the demand involved actual damages, a formal assessment of damages was required. It appears that the court had power to make this assessment itself without the aid of a jury,[45] but the usual practice was to proceed by means of a writ of inquiry directed to the sheriff, under which that officer or his deputy, with a jury, tried the

[44] Rashleigh v. Salmon, 1 H.Black. 541, 126 E.R. 147 (1789); Andrews v. Blake, 1 H.Black. 529, 126 E.R. 304 (1790); Longman v. Fenn, 1 H.Black. 541, 126 E.R. 311 (1791); Shepherd v. Charter, 4 T.R. 275, 100 E.R. 1016 (1791); Christian's note to 3 Blackstone, Comm. (Sharwood's ed. 1860) *398; 1 Tidd, Practice (9th ed. 1828) 570, 571.

[45] Beardmore v. Carrington, 2 Wils. 244, 248, 95 E.R. 790 (1764); Bruce v. Rawlins, 2 Wils. 61, 62, 95 E.R. 934 (1770); Whitaker v. Harrold, 17 L.J. (N.S.) Com.Law, Q.B. 343, 347 (1848); Raymond v. Danbury & Norwalk R.R. Co. 14 Blatch, 133, Fed. Cas. No. 11,593 (1877).

question of damages, subject, as Blackstone says, "to nearly the same laws and conditions as the trial by jury at *nisi prius*." [46] When a verdict had been reached [47] determining the amount of the damages, this was reported back to the court by means of the sheriff's return to the writ, and final judgment normally followed for the amount so found.

From the mode of proceeding thus outlined the American common-law systems did not widely depart. Provision was sometimes made for rendition of default judgment, in the case of liquidated demands, by the clerk of the court who made any necessary computation of interest and the like.[48] Again, under the affidavit of merits practice,[49] where the defendant failed to appear or to take the prescribed steps in defense, judgment upon the demand was usually to be entered for the amount specified in the plaintiff's affidavit of claim. For assessment of damages, following interlocutory judgment, the writ of inquiry directed to the sheriff was in considerable use until approximately the end of the first half of the 1800s, but this proceeding has now generally given way to an assessment by the court with or without a jury.

In the English chancery the effect of what corresponded to the common-law default was not dissimilar to that of the latter. It appears from the observations of Lord Chancellor King in *Hawkins* v. *Croke* (1730) [50] that originally the complainant was required to make proof, although the bill was taken as confessed, but that this requirement was discontinued,

[46] 3 Blackstone, Comm. * 398. Exceptionally the Chief Justice or a judge of assize might sit with the sheriff, but only as his assistant. 1 Tidd, Practice (9th ed. 1828) 576; 1 Sellon's Crompton, Practice, (Am. ed. 1813) * 354.

[47] For errors and irregularities in the proceeding, the remedy was not by motion for new trial but by motion to set aside the inquisition. 1 Tidd, *op. cit.* 582; 1 Sellon's Crompton, *op. cit.* * 357.

[48] See *e.g.*, (N.Y.) Fenton v. Garlick, 6 Johns. 287 (1810); (S.C.) Murray's Admrs. v. Alston, 1 Mill, Const. 128 (1817). Under the practice established in Virginia at an early day and still obtaining there and in West Virginia, the clerk, in case of default for non-appearance, enters a conditional judgment, and, unless the defendant appears and defends by the next rule-day, this judgment as confirmed by the court and with or without an assessment of damages, as the case requires, is followed by final judgment. 1 Robinson, Practice in the Courts of Law and Equity in Virginia (1832) 169. For this practice as currently applied in Virginia, see Burks, Pleading and Practice in Actions at Common Law (3d ed. 1934) § 49.

[49] *Supra*, Chap. XVI, § 1.

[50] Mosely 383, 388, 25 E.R. 453.

and under the current practice of the court the decree *pro confesso* was like a judgment of *nil dicit* at common law: it "binds the defendant as to the truth and cuts him out of any defence." As expressed by Chancellor Sandford of the New York Court of Chancery, in a passage frequently quoted, the principle to be gathered from the English cases, in keeping with this rule, is that "when the allegations of a bill are distinct and positive, and the bill is confessed, such allegations are taken as true, without proof. Where the allegations of a bill are indefinite, or the demand of the complainant is in its nature uncertain, the certainty requisite to a proper decree must be afforded by proofs." [51] Accordingly where such proof was required or where ascertainment of the manner of relief due the complainant necessitated the making of inquiries, the taking of accounts, or the like, the court usually proceeded by means of a reference to a master in chancery, on the basis of whose report, if approved by the court, a final decree could be pronounced for the complainant. Upon obtaining leave of court for the purpose the defendant was entitled to have notice of the proceedings before the master and to appear and participate therein,[52] so far as consistent with his confession of the allegations of the bill.

These principles were followed by the American chancery systems without much change. "A confession of facts properly pleaded," said the Supreme Court of the United States, "dispenses with proof of those facts, and is as effectual for the purposes of the suit as if the facts were proved; and a decree *pro confesso* regards the statements of the bill as confessed." [53] In some jurisdictions, however, there was a tendency to require proof as a general rule; in others the matter was left to the discretion of the court. [54] But the analogy to the common-law

[51] Williams v. Corwin, 1 Hopkins Ch. 471, 476, 477 (1824). The decision of the court was rendered upon an exhaustive examination of the English authorities by a master of the court (Mr. Hoffman, the author of Hoffman's Chancery Practice) which forms a valuable repository of the learning upon the present topic.

[52] 2 Daniell, Chancery Practice (1840) 805.

[53] Thomson v. Wooster, 114 U.S. 104, 110, 5 S.Ct. 788 (1885).

[54] See 1 Daniell, Chancery Practice (3d Am. from 3d Eng. ed. 1865) 506, note 4; Ill. Chancery Act, § 18, Ill. Rev. Stat. 1931, c. 22, § 18 (now repealed); N.J. Stat. Ann. 1939, § 2:29-45; Md. Gen. Equity Rules 1941, Rule 16, Md.

interlocutory judgment, to be followed by an assessment of damages,[55] characterized the procedure throughout, and left the defendant free to take all necessary steps to safeguard his interests so long as he did not dispute the truth of the definite allegations of the bill.[56] Thus the defendant "is not precluded from contesting the sufficiency of the bill, or from insisting that the averments contained in it do not justify the decree." [57]

The unified procedure, both in America and in England, conforms in essence to the modes of ascertainment of the older systems. A considerable number of the codes, commencing with the New York original, provide for entry of judgment by the clerk in the case of liquidated demands. A provision of this sort appears in the Federal Rules of 1938, as applicable when the demand is "for a sum certain or for a sum which can by computation be made certain." (Rule 55(b)(1)). In respect of other cases the code legislation and its congeners usually provide for attending the default by proceedings before the court, which is empowered to do substantially the same things as could a court of law or equity under the former régime, subject in some jurisdictions to the right of the plaintiff, suing on a common-law demand, to require that the assessment of damages be had by a jury.[58] In this regard the Federal Rules provide that if "it is necessary to take an account, or to determine the amount of damages or to establish the truth of any averment by evidence or to make an investigation of any other matter, the court may conduct such hearings or order such references as it deems necessary and proper and shall accord a right of jury trial to the parties when and as required by any statute of the United States." (Rule 55(b)(2)).[59]

Ann. Code (Flack, 1939) 1947 Cum. Supp. p. 2012.

55 Hawkins v. Croke, *supra,* Mosely 383, 388; Thomson v. Wooster, *supra,* 110-111.

56 On this matter, see 1 Whitehouse, Equity Practice (1915) § 193, pp. 367-368.

57 Ohio Central RR. Co. v. Central Trust Co. of N.Y., 133 U.S. 83, 91, 10 S.Ct. 235 (1890). It should be noted that the English Chancery Orders of 1845 contained a provision permitting the defendant, if he waived all objection to the order taking the bill as confessed, to appear at the hearing of the cause, "to argue the case upon the merits as stated in the bill." Ord. LXXXII, Sanders, Orders in Chancery, Vol. I, Pt. II (1845) p. 1008.

58 See on this subject note, 20 L.R.A. (N.S.) 1.

59 There is no general right in the federal system to assessment of dam-

Adaptation of both these provisions appears in the recent rules of Delaware (1947), New Jersey (1948) and Utah (1949),[60] while the second has been domesticated in Arizona (1939), Colorado (1941) and New Mexico (1942).[61]

Under the present English practice, where the writ is endorsed as for a liquidated demand, judgment may be entered forthwith for a failure to appear or for a failure to defend after appearance.[62] These judgments are entered in what would correspond to the clerk's office in American courts,[63] and as a matter of course, except in money-lender's actions where leave of a master of the court is required. If the writ is endorsed as for a claim of pecuniary damages or for the detention of goods, there is an interlocutory judgment similarly entered in case of like default, and this is followed by an assessment of damages or of value or of both as the case may be.[64] The assessment is made by a sheriff's jury under a writ of inquiry (in the King's Bench Division only), by a master of the court, or by an official referee,[65] as determined usually by the master specially charged with practice matters. Final judgment is then rendered in accordance with the assessment.[66] But "where the action is of such a kind that originally (*i.e.*, before the Judicature Acts) it could only have been brought in the Court of Chancery (*e.g.*, a claim for an injunction to restrain a nuisance or a breach of covenant) the procedure is different." [67] Here the plaintiff upon failure of the defendant to appear must file

ages by a jury on default. Raymond v. Danbury & Norwalk RR. Co., 14 Blatch. 130, Fed. Cas. No. 11,593 (1877).

60 Del. Rules of Superior Court, Rule 55(b)(1) and (2); N.J. Rules Civ. Pract., Rule 3:55(a) and (b); Utah Rules Civ. Proc., Rule 55(b)(1) and (2).

61 Ariz. Code Ann. 1939, § 21-1206 (Rules Civ. Proc., Rule 55(b)); Colo. Rules Civ. Proc., Rule 55(b)(2) in Colo. Stat. Ann. 1935, 1941 Replacement Vol. I; N.M. Stat. Ann. 1941, § 19-101(55)(b).

62 O. XIII, r. 3; O. XXVII, r. 2.

63 Specifically, for the Chancery Division, in the Chancery Registrar's office; for the King's Bench Division, "in the judgment-room, Action department, Central Office" of the Royal Courts of Justice. Annual Practice 1949, I, p. 2238.

64 O. XIII, r. 5; O. XXVII, r. 4.

65 *Ibid.;* O. XXXVI, rr. 57, 57A; Annual Practice 1949, I, p. 170, note to O. XIII, r. 5; p. 671, note to O. XXXVI, r. 57.

66 Error in the assessment under a writ of inquiry is no longer challenged by motion to set aside the inquisition as at common law (*supra,* note 47), but by motion for new trial addressed to the Court of Appeal. See William Radam's Microbe Killer Co. Ltd. v. Leather [1927] 1 Q.B. 85 (C.A.).

67 Odgers, Principles of Pleading and Practice (13th ed. 1946) 47.

a statement of claim, and the action may proceed as if the defendant had appeared.[68] The defendant may still appear and deliver his defense within the prescribed number of days from the filing of the statement of claim.[69] Should he fail to do so, or if without failure to appear, his default consists of failure to defend within the time appointed by the Rules, the plaintiff may move for judgment, "and such judgment shall be given as upon the statement of claim the court or a judge shall consider the plaintiff to be entitled." [70]

Just as it was the rule at common law and essentially so in the English chancery procedure, so now it remains the case generally in the American jurisdictions that the defaulted defendant continues to exercise all rights of defense not inconsistent with the admission of the plaintiff's cause of action or factual ground of his claim for relief. For example, in the matter of assessment of damages, he may appear and cross-examine the plaintiff's witnesses, object to the introduction of improper evidence, introduce evidence in reduction of the amount claimed, be heard upon the question of the measure of damages, and in general take all steps that would be open to him on a normal trial, so long as he does not go beyond the theme under examination. Nor is the case substantially different under the present English system.

§ 3. Judgments by Confession

At common law, "where the defendant has no available defence to make to the action, it is usual for him, instead of proceeding to trial, or of allowing judgment to pass against him by default, to give the plaintiff a *cognovit* or written confession of the action, usually upon condition that he shall be allowed a certain time for the payment of the debt or damages, the amount of such debt or damages being first ascertained or agreed upon." [71] Where this was done after plea, the plea was withdrawn, and the case was spoken of as one of *cognovit actionem, relicta verificatione*.[72] The ensuing judgment was

[68] O. XIII, r. 12; Odgers, *loc. cit.*

[69] Odgers, *op. cit.* 48.

[70] O. XXVII, r. 11; Annual Practice 1949, I, p. 470.

[71] 2 Archbold, Practice of the Court of King's Bench (2d ed. 1826) 16.

[72] 1 Tidd, Practice (9th ed. 1828) 559.

the technical judgment by confession of the common law. But another form of confessed judgment was that known as a judgment upon warrant of attorney.[73] This had place pursuant to the long standing commercial usage whereby the debtor, as collateral security to his written obligation, executed a warrant of attorney, authorizing one or more attorneys to appear for him in an action at the suit of the creditor, confess judgment or suffer judgment to go by default and execute a release of errors, all without service of process.[74] "How or when," says Chitty, writing in 1834, "this peculiar security for a debt, authorizing a creditor, as it were *per saltum,* to sign a judgment and issue execution, without even issuing a writ, was first invented does not appear, but it has now become one of the most usual collateral securities on loans of money, or contracts to pay an annuity, and for debts, but usually accompanied with some other deed or security." [75] The origin of the practice still remains to be discovered, but it is highly probable that it had its roots in the *instrumenta guarentigiata* or *confessionata*[76] of the commercial cities of medieval Italy, and that its principle, like that of certain other mercantile institutions,[77] was introduced in England by the Lombard merchants who, as Pollock and Maitland tell us, "have brought with them precedents for bonds, lengthy, precise and stringent forms, which they compel their English debtors to execute." [78]

Both these forms are variously reflected in American procedure. Adapting the first to use before the bringing of an action, the New York Code of 1848 [79] provided for the entry of judgment by confession without action "either for money due or to become due, or to secure any person against contingent liability, on behalf of the defendant, or both . . . ," upon the filing of a statement in writing signed and sworn to by the debtor. The statement was required to set forth the

[73] 2 Archbold, *op. cit.* 19.

[74] *Ibid. loc. cit.;* 1 Tidd, *op. cit.* 545.

[75] 2 Chitty, General Practice (Am. ed. 1836) 334.

[76] Engelmann-Millar, History of Continental Civil Procedure (1927) 10, 499.

[77] As insurance and bills of exchange. Mitchell, Law Merchant (1904) 21; Beawes, *Lex Mercatoria* (ed. of 1787) 8, 292, 448.

[78] 1 Pollock and Maitland, History of English Law (2d ed. 1899) 219-220; Mitchell, *op. cit.* 109.

[79] §§ 335, 336.

amount for which judgment might be entered, as well as to show concisely the facts originating the debt or contingent liability. This manner of provision found wide acceptance in the code States, and, with or without modification, obtains today in California, Idaho, Iowa, Minnesota, Missouri, Montana, New Mexico, North Carolina, North Dakota, Oregon, South Carolina, South Dakota, Utah, and the Territory of Alaska, as well as in New York.[80] Other jurisdictions similarly but in different terms provide for judgment without suit upon the defendant's written confession, while two, at least, Kentucky and Arkansas, insist for the purpose upon the debtor's personal appearance in open court.[81]

The proceeding under warrant of attorney also finds recognition, but is present on its common-law basis in a minority only of the American jurisdictions. The harshness of the remedy has tended in increasing measure to bring about the cessation or restriction of its use. Thus warrants of the kind are declared void by statute in Alabama, Florida, Indiana, Kentucky, Mississippi, Montana and Tennessee.[82] A like result has been reached by judicial decision in Missouri [83] and West Virginia.[84] Texas, without express declaration of invalidity, makes them unlawful,[85] and Massachusetts provides for the annulment on motion of a judgment entered on such a warrant, without service of process, unless there has been specified notice to the defendant of the intention to enter the judgment.[86] Less

[80] Cal. Code Civ. Proc. (Deering, 1949) § 1132 *et seq.;* Idaho Code Ann. 1949, § 10-901 *et seq.;* Ia. Code 1946, § 676.1 *et seq.;* Minn. Stat. 1945, § 548.22; Mo. Rev. Stat. Ann. 1942, § 1259 *et seq.;* Mont. Rev. Codes Ann. 1947, § 93-9401 *et seq.;* N.C. Gen. Stat. 1943, § 1-247 *et seq.;* N.D. Rev. Code 1943, § 28-1001 *et seq.;* N.M. Stat. Ann. 1941, § 19-909 *et seq.;* N.Y. Civ. Pract. Act (Clevenger, Annual Practice, 1950) § 540 *et seq.;* Ore. Comp. Laws Ann. 1940, § 6-405 *et seq.;* S.C. Code 1942, § 670 *et seq.;* S.D. Rev. Code 1939, § 37.0301 *et seq.;* Utah Code Ann. 1943, § 104-33-1 *et seq.;* Alaska Comp. Laws Ann. 1949, § 57-4-1.

[81] Ky. Code Pract. in Civ. Cases (Carroll, 1948) § 381 *et seq.;* Ark. Stat. Ann. 1947, § 29-301 *et seq.*

[82] Ala. Code 1940, Tit. 20, § 16; Fla. Stat. 1949, § 55.05; Ind. Stat. (Burns, 1933), 1946 Replacement Vol. II, § 2-2904; Ky. Rev. Stat. 1948, § 372.140; Miss. Code Ann. 1942, § 1545; Mont. Rev. Codes Ann. 1947, § 13-811; Tenn. Code Ann. (Williams, 1934) § 8848.

[83] First Nat. Bank of Kansas City v. White, 220 Mo. 717, 120 S.W. 36 (1909).

[84] Farquhar & Co. v. Dehaven, 70 W.Va. 738, 75 S.E. 65 (1911).

[85] Tex. Rev. Civ. Stat. (Vernon, 1936) Art. 2224.

[86] Mass. Ann. Laws, 1933, c. 231, § 13A.

drastic, but almost as dissuasive is the rule that the warrant is effectual only when executed after the indebtedness secured has become due.[87] Other discouraging requirements prescribe execution of the warrant in the same manner as a conveyance of land or as a deed,[88] or that the warrant be physically separate from the instrument evidencing the indebtedness.[89] Virginia requires that a warrant incorporated in a note or bond specifically name the person empowered and the clerk's office in which the judgment is to be confessed.[90] Moreover, Virginia, as well as Maryland, provides for notice to be given the defendant of the entry of the judgment.[91] In most of the jurisdictions having statutes on the New York pattern the effect is to exclude the warrant practice.[92] In some, however, the warrant practice is adjusted to the provisions of such statutes.

The warrants usually employed are substantially in the common-law form, frequently with the addition of a provision for attorney's fees. Commonly they appear, where the law permits, as embodied in promissory notes and leases. The promissory note containing such a warrant is the "judgment note" of commercial usage in the acquiescent jurisdictions. In the entry of the judgment it is everywhere the rule, as it was at common law, that the terms of the warrant must be strictly pursued. The judgment, itself, is entitled to all the jurisdictional presumptions attending a judgment rendered on service of process. But it may always be opened on motion and the defendant allowed to defend, if he is able to show by affidavit the existence of a good defense on the merits to all or a part of the plaintiff's demand; in its order of opening it is usual for the court to direct that the judgment stand as security pend-

[87] Ariz. Code Ann. 1939, § 21-1218; N.M. Stat. Ann. 1941, § 19-916.

[88] Kan. Gen. Stat. Ann. 1935, § 60-3111; Okla. Stat. 1941, Tit. 12, § 690; Va. Code Ann. 1942, § 6130a, Va. Code Ann. 1950, § 8-359 (other than warrants in a note or bond)

[89] N.J. Stat. Ann. 1939, § 2:27-266, see § 2:27-271; Mich. Stat. Ann. 1938, § 27.1434.

[90] Va. Code Ann. 1942, § 6130a, Va. Code Ann. 1950, § 8-362.

[91] *Ibid. loc. cit.;* Md. Gen. Rules Pract. & Proc. 1947, Part 3, Subd. II, Rule 1, Md. Ann. Code (Flack, 1939) 1947 Cum. Supp. p. 2048.

[92] See *e.g.,* U.S. Fidelity & Guaranty Co. v. Schickler, 199 App.Div. 74, 191 N.Y.S. 194 (1921). For the opposite view, see the well-considered case of First Nat. Bank of Las Cruces v. Baker, 25 N.M. 208, 180 Pac. 291 (1919).

ing the determination of the issues. In thus dealing with the judgment the court is not bound by the rule of finality applying to judgments in general:[93] the judgment may be opened even after the expiration of the term or the attainment of the substituted point of finality, so long as the defendant has sought the relief without undue delay.[94] This follows from the common-law principle which, responding to the dictates of justice, conceded to the court a species of equitable jurisdiction over such judgments.[95]

The American trend toward discountenancing the warrant to confess judgment accords with the tendency in England. By statute it is there provided that the instrument containing the warrant shall be witnessed by a solicitor named by the debtor and attending at his request to inform him of the legal effect of his act.[96] And, while provision continues to obtain with reference to the signing of judgment by virtue of such warrants,[97] we are told that "after the Acts of 1860 and 1864, whereby judgments ceased to operate as a charge on the debtor's land, this method of securing a debt became almost obsolete." [98]

§ 4. Judgments in Rem

As opposed to the ordinary judgment, based upon jurisdiction of the person and, if for money, enforceable out of the estate at large of the defendant—the judgment *in personam*—stands the judgment *in rem*, restricted in its operation to the particular thing in question. The judgment *in rem* in the fullest sense of the term is one rendered in a proceeding in which the thing itself occupies the position of defendant, as exemplified by an admiralty suit against a vessel, under the American practice,[99] or by a proceeding on the part of the Government for

[93] See *infra*, Chap. XXII, § 1.

[94] Lake v. Cook, 15 Ill. 353 (1854); Kloeckner v. Schafer, 110 Ill.App. 391 (1903); Kolmar Inc. v. Moore, 323 Ill. App. 323, 55 N.E. 2d 524 (1944); 49 C.J.S. 582.

[95] 2 Chitty, *op. cit.* 333.

[96] 32 & 33 Vict. c. 62, § 24; 22 & 23 Geo. V, c. 37, § 81(2).

[97] Practice Masters' Rules, Rule 25, Annual Practice 1949, I, p. 2237.

[98] Williams, Personal Property (18th ed. 1926) 247, note c.

[99] Here the present English admiralty practice differs. Hughes, Admiralty, (2d ed. 1920) 402. There is a writ of summons ordinarily running against "the owners and parties interested," which is normally followed by a warrant of arrest for the seizure of the vessel. Annual Practice 1949, I, pp. 13, 50, II, pp. 2520, 2522.

violation of the customs laws in which the offending articles occupy this position. "The court acquires jurisdiction over the property in such cases by its seizure, and of the subsequent proceedings by public citation to the world, of which the owner is at liberty to avail himself by appearing as a claimant in the case." [100] And the judgment of condemnation is binding as against the world. But cases of this description belong to special procedures which are outside the scope of the present inquiry.

In the general procedure of civil causes, "there is, however, a large class of cases which are not strictly actions *in rem,* but are frequently spoken of as actions *quasi in rem,* because, though brought against persons, they only seek to subject certain property of these persons to the discharge of the claims asserted. Such are actions in which the property of non-residents is attached and held for the payment of debts due by them to citizens of the State, and actions for the enforcement of mortgages, and other liens. Indeed, all proceedings having for their sole object the sale or other disposition of the property of the defendant to satisfy the demand of the plaintiff, are in a general way thus designated. But they differ, among other things, from actions which are strictly *in rem,* in that the interest of the defendant is alone to be affected, that citation to him is required, and that judgment therein is only conclusive between the parties." [101] Within this category come not only cases where it is sought to make the property answerable in respect of pecuniary demands of the plaintiff, but also actions directed to the adjudication of the title or status of the property or a claim of interest therein, including suits to establish title, to remove clouds on the title, for partition, and the like, so far as the law of the particular jurisdiction has vested the court with power to make such adjudication, without dependence on jurisdiction of the person.[102]

[100] Freeman v. Alderson, 119 U.S. 185, 187, 7 S.Ct. 165 (1886).

[101] *Ibid.* 187, 188.

[102] Pennoyer v. Neff, 95 U.S. 714, 733-734 (1877); Arnt v. Griggs, 134 U.S. 316, 10 S.Ct. 557 (1890); Hill v. Henry, 66 N.J.Eq. 150, 154, 57 Atl. 554 (1904); Amparo Mining Co. v. Fidelity Trust Co. 74 N.J.Eq. 197, 71 Atl. 605 (1908); Gassert v. Strong, 38 Mont. 18, 30-32, 98 Pac. 497 (1908); State *ex rel.* South Brevard Drainage Dist. v. Smith, 126 Fla. 72, 75, 170 So. 440 (1936). And see note, 126 A.L.R. 664.

In cases of this description, so long as the property is within the jurisdiction, has been seized as in attachment, or in other cases has been sufficiently described in the complaint, and there has been given to the defendant such statutory notice, by publication or otherwise, as complies with the requirements of due process of law, the conditions are present for the exercise of this manner of jurisdiction.[103] The judgment is thus one *in rem,* although the proceeding is in form one *inter partes.* If, in the course of the proceeding, jurisdiction of the defendant's person is acquired, either by his voluntary appearance or otherwise, it may happen that the judgment imposes as well a personal liability upon the defendant. This is not uncommon in cases of attachment.

Definite segregation of the group of proceedings thus labelled *quasi in rem* is a purely American development, contributed to in important measure by the general use of attachment on mesne process, influenced by the political relationship of the States to one another, and resting on the exigencies of due process of law under the Federal Constitution. It is not met with in the English practice. For one thing, there being no attachment on mesne process under the existing English law, an important incentive to recognition is absent. As appears in a former place,[104] service under the English Rules may be substituted service where the situation so requires, or in certain cases particularly specified may be service outside the jurisdiction. But every such service, bindingly effected, stands on the same basis as personal service within the jurisdiction. In other words, once there is service as authorized by the Rules, either substituted service or service outside the jurisdiction, it will

[103] The essential elements of an action *quasi in rem* are: "(1) a *res* located within the territorial limits of the state in such a way that the state can, if it see fit to do so, exercise absolute power to control and dispose of it. (2) A course of judicial procedure, the object and result of which are to subject the *res* to the power of the state, directly by the judgment or decree which is entered as distinguished from a course of procedure which only affects or disposes of the *res* by compelling a party to the action to control or dispose of the *res* in accordance with the mandate of the judgment or decree. (3) A course of judicial procedure on its face directed specifically toward the *res* so as to disclose this *res* to the defendant when reasonably notified of the action. . . ." Amparo Mining Co. v. Fidelity Trust Co. *supra,* 201-202.

[104] *Supra,* Chap. VIII, § 2.

support whatever manner of judgment is called for by the particular case, whether this involves jurisdiction *in rem* or *in personam*.

Again, there are certain proceedings *inter partes*, directed to the end of "changing or declaring the status of either one or both of the parties to the action," [105] in which the status in question is the *res* upon which the court is empowered to act. The most conspicuous instance of the kind is the suit for divorce. Here, too, when the court has jurisdiction over the *res*, in this case the status, it may proceed to valid adjudication, although notice to the defendant, given in the manner provided by law, has not been personal service. So far the proceeding resembles that of the actions *quasi in rem*. But an important difference exists in the circumstance that the judgment as to the status is binding upon all the world,[106] at least within the jurisdiction of rendition. The English law in the present respect is not materially different from our own. Thus a decree of divorce in proper cases may be rendered on substituted service or service outside the jurisdiction,[107] and when absolute "is a judgment *in rem*, binding *inter partes* and against the whole world, so far as the English jurisdiction is concerned." [108]

§ 5. The Declaratory Judgment

More especially because applications, though isolated and often in an unrevealing form, of what in reality is the principle of the declaratory judgment have been part of our equity tradition, it is a reproach to the Anglo-American administration of civil justice that it has been so tardy in coming to an avowed and definite recognition of that principle. The ordinary judgment or decree, rendered in favor of a plaintiff, embodies essentially two elements, first, a determination of right, implied for the most part in actions of a common-law nature, but for equitable actions generally in express form, and, secondly, an award, effectuable by state-provided means, of the relief to

[105] Hilton v. Snyder, 37 Utah 384, 388, 108 Pac. 698 (1910).

[106] Am. Law Institute, Restatement of the Law of Judgments (1942) § 74.

[107] Matrimonial Causes Rules 1937, rr. 8(2), 9.

[108] Browne and Latey, Law and Practice in Divorce and Matrimonial Causes (11th ed. 1931) 135.

which the verified right entitles. The declaratory judgment, on the other hand, concerns itself only with the determination of right, and is in order where the situation is not ripe for anything more than that determination. Its virtue thus lies in marking out for the parties, when the case so requires, the path which they may lawfully follow, instead of compelling them to wait for judicial action until missteps have occasioned damage or loss—in "enabling a plaintiff assailed by doubt and uncertainty arising from adverse claims or clouds, to avoid the resulting peril and insecurity by obtaining an authoritative adjudication of his rights, before risking disaster by acting on his own assumption or guess or incurring prejudice by not acting because of fear of consequences." [109]

Basically this institution represents an extension of the field of actions, involving, as it does, the recognition of a purely declaratory action, *i.e.*, one looking to a declaration of rights without any concomitant adjudging of relief, but in current Anglo-American usage the accent is placed upon the product of the action rather than upon the action itself. Of Roman-law lineage, it became an important feature of the medieval Romano-canonical procedure, and subsequently entered into the Scottish law, whence it was introduced into England by legislation of the 1850s,[110] particularly the Chancery Practice Amendment Act of 1852.[111] Failing at first of complete domestication through the ultra-conservatism of judicial construction, it finally attained to decisive and sweeping allowance in the Rules of 1883, which vested the court with power to "make binding declarations of right whether any consequential relief is or could be claimed or not." [112] This provision remains in force as supplemented by others permitting application for the declaration in certain cases to be made by the expedited procedure of originating summons.[113]

American acceptance of the principle thus crystallized did not get well under way until the third decade of the 1900s. But thanks especially to the writings of Professors Borchard

[109] Borchard, Declaratory Judgments (2d ed. 1941) 931.

[110] History of the institution in Borchard, *op. cit.* 87 *et seq.*

[111] 15 & 16 Vict. c. 86, § 50.

[112] R.S.C., O. XXV, r. 5.

[113] R.S.C., O. LIVA.

and Sunderland, its subsequent progress has evidenced a reception of the institution, resembling in rapidity and much exceeding in extent, that which attended the code movement in the middle years of the last century. By 1939, as we learn from Professor Borchard's encyclopaedic treatise, statutory recognition of the declaratory judgment had come about in some forty American jurisdictions other than the federal. Twenty-five of these jurisdictions had adopted the model act prepared by the National Conference on Uniform State Laws, and in all, except Massachusetts, South Carolina and Florida where it limited itself to the construction of written instruments, the declaratory power established has been of general application.[114] Since the time mentioned at least five others have been added to the list of adherent jurisdictions, namely, Maine (1941), West Virginia (1941), Georgia (1945), Illinois (1945), and Louisiana (1948);[115] of these the first two follow the Uniform Act.

In the federal sphere the doubt which had existed, especially in view of *Willing* v. *Chicago Auditorium Association* (1928),[116] as to whether a proceeding of this kind could be deemed to involve a "case" or "controversy" within the meaning of Art. III of the Federal Constitution, was effectually removed by *Nashville, Chattanooga & St. Louis Railway Co.* v. *Wallace*,[117] decided in 1933. With the way thus opened a federal declaratory judgment statute was adopted in 1934. At first of general application, this in the succeeding year was amended so as to exclude from its purview questions of federal taxation.[118] Without material change these provisions, in the light of the supervening Federal Rules, were the subject of revision in the act of June 25, 1948.[119] Under the Federal Rules the application for a declaratory judgment, pursuant to the statute, is to be in accordance with their provisions. The Rules

[114] Borchard, *op. cit.* 132-133, with statutory citations. The forty included Puerto Rico and the Philippines.

[115] Me. Laws 1941, c. 233, Me. Rev. Stat. 1944, c. 95, §§ 38-50; W.Va. Laws 1941, c. 26, W.Va. Code Ann. 1949, §§ 5516(1)-5516(16); Ga. Laws 1945, p. 137; Ill. Laws 1945, p. 1149, Ill. Rev. Stat. 1949, c. 110, § 181.1; La. Laws 1948, Act No. 431.

[116] 277 U.S. 274, 48 S.Ct. 507.

[117] 288 U.S. 249, 53 S.Ct. 345.

[118] 48 Stat. 955, 49 Stat. 1027, 28 U.S.C. § 400 (1946).

[119] U.S. Code, Tit. 28, as revised in 1948, §§ 2201, 2202.

also declare that "the existence of another adequate remedy does not preclude a judgment for declaratory relief in cases where it is appropriate." (Rule 57). Moreover, they recognize that the application for a declaratory judgment may be the subject of the summary judgment procedure. (Rule 56(a) (b)).

A question which tends to give some trouble in the American jurisdictions is that of the right of trial by jury. Expressly recognized by the federal statute before the revision of 1948 for "issues of fact triable by jury," and continuingly by the Federal Rules for "any issue triable of right by a jury," this right obtains to a like extent under the Uniform Act and the declaratory statutes generally.[120] It is everywhere acknowledged that the declaratory action is *per se* neither legal nor equitable; and the statutes themselves afford no key to determining whether the issues in a given case are to be regarded as legal in the sense that they are triable by jury or equitable in the sense that they are triable by the court. In the effort to reach a solution of the problem, it is held that if the right asserted by the plaintiff in the declaratory action is one which, if asserted as a defense in an action brought by the now defendant against the now plaintiff, would create an issue triable by jury, that same issue arising in the declaratory action is equally attended with the right of jury trial.[121] "In such a proceeding," says the court, "although the parties are reversed in their position before the court, that is, the defendant has become the plaintiff and *vice versa,* the issues are ones which in the absence of the statute for declaratory relief would be tried at law by a court and jury. In such a case there is an absolute right to a jury trial unless a jury has been waived."[122] Satisfactory as this result undoubtedly is in the particular circumstances, it is

[120] 48 Stat. 955, 28 U.S.C. § 400 (1946); Fed. Rules Civ. Proc., Rules 57, 38(b), 39(a); Borchard, *op. cit.* 401.

[121] Aetna Casualty & Surety Co. v. Quarles (C.C.A. 4) 92 Fed.2d 321 (1937); Pacific Indemnity Co. v. McDonald (C.C.A. 9) 107 Fed.2d 446 (1939); Hargrove v. Am. Central Ins. Co. (C.C.A. 10) 125 Fed.2d 225 (1942); Dickinson v. General Accident Fire & Life Assurance Corp. Ltd. (C.C.A. 9) 147 Fed.2d 396 (1945).

[122] Pacific Indemnity Co. v. McDonald, *supra,* at 448. See comment on this case (1940) 28 Cal.L.Rev. 638; (1940) 35 Ill.L.Rev. 339.

far from yielding a formula capable of general application, and such a formula has not yet made its appearance. Fortunately, however, cases of the kind are of infrequent occurrence, more especially because of the disposition to waive jury trial,[123] and from a practical standpoint, therefore, the difficulty is not a highly serious one.

Allowance made for the matter just mentioned, the institution as implanted in the American jurisdictions has worked well and vindicated in full measure the hopes placed upon it.[124] With its "enormous and far-reaching possibilities in preventive relief,—prevention not merely of threatened wrongs but prevention of uncertainty and misunderstanding in the assertion of rights," [125] it cannot fail within a short day to find acceptance in the very few still reluctant quarters and thus to become an integral part of the remedial system in every American jurisdiction.

123 See Borchard, *op. cit.* 403.

124 For the more recent course of decision in general under the statutes, see (1949) Developments in the Law: Declaratory Judgments 1941-1949, 62 Harv.L.Rev. 787-885.

125 Sunderland, A. Modern Evolution in Remedial Rights,—The Declaratory Judgment (1917) 16 Mich.L.Rev. 69, 89.

Chapter XXII

NON-APPELLATE RECOURSE AGAINST JUDGMENTS

§ 1. Criteria of Judgment-Finality

Although in a strict sense no judgment is final until it has survived proceedings for appellate review or the time for such proceedings has passed, the term "final" is commonly applied to the definitive judgment in the action. But the finality with which we are here concerned is that which exists in respect of the judgment when it is no longer open to substantial change by the court of rendition,—when, in other words, it has passed beyond the control of that court,—except by the invocation of some special form of remedy provided for the purpose.

By the traditional rule of the common law a judgment remained within the control of the court of rendition, with power to alter it in form or substance, until the lapse of the term of court at which it was rendered. During this period it was said to be *in fieri,* or, as otherwise expressed, "in the breast of the court." But, in the words of Coke, "when that terme is past, then the record is in the roll, and admitteth no alteration, averment or proofe to the contrarie."[1] Clerical misprisions might be amended by force of certain early statutes, where there was "something to amend by," as, for example, the notes of the judge,[2] and for matters of substance there existed an important exception to the general rule in a proceeding to correct a certain limited class of errors of fact, the writ of error *coram nobis.* The rule in question had no application to interlocutory orders or judgments, which remained subject to control of the court until expiration of the term at which final judgment was entered.[3]

1 Co. Litt. 260a.

2 1 Tidd, Practice (9th ed. 1828) 712-713.

3 For unorthodox departure from the general rule, see Cannan v. Reynolds, 5 El.&Bl. 301, 119 E.R. 493 (1855),

In the High Court of Chancery, on the other hand, the same terms of court, while observed for some purposes,[4] had no such relation to finality of adjudication as obtained in the common-law courts. Here the decree became final in the present sense when it was formally enrolled—a step which usually involved some delay after the decree had been actually pronounced.[5] Until enrollment of the decree the Chancellor "may rehear, alter, change, or reverse it," [6] but once enrolled, unless appealed, it was normally withdrawn from change other than the correction of merely clerical mistakes, except as a result of an independent proceeding, here usually the bill of review. Interlocutory orders not touching the merits might "not only be altered, but even discharged on good cause by special direction of the court," [7] during the progress of the cause. But capable of enrollment, and so of being withdrawn from change were interlocutory decrees of a final nature, as well as decretal orders "conclusive of any of the rights of the parties to the cause." [8] There was, however, such a thing as vacating an enrollment. This highly exceptional measure might be taken for irregularity in the enrollment itself, and it would appear that "where the case has not been heard upon the merits, the Court will exercise a discretionary power of vacating an inrolment and of giving the party an opportunity of having the merits of his case discussed." [9]

In the American jurisdictions the common-law courts from the outset everywhere followed the rule which marked the expiration of the judgment term as the point of finality; more recent times have witnessed some departure from the rule. In equity, however, there was not the same observance of English precedent. For the most part equity was administered under the same term-regimen as at law. Accordingly, most of the chancery jurisdictions, including the federal, applied the common-law rule to equity decrees, making their finality de-

and the American cases cited in 1 Freeman, Judgments (5th ed. 1925) §§ 198, 232.

[4] See 2 Harrison, Chancery Practice (8th ed. 1796) 507-510.

[5] See 2 Daniell, Chancery Practice (1840) 679 *et seq.*

[6] 2 Maddock, Chancery Practice (4th Am. ed.) *464.

[7] 2 Harrison, *op. cit.* 141; 2 Daniell, *op. cit.* 678.

[8] 2 Daniell, *op. cit. loc. cit.*

[9] *Ibid.* 684.

pend upon the lapse of the term. To reconcile this rule with orthodox chancery practice, it was said that the decree, after proper signature and filing, is "to be considered as taken and enrolled" with the ending of the term at which it was made.[10] But in some States there was a closer adherence to the English model. This was particularly true of the New York Court of Chancery, where the actual enrollment, simplified from the original, and taking place after thirty days from the entry of the decree in the minutes, signified the point of finality.[11] New Jersey[12] and Delaware[13] also fell within this group, but deemed enrollment forthwith effected by entry and signature.[14] Whether the enrollment was thus constructive or actual, it attached the same finality to the decree as did the formal enrollment of the English chancery.

In the later development of American procedure the common-law rule has played the major rôle, under the codes as well as otherwise. But the unequal operation of that rule, which was as applicable to a judgment entered on the last day of the term as to one entered on the first, has induced in various quarters the substitution of a stated number of days, reckoning from the date of the judgment, during which the judgment remains within the control of the court, as in Alabama,[15] Illinois,[16] and New Mexico,[17] where thirty days is the period thus fixed, in Kentucky, where for certain circuit courts "having continuous sessions" a sixty-day period is similarly prescribed,[18] or in Texas, where for certain civil district courts thirty days is again the period appointed, here running

10 Burch v. Scott, 1 Gill &J. (Md.) 393, 426 (1829). Story observes that "in most of the state courts of equity in America, and certainly in the courts of the United States, all decrees in equity as well as judgments at law, are matters of record, and are deemed to be enrolled, as of the term of the court at which they are passed, whether actually enrolled or not." Story, Equity Pleadings (10th ed. 1892) § 403.

11 1 Hoffman, Chancery Practice (1834) 573.

12 See Carpenter v. Muchmore, 2 McCart. (15 N.J.Eq.) 123 (1862).

13 Cochran v. Couper, Admr., 2 Del. Ch. 27, 30 (1837).

14 The States accepting the principle of actual enrollment, however simplified, rather than the expiration of the term, as an index of finality, came to include Michigan (Mich. Stat. Ann. 1938, § 27.1446) but here there may be a petition for rehearing within two months, and where based upon newly discovered evidence, within four months after enrollment. Mich. Court Rules 1931, 1933, Rule 48.

15 Ala. Code 1940, Tit. 13, § 119.

16 Ill. Rev. Stat. 1949, c. 77, §§ 82-84.

17 N.M. Stat. Ann. 1941, § 19-901.

18 Ky. Rev. Stat. 1948, § 451.130.

from the rendition of judgment or the overruling of a motion for new trial.[19] In some jurisdictions, however, the judgment is final as soon as entered, subject only to the special means of recourse provided by law. This is true in Massachusetts, where, terms no longer obtaining, it is "the established principle that after the entry of a final decree in equity, as after the entry of a final judgment in a suit at law, the case is finally disposed of by the court," [20] in the present sense. A similar rule obtains in other States which have discarded terms. Thus in Washington it is held that, subject to the statutory right of vacation for specified cause, "judgments have the quality of a common-law judgment after term, immediately upon their rendition and entry of record." [21] So in California a judgment regularly entered can be reviewed and set aside only in the manner provided by statute.[22] A like principle governs in Montana.[23] But where terms have been retained, or where there has been substituted a statutory period for the exercise of the common-law control, it is generally true that this control is not impaired by the presence of statutory or rule-provided means of recourse. The case, however, appears to be otherwise under the Federal Rules, certainly since the amendments of 1946.[24]

[19] Tex. Rules Civ. Proc. (Vernon, 1942) Rule 330(l).

[20] White v. Gove, 183 Mass. 333, 340, 67 N.E. 359 (1903).

[21] State *ex rel.* McConihe v. Steiner, 58 Wash. 578, 582, 109 Pac. 57 (1910); McCaffrey v. Snapp, 95 Wash. 202, 206, 163 Pac. 406 (1917).

[22] Holtum v. Greif, 144 Cal. 521, 524, 78 Pac. 11 (1904); United Railroads v. Superior Court, 170 Cal. 755, 760, 151 Pac. 129 (1915).

[23] Oregon Mortgage Co. v. Kunneke, 76 Mont. 117, 124, 245 Pac. 539 (1926); Whitbecker v. Montana Central Ry. Co. 21 Mont. 102, 52 Pac. 1098 (1898).

[24] As originally adopted, Rule 6(c) declared that "the period of time provided for the doing of any act or the taking of any proceeding is not affected or limited by the expiration of a term of court." From this, together with certain other provisions as to time, not, however, express to the present point, and also specific provision for relief against the judgment, there was ground for concluding that there had been abrogated the power of control formerly residing in the court until the end of the term, although a different view seems to have been taken in Bucy v. Nevada Construction Co. (C.C.A. 9) 125 Fed.2d 213 (1942). Moore and Rogers, Federal Relief from Civil Judgments (1946) 55 YaleL.J. 623, 628-629, 640. Further support for this opposite view was to be found in Hill v. Hawes, 320 U.S. 520, 524, 64 S.Ct. 334 (1944) and Boaz v. Mutual Life Ins. Co. of N.Y. (C.C.A. 8) 142 Fed. 2d 321, 322 (1944). Now, however, Rule 6(c) has been amended so as to provide that the time which it mentions is not to be affected by "the con-

What thus has been said concerning the principles of judgment-finality is subject to certain qualification when it comes to the matter of judgments by default. This will be considered in a later section of the present chapter.

Correction of clerical errors, after the term or other time-measure of finality, is everywhere the rule in the American jurisdictions. The common-law and classic chancery scope of correction has been amplified and liberalized by the various statutes of amendments. Assuming that the mistake or error has been properly demonstrated, every correction essential to make the judgment record register faithfully the judgment actually pronounced may thus be made, and for this purpose the judgment remains indefinitely open, so long as the rights of third persons are not thereby prejudiced. An advanced type of legislation in this regard is that appearing in the Federal Rules, which provide that "clerical mistakes in judgments, orders or other parts of the record and errors therein arising from oversight or omission may be corrected by the court at any time of its own initiative or on the motion of any party and after such notice, if any, as the court orders." (Rule 60 (a)).[24a]

Similar correction is permissible under the English Rules,[25] but it is to be particularly remarked that in no other way, save in the case of default judgments, do these permit the judgment to be changed after its entry. As the court no longer follows the term-regimen, the old term-rule of the common law has gone by the board; moreover, there is nothing corresponding to the old chancery enrollment. The judgment is

---

tinued existence or expiration" of the term. Citing the cases above mentioned, the Advisory Committee has explained that "the purpose of the amendment is to prevent reliance upon the continued existence of a term as a source of power to disturb the finality of a judgment upon grounds other than those stated in these rules." Note to amendment of Rule 6. Federal Rules of Civil Procedure, West Publishing Co. (1947) p. 14.

24a An amendment of 1946 added here the following: "During the pendency of an appeal, such mistakes may be corrected before the appeal is docketed in the appellate court, and thereafter while the appeal is pending may be so corrected with leave of the appellate court."

25 "Clerical mistakes in judgments or orders, or errors arising therein from any accidental slip or omission, may at any time be corrected by the court or a judge on motion or summons without an appeal." O. XXVIII, r. 11.

final in the sense we are considering, from the time of its entry, and there is no analogue of the American statutory motion to vacate. And, by an even wider departure from former principles, the same quality of finality is attached to interlocutory orders. As stated by the editors of the Annual Practice, the general rule is that "the court has no power under any application in the action to alter or vary a judgment after it has been entered, or an order after it has been drawn up, except so far as is necessary to correct errors in expressing the intention of the court." [26] Under proper circumstances, such as in a former day would have founded resort to the Court of Chancery, an aggrieved party can obtain relief from a judgment or order, but this would involve a fresh proceeding, that is to say, an action to impeach the judgment or order in question.[27]

§ 2. Common-Law Means of Recourse

After the lapse of the term, as has been indicated, the common-law court exercised a narrow measure of control over its own judgment, by virtue of the writ of error known as *coram nobis* in the King's Bench and *coram vobis* [28] in the Common Pleas, the former, however, being the term usually employed in America. The suing out of the writ, which occurred *ex parte*,[29] was in essence an application to the court of rendition to revoke its judgment for certain errors of fact not appearing in the record of the proceeding and not chargeable in any wise to the process of adjudication,—such an error as, for example, would appear "if it turns out that a woman plaintiff who sued as a *feme sole* was, in fact, a *feme covert*, or that an infant plaintiff has sued by attorney instead of guardian, or if judgment is signed after the death of one of the parties, and more than two terms after verdict." [30] Here belonged, also, certain cases of "error in the process, or through the default of the clerks." [31] The proceeding, it was

[26] Annual Practice 1949, I, p. 497.

[27] See *ibid.* p. 498.

[28] From the reference in the writ to errors *"quae coram nobis* (or *vobis*) *resident."* 2 Tidd, Practice (9th ed. 1828) 1136, 1137.

[29] 1 Archbold, Practice of the Court of King's Bench (2d ed. 1826) 276.

[30] Watkin Williams, Principles and Practice of Pleading (1857) 214. See also U.S. v. Mayer, 235 U.S. 55, 68, 35 S.Ct. 16 (1914).

[31] 2 Tidd, *op. cit.* 1137.

said, lay before the court of rendition rather than a higher tribunal, because "error in fact is not the error of the judges, and therefore the reversing of a judgment given by them which is only erroneous in matter of fact is not reversing their own judgment." [32] It was in the nature of a new action in which the complaining party was plaintiff, it involved an assignment of errors, corresponding to a common-law declaration, to which the defendant pleaded or demurred, and the ensuing issues were decided in the usual way, issues of law being heard by the court and issues of fact tried by jury. It resulted in a judgment which, if for the plaintiff, "recalled" the previous judgment, or if for the defendant, affirmed that judgment.[33]

Error *coram nobis* found lodgment in the practice of the American common-law courts, but generally took the form of a motion directed to the setting aside of the judgment for the error in question.[34] Nor did it disappear with the adoption of the codes, but was retained as part of the common-law inheritance in various of the code jurisdictions. Frequently the field of the proceeding has been absorbed in that of certain statutory motions to vacate the judgment. It seems, however, to be the general rule that where the proceeding has not, either expressly or by necessary implication, been abrogated by statute, it continues to be available.[35] Where employed, an affidavit in support of the motion, or as an alternative to the motion and affidavit, a sworn petition takes the place of the old assignment of errors. Defense in point of fact is made by counter-affidavit and defense in point of law by the same manner of legal objection as in ordinary actions. It cannot be said, however, that the old right of jury trial is uniformly preserved; more usually, on the analogy of other motions to vacate, the issues of both law and fact are determined by the court. For the most part, employment of the proceeding has

[32] Impey, *Instructor Clericalis* (3d ed. 1786) 561.

[33] 1 Archbold, *op. cit.* 279-281.

[34] "It cannot be questioned that the appropriate use of the writ of error *coram nobis* is to enable a court to correct its own errors; those errors which precede the rendition of judgment. In practice the same end is now generally attained by motion, sustained, if the case require it, by affidavits." Pickett's Heirs v. Legerwood, 7 Pet. (32 U.S.) 144, 147 (1833).

[35] Smith v. Kingsley, 19 Wend. (N.Y.) 620 (1838); Sanders v. State, 85 Ind. 318, 326, 327 (1882).

always been exceptional,[36] though in a number of States it has found statutory recognition. Judging by the comparative volume [37] of decisions involving the remedy, its current employment in civil cases looms largest in Illinois, Missouri and Tennessee. In Illinois it is the subject of a statutory provision which, abolishing the writ, declares that all errors of fact, "which, by the common law, could be corrected by said writ," may be corrected by motion in writing made within five years from the rendition of final judgment,[38] and notwithstanding the steps toward unified administration of law and equity here taken in 1933, is still, principally because of the statutory language, applicable only to common-law causes.[39] Missouri has no statute of the kind, but recognizes the writ or (as is the common practice) a motion in the nature of the writ based upon the common-law grounds.[40] In this State, however, application of the proceeding appears to be extended to equity judgments and decrees.[41] And no limitation period is prescribed.[42] In Tennessee, again, there is a statute which breaks new ground for the proceeding.[43] It provides that judgments may be reversed on writ of error *coram nobis,* obtained on petition to be filed within one year from the date of the judgment. The relief thus to be sought "is confined to errors of fact occurring in proceedings of which the person seeking relief has had no notice, or which he was prevented by dis-

[36] It should, however, be noted that in recent years it has come into increased favor for the challenge of criminal judgments. State v. Calhoun, 50 Kan. 523, 32 Pac. 38 (1893) is a spectacular instance of the kind. But even in this application the proceeding is classed as a civil one.

[37] See the table of cases by jurisdictions subjoined to Orfield, the Writ of Error Coram Nobis in Civil Practice (1934) 20 Va.L.Rev. 423, 438. This article is highly informative as to the American decisions and constitutes a most valuable contribution to the literature of error *coram nobis.*

[38] Ill. Civ. Pract. Act 1933, § 72; Ill. Rev. Stat. 1949, c. 110, § 196. In Virginia and West Virginia it is provided by statute, apparently applying to both common-law judgments and equity decrees, that errors correctible by the writ may be corrected on motion. Va. Code 1942, § 6329; Va. Code Ann. 1950, § 8-485; W.Va. Code Ann. 1949, § 5756.

[39] Frank v. Salomon, 376 Ill. 439, 34 N.E.2d 424 (1941); Pedersen v. Logan Square State & Savings Bank, 377 Ill. 408, 36 N.E.2d 732 (1941).

[40] Reed v. Bright, 232 Mo. 399, 409, 134 S.W. 653 (1911).

[41] See State *ex rel.* Potter v. Riley, 219 Mo. 667, 118 S.W. 647 (1909); Reed v. Bright, *supra.*

[42] State *ex rel.* v. Riley, *supra,* 683.

[43] Tenn. Code (Williams, 1934) §§ 8971-8979.

ability from showing or correcting, or in which he was prevented from making defense by surprise, accident, mistake or fraud without fault on his part." It is undoubtedly the case that the statute does not cover all the ground of the common-law writ, but, on the other hand, it extends to relief of a purely equitable nature, wholly foreign to the old proceeding. Moreover, the statutory proceeding is applicable to equity decrees as well as common-law judgments, since the judgments made subject to its operation include those of the chancery courts.

It is to be added that the occasional but by no means inconsiderable use of the common-law proceeding in its motion form, obtaining from the outset in the federal courts, was not terminated by the Rules as originally adopted; its availability in respect of common-law judgments, after the taking effect of the Rules was judicially recognized in several cases.[44] But now the amendments of 1946, as part of the provisions relating to relief from judgments (Rule 60(b)), provide in terms that the writ here in question (as also the writ of *audita querela*, bills of review and bills in the nature of bills of review [45]) is abolished and declare that "the procedure for obtaining any relief from a judgment shall be by motion as prescribed in these rules or by an independent action." Inasmuch as the enumerated grounds of such motion [46] seem fully wide enough to cover those traditionally attaching to error *coram nobis*, it would appear that the motion in the nature of that writ continues to be available, although losing it distinctive name.

More particular reference should be had in the present connection to the common-law writ of *audita querela*.[47] This lay to enable the aggrieved defendant to bring forward matter in discharge of the judgment and defeasance of the execution. It was proper when the party "has matter to shew that such execution ought not to have issued, or should not issue, against

[44] See Moore and Rogers, Federal Relief from Civil Judgments (1946) 55 YaleL.J. 623 at 634 *et seq.* and cases cited, especially Prevenden v. Hahn, 36 F.Supp. 952 (S.D.N.Y. 1941).

[45] See *infra*, § 3 of the present Chapter.

[46] *Infra*, § 4 of the present Chapter.

[47] So called from the words of the writ: *audita querela defendentis*, "the complaint of the defendant having been heard."

him." [48] Blackstone tells us that "it seems to have been invented lest in any case there be an oppressive defect of justice, where a party who hath a good defence is too late to make it in the ordinary forms of law." [49] Normally the matter in question was such as arose after judgment, the simplest instance of which would be payment of the judgment, coupled with the refusal of the judgment creditor to acknowledge satisfaction of record. But on occasion the proceeding was available in respect of matter in discharge of the defendant's liability arising before judgment, where he had had no chance to plead it in the cause, as where after verdict the plaintiff had released the defendant but had nevertheless signed judgment.[50] Besides the relief from execution, the proceeding, being in the nature of an action of trespass also gave damages to the aggrieved party "if the execution be without right." [51]

By the time when Blackstone wrote the writ had become largely displaced by summary motion.[52] In American practice, both State and federal, the motion, whether identified or not as a motion in the nature of *audita querela,* has been the means usually substituted for the old writ. As so identified, it survived under the Federal Rules as originally adopted.[53] As regards the abolition of the writ by the amendment of 1946 to Rule 60(b) this appears to have done no more than disestablish the writ itself. In view of the provision for relief by motion existing under the amended rule and particularly its recognition of release or discharge of the judgment or the vacation or reversal of a judgment constituting the basis of the judgment in question as a ground of such motion, it seems clear that the substance of the remedy remains as a matter for motion.

But the writ itself has come to employment in a number of

[48] 2 Wms. Saund. (6th ed. 1845) 148, note 1.

[49] 3 Blackstone, Comm. * 406.

[50] 2 Wms. Saund. *loc. cit.* "If a release be given after the *nisi prius* and before the day in bank, he can't plead it, for there is a verdict already in the cause, and upon another plea; and therefore the cause is determined; so that he is put to his *audita querela* to hinder the execution of the judgment." Gilbert, History and Practice of the Court of Common Pleas (1737) 83.

[51] 2 Wms. Saund. *loc. cit.*

[52] 3 Blackstone, Comm. * 406.

[53] Moore and Rogers, Federal Relief From Civil Judgments (1946) 55 Yale L.J. 623 at 637, 653, 661.

jurisdictions. Indeed, it finds statutory regulation in Massachusetts, Maine and Vermont.[54] The statutes of Massachusetts and Maine provide for the concomitant award of damages under the writ, and the same manner of relief is authorized by judicial decision in Vermont.[55] This manifestly is something which is foreign to the motion practice. In the States named, as at common law, issues of fact arising in the proceeding are triable by jury. Elsewhere the same rule has been recognized as applicable under the substituted motion,[56] but it is probably true that in the greater number of instances it has been either waived or overlooked. In this country the writ has not always been confined to its common-law ambit, that is to say, the showing of circumstances operating in discharge of the judgment or in avoidance of execution proceedings. Here and there it has in some degree encroached upon the common-law province of error *coram nobis* or otherwise transcended its orthodox limits,[57] and thus to some extent become a means of recourse against the judgment itself. As pointed out by Mr. Freeman, this tendency seems especially pronounced in Vermont.[58]

The modern English practice forbids any proceeding by *audita querela* but provides in its stead for an application by the party against whom the judgment has been given "for a stay of execution or other relief against such judgment, upon the ground of facts which have arisen too late to be pleaded." [59] It thus approximates the practice in the majority of the American jurisdictions.

[54] 8 Mass.Ann.Laws 1933, c. 249, §§ 1-3; Me. Rev. Stat. 1944, c. 114, §§ 1-7; Vt. Stat. 1947, §§ 1523, 2148-2154. See also Fla. Stat. 1949, § 52.20.

[55] Stone v. Seaver, 5 Vt. 549 (1833).

[56] Lillie v. Dennert (C. C. A. 6) 232 Fed. 104, 106 (1916). Here it is said, with citation of cases: "Under the established modern practice allowing a motion to enter satisfaction of a judgment at law, by reason of its payment or discharge, as a substitute for the ancient writ of *audita querela*, the trial of controverted issues of fact arising under such motion, is ordinarily to be had in the same manner as under such writ, that is, by jury trial, to which several state courts have held the parties are entitled as a matter of right." See also Ala. Code 1940, Tit. 7, § 573.

[57] See 1 Freeman, Judgments (5th ed. 1925) § 257.

[58] "In Vermont," he says, "it seems to be employed with more frequency than elsewhere, and to answer as a specific for all sorts of mischiefs not otherwise provided against." *Loc. cit.* p. 519.

[59] O. XLII, r. 27.

§ 3. Equitable Means of Recourse

As against decrees after enrollment the English chancery provided an effective means of recourse in the bill of review. This remedy had its established basis in an ordinance of Lord Chancellor Bacon, dating from 1618, which made it applicable in two situations. The first was where there was error of law apparent in the body of the decree, the second, where since the decree new matter had arisen or there had come to light new proof "which could not possibly have been used at the time when the decree passed." In the first situation, the bill might be exhibited without leave of court, but in the second, only pursuant to leave, given upon a showing by affidavit that the new matter or proof was not available at the time of the decree.[60] There was also recognized a bill in the nature of a bill of review having place in conjunction with a petition for rehearing. Under the practice of the court there was in order a petition for rehearing before the actual rendition of the decree, and by the like means, after rendition, but where the decree had not been enrolled, the same manner of relief could be had as by a bill of review after the enrollment. In the latter case, however, where the petition was founded upon the discovery of new matter, it had to be supported by appropriate allegation and prayer in the form of a bill. This, then, was the case of the bill in the nature of a bill of review, more accurately spoken of as a supplemental bill in the nature of a bill of review. For its exhibition leave of court was required as in the case of a bill of review proper based upon the like ground.[61] Since the practice of enrollment had come to be discontinued in considerable measure before the opening of the 1800s,[62] the bill in the nature of a bill of review assumed proportionate importance in the classic chancery procedure. Apart from these proceedings, the Court of Chancery exercised a well-established jurisdiction to set aside its own decrees on

[60] Sanders, Orders in Chancery, Vol. I, Part I (1845) 109; Cooper, Equity Pleading (Am. ed. 1813) 89-92.

[61] Mitford, Chancery Pleadings (5th ed. 1847) 108 *et seq.;* Cooper, *op. cit.* 93-94; 2 Maddock, Chancery Practice (4th Am. ed. 1832) * 537-* 538.

[62] Under date of 1809, Cooper, *op. cit.* 88, speaks of enrollment of decrees as "being now much disused" and of the bill of review proper as being "little known in practice."

those gounds which, appealing to it as a court of conscience, would prompt it to undo transactions in general. It would thus act, for example, where the decree had been brought about by fraud, without fault or negligence on the part of the injured party. In such a case the application took the form of a bill to impeach the decree for the fraud or other inequity relied upon.[63]

But chancery, also, where equitable principles demanded, could afford relief against judgments of the common-law courts. While the Court of Chancery, as a coördinate branch of judicature, obviously had no power to set aside or otherwise directly interfere with a common-law judgment, it was enabled through its process of injunction directed against the person of the successful litigant, to nullify the effect of the judgment, by enjoining him from the issuance of execution upon it, or from realizing upon execution already issued, or otherwise profiting through the judgment's existence.[64] It was with respect to this power that there occurred the historic controversy whose leading protagonists were Sir Edward Coke and Lord Ellesmere—a controversy which was settled by James I in favor of the chancery jurisdiction.[65] And in the established exercise of this power the chancery would thus interfere in very clear cases where there existed circumstances which would render it against conscience for the judgment to be carried into effect, as where, on the one hand, the judgment had been obtained through fraud, surprise, accident or mistake, or where, on the other, there had existed a good defense to the judgment-action on equitable grounds which the common-law court was unable to take into consideration.[66] Always es-

[63] Cooper, *op. cit.* 96 *et seq.;* Mitford, *op. cit.* 112 *et seq.;* 1 Maddock, *op. cit.* * 300.

[64] It could even coerce the judgment creditor to satisfy the inequitable judgment. Said Lord Chancellor Hardwicke in Barnesley v. Powel, 1 Vesey Sr., 284, 288, 27 E.R. 1034 (1749): "Though this court cannot set aside a judgment of a common law court obtained against conscience, yet it will decree the party to acknowledge satisfaction on that judgment, though he has received nothing; because nothing is due." But usually the same result was reached by a perpetual injunction against realizing on the judgment.

[65] See Scott and Simpson, Cases and other Materials on Judicial Remedies (1946) 603-611.

[66] 1 Maddock, *op. cit.* * 300 note 1; 4 Pomeroy, Equity Jurisprudence (4th ed. 1919) § 1364.

sential to this exercise were the meritorious character of the complainant's case and his freedom from fault and from undue delay in exhibiting his bill.

In the United States the courts of chancery jurisdiction, where the grant of this was adequate,[67] succeeded to these powers and broadly exercised them. As may be seen from the classic work of Story on Equity Pleadings,[68] first appearing in 1838, bills of review and bills to impeach decrees in equity for fraud and kindred causes became familiar instrumentalities of American chancery procedure. So also did bills to impeach judgments at law on similar grounds, and bills to effectuate equitable defenses as against such judgments. It is to be noted, however, that a difference from the English practice in the mode of formulating decrees, freeing them from reciting the proceedings to the same extent as in that practice, cancelled the requirement that in the case of a bill of review for error of law, the error must appear in the body of the decree, and rendered it sufficient that the error appear in the pleadings, taken in conjunction with the decree; but error appearing only from a consideration of the evidence remained beyond the reach of the bill.[69] Again, by reason of the rule obtaining in most jurisdictions that the decree was to be taken as enrolled upon the lapse of the term, and the simplification of enrollment elsewhere, the bill in the nature of a bill of review, as employed in the High Court of Chancery, ceased to be adapted to the American practice,[70] and yielded its place to the bill of review proper. In later times, the term "bill in the nature of a bill of review" has been commonly applied to a bill to impeach a decree for fraud, accident or mistake.[71] So long, however, as the American jurisdictions retained the separate administration of law and equity, recourse in equity against

[67] For the development of chancery jurisdiction in the United States, see Wilson, Courts of Chancery in the American Colonies (1884) 18 Am.Law Rev. 226, reprinted in 2 Select Essays in Anglo-American Legal History (1908) 779; and Gager, Equity, in Two Centuries Growth of American Law (1701-1901) Yale Bicentennial Publications (1901) 115, 129-144.

[68] (10th ed. 1892) § 403 *et seq.*

[69] See Whiting v. Bank of U.S. 13 Pet. (38 U.S.) 6, 13, 14 (1839).

[70] See Dexter v. Arnold, 5 Mason 303, Fed. Cas. No. 3856 (1829). For the simplified enrollment in the New York practice, see 1 Hoffman, Chancery Practice (1834) 573.

[71] 1 Whitehouse, Equity Practice (1915) §§ 151, 152.

decrees and judgments stood on substantially the basis marked out by the practice of the English chancery, and this continues to be largely true of those jurisdictions where the separate administration is still the rule. Variation in detail has occurred, as exemplified by the Michigan Court Rule of 1931, superseding the bill of review by a petition for rehearing.[72] Some narrowing of scope, some substantial lessening of the employment of the means described above there unquestionably have been. The increased facility of appeal or other forms of appellate review, as an alternative to the bill of review for error of law, the presence of means of recourse provided by statute or rule of court, and the latter-day recognition, in most of these jurisdictions, of the right to plead equitable defenses in common-law actions, have all contributed in a greater or less degree to limit the necessity for resort in the present regard to the classic instrumentalities of equity practice.

But even in those jurisdictions where the administration of equity is no longer distinct, the equitable means of recourse have in large measure survived, though more often than not parting with their traditional names. In the federal system, the Rules of Civil Procedure, as originally adopted, left intact the equitable avenues previously obtaining; and the bill of review, as well as the bill to impeach a judgment, whether of an equitable or legal nature, continued to be available under the generic name of civil actions.[73] And, while the amendments of 1946 to Rule 60(b) in terms abolished "bills of review and bills in the nature of bills of review," the substance of such proceedings would appear to remain unaffected, as coming within the saving clause of the amended rule with respect to the power of the court to entertain an independent action, in the cases specified, for relief from the judgment.[74] The bill of review remains in active use in Illinois, as against equity decrees.[75] It is recognized as available in California,[76] and

[72] Mich. Court Rules 1931, 1933, Rule 48, §§ 1, 4, Searl Mich. Court Rules Ann. (4th ed. 1933) pp. 313-314, 1948 Cum. Supp. p. 97.

[73] Moore and Rogers, Federal Relief from Civil Judgments (1946) 55 YaleL.J. 623 at 633, 639, 677 *et seq.*

[74] See *infra,* § 4 of the present Chapter.

[75] Wood v. First Nat. Bank of Woodlawn, 383 Ill. 515, 50 N.E.2d 830 (1943); Koberlein v. First Nat. Bank

provided for in Texas.[77] It has been absorbed in Indiana by the statutory complaint in review.[78] It stands nominally abolished by statute in Oregon,[79] and is discountenanced in New York.[80] As for relief against judgments, corresponding to that grantable on bills to impeach judgments for fraud or the like, this branch of equity jurisdiction continues to be exercised in the State jurisdictions of unified procedure through the medium of an independent action, at least where other means, and in particular statutory motions, do not furnish an adequate remedy. The same may be said in general of the relief formerly grantable by bill of review where this is not recognized *eo nomine*.

In a few jurisdictions the courts without specific statutory authority, administer certain equitable relief from judgments after their attainment of normal finality, through the medium of a motion in the judgment-cause, thus relieving the aggrieved party from the necessity of resorting to an independent action. This is notably the case in New York.[81] Such a step represents a sufficiently natural development for courts of unified procedure, but it is a remarkable circumstance that in more than one jurisdiction retaining the partition between law and equity, a non-statutory power to grant similar relief, on mo-

---

of St. Elmo, 376 Ill. 450, 34 N.E.2d 388 (1941); J. B. Inderrieden Co. v. Gill, 373 Ill. 180, 25 N.E.2d 796 (1940); Elieff v. Lincoln Nat. Life Ins. Co. 369 Ill. 408, 17 N.E.2d 47 (1938); Knaus v. Chicago Title & Trust Co. 365 Ill. 588, 7 N.E.2d 298 (1937).

[76] San Joaquin & King's River Canal & Irrigation Co., Inc. v. Stevinson, 175 Cal. 607, 166 Pac. 338 (1917).

[77] Tex. Rev. Civ. Stat. Ann. (Vernon, 1936) Art. 2092(30), 4328; Tex. Rules Civ. Proc. (Vernon, 1942) Rule 330(l); Smith v. Rogers, Tex. Civ. App. 129 S.W.2d 776 (1939); Griffith v. Tipps, Tex. Civ. App. 69 S.W.2d 846 (1934).

[78] Ind. Stat. Ann. (Burns, 1933) 1946 Replacement Vol. II, §§ 2-2604, 2605, 2606; Nealis v. Dicks, 72 Ind. 374 (1880).

[79] Lachele v. Oregon Realty Exchange Investment Co. 121 Ore. 582, 589, 256 Pac. 646 (1927). Here it is said: "It is the form of the bill that has been abolished. The same result is now obtained upon application by motion or petition to correct obvious mistakes or by original suit when the error is not apparent on the record."

[80] O'Neil v. Meccia (In re Gray's Will) 169 Misc. 985, 988, 8 N.Y.S.2d 850 (1939); Crouse v. McVickar, 207 N.Y. 213, 100 N.E. 697 (1912).

[81] See Manahan v. Petroleum Producing & Refining Co. 198 App.Div. 192, 189 N.Y.S. 127 (1921) and cases cited. In this connection Mr. Freeman observes that "in New York judgments seem to be regarded not as inviolate and enduring testimonials, but as temporary structures, to be torn down, remodeled or rebuilt whenever the builders feel competent to improve the original workmanship or design." 1 Freeman, Judgments (5th ed. 1925) § 198.

tion, from common-law judgments is exercised on the common-law side. Maryland and New Hampshire exhibit this anomaly.[82] The case can only be regarded as one of assumption by the common-law courts of equitable jurisdiction *pro hac vice,* and, indeed, is substantially placed on this ground by the Maryland courts.[83]

§ 4. Statutory Means of Recourse [84]

Simplified measures, in lieu of or as supplementing the traditional common-law and equity means of relief from judgments, have been the subject of much legislation on the part of the American jurisdictions since the outset of nineteenth century reform. The New York Code, as amended in 1849, set on foot one type of these measures in the provision that the court might in its discretion and on such terms as might be proper, "at any time within one year after notice thereof, relieve a party from a judgment, order, or other proceeding taken against him through his mistake, inadvertence, surprise, or excusable neglect . . ." [85] This provision has been retained in the New York Civil Practice Act substantially in its original form.[86] Most often with a different time-limitation, but with slight variation otherwise, it has entered into the codes of Alaska, California, Idaho, Indiana, Minnesota, Montana, Nevada, North Carolina, North Dakota, Oregon, South Carolina, South Dakota, and Wisconsin.[87] The time-limitation in some instances follows the original; in others it runs all the way from ninety days to two years. The same measure, based upon its version in the California Code, has found place in the Federal

[82] Cases cited in 1 Freeman, *op. cit.* § 198.

[83] Tiernan v. Hammond, 41 Md. 548 (1875); Kemp v. Cook, 18 Md. 130 (1861). The result, however, is in line with the aberrant English rule appearing in Cannan v. Reynolds (1855) *supra,* note 3 of the present Chapter.

[84] Under this head is included relief provided for by general rules of court.

[85] § 173.

[86] N.Y. Civ. Pract. Act (Clevenger, 1950) § 108.

[87] Alaska Comp. Laws Ann. 1949, § 55-5-77; Cal. Code Civ. Proc. (Deering, 1949) § 473; Idaho Code Ann. 1949, 5-905; Ind. Stat. Ann. (Burns, 1933) 1946 Replacement Vol. II, § 2-1068; Minn. Stat. 1945, § 544.32; Mont. Rev. Codes Ann. 1947, § 93-3905; Nev. Comp. Laws 1929, § 8640; N.C. Gen. Stat. 1943, § 1-220; N.D. Rev. Code 1943, § 28-2901; Ore. Comp. Laws Ann. 1940, § 1-1007; S.C. Code 1942, § 495; S.D. Code 1939, § 33.0108; Wis. Stat. 1949, § 269.46.

Rules, where, as will later appear, it forms part of the wider provisions for relief there obtaining since the amendments of 1946.

Another and more comprehensive measure seems to have had its origin in the Ohio Code of 1853. As there appearing, it authorized the court to set aside or modify its own judgment after the term in nine cases which may be thus summarized: (1) by the grant of a new trial for newly discovered evidence; (2) by the grant of a new trial where the defendant was constructively summoned; (3) for mistake, neglect or omission of the clerk, or irregularity in obtaining the judgment; (4) for fraud practiced by the successful party in obtaining the judgment; (5) for erroneous proceedings against an infant, married woman or person of unsound mind where the condition of such defendant does not appear in the record, nor the error in the proceedings; (6) for the death of one of the parties before the judgment; (7) for unavoidable casualty or misfortune preventing the party from prosecuting or defending; (8) for error shown by an infant within twelve months after attaining full age; (9) for taking judgment on warrant of attorney for more than was due, without notice to the defendant. Different time-limitations were set for invoking relief according to the particular ground, the longest being a period of three years applicable to the third and fourth grounds. Proceedings on the first and second grounds were to be by motion for new trial as elsewhere provided. Those on the third ground, that of mistake, neglect or omission of the clerk, or irregularity were to be by motion; while those on the fourth to the ninth grounds inclusive were to be by petition and summons in the nature of an independent action.[88] Apart from mention of the married woman in the fifth ground, which for an obvious reason has in most instances been eliminated, some variation in arrangement or in the enumeration of grounds, or some addition to or subtraction from these may appear from jurisdiction to jurisdiction, with readjustment of the matter of time-limitation, but this statute in its general pattern is presently a part of the procedural

[88] § 534 *et seq.*, Ohio Laws, Vol. 51, pp. 150, 151.

legislation of Arkansas, Kansas, Kentucky, Nebraska, Ohio, Oklahoma, Washington and Wyoming,[89] and has been largely drawn upon by the recent Iowa Rules.[90]

A third class of legislation, but one whose constituent statutes differ widely among themselves, affords what is usually a more general form of relief, by providing for a review of the judgment by the court of rendition. Thus Wisconsin provides that "all judgments and court orders may be reviewed by the court at any time within sixty days from service of notice of entry thereof, but not later than sixty days after the end of the term of entry thereof." [91] So, under a Minnesota statute, the court has discretionary power to modify or set aside most judgments at any time within one year after notice thereof "for good cause shown." [92] In effect, therefore, these two statutes continue the common-law control, otherwise elapsing with the term, until the expiration of the period thus fixed. Again, in Rhode Island, it is provided that in the case of judgments by default and judgments entered by mistake, as also in the case of all equity decrees, the court of rendition "shall have control over the same for the period of 6 months after the entry thereof," and may for cause shown set aside such judgments and decrees and take other proper steps in the premises.[93] Indiana, laying hold of the bill of review, has converted it into a proceeding applicable to judgments in general. The resultant "complaint in review" may be instituted "for any error of law appearing in the proceedings and judgment, within one year; or for material new matter discovered since the rendition thereof, within three years; or for both causes, within one year, after the rendition of the judgment, and without leave of court." [94] Here belongs also the Massachusetts writ of review, in respect of "final judgment in a civil

[89] Ark. Stat. Ann. 1947, § 29-506 *et seq.;* Ky. Code Pract. in Civ. Cases (Carroll, 1948) § 518 *et seq.;* Kan. Gen. Stat. Ann. 1935, § 60-3007 *et seq.;* Neb. Rev. Stat. 1943, § 25-2001 *et seq.;* Ohio Gen. Code (Page, 1938) § 11631 *et seq.;* Okla. Stat. 1941, Tit. 12, § 1031 *et seq.;* Wash. Rev. Stat. (Remington, 1932) § 464 *et seq.;* Wyo. Comp. Stat. Ann. 1945, § 3-3801 *et seq.*

[90] Ia. Rules Civ. Proc. 1943, Rules 252, 253, in Ia. Code 1946, Vol. II, pp. 2171, 2172.

[91] Wis. Stat. 1949, § 252.10.

[92] Minn. Stat. 1945, § 544.32.

[93] R.I. Gen. Laws Ann. 1938, c. 535, § 2.

[94] Ind. Stat. (Burns, 1933) 1946 Replacement Vol. II, § 2-2605.

action," issued on petition filed within one year after rendition or knowledge of the judgment,[95] and addressed to what is largely the discretionary power of the court.[96] As an alternative, where the execution has not been satisfied in whole or in part, there is provided the more summary remedy of petition to vacate, to be filed within one year after judgment, and likewise addressed to the discretion of the court.[97] Both these proceedings are in the nature of separate actions. A similar separate action is the Maine writ of review for civil actions, also issuable on petition.[98] This originally had the broad scope responding to its name,[99] but was subsequently limited to certain special cases,[100] which include *inter alia* the existence of perjury on the trial, as shown either by the discovery of new evidence or the perjured witness's conviction of the offense, as also the situation where it appears that through fraud, accident, mistake or misfortune justice has not been done and that a further hearing would be just and equitable. In the first case the petition must be presented within three years, in the second within six years after the judgment. Provision is even made for a second review on petition filed within three years after judgment on the first, "when the court thinks that justice requires it, and on such terms as it imposes." [101]

"Irregularity," it will be noticed, is among the grounds specified in the Ohio type of statute. It also finds recognition outside the jurisdictions adherent to this type, as in New York,[102] Missouri,[103] Michigan [104] and New Mexico.[105] In some jurisdictions it is considered that the setting aside of a judg-

[95] 9 Mass.Ann.Laws 1933, c. 250, § 22.

[96] Burt v. Hodsdon, 242 Mass. 302, 136 N.E. 108 (1922); Robinson v. Lyndonville Creamery Association, 284 Mass. 396, 188 N.E. 248 (1933).

[97] 9 Mass.Ann.Laws 1933, c. 250, § 15; Skillings v. Mass. Benefit Association, 151 Mass. 321, 23 N.E. 1136 (1890); Ryan v. Hickey, 240 Mass. 46, 132 N.E. 718 (1921).

[98] Me. Rev. Stat. 1944, c. 110, § 1 *et seq.*

[99] Inhabitants of Thomaston v. Starrett, 128 Me. 328, 147 Atl. 427 (1929).

[100] Pierce v. Bent, 67 Me. 404 (1877); Donnell v. Hodsdon, 102 Me. 421, 67 Atl. 143 (1907).

[101] § 6.

[102] N.Y. Civ. Pract. Act (Clevenger, 1950) § 521.

[103] Mo. Rev. Stat. Ann. 1942, § 1267; Thomas v. Boatright, 217 Mo.App. 273, 263 S.W. 464 (1924); Cross v. Gould, 131 Mo.App. 585, 110 S.W. 672 (1908).

[104] Mich. Stat. Ann. 1938, § 27.1433.

[105] N.M. Stat. Ann. 1941, § 19-101 (60) (d).

ment on this ground, even after the attainment of normal finality, does not depend on the statute, but appertains to the inherent power of the court.[106] In Tidd's Practice, "irregularity" is defined as "the want of adherence to some prescribed rule or mode of proceeding; and it consists, either in omitting to do something that is necessary for the due and orderly conducting of a suit, or doing it in an unreasonable time or in an improper manner." [107] But the irregularity which the author had here in question was one concerned with the proceedings in advance of judgment; [108] it does not appear that at common law irregularity, as such, was ever a ground for setting aside a judgment after the term, where jurisdiction of the defendant had been properly obtained. Precisely what departures from proper procedure will now be regarded as cause for interference on this ground does not admit of categorical statement. "The irregularities which have been treated as sufficient to justify the vacations of judgments," says Mr. Freeman, "are very numerous, and it is not possible to prescribe any test by which, in all jurisdictions, to determine whether a particular irregularity is such as to require the vacation of a judgment." [109] It may, however, be said in general that the irregularity must be one which distinctly prejudices the interests of the complaining party and has not been waived by any conduct on his part.[110]

Mention may also be made of certain miscellaneous measures for statutory relief existing in the State procedures. New York, in addition to the statutory remedy before noted, gives place to a motion, available within two years from the filing of the judgment roll, to set aside a judgment "for error of fact not arising upon the trial." [111] This, while undoubtedly covering the ground of the common-law writ of error *coram nobis*, is of much wider application, and extends to judgments in equitable proceedings as well as to those at law.[112] In

[106] 1 Freeman, Judgments (5th ed. 1925) § 217; Clark v. Scovill, 198 N.Y. 279, 91 N.E. 800 (1910); Cross v. Gould, *supra*.

[107] 1 Tidd, Practice (9th ed. 1828) 512.

[108] See *ibid.* 513 *et seq.*

[109] 1 Freeman, *op. cit.* § 218.

[110] See *ibid. loc. cit.*

[111] N.Y. Civ. Pract. Act (Clevenger, 1950) §§ 522-529.

[112] See Byrnes v. Byrnes, 109 App.

some jurisdictions perjury on the trial has been added as a ground in what we have referred to as the Ohio type of statute.[113] In the same connection is to be noted the Minnesota statutory action to set aside a judgment obtained "by means of perjury, subornation of perjury, or any fraudulent act, practice or representation of the prevailing party," which is to be commenced within three years after discovery.[114] Like relief may be obtained in Georgia on motion, where the judgment was rendered "in consequence of corrupt and wilful perjury," and the offending witness has been convicted of the crime; three years from the rendition of the judgment is here the limitation-period.[115] And in New Hampshire it is provided that within a like period, on petition by any interested party, "a new trial may be granted in any case when through accident, mistake or misfortune justice has not been done and a further hearing would be equitable." [116]

We may appropriately conclude the present account of American regulation by recurring to the Federal Rules. As originally adopted, Rule 60(b), dealing with relief from other than clerical mistakes, contained only the measure before referred to, for relief on the ground of "mistake, inadvertence, surprise, or excusable neglect," which was obtainable by motion to be made within a reasonable time not to exceed six months after the judgment. But by the amendments of 1946, there has been extensive addition to this ground. As it now stands, the rule in question provides that "on motion and upon such terms as are just, the court may relieve a party or his legal representative from a final judgment, order, or proceeding for the following reasons: (1) mistake, inadvertence, surprise, or excusable neglect; (2) newly discovered evidence which by due diligence could not have been discovered in time to move for a new trial under Rule 59(b) [motion to be served within ten days after judgment]; (3) fraud (whether heretofore denominated intrinsic or extrinsic), misrepresentation,

Div. 535, 96 N.Y.S. 306 (1905); Emmet v. Runyon, 139 App.Div. 310, 123 N.Y.S. 1026 (1910); Anderson v. Anderson, 164 App.Div. 812, 150 N.Y.S. 359 (1914); Boslov v. Boslov, 177 Misc. 817, 31 N.Y.S.2d 970 (1941).

113 *E.g.*, Ohio Gen. Code (Page, 1938) § 11631.

114 Minn. Stat. 1945, § 548.14.

115 Ga. Code 1933, §§ 110-706, 3-702.

116 N.H. Rev. Laws 1942, c. 398, §§ 1, 2.

or other misconduct of an adverse party; (4) the judgment is void; (5) the judgment has been satisfied, released, or discharged, or a prior judgment upon which it is based has been reversed or otherwise vacated, or it is no longer equitable that the judgment should have prospective application; or (6) any other reason justifying relief from the operation of the judgment. The motion shall be made within a reasonable time, and for reasons (1), (2) and (3) not more than one year after the judgment, order, or proceeding was entered or taken." In respect of the other reasons "reasonable time" stands unqualified. Further provision of the amended rule reserves to the court the power "to entertain an independent action to relieve a party from a judgment, order, or proceeding, or to grant relief to a defendant not actually personally notified as provided in [the relative Federal statute],[117] or to set aside a judgment for fraud upon the court." The amended Rule thus concludes: "Writs of *coram nobis, coram vobis, audita querela,* and bills of review and bills in the nature of a bill of review, are abolished, and the procedure for obtaining any relief from a judgment shall be by motion as prescribed in these rules or by an independent action."

Rule 60(b) in its original form has been adjusted to the procedures of Arizona (1939) and Colorado (1941), and, plus its amendment, to that of New Mexico (1942, 1949).[118] In its amended form, with some adaptation, it has been taken over by Delaware (1947), New Jersey (1948) and Utah (1949).[119]

When it is considered that, under the present English Rules, outside of the case of judgments by default for want of ap-

[117] Here was designated Section 57 of the Judicial Code U.S.C. Tit. 28, § 118. In consequence of the 1948 revision of Tit. 28 of the Code, this designation was changed by amendment of 1948 to "Tit. 28 USC, § 1655." The section in question provides for service on absent defendants in actions to enforce liens or claims or to remove incumbrances, liens or clouds upon title, in respect of real and personal property.

[118] Ariz. Code Ann. 1939, § 21-1502; Colo. Rules Civ. Proc. 1941, Rule 60(b), in Colo. Stat. Ann. 1935, Replacement Vol. I, 1941; N.M. Stat. Ann. 1941, and 1949 Cum. Supp. to Vol. II, § 19-101(60)(b).

[119] Del. Rules of Superior Court 1947, Rule 60(b), Rules of Court of Chancery 1947, Rule 60(b); N.J. Rules Civ. Pract. 1948, Rule 3:60-2; Utah Rules Civ. Proc. 1949, Rule 60(b).

pearance (the substitute for *audita querela* apart), there is nothing provided in the nature of a motion to vacate the judgment, and that, without appeal, no relief can be had from it in a proper case, except by a fresh action, we are left with the conviction that American civil procedure is for the most part richly provided with simplified means of overcoming injustice in the instant regard. Indeed, one is tempted to think that in some respects we have gone too far in the present direction. This is particularly true of the Federal Rules in point of their omnibus provision which, following the enumeration of specific grounds, allows a motion to vacate for "any other reason justifying relief from the operation of the judgment," and this without definite time-limitation—a concession which would seem to leave the stability of the judgment too largely dependent upon the judicial discretion.

§ 5. Recourse against Judgments by Default

Obtaining in certain of the Continental systems, notably in those of France and Germany, is the principle that a judgment by default may be set aside as a matter of course by means of the proceeding appropriated to this purpose.[119a] In the Anglo-American systems the defaulted defendant is not treated with the same degree of indulgence. Other than in the case where it is based upon some form of notice not amounting to personal service, the default judgment in the American jurisdictions, with some exception, attains finality to the same extent and upon the same conditions as a judgment rendered upon contest. While it may be opened or set aside upon a showing of a meritorious defense, coupled with an excuse for failing to defend, this, by the rule most usually followed, must occur before the expiration of the term or substituted period, or pursuant to motion made within the time thus limited. But all default judgments have the benefit of those means of recourse open to judgments in general, whether according to common-law or equitable principles or by authority of statute or rule of court. Under the existing English Rules, however,

[119a] The French *opposition,* the German *Einspruch.* See Engelmann-Millar, History of Continental Civil Procedure (1927) 776, 612, 626.

the finality of default judgments stands upon a somewhat different basis, as will later be noticed.

At common law the final judgment by default had no distinctive status in the present respect: the end of the term marked the cessation of the court's ordinary power of control over it. So, in the English chancery, a final decree *pro confesso* was equally conclusive after enrollment, where jurisdiction of the person had been obtained in the normal manner. But, for chancery, the statute of 1732, supplying a gap in the methods of process,[119b] had established exceptionally a special manner of service. Under its terms a defendant who had gone out of the realm or had otherwise absconded to avoid the service of process might be notified of the pendency of the cause by certain measures of publication, as a basis for a decree *pro confesso*. Nevertheless, liberal provision was made for enabling him to appear after the final decree and petition for a rehearing. If, returning, he should be served with a copy of the decree at any time within seven years after its date, he had six months from the time of service thus to appear; otherwise the whole period of seven years was open to him for the purpose.[120]

This principle of constructive service of process, as has been seen, was followed for equity procedure in America, and obtains today in all the chancery jurisdictions, as applicable to the case of defendants who are non-residents or are otherwise unavailable for service within the jurisdiction. By the original New York Code the same principle was applied to civil actions in general.[121] Restricted by amendment of 1849 to the cases particularly specified, it was then provided that, except for divorce actions, the defendant might, upon sufficient cause shown, "be allowed to defend after judgment, or at any

119b See 9 Holdsworth, History of English Law (1926) 350; and *supra* Chap. VIII, § 2, and Chap. XXI, § 2(a).

120 5 Geo. II, c. 25.

121 In this connection the Commissioners who prepared the draft of the code observed that "in suits at common law personal service has been heretofore required, while in suits in equity, an advertisement has been allowed against absent defendants, when personal service could not be made. Uniformity in this respect is now necessary. We see no reason why the rule prevailing in equitable cases should not be extended to all. Such a rule prevails in several of the states." First Report of the Commissioners (1948) p. 135.

time within one year after notice thereof, and within seven years after its rendition, on such terms as shall be just." [122] The pattern thus set was influential in the ensuing code movement and today the codes in general contain similar provisions, Provisions of the same character likewise obtain elsewhere over and beyond those existing in the chancery jurisdictions. Very often in such provisions there is the same acceptance, as in New York, of the idea coming from the English statute, of a time at large set for appearance, capable of being reduced to a shorter period by written notice of the judgment being actually brought to the defendant's attention. There is much variation here, as there is in the chancery jurisdictions, with respect to the measure of time. Thus, on the one hand, the period of seven years after judgment or one year after notice, still retained in New York,[123] is followed in South Carolina [124] and South Dakota,[125] while, on the other, we find Iowa [126] and Colorado [127] allowing a flat period of only six months, and Utah,[128] until its Rules of 1949, a like period of but ninety days. In between, the legislative fancy has permitted itself free play. Five years, three years, two years, with or without provision for reduction by notice, and one year, are all represented. The periods most favored seem to be three years and one year. Variation also occurs as to the classes of cases to which this mode of service applies, but with some exception as to proceedings against resident defendants who cannot be found within the jurisdiction, these cases are manifestly reducible to proceedings involving a *res* within the jurisdiction,—such as are compendiously indicated in the Illinois statute which permits this manner of service "in any civil action affecting property or status within the jurisdiction of the court, . . . or in any action at law to revive a judgment or decree." [129] The New York exception as to defense after judg-

[122] Code of 1848, § 114; Code of 1849, § 135.

[123] N.Y. Civ. Pract. Act (Clevenger, 1950) § 217.

[124] S.C. Code 1942, § 436.

[125] S.D. Code 1939, § 33.0815.

[126] Ia. Rules Civ. Proc. 1943, Rule 251, in Ia. Code 1946, Vol. II.

[127] Colo. Rules Civ. Proc. 1941, Rule 60(C)(b), in Colo. Stat. Ann. 1935, 1941 Replacement Vol. I.

[128] Utah Code Ann. 1943, § 104-14-4, superseded by a following of Federal Rule 60(b): see *supra* note 119.

[129] Ill. Civ. Pract. Act § 14, Ill. Rev. Stat. 1949, c. 110, § 138.

ment in divorce actions is repeated in perhaps a majority of the codes;[180] some of these also expressly protect the interests of *bona fide* purchasers under the judgment; and a few of the Western jurisdictions increase the regularly allowed period where the proceedings involve the title or possession of land. In the federal legislation the only statute of the kind is that referred to in Federal Rule 60(b); it applies in the case of defendants not found within the district where the action is one "to enforce any lien upon or claim to, or to remove any incumbrance or lien or cloud upon the title to, real or personal property within the district." The period here allowed for the defendant's appearance is one year.[181]

We have indicated that, apart from the case of constructive service, relief from default judgments does not generally stand upon any broader basis than relief from judgments on contest. But in some jurisdictions the situation is otherwise. Thus in New Mexico it is specially provided that any default judgment may be set aside for cause upon motion filed within sixty days after its rendition.[182] Connecticut, by a similar provision, permits such a judgment or decree to be set aside or opened within four months after its entry, upon a showing of reasonable cause and a reasonable excuse for not appearing.[183] Rhode Island provides for the court's retention of control over default judgments (along with judgments entered by mistake and equity decrees) for a period of six months after entry, within which time they may be set aside for cause.[184] Iowa, by a provision of its rules, overlapping somewhat upon those with reference to judgments in general,[185] specifically declares that a default judgment may be set aside for "mistake, inadvertence, surprise, excusable neglect, or unavoidable casu-

180 In Indiana, it may be noted, a period of two years is limited in divorce actions for defense after judgment on constructive service (Ind. Stat. Ann. (Burns, 1933) 1946 Replacement Vol. II, § 3-1224) as opposed to the five-year period applicable under the same circumstances to judgments in general (*ibid.* § 2-2601).

181 U.S. Code, Tit. 28, § 1655, formerly § 118. See *supra*, note 117 of the present Chapter.

182 N.M. Stat. Ann. 1941, § 19-101 (60) (c).

183 Conn. Gen. Stat. 1949, § 7963.

184 R.I. Gen. Laws Ann. 1938, c. 535, § 2.

185 Ia. Rules Civ. Proc. 1943, Rules 251, 252, 253, in Ia. Code 1946, Vol. II.

alty," upon motion promptly made after discovery of the ground and not more than sixty days after entry of the judgment.[136] So, also, the default judgment has sometimes the benefit of a special proceeding in review before the court of rendition, with a period of greater or less extent for its institution. This is the case in Missouri, Massachusetts, Maine and Vermont.[137]

Under the existing English practice the court holds an exceptionally free hand over default judgments. It is provided that when judgment is entered for default of appearance, "it shall be lawful for the Court or a Judge to set aside or vary any such judgment upon such terms as may be just," [138] and, again, that "any judgment by default . . . may be set aside by the court or a judge, upon such terms as to costs or otherwise as such court or judge may think fit." [139] Nor is there here any express time-limitation imposed. The relief sought must not work any irreparable injury to the plaintiff, otherwise the matter, including the question of delay, rests wholly in the discretion of the court.[140]

§ 6. Collateral Attack

A judgment may fail to accord with law either because it is erroneous or because it is void. Error is present when the court, possessed of full power to render the judgment, comes to a wrong conclusion. On the other hand, a judgment is void when that power is lacking.[141] The lack exists if the judgment emanates from an organ that is not a properly constituted judicatory, or if there is absent jurisdiction either of the person or of the subject-matter, or if the judicatory has not been

[136] *Ibid.* Rule 236.

[137] Mo. Rev. Stat. Ann. 1942, §§ 1247, 1249; Mass. Ann. Laws 1933, c. 250, §§ 21, 22; Me. Rev. Stat. 1944, c. 110, § 1(I); Vt. Stat. 1947, § 2142.

[138] R.S.C., O. XIII, r. 10.

[139] R.S.C., O. XXVII, r. 15.

[140] Atwood v. Chichester, 3 Q.B.D. 722, C.A. (1878); Davis v. Ballenden, 46 L.T. 797, C.A. (1882).

[141] "The line which separates error in judgment from the usurpation of power is very definite; and it is precisely that which denotes the cases where a judgment or decree is reversible only by an appellate court, or may be declared a nullity collaterally, when it is offered in evidence in an action concerning the matter adjudicated, or purporting to have been so." Voorhees v. Bank of U.S., 10 Pet. (35 U.S.) 449, 474-475 (1836).

vested with authority to render the particular judgment.[142] Under some circumstances, also, a judgment is deemed void, although externally meeting the requisites of validity, if it appears that the proceedings leading to it are violative of basic principles of due process of law. Conspicuous here are cases in which, although there has been due jurisdictional notice to the defendant, the court nevertheless has refused him the opportunity to be heard.[143] On the ground that the refusal is "in legal effect the recall of the citation," [144] or that, as jurisdiction is the right to hear and determine, the court in determining without a hearing is not in the exercise of jurisdiction,[145] or simply that, by the arbitrary refusal of the court, "jurisdiction is abdicated or lost," [146] these cases have been assigned to the category of invalidity arising from lack of jurisdiction. The correctness of their result in holding the judgment void, rather than flagrantly erroneous, while no longer open to actual question, may admit of serious doubt from the standpoint of scientific consistency.[147]

In Continental law generally a judicial judgment affected with nullity continues to be regarded as binding until set aside by the proceeding appointed for the purpose. The case was

142 1 Freeman, Judgments (5th ed. 1925) § 325; Van Fleet, Collateral Attack (1892) § 16.

143 Windsor v. McVeigh, 93 U.S. 274 (1876); Hovey v. Elliot, 167 U.S. 409, 17 S.Ct. 841 (1897); Coe v. Armour Fertilizer Works, 237 U.S. 413, 35 S.Ct. 625 (1915). Windsor v. McVeigh, the leading case, was an action of ejectment in which the plaintiff claimed a life estate in certain premises, and the defense was based upon a marshal's deed, issued in 1864, under a decree of condemnation of the premises, purporting to be authorized by an act of Congress of 1862, directed against persons in rebellion. In the condemnation proceedings proper process of monition had been issued and published against all persons interested. The now plaintiff had appeared in such proceedings by counsel and filed his claim and answer to the libel of condemnation. But, pursuant to motion of the district attorney, the court had stricken the claim and answer from the files on the ground that, as appeared from the answer, the claimant was at the time of its filing "a resident within the city of Richmond, within the Confederate lines, and a rebel." And, without giving the claimant any further opportunity to be heard, the court had immediately entered the decree of condemnation. The Supreme Court held that, because of the right to a hearing, the decree was void.

144 Windsor v. McVeigh, *supra,* at 278.

145 *Ibid.* at 283-284.

146 Note, 39 L.R.A. 449.

147 In 1 Black, Judgments (2d ed. 1902) § 226, with particular reference to Windsor v. McVeigh, is expressed the author's lack of conviction that "irregularities in the action of the court, even so gross as those mentioned, can properly be said to deprive it of all jurisdiction and make its decision a mere nullity."

otherwise in the Roman law, where the null judgment was deemed legally inexistent. And, by a strange turn of history, the same thing is true in the Anglo-American law. With us the void judgment is ineffective for any purpose and may be disregarded. It may, however, be formally set aside on review or through any other appropriate means of recourse directly levelled at it, just as would be a judgment which is merely erroneous, that is to say, on direct attack. But, more important in the present connection, it may also be set aside or held for naught whenever, in the course of any subsequent litigation of a different description, the occasion arises. Hence there is recognized what is known as collateral attack. This term does not denote a specific means of recourse: it simply indicates the time and manner in which, under particular circumstances, objection is taken to the validity of the judgment. Collateral attack thus has place where the void judgment is impeached in a collateral proceeding, as, for example, where A brings ejectment against B, claiming title by virtue of a sheriff's deed issued under a money judgment against B, and B, by way of defense, asserts that the judgment was void and that therefore the sheriff's deed conveyed nothing to A. It would likewise be a case of collateral attack if, instead, B had taken the initiative and brought an action to set aside the sheriff's deed to A, on the ground of the invalidity of the judgment,—for here B is not directly impugning the judgment, but is doing so only as incidental to the object of his action, that of setting aside the sheriff's deed. Or, again, A sues B, a sheriff, for wrongful seizure of A's goods. B answers that he seized the goods by virtue of an execution issued upon a judgment against A in favor of one C. In reply, A collaterally attacks the judgment by asserting that it is void for want of jurisdiction. Accordingly, the frequently repeated distinction between direct attack and collateral attack consists essentially in this, that direct attack exists when the judgment is assailed by the specific means expressly provided by law for the purpose, while collateral attack is present when the judgment is impugned in some proceeding looking to another end.[148] While in various

[148] Van Fleet, *op. cit.* § 3; 1 Freeman, *op. cit.* § 306; 1 Black, *op. cit.* § 252.

jurisdictions other factors find place in the allocation of a given attack to one class or the other, the distinction thus expressed represents the doctrine usually accepted, lending itself, as it does, to comparative ease of application. Of the rubric "collateral attack" no mention will be found in any of the English decisions or legal writings. The basis of the concept is present in the modern English law, as it was in the old law from which we derived it. But it was left to the American courts to expand this branch of the law in a measure far exceeding that which was either possible or needed under the English judicial system, and to assign to the concept the convenient name which has long been familiar to all American lawyers.

By the general rule applicable to judgments of courts of record,[149] collateral attack is open to parties or privies only when the invalidity appears on the face of the record. In determining whether the invalidity is thus disclosed there comes into play the matter of jurisdictional presumptions. The record of a court of record is entitled to the fullest presumption of regularity, and unless it appears from the record itself that jurisdiction was lacking, there is no room for collateral attack. Judgments of courts which are not courts of record stand on a different basis. They are entitled to no jurisdictional presumptions, and all jurisdictional facts must appear in what corresponds to the record.[150] A similar rule, qualifying in perhaps most jurisdictions the general rule as to judgments of courts of record, applies where the judgment of such a court is ren-

[149] The distinction here involved is frequently phrased as that existing between superior and inferior courts, as it was at common law, or between courts of general jurisdiction and courts of limited jurisdiction. But in the American judicial system certain inferior courts may be courts of record entitled to the jurisdictional presumptions, and courts of limited jurisdiction, as, for example, the Federal district courts (McCormick v. Sullivant, 10 Wheat. (23 U.S.) 192 (1825)) may be courts of general jurisdiction within their particular field. Under the circumstances the contrast is best presented as between courts of record and courts not of record. See 1 Freeman, *op. cit.* § 374.

[150] "And the rule for jurisdiction is, that nothing shall be intended to be out of the jurisdiction of a superior court, but that which specially appears to be so; and, on the contrary, nothing shall be intended to be within the jurisdiction of an inferior court but that which is expressly so alleged." Peacock v. Bell, 1 Wms. Saund. 73, 74d (1666); Anon. 1 Freem.K.B. 314, 89 E.R. 232; Winford v. Powell, 2 Ld.Raym. 1310, 92 E.R. 357 (1712).

dered in the exercise of a special statutory power, not according to the course of common-law or equity procedure or their reformed substitute, as in the case of attachment on mesne process of property of a non-resident, or in that of eminent domain proceedings: here the usual jurisdictional presumptions do not obtain, and the record must show all the facts or at least the principal facts essential to the exercise of the jurisdiction.[151] But, with respect to judgments of courts of record, another principle must be noted. Since jurisdiction is the power to hear and determine, it includes the power on the part of the court to determine the question of its own jurisdiction. Accordingly, if it appears from the record that the jurisdictional question was adjudicated by the court, the judgment will not be regarded as void even if the adjudication in favor of the jurisdiction is wrong.[152] The case therefore is one of error, subject only to direct attack. Until lately it was generally considered essential to such an adjudication that the question of jurisdiction should have been definitely litigated in the proceedings under scrutiny. But more recent decision of the Supreme Court appears to have seriously trenched upon this doctrine. In *Chicot County Drainage District* v. *Baxter State Bank,*[153] decided in 1940, the case was this: A decree in bankruptcy had been entered by the District Court under the Municipal Debts Readjustment Act of 1934, approving a plan of readjustment of indebtedness of the Drainage District, pursuant to which the cancellation of certain bonds of the District had been effected. In a suit brought in the same District Court upon a number of these cancelled bonds the District pleaded the decree in question, to which it was replied that the decree was void, inasmuch as the statute purporting to authorize it had later been declared unconstitutional by the Supreme Court in a case arising elsewhere. The District Court on this

[151] Galpin v. Page, 18 Wall. (85 U.S.) 350 (1873); Applegate v. Lexington & Carter County Mining Co. 117 U.S. 255, 6 S.Ct. 742 (1886); Cobe v. Guyer, 237 Ill. 516, 86 N.E. 1071 (1908); Ill. Cent. RR. Co. v. Hasenwinkle, 232 Ill. 224, 83 N.E. 815 (1908).

[152] Stoll v. Gottlieb, 305 U.S. 165, 59 S.Ct. 134 (1938); U.S. to the use of Hine v. Morse, 218 U.S. 493, 31 S.Ct. 37 (1910); Louisville Trust Co. v. Comingor, 184 U.S. 18, 22 S.Ct. 293 (1902).

[153] 308 U.S. 371, 60 S.Ct. 317 (1940).

ground held the decree void for lack of jurisdiction and was sustained by the Circuit Court of Appeals. But the Supreme Court took a different view. It ruled that, although the question of jurisdiction had not been raised or specifically decided in the lower court, that court, in the exercise of its power to determine its own jurisdiction, had by the entry of the decree necessarily determined in favor of the jurisdiction, and that the decree therefore was valid. In a subsequent case at the same term, the court took occasion to say that "in the Chicot County case no inflexible rule as to collateral objection to judgments in general was declared. We explicitly limited our examination to the effect of a subsequent invalidation of the applicable jurisdictional statute upon an existing judgment in bankruptcy. To this extent the case definitely extended the area of adjudications that may not be the subject of collateral attack." [154] Despite this caveat, the implications of the Chicot County case are not yet measurable. Whether and to what degree the departure will permit itself to be carried further is a question that no one can presently answer.[155]

A judgment may be attacked collaterally by one who is neither party nor privy, if he is able to show the requisite prejudice to his interest. And, by the rule usually followed, since as to the third party the judgment is *res inter alios acta,* such a third party is not restricted, as is the party or privy, to the situation where the invalidity appears of record. Thus a judgment creditor, in an action to subject assets of his judgment debtor to the lien of his judgment may show by extrinsic evidence that a judgment of prior date against the same debtor is void for lack of jurisdiction, although jurisdiction purports to be shown by the judgment record. Most cases of collateral

[154] U.S. v. U.S. Fidelity & Guaranty Co. 309 U.S. 506, at pp. 514-515, 60 S.Ct. 653 (1940). The court continued its characterization of the case under discussion by saying that there "no examination was made of the susceptibility to such objection of numerous groups of judgments concerning status, extra-territorial action of courts, or strictly jurisdictional and quasi-jurisdictional facts. No solution was attempted of the legal results of a collision between the desirable principle that rights may be adequately vindicated through a single trial of an issue and the sovereign right of immunity from suit."

[155] For comment on the Chicot County case, see Boskey and Braucher, Jurisdiction and Collateral Attack: October Term, 1939 (1940) 40 Col.L. Rev. 1006; and notes (1940) 49 Yale L.J. 959; (1940) 53 Harv.L.Rev. 65; (1940) 28 Georgetown L.J. 1006.

attack by third persons, however, are those asserting that the judgment in question was procured by fraud or collusion. On this ground direct attack only is open to the party or privy, but the third person, with the proper interest, is entirely free to establish on collateral attack the fraud or collusion by any competent evidence.

What has been said as to the limitations upon collateral attack applies to domestic judgments. Foreign judgments, on the other hand, coming in question in the domestic forum, are always subject to inquiry as to the jurisdiction, no matter how regular they are on their face, and so are judgments of sister States, despite the full faith and credit clause of the Constitution. In both cases the lack of jurisdiction may be shown by extrinsic evidence.[156]

[156] Thompson v. Whitman, 18 Wall. (85 U.S.) 457 (1873); Old Wayne Mutual Life Association v. McDonough, 204 U.S. 8, 15, 27 S.Ct. 236 (1907); Williams v. North Carolina, 325 U.S. 226, 228-229, 65 S.Ct. 1092 (1945).

With reference to the matter of jurisdiction on collateral attack, a State judgment coming in question in a federal court stands on the same basis as does a sister State judgment in the domestic forum. Cooper v. Newell, 173 U.S. 555, 19 S.Ct. 506 (1899). As regards a federal judgment coming in question in a State court, some States treat it in the same manner as a sister State judgment; others give it in this respect the same advantages as a domestic judgment. See 3 Freeman, *op. cit.* § 1472.

CHAPTER XXIII

EXECUTION: INITIAL CONSIDERATIONS

Executio est fructus et finis legis [1] says the ancient maxim of the common law. It is the means whereby the judgment is enforced, for (voluntary compliance apart) only in exceptional cases, as in that of a judgment vesting title or fixing status, or notably in that of the declaratory judgment, does the judgment of itself fully attain its end. In the Roman law execution came about only as the result of an action based upon the judgment, the *actio judicati;* but in the Anglo-American law, as in the modern law generally, the judgment normally carries with it the right to execution, usually in express terms.[2] While the word "execution" in a large sense denotes the whole process of enforcing the judgment, it applies in a narrower and more technical sense to the several writs, constituting, for the most part, directions to the sheriff or other court officer, which are addressed to the purpose of enforcement. And these vary according to the particular object sought to be accomplished by the judgment and the particular measures to be employed in this accomplishment.

The history of our law is sharply marked by the difference in the mode of enforcing judgment existing between the common-law and equity jurisdictions. At common law the judgment in ordinary actions is not a direct command to the party; the court speaks objectively: "it is considered that A recover of B such and such" is its usual formula. The impersonal quality of the judgment is reflected in the several writs whereby the sheriff is directed to realize the recovery, for at common law none of these proceeds on any theory that the party, by failing to comply becomes guilty of a contempt of the court.

1 Co. Litt. 289 b.

2 There exist, however, exceptional cases in which a new action is necessary to enforcement, such as the action to revive a dormant judgment or the equitable action to carry a decree into execution. Foreign judgments and judgments of sister States, under the present state of American law, likewise require an action for their enforcement.

In equity, on the other hand, the jurisdiction is *in personam;* the order or decree of the court is a direct command to the party, disobedience of which constitutes a contempt of the court. Equity took over in essence the principle of the ecclesiastical courts, under which "it mattered not whether a party was to be required to take some necessary step in a suit, or to pay a sum of money found to be due to his adversary, or to pay costs, or to perform some more specific duty to his adversary, or to refrain from committing some wrong against him: in either case he was first ordered by the court to do or refrain from doing the thing in question; if he refused obedience, he was pronounced contumacious . . ." [3] To be sure, the chancellors came in the course of time to exercise certain powers with reference to the property of a contumacious defendant, limited, however, in character and never paralleling those available to the common-law court in the enforcement of its judgments. Narrow as they were, these powers were originally looked at askance by the common-law courts and their use never assumed any such proportions as to lessen the significance of the rule that equity enforced its orders through the actual coercion of the person.[4] That coercion involved the imprisonment of the contumacious defendant until he rendered obedience to the court's order. It might be suggested that here was little difference between the two systems, in respect of money judgments and decrees, since, by virtue especially of certain early statutes, imprisonment of a judgment debtor for failure to satisfy a judgment might also occur at common law. But the respective characteristics of the formulated decree and the judgment are impressed upon the mode of their enforcement. The equity decree is a personal command, and its disobedience entails the imprisonment for offense to the dignity of the court. On the other hand, just as the common-law judgment is an impersonal thing, so in its enforcement there is the same element of impersonality. If the judgment debtor fails to satisfy the judgment, imprisonment may be the consequence, but this condition is a purely objective one. The debtor is regarded as failing to meet the condition: he is in no primary sense

[3] Langdell, Summary of Equity Pleading (2d ed. 1883) §§ 42-43.

[4] *Ibid.* § 43.

regarded as disobeying a command of the court or as infringing its dignity. But the distinction between the two systems stands out more clearly if we turn to the case of a chattel as the subject of adjudication. Under special circumstances equity may make a decree requiring the defendant to deliver a given chattel to the plaintiff and in the event of disobedience imprison him until he makes the delivery. Quite different is the case at common law. Here, by the 1700s, the only action in which a definite duty can be imposed upon the defendant to deliver to the plaintiff a specific chattel is the action of replevin. In this the duty to deliver can be imposed by a judgment of recovery. This duty, however, is attended by no such means of enforcement as obtain in equity. In the older law, there were certain indirect means of exerting a leverage upon the defendant to make the delivery, but if these are unavailable or the defendant stands out, nothing can be done to enforce the specific duty. Certainly no imprisonment of the recalcitrant defendant is here permissible.

In the modern law many changes have supervened affecting the relation between the common-law and equitable modes of enforcing judgment. The unification of procedure has brought with it unification of the process of execution so far as consistent with the difference in character and object of the judgments rendered in the exercise of the one jurisdiction and the other. And, even where unification of procedure in general has not been attained, the equitable judgment has been clothed with a large measure of the executory authority formerly appertaining to the common-law courts; money judgments, for example, are now for the most part executed by the like process, whether of common-law or equitable emanation. From a substantive standpoint the equitable jurisdiction has everywhere to a greater or less degree been enlarged by statute so as to enable it in particular instances to proceed definitely *in rem,* with corresponding effect upon the matter of execution. But over against these accretions to the equitable power must be set the highly important fact that the contempt power of equity has undergone material reduction of ambit and no longer plays the same part as it did once in the enforcement of equitable judgments.

CHAPTER XXIV

EXECUTION OF MONEY JUDGMENTS

§ 1. THE ENGLISH BACKGROUND

For the enforcement of money judgments systems of law at different times and in different ways have had resort to measures directed against the person, the personal property or the real property of the debtor. At the outset the common law was severely handicapped in its choice of measures by the presence of the feudal system. Except where the Crown was the judgment creditor, or where the wrong vindicated by the judgment involved a breach of the King's peace, as in trespass *vi et armis,* seizure of the debtor's person by way of coercion to pay the debt, signifying, as it did, subtraction of the vassal from his obligation of service, was not to be countenanced. So, too, seizure of the debtor's land or any exclusion of him from its possession would dislocate the feudal tenure under which he held, and was likewise out of the question. Resort must therefore be had to the debtor's personal property. Two forms of writ were in use for this purpose. One was the writ of *fieri facias,* so called from its command to the sheriff that "you cause to be made" the amount of the judgment out of the goods and chattels of the debtor. The other was the writ of *levari facias,* commanding the sheriff that he cause to be levied the judgment debt upon the lands and goods of the debtor; by virtue of which the officer was enabled to seize the goods and receive the rents and profits of the land, though without taking possession of the latter, until the debt was satisfied.[1] But in the 1200s the slowly growing commercial interests of the kingdom produced a widening of the creditor's rights. A significant development in the matter of execution against property proceeded from the Statute of Westminster II (1285).[2] This provided that in case of a money judgment, "it shall be in the

[1] 3 Blackstone, Comm. * 417.

[2] 13 Edw. I, c. 18.

election" of the creditor to have a writ of *fieri facias,* "or that the sheriff deliver to him all the chattels of the debtor (saving only his oxen and the beasts of his plough) and one-half of his land, until the debt be satisfied by a reasonable price or extent." There was thus created a new writ, called from the words of the statute and the record entry of the creditor's election to employ it, a writ of *elegit.* Under its authority the sheriff first seized the chattels, and, after their appraisement, delivered them or so much of them as necessary to meet the debt, to the creditor at their appraised value. If the debt still remained unsatisfied, the sheriff then installed the creditor in possession of one-half of the land, until its income produced the requisite satisfaction. Accordingly, in the subsequent history of common-law execution, the writ of *levari facias* was largely laid aside, yielding to the superior efficacy of the *elegit.*

But, as another widening of the creditor's rights, there also appeared in the 1200s the beginning of that extension of the right of execution against the person to actions other than those involving a breach of the peace, which was later to assume sweeping proportions. The Statute of Marlbridge (1267) [3] inaugurated the extension by authorizing arrest on initial process in actions of account. In a former place it has been indicated that, with this beginning, the same right of arrest on initial process, in part by fiction, but principally as the result of subsequent legislation, was extended to other actions until it became available in the generality of personal actions.[4] This general use of the *capias ad respondendum* as initial process probably dates from the time of Elizabeth.[5] Now, whenever the right to arrest on mesne process thus existed, it followed that the successful plaintiff had the right to execution against the person of his judgment debtor.[6] The writ here employed was that of *capias ad satisfaciendum,* command-

[3] 52 Hen. III, c. 23.

[4] *Supra,* Chapter VIII, § 1.

[5] 3 Reeves, History of the English Law (ed. Finlayson, 1869) 757-758, cited in 9 Holdsworth, History of English Law (1926) 250, note 2.

[6] "Where *capias* lies in process, there, after judgment, *capias ad satisfaciendum* lies." Harbert's Case, 3 Co. Rep. 11, 12 (1584). It lay equally where the arrest was by virtue of bill in the King's Bench, for this had the same effect as a *capias ad respondendum.* 1 Sellon's Crompton, Practice (Am. ed. 1813) *513.

ing the sheriff to take the body of the debtor to satisfy the judgment. This meant that the debtor must be taken, as the old expression went, into *arcta et salva custodia,* without cease or limit, until the debt was paid or otherwise discharged. For his maintenance, unless he had dishonestly secreted assets, he had to depend upon the charity of his friends or the benevolence of his creditors. Some slight measures of relief to the debtor were afforded by statute in the 1600s and 1700s,[7] but the basic evils of the system long continued to blacken the pages of English legal history, as the reader of Dickens need hardly be reminded. This form of execution was barred to the creditor who had already partially satisfied his judgment by *elegit,*[8] but the principal deterrent to its use lay in the fact that the taking of the debtor's person operated as a satisfaction of the debt, and recourse could no longer be had to any property of his that might later come to light.

The jurisdiction of the English chancery, in the nature of things, did not extend to ordinary money demands, but orders and decrees for the payment of money were of highly frequent occurrence as occasioned by the relief or part of the relief awarded to suitors in the adjudication of controversies arising on equitable grounds. Enforcement of such orders proceeded on a principle wholly different from that of execution in the common-law courts. It involved first a writ of execution *eo nomine* (the writ *de executione judicii*)[9] directed not to the sheriff but to the debtor, repeating the essential part of the order or decree, and commanding its fulfillment. If unavailing, this was followed by a writ of attachment of the person for contempt, directed to the sheriff, and, finally, should the case so require, by a writ of sequestration, appointing commissioners to sequester the lands and personal estate of the debtor.[10] Power of the chancery to issue this writ (which, with a different purpose, was also an important link in the chain

[7] 8 Holdsworth, *op. cit.* (1925) 234-236; 11 *id.* (1938) 595 *et seq.*

[8] 1 Archbold, Practice (2d ed. 1826) 302.

[9] See Huston, Enforcement of Decrees in Equity (1915) 77.

[10] Barton, Suit in Equity (1796) 207-208; Evidence of Mr. Bickersteth before Chancery Commission of 1826, as appearing in 9 Holdsworth, *op. cit.* (1926) 352.

of process to compel appearance)[11] had met resistance on the part of the common-law judges, who maintained that it transcended the limits of the chancery jurisdiction to act *in personam,*[12] but had become definitely settled before the beginning of the 1700s.[13] Under the writ the sequestrators "may take possession of the real and personal estate of the party, and receive the rents, issues, and profits of the same, until he has fully performed the decree."[14] The income thus collected was to be applied to the satisfaction of the creditor's adjudicated demand. When authorized by order of court the sequestrators might sell personal property other than that "which passes by title and not by delivery,"[15] and similarly apply the proceeds. As at common law, and by a stronger reason, there could be no sale of the land.

From the dualism of jurisdiction flowed the consequence, but slightly disturbed by a provision of the Statute of Frauds in 1676, that the common-law process of execution ran only against such property of the debtor as was recognized by the common-law courts, that is to say, his legal estates or interests. Equitable estates or interests were beyond its reach, for these existed only in the contemplation of the court of equity. That provision of the Statute of Frauds[16] did indeed seek to subject trust estates in land to common-law execution, but by its terms it was confined to freehold interests, and, as construed by the courts, it was even then applicable only to " 'cases where the *cestui que trust* is entitled to the full and exclusive enjoyment of the estate, the legal title to which is vested in another'—in other words a dry trust of infrequent occurrence."[17] But common-law judgments in their relation to the debtor's assets were given full recognition by the court of equity whenever occasion arose in the exercise of its own peculiar jurisdiction. Indeed, equity would lend its aid to the enforcement of common-law judgments through its own processes against interests of the debtor, in respect of which

[11] *Supra,* Chapter XXI, § 2 (*a*).

[12] Gilbert, *Forum Romanum* (ed. Tyler, 1874) 18, 77.

[13] See Colston v. Gardner, 2 Cha. Cas. 43, 22 E.R. 838 (1680).

[14] 2 Maddock, Chancery Practice (4th Am. ed. 1832) *471.

[15] 2 Daniell, Chancery Practice (1840) 715; Shaw v. Wright, 3 Ves. Jr. 22, 23 (1795).

[16] 29 Car. II, c. 3, § 10.

[17] Glenn, Rights and Remedies of Creditors (1915) § 9, citing Freeman, Executions, § 187.

common-law processes were powerless or inadequate. Of high importance in this connection was the jurisdiction which it exercised to set aside the debtor's conveyance of property in fraud of his creditors, and to render this property available for the satisfaction of the creditors' judgments—a jurisdiction which was invoked by what was known as a judgment creditor's bill or a bill in aid of execution.

Such, in its major outlines, was the case in England at the opening of the nineteenth century. For common-law judgments the writs of *fieri facias* and *elegit* as against property, supplemented on occasion by equitable aid, the writ of *capias ad satisfaciendum* as against the person, with its unhappy potentiality of life imprisonment; for equity decrees the contempt process, involving attachment of the person and sequestration of assets: these were the instrumentalities which the law placed at the disposal of the creditor for the collection of his money judgments.

§ 2. Normal Execution against Property

America inherited the writ of *fieri facias,* as the instrumentality of execution against personal property, and continues so to employ it, in some jurisdictions under that name, in most, however, and especially those of the codes, under the general designation of a "writ of execution." At common-law the writ bound the goods and chattels of the debtor from the date of its *teste,* that is to say, the date expressed as that of its issue, and this usually was the first day of the term, thus often prior to the actual date of the judgment.[18] The injustice of such a practice gave rise to a provision of the Statute of Frauds,[19] declaring that "no writ of *fieri facias* or other writ of execution shall bind the property of the goods [of the party] against whom such writ is sued forth, but from the time that such writ shall be delivered to the sheriff, under-sheriff or coroners to be executed." This provision was for the benefit of purchasers and did not affect the situation as between the parties.[20] By reënactment of this provision or otherwise

[18] 1 Archbold, Practice (2d ed. 1826) 284.

[19] 29 Car. II, c. 3, § 16.

[20] 2 Tidd, Practice (9th ed. 1828) 1000.

the rule thus laid down obtains in a majority of the American jurisdictions: the lien of the execution dates from the delivery of the writ to the officer. In many, however, the commencement of the lien is postponed until there has been an actual levy on the goods. In some others, as in New York,[21] the statute, while making the execution a lien from the time of its delivery to the sheriff, provides for the protection of *bona fide* purchasers without notice until actual levy. The time of issuance of the writ is differently regulated: in some jurisdictions it may issue immediately after the judgment; in others it must await the lapse of a variously specified period from the time of judgment. It is made returnable within a designated number of days—sixty days is here a common measure—or at the next term, or the like. At the expiration of the period thus limited, if unexecuted, it usually loses all effect, but successive executions may issue as occasion requires so long as the judgment continues in active life. Except in a very few jurisdictions, the lien of the judgment itself extends only to realty, and so far as personal property is concerned the only lien acquired by the creditor in the process is the lien of the execution.

Subject to the lien of the execution is of course tangible personal property, including growing or harvested crops. Terms for years were regarded as chattels at common law and so subject to *fieri facias*. In the United States, however, for the most part, leasehold interests are so regarded for the purposes of execution only when the unexpired term does not exceed a given number of years—five years in New York[22] and Illinois,[23] two years in a number of other jurisdictions. Choses in action in some jurisdictions may be levied upon and sold on execution, but by the more general rule they are attainable only by process of garnishment or, under proper circumstances, by resort to equitable aid. In all or most jurisdictions shares of corporate stock have become subject to execution by various modes of proceeding. Under the Uniform Stock Transfer Act, however, by a provision of fairly general adoption, it is essential to the levy that the certificate

21 N.Y. Civ. Pract. Act (Clevenger, 1950) §§ 679, 683.

22 *Ibid.* § 708.

23 Ill. Rev. Stat. 1949, c. 77, § 3.

"be actually seized by the officer . . . , or be surrendered to the corporation which issued it, or its transfer by the holder be enjoined." [24] Equitable interests in chattels may in some quarters be subjected to direct execution,[25] but more usually their realization for the benefit of the creditor still requires the coöperation of equity.

The officer may or may not be required by statute to make upon the debtor a demand for payment before proceeding to levy the execution.[26] The levy itself always involves an assertion of control by the officer over the property, the particular acts of control depending upon the character of the property and upon what, for this purpose, may be prescribed by statute. In its simplest form, that of levy upon tangible property other than growing crops, the control, initiated by express or implied declaration of intention to take, is actuated by reduction of the goods to the officer's possession, either by manual seizure or by installing a custodian in the premises in which they are situated to represent him in possession pending sale. "The practice in the different States of the Union differs somewhat," said the Supreme Court of Illinois, "but all agree that the property must be within the power and control of the officer when the levy is made, and he must take it into his possession in a reasonable time thereafter . . . and in such an open, public, and unequivocal manner as to apprise everybody that the property has been taken in execution." [27] Once the levy is made, statutes frequently give the debtor the right to select the particular articles, sufficient for satisfaction, which he prefers to have taken and sold.[28] Normally the levy is followed by sale. By a discarding of the common-law rule which permitted the sheriff to use his own discretion as to the manner of sale,[29] the sale in the American jurisdictions is everywhere at public auction. Public notice of the time and place of the sale is given for a specified number

[24] § 13: 6 U.L.A. (1922) p. 17.

[25] 1 Freeman, Executions (3d ed. 1900) § 116.

[26] 2 *id.* § 257.

[27] Minor v. Herriford, 25 Ill. 344, 346 (1861); 2 Freeman, *op. cit.* § 260.

[28] 2 Freeman, *op. cit.* § 258.

[29] Caldwell v. Eaton, 5 Mass. 399, 402 (1809). "And if either party desired to sell at auction he must bear the expense of it, which formed no part of the sheriff's account." *Ibid.* 402.

of days, usually by posting of notices in designated public places. The sale is conducted by the officer or his deputy, and the property normally goes to the highest bidder for cash. Whether provided for or not, no bill of sale or other conveyance from the officer is necessary to the purchaser's title, for this sufficiently appears from the record of the levy and sale contained in the officer's return to the execution.[80]

If we turn now to the matter of real property, we see that the common-law rule which immunized lands from sale on execution was departed from in the colonial era. "In Massachusetts, as early as 1696, and in Pennsylvania, as early as 1700 and 1706, lands were, by colonial statutes, rendered liable to sale on execution." [81] But the departure assumed wider proportions with an act of Parliament of 1732 [82] which, avowedly for the benefit of "his Majesty's subjects trading to the British plantations in America," exposed real estate in those colonies to the like process of execution as had applied to personal property. Apparently the innovation of the statute marched in most quarters with local inclination,[83] and the writ of *fieri facias* was generally made to run against the lands and tenements as well as the goods and chattels of the debtor. Although some exceptions here existed, notable among which was the case of Virginia,[84] long continuing to adhere

80 Floyd v. Goodwin, 9 Yerg. (16 Tenn.) 483, 496 (1835); Kennedy v. Clayton, 29 Ark. 270, 276 (1874).

81 4 Kent, Commentaries on American Law (ed. Holmes, 1873) *430.

82 5 Geo. II, c. 7, § 4.

83 As to Maryland, for example, it has been said that "the peculiar circumstances of the province; the scarcity of money, and the small proportion of personal to real estate seem to have given rise to a wish among the people that land should, in some way, be made entirely subject to be seized and sold for the satisfaction of debts." The act of 1732 "removed a long train of difficulties and inconveniences, and was accordingly adopted almost immediately without opposition and entirely." Coombs v. Jordan, 3 Bland Ch. (Md.) 284, 303, 305 (1831). As to New York the following observation may be noted: "Previous to the statute of 5 Geo. II, c. 7, no judicial sales of land could be made here, under any common-law process; and whether the *elegit* was ever introduced in practice is doubtful, as the small value of the incomes of real estates afforded little inducement to resort to it, as a means of satisfying a debt due upon a judgment; but, upon the passing of that statute, though professedly intended to enable British subjects in England to sell real estates on execution in the colonies, in order to satisfy the debts due to the former, it received a liberal construction here, which extended it to all judgments . . ." Catlin v. Jackson, 8 Johns. (N.Y.) 520, 547 (1811).

84 "In Virginia, that section which subjected lands to the payment of debts,

to the writ of *elegit,* there was thus founded the principle which, crystallized and developed by local legislation throughout the years, now obtains generally in the American jurisdictions, by which the debtor's lands are available for sale on execution. The same form of writ, under the same rules as to issuance and return, whether known as a *fieri facias* or simply as a writ of execution, applies to both classes of property. At the present day some exceptions to this general practice are still existent. Thus, in Virginia the writ of *fieri facias,* save where the Commonwealth is the creditor, runs only against personal property.[35] The writ of *elegit* was in 1849 made to apply to the whole instead of one-half of the debtor's real property,[36] but was finally abolished in 1872.[37] Sale of the realty, however, may only be had by an equitable proceeding, and is conditioned upon a showing that the income for five years will not be sufficient to satisfy the debt.[38] Substantially the same system prevails in West Virginia.[39] In certain of the New England States there obtains the practice of causing the land to be valued by three appraisers and then setting off or allocating so much of it to the creditor at the appraised value as is sufficient to satisfy the debt, or all of it in partial satisfaction if its value does not equal the debt. Connecticut follows this practice to the exclusion of sale.[40] New Hampshire does likewise, though providing for the sale of certain equitable interests.[41] Massachusetts[42] and Maine,[43] on the other hand, permit the execution to proceed either by the same method of allocation or by way of sale. A markedly different practice is that which is followed in Pennsylvania.[44] Here, the officer, after levying upon the land under the writ of *fieri*

---

was rejected and nullified, as an unconstitutional encroachment upon her sovereign rights." Coombs v. Jordan, *supra,* at 307.

[35] Va. Code 1942, § 6485; Va. Code Ann. 1950, § 8-406.

[36] Hutcheson v. Grubbs, 80 Va. 251, 255 (1885). The same step had already been taken in England by 1 & 2 Vict. c. 110, § 11 (1838).

[37] Va. Laws 1871-72, c. 373, § 462; Price v. Thrash, 30 Gratt. (71 Va.) 515, 526 (1878).

[38] Va. Code 1942, § 6472; Va. Code Ann. 1950, § 8-391.

[39] W.Va. Code 1949, §§ 3784, 3785, 3769.

[40] Conn. Gen. Stat. 1949, §§ 8093, 8115.

[41] N.H. Rev. Laws 1942, c. 401, §§ 1, 7, 19.

[42] 8 Mass.Ann.Laws 1933, c. 236, §§ 6, 7, 23, 26.

[43] Me. Rev. Stat. 1944, c. 157, §§ 1, 5, 31.

[44] Pa. Stat. Ann. (Purdon, 1931) Tit. 12, §§ 2381, 2382, 2411, 2412, 2441.

facias, summons an inquest of six men who proceed to ascertain whether the rents and profits of the land would be sufficient to satisfy the judgment debt within seven years. If the inquest finds in the affirmative, it then assesses the value of such rents and profits, and, upon the return of the inquest, the creditor is awarded a writ of *liberari facias,*[45] whereby he is put in possession of the land to be held by him until the debt is satisfied. Should, however, the inquest find in the negative, then resort is had to the extreme measure: the officer sells the land under a writ of *venditioni exponas*[46] for the purpose of satisfying the judgment.

Whether the judgment is thus enforced out of property by sale or otherwise, it is nearly everywhere the rule, in keeping with the principle marking the writ of *elegit* at common law, that the personal property of the debtor must first be resorted to;[47] this, as is frequently said, is the primary fund for the satisfaction of the judgment debt. In Illinois, however, precisely the contrary is true, the statute prescribing that "personal property shall be last taken."[48] And exception also exists in the case of the Virginia sale by equitable proceedings.[49]

An important distinction between the process of execution against personalty and that against realty is that in the latter case, by the rule generally obtaining, a lien upon the property arises from the judgment itself. In England, after the Statute of Westminster II, the judgment bound the lands of the debtor, so that the writ of *elegit* was leviable upon them in the hands of a subsequent purchaser. The right to sue out an *elegit* thus gave to the creditor what was in effect, though not definitely in name, a lien upon the lands.[50] The judgment lien, however,

45 Commanding the officer that he deliver the land to the creditor; founded on the common-law writ of *liberate* used as part of the execution process against land in the case of judgments on a statute staple or on a recognizance in the nature of a statute staple: see 2 Tidd, Practice (9th ed. 1828) 1087.

46 A common-law writ commanding the officer that he expose goods for sale, here in adapted use. Its normal purpose was to require the officer to sell the goods levied upon, when his return to the execution showed that they remained in his hands unsold for want of buyers. 2 Tidd, *op. cit.* 1020.

47 2 Freeman, *op. cit.* § 279.

48 Ill. Rev. Stat. 1949, c. 77, § 11.

49 Stovall v. Border Grange Bank, 78 Va. 188 (1883).

50 Rankin v. Scott, 12 Wheat. (25 U.S.) 177, 179 (1827); Borst v. Nalle, 28 Gratt. (69 Va.) 423, 428-429 (1877); Coombs v. Jordan, 3 Bland Ch. (Md.) 284, 298 (1831).

as we know it in this country, is an American development, principally the creation of statute. An early enactment of the kind was the New York statute of 1813 which, in providing that the debtor's lands, tenements and real estates should be subject to sale on execution of judgment, declared that "the said judgment shall be a lien on such lands, tenements, and real estates." [51] This manner of lien which, without giving any property or right in the land itself, "confers a right to levy on the same, to the exclusion of other adverse interest, subsequent to the judgment," [52] has accordingly come to acceptance in all but a minority of the American jurisdictions. In Kentucky no such lien is recognized, the private creditor being relegated to the lien of his execution,[53] as is elsewhere the rule in the case of personal property. So, also, in Massachusetts, Maine, Connecticut, Vermont, New Hampshire and Rhode Island, the case in this respect is not far removed from what it was in the time of Chancellor Kent, namely, that "the judgment is no lien, and the lands are not bound until execution issued; but as a substitute for this apparent want of due protection to the creditor, the land may be attached, in the first instance, on mesne process, and that creates a valid lien." [54] In Connecticut, however, provision is now present for making the judgment a lien by filing the prescribed statutory affidavit in the proper office.[55]

At common law ordinarily "the judgment, by general intendment of law, has relation to the first day of the term whereof it is entered." [56] Here, again, the Statute of Frauds [57] changed the old rule, providing that as to *bona fide* purchasers the judgment should be effective only from the date of its signing, which was to be specially noted in the margin of the record. In the American jurisdictions the commence-

[51] Hulbert v. Hulbert, 216 N.Y. 430, 438, 111 N.E. 70 (1916).

[52] *Per* Story, J., in Conard v. Atlantic Insurance Co., 1 Pet. (26 U.S.) 386, 443 (1828).

[53] Ky. Rev. Stat. 1948, § 426.120.

[54] 4 Kent, Commentaries on American Law (ed. Holmes, 1873) *435. In these States attachment on mesne process is usually a matter of course, unlike the case in most other jurisdictions, where it depends upon the existence of certain specified grounds. See *infra*, Chapter XXVI, § 1.

[55] Conn. Gen. Stat. 1949, § 7225.

[56] 2 Tidd, Practice (9th ed. 1828) 935, 938.

[57] 29 Car. II, c. 3, §§ 13-15.

ment of the judgment lien is variously regulated. In a few, as in Kansas and Wyoming, the original common-law rule is taken as a guide, and, subject to some exception, the judgment with its lien relates back to the first day of the judgment term;[58] in Michigan no lien arises under most judgments until notice of levy has been recorded, and the lien is then spoken of as the lien of the levy;[59] elsewhere the lien generally commences with the rendition or entry of the judgment or with its docketing, indexing, recording or registration, according to the particular requirement.[60] Much diversity also exists as to the duration of the lien. In some jurisdictions it continues for a stated period—ten years is here often fixed—or it may be throughout the active life of the judgment. In other jurisdictions the duration is in different ways made dependent upon the execution. Thus in Ohio the lien ceases as to other *bona fide* creditors if execution is not levied within one year after rendition of the judgment.[61] In New York the judgment in general is a lien for ten years from the filing of the judgment roll, but execution may issue thereafter during the normal life of the judgment, which is twenty years, and upon the recording of notice of the issuance the judgment lien is resuscitated for the life of the execution.[62] In Illinois, again, the lien of the judgment lasts for seven years from its rendition, or in certain cases from the prescribed filing of a statutory affidavit, but only if execution is sued out before the end of the first year, otherwise, for the residue of the seven-year period, the only lien is that of the execution, issuable during such residue.[63]

Subject to the lien of the judgment are not only such legal estates in land as were available to the judgment creditor at common law, but also estates for years[64] to the extent permitted by statute. Moreover, in most jurisdictions equitable estates have now become subject to the judgment lien. "The general tendency of the American statutes creating and regulating judgment liens," says Mr. Freeman, "is to make such

[58] Kan. Gen. Stat. Ann. 1935, § 60-3126; Wyo. Comp. Stat. Ann. 1945, § 3-4202.

[59] Mich. Stat. Ann. 1938, § 27.1582.

[60] See 2 Freeman, Judgments (5th ed. 1925) §§ 918, 919.

[61] Ohio Gen. Code Ann. (Page, 1938) § 11708.

[62] N.Y. Civ. Pract. Act (Clevenger, 1950) §§ 44, 510, 512.

[63] Ill. Rev. Stat. 1949, c. 77, § 1.

[64] See *supra*, p. 427.

liens a charge upon whatever estate the judgment debtor may have, irrespective of the question whether his title is legal or equitable, perfect or inchoate."[65]

Since, for the most part, the lien upon land is that of the judgment itself, the levy as a prelude to sale does not usually have the same importance as attaches to it in the case of personalty.[66] The levy here involves no actual seizure of the property. "The officer does not disturb the defendant's possession, and, as a general rule, need not go upon the property on which he seeks to levy."[67] In the absence of statutory regulation of the matter, the levy will normally be sufficiently evidenced by the officer's indorsement on the writ. But when the statute speaks, it commonly calls for some form of notice of the levy, describing the property in question, to be recorded in a given public office, or served upon the debtor or the occupant of the land, or for some combination of both methods.[68] The sale, in a number of jurisdictions, is preceded by an appraisement, necessary under statutory provision that the property shall not be sold for less than a given proportion—generally two-thirds—of the appraised value. Notice of the sale, commonly for a longer period than in the case of personalty, is given by newspaper advertisement and by posting in public places, but in some quarters personal notice to the debtor is also required.[69] Exceptionally the statute sometimes requires that the sale be reported to the court and confirmed by its order.[70] Where the institution of statutory redemption is recognized, the officer does not immediately execute a deed to the purchaser, but gives him a certificate of sale, which entitles him to a deed if and when the period of redemption expires without redemption being effected. In other jurisdictions the officer executes a deed to the purchaser forthwith. Again, in those jurisdictions which proceed by the method of setting off the land to the creditor rather than by sale, no deed is issued: the proceedings "operate as a conveyance of the debtor's title, and a payment on the judgment to the amount

[65] 2 Freeman, *op. cit.* § 937.

[66] Otherwise notably in Michigan; see *supra,* note 59.

[67] 2 Freeman, Executions (3d ed. 1900) § 280a.

[68] *Ibid.* §§ 280a, 280b, 281.

[69] *Ibid.* §§ 284, 285, 285a *et seq.*

[70] *Ibid.* § 311.

of the valuation. The return of the officer when recorded passes the title." [71]

The statutory redemption to which reference has just been made obtains in approximately three-fourths of the American jurisdictions. Originating at least as early as the opening years of the 1800s, it affords to the debtor and those claiming under him, including usually junior judgment creditors and incumbrancers, the right as a matter of course to redeem the land from the judgment sale, within a prescribed period, by paying over to the officer the amount for which the property sold with all accrued charges. Commonly it applies to any judgment sale of land, but in Kentucky only where the sale has failed to bring at least two-thirds of the appraised value.[72] The redemption period is variously regulated. Occasionally its terminus is the confirmation of the sale where confirmation is required, but it is usually of more considerable length. In general, the whole period given ranges from six months to two years. Under some statutes there is a period given at large to the debtor and the lien creditors, but more often differentiation is made between them, under a variety of arrangements, as to the time of exercising the right. Thus in Minnesota [73] the debtor has one year within which to act, with five days thereafter being allotted to each of the creditors in the order of priority of their liens. In Iowa [74] the period allowed the debtor is one year, while lien creditors and mortgagees may act after the sixth month and before the end of the ninth month of the year. In New York [75] and Illinois [76] one year is given to debtor and three months thereafter to lien creditors. It is everywhere the rule that the redemption proceedings must be in strict compliance with the statute. Upon the redemption being effected, the fact is evidenced by a certificate of redemption issued by the officer, and the sale thus stands cancelled.

A prominent feature of the law of execution in this country is the liberality with which most of the statutes grant to the

[71] 4 Kent, Commentaries on American Law (ed. Holmes, 1873) *432.

[72] Ky. Rev. Stat. 1948, § 426.530.

[73] Minn. Stat. 1945, §§ 550.24, 550.25.

[74] Ia. Code 1946, §§ 628-3, 628-5.

[75] N.Y. Civ. Pract. Act (Clevenger, 1950) §§ 724, 725, 727, 728.

[76] Ill. Rev. Stat. 1949, c. 77, §§ 18, 20.

debtor exemption of property from levy and sale. In the old law, it will be recalled, the Statute of Westminster II, in according the writ of *elegit,* exempted from its operation the debtor's "oxen and the beasts of his plough." For the writ of *fieri facias,* however, the exemption was negligible: the sheriff, said Holt, C. J., in 1697, "may take anything but wearing clothes; nay, if the party hath two gowns, he may take one of them." [77] But, under the American statutes, there is always exempted a sizable quantum of personal property, frequently specified in much detail, and usually including for the resident head of a family, the family *lares et penates* and the tools of trade or profession, as well as certain domestic animals, sometimes food and fuel for a year, and sometimes, in addition to the specified chattels, related personal property up to a stated value. The extent of such exemption varies greatly according to the local attitude concerning the respective interests of debtor and creditor. In general the Eastern States are the most conservative and the agricultural States of the North West the most liberal. An example of extreme generosity to the judgment debtor is that afforded by North Dakota, where in addition to an ample list of designated chattels, including his crops and grain grown on 160 acres, he is entitled to have as exempt $1500 in selected personal property or in lieu thereof certain specific items of personalty enumerated in the statute.[78] In many States insurance policies on the debtor's life are exempt under differing regulations; a limitation of $5000 in amount is here often set. And everywhere provisions are present exempting a given portion of the debtor's wages or salary.

But over and above the personal property exemption there exists in all but a handful of jurisdictions the institution of homestead exemption [79]—a peculiarly American invention which has found imitation in some foreign countries. This in the usual form gives the debtor who is the head of a family the right to exemption in respect of the dwelling house and its

[77] Hardistey v. Barney, Comb. 356, 90 E.R. 525.

[78] N.D. Rev. Code 1943, §§ 28-2201, 2202, 2203, 2204.

[79] For the origin and progress of this institution, see Vance, Homestead Exemption Laws, in 7 Encyc. Soc. Sci. (1932) 441.

appurtenances, in a few States without limit of value or area, but more commonly only up to a given amount. The limit of value is set at $1000 in a considerable number of States, but it often greatly exceeds this figure. Even $5000 is not altogether exceptional, and in North Dakota the amount is fixed at $8000, with an area of two acres if the land is on a town plat; otherwise the exemption extends to 160 acres without limit of value.[80] Where the value of the homestead exceeds the exemption most of the jurisdictions provide means of enabling the creditor to avail himself of the excess, usually by setting off an appropriate part for sale or by allowing the debtor the amount of the exemption out of the proceeds of sale.[81] It is to be added that the statutes usually exclude from the homestead exemption certain cases of judgment debts, the most important of which are those for taxes, for purchase money of the property in question, and for labor and materials entering into improvement of that property.

§ 3. Execution by Equitable Aid

The English Court of Chancery extended its aid to the judgment creditor principally in two situations. One was where there were equitable estates or interests of the debtor which ought to be applied to the satisfaction of the judgment, as where he was entitled to a trust or equity of redemption;[82] the other where the debtor had made conveyance of his property in fraud of his creditors. The jurisdiction in the one case rested on the ground that the property was beyond the reach of execution at law, the other primarily on the ground of the debtor's fraud.[83] The nucleus of the rules[84] which equity administered in the latter regard was furnished by the Statute

[80] N.D. Rev. Code 1943, § 47-1801.

[81] 2 Freeman, Executions (3d ed. 1900) § 250a.

[82] Adams, the Doctrine of Equity (8th ed. 1890) * 129.

[83] See Beck v. Burdett, 1 Paige Ch. (N.Y.) 305, 308 (1829); Williams v. Hubbard, Walker Ch. (Mich.) 28, 29 (1842).

[84] Glenn, The Law of Fraudulent Conveyances (1931) § 5, where it is said that "at the beginning of the last century the law of fraudulent conveyances was a composite of statutes and decisions. It might better be described as a body of law which had been developed by the courts of common law and equity around the Statute of Elizabeth; the enactment, however, being taken as a norm and not as a mandate."

of Fraudulent Conveyances of 1570,[85] which made such conveyances "void, frustrate and of none effect." Equity was not called upon here to deal with an equitable interest of the debtor, for, however fraudulent the conveyance, it was good as between the debtor and his grantee. But it was void as to the creditor, and equity, when it acted, was freeing the legal estate from the incubus of the transfer.

This jurisdiction of equity, taken over in the United States, has undergone increment in various directions. Thus in the English chancery choses in action, immune from common-law execution, were by its rule as generally understood, equally unavailable to the creditor by equitable aid.[86] Only through bankruptcy or insolvency proceedings or upon the death of the debtor and administration of his estate could they be subjected to the creditor's claim.[87] But in the American jurisdictions, either by judicial departure from the chancery doctrine or by express provision of statute,[88] it has become generally true that choses in action may be reached in equity, if they cannot be made available by levy of execution, garnishment or other statutory procedure. So, too, since the statute of 1570 was construed as applying only to conveyances of legal assets, such things, that is to say, as could be levied upon under common-law execution, it was the chancery rule, as settled in the time of Lord Thurlow, that equity would not interfere with the fraudulent transfer of property not coming within this description.[89] In other words, under the statute, equity would only proceed "by way of helping the creditor to set aside conveyances of physical property." [90] And in this case also Ameri-

[85] 13 Eliz. c. 5, made perpetual by 29 Eliz. c. 5, §§ 1, 2 (1587).

[86] Donovan v. Finn, 1 Hopk.Ch. (N.Y.) 59, 76 (1823); Shaw v. Aveline, 5 Ind. 380 (1854); Greene v. Keene, 14 R.I. 388 (1884); Harper v. Clayton, 84 Md. 346, 35 Atl. 1083 (1896). As a practical matter, the deficiency of English equity in this regard was fairly well counterbalanced by the leverage upon the debtor to disgorge exerted by the specter of imprisonment for debt: see Greene v. Keene, *supra*, at 396.

[87] Glenn, *op. cit.* § 136.

[88] An example is the Illinois statute, apparently patterned upon an early New York enactment, which includes "things in action" among the property out of which equity may decree satisfaction to the judgment creditor. Ill. Rev. Stat. 1949, c. 22, § 49.

[89] Dundas v. Dutens, 1 Ves.Jr. 196, 30 E.R. 298 (1790); McCarthy v. Goold, 1 Ball & B. (Irish Ch.) 387 (1810).

[90] Glenn, *op. cit.* § 136.

can law has in general extended the scope of equitable aid to the creditor, here by enabling him to have set aside the debtor's fraudulent transfer of any species of property in any wise answerable for his debts. [91] In effect, therefore, the interposition of equity in the one respect and the other has become coextensive with the right of the creditor to realize his claim out of the debtor's assets so far as other means of realization are lacking or inadequate.[92]

The aid of equity in these matters is invoked by the suit of the creditor for his own benefit, or on behalf of himself and other creditors similarly situated who may desire to join and contribute to the expense of the suit.[93] This suit, despite the change of nomenclature accompanying the reformed procedure, is still commonly referred to by its chancery name of "judgment creditor's bill" or simply as a "creditor's bill." [94] It is framed in correspondence with what is sought to be accomplished. It may therefore confine itself to the designation of particular equitable interests and pray that they may be made answerable for the judgment. More usually, however, it assumes one of two general forms. In the first, it seeks a complete discovery of the debtor's assets, including, it may be, property fraudulently conveyed, and the subjection by the court of such assets to realization and application to the payment of the judgment. This is the ordinary case of the judgment creditor's bill proper. In the second case, it seeks to have the fraudulent conveyance of described property set aside so that the process of legal execution may proceed without hindrance. Here we speak of a bill in aid of execution. But the suit may very well partake of both characters.[95]

Subject to what will presently be said, the existence of a judgment is a prerequisite in either case. Where this remains the rule, the more general requirement for the creditor's bill

[91] *Ibid.* § 138.

[92] To the advance thus made by the American law the modern English development offers a substantial parallel, as will appear in a later section of the present Chapter.

[93] Edmeston v. Lyde, 1 Paige Ch. (N.Y.) 637 (1829).

[94] In the English chancery the term "creditor's bill" without the appellative was confined to the creditor's suit against the representatives of a deceased debtor, presenting his claim against the estate. Langdell, A Brief Survey of Equity Jurisdiction (2d ed. 1908) 125.

[95] Williams v. Hubbard, *supra.*

proper is that an execution shall have been issued and returned unsatisfied, although various jurisdictions are content with the fact of issuance.[96] For the bill in aid the more reasonable view demands only the showing of judgment,[97] but sundry jurisdictions insist in this case also that an execution shall have been issued or even that it shall have been returned unsatisfied.[98] But the necessity at all of a judgment as a condition precedent to the creditor's suit is tending to disappear. For one thing, the Uniform Fraudulent Conveyance Act,[99] now obtaining in some twenty States, impliedly dispenses with this prerequisite in suits brought under its provisions.[100] Then again, either by express provision or by reliance upon the power of the court, under the reformed procedure, to administer law and equity in the same suit,[101] a like result has been reached in other jurisdictions.[102] In this regard the Federal Rules of 1938, authorizing the joinder of claims, one of which is conditioned upon the successful prosecution of the other, expressly declare that, "in particular, a plaintiff may state a claim for money and a claim to have set aside a conveyance fraudulent as to him, without first having obtained a judgment establishing the claim for money." (Rule 18(b)). As to creditor's suits of a different description, those seeking to reach equitable assets of the debtor, displacement of the old requirement of judgment has also been coming about, but here in a much lesser degree and usually as a result of the permissible joinder of legal and equitable demands, even though one is dependent upon the other, on the same principle as that now recognized by the Federal Rules and put in relief for the case of fraudulent conveyances.

For the most part it is held that the judgment does not constitute a lien on fraudulently conveyed real property, for pending removal of the transfer it is no longer property of

[96] See Note, 23 L.R.A. (N.S.) 1, 10 *et seq.*, 46 *et seq.*

[97] Beck v. Burdett, 1 Paige Ch. (N.Y.) 305 (1829); Miller v. Davidson, 3 Gilm. (8 Ill.) 518 (1846), and cases cited in 2 Pomeroy, Equitable Remedies (2d ed. 1919) § 887, note 87.

[98] See Note, 23 L.R.A. (N.S.) 1, 49 *et seq.*

[99] §§ 9, 10.

[100] American Surety Co. v. Conner, 251 N.Y. 1, 7, 166 N.E. 783 (1929); Glenn, *op. cit.* § 76.

[101] *E.g.*, Vail v. Hammond, 60 Conn. 374, 383, 22 Atl. 954 (1891).

[102] For these jurisdictions, see Bigelow, Fraudulent Conveyances (1911) 152 n. 2; 2 Pomeroy, Equitable Remedies *ut sup.* § 882 n. 62; Glenn, *op. cit.* § 87; 14 Am.Jur. 696.

the debtor.[103] But, as it does in the case of equitable assets, the filing of the bill or complaint operates to give the creditor an equitable lien, particularly important in determining the relative priority of his claim against the real estate in question. It is everywhere well established that the creditor, if he chooses, may cause the fraudulently transferred land to be levied upon and sold under his execution, leaving the question of fraud to be litigated in, for example, an action of ejectment brought by the purchaser. But, apart from the fact that any purchaser here, be it the creditor himself, would in effect be buying a lawsuit and that in consequence this method has never been regarded as affording an adequate remedy, the creditor, save as it may exceptionally be the rule that the levy is effective for the purpose,[104] acquires no lien in the course of this proceeding and is likely, therefore, to find his claim subordinated to that of a junior creditor who has resorted to equity. By the rule more generally followed, however, although the judgment is not regarded as a lien on the property fraudulently conveyed, yet if the property has been attached on mesne process, the attachment will create a lien.[105] And there is authority to the effect that the attaching creditor may maintain a suit to set aside the fraudulent conveyance in advance of the attainment of judgment[106]—a matter obviously that is of importance only where the remedy has not been extended to the simple contract creditor.

With the general end of bringing about satisfaction of the creditor's judgment, the particular manner of relief afforded by equity conforms to the character of the suit. For the judgment creditor's bill proper it normally involves the appointment of a receiver for the debtor's assets, which upon realization by sale or otherwise are applied by the decree of the court to the payment of the creditor's judgment. In the case of the bill in aid, the normal relief is a decree setting aside the

[103] Miller v. Sherry, 2 Wall. (69 U.S.) 237, 17 S.Ct. 827 (1865); In re Estes & Carter (D.C.D.Ore.) 3 Fed. 134 (1880); Union Nat. Bank v. Lane, 177 Ill. 171, 52 N.E. 361 (1898).

[104] See Schelowski v. Pawlowski, 168 Mich. 664, 667, 134 N.W. 997 (1912).

[105] McKinney, Gilmore & Co. v. Farmers' Nat. Bank of Keithsburg, 104 Ill. 180 (1882); Pease v. Frank, 263 Ill. 500, 105 N.E. 299 (1914); 2 Pomeroy, *op. cit.* § 885.

[106] Bigelow, *op. cit.* 156 n. 2 to 152; 37 C.J.S. 1161.

fraudulent conveyance, establishing the creditor's lien and permitting him to pursue his legal process free from the obstruction. In either case it may become necessary to use the process of injunction for the creditor's protection. But the relief follows no stereotyped pattern; the court, as always in equity, adjusts the mode of relief to the exigencies of the situation, so that, even if the case is one of a bill in aid, it may very well be found proceeding by sale of the property, rather than by facilitating legal execution, where the circumstances so require.

§ 4. Supplementary Proceedings

It was a corollary of the general principle on which moved the New York Code of 1848 that in the matter of execution it should seek to telescope in some measure the invocation of equitable aid with the judgment action itself. Something in the nature of a precedent, though narrow in scope, had been introduced by the English provision of 1838, which authorized any judge of the superior courts, on the application of the judgment creditor, to order that government stock, funds or annuities or stock in any public company, owned by the judgment debtor, stand charged with the payment of the judgment.[107] Accordingly the Code, with its original text in this regard materially improved by amendment of 1849, provided for a proceeding supplementary to the judgment, summary in character, by which, without the elaborate mechanism of the creditor's bill, discovery could be had of assets of the debtor to be made available to the creditor. It was initiated by application of the creditor for an order directing the debtor to appear and answer concerning his assets, the making of which was conditioned upon the return of execution unsatisfied or upon issue of execution and proof by affidavit that the debtor had property which he refused to apply to the satisfaction of the judgment. Where it was shown by affidavit that, in the case of a debtor thus refusing, there was danger of his leaving the State or concealing himself, a warrant for his arrest might take the place of the order to appear. An order to ap-

[107] 1 & 2 Vict. c. 110, §§ 14, 15.

pear might also go against third persons, alleged by affidavit to have property of the debtor or to be indebted to him. Provision was made for the examination of the debtor and of such third parties (a corporation through an officer thereof), as well as of witnesses on the part of either party. The judge was empowered to order application toward the satisfaction of the judgment of any of the debtor's assets not exempt from execution. So also the judge was authorized to appoint a receiver of the debtor's property and to forbid the transfer or other disposition of his unexempt property. In case any third person alleged to have property of the debtor or to be indebted to him claimed an adverse interest in the property or denied the debt, the controverted question was to be determined in an action to be brought by the receiver, with the interim power in the judge to forbid a transfer or other disposition of the interest in dispute.[108]

The institution thus set on foot became in some form a part of the procedure in all the code States. Gradually other jurisdictions have availed themselves of its advantages, Illinois, for example, not adopting its limited form of the proceeding until 1941.[109] At the present day, therefore, a proceeding of the kind obtains in all but a small minority of the American jurisdictions. The various statutes, though following the same basic principle of examination for discovery of assets, differ considerably in their provisions. Indeed, in New York itself the early provisions now stand materially recast and amplified.[110] Under the initial system, perhaps due to the influence of the English measure above mentioned, the proceeding was to occur before a judge rather than the court. This, no longer the rule in New York,[111] has been followed in a number of jurisdictions; others, however, place the proceeding before the court, or before the court or a judge as the creditor elects. Everywhere the existence of a judgment is a condition pre-

[108] Code of 1848, §§ 247-257; Code of 1849, §§ 292-302.

[109] Ill. Rev. Stat. 1949, c. 110, § 197 (2), § 259.26A (S.C. Rule).

[110] For the course of the New York statute, see Cohen, Collection of Money Judgments in New York (1935) 35 Col. L.Rev. 1007, 1008; *ibid.* 1196, 1198, 1202.

[111] N.Y. Civ. Pract. Act (Clevenger, 1950) § 786.

cedent, and for a few jurisdictions, now including New York,[112] the unpaid judgment is sufficient to ground the proceeding. In addition to the fact of judgment, some jurisdictions adhere to the original requirement of execution unsatisfied as an alternative to issuance of execution plus affidavit of property;[113] for some there must always be a return of *nulla bona;*[114] while others insist only upon the issuance of execution.[115] As the order for the examination of third persons alleged to have in their hands property of the debtor or to be indebted to him trenches upon the province of garnishment, some jurisdictions omit this feature altogether. Nor is provision for a receiver everywhere included. Frequently absent is provision for arrest of the debtor to avert the danger of his departing the jurisdiction or concealing himself. In general the inquiry extends to all unexempt property of the debtor not available for levy on execution, but in more than one State exception exists with respect to the corpus of trust property proceeding from someone other than the debtor himself.[116]

The commissioners who drafted the New York Code of 1848 announced that the proceeding "is a substitute for the existing remedy by creditor's bill."[117] But even on the showing of their own provisions it was but a partial substitute. And in by far the most of the jurisdictions concerned the institution still stops decidedly short of completely fulfilling the purposes of a creditor's bill.[118] Usually the proceeding confers

[112] N.Y. Civ. Pract. Act (Clevenger, 1950) §§ 773, 775; Md. Ann. Code (Flack, 1939) Art. 75, § 147; N.M. Stat. Ann. 1941, § 19-101 (69 (b)); Colo. Rules Civ. Proc., Rule 69 (d) *et seq.*, in Colo. Stat. Ann. 1935, Replacement Vol. I, 1941.

[113] *E.g.*, Ohio Gen. Code (Page, 1938) §§ 11768, 11769.

[114] *E.g.*, Wash. Rev. Stat. (Remington, 1932) § 613.

[115] *E.g.* Va. Code 1942, § 6503; Va. Code Ann. 1950, § 8-435.

[116] N.Y. Civ. Pract. Act (Clevenger, 1950) § 792; Wash. Rev. Stat. (Remington, 1932) § 637.

[117] First Report of Commissioners (1848) 201.

[118] The case is thus put in Wilson v. Harris, 21 Mont. 374, 407, 54 Pac. 46 (1898): "The courts have not infrequently spoken of such proceedings as a substitute for the creditors' bill, and some have gone to the length of asserting that the creditors' suit in equity has thereby been abolished. By the greater number of courts, and in the majority of cases, however, this extreme view has not been accepted in its entirety, but is modified to the extent of holding that the supplemental proceedings are designed to provide the only remedy, except in matters where the relief sought is beyond the scope of such proceedings, and that in those cases courts of equity yet re-

no jurisdiction to determine any substantial controversy as to ownership of property asserted to belong to the debtor, or as to the existence of indebtedness alleged to be due him. While, under one mode of applying the proceeding, there may be full inquiry into the facts of the controversy, as a matter of discovery,[119] under another the positive assertion of claim or denial of the indebtedness on the part of the third party stops even the inquiry.[120] But, whatever the range of the inquiry, it follows that by the rule generally obtaining the question of the debtor's fraudulent conveyance of property cannot be passed upon here. Every controverted matter of the kind is left to be determined in an appropriate independent action to be brought by the receiver or by the creditor himself as the statute may purpose.[121] This limited scope of the proceeding, however, is not without exception. Notably is this the case in Indiana, Florida and Washington. Indiana originally construed the proceeding as narrowly as most, but in 1879 changed its view and established the doctrine that, with all interested parties joined, as they might be, and on issues raised by appropriate pleadings, the court in the supplementary proceedings is competent to hear and determine "any and all controverted questions between any or all of the parties." [122] In Florida the statute expressly directs itself to the matter of fraudulent transfers of the debtor's property, and in general permits the determination in the proceeding itself of all adverse property claims of third persons who are properly made parties to the proceeding.[123] And in Washington there is explicit provision

tain jurisdiction to entertain the suit by creditors' bill . . . A reasonable degree of accuracy is attained when we say that the supplemental proceedings have, to a great extent, obviated that feature of a creditors' bill which sought a discovery, but that, in so far as the equity suit was and is a bill for relief, the supplemental proceedings cannot be considered as a substitute for it, or as having more than a slight resemblance to it."

119 Lathrop v. Clapp, 40 N.Y. 328 (1869); People *ex rel.* v. Hanbury, 162 App.Div. 337, 147 N.Y.S. 851 (1914).

120 Lewis v. Chamberlain, 108 Cal. 525, 41 Pac. 413 (1895).

121 See 3 Freeman, Executions (3d ed. 1900) §§ 415, 418.

122 Toledo, Wabash & Western Ry. Co. v. Howes, 68 Ind. 458, 463-464 (1879); McMahan v. Works, 72 Ind. 19 (1880). See 3 Freeman, *op. cit.* § 415.

123 Fla. Stat. 1949, § 55.52 *et seq.;* Ryan's Furniture Exchange, Inc. v. McNair, 120 Fla. 109, 162 So. 483 (1935); State *ex rel.* v. Viney, 120 Fla. 657, 163 So. 57 (1935); Richard v. McNair, 121 Fla. 733, 164 So. 836 (1936),

for adjudication in the proceeding of the respective interests of the parties in real or personal property where question arises as to the ownership or right of the debtor, if the adverse claimants are already parties to the proceeding or are made so by appropriate order.[124]

§ 5. Garnishment after Judgment

Similar to the third party notice and order in supplementary proceedings, but attended with certain important differences, is the much older institution of garnishment. As an essential part of the process of foreign attachment, obtaining in England down to comparatively recent times, under the custom of London and other commercial cities, a third person owing money to a defendant residing outside the city or having in his hands goods of such a defendant, might be summoned to disclose and produce these assets, to be applied toward the satisfaction of the plaintiff's demand in an action of debt. This was known as garnishment. It is not to be confused with that common-law garnishment, obsolete from an early day, which consisted of the calling in of a third-party claimant of the chattel in an action of detinue.[125] The only thing in common between the two was the warning (Norman-French *garnir,* "to warn") to the third party, from which the proceeding in either case took its name. Foreign attachment under the custom, with its process of garnishment, never became part of the common law, but utilized as a security measure it was taken over by American legislation in the colonial period, and as corrected and widened constitutes the basis of the attachment statutes prevailing throughout the Union. This, however, is a matter to be considered in a later chapter.[126] For the present, concerning ourselves with the enforcement of judgment, we may note that it was natural enough for the legislator to conclude that

[124] Wash. Rev. Stat. (Remington, 1932) § 638-1; Junkin v. Anderson, 12 Wash.2d 58, 120 Pac.2d 548 (1941). This remedy, in the view of the Washington Supreme court, supersedes the action in equity. Knettle v. Knettle, 164 Wash. 468, 475, 13 Pac.2d 133 (1931). See further as to Indiana, Florida and Washington: Cohen, Collection of Money Judgments: Experimentation with Supplementary Proceedings (1936) 36 Col.L.Rev. 1061, 1087 *et seq.*

[125] *Supra,* Chapter XII, § 2.

[126] *Infra,* Chapter XXVI, § 1.

the same process of garnishment which, under the custom, had been applied in advance of judgment, could be availed of as a means directed toward the satisfaction of a judgment already rendered, independently of any pre-judgment attachment. Such a step was taken by the English Common Law Procedure Act of 1854.[127] But the English provision had long been anticipated by American legislation, this even before the Revolution, as attested by the Maryland acts of 1683 [128] and 1715,[129] as well as by the Delaware statute of 1770,[130] all providing for what was known as attachment on execution, with *scire facias* as summons to the garnishee. In the opening years of the 1800s the proceeding found rapid adoption in jurisdiction after jurisdiction,[131] and under the name of garnishment except in Pennsylvania, where, since the passage of the relative statute in 1836, it has been known as "attachment execution." In certain of the code States it is more or less integrated with the statutory supplementary proceedings,[132] while in the New England States provision for commencing actions as a matter of course by attachment or by garnishment (here called "trustee process") operates to lessen the importance elsewhere appertaining to garnishment after judgment.

From what has been said it is apparent that the proceeding is a purely statutory one. It is ordinarily classed as a proceeding at law and attended with the right of jury trial. In Kentucky, however, the only garnishment after judgment is effected by means of a petition in equity.[133] Throughout the jurisdictions the statutes exhibit variation to some extent with respect to the character of property for which the garnishee

[127] 17 & 18 Vict. c. 125, §§ 61-67.

[128] Archives of Maryland, Vol. VII (1889) p. 608; Proceedings of the Maryland Court of Appeals 1695-1729 (1933) p. xlvi.

[129] Act of 1715, c. 40, § 7; Dorsey's Exr's v. Worthington, 4 H.&McH. 533 (1771); Davidson's Lessee v. Beatty, 3 H.&McH. 594, 617 (1797); Harden v. Moores, 7 H.&J. 4 (1825).

[130] Act of 1770, § 18, Del. Laws (1797) p. 469.

[131] Some of the adoptions at this period were: Alabama, 1818 (Clay's Digest 1843, p. 259); Georgia, 1822 (Prince's Digest, 2d ed. 1837, p. 37); Mississippi, 1827 (Anderson v. Wanzer, 5 How. (6 Miss.) 587, 596, 1841); Pennsylvania, 1836 (Pub. Laws 1836, p. 755, c. 33); Arkansas, 1831 (Walker v. Bradley, 2 Ark. 578, 584, 1840).

[132] *E.g.*, Kan. Gen. Stat. Ann. 1935, § 60-3491; Ind. Stat. Ann. (Burns, 1933) 1946 Replacement Vol. II, § 2-4401 *et seq.;* Neb. Rev. Stat. 1943, § 25-1569; S.C. Code 1942, § 747.

[133] Ky. Code of Pract. in Civ. Cas. (Carroll, 1948) §§ 439, 441.

must respond, but as a rule this does not go beyond debts owed to the debtor by the garnishee and personal property in the garnishees hands belonging to the debtor.[134] Almost everywhere land, as distinguished from its income, is beyond reach of the proceeding.[135] For the most part it is held that the debt owing by the garnishee must be a liquidated one and, even though it be unmatured, one payable unconditionally and, again, that either debt or property must be such that, if sought to be recovered by the debtor himself, it would be the subject of a legal as distinguished from an equitable action. By the general rule the creditor here stands in the shoes of the debtor and is entitled to nothing which could not be recovered in the debtor's own action.[136] But this rule, if carried to its logical conclusion, would bar the creditor from attacking in this proceeding a fraudulent transfer made by the debtor to the garnishee, for, as we know, the debtor himself could not undo such a transfer. Accordingly in the great majority of jurisdictions this case falls without the general rule, and the proceeding is regarded as a proper means of assailing the fraudulent transfer.[137] Again, the principle confining the proceeding to debts or property recoverable by the debtor in an action at law is departed from in various jurisdictions, which recognize the remedy as applicable in respect of certain equitable interests of the debtor.[138]

A prerequisite to the commencement of the proceeding in most States is the issuance of execution on the judgment. Under a majority of the statutes it is further required that the execution be returned *nulla bona,* but others are content with or even require the fact of an execution outstanding.[139] Under the usual method of commencement the judgment creditor files

[134] See Note, 59 L.R.A. 353, 355.

[135] See, however, Citizens' State Bank v. Carda, 47 S.D. 29, 195 N.W. 828 (1923) holding that real estate is a proper subject of garnishment under the South Dakota statute.

[136] This rule finds external reflection in the Illinois practice, where the proceeding is carried on in the name of the debtor (nominal plaintiff) for the use of the creditor (beneficial plaintiff). See Stahl v. Webster, 11 Ill. 511 (1850); Chatroop v. Borgard, 40 Ill. App. 279 (1891).

[137] *Contra:* Chatroop v. Borgard, *supra.*

[138] *E.g.,* Smith v. Gruber Lumber Co. 81 Wash. 111, 142 Pac. 493 (1914); Nat. Surety Co. v. Hurley, 130 Minn. 392, 153 N.W. 740 (1915); Roberts v. First Nat. Bank of So. Md. 157 Md. 36, 145 Atl. 220 (1929). And see Note, 59 L.R.A. 353, 384-386, 392.

[139] See Note, 128 A.L.R. 1153, 1154.

an affidavit alleging the unsatisfied judgment with the necessary facts in relation to the execution, his lack of knowledge of any property of the debtor upon which direct execution can be levied, and his belief that the person now named as garnishee is indebted to the debtor or has property of the debtor in his possession or control. Upon the filing of the affidavit there issues a writ of summons or equivalent notice to the garnishee as defendant in the present proceeding, requiring him to appear and answer. Characteristic of the proceeding are the written interrogatories of the plaintiff to the garnishee; these ordinarily are filed before the answer of the garnishee is due, but in some jurisdictions either these or an oral examination in their stead are used only in case of an incomplete disclosure in the answer.[140] Most commonly the garnishee must respond only as to the situation at the time of service upon him, although in some jurisdictions he is accountable down to the time of answer.[141] In his answer the garnishee should avail himself of all defenses that he could have interposed against the debtor, for, if he fails to do so, he runs the risk of being held liable a second time, in an action by the debtor.[142] If the plaintiff considers that the answer is not in accordance with the facts, he may contest its statements by means of a traverse, and the trial of the issue thus arising is determinative of the garnishee's liability.

Should the garnishee fail to appear or answer, judgment is rendered against him by default. But this judgment can seldom be other than a judgment *nisi* or conditional judgment. As such conditional judgment it is followed by a new warning to the garnishee, which according to the particular practice takes the form of a writ of *scire facias* or of a notice to show cause against the judgment. If the garnishee still fails to appear after service of the writ or notice, the conditional judgment is confirmed and becomes absolute. Appearing, the garnishee, as concerns the merits, stands in the same position with respect to answer and defense as before the conditional judgment.

140 2 Shinn, Attachment and Garnishment (1896) § 631.

141 See 38 C.J.S. p. 404; 4 Am.Jur. p. 653.

142 2 Shinn, *op. cit.* § 623.

When it comes to final judgment against the garnishee, this, in the case of indebtedness found owing from him, is for the amount due on the creditor's judgment or so much thereof as the garnishee's indebtedness extends to cover. Where that indebtedness is not yet matured, the judgment under some statutes must await maturity; under others there is no deferring of the judgment, but execution is stayed until the indebtedness becomes payable. If what is found in the garnishee's hands consists of goods and chattels or choses in action, no money judgment against the garnishee is in order.[143] Normally the judgment will provide that the goods and chattels, or so much of them as is necessary, be surrendered to the sheriff to be levied upon and sold under execution, as may be done also in the case of choses in action where these are subject to levy and sale. But in some jurisdictions the statute invests the court with power to appoint a receiver with power to collect, sell and dispose of such property other than money for the benefit of the creditor, and the final judgment against the garnishee may accordingly direct the delivery of the property in question to the receiver.[144]

Most of the statutes contemplate participation in the garnishment proceeding of third-party claimants of the fund or property under garnishment. Often they permit such a claimant to appear voluntarily for the purpose of asserting his claim. As a rule the garnishee for his own protection is under the duty of disclosing in his answer the existence of any such claim coming to his knowledge.[145] And it is sufficiently common for the statutes to provide for the summoning in of the stranger claimant, where the fact of his claim appears from the garnishee's answer or otherwise, with the consequence that his failure to appear will bar his subsequent assertion of the claim. Thus the proceeding may give rise to a case of intervention, on the one hand, or of medial interpleader, on the

143 *Ibid.* § 687. Unless he should refuse to deliver the property, in which case provision is sometimes made for a money judgment against him, as under the Illinois statute directing that such judgment be for the amount of the plaintiff's judgment. Ill. Rev. Stat. 1949, c. 62, § 25.

144 Ill. Rev. Stat. 1949, c. 62, § 24; Mich. Stat. Ann. 1938, § 27.1861.

145 38 C.J.S. p. 444; 2 Shinn, *op. cit.* § 671.

other.[146] In Illinois, however, the third party's pleading setting up the claim is generally called an "interplea" even in the first case, and there is a strong tendency to apply the term "interpleader" indiscriminately to either case.[147] On this pleading, whatever it be designated, there is formed an issue between the claimant and the plaintiff creditor, with which the garnishee is not ordinarily concerned, to determine the question of the ownership of the fund or property as between the claimant and the debtor. If the claimant succeeds in establishing his right, while there is no uniformity of practice under the different statutes,[148] the more usual judgment, perhaps, as it is the more logical, is one awarding the claimant his costs and discharging the garnishee.[149]

Perhaps the most common use of the proceeding is to reach the wages or salary of employed persons and to render available to the creditor the excess after allowance to the employee of the statutory exemption here obtaining. This field has been the subject of much legislation in more recent years. On the one hand, the tendency has been to impose restrictive conditions upon use of the proceeding, such as requiring written demand to be made upon employer and employee a certain number of days before commencement of the proceeding, and limiting to a very brief period the time during which the employer must hold the unexempt portion of the wages or salary.[150] On the other hand, since, where the creditor's judgment is for a substantial amount, repeated garnishments would often be necessary under the ordinary rules, an opposite tendency has developed in a few jurisdictions which, to relieve the creditor of this manner of burden, have provided for

[146] See *supra*, Chapter XII, §§ 1, 2.

[147] See *e.g.*, Doretti v. Geo. E. Rice Potato Co. 210 Ill.App. 300 (1918); Fry v. Radzinski, 219 Ill. 526, 76 N.E. 694 (1906).

[148] See 38 C.J.S. p. 571.

[149] Walton v. Detroit Copper & Brass Rolling Mills, 37 Ill.App. 264 (1890); Buckingham v. Shoyer, 86 Ill.App. 364 (1900); Carpenter v. McClure, 37 Vt. 127 (1864); Fla. Central & Peninsular RR. Co. v. Carstens, 48 Fla. 72, 37 So. 566 (1904); Garst v. Canfield, 43 R.I. 554, 113 Atl. 865. But see Ill. Rev. Stat. 1949, c. 62, § 12, providing that, if it appears that the claimant is entitled to possession of the property, the court shall order its delivery to him. The constitutionality of such a provision, however, is seriously open to question, as applied to a garnishment after judgment, since the debtor himself is not a party to the proceeding.

[150] *E.g.*, Ill. Rev. Stat. 1949, c. 62, § 14; N.D. Rev. Code 1943, § 32-0903.

making the execution a continuous lien upon a designated portion of the debtor's unexempt income, including his wages or salary, until satisfaction of the judgment is attained.[151]

§ 6. Execution by Sequestration

Since under the prevailing system money decrees in general are now executed in the same manner as money judgments at law, the writ of sequestration as a means of enforcing the former does not figure largely in the American jurisdictions.[152] In most the writ finds no place even with respect to decrees other than for money. In others it obtains by statutory recognition or equity tradition, or is represented by a statutory equivalent, but is a means seldom employed. Usually it is only under special circumstances which justify the continued exercise of the contempt power that the process comes into play to enforce the payment of money. Thus the principal field of its application—in a number of States under special legislative authorization—is in matrimonial actions. Here it finds occasional employment, as against a contumacious husband, to enforce orders for the payment of alimony, by bringing about a seizure of so much of his estate as is necessary for the purpose.[153] Sometimes a receiver takes the place of the traditional commissioners. In any case the sequestration is directed toward satisfying the order in question out of the rents and profits of the sequestered real estate and, at least to the same extent as in the English chancery, out of the proceeds of sale or other disposition of the personal property, under the court's direction. In New York, however, it is provided that where it becomes necessary, the court may authorize the receiver to mortgage or sell the real estate.

[151] N.Y. Civ. Pract. Act (Clevenger, 1950) § 684; Ind. Stat. Ann. (Burns, 1933) 1946 Replacement Vol. II, § 2-4406. In neither case, however, does the proceeding conform to the common type of garnishment. That in New York is a specialized form of execution levy, the execution in such case being known as a "garnishee execution," and that in Indiana is part of the statutory supplementary proceedings.

[152] For sequestration as a means of security, see *infra,* Chapter XXVI, § 4.

[153] See Wightman v. Wightman, 45 Ill. 167 (1867); Ark. Stat. Ann. 1947, § 34-1212; D.C. Code 1940, § 16-410; Mo. Rev. Stat. Ann. 1942, § 1519; Haw. Rev. Laws 1945, § 12228; N.J. Stat. Ann. 1939, § 2:50-37; N.Y. Civ. Pract. Act (Clevenger, 1950) §§ 1171, 1171-a.

It is to be mentioned that the term "sequestration" is at times used by the statutes to designate certain forms of executional seizure unconnected with the equity writ. In particular, the name in several jurisdictions is applied to a special statutory proceeding, based on an unsatisfied judgment against a corporation, looking to seizure of its assets and their application to the payment of the judgment[154]—in effect a species of creditor's suit or supplementary proceedings.

§ 7. Execution by Judicial Sale

A sufficiently common type of execution, distinct from that depending on a writ, is execution by judicial sale,[155]—the case, that is to say, of sale directly ordered by the judgment itself for the purpose of enforcing payment of a pecuniary sum, where this is secured by a lien on property recognized by the judgment. Such is the case in the equitable action[156] to foreclose a real estate mortgage (or its substitute trust deed) according to the method more usually followed, under which "the proceeding is in effect an execution for the mortgage debt against the mortgaged land."[157] By the normal practice of the English chancery, the suit to foreclose a mortgage envisaged a decree providing for the ascertainment of the amount of the mortgage debt, allowing the mortgagor a stated time, commonly six months, to pay it, and ordering that in default of payment of the indebtedness and costs, he stand foreclosed

[154] Fla. Stat. 1949, § 55.24; Pa. Stat. Ann. (Purdon, 1931) Tit. 12, § 1331; Minn. Stat. 1945, § 316.05.

[155] A judicial sale "is, in contemplation of law, a sale made *pendente lite;* a sale in court, and the court is the vendor . . . In a legal sense, the sale is made by the court itself in enforcement of its own orders and decrees, wherein is described the property to be sold . . . Such sale is unlike a sheriff's sale on ordinary common law or statutory execution, which is a *ministerial* and not a *judicial* act; and in making which the law regards the officer, and not the court, as the vendor." Rorer, Judicial and Execution Sales (2d ed. 1878) §§ 1, 9.

[156] For foreclosure of real estate mortgages by means other than suit, see 3 Jones, Mortgages of Real Property (8th ed. 1928) §§ 1600 *et seq.*, 2230 *et seq.* The ordinary action to foreclose is the equitable one, although in a few jurisdictions proceedings at law are used for the purpose, the writ of entry in certain of the New England States (*ibid.* § 1648 *et seq.*) and *scire facias sur mortgage* in Pennsylvania (*ibid.* § 1734). In Illinois the proceeding by *scire facias* is provided for by statute (Rev. Stat. 1949, c. 95, §§ 18-22) but has long been completely out of use.

[157] Sedgwick v. Fish, 1 Hopk.Ch. (N.Y.) 594 (1824).

of all right of redemption, the mortgagee in that event becoming the absolute owner of the land, legal title to which had been vested in him by the mortgage. Only in exceptional instances did the court exercise the power of ordering a sale.[158] This course of practice was not departed from in England until the Chancery Practice Amendment Act of 1852,[159] which, under some restriction, authorized sale of the land as the general mode of proceeding. But, in the United States outside of the New England jurisdictions, foreclosure by judicial sale had become the normal rule by the end of the first quarter of the 1800s, and in certain jurisdictions at a much earlier date.[160] The older method, however, which has come to be known as "strict foreclosure" still finds some footing. In Connecticut and Vermont[161] it continues, at least in principle, to be the ordinary method of foreclosure by equitable action. In a number of other jurisdictions it may be resorted to under special circumstances, as in Illinois, "where it appears that the property is of less value than the debt for which it is mortgaged, and the mortgagor is insolvent, and the mortgagee is willing to take the property in discharge of his debt."[162] In others, again, and perhaps a majority, necessarily including all those subscribing in its entirety to the so-called lien theory of the mortgage, strict foreclosure is not allowed at all, its place being completely taken over by the method of judicial sale.[163]

[158] Lansing v. Goelet, 9 Cow. (N.Y.) 346, 371 *et seq.* (1827); 4 Kent, Commentaries on American Law (ed. Holmes, 1873) * 180; 1 Glenn, Mortgages (1943) § 59.1.

[159] 15 & 16 Vict. c. 86, § 48.

[160] For New York it seems to have antedated a recognitive statute of 1813. Lansing v. Goelet, *supra,* at 365, 392, *per* Jones, Ch., assigning to the Court of Errors the reasons for his decree in the Court of Chancery. Indeed, in the same case it was said by Senator Oliver, delivering the opinion of the Court of Errors that "in this State sales of mortgaged premises, by the Court of Chancery, are believed to be coeval with the organization of that court under the constitution of 1777." *Ibid.* at 401. And, for Georgia, sale under judgment as the general mode of proceeding was established by the Judiciary Act of 1799, § 17. Prince's Digest (1822) p. 209. See also Hord v. James, 1 Overton (Tenn.) 201 (1805); Fleming v. Sitton, 1 Dev.& Bat.Eq. (21 N.C.) 621, 623 (1837); Mussina v. Bartlett, 8 Port. (Ala.) 277, 288 (1838).

[161] 3 Jones, *op. cit.* §§ 1967, 1985.

[162] Carpenter v. Plagge, 192 Ill. 82, 99, 61 N.E. 530 (1901).

[163] For the rule in different States, see 3 Jones, *op. cit.* §§ 1964-1987; 1 Glenn, *op. cit.* § 67 *et seq.*

The same manner of execution by judicial sale obtains in the enforcement of mechanics' liens, vendors' liens and various other liens upon realty, where this occurs by action.[164] Whether the case is that of mortgage foreclosure or foreclosure of any other lien, the sale, pursuant to direction of the judgment, and after due notice given, is had at public auction and is conducted usually by a master or commissioner of the court, sometimes by the sheriff or even the clerk of the court. Its regimen, in respect of notice, bidding and conduct in general, presents few points of difference from that of an execution sale. But, conformably to the principle governing judicial sales in general, and thus differing from the rule more commonly applying in the case of execution sales, the sale is ineffective for any purpose until confirmed by an order of the court after report of sale made to it by the officer.[165] Since the court is here regarded as the vendor and the selling officer as merely its agent, it has a very wide discretion as to granting or withholding its approval.[166] The purchaser at the sale receives from the officer an interim certificate of sale or an immediate deed, as the local rule may prescribe. The proceeds of the sale are applied to the satisfaction of the mortgage or other lien debt and accrued costs. If any surplus remains after payment of the debt with incident charges, and the satisfaction of any other liens established in the suit, it goes to the mortgagor or lienee. In the case of mortgage foreclosure, if a deficiency is left after application of the proceeds to the amount due the mortgagee, and the mortgagor is personally liable on the promissory note or other obligation secured by the mortgage, the earlier rule, following that of the English chancery,[167] relegated the mortgagee to his action at law for the recovery of such deficiency. But now the statutes generally authorize the court in the foreclosure proceeding to render judgment for the amount of the deficiency against the mortgagor or any other

164 Cases may exist of foreclosure of liens upon personalty by judicial sale. Thus in some States chattel mortgages or at least certain kinds of chattel mortgages can be foreclosed only by action.

165 Rorer, *op. cit.* § 106.

166 *Ibid.* § 108; Miller v. Miller, 332 Ill. 177, 180, 163 N.E. 343 (1928).

167 See Orchard v. Hughes, 1 Wall. (68 U.S.) 73, 77 (1864).

defendant thus personally liable, provided that personal service of process has been had upon him in that proceeding. This judgment in point of execution stands on the same basis as any money judgment at law except that it may not be enforced against the land already sold.

In those jurisdictions which provide for a statutory redemption from execution sales of real estate, a like right is accorded in respect of sales under judgments of mortgage foreclosure, and usually under the same conditions. As regards such a right in the case of foreclosure of other liens on real estate, it may be said that while in some jurisdictions redemption is here permitted by virtue of a general provision,[168] in others the existence of the right depends upon the statutory regulation of the particular lien.

§ 8. Execution against the Person

In the pre-Revolutionary era the English process of execution against the person was generally followed in the American jurisdictions.[169] But the mounting opposition to imprisonment for debt which, in England could not make itself decisively felt until 1869,[170] was, under the different social and economic conditions prevailing in America, enabled to translate itself into law at a much earlier date. Thus, on the very heels of the Declaration of Independence, the Pennsylvania constitution of 1776 [171] declared that "the person of a debtor, where there is not a strong presumption of fraud, shall not be continued in prison, after delivering up, *bona fide,* all his estate real and personal, for the use of his creditors, in such manner as shall be hereafter regulated by law." The like declaration followed on the part of the North Carolina constitution of 1776 [172] and the Vermont constitution of 1777.[173] After the conclusion of the War of Independence, the prohibition in almost identical terms was embodied in the constitutions of Ken-

[168] *E.g.,* Ill. Rev. Stat. 1949, c. 77, §§ 16, 18; Ala. Code 1940, Tit. 7, § 727; Ariz. Code Ann. 1939, § 24-303.

[169] 2 Kent, Commentaries on American Law (ed. Holmes, 1873) * 398.

[170] 32 & 33 Vict. c. 62, § 4 *et seq.*

[171] Plan or Frame of Government, § 28.

[172] Chap. II, Constitution or Form of Government, XXXIX.

[173] Plan or Frame of Government, § XXV.

tucky (1792),[174] Tennessee (1796),[175] Georgia (1798),[176] Ohio (1802),[177] Indiana (1816),[178] Mississippi (1817),[179] Illinois (1818),[180] and Alabama (1819).[181] Subsequent constitutions have registered the prohibition in similar terms or otherwise. Most commonly they expressly except from the interdiction the case of fraud. But some are literally or substantially in terms of absolute prohibition of imprisonment for debt, as those, presently in force, of Maryland (1867),[182] Tennessee (1870),[183] Texas (1876),[184] Georgia (1877),[185] Mississippi (1890),[186] Alabama (1901),[187] and New Mexico (1911).[188] Not all the State constitutions[189] contain a declaration of the kind, and this is the case in New York,[190] but in its absence the prohibitory rule is to be collected from the statutes or exists by necessary inference from other constitutional provisions.

By the interpretation generally obtaining the constitutional prohibition does not apply to judgments for torts, it being considered that imprisonment under such a judgment is not imprisonment for debt.[191] And where the prohibition has been left to the legislature, the same principle is followed. In a few States, therefore, execution against the person may issue on any tort judgment.[192] For the most part, however, it is here confined to specified cases, such as where wilfulness, malice, breach of duty by a public officer, or some other aggravating circumstance has entered into the commission of the tort, or where this involves conversion of money or personal property. Even for tort judgments it is sometimes available only when there is danger of the debtor's estate being put beyond the

174 Art. XII, § 17.
175 Art. XI, § 18.
176 Art. IV, § 7.
177 Art. VIII, § 15.
178 Art. I, § 17.
179 Art. I, § 18.
180 Art. VIII, § 15.
181 Art. I, § 18.
182 Art. III, § 38.
183 Art. I, § 18.
184 Art. I, § 18.
185 Art. I, Sec. I, Par. XXI.
186 Art. 3, § 30.
187 Art. I, § 20.
188 Art. 2, § 21.
189 For the several State constitutions to 1908, see Thorpe, Federal and State Constitutions etc. (1909) Vols. 1-9.
190 See Reeves v. Crownshield, 274 N.Y. 74, 8 N.E.2d 283 (1937).
191 Note, 34 L.R.A. 634, 640; 33 C.J. S. 768; In re Petition of Blacklidge, 359 Ill. 482, 195 N.E. 3 (1935).
192 R.I. Gen. Laws 1938, c. 552, § 11; Me. Rev. Stat. 1944, c. 107, § 46; Conn. Gen. Stat. 1949, §§ 8112, 8114, Campbell v. Klahr, 111 Conn. 227, 149 Atl. 770 (1930).

reach of his creditors. In the case of judgments founded on contract, fraud in various manifestations finds place as a basis for execution against the person. A frequent ground is fraudulent transfer or concealment of property or the absconding of the debtor, accomplished or feared; less common, perhaps, but fairly prevalent, is fraud in the contracting of the indebtedness. In some jurisdictions judgments in actions for breach of promise of marriage are here included, as are judgments for money lost at gaming. Under many statutes, the body execution must be authorized by the judgment or may be issued only by an order of court. It is often a condition of its issuance that a property execution shall have been returned unsatisfied. And rules very widely obtain exempting women from this manner of execution, either altogether or except in designated cases.

Some idea of the diversity to be found among the statutes as to the grounds of body execution may be had by comparing the situation in California with that in Illinois. The California statute [193] which, with some variations, has been reproduced in Nevada, Oregon, Idaho and Montana,[194] provides for arrest on mesne process, and by consequence on execution against the person:

> (1) In an action for the recovery of money or damages on a cause of action arising upon contract, express or implied, when the defendant is about to depart from the state with intent to defraud his creditors.
>
> (2) In an action for a fine or penalty, or for money or property embezzled, or fraudulently misapplied, or converted to his own use, by a public officer, or an officer of a corporation, or an attorney, factor, broker, agent, or clerk, in the course of his employment as such, or by any other person in a fiduciary capacity; or for misconduct or neglect in office, or in a professional employment, or for a willful violation of duty.
>
> (3) In an action to recover the possession of personal property unjustly detained, when the property or any part thereof, has been concealed, removed, or disposed of, to prevent its being found or taken by the sheriff.

[193] Cal. Code Civ. Proc. (Deering, 1949) § 479.

[194] Nev. Comp. Laws 1929, § 8644; Ore. Comp. Laws Ann. 1940, § 7-301; Idaho Code Ann. 1949, § 8-102; Mont. Rev. Codes Ann. 1947, § 93-4002.

(4) When the defendant has been guilty of a fraud in contracting the debt or incurring the obligation for which the action is brought; or in concealing or disposing of the property, for the taking, detention, or conversion of which the action is brought.

(5) When the defendant has removed or disposed of his property, or is about to do so, with intent to defraud his creditors.

In Illinois, on the other hand, the grounds of execution against the person are not the same as those warranting arrest on mesne process. The statute allows execution against the person in but two cases: (1) on any judgment either in contract or in tort, where the debtor has refused to deliver up his estate for the benefit of his creditors, and (2) on tort judgments where malice is the gist of the action and it shall so appear from a special finding of the jury or, in non-jury cases, of the judge.[195]

Statutes making provision in respect of the debtor's discharge from imprisonment generally agree in requiring the debtor to apply for and submit to an examination. But they vary greatly in point of their further requirements. In California, for example, the debtor is entitled to his discharge in any case of body execution upon showing to the satisfaction of the court that he is unable to pay the judgment, and taking the prescribed oath to the effect that he has no property to the amount of $50, except such as is exempt, and has not fraudulently disposed of any of his property.[196] In Illinois, again, discharge may be effected under the Insolvent Debtors Act where the ground of body execution is the debtor's refusal to surrender his estate. In that case there is a jury trial of the charge of refusal, and if the jury finds in favor of the debtor his discharge follows. If, on the contrary, its verdict is against him, he is then to submit a schedule of all his estate and of his debts then owing, verifying it by the statutory oath. The truth of this may be disputed, but if, after a hearing, it is found correct by the court, it is made the duty of the debtor to assign all his unexempt estate, or so much thereof as is necessary to

195 Ill. Rev. Stat. 1949, c. 77, § 5, 65.

196 Cal. Code Civ. Proc. (Deering, 1949) § 1143 *et seq.* In the New England States statutes of this type are commonly termed "Poor Debtors Acts."

pay his debts, to a judicially appointed assignee, who then realizes upon the property and makes due distribution to the plaintiff and other creditors. Upon production of the receipt of the assignee for the property and the debtor's books and accounts, the debtor is entitled to an order of discharge.[197] Where, however, the execution is in a tort action with malice specially found as the gist of the action, the defendant is not entitled to relief under the act.[198] Unless and until he pays the judgment, he must remain under imprisonment for the period of six months, set by statute as the limit of imprisonment for all execution debtors except those who, coming within the terms of the Insolvent Debtors Act, refuse to schedule as therein provided.[199]

As a condition of the debtor's imprisonment it is usually required that the creditor pay the jailer for the prisoner's subsistence, it being often provided that this shall be done weekly in advance.[200] In England, under the later common law, a civil prisoner might be "allowed, on giving security to the marshal or warden, the benefit of the rules of the King's Bench or Fleet prison, or of living within certain limits, out of its walls." [201] In some of the older States place is given to the same manner of privilege, upon the debtor giving to the proper official a so-called prison-limits bond with sufficient security. The prison limits, bounds or liberties, as they are variously termed, ordinarily comprise a considerable area, frequently embracing the town or county in which the prison is situated. In New Jersey, for example, the county is established by statute as the prison limits.[202] Within the limits thus fixed the prisoner has normally entire freedom of movement. But if he leaves these limits, for however short a time, the case is one of escape, inviting the forfeiture of the bond for the benefit of the creditor.[203]

[197] Ill. Rev. Stat. 1949, c. 72, § 1 *et seq.*

[198] In re Petition of Blacklidge, *supra.*

[199] Ill. Rev. Stat. 1949, c. 77, § 68.

[200] *E.g., ibid.* c. 72, §§ 29, 33; Cal. Code Civ. Proc. (Deering, 1949) § 1154.

[201] 1 Tidd, Practice (9th ed. 1828) 373.

[202] N.J. Stat. Ann. 1939, § 2:37-1.

[203] This procedure in New York is the theme of Arthur Train's ingenious tale "The Liberty of the Jail" in "Mr. Tutt's Case Book" (1936) pp. 549-572.

Apart from execution against the person in the sense above considered, imprisonment of a debtor may sometimes occur by attachment of his body in the case where his failure constitutes a contempt of court. As has been seen, equitable money judgments, being now executory by the same means as judgments at law, are no longer enforceable in general by the contempt process. But in exceptional cases, where the failure to pay carries with it more than ordinary offense to the canons of justice, some special stigma of inequity, enforcement of money orders and judgments may still to some extent command use of that process, at least where other means of enforcement are inadequate. Orders for the payment of alimony usually fall into this category.[204] So, also, do orders or judgments directing payment by trustees of trust moneys,[205] as well as those requiring payment by receivers and other court officers of money coming to their hands in the course of their duties.[206] But, even in such cases, the attachment cannot be supported unless the failure to pay amounts to a wilful disobedience of the order or judgment, or the debtor has wilfully put it out of his power to obey: the contumacy of the debtor must be beyond question.[207] It is to be added that, while the situation is not without some note of dissent, it is generally held that imprisonment under such circumstances does not infringe the prohibition of imprisonment for debt.[208]

In the same connection notice must be taken of a statutory measure adopted of recent years in certain States which had come to be impressed with the insufficiency of their pre-existing processes for the collection of debts—a development which finds some precedent in the English act of 1869.[209] Under this measure, as appearing in the statutes of Rhode Island, Massachusetts and New York,[210] it is in substance the rule that where,

[204] See Note, 76 A.L.R. 390, 392.

[205] People v. La Mothe, 331 Ill. 351, 163 N.E. 6 (1928); Note, 60 A.L.R. 322.

[206] Rapalje, Contempt (1884) §§ 15, 17.

[207] Note, 76 A.L.R. 390; People v. La Mothe, *supra*.

[208] Note, 30 A.L.R. 130; Note, 60 A.L.R. 322, 323.

[209] 32 & 33 Vict. c. 62, § 5.

[210] R.I. Gen. Laws 1938, c. 555, §§ 1-3, dating from 1915; 7 Mass. Ann. Laws 1933 and 1949 Cum. Supp. c. 224, § 16, dating from 1927; N.Y. Civ. Pract. Act (Clevenger, 1950) § 793, dating from 1935. By Massachusetts amendment of 1943 the support allowance is to be not less than $20 per week for the head of a family.

in supplementary proceedings, it is disclosed that the debtor is in receipt of income, from whatever source, out of which he could make partial payments on the judgment, the court is authorized, after due allowance for the reasonable support of the debtor and his family, to order that he pay the judgment debt in installments from time to time. Failure to pay as ordered is declared a contempt of court, for which, as in other cases of contempt, the contemnor may be attached and committed to prison. In *Reeves* v. *Crownshield* (1937) [211] the constitutionality of the New York provision was attacked, principally on the ground that, although the State constitution contained no prohibition of imprisonment for debt, the like prohibition followed from the due process clauses of the State and Federal constitutions. But the Court of Appeals held no case of imprisonment for debt was here presented. "To compel the judgment debtor to obey the order of the court," it said, "is not imprisonment for debt, but only imprisonment for disobedience of an order with which he is able to comply. His refusal is contumacious conduct, the same as a refusal to obey any other lawful order of the court." [212]

§ 9. The Modern English Development

In the English procedure of the present day the writs of *fieri facias* and *elegit* continue in use, and, since the Judgments Act of 1838,[213] have been the principal forms of execution upon money judgments, as well those attributable to the equitable powers of the court as to its legal powers. But by that act of 1838 the writ of *elegit* was made applicable to the whole, instead of the old moiety, of the debtor's land,[214] and in 1883 [215] it ceased to concern itself with chattel property. The writ of *fieri facias* runs not only against tangible personal property to which the debtor has legal title, but also against that in

211 274 N.Y. 74, 8 N.E.2d 283.

212 At pp. 79-80.

213 1 & 2 Vict. c. 110, § 18. "A judgment for the recovery by or payment to any person of money may be enforced by any of the modes by which a judgment or decree for the payment of money of any court whose jurisdiction was transferred by the Supreme Court of Judicature Act, 1873, might have been enforced at the time of the passing thereof." O. XLII, r. 3.

214 1 & 2 Vict. c. 110, § 11.

215 Bankruptcy Act 1883, 46 & 47 Vict. c. 52, § 146.

which he has the whole beneficial interest.[216] Moreover, since 1838,[217] it authorizes levy upon money or banknotes, cheques, bills of exchange, promissory notes, bonds, specialties or other securities for money, belonging to the debtor. The writ binds the personalty from the time of its delivery to the sheriff, but as to *bona fide* purchasers it is effective only against those who have had notice that the particular writ, or any other for the seizure of the debtor's goods, has been so delivered and remains unexecuted in the sheriff's hands.[218] Sale by the sheriff of goods seized, where the execution is for more than £20, is now at public auction after advertisement, unless the court otherwise orders.[219] Where the property seized consists of money or banknotes, these or so much of them as is necessary are paid over to the judgment creditor; where it consists of securities, the sheriff holds them as security for the judgment debt, and is authorized to realize upon them for the benefit of the creditor, the latter providing the officer with a proper indemnity bond.[220] The only property of the debtor exempt from execution is the wearing apparel and bedding of himself or his family, and the tools and implements of his trade, the whole not to exceed £5 in value.[221] The judgment may also be enforced against the debtor's interest in designated government funds and in company stock or shares. This, however, is not done through a writ of execution, but by means of an application to the court for a charging order, on a showing of the unpaid judgment and of the debtor's title. The order, when made after a hearing, gives the judgment creditor the same remedies as if the charge had been granted by the debtor himself, but the creditor may not proceed toward realization until after the lapse of six months from the date of the order;[222] although by means of a judicial stop order he may cause to be restrained meanwhile the payment of dividends to the debtor.[223]

216 Annual Practice 1949, I, p. 827.

217 1 & 2 Vict. c. 110, § 12.

218 Sale of Goods Act 1893, 56 & 57 Vict. c. 71, § 26.

219 Bankruptcy Act 1883, 46 & 47 Vict. c. 52, § 145.

220 1 & 2 Vict. c. 110, § 12.

221 8 & 9 Vict. c. 127, § 8.

222 1 & 2 Vict. c. 110, §§ 14, 15; 3 & 4 Vict. c. 82, § 1.

223 Walls v. Jeffereys, 3 Mac.&G. 372, 42 E.R. 305 (1851); Annual Practice 1949, I, p. 886.

Concerning the subjection of land to the judgment, while it was provided by the Judgments Act of 1838 that the judgment should be a charge upon the land in respect of both legal and equitable interests, it is now the rule, after a considerable volume of interim legislation,[224] that the judgment itself is not a charge upon the land, nor is the writ of *elegit,* unless the writ is registered as provided by statute. When the writ is thus registered, the judgment becomes an equitable charge upon the land of the debtor, whether his estate is legal or equitable, binding it as against subsequent purchasers and incumbrancers.[225] Under the *elegit* the creditor is normally given the right to possession of the land, after inquisition, substantially as at common law he was given possession of a moiety, and becomes entitled to hold the land as tenant by *elegit,* receiving the rents and profits until his judgment is satisfied. But in 1864 [226] occurred the important change in the law by which the *elegit* creditor was authorized to apply for a sale of the land. Application for sale is now made by way of originating summons in the Chancery Division.[227] The sale may be had forthwith once the creditor is in possession, but if possession has not been delivered to him under the writ,[228] then the sale must await the expiration of one year from the date of the judgment.[229]

As regards equitable aid in the setting aside of fraudulent conveyances, there no longer survives the old rule limiting such relief to cases where the property is of a character subject to legal execution. It has been rendered obsolete by the march of legislation in extending the creditor's right of execution-realization to property of his debtor not before available to him.[230]

[224] For an account of this, see Williams, Real Property (23d ed. 1920) 291 *et seq.*

[225] Law of Property Act 1925, 15 Geo. V, c. 20, § 195(1)(3).

[226] Judgments Act 1864, 27 & 28 Vict. c. 112, §§ 4-6.

[227] O. LV, r. 9B.

[228] "If the interest of the debtor is equitable and therefore not extendible under the writ it can be reached by process of equitable execution." Annual Practice 1949, I, p. 835. See *infra,* p. 466.

[229] Law of Property Act 1925, § 195 (3)(ii); Annual Practice 1949, I, pp. 1217-1218.

[230] Probably the operation of no statute has been affected so much by subsequent legislation as that of 13 Eliz. c. 5. Property which was not originally within the reach of creditors has from time to time been brought within their reach, and whenever that has been

Moreover, the necessity for a judgment or lien as a condition of relief against fraudulent alienation no longer obtains, it being held by the Court of Chancery in 1869 that "it is not necessary that a creditor should have a lien or charge on the property" to maintain an action of this kind,[231] although in its absence realization for the creditor by sale or otherwise will depend upon further proceedings. The basis of the law of fraudulent conveyances is now furnished by a provision of the Law of Property Act 1925, which declares as the general rule that "every conveyance of property, made whether before or after the commencement of this Act, with intent to defraud creditors, shall be voidable, at the instance of any person thereby prejudiced." [232] Apart from the question of fraudulent alienation, equitable aid is extended to the creditor under traditional principles where impediment exists to legal execution.[233] But when circumstances require, resort to legal process may be altogether dispensed with. As a precondition of equitable aid this has ceased to be imperative since the Judicature Act of 1873, and the court now has "power to grant an equitable remedy without the necessity of first exhausting the legal remedy against the legal property." [234]

Corresponding to our garnishment after judgment is the measure in relation to debts owed the judgment debtor, introduced by the Common Law Procedure Act of 1854.[235] It is officially styled "attachment of debts," but the debtor of the judgment debtor is spoken of as the "garnishee" and the initial order is a "garnishee order." Unlike the garnishment of the American statutes, it is concerned, as the name implies, solely with pecuniary indebtedness owed the judgment debtor and does not seek to reach other property of his in the hands

done, the Courts have been prompt to recognize that such other property can be disposed of fraudulently as against creditors, that is, to delay, hinder, or defraud them in pursuing newly conferred rights of proceeding." Kekewich, J., in Ideal Bedding Co. Ltd. v. Holland, [1907] 2 Ch.D. 157, 166. See also Stokoe v. Cowan, 28 Beav. 637, 54 E.R. 775 (1861); Edmunds v. Edmunds, [1904] P. 362, 375.

231 Reese River Silver Mining Co. v. Atwell, 20 L.T. (N.S.) 163, 164, L.R. 7 Eq. 347, *per* Lord Romilly, M.R. (1869).

232 15 Geo V, c. 20, § 172.

233 See Cheshire, Modern Law of Real Property (5th ed. 1944) p. 745.

234 Stirling, L. J., in Hills v. Webber, 17 T.L.R. 513, 514, C.A. (1901); *Re* Whiteley, 56 L.T. (N.S.) 846 (1887).

235 17 & 18 Vict. c. 125, §§ 61-67.

of the garnishee. It does not require previous issue of execution on the judgment; the fact of the unsatisfied judgment is sufficient. It proceeds by an order, made on *ex parte* application supported by affidavit, attaching all indebtedness of the garnishee to the judgment debtor and calling upon the garnishee to show cause why he should not pay such indebtedness to the judgment creditor. After service of the order upon the garnishee and the judgment debtor or his solicitor, if the garnishee fails to appear or does not dispute his liability, the court may order execution to issue, to be levied against the amount due from the garnishee. If appearing, the garnishee disputes his liability, there is a hearing at which the disputed liability is determined. Any other person suggested by the garnishee as claiming the debt or an interest therein may be ordered to appear and present his claim, and the resulting issue between such other person and the judgment creditor is similarly determined. In the usual case of the garnishee being found liable to the judgment creditor, the order *nisi* becomes absolute and the garnishee is ordered to pay to the judgment creditor the indebtedness in question or so much of it as is sufficient to satisfy the amount due on his judgment.[236]

The field which in the majority of the American jurisdictions finds itself assigned to statutory supplementary proceedings is in England occupied by two distinct measures, both steps in the judgment action. One is the examination for discovery in aid of execution, ordered on application of the judgment creditor, in the course of which the judgment debtor or any third person may be examined as to the debtor's means of satisfying the judgment.[237] This proceeding is confined to the discovery of assets. The other is the appointment of a receiver by way, as it is said, of equitable execution.[238] This, in a limited way, represents invocation of the traditional equitable aid in enforcement of the judgment, and is accordingly in order where the judgment debtor has assets which cannot be reached by the ordinary means of execution.[239] As in most of

[236] O. XLV, rr. 1-9; Annual Practice 1949, I, p. 858 *et seq.*, II, p. 2693 *et seq.*

[237] O. XLII, rr. 32-35.

[238] O. L, rr. 15A-22.

[239] See Annual Practice 1949, I, pp. 961, 964-965.

the American systems, the proceeding thus set on foot does not contemplate the determination of substantial controversies as to title to property; these, it would appear, must be left to an independent action brought by the judgment creditor. Thus a considerable area is left for resort to equitable aid by actions in the nature of the old judgment creditor's bill or bill in aid of execution, particularly where it is sought to set aside a conveyance or transfer in fraud of creditors.

The writ of sequestration, continuing to be employed occasionally in the exercise of the contempt power, may issue against the debtor's real and personal estate, where there has been clear disobedience of a judgment or order to pay money into court or to pay money to a given person within a limited time.[240] So, too, in the case of a corporation wilfully disobeying any judgment or order, the writ is available against the corporate property or the property of its directors or officers; here, however, it is issued only by leave of court.[241] The procedure under the writ in either case is substantially that of the former Court of Chancery.[242]

Execution against the person retains but a slender foothold. Under the storm of censure which it had come to encounter, the institution of imprisonment for debt was finally abolished by the Debtors Act of 1869,[243] except as to debts, "the incurring of which," in the words of Lord Chancellor Hatherley, "was in some degree worthy of being visited with punishment." [244] The exceptions thus made by the statute include the case of a debtor who defaults in the payment of any debt or installment of any debt—the act giving power to direct payment in installments—"due from him in pursuance of any order or judgment" of a competent court. In this case the condition of imprisonment, which cannot be longer than six weeks, is that it be "proved to the satisfaction of the court that the person making default either has or has had since the date

240 O. XLII, r. 4; O. XLIII, r. 6, the latter speaking of failure to pay money into court "or to do any other act in a limited time."

241 O. XLII, r. 31.

242 See Odgers, Principles of Pleading and Practice (13th ed. 1946) 296-297.

243 32 & 33 Vict. c. 62.

244 In Middleton v. Chichester, L.R. 6 Ch.App. 152, 156 (1871). See also Marris v. Ingram, 13 Ch.D. 338, 343 (1879).

of the order or judgment the means to pay the sum in respect of which he has made default, and has refused or neglected, or refuses or neglects, to pay the same." [245] By the Debtors Act of 1878 the court was given certain discretionary power in the administration of this provision.[246] Steps are taken to enforce the provision by means of a so-called "judgment summons," [247] issuable either in the High Court (under authority of a judge exercising jurisdiction in bankruptcy), or more usually [248] in the County Court which has jurisdiction thus to proceed in respect of judgments and orders of the High Court, as well as of its own. In the High Court the amount due on the judgment or order is not to be less than £50, except in divorce actions or under special circumstances; and the summons cannot issue without a judge's order.[249] Personal service of the summons must be had upon the judgment debtor, save that in the High Court substituted service may sometimes be deemed sufficient.[250] If the court finds that the situation is one for the application of the provision—and in the case of installments this can only be for such as are in arrear—it makes an order of committal under which the imprisonment is effected.[251] Payment of arrears of alimony may be thus enforced.[252] Except in this case, for such arrears are not a debt provable in bankruptcy, the court, under a provision of the Bankruptcy Act of 1914,[253] if convinced that the judgment debtor is actually insolvent, may, instead of committing him, make a receiving order against him, with the consent of the creditor. This has the effect of an act of bankruptcy and affords "a speedy means of putting the defaulter through the bankruptcy process." [254] Again, in the County Court, where the judgment debtor is able to show that his total indebtedness amounts to no more than £50, the court, in lieu of an order of committal, may

[245] 32 & 33 Vict. c. 62, § 5. On this exception generally, see Bundy v. Motor Cab Owner Drivers' Association, 143 L.T. 334, 336 (1930).

[246] 41 & 42 Vict. c. 54, § 1.

[247] Annual Practice 1949, I, p. 786; County Court Rules 1936, O. XXV, rr. 33-66.

[248] Odgers, *op. cit.* 298.

[249] Annual Practice 1949, I, p. 786; Ringwood, Principles of Bankruptcy (16th ed. 1930) 278.

[250] Ringwood, *op. cit.* 280.

[251] 2 Halsbury, Laws of England (2d ed. 1931) 448, 455.

[252] Linton v. Linton, 15 Q.B.D. 239, C.A. (1885).

[253] 4 & 5 Geo. V, c. 59, § 107; Ringwood, *op. cit.* 35.

[254] Ringwood, *op. cit.* 276.

make what is known as an administration order.[255] The latter brings about a simple proceeding "analogous to bankruptcy in that it is a means of distributing the debtor's assets among his creditors, and of freeing him from liabilities which he is unable to meet. Beyond that it does not go." [256]

The other exceptions to the abolition of imprisonment for debt existing under the Debtors Act of 1869 are of limited application and rest upon the nature of the liability giving rise to the judgment or order. Among them are the case of default on the part of a trustee or other fiduciary ordered to pay money in his possession or under his control, and certain cases of non-compliance on the part of solicitors with orders to pay money. For cases of the kind the term of imprisonment may extend to one year. In the relative procedure the commitment is here effected under a writ of attachment [257] of the person.

The underlying theory of all the exceptions admitted by the act is that they involve a disobedience of a judgment or order amounting to a contempt. Exercise of the contempt power against the person in respect of the non-payment of money may occur outside the statute, in respect of a judgment or order against a corporation. For here the Rules provide that such a judgment or order, wilfully disobeyed, may by leave of court be enforced by sequestration, as above mentioned, "or by attachment against the directors or other officers" of the corporation.[258]

[255] Bankruptcy Act 1883, § 122; County Courts Act 1934, 24 & 25 Geo. V, c. 53, §§ 149-157.

[256] Ringwood, *loc. cit.*

[257] See Annual Practice 1949, I, pp. 846-847.

[258] O. XLII, r. 31.

CHAPTER XXV

EXECUTION OF OTHER THAN MONEY JUDGMENTS

§ 1. IN PROPERTY ACTIONS OF COMMON-LAW DERIVATION

(*a*) In the old real actions, whether droitural or possessory, judgment for the demandant was enforced by the writ of *habeas facias seizinam,* so called "from the command to the sheriff, in the writ, that he cause the demandant to have seizin of the tenements recovered." [1] Ejectment, however, which, as we know, came to supplant the real actions almost altogether for the trial of title to land in the common-law courts, was in theory an action to recover possession, and accordingly the means of enforcing its judgment was the writ of *habere facias possessionem,* in later days commonly spoken of as a writ of possession,[2] commanding the sheriff to put the plaintiff in possession.

None of the real actions found any but transitory footing in America, apart from the practice in New England. There place was given at an early day to simplified versions of certain of these actions, and today in Massachusetts,[3] Maine [4] and New Hampshire [5] the old writ of entry, as remodelled by statute or practice is still a recognized remedy for the recovery of land.[6] Elsewhere the American jurisdictions have subscribed in general to the pattern set by common-law ejectment, with many variations in detail. For the States which adhere to the divided administration of law and equity the remedy is usually a statutory form of common-law ejectment, long since stripped

[1] Stearns, A Summary of the Law and Practice of Real Actions (2d ed. 1831) *245-246.

[2] 2 Tidd, Practice (9th ed. 1828) 1244.

[3] Mass. Ann. Laws 1933, c. 237.

[4] Me. Rev. Stat. 1944, c. 158, §§ 1-47.

[5] See Salisbury Beach Associates v. Littlefield, 89 N.H. 447, 200 Atl. 777 (1938).

[6] See as to these actions generally Hepburn, Writ of Entry, 20 C.J. 1276; Finley, Real Actions, 52 C.J. 1160.

of the fictitious features by which that action was characterized.[7] In one or two jurisdictions, however, the fictitious proceeding, though seldom used, appears not to have been wholly ousted by the statutory one.[8] Under the code procedure, the remedy, though commonly referred to as ejectment, is an action formally styled as one for the recovery of real property or for the recovery of possession of real property. Further to be mentioned is the action of trespass to try title. This had its rise in South Carolina in 1791, as furnishing a simplified equivalent of ejectment, and was later employed in Alabama, but now is confined to Texas. It presents a marked similarity to statutory ejectment.[9] On the whole it is substantially true, as observed in the admirable work of Sedgwick and Wait, that the essential principles governing the various remedies employed in the United States for the recovery of land "constitute practically one general method of procedure disguised under a variety of names." [10] And in this procedure, generally, the judgment of recovery is enforced by a writ of possession (in the Massachusetts action of writ of entry represented traditionally by a writ of seizin [11]) under which the sheriff installs the plaintiff in possession, doing all acts necessary for the purpose, including the removal of persons holding without authority of law.[12]

In England, after the more or less nominal survival of the real actions had, with slight exception, been swept away by a statute of 1833,[13] the fictions attending common-law ejectment definitely came to an end under a provision of the Com-

7 This reform commenced in the first half of the 1800s. In Illinois, for example, it dates from 1845. Rev. Stat. 1845, c. 36, § 6.

8 See Ga. Code 1933, § 33-111; Georgia Iron & Coal Co. v. Allison, 116 Ga. 444, 42 S.E. 794 (1902); Ala. Rules of Practice in the Circuit and Inferior Courts of Common Law Jurisdiction (in Ala. Code Ann. (1940) Appendix to Tit. 7) Rule 24; Ala. State Land Co. v. Matthews, 168 Ala. 200, 207, 53 So. 174 (1910).

9 Sedgwick and Wait, Trial of Title to Land (2d ed. 1886) § 81 *et seq.;* McTarnaghan, Trespass To Try Title, 63 C.J. 1150; Martin, Civil Procedure at Common Law (1905) §§ 172-173.

10 Sedgwick and Wait, *op. cit.* § 92. For the most part the plaintiff, to recover in actions of the kind, must be equipped with a legal title. But in certain of the code States as well as in Pennsylvania, (see 18 Am. Jur. pp. 23-24), and under the trespass to try title of Texas, he may recover on the strength of a full equitable title.

11 See Mass. Ann. Laws 1933, c. 237, §§ 29, 37, c. 214, § 41.

12 See Sedgwick and Wait, *op. cit.* § 550 *et seq.*

13 3 & 4 Will. IV, c. 27, § 36.

mon Law Procedure Act of 1852.[14] Under the present Rules the corresponding remedy is the action to recover land or its possession to which the term "ejectment" still informally clings. The order or judgment of recovery is "enforced by writ of possession in manner immediately before the 1st November, 1875, used in actions of ejectment in the superior courts of common law." [15]

(*b*) For the recovery of specific personal property the common law, in practical usage, provided the two actions of detinue and replevin. Detinue lay for unlawful detention of the goods. Originally restricted to wrongful detention after lawful acquisition, it latterly was extended, as the effect of judicial decision, to detentions arising from tort.[16] But its judgment in favor of the plaintiff did not provide for an outright recovery of the chattels. It directed that he recover them, but that "if he cannot again have the said goods," then that he recover a named sum of money, being their value as fixed by verdict of the jury, together with damages for their detention. Accordingly, "the execution authorized the sheriff to distrain the goods and chattels of the defendant if he did not return the goods or pay a certain sum of money." [17] Replevin, on the other hand, concerned itself only with such detention as was consequent upon an unlawful taking, and appears to have been employed scarcely at all, in cases other than those of illegal distress, until the early 1800s.[18] Since a judgment for the plaintiff simply confirmed him in possession of the goods delivered to him at the outset of the action, the only execution he required was one for damages and costs. But where judgment had gone against the plaintiff, the defendant was normally entitled to a return of the goods. This was enforced by the writ of *retorno habendo*, commanding the sheriff to cause the goods to be delivered back to the defendant, it being added, where the judgment was on verdict or demurrer: "to hold to him irreplevisable forever." [19]

[14] 15 & 16 Vict. c. 76, § 158 *et seq.*

[15] O. XLVII, r. 1.

[16] Gledstane v. Hewitt, 1 Cr.&J. 565, 148 E.R. 1548 (1831).

[17] *In re* Scarth, L.R. 10 Ch.App. 234, 235 (1874).

[18] See 3 Street, Foundations of Legal Liability (1906) 217-218.

[19] 2 Tidd, Practice (9th ed. 1828) 1038.

While in America the common-law action of detinue continues to be at least theoretically available in some quarters and in some others has lent its name to a statutory action of like object, the emphasis is mainly on the remedy of replevin. The contrary is true in the existing English procedure. Here replevin has become all but negligible, and the emphasis is laid upon the reformed action of detinue. In this the judgment is still in the alternative,[20] but it is no longer the case that the value need be assessed before judgment.[21] The practice as to execution [22] is based upon a provision of the Common Law Procedure Act of 1854,[23] which changed the common-law rule by vesting power in the court to "order that execution shall issue for the return of the chattel detained, without giving the defendant the option of retaining such chattel upon paying the value assessed." Accordingly, the successful plaintiff, if he wishes to exclude the defendant from such retention, may, without assessment of value, obtain by leave of court the issuance on the judgment of a writ of delivery, requiring that the sheriff cause the chattel to be returned to him.[24] If necessary the return may be coerced by distraint upon the defendant's land and goods,[25] or by resort to the contempt process.[26] On the other hand, the plaintiff, armed with his judgment, may have the value assessed by appropriate procedure,[27] in which case he is entitled either (i) by leave, to a writ of delivery commanding the sheriff to cause the return of the chattel, or, if it cannot be found, to make the amount of the assessed value and damages out of the defendant's goods and chattels, or (ii) without leave, to an ordinary writ of *fieri facias* for the assessed value and damages.[28]

As for replevin, further consideration of its execution process, both at common law and in its later development, will more aptly find place in connection with other features of the action to be noticed in our next chapter.

20 Annual Practice 1949, I, p. 170.

21 Hymas v. Ogden [1905] 1 K.B. 246, C.A.

22 O. XLVIII, r. 1.

23 17 & 18 Vict. c. 125, § 78.

24 Annual Practice 1949, *loc. cit.*

25 O. XLVIII, r. 1.

26 Hymas v. Ogden, *supra.*

27 *I.e.,* by writ of inquiry directed to the sheriff or by proceedings before a master or official referee. Annual Practice 1949, I, pp. 170, 671-672.

28 Annual Practice 1949, I, p. 170.

§ 2. In Equitable Actions for Non-Pecuniary Relief

"A decree is not like a judgment in the King's Bench or Common Bench, for such a judgment binds the right of the party; but a decree does not bind the right, but only the person to obedience, so that if the party will not obey, then the Chancellor may commit him to prison until he will obey, and this is all that the Chancellor can do." So spoke Serjeant Knightly in 1535,[29] expressing thus pithily the original principle of execution in chancery, namely that the sole means of enforcing its decrees was by the use of the contempt power against the person. Although something of this has already been seen, especially in connection with money decrees,[30] it stands forth with particular vividness in the class of cases now coming under discussion. But whatever the character of the decree, whether it ordered the payment of money or the doing or not doing of specific acts within the ever-widening circle of equity adjudication, the principle was always the same,—the decree was purely an exercise of jurisdiction *in personam,* enforceable by imprisonment as a means of coercing obedience.

For the execution of decrees in relation to specific acts the enginery of contempt was brought to bear by the same succession of steps as in the case of a money decree. The succession was initiated by the writ *de executione judicii,* directed to the defendant. Then, in case of continued disobedience, came the process of attachment under which the defendant was taken into custody. From the 1600s on [31] there was the further step of sequestration, if the disobedience persisted. And in addition, for the manner of decree now in question, the writ of injunction could be brought into play where the exigencies of enforcement so dictated. While it was maintained by the chancery that the writ of sequestration was only a personal process to enforce a personal duty,[32] the fact that the con-

[29] In Y.B., Trin. 27 Hen. VIII, f. 15, pl. 6, quoted in Ames, Cases in Equity (1904, 1923) 2, note 1.

[30] *Supra,* Chapter XXIV, § 1.

[31] Sequestration is provided for in Lord Chancellor's Ordinances of 1618-19, §§ 27, 29, 30. Strenuous attack upon the institution came to a head in Hide v. Pettit, 1 Ch.Cas. 91, 22 E.R. 709 (1667), where it was held by the chancery that sequestrations "were a necessary process of this court."

[32] Bligh v. Earl of Darnley, 2 P. Wms. 619, 24 E.R. 886 (1731); Wharam v. Broughton, 1 Ves.Sr. 180, 27 E.R. 969 (1748).

temnor's estate was seized as a species of pledge evidences that in the use of this process, however it might lack the properties of common-law execution, chancery was departing from the strait confines of an acting *in personam.*

But another departure of a similar nature appears at a somewhat earlier date. This occurred in cases where it had fallen to the chancery to adjudicate the title to land. The court manifestly could not, as could a court of law, through the operation of its judgment, "bind the right" and vest the legal title in the successful litigant; in this regard what it could do, and habitually did, was to command the other party to execute a proper conveyance to the victor. But now it began, in the time of Elizabeth,[83] to put the latter in possession of the land by appropriate process. "Where the decree is for land," says Bohun, writing in the early 1700s, "and the party remains obstinate after his imprisonment, the court usually grants an injunction for the possession thereof to be yielded up to the party, for whom the decree was; and if this be disobeyed after it is served, and oath made thereof, the court doth in that case grant a commission to some justices of peace to put the other party in possession. And if need be, a writ of assistance may be had, which is directed to the sheriff, and commands him to be aiding and assisting (to the justices) in putting the party in possession." [84] Such was the origin of the well-known writ of assistance. Soon the commission to justices was to be altogether supplanted by that writ, the issue of which, however, was reached by the sequential progress characterizing the contempt process in general. As it appears for the present case in the late 1700s, the sequence was (*a*) a writ of execution of the decree or order for possession; (*b*) a writ of attachment for disobedience of the decree or order which, nevertheless, by this time is *pro forma* only and is not executed; (*c*) a writ of injunction to deliver possession; and (*d*) possession still being refused, the writ of assistance itself.[85]

83 Huston, Enforcement of Decrees in Equity (1915) 80. See Bacon's Ordinances of 1618-19, § 9, providing for a commission to place the party in possession.

84 *Cursus Cancellariae* (2d ed. 1723) 368.

85 Dove v. Dove, Dick. 617, 21 E.R. 411 (1783).

By virtue of the writ the sheriff was to "cause the aforesaid plaintiff to have without delay full, pacific and quiet possession of all and singular the premises aforesaid."[36] Despite the possession thus acquired, however, the plaintiff was still without legal title, and could not obtain it unless and until his opponent should obey the command of the decree, if necessary by compulsion of personal imprisonment.

Thus the contempt power exercised against the person, as reinforced by the limited means of direct interference with property represented by the writ of sequestration and the writ of assistance, constituted the full measure of decree-enforcement in the English chancery before the coming of nineteenth century reform, and accordingly the basis of execution inherited by the chancery jurisdictions in America. But in no field of procedure does the modern development in both countries exhibit any more pronounced changes than have here supervened. That development has succeeded in subtracting from the domain of contempt-enforcement by far the greater proportion of the area which it formerly embraced. For money decrees, as has been noted, there has been everywhere substituted, with but few exceptions, the process of execution appropriate to common-law judgments. And in respect of decrees, also, for other than pecuniary relief legislation has largely rendered unnecessary enforcement by the contempt process in most of the cases where it once was indispensable. This has come about by expressly lodging in the equity courts a certain measure of jurisdiction *in rem,* and by giving them the power to do by the decree itself, or through its operation, those things essential to its fulfillment, which in an older day it could accomplish only through the agency of the party against whom the decree ran, acting under the lash of coercion. Legislation of this sort began in America. For, "even before the opening of the nineteenth century Maryland (1785) and New Jersey (1799), and in its first decade Tennessee (1801), Connecticut (1801), and Ohio (1810) enacted statutes to give to their courts administering equity the right to transfer titles directly by the decree they rendered.

[36] Bohun, *op. cit.* 373-374.

The earliest statute of all seems to be that of Maryland in 1785."[37] Moreover, Kentucky in 1808 and Virginia in 1818 accomplished the same result by providing for the execution of the commanded conveyance by an officer of the court in case of the party's failure to obey.[38] Other States followed in the same legislative path, sometimes employing the method of direct vesting by the judgment, sometimes that of conveyance by a master, commissioner or other officer of the court, or other appointed person, sometimes permitting a choice of the two methods, until at the present day there are but few American jurisdictions that fail to provide for the exercise of this manner of power.[39] Most of the statutes in question apply to the case of personal as well as real property.[40]

The English advance in this direction did not come until the Contempt of Court Act of 1830. This evinced considerably more reluctance to relinquish the traditional contempt process than had done its American predecessors. For, while giving the court power to authorize a master to execute the ordered conveyance, in lieu of the disobedient respondent, and providing that the conveyance thus made should in all respects have the same force and validity as if made by the respondent himself, it contemplated his imprisonment under the contempt process, and postponed the exercise of the new power until a second refusal to obey, occurring after the expiration of two calendar months from the time of the respondent's committal.[41] But this use of the contempt process as a necessary preliminary was not to endure. After the Judicature Acts of 1873 and 1875, the Rules of 1883, adapting a provision which had appeared in the Common Law Procedure Act of 1854[42] in its regulation of mandamus, provided that in case of disobedience of a mandatory order, injunction, or judgment for specific performance, "the court or a judge, besides or instead of proceedings against the disobedient party for contempt, may

[37] Huston, *op. cit.* 16-17.

[38] *Ibid.* 19.

[39] *Ibid.* 19-21. For the particulars see in addition to Professor Huston's book, and as supplementing its account, the timely article of Leighton, Development of the In Rem Powers of Courts of Equity (1947) 5 Nat.BarJourn. 1, 30 note 111.

[40] See the statutes in Huston, *op. cit.*, Appendix, 157 *et seq.*

[41] 11 Geo. IV & 1 Will. IV, c. 36, § 15(15).

[42] 17 & 18 Vict. c. 125, § 74.

direct that the act required to be done may be done so far as practicable by the party by whom the judgment or order has been obtained, or some other person appointed by the court or judge, at the cost of the disobedient party. . . ."[43] And in 1884, an amendment to the Judicature Acts complemented and widened the authority of the court in the present regard by declaring that "where any person neglects or refuses to comply with a judgment or order directing him to execute any conveyance, contract, or other document, or to indorse any negotiable instrument," the court might order, with or without terms, that the act in question be done by such person as it might nominate for the purpose, with the same effect as if done by the party originally directed,[44]—a provision now appearing with slight verbal change in the Consolidated Judicature Act of 1925.[45] But, with respect to conveyances of land, the preferred method of enforcement is that of the exercise of the court's vesting power.[46] This, given in specified cases of trust by legislation beginning in 1850 and culminating in the Trustee Act of 1925,[47] has since the act of 1893[48] become available in cases outside the realm of technical trusts by the provision (as it now appears in the 1925 act) that "generally where any judgment is given for the conveyance of any interest in land, either in cases arising out of the doctrine of election or otherwise, the court may declare that any of the parties to the action are trustees of the land or any interest therein or any part thereof within the meaning of this Act," and make a vesting order accordingly.[49]

Apart from their mode of arriving at vesting orders, the more recent English provisions have not been without influence in America. The Federal Equity Rules of 1912,[50] with relation to "a mandatory order, injunction or decree for specific performance" contained a provision following rather closely that of the English Rules. And now Rule 70 of the Federal Rules of 1938, apparently profiting also by the Judicature Acts amendment of 1884, embodies the same canon in its

[43] O. XLII, r. 30.
[44] 47 & 48 Vict. c. 61, § 14.
[45] 15 & 16 Geo. V, c. 49.
[46] Jones v. Davies, W.N. 1940, 174.
[47] 4 Halsbury, Statutes of England (2d ed. 1948) 647-648.
[48] 56 & 57 Vict. c. 53, § 31.
[49] 15 Geo. V, c. 19, § 48.
[50] Rule 8.

sweeping provision that "if a judgment directs a party to execute a conveyance of land or to deliver deeds or other documents or to perform any other specific act and the party fails to comply within the time specified, the court may direct the act to be done at the cost of the disobedient party by some other person appointed by the court and the act when done has like effect as if done by the party." But the same Rule, addressing itself to the matter of vesting, finds no necessity of resorting to the English convention of trusteeship and follows, instead, the precedent of forthright vesting set by State legislation. "If real or personal property," it declares, "is within the district, the court, in lieu of directing a conveyance thereof may enter a judgment divesting the title of any party and vesting it in others and such judgment has the effect of a conveyance executed in due form of law."

Neither in England nor America, whether expressly so recognized by the relative legislation or not, does the presence of provisions authorizing the court to vest titles directly or indirectly or to accomplish other acts in despite of the disobedient respondent deprive it of the power, in case of need, to make use of the contempt process in compelling obedience. Attachment of the person and sequestration of his estate thus continue to be available, although the latter is seldom resorted to on either side of the Atlantic. The English Rules provide for both as means of enforcing "a judgment for the recovery of any property other than land or money," and also that "a judgment requiring any person to do any act other than the payment of money, or to abstain from doing anything, may be enforced by writ of attachment or by committal." [51] And sequestration is again authorized under the terms of the Rule making it available where there has been disobedience of a judgment or order directing the party to pay money into court "or to do any other act in a limited time." [52] So also Federal Rule 70, with reference to the judgment for the performance of specific acts, provides that "on application of the party entitled to performance, the clerk shall issue a writ of attachment or sequestration against the property of the disobedient party to compel obedience to the judgment. The

[51] O. XLII, rr. 6, 7.

[52] O. XLIII, r. 6.

court may also in proper cases adjudge the party in contempt." [53] With respect to delivery of possession, a writ of possession is in England generally substituted for the writ of assistance, although in particular cases the latter may still be employed.[54] Federal Rule 70 in this connection provides that "when any order or judgment is for the delivery of possession, the party in whose favor it is entered is entitled to a writ of execution or assistance upon application to the clerk." Both in England and in America the writ of assistance has been exceptionally recognized as applicable to the case of chattels.[55] Under the English practice, as commonly enough in our own, there is no *writ* of injunction [56]—an innovation which goes back to the New York Code of 1848.[57] In a number of the States, the writ is retained. But, be it effectuated by writ or by service of order, the injunction may always be utilized, where occasion demands, as a further means of enforcing the judgment.

Federal Rule 70, *mutatis mutandis,* has been adopted by Arizona (1939), Colorado (1941), New Mexico (1942), Delaware (1947) and Utah (1949).[58] But, after all, its provisions reflect in the main what is permitted by the usual State practice. Whether resting on statute, rules of court, or the judicial acceptance of established equity usage, measures of the kind, in a greater or less degree, are in general open to the courts throughout the American jurisdictions. For otherwise would be falsified the principle that "where the court possesses jurisdiction to make a decree, it possesses the power to enforce its execution." [59]

[53] It appears from the Advisory Committee's note that "attachment" is here used as an alternative designation for "sequestration." See Federal Rules of Civil Procedure (West Publishing Co. 1947) p. 155. Moreover, the Rule seems to overlook the fact that by the traditional doctrine the party must be in contempt before sequestration is ordered.

[54] Annual Practice 1949, I, p. 897.

[55] Wyman v. Knight, 39 C.D. 165 (1888); Hooper v. Yonge, 69 Ala. 484, 486 (1881); Commonwealth *ex rel.* v. Lewis, 253 Pa. 175, 185, 98 Atl. 31 (1916).

[56] O. L, r. 11.

[57] § 191.

[58] Ariz. Code Ann. 1939, § 21-1614; Colo. Rules Civ. Proc. 1941, Rule 70, in Colo. Stat. Ann. 1935, Replacement Vol. 1, 1941, p. 258; N.M. Stat. Ann. 1941, § 19-101(70); Del. Rules of Court of Chancery 1947, Rule 70(a); Utah Rules Civ. Proc., Rule 70.

[59] *Per* Field, J., in Montgomery v. Tutt, 11 Cal. 190 (1858), quoted in Root v. Woolworth, 150 U.S. 401, 412, 14 S.Ct. 136 (1893).

Chapter XXVI

SECURITY MEASURES ANTICIPATORY OF EXECUTION

§ 1. Attachment on Mesne Process

While the term "attachment" has varied applications in the field of civil procedure, in respect of person and property, what we here must consider is that form of attachment—in America usually spoken of as "attachment" *simpliciter*—which consists in the judicial seizure of property of the defendant, or its reduction otherwise to judicial control, at the outset or during the pendency of an action on a money demand, so that it may be held to answer a judgment for the plaintiff if and when this is recovered. The story of this manner of proceeding is in the main that of an English institution which, by reason of its adventitious weaknesses, finally withered and died on English soil, but which, transplanted in America, shorn of those weaknesses and cultivated with care, has blossomed and flourished, to become an almost indispensable constituent of our procedural systems. That English institution found no place in the common law; it was the practice of foreign attachment existing by virtue of borough custom and especially under the local custom of London,[1] by which in its original form the creditor was exceptionally advantaged with respect to a "foreign" debtor—and this meant one dwelling outside the city—or with respect to a local debtor who had absconded. The suggestion advanced by certain of the older writers [2] that in London this practice represented a survival of the law in force

[1] The practice existed in various other trading centers, including Bristol, Exeter and Lancaster (Pulling, Customs of London (2d ed. 1849) 188), but it is to the custom of London that the American development has principally looked.

[2] Pulling, *op. cit. loc. cit.;* Locke, Law and Practice of Foreign Attachment (Am. ed., Law Library, Vol. 78, 1854) * 1; 2 Reeves, History of English Law (ed. Finlason, 1869) 29, note (a).

at the time of the Roman occupation of Britain may be dismissed as something out of the realm of legend. In all likelihood its origin is common with that of the corresponding institution on the Continent, which developed out of the medieval fusion of Germanic and Roman principles in the commercial cities of northern Italy.[3] The particular product of this fusion, disseminated through mercantile intercourse and established in the principal trading centers of the Continent, could hardly have failed to reach England, and especially London, by the same process, in view of the volume and variety of trade which medieval England carried on with merchants from beyond the seas.[4]

As certified by the Recorder of London in 1482, it was the custom that "if a plaint be affirmed in London before &c. against any person, and it be returned *nihil,* if the plaintiff will surmise that another person within the city is a debtor to the defendant in any sum, he shall have garnishment against him to warn him to come in and answer whether he be indebted in the manner alleged by the other; and if he comes and does not deny the debt, it shall be attached in his hands, and after four defaults recorded on the part of the defendant, such person shall find new surety to the plaintiff for the said debt; and judgment shall be that the plaintiff shall have judgment against him, and that he shall be quit against the other, after execution sued out by the plaintiff." [5] The proceeding extended to goods and chattels in the hands of the garnishee as well as to money debts.[6] It was available only in actions of debt, the most common form of which, as used in the English local courts, was the action of *concessit solvere.*[7] The defendant was entitled to appear and contest the plaintiff's claim, but only by putting in special bail or surrendering his person; in either case the attachment was at an end; [8] for in theory the pro-

[3] See Wach, *Der Arrestprozess* (1868) 33 *et seq.,* 87 *et seq.*

[4] See Bewes, Romance of the Law Merchant (1923) 94 *et seq.,* 132 *et seq.*

[5] Bowser v. Colins, Y.B. Mich. 22 Edw. IV, f. 30, pl. 11; Williams' note to Turbill's Case, 1 Wms. Saund. 67. See also the description in *Liber Albus* (transl. Riley, 1861) 183.

[6] Bohun, *Privilegia Londini* (3d ed. 1723) 261; *Liber Albus, loc. cit.*

[7] For *concessit solvere,* see 1 Wms. Saund. 68, note 2.

[8] *Ibid.* 67, note 1.

ceeding was directed towards enforcing the defendant's appearance. After the four recorded defaults by the defendant, a *scire facias* issued against the garnishee, and "if he acknowledges the debt due from him to the defendant, and the plaintiff swears his debt from the defendant, and finds pledges to return the money attached, if the defendant disprove the original debt within a year and a day, the plaintiff shall have judgment and execution for the money in the hands of A [the garnishee] and shall acknowledge satisfaction for them upon record," [9] to the extent, that is to say, of his claim as established. Should the garnishee contest his liability to the defendant, there was a jury trial of the issues, the verdict, if for the plaintiff, fixing the amount of the garnishee's indebtedness. In case of goods in the garnishee's hands, the value was fixed by appraisement, viz., by sworn appraisers if the garnishee failed to appear, otherwise by jury—originally, it would appear by a new jury after judgment of appraisement, later by the jury which tried the issues—and the value fixed was treated as money in the hands of the garnishee.[10] The proceeding was thus essentially a garnishment; no provision appears to have existed for direct seizure of goods except in the one case where these had been left in locked premises with no person in charge. Here the premises were put under seal, and a seizure followed in four days. In this case the proceeding was spoken of as a "sequestration." [11]

As has often been true in the history of courts of justice, the desire to expand jurisdiction brought about disfigurement of practice. By the 1800s the institution had ceased to respect its original compass. For, under date of 1849, we are told that "this remedy by attachment is not confined to citizens or even residents within the city; it is a common process, open to any person when his debtor has property within the jurisdiction of the court, whether the parties themselves reside or the debt

[9] Com. Dig. Attachment A (4th ed. 1800, Vol. I, p. 580).

[10] Description of the practice in special case stated by arbitrator in London Joint Stock Bank v. Mayor &c. of London, as appearing in report of the case in the Court of Appeal, L.R. 5 C.P.D. 494, 498 (1880). See also Bohun, *op. cit.* 257.

[11] Bohun, *op. cit.* 281-282; *Lex Londoniensis* (1680) 38-40; Pulling, *op. cit.* 192.

arose in London or not . . ." [12] Again, whatever may have been the original usage as to process against the defendant, it is clear, as the custom emerges in later days, that no notice at all was given him. In 1880 it appeared beyond question that this had been the practice for at least two centuries. To be sure, the record always recited the summons to the defendant, the four returns of *nihil* and the four defaults of the defendant, but these recitals had come to be pure fictions.[13] It is difficult to understand how the proceeding continued to move on this basis, especially in view of a decision of the Common Pleas in 1772, declaring that the failure to give notice to the defendant was "contrary to the first principles of justice." [14] But move on this basis it did until it experienced the impact of two decisions of the House of Lords, the one in 1867, the other in 1881. The first of these was *Mayor &c. of London* v. *Cox,* error to the Exchequer Chamber, in an action of prohibition, where, from the point of pleading decided, it followed that the city court "had no jurisdiction to proceed in foreign attachment in a case where no one of the parties is a citizen or a resident in the city, and where neither the debt sued for, nor the debt alleged to be due from the garnishees to the defendants arose within the city." [15] The

[12] Pulling, *loc. cit.*

[13] Statement of special case, and judgment of Baggallay, L. J., in London Joint Stock Bank v. Mayor &c. (Court of Appeal) *supra,* 499-500, 502-503.

In the report of the Municipal Corporation Commissioners, appointed in 1834, dealing with the institutions of the City of London, after reference to the circumstance that the defendant was solemnly called at four several courts, prior to the summoning of the garnishee, it is said: "In ancient times, therefore, when the custom was strictly adhered to, every possible precaution was taken to give notice to the defendant of the intended proceeding against his property; and unless he was actually absent from the country (in which case he might, on his return within a year and a day, resort for his protection to the securities given by the plaintiff for restoring the goods) it was scarcely possible he should not be informed of it. But the present practice is to give no notice of any kind to the defendant." Quoted by Locke, *op. cit.* Introd. p. xxiv.

Indeed, in Tamm v. Williams, 3 Doug. 281, 283, 99 E.R. 655 (1783), there appears the following observation of Lord Mansfield: "The very essence of the custom is, that the defendant shall not have notice; because it is a proceeding against an absent man, who cannot be found, and has nothing to be summoned by. It is a proceeding in rem, like confiscations in the Exchequer."

[14] Fisher v. Lane, 3 Wils. 297, 302-304, 2 Wm. Black. 834, 96 E.R. 492 (1772).

[15] L.R. 2 H.L. 239, 293 (1867).

second was *London Joint Stock Bank* v. *Mayor &c. of London,* an appeal from the Court of Appeal, in another action of prohibition; here the House of Lords held that garnishment, under the custom, did not lie against a corporation, and also approved the view of the Court of Appeal that, as the record allegations of summons and default had been admitted to be pure fictions, the custom had been violated and the proceeding was invalid.[16] These cases, however unnecessarily, were fatal to the practice. As their result, its use was tacitly discontinued, and the entire institution thus came to an end.[17] Very little in the way of legislation would have been required to reform it and convert it into a useful mode of proceeding consonant with the dictates of due process of law, but no such legislation ever came about. And with the disappearance of the local proceeding, England today is wholly without anything in the nature of that attachment of property on mesne process so familiar to us in America.[18]

In America the principle of foreign attachment made particular appeal to the colonies. Their dependence in large degree upon trade overseas and with each other, and the comparative ease with which a local debtor might translate himself into another English-speaking jurisdiction to escape his creditors, cogently demanded such a proceeding. "The attachment process for reaching the property of absconding and absent and nonresident debtors," says Chancellor Kent, "was a favorite measure of justice with the colonial legislatures; but in respect to nonresident debtors, was strongly opposed by the governor and council in some of the states, as being different from the mode of recovery allowed in like cases in England. Royal instructions were communicated to the colonial governors, to refuse assent to such attachment laws . . ."[19] Despite this opposition, the process succeeded in intrenching itself from

16 L.R. 6 App.Cas. 393, 398, 413 (1881).

17 22 Halsbury, Laws of England (2d ed. 1936) 266, note i. And see Anon., Foreign Attachment (1880) 15 Law Jour. 192.

18 The only attachment of property under the present English system is the attachment of debts after judgment, introduced by the Common Law Procedure Act of 1854; see *supra,* Chapter XXIV, § 9.

19 2 Kent, Commentaries on American Law (ed. Holmes, 1873) * 403, note (*a*).

an early day, both as to non-residents and absconders, so that "attachments became part of the general pattern of business practices sanctioned by the courts in favoring creditors, particularly local creditors, and the mercantile class generally." [20] Beginning in the late 1600s, statutes thus directed against absent or non-resident debtors, and looking to attachment on mesne process of their property in the hands of third persons made their appearance throughout the colonies.[21] Instances of the kind are those of Maryland in 1683,[22] South Carolina in 1693,[23] Pennsylvania in 1699,[24] Massachusetts in 1708,[25] and New Hampshire in 1718.[26] But in the New England jurisdictions this variety of attachment, with process against third persons, assuming usually the name of "trustee process" became adjunct of the so-called "common attachment," a system, that is to say, already in existence and available as a matter of course against defendants generally in common-law actions for the recovery of money, whereby tangible property in their own possession could be provisionally taken at or after the commencement of the action as security for the plaintiff's claim.

As regards this common attachment, Massachusetts, as early as 1644, had provided that "it shall be the liberty of every plaintiff to take out either summons or attachments against any defendant." [27] At the outset the attachment here in question was no more than that of the common law,[28] a

[20] Morris, Introd. to Select Cases of the Mayor's Court of New York City, 1674-1780 (1915) 19-20.

[21] Of particular value in this connection is the informative article of Mussman and Riesenfeld, Garnishment and Bankruptcy (1942) 27 Minn. L.Rev. 1, 17 *et seq.*

[22] Proceedings and Acts of Md. Gen. Assembly, Oct. 1678–Nov. 1683, 7 Md. Archives (1889) 606; Proceedings of Md. Court of Appeal, 1695-1729 (1933) Introd. p. xlvi.

[23] Act No. 100 of May 20, 1693, 2 S.C.Stat. (1837) p. 78. Its text does not appear, the editor stating that the original act is "not now to be found." Apparently its essentials passed into the repealing act of 1712, Act No. 324, 2 S.C.Stat. p. 588.

[24] Law of May 20, 1699, Charter & Laws of Province of Pa. (1873) 289.

[25] Acts of 1708-09, c. 7, 1 Acts & Resolves of the Province of Massachusetts Bay (1869) 629.

[26] Act of May 14, 1718, 2 Laws of N.H. (1913) 315.

[27] Colonial Laws of Mass.—from ed. of 1672—(1887) 7; Charter & General Laws of the Colony and Province of Massachusetts Bay (1814) 49.

[28] *Per* Parsons, C. J., in Bond v. Ward, 7 Mass. 123, 128 (1810).

means of coercing the defendant's appearance, without furnishing any security for the plaintiff's demand.[29] But in 1659

[29] Apart from the cases in which the action was initiated by *capias*, attachment at common law was the first process in actions of trespass; in most other personal actions it followed a failure to heed the summons. If the attachment was not effective in compelling appearance of the defendant, it was succeeded by distress infinite, which "is a process to distrein him continually after, till he do appear, by certain of his goods, and profit of his lands, or as we use to say, issues, which he loseth if he appear not." Finch, Law (1678) 352. There was no forthright seizure of the defendant's property; at first there was usually no more than a nibble at it. It was said in 1697, *per* Powell, J., in the King's Bench, that "a single thing only can be attached," the Chief Justice remarking in the same case that "it ought to be a reasonable distress to compel the defendant to appear." Hargrave v. Ward, 2 Lutw. 1452, 1457, 125 E.R. 801. And a century later, Lord Ellenborough, referring with approval to the statement in 4 Comyn's Digest, tit. Process, Distringas, D 7, that "the issues returned upon a distringas ought to be reasonable; in a personal action so much as may be the charge of the process," observed that "it was so much of course that the distringas should at first only issue for 40s, that no more ought to be levied by the sheriff in the first instance." Bloxam v. Surtees, 4 East 162, 163, 102 E.R. 702 (1803). For succeeding distresses the amount of the issues was increased in the discretion of the court (1 Tidd, Practice, 9th ed. 1828, 110-111, 155) and the process of distress might thus go on, the defendant, in the words of Blackstone, "if he had any substance, being gradually stripped of it all by repeated distresses." 3 Comm. *281. Originally and in theory the issues were forfeited to the Crown (Dalton, Office and Authority of Sheriffs, ed. of 1682, 156), but latterly it became the practice to utilize them for the payment of costs occasioned to the plaintiff. Whether or not this practice antedates the statute of 1769 (10 Geo. III, c. 50, §§ 3, 4) is uncertain, but by that act it was declared that the court "may order the issues levied from time to time to be sold, and the money arising therefrom to be applied to pay such costs to the plaintiff as the said court shall think just, under all the circumstances, to order; and the surplus to be retained until the defendant shall have appeared, or other purpose of the writ be answered," and also "when the purpose of the writ is answered that then the issues shall be returned; or if sold, what shall remain of the money arising by such sale shall be repaid to the party distrained upon." One is struck with the pronounced tenderness thus displayed toward the recalcitrant defendant, but the remarkable thing about this whole development is that it never once entertained the thought that the property seized should be turned to account as a means toward satisfying a judgment in favor of the plaintiff.

That this thought should have come to the Massachusetts colonists and been definitely acted upon in a day even before the English law had authoritatively treated the issues as answerable for the plaintiff's costs may be accounted for by considerations of common sense and practical utility. But its explanation may also lie elsewhere. It is undoubtedly true that the English law with which the New England colonists had any familiarity was not the law administered by the superior courts in London, but that applied by the local courts of their former places of residence: see Goebel, King's Law and Local Custom in Seventeenth Century New England (1931) 31 Col. L.Rev. 416, 417, 420, 448; Farrell, Introd. to Superior Court Diary of William Samuel Johnson, 1772-1773 (1942) p. xxvi (Connecticut). Now it was provided that "henceforth all goods attached upon any action shall not be released upon the appearance of the party, or judgment given, but shall stand engaged until the judgment or the execution granted upon the said judgment be discharged." [80] The capstone of the transformation came by a statute of 1701, which enacted that the property attached should not be released until the expiration of thirty days after judgment for the plaintiff, "to the intent that he may take the same by execution, for satisfying of such judgment in whole or in part, so far as the value thereof can extend, if he think fit, unless the judgment be sooner or otherwise satisfied, any law, usage or custom to the contrary notwithstanding." [81] The system thus set on foot was ultimately followed, with local differences of detail, by all the New England jurisdictions, including Connecticut,[82] although the latter in its earlier history [83] had set its face against attachment other than in certain cases especially threatening security of the plaintiff's claim. Subject to the attachment process so recognized were not only the defendant's goods and chattels but also his lands after these had become liable to execution for debt.

---

these local courts made much use of attachment and distress as part of their process, and we are told that distress "was regarded as a means of satisfaction . . . The borough distress, whether extra-judicial as against a foreigner, or taken by leave of the officer of a court as against a burgess, resembled rather a seizure in execution than a distress for rent arrear. But it was not, like a seizure in execution, an immediate means of satisfaction. A year and a day had to elapse before sale and satisfaction could follow." Bateson, Introd. to 2 Borough Customs, Selden Society, Vol. 21, p. xlviii. With such a source in their recollections of the home procedure, it is easy to see how the Massachusetts colonists could find in it confirmation of the practical idea that the attachment of property should serve, not as a mere leverage to compel appearance, but as an actual means of satisfying the potential judgment, and proceed accordingly to construct on its basis their own system, prescribed by their own discernment as adapted to local conditions and needs. Nor can we suppose that like explanation of the origin of the practice may not hold true elsewhere in the colonies.

[80] Mass. Colonial Laws, *supra*, 144; Mass. Charter & General Laws, *supra*, 192.

[81] Acts of 1701-02, c. 5, § 11, 1 Mass. Bay Acts & Resolves, *supra*, 466.

[82] 2 Swift, System of Laws of the State of Connecticut (1796) 177, 189. "Prior to 1805 the right to proceed by attachment on the original process had been extended, and such process was allowed in all cases, and applied to residents as well as nonresidents or absconding debtors." Barber v. Morgan, 84 Conn. 618, 622, 80 Atl. 791 (1911).

[83] Code of 1650 (Andrus, 1822) 22.

Alongside the common attachment, and authorized it might be by the same writ, there moved the garnishment or trustee process, by which goods and credits in the hands of third persons could be reached. This, as an emanation of foreign attachment, was originally restricted to the case of absent or absconding debtors. But in 1795 [34] Massachusetts extended it to the case of debtor-defendants generally, though not altogether in the same circle of actions as those subject to common attachment; and subsequently much the same step was taken by the other New England jurisdictions.

The system of common attachment, with a single exception later to be mentioned, confined itself to New England. On the other hand, the attachment on special grounds, from its colonial beginnings as foreign attachment, found increasing foothold elsewhere. As an integral part of its process, it permitted the garnishment of money or goods in the hands of a third person, as under the custom of London, as well as direct levy upon property personal and real. With considerable variation in point of grounds and sundry divergencies in practice, it obtains today through the length and breadth of the American jurisdictions outside the area of the New England system.

Accordingly the American jurisdictions here fall into two main groups. The one embraces the New England States, viz., Massachusetts, Maine, Connecticut, New Hampshire, Rhode Island and Vermont, where attachment on mesne process stands available in money actions generally, having its supplement in the trustee process. This group may also be taken measurably to include the Territory of Hawaii,[35] as a result, we may conjecture, of New England missionary influence. The second group consists of all the other jurisdictions; in these attachment, as before indicated, is always conditioned upon the existence of special grounds designated by statute.

In this second group two subordinate groups are encountered. In the larger of these, the usual grounds, variously phrased, are non-residence of the defendant or the fact that

[34] Mass. Laws 1794, c. 65 (Act of Feb. 28, 1795), 1 Mass. Gen. Laws to 1822 (1823) p. 464.

[35] Haw. Rev. Laws 1945, §§ 10142 *et seq.*, 10301 *et seq.* The first Hawaiian attachment statute appears to be that of May 18, 1841. Shillaber v. Waldo, 1 Haw. 21, 23 (1847).

the defendant is a foreign corporation, the defendant's evasion of process, his departure or intention to depart from the jurisdiction to the injury of his creditors, his fraudulent concealment of property or removal of it from the jurisdiction accomplished or intended, or his conveyance of or intention to convey property in fraud of his creditors. Under many statutes the fraudulent contracting of the debt is also a ground. In this category, the proceeding, given the statutory ground, is available in contract actions generally for the recovery of money, while various of the included jurisdictions permit it also in actions of tort for money damages. For most of the jurisdictions of unified procedure the money demand may be of either a legal or an equitable nature, and in certain of the jurisdictions of divided procedure the remedy is specially extended to equitable money actions.

The lesser of the two subordinate groups, consisting of California, Nevada, Arizona, Oregon, Montana, Idaho and Alaska, stands on a different basis from the other in respect of a provision concerning the contract in suit, which apparently had its inception in the California Practice Act of 1851.[86] Thus the present California Code of Civil Procedure authorizes the proceeding in an action upon a contract, express or implied, or for damages arising from a wrongful injury to property within the State, where the defendant is a non-resident, has departed from the State, cannot be found within the State or conceals himself to avoid service. But it also—and this is the distinctive trait of the second subordinate group—makes the proceeding available "in an action upon a contract, express or implied, for the direct payment of money, where the contract is made or is payable in this State, and is not secured by any mortgage, deed of trust or lien upon real or personal property, or any pledge of personal property; or, if originally so secured, such security has, without any act of the plaintiff or the person to whom the security was given, become valueless."[87] In California, therefore, it is sufficient to ground the proceeding, regardless of the defendant's resi-

[86] Cal. Pract. Act 1851, § 120, Cal. Laws 1851, p. 68.

[87] Cal. Code Civ. Proc. (Deering, 1949) § 537.

dence, and without other special cause, if the contract in suit is of the description just quoted. The provision thus characterizing the contract, with or without incidental variations, appears in all the jurisdictions of this category.[38] And in all the same principle obtains, namely, that given a contract of the kind described, without more, there is present one of the grounds of attachment.[39]

A further word will later be said concerning the New England system. For the present we may look at the typical features of the procedure in the attachment on special grounds. First, it usually involves an affidavit setting forth the nature of the plaintiff's demand and the amount claimed to be due, and also bringing the case within the ground relied upon, ordinarily by stating this in terms of the statute.[40] The exceptional practice of a few Eastern States apart,[41] there must always be presented, along with the affidavit, a bond in the sum appointed by the statute, often double the amount of the demand, conditioned for the due prosecution of the proceeding, and the payment of costs and damages in case it cannot be supported. Based on the affidavit and bond there issues the attachment process, more generally spoken of as a writ of attachment, but in New York and some other States called a warrant of attachment. In most of the jurisdictions the issuance is the act of the clerk without a preceding judicial order; elsewhere, as in New York,[42] an order of the court or of a judge is required. The writ or warrant directs the sheriff

[38] Nev. Comp. Laws 1929, § 8703; Ariz. Code Ann. 1939, § 25-101; 1 Ore. Comp. Laws Ann. 1940, and 1943 Pocket Part, § 7-201; Mont. Rev. Codes 1947, § 93-4301; Idaho Code Ann. 1949, § 8-501; Alaska Comp. Laws 1949, § 55-6-61.

[39] Utah requires a showing that the indebtedness claimed in attachment is an unsecured one, but this merely as a circumstance that must exist before resort to any of the specified grounds. Utah Rules Civ. Proc. 1949, Rule 64 C(a).

[40] See on this point Drake, Attachment (7th ed. 1891) §§ 84 *et seq.*, 97 *et seq.*

[41] The Delaware practice is perhaps closest to that under the custom of London. No preliminary bond is here required, although, as under the custom, security is exacted before the creditor may receive the proceeds of the attachment. Moreover, down to 1917, the custom was substantially followed in requiring the defendant to furnish security as a condition of appearance and defense—a requirement held not to be violative of due process of law in Ownbey v. Morgan, 256 U.S. 94, 41 S.Ct. 433 (1921).

[42] N.Y. Civ. Pract. Act, § 902 *et seq.*, Rules Civ. Pract., Rule 84 (Clevenger, 1950).

to attach property of the defendant to the amount of the plaintiff's claim, but may also direct him to summon the defendant, as well as to summon third persons as garnishees, if the particular practice so dictates, instead of using separate writs for these purposes. Subject to attachment is such real or personal property as is liable to execution, and in general there is no requirement that personal property be first taken. The attachment of realty is effected in much the same manner as is the levy of execution thereon, usually by the filing with the designated public officer of a proper certificate or a copy of the writ and return. Provision is commonly made for the sale of perishable property taken on attachment; other personal property normally remains in the custody of the officer pending developments in the case. The defendant ordinarily may regain possession of the attached personal property by giving bond. Two types of such bonds are in use. The one is the so-called forthcoming or delivery bond, conditioned for the production of the attached property to meet a judgment for the plaintiff; the other, sometimes spoken of as a bail bond, is conditioned for the payment of the judgment, and, on approval, necessarily operates to dissolve the attachment. This second type is equally applicable in the case of the attachment of realty.

Service upon the defendant is demanded by due process; from the earliest times the American systems have sedulously required that he be properly notified of the proceeding. If personal service of the writ or summons cannot be made, then resort is had to constructive or substituted service, according to the particular mode prescribed by the statute. In the American jurisdictions generally,[42a] the defendant is free to appear without any such condition as obtained under the custom of London, but his appearance does not operate, as it did there, to release the attachment. The attached property or the forthcoming bond given in its stead remains as security for the plaintiff's claim, while in the case of the other form of bond, it is the bond itself and not the appearance that releases the attachment.

[42a] But see Ownbey v. Morgan, *supra*.

As the validity of the attachment depends upon the existence of the ground alleged, it is always open to the defendant to contest such existence. The proceeding, therefore, may develop two sets of issues, the one dealing with the existence of the asserted ground, the other consisting of the issues in chief. So far as these involve questions of fact, the two may be the subject of separate trials—the former properly being tried first—or may be submitted to the court or jury together, according as the local practice enjoins. When a defendant not personally served has appeared without reservation, he has obviously given the court jurisdiction over his person, opening the way to a personal judgment against him. But, as it is in his interest to defeat the attachment, he is always entitled to dispute the ground alleged. In the absence of personal service upon him, however, the defendant in many quarters may appear specially or conditionally for the sole purpose of such an attack, without submitting to the jurisdiction generally.[43] In either case, success in disproving the ground relied upon brings the attachment phase of the action to an end; otherwise the attachment stands. Dependent upon considerations of the kind, when it comes to judgment for the plaintiff, this may be in essence, if not in form,[44] (*a*) a judgment *in rem* supporting the attachment and authorizing satisfaction of the proved demand out of the attached property or its proceeds; (*b*) a judgment which is *in personam* and at the same time is one *in rem* upholding the attachment with like authorization; or (*c*) a judgment *in personam* only. So far as the judgment is personal it affords a basis for the issuance of a general execution against the defendant's property at large; so far as it supports the attachment and to this extent is *in rem,* it is enforceable only by a special execution directed against the property attached. The attachment which is found to be supported has created a lien upon the attached property, real or personal, which takes priority from the date of the levy, while a personal judgment can take no priority of lien in advance of its date.

43 See Drake, *op. cit.* §§ 112, 414; 1 Shinn, Attachment and Garnishment (1896) § 442; 7 C.J.S. 619.

44 In some States the judgment in all these cases takes the same form, that is to say, the form of a personal judgment, but has no other operation than if its effect had been actually spelled out in the manner above indicated. See 1 Shinn, *op. cit.* § 453; 6 C.J. 484.

In case of garnishment in the attachment suit, the *res* which is the subject of attachment is the claim of the defendant against the third person, the garnishee, and jurisdiction to deal with it is basically governed by the same principles as govern the attachment levy on tangible property. Service of the garnishment writ, however, does not effect a lien on specific property in the hands of the garnishee, as does the levy upon tangible property attached: it only creates for the plaintiff "such a lien as gives him the right to hold the garnishee personally liable for it or its value, and to restrain the garnishee from paying his debt to the defendant." [45] Thus, if the plaintiff succeeds, his right to satisfaction out of the *res,* that is to say, the demand of the defendant against the garnishee, is effected normally by a personal judgment against the garnishee; but if specific property is surrendered by the garnishee pursuant to judgment, the plaintiff's right becomes enforceable against the property itself now in the hands of the officer.

In the main, the proceedings against the garnishee follow the same course as we have seen in the case of garnishment after judgment. The garnishee, properly served, is required to answer and make disclosure, may contest his liability, and is entitled to the benefit of conditional judgment precisely as in that case. Certain differences of procedure necessarily arise from the fact that the garnishment here is a measure taken in the attachment proceeding, and is thus collateral and ancillary to the prosecution of a yet unadjudicated demand of the plaintiff against the defendant. The right of the plaintiff in respect of the garnishee, just as his right in respect of property taken on the attachment, therefore depends upon the establishment of his claim. And such establishment, accordingly, may come by way of personal judgment against the defendant, if jurisdiction has been obtained over his person, otherwise by a judgment supporting the attachment, a judgment against the defendant *in rem.* In either case, it is the usual rule that no final judgment can go against the garnishee until after judgment against the defendant.

What has been said in a former place [46] regarding partici-

[45] Drake, *op. cit.* § 453.

[46] *Supra,* Chapter XXIV, § 5.

pation of third party claimants in the case of garnishment after judgment applies likewise to garnishment before judgment. But, as authorized by statute, there may be such participation also in the matter of attachment of tangible property. Here the usual form is that of intervention, and occurs by way of a sworn petition or an affidavit setting forth the third party's claim. This is frequently called an "interplea." There appears, however, in this case, to be no room under the statutes for such a true interpleader as exists in the case of the medial interpleader in garnishment. On the petition or affidavit issues are formed between the plaintiff and the claimant as to the property right asserted by the latter, and are decided in the usual way. If the intervenor prevails, there is a judgment awarding him the property claimed, with costs, and in a few jurisdictions, with damages,[47] and the attachment so far as regards that property is dissolved.

In the existing law of the New England States the common attachment, without special grounds, is available generally in all actions for the recovery of money, both legal and equitable, and whether sounding in contract or in tort.[48] Its use in equitable actions is in Rhode Island conditioned upon an order of court, and the same is true of one form of commencing the suit in Massachusetts.[49] In Rhode Island, exceptionally, attachment in tort actions is permitted only in the case of nonresident defendants,[50] and this State also stands apart in requiring for all cases an affidavit that the plaintiff's claim is just and that he expects to recover an amount sufficient to give the court jurisdiction.[51] Vermont exacts a preliminary bond in the form of a recognizance,[52] but none of the others discloses such a requirement, although provision appears to the effect that in case of doubt as to the ownership of the personal property in question or its liability to attachment, the sheriff

47 Note, 66 A.L.R. 908, 911.

48 See Mass. Ann. Laws 1933, c. 223, §§ 16, 42, c. 214, § 7; Me. Rev. Stat. 1944, c. 99, §§ 2, 24, 60, c. 95, § 10; Conn. Gen. Stat. 1949, § 8022; N.H. Rev. Laws 1942, c. 386, § 4, c. 388, § 1, c. 371, § 16; Vt. Stat. 1947, §§ 1522, 1524; R.I. Gen. Laws Ann. 1938, c. 546, §§ 1-4: see also c. 514, § 11.

49 R.I. Gen. Laws Ann. c. 546, § 4; Mass. Ann. Laws 1933, c. 214, § 7.

50 R.I. Gen. Laws Ann. 1938, c. 546, § 5.

51 *Id.* c. 546, § 1.

52 Vt. Stat. 1947, § 1528. The same requirement applies to the issue of summons.

is entitled to require security for his indemnity.[53] The property attached stands as security for the plaintiff's demand for a specified period after judgment in his favor. Thirty days is the period more commonly appointed for the case of personal property; for the case of realty the period, variously fixed, is usually longer, sometimes much longer.[54] The defendant may generally obtain release of the attached property by furnishing substituted security.[55]

Garnishment continues to be effected by the so-called "trustee process," which, however, in Connecticut, still bears the statutory designation of "foreign attachment." [56] As before mentioned, this no longer requires any special grounds, but is not as closely integrated with attachment of property in the defendant's own possession as is garnishment in most of the American jurisdictions. For one thing, it will not everywhere lie in the same cases as common attachment. In Massachusetts, for example, it is excluded in actions for malicious prosecution, slander or libel and assault and battery, as well as in replevin.[57] Again, by recent enactment of the same State, there has been established for it the requirement, with certain exceptions, that the plaintiff furnish bond for the protection of the defendant in respect of costs and damages where the demand exceeds $1000.[58] The trustee (garnishee) is always required to make disclosure on the same principle as obtains in other forms of garnishment, and for this purpose may be subjected to examination. But the right to contest the trustee's answer is not everywhere on the same basis. Thus in Maine, New Hampshire and Vermont provision is made for taking issue on the answer,[59] but in Massachusetts the statute limits the counter-allegations of the plaintiff to material facts "not stated or denied" by the trustee,[60] while in Rhode Island the liability

[53] Mass. Ann. Laws 1933, c. 223, § 45A; Me. Rev. Stat. 1944, c. 105, § 7; Vt. Stat. 1947, § 2305.

[54] See *e.g.,* Mass. Ann. Laws 1933, c. 223, § 59, 1949 Supp. to Vol. VII, c. 223, § 114A; Vt. Stat. 1947, § 2289.

[55] *E.g.,* Mass. Gen. Laws 1933, c. 223, §§ 120-125.

[56] Conn. Gen. Stat. 1949, c. 394.

[57] Mass. Ann. Laws 1933, c. 246, § 1, as amended, 1949 Supp. to Vol. VIII.

[58] *Ibid.*

[59] Me. Rev. Stat. 1944, c. 101, §§ 30, 31; N.H. Rev. Laws 1942, c. 412, §§ 13, 17-20; Vt. Stat. 1947, §§ 1829, 1830; as to Connecticut, see Gen. Stat. 1949, § 8079.

[60] Mass. Ann. Laws 1933, c. 246, § 16.

of the answering trustee, in the trustee proceeding, must result from his own disclosure.[61] In certain of these States a proceeding by *scire facias* plays an important part in effecting the plaintiff's relief. Thus "in Massachusetts, Connecticut and Maine, a judgment charging the trustee does not bind the trustee personally." [62] For this purpose resort must be had to a writ of *scire facias*.[63] As to Connecticut, it is properly said that the hearing of the disclosure "is an informal proceeding which is merely preliminary to the bringing of a *scire facias*." [64] In Rhode Island it is the action on the case which performs the office of a supplementary remedy. For here the order charging the trustee is not a judgment in the full sense: it merely affords the basis for an action on the case in which the liability of the trustee is definitively adjudicated.[65] So, also, an action on the case lies for damages occasioned to the plaintiff by a false answer on the part of the trustee.[66] But everywhere the effectuation of the plaintiff's right against the trustee, however accomplished, just as does the realization of the attachment by levy, depends upon a judgment against the defendant, which, on substantially the same principles as obtain in other American jurisdictions, may be either a personal judgment, based on jurisdiction of the defendant's person or a judgment *in rem* affecting only the property here involved.

The Hawaiian derivative of the New England system has in various respects followed a way of its own. Its general method is indicated in the subjoined note.[67]

61 R.I. Gen. Laws Ann. 1938, c. 550, § 4.

62 McConnell, Trustee Process (1886) § 390.

63 Mass. Ann. Laws 1933, c. 246, § 45; Me. Rev. Stat. 1944, c. 101, § 67; Conn. Gen. Stat. 1949, § 8125.

64 McConnell, *op. cit.* § 481.

65 R.I. Gen. Laws Ann. 1938, c. 550, §§ 4, 6, 11; McConnell, *op. cit.* §§ 362, 480.

66 R.I. Gen. Laws Ann. 1938, c. 550, § 10. A similar action is recognized in Massachusetts (c. 246, § 19) and Maine (c. 101, § 77).

67 Here the plaintiff may have a writ of attachment issued with the approval of the court "in any action upon a contract, express or implied." (Haw. Rev. Laws 1945, §§ 10142, 10147). Precondition, however, is the filing of an affidavit of the indebtedness claimed, stating also that the step is not being taken in hindrance or delay of any creditor, and with it a proper bond. (§§ 10143, 10144). Garnishment lies at the suit of "any creditor" (§ 10301), and has much the same nature of independence in relation to attachment by levy as characterizes the trustee process in New England. Thus it requires no preliminary affidavit or bond, but merely a request in the plaintiff's pleading. The order made in accept-

§ 2. The Replevin Process

In the action of replevin, which we have already had occasion to glance at in connection with execution, the common law afforded the plaintiff a very substantial means of security in anticipation of judgment, with respect to his claim for the specific recovery of chattels wrongfully taken and detained, since it aimed at putting him in possession of the chattels at the outset of the action, upon his giving the requisite security. This action, arising as a counter-instrumentality to the primitive institution of seizure of pledge, *i.e.*, distress, has its name from the judicial repledging (*replegiare*) which it involved, and at common law was employed as a remedy for unlawful distresses—usually of cattle—so much so that Blackstone,[68] with others, mistakenly supposed that it was available in no other cases.[69] Accordingly its procedure was strongly marked by various peculiarities having their source in the feudal relation between landlord and tenant.[70] At the outset, the action was commenced by original writ issued out of the chancery, which commissioned the sheriff as judge of the county court to hear the cause in that court. But to obviate the delay necessitated by resort thus to London, frequently grievous in the then conditions of travel, the Statute of Marlbridge in 1267 [71] permitted the proceedings to be begun locally by plaint to the sheriff. In either case the replevy of the chattels was effected under the sheriff's precept to his bailiff, which also commanded attachment of the defendant's goods by way of process for his appearance.[72] In either case, also, the action might be removed to the King's Bench or Common Pleas, at the instance

ance of the garnishee's disclosure appears to be treated as a judgment against him. (See Bishop Trust Co., Ltd. v. Hilo Pineapple Co., Ltd. 27 Haw. 749 (1924); Bishop Trust Co., Ltd. v. Furstenburg, 28 Haw. 528 (1925)). But, if the garnishee disputes the indebtedness alleged by the plaintiff, no order can be made against him, and the question must be left for determination in an independent action. (Davies & Co., Ltd. v. Hilo Pineapple Co. 27 Haw. 651 (1923)).

[68] 3 Blackstone, Comm. * 146; 2 Sellon's Crompton, Practice of the King's Bench and Common Pleas (Am. ed. 1813) * 153.

[69] See 3 Street, Foundations of Legal Liability (1906) 217-218.

[70] Daggett v. Robins, 2 Blackf. (Ind.) 415, 417 (1831). See 2 Pollock and Maitland, History of English Law (2d ed. 1899) 578.

[71] 52 Hen. III, c. 21.

[72] Gilbert, Distresses and Replevins (1757) 86.

of either party, by writ of *pone* for proceedings by original writ, by writ of *recordari facias loquelam* (abbreviated to *refalo*) for proceedings by plaint.[73] Removal was always essential where the freehold came in question—as it frequently did in case of distress damage feasant—for this question the sheriff had no power to try.[74] Ultimately, however, removal was to become a usual practice in all contested cases. In the beginning, the security required of the plaintiff consisted only of pledges to prosecute the action, but in 1285, by the Statute of Westminster II,[75] there was added the highly important requirement of pledges for the return of the chattels, should this be adjudged.

Especially reflecting the indirection of legal method characteristic of the older day were in replevin the writ *de proprietate probanda* and the process *in withernam*. Certain differences of procedure existed between the two kinds of replevin in these respects, but as replevin by plaint was in later practice to supersede altogether replevin by writ,[76] we speak here only with reference to the former. The writ *de proprietate probanda* was in order where the defendant asserted a claim of title to the property in question. Once he did so, the matter came to a standstill until there could be procured from the chancery the writ named, which authorized the sheriff to proceed. Under the writ the sheriff held an inquest of office by means of a jury, which passed upon the claim. If it found against the claim, the sheriff was to make deliverance of the chattels to the plaintiff, subject to the defendant's right to remove the proceedings and litigate the question above. But "if the inquest of office find for the defendant, there is an end of the replevin by plaint, because the property is found for the defendant, and so no redeliverance can be made by the sheriff." [77] The process *in withernam* was brought into play by inability of the officer to replevy the chattels. If the bailiff made return that the defendant had removed the chattels from the jurisdiction, in technical language had "eloigned" them—a common

[73] *Ibid.* 129; 2 Sellon's Crompton, *op. cit.* * 160.

[74] Gilbert, *op. cit.* 70.

[75] 13 Edw. I, c. 2.

[76] Replevin by plaint "is the only kind known in practice." Stephen, Pleading (1824) 20, note m.

[77] Gilbert, *op. cit.* 124-125.

case was that of driving cattle out of the country—or had concealed the chattels, the sheriff, after determining the truth of the return by inquest of office, could issue his *capias in withernam,* which directed the bailiff to seize equivalent chattels of the defendant to be held as a distress, until he surrendered the chattels in suit.[78] "And if he will not award a *withernam,* the plaintiff may have a writ out of chancery, directed to the sheriff, rehearsing the whole matter, and commanding him to award a *withernam.*" [79] A remedy, alternative to the *withernam* process, was at one time open to the plaintiff where the proceedings had been removed to the superior court. By framing his declaration in the *detinet,* as distinguished from its ordinary framing in the *detinuit,* and thus alleging that the defendant presently *detains* the chattels, the plaintiff, when he prevailed, was entitled to a judgment for their value, in addition to the usual damages, and this, says Baron Gilbert, writing in 1757, "is a shorter way than to sue a *withernam* and *cap.* for return of the beasts." [80] But this sensible practice failed to survive, Serjeant Williams in his notes to Saunders' Reports speaking of it as "long since obsolete." [81]

Another peculiar feature of the old action was the writ of second deliverance. This writ, owed to the Statute of Westminster II, was occasioned by the circumstance that replevin was no exception to the rule which permitted a plaintiff, after nonsuit, to commence his action anew, nor did it make any difference that a return of the chattels had been adjudged to the defendant. The result, in the words of the statute, was that the chattels could "be replevied twice or thrice, and infinitely." Accordingly it was provided that the sheriff was not to make delivery in the renewed action except under the special writ in question, issued out of the superior court; that the defendant was to appear in that court, where the case was to be tried; and that if there a return should be adjudged to the defendant, whether in consequence of nonsuit or otherwise,

[78] *Ibid.* 93, 103.

[79] 2 Sellon's Crompton, *op. cit.* * 159.

[80] Gilbert, *op. cit.* 168.

[81] 1 Wms. Saund. 347*b.* "Of late years, no action has been brought in the *detinet,* though there is much curious learning in the old books concerning it." Buller, Nisi Prius (Am. ed. 1806) 52. And see Fletcher v. Wilkins, 6 East 286, 102 E.R. 1295 (1805).

such return should be adjudged irreplevisable forever.[82] The writ of second deliverance, however, lost much of its importance as the result of a statute of 1665 relating to distress for rent. The statute in effect displaced the writ in replevins arising from distresses of the kind and pending in or removed to the superior courts, by providing for a special mode of proceeding in such cases. Under this, either in the event of nonsuit or his prevailing on demurrer or verdict, the defendant claiming the right to hold the replevied chattels was entitled to have a money judgment in the replevin suit itself for the amount of the rent due or so much thereof as was represented by the value of the replevied chattels. In that case the plaintiff kept the chattels in question.[83]

The idiosyncrasies of replevin were carried into the field of pleading. The defensive allegation admitting the plaintiff's property in the chattels, but asserting the defendant's right to take and detain them as security, was known, not as a plea, but as an avowry or cognizance—an avowry where it alleged the right as one existing in the defendant himself, a cognizance where the right was alleged as that of a third party, by whose command or authority the defendant had acted. Moreover, the plaintiff's response of fact to either was termed not a replication but a plea. And to the same extent as in the case of pleas to the action, the statute of 1705 [84] permitted the use of more than one such plea. The special regulation thus obtaining arose from the fact that the defendant here was in a certain sense advancing a counter-action, looking to the return of the chattels in question, it being commonly said, in respect of this and other incidents of the action, that both parties are actors in replevin.[85]

In view of the general practice of removal, the judgment was normally that of a superior court. To what has been said in a former chapter concerning its general character and that of the execution process it may be here added that if to the

[82] 13 Edw. I, c. 2; Gilbert, *op. cit.* 233-236.

[83] 17 Car. II, c. 7; Gilbert, *op. cit.* 244-246; 2 Sellon's Crompton, *op. cit.* * 179-* 184.

[84] 4 Anne, c. 16, § 4.

[85] See 1 Chitty, Pleading (11th Am. ed. 1851) * 165; 2 Sellon's Crompton, *op. cit.* * 164.

writ of *retorno habendo,* for restoration of the chattels to a victorious defendant, the officer made return that they had been eloigned, the common law in this case, as well as in that of the initial replevy, permitted resort to the *capias in withernam* to compel their surrender, that is to say, by seizure of chattels belonging to the plaintiff.[86] This means, however, does not seem to have been often employed.[87]

Apart from the notable reformatory statute of 1738,[88] requiring *inter alia* that the sheriff in all replevins of distress for rent take from the plaintiff a bond with two sureties in double the value of the goods distrained, conditioned for prosecution of the action and eventual return of the chattels, the English law rested in the main upon the basis above outlined until the middle of the 1800s. But, commencing with the act of 1846 [89] establishing the new system of County Courts and the amendatory act of 1856,[90] the procedure of replevin has been radically recast. It is now regulated by the County Courts Act of 1934 [91] and the County Court Rules of 1936. The action continues to be confined to the case of illegal distress and other unlawful takings. It is normally dealt with in the County Court, but may be instituted either in the court, subject to removal by the defendant to the High Court, or originally in the High Court, although invocation of the latter is in either case under special restrictions in point of subject-matter and with respect to the matter of security. Since 1856, however, the plaintiff before commencement has to apply to the Registrar of the County Court, who alone is authorized to cause the goods to be replevied, upon the plaintiff giving the requisite security, conditioned among other things to commence and prosecute the action, the commencement to be within one week if he sues in the High Court, within one month if he sues in the County Court. The judgment, if for the plaintiff, follows the old principle [92] of being for damages only; if for the defendant, supporting his right to possession, it is regulated according to

[86] Gilbert, *op. cit.* 116, 122; 2 Sellon's Crompton, *op. cit.* * 186.

[87] For other remedies open to the defendant, see 1 Wms. Saund. 195*a*, 195*b*.

[88] 11 Geo. II, c. 19, § 23.

[89] 9 & 10 Vict. c. 95, §§ 119-121.

[90] 19 & 20 Vict. c. 108, §§ 63-68.

[91] 24 & 25 Geo. V, c. 53, §§ 101-103.

[92] Gilbert, *op. cit.* 223.

the situation. In cases of distress for rent or to enforce any other money demand, it is for a return of the chattels if the defendant so requests, for their assessed value if this is less than the amount of the demand, or for the amount of the demand if this is less than the value so found. In cases of distress damage feasant, it is for a return, or upon request of the defendant, in the alternative for a return or for the amount of damages sustained by the defendant. In cases other than those of distress, where the defendant justifies the taking, it is for a return.[93] The return is enforced by warrant of delivery in the County Court, by writ of delivery in the High Court.[94] But, owing in part at least to the importance achieved by the modernized action of detinue, replevin, despite its meticulous regulation, does not appear to be a popular remedy in present-day England. It is said, under date of 1948, that "actions of replevin are now extremely rare," and reference is made to cases in 1912 and 1934 as two of the latest reported instances of the action.[95]

In the United States replevin is closely regulated by statute. The development in general has broadened the scope of the remedy by appropriating it to the case of any unlawful detention of tangible personal property, whether tortiously taken or not. Otherwise it has followed in the main one of two courses. Under the one, replevin remains a distinct action, but as regards the court of commencement stands on a par with other actions, our localized administration of justice obviating the need of any such system as obtained at common law. Under the other, replevin has been reduced to the status of an ancillary proceeding, as an adjunct of a statutory action for the recovery of personal property. This is the so-called proceeding of "claim and delivery," originating in the New York Code of 1848,[96] which obtains in most of the code jurisdictions and in some others,[97] although not always

[93] County Court Rules 1936, O. 33.

[94] *Ibid.* O. 25, r. 74; R.S.C., O. XLVI, r. 6.

[95] 5 Halsbury's Statutes of England (2d ed. 1948) p. 81, note to § 101, County Courts Act of 1934.

[96] § 181 *et seq.*

[97] As to non-code States, see Ala. Code 1940, Tit. 7, § 918; Va. Code Ann. 1942, § 5797 *et seq.;* Va. Code Ann. 1950, § 8-586 *et seq.;* W.Va. Code Ann. 1949, § 5463 *et seq.*

under that name.[98] In this form of procedure the plaintiff, at the time of commencing his action, or within a designated period thereafter—originally and still for the most part, until answer, but in some jurisdictions, until judgment [99]—may, upon proper affidavit and security, obtain the delivery to him of the goods in question, and the cause then proceeds as in replevin proper. But if the plaintiff does not avail himself of this ancillary remedy, the action simply remains one for the specific recovery of the goods, in which his relief necessarily awaits the final judgment. From this general course of development Georgia and Texas stand definitely apart. In the former the office of replevin is measurably performed by the institutions of bail trover and possessory warrant,[100] in the latter by the writ of sequestration [101] (adopted under Louisiana influence) and the statutory proceeding of trial of right of property.[102]

The replevin proceedings are initiated by an affidavit, representing the common-law plaint to the sheriff.[103] Its contents are variously regulated, but, as a rule, it is required to allege the plaintiff's lawful possession of the property described and that this has been unlawfully detained by the defendant. Very

[98] See Shinn, Replevin (1899) § 57.

[99] Until judgment, is now the rule in New York. N.Y. Civ. Pract. Act (Clevenger, 1950) § 1094.

[100] In Georgia, where trover lies for the specific recovery of chattels, the plaintiff is entitled to an ancillary proceeding not unlike that of claim and delivery, but only upon affidavit that he has reason to apprehend that the goods will not be forthcoming to meet the judgment. Where this is used the action is spoken of as bail trover, from the fact that the defendant is put under bail to produce the goods. Failing this bail, the goods are delivered over to the plaintiff, upon security, to await the outcome of the case. Ga. Code 1933, c. 107-2. The possessory warrant introduces a summary proceeding looking to restoration of the *status quo*. It issues at the instance of a plaintiff, from whose lawful possession chattels have been taken by fraud, violence or otherwise, for the arrest of the defendant as well as the seizure of the property. Upon trial, which is limited to the question of possession, the property may be delivered to the successful plaintiff if he gives proper security for its forthcoming in any action to be brought by the opposite party within four years. Code, cc. 82-1, 82-2.

[101] See *infra,* § 4 of the present Chapter.

[102] See Shinn, *op. cit.* § 59. In the proceeding of trial of right of property, any claimant of personal property levied upon under a writ of execution or attachment or other writ, to which he is not a party, may upon affidavit and bond cause the property to be delivered to him ("replevied" is the term ordinarily used) to be held until the claim is adjudicated in the course of the proceeding. Tex. Rules Civ. Proc. (Vernon, 1942) Rules 717-736.

[103] Anderson v. Hapler, 34 Ill. 436 (1864); Wells, Replevin (1880) § 654.

commonly it is also required to state that the property has not been taken under any execution, attachment or other judicial process issued against the plaintiff or for any tax, assessment or fine levied against him or against the property. Sometimes, with a view to the matter of bond, it must state the value of the property sought to be replevied. Before the writ of replevin issues on the basis of the affidavit, or at least before it is executed,[104] the plaintiff has to give bond to the sheriff,[105] usually in double the value of the property in question, conditioned on the old principle for prosecution of the action and for return of the goods in case this is awarded, as well as to such further effect as the statute may prescribe. Under the writ, which also more usually serves as a summons for the defendant's appearance, the sheriff proceeds to seizure of the goods and delivers them to the plaintiff pending further proceedings. In by far the majority of the jurisdictions, however, provision is made for release of the goods to the defendant upon the latter giving the requisite security.[106]

What if the officer, by reason of their concealment or removal on the part of the defendant, is unable to take the goods on the replevin writ? While instances of the use of the *capias in withernam* appear in a few of the older cases,[107] this as mesne process has long been laid aside. In a number of jurisdictions direct measures may be employed against the defendant to compel the surrender of the property. Thus in some the existence of ground for fearing in advance the defendant's frustrative conduct may be cause for his arrest,[108] but, as in

[104] See Shinn, *op. cit.* §§ 354, 367.

[105] This bond is largely modelled upon that prescribed by the English statute of 1738. Wells, *op. cit.* § 386.

[106] Under the peculiar practice obtaining in Mississippi, the goods are seized pursuant to the writ prior to the giving of bond. The defendant is then entitled to obtain their release by furnishing bond. If he fails to do so within two days after the seizure, the plaintiff may obtain delivery by giving bond on his part. If, however, it appears from the plaintiff's affidavit that the goods have been unlawfully taken from his actual possession within thirty days, the plaintiff has the preference over the defendant in respect of the two-day period. Miss. Code Ann. 1942, § 2849 *et seq.*

[107] McColgan v. Huston, 2 Nott & McC. (S.C.) 444 (1820); Swann v. Shemwell, 2 Har.&Gill (Md.) 283 (1828); Bennett v. Berry, 8 Blackf. (Ind.) 1 (1846).

[108] See *e.g.,* N.Y. Civ. Pract. Act (Clevenger, 1950) § 826; Cal. Code Civ. Proc. (Deering, 1949) § 479; Ark. Stat. Ann. 1947, § 34-2112.

other cases of civil arrest on mesne process this involves the plaintiff furnishing appropriate bond. Elsewhere to a limited extent such provision is made that, after a showing of the concealment or other obstructive conduct by the officer's return or otherwise, the defendant may be cited for contempt.[109] Procedure of the kind, however, remains exceptional. But the plaintiff who may be thwarted by the defendant's misbehavior in this regard is in much better case than he was at common law. For not only may he usually proceed outright for a money judgment under the original or amended pleadings, but it is widely the rule that if he succeeds in the action he is entitled to a judgment in the alternative for the property or for its value if the property cannot be found.

The rule of alternative judgment usually applies to the prevailing of the defendant where it is apposite, as well as to the prevailing of the plaintiff. The basis for its existence in most of the code jurisdictions appears to have been furnished by the New York Code, as amended in 1849, in the provision that "in an action to recover the possession of personal property, judgment for the plaintiff may be for the possession, or for the recovery of possession, or the value thereof, in case a delivery cannot be had, and of damages for the detention. If the property have been delivered to the plaintiff, and the defendant claim a return thereof, judgment for the defendant may be for a return of the property, or the value thereof, in case a return cannot be had, and damages for taking and withholding the same." [110] Variants of the rule appear in different quarters. Thus the successful party under some statutes is given the right to elect between a judgment for the property and one for its money value.[111] And in Illinois the alternative judgment is confined to the case of a successful defendant who has held the property for a money claim, and is for the amount of the claim with damages, if paid within a given time, other-

[109] See Ind. Stat. Ann. (Burns, 1933) 1946 Replacement Vol. II, §§ 3-2707, 3-2709 *et seq.;* Minn. Stat. 1945, § 565-08; Ia. Code 1946, § 643.11; Ky. Code Pract. Civ. Cas. Ann. (Carroll, 1948) § 193.

[110] N.Y. Code 1849, § 277.

[111] See Mich. Stat. Ann. 1938, §§ 27.-1841, 27.1842; Mo. Rev. Stat. Ann. 1942, §§ 1798, 1799, 1801.

wise for return of the property.[112] Perhaps because of the extensive use of the alternative judgment in the jurisdictions generally, the statutes do not widely disclose provision for the case of enforcing specific delivery under the judgment where the property has been put beyond reach of the officer—a matter to be distinguished from that of enforcing the provisional delivery under the replevin writ. But in some of the New England States there is here recognized a descendant of the old *capias in withernam* in the writ of reprisal, under which goods and chattels of the offending party may be seized,[113] and Maryland similarly recognizes a writ "in the nature of a writ of *capias in withernam*" for the same purpose.[114] Again, simpler proceedings by way of distraint are not unknown,[115] nor is the use of the contempt process in this case without authorization.[116]

Although inability to force specific surrender of the property in question, either on the replevin writ or pursuant to judgment, is rarely calculated to work an intolerable injustice, in view of the substituted pecuniary relief usually attainable, yet if the party entitled wants the specific property itself, the law ought to enable him to have it, if this is at all possible. The power which the adverse party here largely retains to set at naught the delivery process should be definitely suppressed. The remedy lies in a wider adoption of the contempt process. An attempt in this direction made about ten years ago by the rules of the Municipal Court of Chicago failed on the ground that it was beyond the rule-making power of the court, since no such method was contemplated by the replevin statute.[117] No doubt the result was correct under the particular system. The occasion might well have prompted the enactment of a general statute to similar effect, but this, unfortunately, has not yet come about. Equity has long exercised the power of awarding the specific recovery of chattels having "a cer-

[112] Ill. Rev. Stat. 1949, c. 119, § 22.

[113] Vt. Stat. 1947, § 1969; Me. Rev. Stat. 1944, c. 112, § 17. This writ was formerly employed in Massachusetts. Parker v. Simonds, 8 Metc. (49 Mass.) 205 (1844).

[114] Md. Ann. Code (Flack, 1939) Art. 75, § 128.

[115] Ala. Code 1940, Tit. 7, § 924.

[116] Ariz. Code Ann. 1939, § 27-1610; Md. Ann. Code (Flack, 1939) Art. 75, § 128.

[117] Universal Credit Co. v. Antonsen, 374 Ill. 194, 29 N.E.2d 96 (1940).

tain special, extraordinary, and unique value impossible to be compensated for in damages," [118] and enforcing their discovery, production and delivery by means of the contempt process. Massachusetts, indeed, allows such a remedy in any case of goods "taken or detained from the owner, and so secreted or withheld that they cannot be replevied." [119] Particularly in view of the widely established and ever-increasing unification of legal and equitable procedure, there is accordingly no good reason why the common-law tradition should stand in the way of empowering the courts everywhere to employ the contempt process in cases of the present kind.[120]

The old writ of second deliverance has never had any place in the American scene.[121] And, to some extent, the plaintiff who suffers a nonsuit, even after delivery of the goods to him, may still, upon return pursuant to judgment, commence his action anew.[122] But, for the most part, by invocation of the principle that both parties are actors in this action, it is held that once the goods have been delivered to the plaintiff, he can no longer, by taking a voluntary nonsuit, cut off the defendant's right to an adjudication on the merits of his claim to the goods.[123] Hence the plaintiff is either debarred altogether from taking a nonsuit after this point,[124] or else the defendant, regardless of the nonsuit, is entitled to proceed to hearing and judgment.[125] Only where the defendant fails to avail himself of the right thus open to him does there arise the possibility of a fresh action on the part of the plaintiff. In any event, liability on the replevin bond—a much more adequate security than the common-law pledges—generally operates as an effective deterrent of vexatious repetition of the action.

[118] 1 Pomeroy, Equity Jurisprudence (4th ed. 1918) § 177.

[119] Mass. Ann. Laws 1933, c. 214, § 3.

[120] See note on Universal Credit Co. v. Antonsen, *supra,* (1941) 35 Ill.Law Rev. 988.

[121] See Daggett v. Robins, 2 Blackf. (Ind.) 415 (1831).

[122] 2 Freeman, Judgments (5th ed. 1925) § 893; Walbridge v. Shaw, 7 Cush. (61 Mass.) 560 (1851); Peterson v. Kissell, 148 Ia. 516, 125 N.W. 808 (1910).

[123] Shinn, *op. cit.* § 694; Wells, *op. cit.* § 516. See Note, 2 A.L.R. 200.

[124] Crump v. Branning, 74 Fla. 522, 77 So. 228 (1917); Vose v. Muller, 48 Neb. 602, 67 N.W. 598 (1896).

[125] Security State Bank v. Hubbard, 170 Okla. 502, 38 Pac.2d 16 (1935); Thomas v. First Nat. Bank, 32 Okla. 115, 121 Pac. 272 (1912).

As a rule a third person claiming possession of the replevied property may assert his claim by intervening in the action, usually, but not always,[126] as an optional remedy. In the larger number of jurisdictions the right so to intervene depends upon provisions applying to property actions in general. But there exist also not a few special provisions in the replevin statutes regulating the matter of intervention.[127] Under most of these the third party, usually before the goods have been delivered over by the sheriff, may obtain possession of the property upon giving the prescribed bond, to be held by him pending adjudication of the questions in suit. It should also be noted that with local variations there very frequently occurs[128] a provision, which apparently had its origin in an 1849 amendment of the New York Code,[129] to the effect that, upon the filing with the sheriff of an affidavit of claim by a third party, the sheriff may withhold delivery from the plaintiff unless the latter furnishes him with a bond of indemnity against the claim thus advanced. And in New York it is now expressly declared that, failing the bond of indemnity, it is within the discretion of the sheriff to deliver the property to the claimant "without incurring any liability to the plaintiff by reason of so doing."[130]

§ 3. Conservation by Receivership

Foremost in importance of all the means provided for assuring that the parties entitled shall enjoy the fruits of the litigation is the equitable jurisdiction to appoint a receiver. Of this many-branched instrumentality, reaching into the most diverse fields of business and affairs, our purpose here permits only the briefest mention. It was the rule of the English

126 See Miss. Code Ann. 1942, § 2864.

127 *E.g.*, Miss. Code Ann. 1942, *loc. cit. et seq.;* Ala. Code 1940, Tit. 7, § 932; Pa. Stat. Ann. (Purdon, 1931) Tit. 12, § 1826; N.C. Gen. Stat. 1943, § 1-482; Ill. Rev. Stat. 1949, c. 119, § 22a.

128 As Idaho Code Ann. 1949, § 8-311; Ky. Code Pract. Civ. Cas. (Carroll, 1948) § 191; Mont. Rev. Codes Ann. 1947, § 93-4115; Nev. Comp. Laws 1929, § 8690; Colo. Rules Civ. Proc., Rule 104(j) in Colo. Stat. Ann. 1935, 1941 Replacement Vol. I; Ark. Stat. Ann. 1947, § 34-2111; Wash. Rev. Stat. Ann. (Remington, 1932) § 716; Ore. Comp. Laws 1940, § 7-411; N.D. Rev. Code 1943, § 32-0710; S.D. Code 1939, § 37.3805; Utah Rules Civ. Proc. 1949, Rule 64B(i); S.C. Code 1942, § 563.

129 N.Y. Code 1849, § 216.

130 N.Y. Civ. Pract. Act (Clevenger, 1950) § 1107.

chancery from an early day that, if property in litigation was in danger of being lost or destroyed, the court would interfere to prevent it, if no legal remedy was sufficient for the purpose.[131] A principal means to this end was the appointment of a receiver for the property in question. This rule, broadened and amplified, continues to control in the Anglo-American jurisdictions. Appointed by the court on application of the party, the receiver is the representative of the court and not of any of the parties. Through his agency the court "takes possession of the property which is the subject of the suit, preserves it from waste or destruction, secures and collects the proceeds or profits, and ultimately disposes of them according to the rights and priorities of those entitled." [132] Absence of legal remedy is always a condition of the measure, as is also a proper showing of the danger apprehended, together with that of the interest of the applicant in the property involved. These conditions satisfied, the appointment is usually a matter for the discretion of the court.[133] Apart from statutory exceptions,[134] no bond is generally required of the applicant, but the receiver himself must ordinarily give bond for the faithful discharge of his duties.[135]

Resting on this basis, "the law of receiverships has in recent years rapidly developed and with constantly widening scope. Indeed in no other branch of equity jurisdiction has there been such an adaptation of equitable principles to the requirements of commercial advancement. This development has taken place through the action of the chancery courts themselves, and, perhaps to a greater extent, through the extension by statutory enactments of the remedial action to subjects not within the original equitable scope. Especially has this been true in respect of the winding up of corporations and the administration of their assets. Statutes in many states and acts of Parliament in England provide for liquidating the affairs of corporations through receivers and define their powers,

[131] Mitford, Chancery Pleadings (5th ed. 1847) 158; 2 Story, Equity Jurisprudence (14th ed. 1918) § 1145.

[132] Beverley v. Brooke, 4 Gratt. (Va.) 187, 208 (1847).

[133] High, Receivers (4th ed. 1910) §§ 4-8.

[134] *E.g.*, Ill. Rev. Stat. 1949, c. 22, § 54; Ala. Code 1940, Tit. 7, § 1158.

[135] See High, *op. cit.* § 118 *et seq.*

duties and liabilities. These statutes generally provide for the presentation and allowance of the claims of creditors and, in some cases, define who are creditors."[136] While pronounced expansion of the institution has thus appeared on both sides of the Atlantic, that in the United States has probably been the wider, reflecting the wider range of American economic development.[137]

Such is the case of the equity receivership, confined to equity litigation. But the statutes often provide for the appointment of a receiver in purely statutory proceedings, as, for example, in garnishment, where collection of assets and adjustment of claims require, for the assistance of the court, more than the ordinary course of procedure. Receivers of this kind, however, enjoy only such powers as are definitely conferred upon them by the statute.

§ 4. Interim Sequestration as a Security Measure

The writ of sequestration as employed in the English Court of Chancery was confined to the purpose either of enforcing appearance or of enforcing orders and decrees for the payment of money.[138] Except as incident to such purpose, it had no office of safeguarding property in litigation. Yet it has been said that the appointment of a receiver is in the nature of a sequestration,[139] and it might easily have become the rule in the development of American equity jurisdiction that the danger of loss or destruction of the subject-matter in litigation would in proper cases afford a basis for the writ in question, either in lieu of or as an alternative to the appointment of a receiver. Such a result, indeed, has not lacked decision in its support,[140]

136 Pennsylvania Steel Co. v. New York City Ry. Co. (C.C.A. 2) 198 Fed. 721, 736 (1912).

137 For the English law of receivers in general, see Kerr, Receivers (10th ed. 1935).

138 Steam Stone-Cutter Co. v. Sears (C.C.D.Vt.) 9 Fed. 8, 9 (1881).

139 Beverley v. Brooke, 4 Gratt. (Va.) 187, 208 (1847); and see 1 Spence, Equitable Jurisdiction of the Court of Chancery (1846) * 378.

140 Parker v. Grammer, 62 N.C. 28 (1866); Dean v. Boyd, 86 Miss. 204, 38 So. 297 (1905). In the former case it is said that "where there is reason to apprehend that the subject of a controversy in equity will be destroyed, or removed or otherwise disposed of by the defendant, pending the suit, so that the complainant may lose the fruit of his recovery, or be hindered or delayed in obtaining it, the court, in aid of the primary equity, will secure the fund

but the general rule calls instead for a receivership in consonance with the traditional principle. Nevertheless, the idea that the writ of sequestration is here in order is in Mississippi recognized by statute. This provides that, where a bill in chancery is filed with reference to personal property, a writ of sequestration will issue upon the plaintiff filing a proper affidavit and giving bond in double the value of the property. The affidavit is required to show the plaintiff's belief on good ground that the property is in imminent danger of removal from the State, of concealment beyond the reach of process or of transfer so as to defeat the plaintiff's right.[141]

Much broader in scope, but wholly distinct in origin is the writ of sequestration as obtaining in Texas. This is derived from the Louisiana practice and ultimately from the Spanish and French laws. Under the Texas statute it is available in eight cases, seven of which expressly proceed on the ground of apprehended injury to or loss of property to the detriment of the plaintiff. In sum, these embrace suits for divorce by a married woman who fears such injury or loss by acts of her husband in respect of her separate property or of the common property, and suits to recover the title or possession of real or personal property, or for the foreclosure of mortgages or liens on real or personal property, where the fear exists on the part of the plaintiff respecting the property in suit. The eighth case, concerning real property only, is that of suits to try title, to remove clouds on title, to foreclose liens or for partition, where the defendant is a non-resident of the State. To obtain issuance of the writ the plaintiff is required to make affidavit of the particular ground, including therein a description of the property and certain other data prescribed by rule. And as a further condition of the issuance he is obliged to file a bond with two sureties in at least double the value of the property in question.[142]

---

by the writ of sequestration, or the writ of sequestration and injunction, until the main equity is adjudicated at the hearing of the cause." (pp. 28-29).

[141] Miss. Code Ann. 1942, § 1328 *et seq.* The court, however, holds that the writ is available independently of the statute. Dean v. Boyd, *supra,* at 208; Lee v. Lee, 135 Miss. 865, 875, 101 So. 345 (1924).

[142] Tex. Stat. (Vernon, 1936) Art. 6840; Tex. Rules Civ. Proc. 1941 (Ver-

While the Mississippi statute is undoubtedly of equitable descent, we may suspect that the Louisiana influence had something to do with its procedure. For both in Mississippi and in Texas, as under the Louisiana practice,[143] if the defendant, from whose possession the property has been taken by the sheriff, does not obtain its release to him by the giving of a prescribed bond within a stated number of days, the right to secure interim possession then inures to the plaintiff upon the giving by him of a corresponding bond.[144] If no bond is given by either party, the property remains in the custody of the sheriff to await adjudication of the controversy, unless it be perishable, in which case provision is made for its sale and the substitution of the proceeds. But either party, upon giving

---

non, 1942) Rule 696 *et seq. In extenso* the grounds are:

"(a) When a married woman sues for divorce, and makes oath that she fears her husband will waste her separate property, or their common property, or the fruits or revenues produced by either, or that he will sell or otherwise dispose of the same so as to defraud her of her just rights, or remove the same out of the limits of the county during the pendency of the suit.

"(b) When a person sues for the title or possession of any personal property of any description, and makes oath that he fears the defendant or person in possession thereof will injure, ill-treat, waste or destroy such property, or remove the same out of the limits of the county during the pendency of the suit.

"(c) When a person sues for the foreclosure of a mortgage or the enforcement of a lien upon personal property of any description, and makes oath that he fears the defendant or person in possession thereof will injure, ill-treat, waste or destroy or remove the same out of the county during the pendency of the suit.

"(d) When any person sues for the title or possession of real property, and makes oath that he fears the defendant or person in possession thereof will make use of his possession to injure such property, or waste or convert to his own use the fruits or revenue produced by the same.

"(e) When any person sues for the title or possession of any property from which he has been ejected by force or violence, and makes oath of such fact.

"(f) When any person sues for the foreclosure of a mortgage or the enforcement of a lien on real estate, and makes oath that he fears the defendant or person in possession thereof will make use of such possession to injure such property, or waste or convert to his own use the timber, rents, fruits or revenue thereof.

"(g) When any person sues to try the title to any real property, or to remove cloud upon the title to such real property, or to foreclose a lien upon any such real property, or for a partition of real property and makes oath that the defendant or either of them in the event there be more than one defendant, is a nonresident of this State."

143 Louisiana Code of Practice (Dart, 2d ed. 1942) Art. 279.

144 Miss. Code Ann. 1942, §§ 1332, 1333; Tex. Rules Civ. Proc., Rules 701, 708.

bond, may obtain possession at any time before sale or after sale may receive the proceeds.[145]

Outside of sequestration to compel appearance or to enforce orders and decrees for the payment of money, the American statutes elsewhere afford little recognition to the remedy. Pennsylvania, however, furnishes an example of the kind of sequestration here under discussion in permitting a remainderman or reversioner to obtain on petition the appointment of a sequestrator for the rents, issues and profits of the land in question as against a tenant for life or for years under duty to pay taxes and assessments and make repairs, who has failed to do so—a result which the tenant may avert by giving security as fixed by the court.[146] So, also, in the same State a writ of sequestration is in order as against a trustee who is wasting or otherwise disposing of trust property, or is about to abscond and remove such property from the jurisdiction. Under the writ the sheriff takes possession of the property and holds it subject to the order of the court, being authorized first to require of the applicant an indemnity bond. But execution of the writ may be prevented by a forthcoming bond on the part of the trustee.[147]

In some of the States maintaining the divided jurisdiction of law and equity, attachment on mesne process, ordinarily appurtenant to actions at law, is available to a greater or less extent in equity suits on money demands. In a few others, however, the counterpart of attachment is found in a writ of sequestration. This is particularly true in Vermont where the statute authorizing such sequestration in chancery proceedings,[148] which dates from 1797,[149] is authoritatively said to have been adopted "to conform the proceedings in chancery to those in the court of law, in regard to securing the ultimate judgment of the court, by a previous attachment of the property." [150] Until superseded by the unifying rules of 1948, there

[145] Miss. Code Ann. 1942, § 1334, (here extraordinary expense of preserving the property may also be ground for sale); Tex. Rules Civ. Proc., Rule 710 *et seq.*

[146] Pa. Stat. Ann. (Purdon, 1931) Tit. 68, §§ 251, 253.

[147] *Ibid.* Tit. 20, § 2399.

[148] Vt. Stat. 1947, § 1297.

[149] Steam Stone Cutter Co. v. Jones (C.C.D.Vt.) 13 Fed. 567, 576 (1882).

[150] Peck v. Crane, 25 Vt. 146, 147 (1853). "It is apparent that this writ of sequestration is merely an attach-

obtained in New Jersey a statute of the same nature, under which the court of chancery, where a money decree was prayed, issued the writ when it was made to appear by affidavit that the defendant was a non-resident and had property within the jurisdiction, the purpose of the writ being effectuated by the usual means of service upon non-residents.[151] A similar use of the writ still appears in Delaware. The statute, while directed primarily toward compelling the appearance of defendants who are non-residents or are believed on just grounds to be avoiding service, by seizure of their property under the writ, subjects the defendant and his property to substantially the same consequences as under the ordinary attachment on mesne process.[152] A salient distinction between these cases of sequestration in the nature of attachment and the case of sequestration proper is that the former, like attachment, effects a lien on the property involved, whereas the latter is intended to preserve the property for the benefit of all the parties pending final adjudication.

---

ment by mesne process in an equity suit." Steam Stone Cutter Co. v. Jones, *supra,* at 576.

[151] N.J. Stat. Ann. 1939, §§ 2-29:89, 2-29:97; and see Frank v. H. E. Salzburg Co. 102 N.J.Eq. 107, 104 Atl. 241 (1928). Both provisions having been repealed in 1948, sequestration no longer obtains "except to enforce a judgment or order of the court." N.J. Rules Civ. Pract., Rule 3-72:6.

[152] Del. Rev. Code 1935, § 4374; Del. Rules of Court of Chancery 1947, Rule 64. See Wightman v. San Francisco Bay Toll-Bridge Co. 16 Del.Ch. 200, 142 Atl. 783 (1928); Skinner v. Educational Pictures Securities Corporation, 14 Del.Ch. 417, 129 Atl. 857 (1925).

INDEX

INDEX